TOUCHSTONE

THE WORLD OF THE PAST

VOLUME I

EDITED, WITH AN INTRODUCTION

AND INTRODUCTORY NOTES, BY

JACQUETTA HAWKES

A TOUCHSTONE BOOK
PUBLISHED BY SIMON AND SCHUSTER

IN MEMORY OF

Leonard Woolley

a brilliant excavator
and a writer of imagination

Editor's Preface

THE CHOICE of extracts for this anthology has been determined first of all by the quality of the writing. Happily there was an abundance of enjoyable literature to choose from, for while very few of those who have written about archaeology were professional authors, many had exceptional gifts enabling them to write well. Men and women whose natures led them into archaeological pioneering were likely to be imaginative, unconventional and open-eyed. Quite often their minds were enlivened with a broad seam of eccentricity. Moreover, their extraordinary adventures and discoveries gave them something urgent to say, and this urgency lent them style.

In making the selection I had to respect a second consideration. An anthology on this scale ought as far as possible to cover all the main centres of archaeological interest throughout the world, and also to illustrate the development of knowledge in each province.

In balancing literary merit against subject matter, there was bound to be some conflict of interests. Certain regions, such as Mesopotamia, have a mass of excellent archaeological literature available in English; others, such as India and China, are short of it. Again, when seeking to show the growth of knowledge, one finds that it is exactly when information begins to be precise and coherent that good writing becomes exceptional. The early humanist explorers are often contemptuously treated by modern scientists for their carelessness and addiction to treasure-hunting. But at least they took the trouble to communicate gracefully or vigorously with their fellows. Modern archaeologists, on the other hand, are inclined to think that literary skill will diminish, and unnecessary jargon enhance, their scientific reputations.

For this reason in recent years a division has widened between the original research workers who too often wish to remain unintelligible to the general reader, and the untrained popularisers who are perhaps too easily intelligible, and who are not writing out of their own knowledge and experience. I have tried to avoid both extremes, and, fortunately, enough good archaeologists have recognized the need to write for the ordinary intelligent public generally to enable me to do so.

If there are still some small gaps in the anthology caused by the lack of suitable material, I hope to have made them good in my Introduction. In it I have given an outline of the history of antiquarian and archaeological discovery which should enable readers to learn something of the work of individuals who made great contributions to knowledge but who published little, or who could not write enjoyably, or whose writings are not available in the English language.

When planning *The World of the Past* in advance, I drew up a standard list of topics for each part, supposing that I could achieve a monumental regularity of form. When it came to making the actual selection, however, I soon realized that such uniformity could not be achieved—and indeed was not even desirable. The literature was, of course, as variable as the history and natural conditions of the different regions and periods involved.

Finally I found it best to begin with two parts presenting the evolution of man and the development of his culture for as long as it has a universal meaning—that is to say the history of the early hunting cultures and of the origins and spread of farming. For later periods I used regional groupings, allowing the plan of each regional section to be decided by the nature of the material available. For example, in Egypt the content of the art and the survival of vast quantities of ordinary human possessions demanded that emphasis should be placed on the lives of the ancient Egyptians, while in Mesopotamia it seemed inevitable to follow the dramatic development of archaeological knowledge as excavators cut deeper and deeper into the past.

It remains to mention a few points of editorial detail. Nearly all footnotes have been left out, as they can seldom appeal to the general reader. Exceptionally, however, where they are of interest, they have been included in the text. The spelling of proper names varies according to the period, nationality and whim of the authors. It seemed to me contrary to historical propriety to standardize these spellings, with a few exceptions; but in order to avoid confusion the most usually accepted modern version has been inserted in brackets after the first appearance of the original form. Editorial insertions also appear in brackets.

I believe that a diligent reading of these volumes will give something approaching a history of archaeology and of archaeological knowledge. But I should be sad indeed if all readers had to be so zealous. I think hardly less well of those adventurers who prefer to sample at random. They will be able to savour unusual juxtapositions, to compare the greatest moments of archaeological discovery of all times and countries, and to contrast various accounts of famous monuments written over many centuries—occasionally over millennia. Anyway, I hope that both kinds of reader, the serious and the casual, will find their appropriate pleasures.

JACQUETTA HAWKES

Contents

II : THE OLD STONE AGE AND THE EVOLUTION OF MAN

III : THE NEW STONE AGE AND THE BEGINNINGS OF FARMING

IV : MESOPOTAMIA AND PALESTINE

V : THE EGYPTIAN WORLD

List of Plates

PLATE

PLATE

Maps

ACKNOWLEDGMENTS

The drawing on p. 207 is from the Preface to *Beyond the Bounds of History* by Abbé Henri Breuil, London, 1949. Reprinted by kind permission of the publisher, T. V. Boardman & Co. Ltd. The drawing on p. 384 is from *History Begins at Sumer* by S. N. Kramer, 1956 (published in London by Thames and Hudson, Ltd., and in Indian Hills, Colorado, under the title *From the Tablets of Sumer*, by the Falcon's Wing Press). Reprinted by kind permission of both publishers.

THE
WORLD
OF THE
PAST

INTRODUCTION

Archaeology: Purposes and Pleasures

TRAVELLERS' tales have always found listeners. Whether it was Pytheas the Greek, home from his dim and misty voyage round the British Isles, Marco Polo back from the court of the Great Khan, Columbus from America, Cook from the Pacific or Gagarin and Glenn from outer space, their fellows have drawn round to hear tell of the strange things they have seen. In particular (and here the astronauts are at a disadvantage) men have delighted to learn about the ways of unknown races in order to compare these ways with their own—to wonder and to laugh at the foreigners' preposterous manner of eating and dressing, of marrying and burying, or at their peculiarities of skin colour, features and hair.

Almost exactly the same kind of curiosity and wonder have been roused by the discoveries of individuals who have explored not in space but in time. Layard and Schliemann, Botta and Mariette, Stephens, Evans and Woolley are all famous for having brought back news of unknown peoples—of peoples who did not live far away, but long ago. And although they may be felt to have lost something in being denied encounters with living men and women, they also gained immeasurably in having ventured into the past. For one thing, almost everyone has a nostalgia for the past—whether it is his own past or that of mankind. But also, while living "barbarians" and "savages" ("Ancient Britons" equally with Australian aborigines) were always felt to be oddities on the fringes of history, it was often clear that the remains of forgotten cultures recovered by the spade lay at the roots of our own civilization; were a part of the central development of world history.

There are two strong justifications for beginning an introduction to archaeology with this analogy between explorations in space and time. The first and most obvious is that until recent times the two overlapped and were sometimes almost identical. This will become evident in the anthology itself. Herodotus, for example, is rightly accepted as the Father of History, yet what is now of interest to archaeology is not his heroic account of the Persian Wars, but the enthralling digressions in which he describes the many peoples inhabiting the background of his scenes. These digressions, which evidently fascinated him as much as they have fascinated his readers ever since, were generally the fruits of his own travels—or those of his many informants. It will be found, too, that many of the extracts dating from the seventeenth to the early nineteenth century come from the books of men who were first and foremost simply travellers. They noted the antiquities they saw, might even on occasion, like Stephens, stop to do a little digging, but their accounts show an equal interest in the living Arabs, Egyptians, or Mexicans who entertained or robbed them, or in the other adventures they experienced in the course of their journeys. They were archaeologists only by the way.

The second and more significant justification for the use of the analogy is that it illumines what should be the best aims of archaeology. An immense amount of labour, skill and ingenuity goes into excavation and the study of antiquities, but unless they result in the resurrection of life, all this effort is largely vain. This has been insisted upon again and again by leading archaeologists. Sir Mortimer Wheeler has written ". . . the archaeologist is digging up, not *things*, but *people*. Unless the bits and pieces with which he deals be alive to him, unless he have himself the common touch, he had better seek out other disciplines . . ." Professor Grahame Clark puts it like this: "It is true that your archaeologist is compelled by circumstances to rely upon the material remains surviving from the people he is studying to arrive at any idea of their daily life; yet however much he may be preoccupied with things, often in themselves unattractive, he is really interested all the time in people." Professor Clark perhaps too easily assumes that this *is* so rather than that it *should be* so. There are only too many lesser practitioners in the subject who—whether because they lack "the common touch" or simply imagination—seem only too ready to use ever more meticulous techniques to pile up ever larger mounds of almost meaningless information.

In fact the insistence on the human values of archaeology is far more necessary today than it was in the past. Modern excavators condemn their predecessors out of hand for their lack of scientific methods and aims. But at least the old antiquaries and such early diggers as Layard were working directly to enrich their own cultures. Thus sculptures brought home from the Grand Tour might represent ignorant pillage, but they beautified fine houses and gardens. Classical remains unscientifically studied by such men as the Adam brothers led to a happy revolution in architecture and interior decoration. The observations on Egyptian art brought back by the learned gentlemen accompanying Napoleon's armies to the Nile gave rise to all the delicious Egyptianate fantasy of the *Empire* style. Layard and Botta's discoveries in Assyria introduced a new art to all the educated public of Europe as well as putting new heart into Bible students. In this last they may be said to have countered the almost simultaneous discoveries of the scientists who were establishing the reality of antediluvian man and setting fundamentalist Christianity in turmoil. No, it is only today, when science can fill many pages with statistical tables giving the angles of percussion of flint implements and the like, that it has to be insisted that archaeology is first and foremost a handmaid of history.

For I must expand a little on the statements of Sir Mortimer Wheeler and Professor Clark. While certainly archaeologists must always concern themselves with revealing people and their daily lives, I believe that they must also be shown in the context of *history*—that is to say of change and development. Quite static studies of a family of Palaeolithic cave dwellers or of Basket Maker Indians are interesting in themselves, certainly, because of the special lure of the past. Yet one has to ask whether it is reasonable to devote so much time to them, when nobody is taking anything like the same trouble to discover and record the details of modern life—say of an agricultural worker in his cottage, of a National Service man in his barracks, or a millionaire in his penthouse. No, the interpreter of archaeological discovery must not be content with static description. He can show us a vast spectacle of movement in time, of cultures and civilizations each unique in form and style, growing, flowering, and dying. He can enable us to make comparisons between all these endlessly various manifestations of human creativity, and between them and our own. Above all, archaeological discovery can give a sense of the continuity of past and present. Despite the terrible extravagance of human affairs, the often-repeated tragedies of degeneration and destruction (which excavation has revealed to us even more clearly than written history), the long vista which we now command, from the days of the apemen to our own, enables us to watch past effort and achievement accumulating to form the present. Archaeology has revealed the cultural evolution of man.

If these are some of the aims and purposes of our subject, it also has its more spontaneous gifts and pleasures, no less important but less solemn. It has enormously enriched the art treasury of the world. Thousands of works of art, each an expression of the style of its age and place, have been unearthed and offered for our enjoyment. To enter museums where such treasures are best displayed, often the products of civilizations completely unknown a century ago, can be a most moving experience. They are ancient, yet come to us pristine from the imaginations that created them.

Finally, there is the pleasure which archaeology brings to its own devotees. It is a subject, as these volumes will show, which happily bridges the chasm between the arts and sciences. It also offers equal opportunities to work indoors and out of doors, to the man of action and the man of thought or scholarship. There may be the adventure of going into remote places, of setting up camp far from the modern world and getting to know the native people in a way quite impossible for the ordinary traveler. Several excavators, particularly those writing in the nineteenth century, have left full and affectionate portraits of workmen, foremen and local worthies. Then, whatever the more austere type of modern scientific excavator may say, there is the extraordinary excitement of seeing what is going to turn up next. It is true that day after day workers may be tied to boring routine, often tormented by heat, flies, and dust—or, in Europe, by rain and mud. But then *something* shows in the trench or pit, it is followed up with trowel and knife and brush, it takes shape, and is finally laid bare. This kind of dramatic experience extends all the way from the uncovering of some quite humble object to the great moments of archaeology such as the unearthing of the Sutton Hoo Treasure (p. 449, II), the descent into the pyramid tomb at Palenque (p. 629, II) and the opening of the inner burial chambers of Tutankhamen in the Valley of the Kings (p. 501, I).

History

Men have probably been interested in the past, and more particularly in origins, ever since they have been capable of conceptual thought. But for a very long time there was no attempt to look back objectively and rationally, much less to try to recover past events through their material remains. Instead, men explained their origins imaginatively, making their creation stories part of their religious beliefs. The resulting myths were historical only in so far as they were emanations of the human psyche. The Babylonians told how the creator, Ea, made men from the blood of the erring divinity, Klingu, in order that they might serve as slaves for the gods; one Egyptian myth tells how men were first shaped on a potter's wheel by the ram-god Knum; according to the Shilluk the original man was born of a white cow which came up from the Nile; the Pueblo Indians believe that mankind climbed from the underworld through the opening of Shipapu. In the ancient world how astonished they would have been to learn that the Hebrew version of the creation story as told in *Genesis* was to cause violent resistance to the findings of science thousands of years later.

A more objective approach to a study of man began, as has been seen, with the observations made by travellers and foreign visitors. Thus Egyptian artists of the New Kingdom distinguished in feature and colouring between four racial types. They depicted Semites in yellow, Negroes in black, Europeans in white (with blue eyes and fair beards) and Egyptians in red. As the Egyptians came to have closer contacts with the Mediterranean cultures, they also distinguished a number of maritime peoples by name and dress. It might be said that the first recorded excavation, too, was carried out in New Kingdom Egypt—but its purposes were not scientific. A slab of red granite set between the paws of the Great Sphinx at Gizeh records how the Pharaoh Thutmose IV, before he came to the throne, fell asleep in the shadow of the Sphinx and dreamed that the Sun God which it represented promised to make him Pharaoh if he would clear away the sand that had buried the lower part of the monument. This (evidently) Thutmose did, setting up the stela as a kind of excavation report.

The really great advance, as in so many other fields of thought and knowledge, began with the Ionian Greeks. Homer, himself an Ionian Greek, in his epics was looking back at a bronze-using society, and his work contains much that is of interest to archaeologists (p. 5 ff., II), but his real importance in any history of "the study of mankind" lies in the powerful influence he had on Greek modes of thought.

Homer, by his completely unsuperstitious outlook on life, by his lack of reverence for the conventional deities of Greek religion and by his emphasis on the fundamental beauty of existence, had shaped a strange moral system which not only deeply appealed to the Greek mind but shaped its course. . . . Homer acted as a purge for all that was barbaric and retrogressive in a barely established society. . . . Homer rationalized a world that was waiting for philosophy.[1]

Hesiod, who followed Homer still within the eighth century B.C., set out in his great poem, *Works and Days*, a succession of Five Ages (p. 53, II) that might be called the first chronological system for human history. It is true that his Ages of Gold and Silver were entirely philosophic and poetic in meaning, but he seems to have known as an historical fact that bronze was used before iron, and to have given expression to genuine "folk memories" of Minoan civilization and its fall.

The later philosophers and scientific observers who flourished in Miletus and other rich mercantile cities of Ionia had the detached curiosity of the scientific spirit. Untrammelled by theological traditions or beliefs in special divine creation, they were the
‸‸‸‸‸‸‸‸‸‸‸‸‸‸‸‸

[1] Stanley Casson: *The Discovery of Man*. London. Hamish Hamilton; 1939, pp. 41-2.

first human beings to use their intellects freely and to look at
their species as a part of the natural universe. Food for their liberal
thought was provided by the commercial interests of their country.
After the eighth century B.C. seaborne trade increased, and ships'
officers and educated passengers pooled the knowledge they had
acquired, to produce handbooks for mariners, with titles such as
Guide Book to the Red Sea. These curious books, known generally
as "Sailings Round," came to include all kinds of practical information about the inhabitants of the coasts described. Maps, too, were
engraved—as is known from the passage in Herodotus where
Aristagoras of Miletus goes to see the king of Sparta and takes
with him "a bronze tablet on which was engraved a map of the
whole earth with all the seas and rivers."

The Ionian thinkers accepted the principles of evolution—even
though it was, of course, on a speculative basis. Anaximander and
Archelaus, both citizens of Miletus, stated them most clearly.
Anaximander proclaimed that "Man was produced in the first instance from animals of a different sort," and "Animals came into
existence by a process of evaporation by the sun: but man came
into existence in the likeness of another animal, in the first instance a fish." Archelaus, whose ideas are of particular interest
because he was one of Socrates's teachers, described how "when
the earth became warm in the beginning" a great variety of short-
lived animals (presumably he meant invertebrates) came into
being in the slime. "But afterwards interbreeding occurred among
them and men were separated off from the rest . . . And reason
is implanted in all animals alike: for each according to his bodily
frame uses it, one more slowly, another more quickly." Such liberal
thinking, with its ability to look at man quite steadily as a part
of nature, was hardly to be known again for two and a half millennia. And it is astonishing how near these two scientific philosophers came to guessing the facts of evolutionary history as they
were to be established by Darwin and his successors.

Among those Ionians whose interests were above all in the study
of man—who were serving the ideal of their colleague Heraclitus
when he said "All men have the capacity to understand themselves and so to be wise"—the greatest was Herodotus. Born in
about 485 B.C. at Halicarnassus (then about one day's journey
from Miletus), he seems to have spent much of his twenties and
thirties travelling. His tremendous journeys ranged between European Greece and Babylon and Susa, between Egypt and the mouth
of the Dnieper. He resided in many of the lands he visited, dili-
gently collecting information. Although his romantic temperament
made him sometimes too credulous of the tales of his informants
(particularly when they concerned the past), his own observations

were careful and he did his best to sift the evidence. He was almost free from racial prejudice or nationalism, but was filled with wonder and delight at the variety of mankind and its ways of life. This enthusiasm he conveyed in the brilliant descriptive passages of his *History*—written in "sweet, pure and flowing"[2] Greek.

While it is true that Herodotus is at his most unreliable when recording what people told him about their past history, the sights which he himself saw have now become for us the material of archaeology. His account of a royal Scythic burial, for example, has been accurately confirmed by modern excavations—providing the best "double-take" of this kind that is ever likely to occur. No wonder, then, that Herodotus is the earliest author to be extensively represented in this anthology. His younger contemporary, Thucydides, deserves a place because in the introduction to his *History of the Peloponnesian War* he gives a brief prehistory of the Greeks which includes the very first recorded instance of archaeological method being used to reconstruct history (p. 111, I). Yet in general, of course, he wrote history as the heroic exemplar—the kind of history which was to prevail for so long and which lies at the opposite extreme from that arrived at through "the common touch" of archaeology.

Herodotus's detached, anthropological approach to the study of mankind had no worthy development. Ionia was weakened by her struggle against the Persians, and her science must have received an exceptionally severe blow in the destruction of Miletus itself. As the centre of Greek intellectual life shifted to Athens, ethics and metaphysics largely displaced the natural sciences as the dominant interest; philosophical speculation was preferred to observation. In some part of his work, Aristotle was an exception to this—indeed, he may have acquired his scientific attitude during the long stay he made in Ionia as a young man. His biological work, ignored during the Middle Ages when his authority in other fields was paramount, shows Aristotle at his best as a scientist. His former pupil, Alexander the Great, urged him on in these researches into "the nature of animals." The Elder Pliny says that Alexander "placed at his disposal some thousands of men in every part of Asia and Greece, among them hunters, fowlers, fishermen, park-keepers, herdsmen, beekeepers, as well as keepers of fishponds and aviaries, in order that no creature might escape his notice."

Aristotle has not left us any scientific study of the human species, but his work on animals was seen as a part of the investigation of man. Indeed, some historians of science have liked to link Aristotle with another almost equally great man who followed him in the same field—Charles Darwin. For this reason it is interesting

---
[2] Quintilian.

to read what the eminent Victorian thought of his precursor when, evidently quite belatedly, he came upon his biological writings.

"From quotations I had seen I had a high notion of Aristotle's merits, but I had not the remotest notion of what a wonderful man he was. Linnaeus and Cuvier have been my two gods, though in very different ways, but they were mere schoolboys to old Aristotle."[3]

This recognition, naive and intimate, of the author of the *History of Animals* by the author of the *Origin of Species,* seems to make nothing of the gulf of over two thousand years that lay between them.

The Phoenicians, who had been colonists before the Greeks, lacked the lively Greek curiosity about what they saw; so too did their Roman successors. Of all the administrators, engineers, and soldiers who worked throughout the Roman Empire, few indeed have left records of the conquered peoples they must have known so well. Nor did Roman thinkers and men of letters serve us much better. Lucretius, the didactic poet of the second century B.C., has, it is true, been hailed as a pioneer of archaeology; but this is rather too large a claim. The passages in his *De rerum natura* describing the cultural evolution of mankind (p. 707, II) can be likened to those in which Hesiod set out his Five Ages, but further rationalized and strengthened with some remarkably good guesses. He might be said to have anticipated the Three Age system of the Scandinavians (p. 31, I), but his ideas were based on tradition and philosophical speculation, not on material evidence.

Julius Caesar and Tacitus, two men who did think it worth while to record something of what they had seen, or heard about, the extremities of the Empire, wrote enough to make us almost resentful that there were not a dozen others to equal them. Caesar's references to the Gauls and Britons (p. 414, II) are very much the asides of a military historian, yet they are factual and unslanted and so give valuable information about these Celtic peoples—who, for all their misfortunes, still survive in western Europe, still speak their own languages and treasure their cultural traditions. Archaeology has often corrected inaccurate or biased historical records, but occasionally has been proved wrong in its turn. Julius Caesar has won such a vindication. Among his comments on Britain he said that "the people of the interior do not, for the most part, cultivate grain, but live on milk and meat and are clothed in skins." British archaeologists long denied this barbarous picture, for they had found plenty of evidence that the Britons enjoyed a far more civilized existence in the last century B.C. But more exact research has now shown that there was a very great difference in the

---

[3] From a letter to the naturalist William Ogle, 1882.

"British Way of Life" north and south of the Jurassic Belt that runs obliquely across central England. It seems to be a fact that before the Roman Conquest the northerners hardly practised agriculture but were pastoralists, perhaps even semi-nomadic pastoralists. They therefore would have lived on meat and milk and probably, "for the most part," dressed in skins.

The full title of Tacitus's *Germania* is *Concerning the Geography, the Manners and Customs, and the Tribes of Germany.* This sounds very much like a detached anthropological study, yet it was both more than that, and not precisely that. It is written in a very ornate style which suggests a cultivated gentleman displaying his literary accomplishment. Moreover, whatever Tacitus's main purpose in writing it, the *Germania* often seeks to shame the sophisticated Romans by lauding the simple, stalwart virtues of an unlettered people. At times Tacitus is quite clearly holding up the image of the Noble Savage.

Yet the book is the first deliberately planned and painstakingly executed study of a single people, and is virtually our only written source of information about the ancient Germans. It shows in embryo the type of culture and society that was to prevail throughout western Europe in the Middle Ages.

No other work surviving from classical Rome can compare in value with the *Germania* for a student of early man. Ptolemy, an Egyptian-born Greek of the second century A.D., made a remarkable contribution to science, bringing together the geographical knowledge of the ancient world. But unhappily he worked and thought essentially as a mathematician, so that although the coasts whose positions he calculated with widely-varying accuracy stretched from end to end of the known inhabited world, he tells us almost nothing of the inhabitants.

When the classical world came gradually and piecemeal to an end it had accomplished much in the study of mankind by man. Greek genius had succeeded, for the first time in what was already the long history of civilization, in developing free and fearless intellectual enquiry. The Greeks were fascinated by the problems of the origins of life, of man and of civilization, and did all they could through observation and speculation to illuminate them. If one wanted to be a little perverse, one could say that they succeeded so well that nothing more was needed for a general, philosophical understanding of human history. One could say that the Ionian theory of man's biological emergence, together with the traditional knowledge of cultural evolution, was sufficient for this understanding.

Yet, even apart from the fact that ideas as vague and generalized as these can hardly be satisfying, the essential weakness was that nothing had been *proved* with the kind of evidence that could convince ordinary men or crush opposing theorists. When at last interpretations similar to those of the Greeks came to the fore again, it was to be overwhelming material proof, supplied by geological fieldwork and archaeological excavation, which was, after a struggle, to silence opposition and turn Adam and Eve into symbolic rather than historical figures.

In the later days of the Roman Empire, growing Christian influence was already discouraging adventurous thought. Soon Europe was to return to a cosmogony of Bronze Age type—indeed of direct Bronze Age origin. Once again men accepted explanations in the form of myths and were content to let their thinking on human history be bounded by the book of Genesis. Greek curiosity did, it is true, remain alive in Byzantium, but was now exercised on the intricacies of theology.

Then, after a millennium of slumber, the old spirit of Greek humanism began to stir once more. Greek manuscripts found their way into the hands of Italian scholars, some derived from Constantinople, some from Greece itself, where the Italian ruling élite often obtained them from the monasteries where they had lain for so long. The Acciajuoli, Florentine Dukes of Athens, added a library to their palace—which stood on the Acropolis itself.

An Italian scholar of this epoch of reawakening is one of a number of men who have been given the title of the Father of Archaeology. This is Cyriac de Pizzicolli, a merchant, born at Ancona as early as 1391. His claim to the title comes from the fact that not only did he travel extensively in unknown regions, visiting ruins, collecting coins and works of art, and—above all—copying inscriptions, but he also ordered the information he collected in a systematic way. His earliest travels took him as far as Egypt, but most of his work was done in Greek lands; he was the first antiquary to visit many great Hellenic sites, including Thebes; the first to copy inscriptions at Delphi. He acquired a manuscript of Herodotus's *Histories* in remote Arcadia. In many of the places Cyriac visited, he fell in with fellow countrymen who shared his interests and they spent days of happy enthusiasm together. One can almost see the "lights of Europe going up one by one," and this great itinerant scholar with his *Commentaries* in his bag was one of the lamp-lighters.

At first the revival of interest in classical manuscripts and the classical world itself did not lead to any serious speculation concerning human origins; consequently there was no immediate clash with the authority of the Roman Church. (The astronomers and mathematicians with their inconvenient discoveries about the solar system were in serious trouble much sooner.) From the fifteenth century on, Popes, Cardinals and all who could afford it began to collect antiquities and enjoy classical art—became, in fact, *dilettanti* in the original, non-pejorative sense of *those delighting in the arts.* As the supply above ground of statues and the like ran out, it was renewed by digging. These tastes spread among the gentry of Europe and reached a new phase with that great eighteenth century figure, Winckelmann, who began the serious historical interpretation of ancient art.

In England "in the year 1734 some Gentlemen who had travelled in Italy, desirous of encouraging, *at home,* a taste for those objects which had contributed so much to their Entertainment *abroad*" founded the Society of Dilettanti. Rich and influential, this society did much to foster the study of classical remains and to improve its standards. In the early 1750's it was behind the painter James Stuart and the architect Nicholas Revett in their arduous survey of Athenian monuments, and published their *Antiquities of Athens.* In 1764 the Society also itself financed an ambitious expedition to the Ionian coasts, the results being published in the important volumes of *Antiquities of Ionia* which appeared between 1769 and 1797. This great work is of particular interest for the influence it had upon the architecture of North America. Greek taste equally with Greek ideas had a strong appeal for a people pressing towards independence—and here was the finest source of inspiration. It can be seen at work in the Ionian porticos of the State Buildings, the Doric façades of many New England houses and generally in much of the Hellenic spirit of the architects both of New England and the Southern States.

In contrast the relatively traditionalist and authoritarian aristocracy of Britain preferred Roman models. The discoveries at Herculaneum and Pompeii (p. 210 ff., II), which were then exciting the cultivated world, together with the architect Robert Adam's survey of the Palace of Diocletian at Spalato (published in 1764) inspired much of the architecture and interior decoration of the great Georgian age.

Some travellers went further afield in their pursuit of antiquity. Robert Wood, for example, was able to publish the *Ruins of Palmyra* in 1753 and the *Ruins of Baalbek* a few years later. Row after row of handsome and well-illustrated volumes, fit ornaments for the libraries of the magnificent country houses of the time, made their stately emergence from the presses during this second half of the eighteenth century. Nor did they cease during the first quarter of the nineteenth, when Lord Elgin and many others were busy in Greece and the Society of Dilettanti dispatched a "Second Ionian Mission." Moreover, although undertaken as a part of the gentlemanly cultivation of taste, this study of classical remains was often intensive, and much of it is now invaluable as a record of treasures since destroyed. It represents a very real contribution to the annals of archaeology.

Away from the Mediterranean and the centres of early civilization, the return to the classical authors had another effect. The English and French and Germans read accounts of their forebears —or at least brief reference to them—which showed them to have been primitive peoples with strange and often barbaric customs. Western and northern Europe was thickly scattered with great constructions in earth and stone of absolutely unknown origin. The country folk had usually attributed these to the devil, to giants or to well-known legendary characters, but now the scholars began to think that they might instead be the handiwork of these Gauls and Celts, these Goths and Germans and other curiously-named barbarians described by Greek and Roman writers.

Such speculations contributed to a vigorous growth of antiquarianism in Renaissance England. Henry VIII appointed as his personal Antiquary one John Leland, who toured the country in the 1530's and '40's, charged by the king to search cathedrals, colleges, and religious houses for manuscripts and antiquities. He was particularly concerned to save from destruction the libraries of the recently-dissolved monasteries. On his tours he made records of ancient monuments—mainly of mediaeval buildings, but including a few of the more conspicuous prehistoric remains that caught his eye.

Leland collected a mass of material and intended, among other equally grandiose projects, to write a great history of British antiquities. But, poor fellow, like many antiquaries and archaeologists since his day, he had amassed more than he could digest. Struggling with his octopus of a task at his house in London's Cheapside, he became mentally deranged, was certified as insane in 1550, and died two years later.

Leland is of great interest as a transitional figure, belonging in part to the Middle Ages, in part to the Renaissance world. During mediaeval times the west European peoples had embraced various legendary national histories that were as fanciful as they were heroic. The British story told how Brutus, a Trojan prince, had come to the islands, given them his name, founded London and defeated the aborigines—a race of giants. In later stages of the chronicle, Kings Lear, Lud, and Coel appear on the scene with a host of other, now less familiar, characters. After the withdrawal of the Romans, Ambrosius, his brother Uther Pendragon, and Uther's son, King Arthur, win great victories over the Saxons (with Merlin's assistance), while Arthur conquers large parts of the continent. In the end, however, the Saxons unjustly triumph and the

British have to withdraw and become the Welsh; but one of their last kings, Cadwallader, before dying in Rome, hears angelic voices promising the return of the Britons and the recovery of their kingdom.

This *British History* was first fully set out by the twelfth century chronicler, Geoffrey of Monmouth, whose skill as a narrator won it immediate popularity. Inevitably, of course, it had to be seen against a background of biblical history. The Trojan lineage of Brutus was traced back to Noah (Japhet was accepted as Founding Father of the European peoples). Right through to the sixteenth century more and more fanciful additions became attached to the story. One version introduces Isis and Osiris, Neptune and Amphitrite as parents and grandparents of King Albion. Then the legend of Joseph of Arimathea's journey to Glastonbury was developed by the brethren there, finally leading to the claim that the British church was founded in A.D. 41. Joseph was soon recognized as an ancestor of King Arthur.

The *British History*, like its counterparts among the continental nations, is a mixture of pure legend with confused historical traditions. Its strength was renewed and its life prolonged because the accession to the English throne of the Welsh line of the Tudors was widely regarded as fulfilling the prophecy made to Cadwallader. Quarterings in coats of arms of Tudor monarchs from Henry VII to Elizabeth I include those of Brutus, Arthur, and other princes from the *British History*. Thus a strong political element entered into the passionate defence of the Brutus story that was waged during the sixteenth and seventeenth centuries.

Leland was a pioneer of the new age in that he went into the countryside and himself examined British antiquities—in this he was like a modest, "barbarian," Cyriac of Ancona. But his personal attachment to the Tudors, his fervent nationalism, made him a champion of the old, impossible mediaeval tale. Thus while Camden and the long line of devoted out-of-door antiquaries who were to make such a fine contribution to the study of the past may be recognized as his descendants, Leland was bound to be in collision with the progressive historians of his age.

True Renaissance scholars such as John Colet (friend of Erasmus) and their successors of the next generation had the learning to expose the mediaeval fantasies for what they were. More significantly, the old Greek spirit of free enquiry had in part at least revived in them; one and all they were ready to question authority.

The first antiquary to show strong scepticism of the *British History* was the Italian-born Polydore Virgil. His treatment of it in his *Historia Anglica* (1534) was so disrespectful that it provoked

Leland to reply with *Assertio Incomparabilis Arturii* and other defences of the ancestral heroes.

Of more importance, however, because already in the direct line of English topographical study, was the work of William Camden. Camden, born the year before Leland's death, was one of the brilliant circle of teachers, scholars and learned Anglican divines of his day. He was a friend of such men as Sir Robert Cotton, John Selden and Archbishop James Ussher. (There is irony in the fact that it should have been Ussher, the enlightened and scholarly Protestant, who calculated the date 4004 B.C. for the Creation, little knowing that it would be blindly defended in the face of scientific discoveries nearly three hundred years later.)

Camden himself was remarkably gifted. He was only twenty-five years old when, in 1586, he published the first edition of his famous *Britannia* (p. 362, II). In it, although he expressed himself with great restraint, he made it quite clear that he shared Polydore Virgil's scepticism concerning the Brutus story. Indeed he put forward his own more rational interpretation, deriving the name Britannia from a Celtic-Greek compound meaning "the land of the painted people," and suggesting that the Britons were an offshoot of the Gauls. Beyond that, of course, he accepted biblical authority, deriving the Gauls themselves from Japhet through his son Gomer. Camden, like Leland, travelled the country visiting ancient monuments. In successive editions his *Britannia* became larger and larger, and in 1610 was first translated into English from the original elegant Latin. It was to be revised and enlarged again and again, appearing in three volumes in 1789 and four in 1806. It remained, in fact, the guide and companion of generation after generation of industrious English antiquaries.

The knowledge and critical good sense of Camden and his friends and their seventeenth century followers finally destroyed faith in the *British History*, but the struggle went on for many decades and makes fascinating reading for anyone interested in clashes between those persistent modes of thought—the mythical and fabulous and the factual and rational. It is of interest, too, as a kind of rehearsal for the great nineteenth century battle over evolution. It led to the defeat of the legendary explanation of the origin of a nation by a sober historical one, just as the later, more profound, controversy led to the replacement of a mythical origin of Man by a scientific one.

Leland and Camden, despite the deep division between them, were founding fathers of a great antiquarian tradition. The enduring passion of the English gentry and nobility for the country life and the management of their estates meant that there were many cultivated individuals scattered throughout the land. It was inevitable that a proportion of them should take an intelligent interest in the antiquities visible on their estates, or in their county or region—often to the extent of writing a more or less learned and reliable account of them. In the seventeenth century there were already half a dozen good county histories written—Dugdale's on Warwickshire being perhaps the best known. The enthusiasm of these men is well expressed in the diary of young Anthony Wood, himself to win fame as historian and antiquary of Oxford:

This summer [of 1656] came to Oxford *The Antiquities of Warwickshire* written by William Dugdale, and adorned with many cuts. This being accounted the best work of its kind that hitherto was made extant, my pen cannot enough describe how A. Wood's affections and insatiable desire of knowledge were ravished and melted downe by the reading of that book.

John Aubrey, a Wiltshire landowner, whom Anthony Wood described as "magotie-headed and sometimes little better than crazed," did some excellent recording work in Surrey and his own county, and was the first person to bring the great Bronze Age sanctuary of Avebury to the attention of the learned.

Some of these true *amateurs* went so far as to send out questionnaires to collect information. One asked, "Are there any ancient sepulchres hereabouts of Men of Gigantic Stature, Roman Generals and others of ancient times?" or "What . . . round heaps of stone or earth cast up in Hills, trench'd round about or otherwise? What fortifications, camps?" Towards the end of the seventeenth century some remarkably systematic work was done, especially by the Welshman, Edward Lhwyd, for the fine Gibson edition of Camden.

There is no question that even as mediaeval fantasies were left behind during the course of the seventeenth century, the study of British antiquities, including prehistoric remains, became increasingly accurate and systematic. Yet still, as among the Ionian Greeks, there was no method of establishing to what age or culture any particular type of monument belonged. One speculative interpretation was as good as another. This can best be illustrated by Stonehenge, the greater part of which we now know to date from the beginning of the full Bronze Age in southern England: about 1,500-1,400 B.C. Because the huge stones of this sanctuary make it strikingly conspicuous (it is indeed the most striking monument of all prehistoric Europe), it has always attracted attention. Already it has its place in Geoffrey of Monmouth's *British History*— which tells how Ambrosius and the wizard Merlin magically transported it from Ireland to Salisbury Plain as a memorial to British nobles slain by the Saxons. As this story (which almost certainly must have embodied some tradition of the fact that the smaller

"bluestones" were in very truth brought from the western extremity
of Wales) became unacceptable to sceptics, Stonehenge was occasionally attributed to the Romans. Then King James I chanced
to see it, and instructed the architect Inigo Jones to make a plan
of the monument and write its history. This he apparently did,
but the findings were published only some time after his death—
and the result was sufficiently surprising. The elaborate plans and
drawings showed these rough-hewn stones as exactly rectangular
columns, and the inner horseshoe settings as perfect circles. This
remarkable "restoration" was in harmony with a text which pronounced Stonehenge to be a temple in the Tuscan order erected
by the Romans in honour of the god Coelus. This thesis was
vigorously countered by Charles II's physician, Dr. Charleton, who
declared with equal certainty and more partisanship that the monument was in fact "erected by the Danes . . . to be a Court Royal,
or a place for the inauguration and election of their Kings." Other
current theories gave readers the additional choice of Phoenicians
and Saxons as architects of Stonehenge. John Aubrey was the first
to attribute it to the Druids, the Celtic priests whose curious combination of barbaric human sacrifice and philosophy had roused the
interest of those who knew their Latin authorities.

This was the view that tended to prevail in the eighteenth century, when it was supported and elaborated by William Stukeley
(p. 21, I)—but by then Stonehenge had become one of the properties of the Romantic Movement. It appears more than once in the
Prophetic Books of William Blake. To put the absolutely regular
elevations of Stonehenge as a temple of the Tuscan order beside
some of the drawings of romantic feeling, in which every stone
is as jagged as a piece of shrapnel and the whole monument in
tempestuous disorder, makes one realize the extent of the subjectivity of vision possible to the committed.

Were the extraordinary stones on Salisbury Plain raised there
by the Phoenicians, the Romans, the Saxons, the Danes—or by
the Druids? No one could say which diagnosis was the more probable—no one could know that they were in fact all quite wrong.
No wonder that when, like so many other travellers, Daniel Defoe
went out of his way to see Stonehenge, he noted down his disapproval of the antiquaries and their fanciful speculations. No
wonder that Dr. Johnson (so wise yet so often wrong) pronounced
that "All that is really known of the ancient state of Britain is
contained in a few pages. We can know no more than what the
old writers have told us."

No one had realized that ancient objects and monuments could
be arranged in cultural groups and often in irreversible sequences
of development and decline. No one had realized that excavation,

by revealing which cultures regularly overlaid other cultures, would make it possible to judge their relative ages. No one could have guessed that it could ever be possible to forge chains of evidence linking these cultures with historic civilizations and so to give them absolute dates.

One of the first recorded excavations to be made in Britain was of a large round barrow on Barham Downs. This dig, which was undertaken at the instruction of Henry VIII and the expense of the Master of the Rolls, and, oddly enough, supervised by one William Digges, was hardly scientific in spirit. The project had, indeed, been inspired by the dream of a shepherd. During the seventeenth century, gentlemen with "heaps of stone or earth cast up in Hills" on their property must occasionally have had the central burial uncovered in order to remove the grave goods. But it was only in the eighteenth century that excavation became a recognized part of the pursuit of the "Ancient Britons." Moreover, although it was generally limited to burials, where there was a good chance of finding objects worthy of display in collectors' cabinets, and although the work was done hastily, and sometimes simply as an entertainment, it did become increasingly purposeful. The excavation of many sites within a limited area, or entire cemeteries (p. 446, II), and the comparison of the finds, at least familiarized antiquaries with distinctive forms of implement in stone, bronze and iron, with various types of pottery, ornaments and other things regularly buried with the dead.

Eighteenth century British antiquarianism, then, was a gentlemanly pastime. As a source of antiquities to display in private collections it might be recognized as a slightly humbler substitute for the collecting of classical works of art then fashionable among the very wealthy. Yet at the same time it can be seen as leading directly towards the more serious researches of the nineteenth century and the scientific methods of the twentieth. It is, indeed, rather pleasing that General Pitt-Rivers, the first scientifically meticulous excavator (p. 87, I), can also be seen as the last of the long line of great land-owning antiquaries who excavated upon their own estates.

Yet although this continuity of development in British antiquarian and archaeological studies is real, it did not follow an altogether straight course. The seventeenth century (which saw the foundation of so many scientific societies in Europe, including the Royal Society in London) was essentially an age of science that had more in common with the Victorian age than with the eighteenth and early nineteenth centuries.

The relationship between the Augustans and the men of the Enlightenment and those of the seventeenth century might, with caution, be likened to that between the Athenians and the Ionians. The beginning of observation and experiment of the earlier age was checked in favour of classicism and philosophy. But the great break, and one which had a deep effect on the study of prehistoric man, was made by the Romantic Movement. As we see it now, this was an upsurge from the unconscious, a strong reaction after the excessive order, moderation and intellectualism of the Enlightenment. Men turned from classical architecture and neat fields to Gothic architecture and wild landscapes, while at the same time allowing their conscious minds to be invaded by all kinds of dark images and love of the horrific. The rugged remains of their prehistoric ancestors, especially monuments built of great stones such as Stonehenge and Avebury and the megalithic tombs, chimed in perfectly with these new tastes, while the idea of associating them with the grizzly human sacrifices of the Druid priesthood provided a strong seasoning of horror. A curious little archaeological incident beautifully illustrates this involvement with Romanticism. Horace Walpole, whose scarifying *Castle of Otranto,* equally with his Gothic fantasies at Strawberry Hill, made him a high priest of the Romantic Movement, was an old friend of Marshal Conway. At a time when Conway was Governor of Jersey, in the Channel Islands, a megalithic tomb of unusual elaboration was discovered there. On his retirement the grateful islanders (evidently thoroughly romanticized) offered him the tomb as a gift. Urged on by Walpole, who wrote, "pray do not disappoint me, but transport the Cathedral of your island to your domain on our continent," he accepted this bulky present, and in 1788 the stones were shipped and re-erected above the Thames—at no very great distance from Strawberry Hill. They were then inscribed with a verse (one would like to think Walpole composed it) describing in lurid words the blood which had flowed on these supposed altars, the screams of the sacrificial victims.

Among all the men involved in the fascinating interplay between British antiquarianism and the Romantic Movement, William Stukeley is by far the most important. His life's work spans the transition from the scientific observation of the seventeenth century, through a phase of classicism to one of romantic imaginings. He was born in 1687, included natural sciences in his studies at Cambridge and was already a careful observer of natural history and also of antiquities. He studied medicine in London, and practiced it for some years first in the country and then again in London. Meanwhile his enthusiasm and charm brought him many eminent and noble friends, and he increased his antiquarian knowledge by each year riding off on a journey through some part of the English countryside. In 1718 he was elected a Fellow of the

Royal Society (Isaac Newton was then President), and at about
the same time was involved in the foundation of the Society of
Antiquaries of London, becoming its first Secretary. The minutes of
the Society begin in the winter of 1717-18 and have been kept ever
since, faithfully reflecting the ups and downs, the changes in philosophy and method, of antiquarian and archaeological studies.

Stukeley was becoming more and more interested in Stonehenge,
which he often discussed with "My Lord Pembroke, in whose neighbourhood the Noble Antiquity stands . . ." He also began to take
note of Avebury, the other great Bronze Age sanctuary lying to the
north of Stonehenge, having probably been attracted to it through
the unpublished descriptions by its discoverer, John Aubrey. It was
very likely from Aubrey, too, that he took the idea that these stone
circles were Druid temples. From 1719 for several following years,
Stukeley made repeated visits to both monuments, taking careful
measurements and making charming and quite accurate sketches.
His most exhaustive work at Stonehenge was in 1723, when he
was there with several choice spirits. He describes how "we took I
believe 2,000 measures. . . . Lord Winchelsea has workt very
hard, and was ravisht with Stonehenge." Financed by Lord Pembroke, Stukeley also at this period excavated some of the many
barrows in the neighbourhood of the sanctuary. He did the work
thoroughly, observing the construction of the mound and even
drawing a transverse section—the first record of this kind in
British archaeology.

All this time Stukeley was planning to publish monographs on
Avebury and Stonehenge. Had he done so when his excellent fieldwork was completed, in the mid-1720's, they would probably have
been models of their kind—worthy of the old seventeenth century
tradition of scientific observation. It is true that he and his distinguished friends were already involved with Druids and other
Celtic fancies. They had formed a Society of Roman Knights for
the study of Roman Britain, each member with a Celtic or Roman
name. (It was extraordinary in admitting women. Mrs. Stukeley
was enrolled as Cartismandua, the Duchess of Hertford as Bunduca
—or Boadicea. The Society of Antiquaries was to resist the sex for
another two centuries.) Stukeley himself was honoured as the
Archdruid and sometimes given the dubiously druidical name of
Chyndonax. Yet all this was light-hearted nonsense—Stukeley at
this time would have attributed Avebury and Stonehenge to the
Druids, but he would have given a reasonably straightforward account of the monuments.

Unhappily, however, publication was delayed, and Stukeley himself underwent a profound change of personality and outlook—a
change which by 1729 led him to take holy orders. The young Dr.

Stukeley looked back to an age of science, the Reverend William Stukeley was a precursor of the Romantic Age that was to come. He meditated more and more upon the Druids, and brought together various old speculations concerning them into a grand theory which soon dominated all his thought. He believed that they were Phoenicians, who had come to Britain in Abraham's day, or even "soon after Noah's flood," introducing a pure patriarchal faith which had ripened into none other than the Church of England. It was they who had built all the stone circles—indeed Stukeley believed that their leader, Tyrian Hercules, raised the ring of Boscawen-Un in Cornwall immediately upon landing.

Studying the plan of the stone circles and avenues at Avebury he persuaded himself that it represented a serpent, a symbol of the deity, "more particularly of the Trinity . . . A snake proceeding from a circle is the eternal procession of the Son from the first cause." When he came to publish *Abury* (Avebury) in 1743 he not only filled the text with the wildest aberrations of this kind, but actually altered his drawing so that the outlying circle at the end of the avenue should appear to have the oval form appropriate to a serpent's head. Stukeley's ruin as a great pioneer field archaeologist was complete.

Yet this man, friend of the nobility, of the Primate of England, of princes and princesses, had an extraordinary influence on his world. The Romantic Movement became permeated with his ideas of druidism, and these Celtic priests, whom he had idealized, conveniently forgetting their barbarity, were recognized as defenders of freedom against Roman authority and so became a part of the canon that was to link the Romantic Movement with the ideas behind the French Revolution.

Not only did the poets Gray and Collins take much from Stukeley, but William Blake was more deeply influenced by him, transforming his ideas concerning the original patriarchal religion of the Druids into his own beliefs in a mystical holy land in Britain. The Prophetic Books, especially *Jerusalem,* are inspired by this idea, while at the same time containing very many direct allusions to particular notions of Stukeley's, such as "Serpent Temples" and the like.

Above all, of course, Stukeley had a lasting influence on everything to do with antiquarianism. Countless grottoes, sham ruins, *al fresco* inscriptions, title pages, knew his influence, while it has proved impossible for all the forces of modern science to expel his Druids from our Bronze Age circles. Indeed a society known as the Ancient Order of Druids founded in the eighteenth Century is still in being, and still assembles in white robes to celebrate the midsummer solstice at Stonehenge.

Romantic antiquarianism has a special interest because never at any other time did the subject have a greater influence on general culture. Yet in a sense it was no more than a flowery side branch of the main stem of development in man's study of his past. As we have seen, ordinary study of classical and local antiquities went on more or less undisturbed. Collecting became broader-based and more orderly—the Ashmolean Museum at Oxford, founded in the seventeenth century, had many additions in the eighteenth; the British Museum was opened to the public in 1759 and grew fast. Travel to ancient places increased and was extended as transport and roads improved. Stukeley himself in his old age belonged to an Egypt Society of gentlemen who had been to the Nile Valley and the Near East. With the nineteenth century all these activities tended to increase, although with the growth of industry and the middle class they passed more into the hands of professional people who banded together into local antiquarian and natural history societies, often with their own museums.

Napoleon's Egyptian campaign increased the interest in that ancient civilization, while the resulting work on hieroglyphs and Champollion's great successes prepared the way for the rediscovery of the ancient world that was to become such an exciting part of men's widening horizons after the middle of the century.

All these studies—of the prehistoric remains of western and northern Europe, of classical antiquity and of the ancient civilizations—could be carried very far without disturbing accepted religious views concerning the origins and earliest history of mankind. All speculation, whether rational or fantastic, could accept Ussher's date of 4004 B.C. for the creation, and scholars need only admire Bishop Lightfoot's greater accuracy when he established the exact day to have been October 23rd of that year. Nor did such studies raise any objections to an ancestry running through the Ark to the Garden of Eden. Since the Renaissance there had been sceptics of all kinds, but the findings of the antiquaries and early archaeologists contributed little to their scepticism. Indeed Stukeley was not the only antiquary who used his learning hotly to refute the "freethinkers."

But other lines of enquiry into the past were bound to lead to a clash and, as the nineteenth century progressed, their affiliation with the old, innocent historical and prehistorical researches became more and more obvious. Thus when the great battle was joined in the 1850's and '60's, there were archaeologists as well as biological evolutionists among the High Command of the scientific host. To understand these other lines of enquiry, it is necessary to look back once more as far as the sixteenth century.

A tremendous shock was administered to thinking men by the

discovery of a New World well stocked with human beings. Having proved the earth to be a sphere, the Greeks had discussed the pro- bable existence of antipodal man, but the early Christian Fathers, preferring to make the earth flat again, had brought such specula- tion to an end. St. Augustine in particular derided the notion of antipodal man with all his powers of sarcasm. For a thousand years views such as his prevailed—and men find it bitterly hard to relinquish ideas held for a millennium. Europeans had thought that they knew the whereabouts of all the descendants of Ham, Shem and Japhet, yet here was a vast inhabited continent alto- gether outside the scheme of things. Could the natives be descended from the First Parents? The Papacy wisely proclaimed that they were, but it was disturbing all the same. Then Magellan's voyage showed beyond doubt that the earth was a globe, and therefore that some of its inhabitants were inescapably antipodal.

Impressions of what the new-found men looked like and how they lived soon began to spread. Probably at first the extraordinary civilizations of Mexico and Peru aroused most wonder, but the primitive Indians also had their appeal. In 1550 a Brazilian tableau was staged at Rouen illustrating the simple, good life of the natives. Montaigne felt that they might be the true representatives of man- kind, living as man should properly live ". . . naked, simply-pure, in Natures lappe . . . with such measure and food as his mother- nurse affoorded him." In England, where reports were mostly of the North American Indians and Eskimos, there was less tender- ness. In about 1585 the Virginia pioneer, John White, published some superb engravings of Indians, mostly Roanoke. He also used them as models for other figures apparently intended to represent primitive Europeans—and with some elaboration of dress, later historians made them serve as Picts, Scots and Ancient Britons. Thus men who were already familiar with descriptions of the barbarian ancestors left by Caesar and Tacitus, used the American Indians to fill out the portrait. It was another of the means used to build a better understanding of the pre-Roman peoples of western Europe and to refute such mediaeval tales as that of the *British History* (p. 15, I).

Early in the seventeenth century, Garcilasso de la Vega, whose mother was a Peruvian of royal stock, wrote a history of the Incas which roused immense interest in a civilization that had flowered unknown to the Christian world. Many Jesuit mission- aries added their researches to this early spring of American Ethnology, while Las Casas, a Dominican monk who spent years studying the customs and antiquities of the Indians, published a book that included exposures of the brutal slaughter and destruc- tion that the Spanish were inflicting on their subjects.

When Sir Richard Rycaut came to issue an English edition of Garcilasso's history, he made a most perspicacious judgment on the origin of the American Indians. He wrote: "Various have been the opinions amongst Historians concerning the Original of these people. They proceeded from the Race of the Northern Tartar, whom they resemble in the shape and air of their features and in their barbarous way of living; but then we must fancie, as some Geographers do, that the West side of America is continent with Tartary or at least disjoyned from there by some narrow strait of which I am well persuaded we have no certain knowledge."[4] Not only does this forecast with most remarkable accuracy the findings of modern science, but it is infused with a scientific spirit that seems far away from poor Stukeley's maunderings of nearly a century later.

Rycaut, for all his foresight, can have had no inkling that this branch of the "Northern Tartars" would prove to have started crossing the "narrow strait" at least ten thousand years before Ussher's date for the Creation. Yet there was a general feeling abroad that the new discoveries both on earth and in heaven were bursting the bonds of the Mosaic cosmogony. The theologians had been obliged to give way again and again after fighting prolonged rearguard actions: they had given way on the sphericity of the globe and the existence of antipodal man; they were already close-pressed on the matter of the earth going round the sun. Were not Adam and Eve and the family of Noah beginning to look very pale in the light from the New World?

An individual whose work expressed the doubts of ordinary people and helped to give them greater coherence, was the French Calvinist, Isaac de la Peyrère. A man of moderate ability but great sincerity and courage, he published in 1655 a book that was his first and last. The fact that it said something men wished to hear is shown by its immediate popularity in Western Europe. In England it appeared under the title *A Theological Systeme upon that presupposition that Men were before Adam.* Not only did he insist that the newly-discovered lands to east and west could not have been peopled by "Adam's posterity," but his knowledge of such Egyptian and Assyrian history as was available convinced him that these peoples legitimately claimed an antiquity greater than any allowed for in Christian teaching. His evasion of the difficulty was a rather lame one. He declared that "Adam was the first and father of the Jews, not of all men." The Gentiles were left free to establish quite other ancestries.

Peyrère's compromise proved unacceptable to the orthodox. It
wwwwwwwwwwwwww
[4] Garcilasso de la Vega: *The Royal Commentaries of Peru,* translated by Sir Richard Rycaut. London, 1679.

was said to contain ideas "diametrically opposed to the Christian faith." Fabricius calls it "profane and impious," and laments that nevertheless it "in a moment has flown over the Christian world." The author was seized by the Inquisition and his book publicly burnt in Paris; he was forced to renounce both his Pre-adamites and his Calvinism and died in a convent, a mentally battered man.

Another line of investigation bound to come into collision with established orthodoxies was that of the human body and its relationship with other animal bodies. Renaissance artists such as Leonardo da Vinci recovered the Greek delight in the body and closely studied its anatomy. This was unobjectionable, but the brilliant Flemish doctor and anatomist, Vesalius, was soon in trouble. His book, *De humani corporis fabrica* (1543), was based on the dissection of a corpse—that of a Spanish grandee, oddly enough. The Inquisition moved in: Vesalius, the greatest man of medicine since Galen, was condemned to death. His sentence was commuted to exile in Palestine and he was later recalled—only to be drowned on the way back to Italy.

Man was not yet able to look at himself with the fearless detachment possible to the Greeks two thousand years before: above all he must never look at himself as one with the rest of nature. Buffon, the great French naturalist, though no systematizer, did place man among other animals as Aristotle and the Ionians had done. He also began an approach to the evolutionary point of view in saying "the less perfect species, those that were more delicate, heavier, less active or less well armed have already vanished, or will vanish with time." Moreover, study of fossils convinced him that Noah's brief flood could not account for them. Life, he estimated, had already existed for 15,000 years on an earth that was 75,000 years old.

Even at that time, in the mid-eighteenth century, the Comte de Buffon got into trouble with the Roman Catholic Church and had to recant his "heresies" in the following words: "I declare that I had no intention of contradicting the text of scripture: that I most firmly believe all therein related about the Creation, both as to order of time and matter of fact."

Linnaeus, on the other hand, born in the same year as Buffon (1707) but in remote and Protestant Sweden, was unopposed. This first great systematizer of living forms firmly classified man with the rest of the animal kingdom. In the earliest edition of *Systema naturae* he appears among the quadrupeds together with the ape and sloth, but in the tenth edition of this immensely influential book, man, apes, lemurs and bats are classified as primates. Man himself is subdivided as *Homo sapiens, Homo ferus, Homo americanus* and so on, an arrangement which reflects the growing familiarity with the variety of mankind that was a result of the exploration of our globe. Under the auspices of Linnaeus, one of his disciples published a strange picture with four figures in line, ranging from a properly simian orang-utan, through an over-human chimpanzee, to two unfortunate women, one hairy, one tailed— belonging to the type of "monster" then often displayed at fairs. A crude and confused piece of work, but one already suggestive of future illustrations of evolutionary principles.

Geological researches were also leading to conclusions unacceptable to religious orthodoxy—and with them must be included the first tentative beginnings of that early Stone Age archaeology that is closely tied to quaternary geology. Men, of course, always observed fossils in the rocks, but as the Creation story told that earth and water were separated on the Third Day while animals were created only on the Fifth, evidence that there had been life when rocks lay below the sea was contrary to scripture. Some men escaped the dilemma by denying that the fossils had ever been living creatures—they were dismissed as "figured stones," perhaps shaped through the influence of the stars. Others preferred to think that they were accounted for by the Flood, while some Italians, familiar with volcanoes, quite sensibly suggested that they had been thrown up by eruptions.

The extraordinary universal genius of Leonardo contributed also to geology: he ridiculed the idea of figured stones and insisted that fossils had been living creatures and therefore that what is now dry land had once been submarine. It was a Dane by birth, Nicholas Steno, who already in 1669 was able to publish a book demonstrating that many sedimentary rocks with their fossil flora and fauna exactly represented the deposits to be expected in various conditions on the sea bed, and also laying down some of the fundamental laws controlling the stratification of these deposits—laws that were to underlie future archaeological, as well as geological, research.

In the following century the Scottish geologist, James Hutton, was able to demonstrate how the stuff of land surfaces must have been constantly eroded and deposited on ocean beds, only to be raised up once more by some agency, which he assumed to work from the earth's interior. He was well ahead of his time in seeing that the formation of the geological record had been the result of natural processes identical with those still in progress.

Meanwhile the stone implements left by prehistoric man were attracting more attention. Conspicuous types, such as flint arrowheads and Neolithic polished axes, had always caught the eye— indeed a Thracian princess of the fifth century B.C. had made a collection of axes from prehistoric sites and had them buried with her, probably for good luck. Usually they were regarded either as freaks of nature—"thunderbolts"—or were attributed to elves and fairies. As late as the seventeenth century some sadly bogus scientific accounts were given of the formation of axeheads in the sky. However, even before this, Mercati, physician to Pope Clement VIII, was saying that the "thunderbolts" were really the arms of primitive men (the emphasis was always on arms rather than on tools). A little later Sir William Dugdale declared that they were "weapons used by the Britons before the art of making arms of brass or iron was known." Peyrère, too, early champion of the Preadamites, recognized stone artifacts for what they were.

Yet still there was no way of judging the age of implements, or distinguishing those of one age from those of another. An early Palaeolithic hand axe was found as early as about 1690, lying in gravel near Gray's Inn Lane in the City of London (p. 141, I). Nearby were the bones of a fossil elephant—and so there was no difficulty in identifying this discovery with the Emperor Claudius, who had brought over elephants at the time of the Roman Conquest of Britain. Presumably the hand axe was accepted as a weapon of the Britons who had then opposed him. So helplessly was even well-informed opinion still at sea!

About a hundred years later, in 1797, another find of tools of the same kind was interpreted with such intelligence that it might have led to an earlier dawn of prehistory had not the words fallen on prejudiced minds. A modest country antiquary, John Frere, working at Hoxne in Suffolk, unearthed a number of hand axes associated with an extinct fauna in a natural stratum twelve feet below the surface. His claim for their great antiquity, "even beyond that of the present world," based on a study of the geological strata in which they lay, was one of the first demonstrations of true archaeological science (p. 142, I). It passed almost unnoticed.

Gradually the opposing forces of tradition and innovation took shape. In general the traditionalists were obliged to support an intermittent, non-consistent view of the universe, because of the need for divine interventions and the special creation of man. Thus in geology they favoured a series of creations, each with a new, more developed assemblage of species and each brought to a violent end. Many held the account of Noah's Flood in *Genesis* to be an historical record of the most recent of these destructions.

In this scheme of things species were immutable; man, made in the likeness of God and with his soul belonging to a distinct spiritual world, was set apart from the rest of creation. The supporters of this view were known as the Catastrophists or Diluvialists (because of their faith in a series of floods).

The opposing army were called Fluvialists. Although they held various views concerning a possible spiritual world, they saw the material world as uniform and steadily evolving—a concept essential to the development of the natural sciences. They believed that the geological happenings recorded in the rocks were essentially the same as those taking place in their own day, and there was no bar in their thinking against a long history for "Antediluvian Man."

With the whole weight of religious authority and conventional thinking behind them, the Diluvialists were in the ascendancy, but with the beginning of the nineteenth century opposition stiffened as the Fluvialists armed themselves with more and more inconvenient evidence. Battle between Catastrophic Diluvialists and Evolutionary Fluvialists was fully joined.

The authority of the former prevailed long enough both on the Continent and in Britain for many discoveries, which, in fact, proved the great antiquity of man, to be either ignored or carefully misinterpreted. It was a Catholic priest, Father MacEnery, who first found proof that men were on earth at the same time as extinct animals. Excavating in Kent's Cavern, Devon, in 1825, he discovered an unmistakable flint implement in association with the tooth of an extinct rhinoceros—both lying in a stratum securely sealed below a layer of stalagmite. Father MacEnery bravely maintained that this proved the coexistence of man with fossil animals known to be of great antiquity, but the Diluvialists would have none of it. Dean Buckland, the first professor of geology at Oxford, declared that the "Ancient Britons" whose remains had been found in the upper levels in the Cavern, had sunk ovens through the stalagmitic floor and that the flint implement had penetrated through one of these holes. Inevitably, then, when the Dean himself made what was in truth the earliest discovery of a Palaeolithic burial—in a sea cave at Paviland in South Wales (p. 186, I)—he refused to recognize his own good fortune. Again he insisted that it was "clearly not coeval with the antediluvian bones of the extinct species" among which it lay, and dated it to Romano-British times.

The story was much the same on the other side of the Channel. Several cave hunters in the south of France found stone tools or human bones associated with extinct fauna, while at much the same time, in the twenties and thirties, Dr. Schmerling conducted long and arduous excavations in caves near Liége. He unearthed human skulls, flint implements and quantities of animal bones including both rhinoceros and mammoth, and declared: "There can be no doubt that the human bones were buried at the same time and by the same cause as the other extinct species." Yet he was ignored. It was a quarter of a century "before even the neighbouring professors of the University of Liége came forth to vindicate the truthfulness of their indefatigable and clear-sighted countryman," as Sir Charles Lyell was later to write with fine indignation.

Only a few years after Schmerling published his results, knowing, as Lyell said, that they would be "unwelcome intelligence, opposed to the prepossessions of the scientific as well as of the unscientific public," two men began observations in the valley of the Somme that were to play a great part in the final battle over the antiquity and evolution of man. In about the year 1835, a dredger working in the river on the outskirts of Abbeville hauled up ancient animal bones and various unmistakable stone implements. These, and particularly an axe in an antler haft, stirred the imagination of Jacques Boucher de Perthes, chief Customs Officer of the town and President of the local *Société d'Émulation*. The finds drew him closer to Dr. Casimir Picard, a young doctor who had not only made serious palaeontological studies at Abbeville, but had also distinguished two stone-using periods, one in which the flints were chipped, and one in which flint or stone was polished. Picard encouraged his patron the Customs Officer to pursue his new scientific interests, and the two worked together until Picard's early death in 1841. Boucher de Perthes now continued alone, and before long was rewarded by himself making a discovery which convinced him that he had proof of the existence of Antediluvian man. In excavations made for a hospital, he took from the same stratum three (as we now know) Palaeolithic hand axes and a chunk of molar tooth of a species of elephant. Yet when he wrote his *Antiquités celtiques et antédiluviennes* and in 1846 submitted it to the Institut de France, asking them to send down a committee of enquiry, his work was treated with scepticism. In particular the geologist Élie de Beaumont used all his influence against the unknown provincial Customs Officer, denying that man could have lived in France at the same time as elephants, and claiming that the flint implements from Abbeville were of Roman date.

The other eminent French scientist who stubbornly maintained the Diluvialist case against all evidence was Cuvier—a great comparative anatomist and in many ways an admirable man, but one who had allowed "prepossessions" to smother his scientific spirit. He died in 1832, but his influence remained.

So the thirties and forties saw a pause in the flow of European thought. The Diluvialists had thrown up a dam (the metaphor is appropriate) that held for a time, in spite of the growing pressure of the evidence piling up behind it. Meanwhile, however, very real progress was being made in archaeological research of a kind which did not rouse immediate theological opposition, but which in the end was to contribute to its overthrow. In England, country antiquaries were emerging from the greatest excesses of Romanticism; in Wiltshire, particularly, a region immensely rich in field monuments, Cunnington and Sir Richard Colt Hoare were excavating many hundreds of barrows and attempting to classify them. Widespread interest is proved by such features as Roach Smith's "Antiquarian Notes" in the *Gentleman's Magazine*. Even textbooks of a kind were appearing, notably *Fosbrooke's Encyclopaedia of Antiquities and Elements of Archaeology*, published in 1822-3. Yet still the pre-Roman period was a blur of "Ancient Britons." No one knew whether any particular prehistoric object or monument dated from ten or a thousand years before the Roman Conquest. Colt Hoare himself, in his huge, sumptuous and well-ordered *History of Ancient Wiltshire* (1810-21), lamented that after ten years' work there was still "total ignorance as to the authors of these sepulchral memorials; we have evidence of the very high antiquity of our Wiltshire barrows, but none respecting the tribes to whom they appertained that can rest on solid foundations."

The means by which archaeologists were to advance from "total ignorance" of prehistory to the remarkable knowledge of today were first established in Denmark. Linnaeus had begun to bring order out of the bewildering array of plant and animal species, and now other Scandinavians were to do the same great service for prehistoric antiquities. Several Danes were involved in the work, but much of the credit goes to C. J. Thomsen. Denmark is rich in conspicuous prehistoric monuments and in marvellously well preserved antiquities from her bogs. Moreover, as her recorded history begins only in the tenth century, there was an added incentive to try to learn more of the national past. As early as 1807, the Government set up a Royal Committee for the Preservation and Collection of National Antiquities, and this body was charged to form and popularize a national museum. Thomsen succeeded to the secretaryship of the Committee in 1816 and became the first curator of the Museum in the same year, a post he held until 1865. Immediately he set to work to sort out the mass of antiquities and "curiosities" which were housed in the University Library at Copenhagen. When the doors were opened to the public in 1819 they found the collection clearly arranged on what has now become so familiar as the Three Age System—that is to say, all objects were assigned to the age of Stone, Brass (Bronze) or Iron in a recognized chronological sequence.

It is perfectly true that antiquaries were familiar from the classical authors with the idea of such Ages, and that many, like Dugdale, had long ago referred to stone implements as having been made "before the art of making arms of Brass or of Iron was known." Nevertheless this was largely theoretical, had never been used for a hard and fast classification of actual antiquities, remaining essentially an idea rather than a classificatory system. With Thomsen and his pupil and successor, Worsaae, it was quite otherwise.

Their Three Ages were based on observation of what objects were found together, and even, on occasion, of stratification—which types were regularly found above or below others. Also the Danes used the method with a proper historical sense, observing, for example, that bronze equipment seemed to appear so abruptly that it must indicate some kind of foreign influx. Even their attempts to estimate precise dates were not very wide of the mark. They were also led in time to a study of typology—the classification of objects by the evolution of their forms—which was to prove perhaps the second most valuable method after stratification for the gradual piecing together of a chronological framework for prehistory. The acceptance of the Three Age system had an effect like the sudden discovery of a map by travellers lost in unknown country. The Danes—and the Swedes, Norwegians and Germans who soon followed their lead—became immediately purposeful; they could see their way now out of that wilderness of "total ignorance."

The first full exposition of the new system was not published until 1836, in a guide book written by Thomsen for the museum at Copenhagen which, by this time, had outgrown the University library and was housed in the Christianborg Palace with a separate room allotted to each Age. Half a dozen years later it was further elaborated in Worsaae's famous *Danmark's Oldtid,* soon bringing light also to England where it was published in 1849 as *The Primeval Antiquities of Denmark.* So, by the middle of the century, the archaeological means for the recall of the prehistoric past had been established and were ready for use in interpreting the remoter periods of prehistory as soon as these had been theologically and scientifically allowed to exist. Together with all the discoveries of the previous decades and the ferment of ideas that accompanied them, they were in fact awaiting the release of the powerful breakthrough that was to have its *annus mirabilis* in 1859.

The main impetus was to come from England. There, while many geologists remained attached to the Diluvialist cause and were still quite capable of supporting it with books and papers such as Hugh Miller's *Footprints of the Creator* and *Geological Evidence in Favour of Revealed Religion,* Sir Charles Lyell and his associates were building up the case of the Fluvialists. In his *Principles of Geology,* Lyell set out clearly and comprehensively his conviction that past geological agencies were essentially identical to, and continuous with, those operating in the modern world, and this uniformitarianism had since been further developed. So the geologists prepared the way for the Palaeolithic archaeologists.

In 1846 excavations were reopened at Kent's Cavern under the direction of William Pengelly; although he confirmed MacEnery's findings that flint implements were contemporary with the bones of the late Pleistocene (Ice Age) animals, the evidence of the Cavern still remained suspect. Then, in 1858, quarrying above Brixham harbour in Yorkshire exposed a number of small caves. There could be no question of these having been disturbed, and a distinguished committee, including both Lyell and Prestwich, was set up to sponsor excavations. Again Pengelly was chosen as director. By extraordinary good fortune this work at the Windmill Hill cave, Brixham, almost a test case for the Fluvialists, met with immediate success. The fossilized bones of lion, mammoth, rhinoceros, reindeer and other Pleistocene fauna lay *on* and *within* a three-inch bed of stalagmite; *beneath* it cave earth contained flints unmistakably shaped by man. No Romano-British "ovens" offered a bolt hole for the Diluvialists. Brixham convinced all those whose minds were accessible to argument.

On the terraces of the Somme science had not stood still either. Boucher de Perthes himself had poured out further publications— of varying quality—and had made one considerable convert. A Dr. Rigollot, an amateur archaeologist of Amiens, had gone to Abbeville to mock, but had stayed to be convinced by what Boucher de Perthes showed him. On his return home, he dug in the gravel pits of the suburb of St Acheul and found implements comparable to those of Abbeville—and again in association with such creatures as rhinoceros and hippopotamus. (Because of the pioneer work of these two men in the Somme valley the names Abbevillian and Acheulian have been given to two of the earliest cultural phases of the Lower Palaeolithic period (p. 139, I), and are now current throughout the world.)

In 1858 Dr. Hugh Falconer, a distinguished English palaeontologist and member of the Brixham Committee, called on Boucher de Perthes on his way to Italy, was impressed by what he saw and on his return to England persuaded Joseph Prestwich to go to inspect the evidence of the Somme gravels for himself. In April of 1859, when Pengelly was still digging at Brixham, Prestwich and John Evans, then a young archaeologist mainly interested in British coins, went to Amiens and Abbeville (p. 147, I). They found the contemporaneity of the early fauna and worked flint implements proved beyond reasonable doubt, and Prestwich immediately threw the whole of his authority into convincing the learned and scientific world. On May 26th he read a paper to the Royal Society with the title "On the Occurrence of Flint Implements, associated with the Remains of Animals of Extinct Species in beds of late Geological Period at Amiens and Abbeville and in England at Hoxne." Prestwich described how the discoveries at Kent's Cavern, Brixham, and now at Abbeville had convinced him of the immense antiquity of man—and was remarkably quick in recalling Frere's long-forgotten finds at Hoxne. Sitting before him at this historic meeting were Lyell, Murchison, Huxley and Faraday. The next month John Evans spoke on the flint implements before the Society of Antiquaries, and later in the summer Sir Charles Lyell, who happened that year to be president of the anthropological section of the British Association, announced in his presidential address that he was "fully prepared to corroborate the conclusions . . . recently laid before the Royal Society by Mr. Prestwich."

In Britain almost the whole scientific world was carried by storm, but in France the dyed-in-the-wool Diluvialists still held out a little longer from the stronghold of the Academy of Science. In 1863 the stubborn Élie de Beaumont said "I do not believe that the human species was contemporaneous with *Elephas primigenius* [mammoth]. In this respect I continue to share M. Cuvier's opinion." It so happened that very shortly afterwards the matter was clinched in an unexpected manner. Lartet, digging in the La Madeleine cave in the Dordogne, found the portrait of a mammoth engraved by a Palaeolithic artist on a mammoth tusk.

It is one of the most remarkable chances in the history of science that Charles Darwin's *Origin of Species* should have been published in 1859, the year of Prestwich's paper to the Royal Society and of the conclusive excavations at Brixham. The geologists and archaeologists had produced incontrovertible material evidence of the presence of man on earth at a then incalculably remote period at the very moment when Darwin published his great biological concept which theoretically demanded a great antiquity for man. It was a perfect piece of scientific dovetailing.

Ideas concerning evolution had, of course, a long history before the appearance of the *Origin of Species*. Even those theorists, however, who were not tied by faith in one or more divine creations, were inclined to believe in the immutability of species. Sir Charles Lyell, whose *Principles of Geology* was in fact one of the two books that set Darwin on his path, and who, as T. H. Huxley said, "was the chief agent in smoothing the road for Darwin" because his uniformitarianism implied organic as well as inorganic evolution, opposed the transmutation of species until converted at last by the *Origin*. Lamarck, on the other hand, had believed there to be no fixity of species but a more or less continuous organic flux in response to changing environment.

Darwin's great importance was due in part to the firmness and clarity with which he set out his general principles, and the many years of minutely detailed study of living and fossil forms that lay behind them, and in part to his brilliant demonstration of natural selection as the means by which the evolution of species could be brought about. The full title of his great book, it should be remembered, is *Origin of Species by Means of Natural Selection or the Preservation of Favoured Races in the Struggle for Life*—a description which makes clear his debt to Malthus. Huxley, who had refused hitherto to accept evolution because he saw that Lamarck and others had failed to show *how* it could come about, was immediately won over by the doctrine of natural selection. He became, as he put it, "Darwin's bulldog."

It is a well known story how Darwin was working infinitely slowly on his evolutionary theory (which he had first set out in two manuscript outlines as early as 1842 and '44) when in the early summer of 1858 the post brought him a manuscript essay from A. R. Wallace, then in the Malay Archipelago. It expressed a theory of the origin of species identical with his own. Writing that same day to Lyell he declared: "I never saw a more striking coincidence; if Wallace had my manuscript sketch written out in 1842, he could not have made a better short abstract!" Poor Darwin! With his extreme moral scrupulousness, he thought it might be wrong to hurry out any statement of his own simply because he had discovered that Wallace was in the field. "It seems hard on me that I should be thus compelled to lose my priority of many years' standing, but I cannot feel at all sure that this alters the justice of the case. First impressions are generally right, and I at first thought it would be dishonourable in me now to publish." However, he was prevailed on to leave the decision to Lyell and other friends. They arranged that, at a meeting of the Linnean Society on July 1st, Wallace's essay should be read simultaneously with a paper by Darwin which included passages from the sketch of 1842. Darwin himself then began work on the *Origin*—which he always regarded as an extract from the massive publication of his researches that he had originally intended. The whole of the first edition was sold on the day of issue, and the public impact was immense. There is no doubt that the bolt from the Malayan blue was a very fortunate one.

Wallace made no allusion whatever to man's role in his scheme. Darwin, who had from the first recognized that *Homo sapiens* must take his evolutionary place among other species, did not deal with the subject in the *Origin,* except to say, "in order that no honourable man might accuse" him of concealing his views, that through a comparative study of the apes "light would be thrown on the origin of man and his history."

This delicacy of approach appears to have made no difference to the public reaction; it was recognized immediately that the creation of the Sixth Day was threatened along with the rest. The *Origin* received some very hostile reviews, and the struggle was intense. The famous clash between Huxley and Bishop Wilberforce, when Disraeli intervened to say that if the choice of ancestors lay between apes and angels, he "was on the side of the angels," took place as early as 1860. (On the other hand Paul Broca said *"j'aimerais mieux être un singe perfectionné qu'un Adam dégón- éré."*) Richard Owen, the leading British comparative anatomist, who had shown some sympathy with Darwinism, could not stand against "the wrath of fashionable orthodoxy" when it was applied to humanity. He announced that man was differentiated from all other animals by the structure of his brain. This distortion roused the intellectual ire of Huxley, who dealt with it in his *Man's Place in Nature*, published in 1863 (p. 161, I). In this widely-read book, Huxley was able to include an account of the Neanderthal skull which had been found a few years before, but had been dismissed by some authorities as that of a congenital idiot. He accepted it as representing the most ape-like known human, pronouncing it to be "more nearly allied to the higher apes than the latter are to the lower." What Carlyle called the "monkey damnification" was complete.

While attacks on Darwinism were fervently maintained in some quarters, the general principles of evolution were well-suited to Victorian scientific optimism. *Homo sapiens* was obviously in the van of universal progress. More unfortunately, the idea of the survival of the fittest was used by some to justify war.

It is a remarkable manifestation of the endless adaptability of the English Establishment, that Lyell, Prestwich and Darwin, three men who did so much to discredit the Mosaic cosmogony and con- found the conventional, were all knighted and all buried in West- minster Abbey.

The great year 1859 can be taken as marking the beginning of the age of archaeological science. Man's simian ancestry was accepted, together with his immense antiquity as a tool-maker. The Three Age system was there as a basis for historical inter- pretation, while stratification and typology had become established methods, and even excavation was improving a little. Archaeolo- gists had been given the temporal space to work in, and the right tools for the reconstruction of man's forgotten history. The next century was to see that reconstruction accomplished with a range and precision which would then have appeared incredible.

Lost Civilizations

During the last phase of the struggle for "Antediluvian Man" there was a simultaneous development in the non-controversial explor- ation of past civilizations. Indeed, although both to some extent relied on excavation and might be seen by the broadminded to have

a single purpose—the recovery of man's past—these two wings of
archaeology, the scientific investigation of origins, and the scholarly and humanistic appreciation of advanced cultures, appeared at
this time to be almost in opposition. The centre of interest for the
humanists had shifted from the Mediterranean of the classical
world to the great valley of the Two Rivers—the Mesopotamia
which we now have to call Iraq; also, though less strongly, to the
Nile Valley, which the cracking of the secret of hieroglyphs had now
brought within the range of history.

This change meant that exploration was focused on regions
involved in Hebrew history—the "lands of the Bible." There is no
doubt that as biblical cities, and texts related to biblical accounts,
were found and identified, many naive and worried people saw
them as opposing the unwelcome advances of the evolutionists.
For those who did not want to distinguish between the religious
myths of south-west Asia and the history of the Hebrew people, the
discoveries in Mesopotamia and Egypt quite simply "proved the
Bible to be true." So the work of the explorers was followed with a
supercharged interest and concern.

Mesopotamia presents unusual conditions for archaeological
excavation. From the hot, dead flat plain of the lower valley which
was the land of the Sumerians and Babylonians, to the cooler,
mountain-lined upper valley which was the land of the Assyrians,
the sites of ancient cities are marked by huge mounds or *tells*.
Owing to the practice of building with sun-dried bricks that quickly
disintegrate and have to be renewed, long inhabited cities rose
higher and higher above ground level, each new building standing
on the ruins of its predecessor. In addition to these unintentionally
formed mounds, most cities possessed one or more temple mounds
or *ziggurats*, artificial mountains built as religious "high places."
(One of these is well know to us as the Tower of Babel.) Large
artificial platforms were also sometimes built for temples and
palaces. So today the cities present to the excavator masses of grey,
compacted dust that are as intimidating in their colossal bulk as
they are depressing in texture and appearance. Nevertheless with
skill and patience it is possible to detect and expose the mud-brick
walls, while the age-long accumulation of deposits offers a stratigraphical book that can be read back through the millennia to the
first foundations of the city.

In the later Assyrian capitals, moreover, the architects, dissatis-
fied with mud and painted stucco, introduced huge slabs of stone
to line the walls and façades of ceremonial buildings, enriching
them with sculpture and inscriptions. It was these alien stones,
completely embedded as they were in the disintegrated mud-brick,
that roused the excitement of the first excavators.

Jewish and Arab tradition had preserved the belief that the series

of mounds and embankments rising from the dead flat landscape
beside the Euphrates near Hilla marked the site of the fabled
Babylon, and the comparable group far away to the north across
the Tigris from Mosul, the site of Nineveh. Already by the end of
the eighteenth century the Pope's Vicar-General in Babylonia, the
Abbe Beaumont, had taken cuneiform-inscribed bricks from the
first site, and the East India Company had commissioned their man
in Basrah to acquire some more. But it was not until the Company
opened a Residency in Baghdad, and in 1808 made a remarkable
young man called Claudius Rich the British Resident there, that
any serious work was done. Rich was one of those human beings
born with a prodigious gift of tongues, and already as a lad in
Bristol his particular interest had been focused on Oriental languages. Because of his attainments he was taken to see the collection of Arabic and Persian manuscripts belonging to the scholar of
Persian, Charles Fox. The boy was delighted with the beautiful
flowing scripts, and Fox was delighted with the intelligent boy; as
a result Claudius became his pupil in Turkish, Arabic and Persian.
The story goes that on meeting a stranger on the hills above Bristol
who proved to be a shipwrecked Turk, young Rich was soon in
fluent conversation with him. During his Residency in Baghdad,
the country was in a most unsettled state, and this together with
his work for the Company made the pursuit of archaeology difficult.
Nevertheless, from the first he took a keen interest and amassed a
considerable collection of manuscripts and antiquities that afterwards went to the British Museum. His first expedition to Babylon
was made in 1811 (p. 324, I). Anyone who has made the journey
in an hour or two along the excellent if dreary motor road may be
surprised that it took the Rich family two days, and that they were
attended by a troop of Hussars, sepoys, a galloper gun and seventy
baggage mules.

Once arrived at Hilla, however, they stayed long enough for
Claudius to make a thorough survey of all the mounds—and the
next year he published his famous *Memoir on the Ruins of
Babylon* (p. 324, I). This, together with a later sequel, roused intense interest and certainly gave the first impetus to the advance of
Mesopotamian archaeology. They even found a place in Byron's
Don Juan: "Though Claudius Rich Esquire, some bricks has got,
and written lately two memoirs upon't." Rich also firmly accepted
the mounds at Mosul as the ruins of Nineveh—which makes it the
more surprising that there was subsequent confusion over this
identification.

The most direct result of Rich's publications was to prompt the
French authorities to appoint a consular agent at Mosul especially
charged to excavate in the local ruins. The man chosen to be the

first excavator of a Mesopotamian *tell* was Paul Emile Botta, a
naturalist and son of an historian. Among the medley of large
mounds to be seen from Mosul across the turbid waters of the
Tigris, those known as Kuyunjik and Nebi Yunus were the largest.
When in 1842 Botta was ready to dig, he at first selected the
latter mound, which is crowned by a Moslem shrine known as the
Tomb of Jonah. Religious opposition was so strong that he had to
transfer to Kuyunjik. He worked there that year and part of the
next without much success, and hearing of sculptured stones turning up at Khorsabad some fourteen miles to the south, he determined to try his luck there instead. Almost at once his trenches
struck what was in fact the palace of the eighth century B.C.
Assyrian king, Sargon II, in his capital of Dur Sharrukin, and he was
uncovering slabs with bas reliefs and cuneiform inscriptions (p.
317, I). With remarkable lack of logic for a Frenchman, he immediately assumed that this rewarding mound, and not those at
Mosul, must be the site of Nineveh. He sent a dispatch to Paris,
"Ninève est retrouvé."

In France enthusiasm was at once aroused by Botta's discoveries,
and especially by the sculptured slabs, magnificent examples of a
hitherto almost unknown art. Money and help were forthcoming
from the Government for continued excavations, and later for the
publication of the five fine volumes of *Monument de Ninève*. Here,
as so often before and since, there was a sad contrast between the
whole-hearted support which Botta won from his government and
the meanness of official British support for an extraordinary young
Englishman who now appeared on the Assyrian scene.

This was Austen Henry Layard. With a cosmopolitan upbringing
and a dashing temperament, he had found reading law in London
an intolerable bore. He accepted the offer of a job in Ceylon. To
satisfy as far as possible a craving for the Orient nourished by
much reading (which included Rich's still seminal *Memoirs*), he
determined to make his way to India by an overland route that
would take him *via* Baghdad through Central Asia. After preparing
themselves rather sketchily by learning a little Persian and Arabic,
and less navigation and medicine, Layard and a friend left England
in 1839. In Central Europe Layard suffered the acute gastritis well
known to all northerners travelling on the cheap, but after his
recovery made his adventurous excursion to Petra (p. 310, I), was
several times robbed, and at last tramped up to the British Consulate in Damascus penniless and stripped of his clothes. (Nearly
forty years later he was to return with all the pomp of an ambassador.) The two Englishmen now went on to Mosul, where Layard
responded with his quick, intuitive imagination to the strange
Assyrian countryside, and had his first view of the *tells* of Nineveh,

Nimrûd and Ashur where his excavations, then unthought, of were so soon to make him famous (p. 293, I).

They sailed down the Tigris to Baghdad, then resumed their journey to India with Layard in Persian dress, his crown shaved and his remaining hair and beard "dyed a deep shining black with henna and rang." But the lure of some of the wildest regions of Persia, together with a persistent interest in the archaeological possibilities of the Mesopotamian *tells*, made him decide to abandon his Indian prospects. He spent the next year or two in further dangerous travel—and indeed was within an instant of being speared to death near Babylon when some Arabs mistook him for a Turk. But for the intervention of a young sheikh, Victorian archaeology would have been deprived of one of its most picturesque and successful figures.

Because by this time Henry Layard had gained an extraordinary insight into the subtle entanglements of Middle Eastern politics, he worked for some time with Sir Stratford Canning, British Ambassador to the Sublime Porte at Istanbul. Luckily, however, he was not immediately swallowed by the diplomatic service, but was, on the contrary, set up by Canning as an archaeologist. In 1845 the Ambassador agreed to finance trial excavations in Assyria, both men having been stirred by Botta's reports from Khorsabad. Layard hurried off to Mosul, and started digging on a very modest scale just three years after Botta's first cut at Kuyunjik.

The site he chose was Nimrûd, about twenty miles down river from Mosul. The Assyrian kings frequently shifted the capital of their powerful, militaristic empire, which is partly why there were so many city mounds to confuse the pioneers of archaeology. Ashur (Qal'at Sharqat) was the earliest, then Nimrûd (the biblical Calah), and after them the more famous Nineveh and Dur Sharrukin. All through his first period of excavation at Nimrûd, Layard was convinced that he was on the site of Nineveh, and so we have the curious situation that both his best-selling work, *Nineveh and its Ruins,* and Botta's *Monuments de Ninève* expressed wrong identifications, while the real site of the famous capital, Kuyunjik, Nebi Yunus and the other mounds at Mosul, was temporarily neglected.

At Nimrûd, Layard almost immediately came upon royal palaces, and during his time there between 1845 and 1847 he extracted the Black Obelisk of Shalmaneser III with its references to Biblical characters, many magnificent bas-reliefs which had lined the chambers of mud-brick palaces, and the great man-headed winged bulls and lions which had guarded their portals. He also began to find the exquisite Nimrûd ivories—to be won in even larger quantities by Max Mallowan over a century later. His first dispatch of antiquities arrived at the British Museum in 1848, but in a somewhat disordered state. While the cases lay on the quay at Bombay, inquisitive members of the British community had opened them, examined the finds, and apparently kept a few of them. An enterprising clergyman had taken squeezes of the Black Obelisk and used them for a lecture. There was a scandal, and thereafter the Bombay authorities saw to it that all consignments for the British Museum were forwarded with unusual speed.

Before he left for England, Layard sampled the Ashur *tell* but left it in disappointment—for the reason, as we now know, that this first capital of the Assyrians had been deserted before the royal architects had begun to incorporate stone sculpture. Layard's crude digging hacked through the mud-brick walls without detecting them, as was shown over fifty years later when Ashur was systematically excavated by a German expedition. He spent the last of his meagre funds (which he was now receiving through the British Museum) on making a sounding at Kuyunjik, the real Nineveh. Here he came to realize that Botta had failed because, unlike the other Assyrian *tells*, this one was buried below later deposits. He dug deeply enough to strike the palace of Sennacherib, which later was to yield rich spoils.

Back in England, the exhibition of the sculptures and inscriptions from Nimrûd, together with the publication of *Nineveh and its Remains*, brought Layard to a pinnacle of fame. He was heaped with public and academic honours, but the British Treasury displayed its customary parsimony towards culture and refused sufficient money for worthy publication, while for himself, as he wryly observed, "As a reward for my various services and for my discoveries, I was appointed an unpaid attaché of Her Majesty's Embassy at Constantinople."

Nevertheless, just enough cash was extracted to provide for a second expedition from 1849-51. Layard now concentrated mainly on Kuyunjik, where in the palace of Sennacherib he came upon the King's Library, two large chambers piled to the depth of a foot or more with cuneiform tablets. When, a few years later, his assistant, Hormuzd Rassam, found what appears to be the remainder of the royal archive in the library of Sennacherib's grandson, Ashurbanipal, the total reached about 24,000 tablets—for the future historian an all but inexhaustible store of Assyrian literature, mythology, science and state affairs. Layard also did some more work at Nimrûd, sampled several other *tells* in the Mosul area, and went south to try his luck at Babylon and Nippur, but he had not the patience, technique nor funds to tackle these vast accumulations of brick and mud-brick ruins. Here was the end of this attractive man's archaeological career. The adventurous lover of the then "mysterious Orient," who had so often been robbed and beaten, who had gone in romantic attire, or barefoot and in rags, and who had roused the whole world with the drama of his discoveries, went home to become, as Sir Henry Layard, an M.P., an Ambassador, and even for a time Under Secretary of State for Foreign Affairs.

Layard had been more a seeker for portable antiquities than an excavator in the modern sense. Partly because he was above all interested in winning museum exhibits, partly because of his impatient temperament, but most of all because of the absurd inadequacy of his funds, his ways of digging were bad even for his time. They might, indeed, be likened to those of a mole. Often he resorted to tunnelling through palaces and temples, following the stone slab walling and leaving the centre of each room entirely unexplored. When, in semi-darkness and without the help of trained draughtsmen, he had copied the sculptures and inscriptions, he filled up his trenches with rubbish from subsequent cuttings, thus preparing a terrible hotchpotch for his successors. Layard himself was apologetic concerning these makeshifts forced upon him by "the smallness of the sum placed at my disposal." No wonder that archaeologists of the next generation were sharply critical; Hermann Hilprecht, director of an American mission excavating in Babylonia towards the end of the century, wrote, "He was thus practically prevented by his own government from making a methodical exploration of Nimrûd. And this lack of method, system and thoroughness unfortunately remained a characteristic feature of most of the following English excavations in Assyrian and Babylonian ruins—a lack felt by nobody more keenly than by Layard, Loftus, and all the other great British explorers."

Quite apart from crudities in excavation, the Mesopotamia of the mid-nineteenth century was hardly ready for archaeology. Again and again Botta, Layard and others were in serious trouble with upstart rulers who tried to boycott their work. Packing and transport of antiquities was primitive. One of Botta's huge bulls from Khorsabad was abandoned on the road to Mosul owing to the collapse of the trolley, and was burnt for gypsum by the local villagers. One of Layard's bulls, the cart having stuck and been left overnight, was damaged by rifle fire from robbers, while a lion was cracked during loading and finally broke in two. Even when the crated antiquities reached the river they were still in danger. More than one consignment went to the bottom, by far the worst disaster of this kind occurring at Kurnah at the head of the Shatt-al-Arab in 1855. Boats and rafts carrying a very large consignment from various Assyrian and Babylonian sites, including two hundred and forty cases from Khorsabad and Nineveh, were deliberately capsized by Arab brigands. This terrible loss is the main cause of the Louvre's relatively poor collection of Assyrian sculpture.

One profoundly important change had taken place between Layard's first and second expeditions: a rapid development in the ability to read cuneiform. It is surprising to recall that when Layard first started to dig he had no notion what inscribed tablets were, referring to them as "bits of pottery decorated in an unusual manner." Yet by the time he lighted upon the King's Library they could be adequately translated. The man who more than any other unlocked this door into a new mansion of human history was Henry Creswicke Rawlinson.

Like Claudius Rich, Rawlinson spent much of his boyhood in Bristol and started on his career with a cadetship in the East India Company. But unlike Rich (who was probably illegitimate) he had a well-to-do father, owner of a Derby winner, while the aunt with whom he lived in Bristol belonged to a distinguished literary circle. On the other hand young Rawlinson did not show precocious linguistic ability, and when posted to India had no knowledge of oriental languages and enjoyed the life of a high-spirited, horse-mad subaltern. Indeed, as he himself records, he "was distinguished in all athletic amusements," and in 1832, while at Poona, he offered "to compete with any rival for a stake of £100, in running, jumping, quoits, racquets, billiards, pigeon-shooting, pig-sticking, steeplechasing, chess and games of skill at cards." He also won a wager by riding seventy-two miles in under four hours.

Yet with the extraordinary vitality and versatility of so many Victorians, this hearty young man also found time to learn two Indian languages and make a serious study of Persian—his interest having apparently been aroused by a friendship he had made, during the long voyage out, with Sir John Malcolm, governor of Bombay and an historian of Persia. He was able to start his own career as an orientalist when a few years later he was sent on a military mission to the Shah. Mr. Seton Lloyd gives a clear account of the early steps in the "cracking" of cuneiform and Rawlinson's part in it (p. 382, I). In 1843 he was delighted to be able to step once again into Claudius Rich's footsteps when he was offered the Residency at Baghdad. Two years later, fresh from his first triumphant season at Nimrûd, Layard spent Christmas with him at the Residency, and these two gifted men quickly made friends—an intimacy which was to prove invaluable when Layard began to find quantities of tablets and inscriptions.

Rawlinson had reached the height of his fame and influence when he returned to Baghdad in 1851 after the publication of *On the Babylonian Translation of the great Persian Inscription at Behistun*. The exuberant young subaltern had by now matured into a formidable personality. Many years later an elderly official told an English visitor in Baghdad how "towards the end of his time here had he taken one dog and put his English hat on his head and sent him to the Sarai, all the people in the bazaar would have made way for him, and bowed to him, and the soldiers would have stood still and presented arms to him as he passed, and the official in the Sarai would have embraced him; and if he had sent another dog with another of his hats across the river to Kazimen, the Shi'ites and the Sunnites would have stopped fighting each other and would have asked him to drink coffee with them."

Unhappily, however, despite this truly extraordinary authority, Rawlinson was not able to impose seemly, let alone scientific, order upon the conduct of excavations, which became his responsibility upon Layard's withdrawal. The Assyrian scene was marred by disgraceful rivalries between Victor Place, the French successor to Botta, and Rassam, a Mosul-born British subject who had to some extent taken Layard's place. Rassam was sometimes little more than an archaeological freebooter, sending gangs of workmen all over the country to likely mounds, to tunnel after museum loot. On sites where the French had concessions there was bound to be trouble—indeed there was an actual battle amid the ruins of Ashur. Still more serious was the contention at Nineveh itself. Rawlinson did his best to lay down a boundary between the French and English concessions at Kuyunjik, but the unscrupulous Rassam went so far as to send across a gang to work secretly at night in the French sector. In this way he found the palace of Ashurbanipal, and when Place most generously conceded it to him, excavated this wonderful treasure house of historical documents and works of art in a peculiarly brutal manner. The famous lion hunt reliefs, now in the British Museum, were whipped out, but little beyond sculpture and tablets was thought worth keeping. No proper records were kept either.

One happy incident was to issue from this deplorable affair. Among the mass of tablets in the lion-hunt gallery were those inscribed with the Assyrian account of the Deluge. They were first identified by George Smith, an ex-banknote engraver who had been recruited to the British Museum and proved to possess an unusual talent for decipherment. Toiling over the endless jigsaw puzzles presented by the Nineveh tablets, he describes how "my eye caught the statement that the ship rested on the mountains of Nizir, followed by the account of the sending forth of the dove." The story of how Smith went out to seek the missing portion of the Deluge story and found it almost immediately (p. 385, I) is one of the best known and most astonishing in the history of archaeology. (It is perhaps less well known that poor George Smith died of dysentery a few years later, seemingly the first archaeologist to meet his death in the field).

Meanwhile, during the archaeological war of Rassam and Place in Assyria, some tentative investigations were being made far away to the south in Babylonia. This region of fertile alluvium at the head of the Persian Gulf had been drained and cultivated by the Sumerians, and brought to a high pitch of prosperity under the Babylonians. But it is a land that can be maintained only by energy and organization, and long before the nineteenth century it had relapsed into marshy misery. At the end of 1849, two Englishmen resolved to ride across deserts and marshes from the Euphrates to the Tigris. To their astonishment, Loftus and Churchill saw all about them signs of former prosperity—the marks of intensive cultivation and hardly numerable city mounds. Among these *tells* were those afterwards identified as Ur, Nippur and Erech. Loftus himself got permission to dig at Erech (the modern name is Warka), and although his puny efforts could not achieve much against so vast a ruin, he did discover, in addition to much later material, a wall ornamented with coloured terra cotta cones, which, although he did not dream of it at the time, had been built by the Sumerians of the fourth millennium B.C.

Later both Loftus and J. E. Taylor, English Vice-Consul at Basrah, took soundings in a number of mounds which were chiefly made notable by their collaboration with Rawlinson. "The Father of Cuneiform" examined their finds and was able to identify no fewer than three cities: Larsa (Ellarsar of the Bible), Ur and Eridu. A French expedition was also in Babylonia at this time digging at Babylon itself and at Kish. They were not very successful—and suffered a final blow when all the finds they had made were lost in the Kurnah disaster.

After this year, 1855, the Crimean War caused a lull in archaeological activity in Mesopotamia. It was just as well, for the splendour of the great pioneer days of Botta and Layard had quickly tarnished. Not only did their immediate successors fail to improve on their methods, they tended to slide into worse ones and to become more openly avaricious. A comparison between these activities and some of the work being done at this time in Europe shows how far the "humanistic" wing of archaeology was behind the scientific so far as technique was concerned. The discoveries in Assyria and Babylonia were made largely by men interested in art and languages, and followed by kindred spirits—and even more enthusiastically by all those eager to find confirmation of Bible history. The discoveries in the caves, bogs and gravels of Europe, on the other hand, were made by men directly under the discipline of geology and biology and in general dedicated to the scientific ideals of exact observation of detail, measurement and the inductive method. Their success against the defenders of the literal truth of a Bronze Age mythology was inevitable. Yet no one can question the extraordinary abilities of the men who first revealed something of the real nature of Assyrian and Babylonian civilization to the modern world, nor deny that the brilliance, versatility, courage and charm of men such as Layard and Rawlinson gave a special quality to their work and made theirs one of the most enthralling chapters in the history of archaeology.

When excavation began to increase once more in the 1870's, methods had hardly improved but there had been a significant gain in understanding of the early history of Babylonia. Jules Oppert, a member of the unsuccessful French expedition to Kish and Babylon, had brilliantly deduced the existence of a very ancient, pre-Akkadian people speaking a non-Semitic language, whom he rightly identified with the Sumerians. (Many inscriptions had been found to refer to rulers of "Sumer and Akkad," and the Akkadians had been recognized as the first Semites in the valley.) The work of the later decades of the nineteenth century was mainly distinguished for beginning the recall of this completely forgotten civilization. The process of probing further and further back into the origins of civilization in the Middle East has continued ever since, culminating in the astonishing discoveries at Jericho (p. 251, I).

Unfortunately Rassam returned among the first post-Crimean swallows and continued his dubious treasure hunting for the British Museum. There were more scuffles, and at Telloh he made a raid against the French comparable to his escapade at Kuyunjik. He did, however, secure some remarkable finds, including the bronze gates of Shalmaneser II, now an ornament of the London collections, and identified the city of Sippar by means of the famous Sun God tablet of King Nabu-apal-idinna.

The excavation which did most to reveal the Sumerians was that of the Frenchman, Ernest de Sarzec, at Telloh. This site, on the Shatt-al-Hai canal, was recommended to de Sarzec, the French Vice-Consul at Basrah, by an Arabian dealer in antiquities who knew it as a source of stone statuettes. De Sarzec dug there intermittently from 1877 to 1900, proving it to be the site of ancient Lagash. Not only did he find many of the promised statuettes, most of which portrayed governors of the city during the third millennium B.C., but he also laid bare much of the city itself. Even if his methods were far from systematic, he was the first Mesopotamian archaeologist to make an effort to explore the greater part of a city. A fellow countryman wrote "C'est Tello qui nous a révélé les Sumériens."

In spite of de Sarzec's relative virtue, by bad luck he encouraged the outbreak of the most disreputable commercialism. It became widely known that he had sold his first collection of antiquities to the Louvre for £5,000. This stimulated secret pillaging by peasants, a hot market for private dealers, and even the sale of stolen finds by workmen on Rassam's and other official excavations.

In 1884 the Americans made their Mesopotamian debut, when the University of Pennsylvania sent out a team to prospect for a promising site. They selected Nippur, a holy city of the Sumerians, and excavations were started there three years later under the direction of John Punnett Peters and Hermann Hilprecht. They found the scale of the place, with its colossal ziggurat, a little daunting. Hilprecht commented "What would our committee at home have said at the sight of this enormous ruin, resembling more a picturesque mountain chain than the last impressive remains of human constructions." Unfortunately, either from excessive principle or ignorance of the ways of the country, Peters failed to put himself under the protection of a local sheikh, paying a modest sum for labour and for safety, but camped on the top of the ziggurat and left things to his Turkish official. The local Afaq tribes were both poor and wild, the workmen had no Arabic-speaking supervisors, thieving began, a thief was shot dead, and Peters, fearful of retaliation, sent for the police. The story of the resulting siege and the burning of the camp is well known (p. 407, I). However, the "committee at home" was undaunted, digging began again in 1890, and although a rather foolish policy of intimidating the Afaq was maintained, excellent results were obtained before the end of the century. In particular, Nippur proved rich in tablets of a mythological and literary character—their decipherment was indeed to engage scholars for over half a century.

Like the French work at Lagash, the American excavations at Nippur represent an advance in that there was serious concentration on a single site. On the other hand, Peters and Hilprecht again resembled de Sarzec in that their actual methods were still quite primitive. The revolutionary advance was left to the Germans, who arrived at Babylon just before the end of the century and worked there until the outbreak of the First World War. Robert Koldewey (p. 331, I) set himself the task of examining the whole architectual and social setting of the Babylonians. He also introduced the careful stratigraphical digging already developed among the more scientific archaeologists in Europe. The Germans at Babylon, in fact, can be seen as the advance guard of modern scientific archaeology in Iraq, which now has such great achievements to its credit.

In Egypt the development of archaeology through the nineteenth century followed much the same course as in Mesopotamia, although the first phase had opened much earlier. A period of pioneer glory, followed by a more or less disreputable scramble for antiquities; then a great struggle for improvement both in aims and methods; and finally the achievement of something like scientific proficiency.

Napoleon's team of one hundred and seventy-five savants and the princely scheme for the publication of their findings in the enormous *Description de l'Egypte* had set an exalted standard. In 1828, six years after his first announcement of his decipherment of hieroglyphs, Champollion, now famous and heaped with honours, went with the Italian professor Ippolito Rosellini to make another great survey of Egyptian art and architecture. This time they penetrated as far as the First Cataract. They recorded many monuments, Champollion made many translations, and on their return they published dignified folio volumes of their drawings. In 1842-5 the French were rivalled by the Prussians, who sent their great scholar Richard Lepsius on yet another surveying expedition which was extended right through Nubia as far as Khartoum. Lepsius made some excavations at Memphis and had the distinction of discovering the inscriptions left by Egyptian copper miners in Sinai. The Prussians followed the tradition, which has given all libraries of Egyptology a special shelving problem, of publishing in the largest possible size. Lepsius's illustrations appeared in the twelve vast tomes of *Denkmäler aus Aegypten*—though the text was long delayed and appeared only posthumously.

The artists attached to this expedition found the difficulty that was also being experienced at about this time in recording Mayan art (p. 520, II). The preconceptions absorbed from their European background gave them, as it were, distorting glasses. Much of their work so far missed the spirit of Egyptian art as to be positively inaccurate.

Meanwhile, side by side with these stately, government-supported expeditions, a number of individuals were at work. One of the most bizarre figures, in a field where the proportion of eccentrics is high, was the Paduan-born Giovanni Belzoni. Six feet seven inches tall and broad in proportion, he originally intended to hide his giant strength in a monastery. The French occupation of Rome frustrated this intention, and after some wandering and a marriage with an Englishwoman of proportionate size, the two of them fell on hard times and had to appear in the role of strong man and woman in fairs and even on the streets of London. Various chances took him to Egypt, where he began to work under the patronage of the British Consul-General, Henry Salt, a traveller and antiquary. Probably his best-known exploit (curiously appropriate to an ex-strong man) was his removal of the colossal bust of Ramses II from Thebes to London, a task which he directed with exceptional skill. (This is the piece of sculpture, now in the British Museum, which is reputed to bring ill luck on all who handle it.)

He also was the first partly to clear the drifted sand from the Great Temple at Abu Simbel, the first to enter the Pyramid of Chephren at Gizeh, and the discoverer of the sepulchre of Sethos (Seti) I—still described in guide books as Belzoni's Tomb.

His methods were unbelievably rough; at his own admission, Belzoni.in a tomb was more destructive than any bull in any china shop. "When my weight bore on the body of an Egyptian it crushed like a band-box. I sank altogether among the broken mummies with a crash of bones, rags and wooden cases . . . I could not avoid being covered with legs, arms and heads rolling from above." He was an unscrupulous collector of antiquities both for his own profit and on behalf of museums. But in this he was no worse than many of his contemporaries, who at this time were filling European galleries with Egyptian plunder. The agents of different nations had battles such as were soon to break out in Mesopotamia. On one occasion when Belzoni had quietly whisked away the Philae Obelisk on behalf of the British Consul, he was held up at gunpoint by the agents of the French Consul, who claimed it as theirs.

In 1823 Belzoni rashly tried to reach Timbuktu from the west coast of Africa, and, after reaching Benin, died of dysentery in a remote village.

Very much more virtuous were the activities of various English-men who laboured to record the monuments. Between 1820 and 1839, for example, Robert Hay led parties of this kind—including Catherwood, the artist who was later to become well known for his work with Stephens among the Maya ruins. Other colleagues were James Burton, and Sir John Wilkinson whose *Manners and Customs of the Egyptians* (p. 561, I) did much to spread an interest in an-cient Egypt among the English public. These English gentlemen evidently enjoyed living in the fashion of the country. A drawing by Lane, one of the Hay artists, shows three of them in a chamber that may be the tomb of Ramses II, dressed in Turkish costume, fezzed, and reclining on carpets to smoke their hookah pipes.

By 1850 most of the known Egyptian monuments had been recorded, albeit imperfectly by modern standards. This was the year in which a new phase of research, comparable with that in-augurated by de Sarzec and Peters in Mesopotamia, is represented by the arrival of the Frenchman, Auguste Mariette.

He was a young official of the Louvre, originally sent to Egypt to collect Coptic manuscripts. On a visit to Sakkara, he saw some ruins submerged in sand which he believed to mark a site described by Strabo. He promptly abandoned his official mission, and began, "almost furtively," to excavate. This was how he came upon the enormous building known as the Serapeum—and how he came to devote the rest of his life to Egyptology.

Although at first he sent many treasures to the Louvre, he became devoted to the idea that the Egyptians should not only be allowed to keep their own antiquities, but also helped to discover and preserve them. Working with the strong support of de Lesseps (creator of the Suez Canal) and Napoleon III, he goaded Said Pasha, the Khedive, into setting up an Egyptian Service of Antiquities with himself as Director. The Khedive, however, was primarily interested in getting what he wanted from Napoleon and "came to the conclusion that he would be more acceptable to the Emperor if he made some show of taking pity on the Pharaohs." He was therefore a most unreliable ally, subjecting Mariette to every kind of inconvenience and humiliation, even to sudden refusals of the funds necessary to complete excavations.

Nevertheless the Frenchman succeeded in using his position to control the commercial plundering of antiquities and to impose some sort of excavation policy. Even if this policy was that no one but Mariette was allowed to dig, at least this prevented the unseemly rivalries that were fought out in Mesopotamia.

He was also determined to provide Egypt with a worthy museum —and indeed the splendid finds that poured in from his own explorations demanded a home. The Khedive was reluctant, and for some time granted him only the most squalid accommodation. The way in which he was finally induced to repent makes an amusing story. In 1859 one of Mariette's excavations discovered the burial of Queen Aahotep near the entrance to the Valley of the Kings at Thebes. Before he could dispatch it to Cairo, a local Mudir seized it, opened the gilded coffin and removed the superb jewellery, mostly the gift of the old lady's royal son. Thinking to find favour with the Khedive by presenting him with the treasure, he embarked for Cairo. Mariette, always a man of decisive action, pursued him in a faster boat, boarded the Mudir's craft and forced him to hand over the jewellery—which he then himself took to Cairo.

The Khedive now showed a more attractive side of his character, for he was amused by this exploit and evidently admired the Frenchman's successful naval action. After choosing a few pieces for himself and one of his wives, he ordered that the rest of the jewellery should be worthily displayed in a new museum. So Mariette got what he wanted, and Egypt possessed the first National Museum and the first National Antiquities Service in the Near or Middle East.

During his thirty years of command, Mariette excavated at very many—far too many—of the outstanding Egyptian monuments. He dug extensively at Memphis, Sakkara and Thebes; he uncovered the Sphinx and the great temples of Dendera and Edfu. He was busy almost everywhere from Tanis in the Delta to Gebel Barkal in the Soudan. In spite of his trouble with the Khedive, and a period of disfavour with the Emperor provoked by his firm refusal to present the Empress Eugénie with a great collection of Egyptian jewels, after she had indicated that she would be willing to receive them, Mariette prospered and died (in 1881) a pasha and weighed down with European honours. They were deserved, for although much of his exploration was done in a slapdash way and left unfinished and unpublished, he rendered an immense service to Egyptian archaeology.

Mariette's work was conscientiously carried on by his successor, Gaston Maspero, who was immediately fortunate in assisting in the discovery of the cache of royal mummies at Deir el Bahari (p. 483, I). He also opened the little pyramid of Unas at Sakkara and revealed its chambers covered with the exquisitely engraved hieroglyphs of the "Pyramid Texts." But the French mantle more truly fell upon an Englishman, William Flinders Petrie, who had arrived in Egypt in the year before Mariette's death.

Petrie was brutally critical of Mariette, perhaps because, like most successors, he took for granted the achievements of his predecessor while dwelling on his weaknesses with the uncharitable stare of a new generation. Petrie himself certainly arrived with high standards for thorough, carefully-recorded and promptly-published excavations, for the exact study of the material and techniques of antiquities, and for using every possible scrap of evidence for the reconstruction of history.

He proved, in fact, methodical and objective in his researches, in spite of the fact that his first interest in Egyptology was inspired by Charles Piazzi Smyth, a close friend of his parents who, while an eminent astronomer, was one of those who believe that the measurements of the pyramids are endowed with mystical or prophetic meaning. His father urged young Flinders Petrie to make a survey at Gizeh in the light of Smyth's notions, and this in time he did, only to find, as he himself put it, "the ugly little fact which killed the beautiful theory." Petrie went to Egypt on his survey mission in 1880; three years later he was made field director for the newly-constituted Egypt Exploration Fund—the enthusiastic secretary of which was Amelia Edwards, she who had steeped Ramses II's face with coffee and whose account of her travels makes such good reading (p. 460, I).

Petrie was not out for spectacular finds—in this he was a little ahead of his contemporaries in Egypt and southwest Asia. Nevertheless he did have some lucky strikes, including the magnificent group of gold objects and other treasure from a tomb at Lahun which is now in the Metropolitan Museum, New York. He also played an important part in the recovery of the Tell el Amarna tablets unearthed by a peasant woman in 1887.

Petrie made three main contributions to Egyptology. One was insistence on methodical excavation and publication and a system which he called Sequence Dating: a way of fixing relative dates based on stratification and on the successive forms of pottery. Another was his pioneer work in comparative archaeology. Excavating in Egypt at Gurob near Heracleopolis in 1889 he found pottery of the Mycenaean age of Greece together with Egyptian objects dating from the late XVIIIth Dynasty—about the fourteenth century B.C. Then the next year at Kahun in the Fayum pottery came to light which with a sure instinct Petrie also attributed to the Aegean, although its like was not to be known until the discovery of the Minoan civilization a decade later. This Kahun pottery was in a much earlier Egyptian context: that of the XIIth Dynasty. Soon after this discovery Petrie went to Athens to see Schliemann's Mycenaean material. He not only saw pottery such as he had found at Gurob, but was also able to point out XVIIIth Dynasty Egyptian influence on the Mycenaean products and even some actual Egyptian imports.

"Cross dating" was thus made possible and gradually a chronological system was established for the northern Mediterranean. This in turn could be extended into Europe until at last it began to be possible to assign at least approximate dates to events in the prehistory of the misty west and north. So the historical light kindled with the decipherment of hieroglyphs was turned upon the darkest corners of the barbarian world. This comparative method, extended from land to land, was to be the only means of absolute dating of non-literate cultures until the recent development of the Carbon-14 and other comparable scientific methods. On the whole the chronology begun by Flinders Petrie has stood up to the scientific testing remarkably well.

Petrie's last outstanding contribution to his subject was his discovery of cultures that had been flourishing in the Nile valley long before the crowning of the first Pharaohs and the unification of Egypt. As with the prehistoric remains in Mesopotamia, to be detected considerably later, these predynastic villages and graves were often more deeply buried, always far humbler, than the evidences of the Pharaonic kingdom, and so for long passed unnoticed. Petrie, with his belief in "realising the importance of everything found," recognized the various peasant groups which had farmed the land during the fourth millennium B.C. and used his Sequence Dating to bring them into order. This was to prove another most repaying field for further research.

Sir Flinders Petrie was like Layard, and unlike Schliemann and Arthur Evans, in that he was himself a poor man and had to work on a very tight budget. That is partly why life in the excavation camps run by him and his wife was notoriously austere. This remarkable couple continued to work into their old age, and may perhaps have become a little overwhelmed by the accumulation of their discoveries. The present writer has heard them criticized almost as severely as Petrie himself criticized Mariette. But there is no question whatever that Petrie was one of the giants not only of Egyptology but of archaeology as a whole. He gave a lead in conscientious and purposeful excavation, attaining standards that might already be known here and there in Europe, but which had certainly not been reached until his day in the far more strenuous circumstances of Egypt and Asia.

In both Mesopotamia and Egypt, archaeologists of the second half of the nineteenth century cut down through time to discover the remains of older peoples behind those of whom at least some faint historical record had survived. The same thing happened in Greece, Asia Minor and Italy, the only difference being that in those classical lands the study of the later, historical antiquities had been pursued far longer and more intensively.

In Italy the first important group of Etruscan tombs, with their strange furnishings and wall paintings, had been stumbled upon in 1827. These were at Corneto, but other cemeteries were soon thrown open at Chiusi, Veii, Cerveteri and Orvieto. It was unfortunate that this happened so early, and that no man of vision or authority appeared to take charge of the situation. As it was, the tombs were often handed over as concessions for commercial exploitation by dealers interested in nothing but the sale of antiquities. The pillage was, in fact, worse than anything that happened outside Europe. So our knowledge of these intruders who seem to have come to Italy from Asia Minor, who were so greatly influenced by the Greeks, and in their turn had so great an influence on their Roman conquerors, has been irremediably diminished.

Yet the cultivated public of Europe was stirred by the discoveries: exhibitions of treasures from the cemeteries were well patronized, distinguished visitors hurried to see the painted tombs for themselves (p. 174, II), and books such as George Dennis's *Cities and Cemeteries of Etruria* (p. 184, II) were eagerly read. So little were the finds understood that the Greek vases found among the grave goods, equally with the cruder local copies, were known as Etruscan vases. Even today in many sale catalogues and country house guides, Greek painted pottery appears under this name. Perhaps because of the powerful effect on the visitor of their great cities of the dead and the atmosphere of the tombs themselves, the Etruscans were considered a mysterious people, a reputation they have never lost, as can be seen from the descriptions by D. H. Lawrence (p. 206, II). It so happens, too, that their script is one of the few which still defies all efforts at decipherment.

A striking improvement in the study of classical remains began after the middle of the century. Pompeii might be said to be one of those archaeological sites that has everything to appeal to the public—dramatic historical associations, works of art, objects of value, cosy remains of everyday life, and at the same time something more than a little horrific in the casts which it proved possible to take of fleeing men and women, the death throes of their pets. Even at the beginning of the century, excavations there had been relatively well conducted, thanks to the intelligent patronage of the Napoleonic rulers—indeed they have been called "the first large planned excavations in history." They were continued under the restored Bourbons, but it was not until 1861 that their direction fell to Giuseppe Fiorelli, who introduced a clear policy to seek not primarily for works of art but for the city itself, and for its unique evidence of the life of Roman citizens. From that time to the present this type of excavation has gone on intermittently at Pompeii, and then again at Herculaneum, until today visits to these sites and to the collections in Naples are among the most fascinating archaeological experiences in the world.

It would demand most exhaustive research to reconstruct a precise history of how more scientific methods began to be accepted by humanist archaeologists at this time. One would have to discover not only interchanges between related disciplines, but contacts of all kinds between individuals working in half a dozen different countries. Perhaps the excavations in Danish bogs and Swiss "lake-dwellings" can be seen as forming a bridge between the scientific tradition of the geologists and Pleistocene archaeologists and the artistic and linguistic interests of the humanists. Certainly it was the thorough-going northerners, and especially the Danes and Germans, who in the end were mainly responsible and whose influence has been seen making itself belatedly felt in lands where more romantic traditions had prevailed.

One of the centres for the new methods was the Aegean, where after 1870 several German and Austrian excavators were at work on classical sites. There was Alexander Conze, for example, a highly conscious exponent of reform, who dug at Samothrace, had it meticulously planned, and published the first excavation report to be illustrated with photographs. Then, in 1875, the German Archaeological Institute, recently taken over by the State, founded a branch at Athens and put Ernst Curtius in charge of great excavations at Olympia. Money, some of it provided personally by the Emperor William, was spent lavishly, even though by this time (1875-80) the Greek government had prohibited the export of antiquities. These excavations of Conze and Curtius and their immediate disciples, with their insistence on full records, on the careful observance of stratigraphy and also in time on the study of pottery, became virtual schools of archaeological method. French and American excavators (notably Bacon and Clark who dug in the Troad) learned from them and carried on their traditions; so did the Greeks themselves.

A young architect who joined the party at Olympia was Wilhelm Dörpfeld. He was to become one of the most enthusiastic exponents of the scientific method, but is probably more widely remembered as an able assistant to one who is perhaps the most famous of all archaeologists—Heinrich Schliemann. It was to be an ideal conjunction: the exact, objective, relatively impersonal and colourless man of scientific outlook, with the man whose imagination and creative energy shed a kind of glory on all that he did, riveting the attention of the world and enhancing the drama of his discoveries with the dramatic force of his own personality.

Schliemann was the son of a Mecklenburg pastor, and grew up in materially poor but intellectually well-furnished surroundings. His father told him tales of Pompeii and also of the Trojan war. In his autobiography he recalls how in 1829, after discussing a picture of Troy in the *Universal History for Children,* young Heinrich, then about seven years old, agreed with the pastor that "some day I should excavate Troy." A little later he wrote a Latin composition on Troy as a Christmas present for his father.

Nevertheless at fourteen he was put into a small town grocer's shop, working long hours at the counter and in the warehouse. He stayed in this depressing employment for over five years, then had a hard time first in Hamburg, then in Amsterdam—indeed he nearly ended his life with Troy undiscovered when the brig on which he was serving as cabin boy was wrecked off Texel. Then his extraordinary ability and will power began to get a grip of his surroundings. He built up a reputation as an agent that took him into a mercantile firm with wide interests. Immediately he set to and learned four languages. Indeed, he proved to have a gift for languages equal to that of Claudius Rich, mastering them in a few weeks. He claimed fluency in no fewer than fifteen. Writing to a schoolboy son many years later he said, "You ought to try to follow the example of your father who in whatever situation always proved what a man can accomplish by unflagging energy alone. During the four years in Amsterdam from 1842 to 1846 I truly performed wonders. My achievements there have never been equalled, and never will be equalled."

The firm then sent him to Russia, where he amassed a fortune as a wholesale merchant specializing in indigo, being considered, as he said with pride, "the slyest, most cunning and most capable of merchants." In 1850 he made a prolonged visit to California in search of one of his brothers. He seems to have been unable to avoid making more money in the boom condition of the West, while California's entry into the Union gave him a present of American citizenship. A photograph taken of him in about 1860, when he held several high positions in St. Petersburg, shows him almost extinguished by a huge, fur-lined coat, its skirts resting on the ground, its cuffs extending far beyond his hands. From the tremendous hairy collar emerges a neat, oval face eclipsed down to the brows by a marvellously glossy top hat.

Yet in reality no man was less dominated by success and self-won grandeur. Many of us have known young men who determined to make money in order to be able to carry out some cherished ambition. But how very few have kept to their plan: either they have failed to make any money, or they have lacked the will to stop making it. Schliemann was inflexibly true to his childhood's dream. In 1856 he learnt first modern and then ancient Greek, and two years later tried to retire from business, setting out on travels that took him as far as the Second Cataract of the Nile. However, in his absence his business faltered, and he had to return to it—only to make such large sums in tea and cotton that at last he was able to sell out completely and free himself for the discovery of Troy.

His self-discipline was still not exhausted, for he resolved first to prepare himself by travel and by a concentrated study of archaeology. For his archaeological cramming he settled in Paris and it would be extraordinarily interesting to know just what he read and saw there, and whom he met. Schliemann has often been seen as a dilettante in the bad sense, but a man of his phenomenal application and powers of memory could easily in those few years have assimilated all that was in the least valuable for him to know. It is true that he did not seek any practical training in excavation, but then there were few men in the late sixties capable of giving him sound instruction. The general principles of excavation, in so far as they had been established, he must have understood, for he strove to apply them when he found himself in the field.

In 1868 and the following year he visited for the first time both famous and little-known sites in Greece and Anatolia—the sites which he had imagined through so many years of commercial life. "I confess," he wrote, "that I could hardly control my emotion when I saw before me the immense plain of Troy, whose image had hovered before me even in dreams of my earliest childhood."

It was in the spring of 1869 that he visited that plain and made his way to the large *tell* of Hissarlik, walking round it watch in hand to check the three circuits of Troy achieved by Achilles and Hector in the course of battle. Soon afterwards he published his conviction that this was indeed the site of Troy.

It was in this year, too, that he acquired a second wife, his first having refused to follow him into the world of archaeology. He set about the business as coolly as he would a deal in indigo. He told his father ". . . since the growth of my passion for the Greek language, I believe I can only be happy with a Greek woman. I will take her, however, only if she has an interest in the sciences." In writing more frankly to his brother he said that he would have an advantage in the hunt because the Greek girls were "as poor as church mice," adding "Thank God, the choice in Greece is large, and the girls as beautiful as the pyramids of Egypt." Finally he chose a very beautiful one, Sophia, from photographs obligingly supplied to him by the Archbishop. She was not in the least like the pyramids of Egypt, but proved almost equally staunch, working strenuously with her husband and assuring that his activities were worthily carried on after his death. She also bore him two children: Agamemnon and Andromache. Schliemann published a photograph of Sophia decked in the Trojan necklace and headdress from what he called "the Treasure of Priam" (p. 23, II).

Having settled his marriage arrangements to his complete satisfaction, Schliemann was now ready to dig, and in 1870 he started work at Hissarlik. During the next three years he put in over eleven months' work there, employing between eighty and one hundred and fifty men. So did the profits from indigo, tea and cotton serve to lay bare the secrets of Troy.

It is sad to have to record the condescension and contempt with which the new but great recruit to archaeology was long treated by leading scholars. Perhaps they could not forget that he had been in a grocer's shop when they were at their studies, perhaps a certain envy of the power of his wealth underlay their condescension toward one who had been in trade. Then it may be that a naive self-admiration in the man (the scholar's conceit is always well concealed) exacerbated their worst feelings. But undoubtedly the antagonism of his learned contemporaries was very largely due to their reluctance to believe that there was a strong historical element in Homer. At that time two rival schools of thought existed, one holding that the poems were a collection of old folk tales put together by minstrels, the other that they came from the imagination of a great poetic genius. The case was disputed hotly, but only from study chairs. No one thought of going out to look for remains of the Homeric age, for both parties were agreed that the epics told of things that had never been on land or sea.

Schliemann, of course, thought otherwise; he went with Homer in his pocket and used it almost as a guide book. His convictions were too simple; they led him to make many mistakes, for his immediate impulse was to assign everything he found to the

Homeric heroes. It is now well known, for example, that "Priam's Treasure" did not come from the Homeric level at Hissarlik and that the Shaft Graves at Mycenae were not the burial places of Agamemnon and the rest, but belonged to an earlier phase of the Bronze Age.

On the other hand Schliemann did discover Troy, did prove the epics to be based on history, did reveal the Bronze Age background to Homer. Moreover the mistakes made by Schliemann's detractors were more absurd than his. Scholars may fight among themselves, but they usually like to turn a more united front on the outside world. Thus the errors of the layman remain exposed in the market place, while the errors of the learned are soon decently interred. Max Müller declared that the historicity of the Trojan war was not to be distinguished from that of the Nibelungs. Nor, regrettably, were the men with field experience any better. Conze went so far as to say that everything found at Troy could be attributed to the classical Greeks, while Curtius made a frightful howler in suggesting that the bearded gold mask found on one of the bodies in the Shaft Graves was a Byzantine portrait of Christ.

It must be admitted that, although they angered him, Schliemann's self-confidence does not seem to have been shaken by these scholarly assaults. As early as 1870 he wrote, "At the moment, as an archaeologist, I am the sensation of Europe and America because I have discovered ancient Troy, the Troy for which the archaeologists of the entire world have searched in vain during the past two thousand years." The first part of this statement is more accurate than the second.

The "Treasure of Priam" was discovered on the last day of the first phase of excavation at Hissarlik. Schliemann was now granted official permission to dig at Mycenae. He was supposed to work with Greek collaborators, but their collaboration was not enthusiastic. When he had first visited this city with its Cyclopean walls and Lion Gate, he had been convinced that the tombs which had been shown to the Greek traveller Pausanias as those of Agamemnon and Clytemnestra were not, as was generally thought, the vaulted "Treasuries" outside the walls, but lay within the citadel itself. He therefore dug inside the Lion Gate, in an area enclosed by a circular wall, and with little difficulty found and cleared the famous Shaft Graves. The "Treasuries," or *tholos* tombs, had been plundered in antiquity, but these burials were untouched, the princely owners still lying with their splendid vessels of gold and silver, their exquisitely ornamented weapons and golden death masks. Because Pausanias had said there were five graves, Schliemann did not look any further, but a sixth subsequently came to light.

The precious things from the Shaft Graves can still be relied upon to astound any visitor to the Athens Museum, where they have been so displayed as to give a dazzling first impact. They were Schliemann's greatest find. But he also explored part of the city and recovered quantities of the handsome painted pottery— the pottery which was to make it possible to date the Mycenaean culture by reference to Egypt (p. 52, I). As always, he was quick to publish his results. In 1876 his *Mycenae* appeared in three languages, the English edition with a preface by W. E. Gladstone. The statesman was a firm admirer and supporter of Schliemann, and in general the German was far more acclaimed in England than in his own country.

In 1879 Schliemann returned to Hissarlik, for Troy was, after all, his first and greatest love. Here he cut down and down through the *tell*, further back into the prehistoric past. He had at first thought that he could detect the remains of seven successive cities of which the Homeric was the second or third. In fact both these levels (which yielded the "Treasure of Priam") date from the early Bronze Age of the third millennium B.C. When the more skilled and experienced Dörpfeld joined Schliemann, he distinguished nine cities with Homer's Troy as the sixth. Because by then they had become so firmly established in Anatolian prehistory, these nine divisions were retained by Carl Blegen and the expedition from Cincinnati University when they returned to Hissarlik in the 1930's. The meticulous American excavators, however, subdivided them into no fewer than forty-six distinct building periods. Most scholars are agreed with Blegen that the beginning of the seventh settlement, dating from the thirteenth century B.C., represents Homeric Troy, but a few are returning to the claims of the sixth.

Extraordinarily different estimates have been made of Schliemann's skill as an excavator. Some have hailed him as one of the pioneers of sound methods, others as a bungling incompetent. Certainly his account (p. 24, II) of how, threatened by the collapse of an overhanging wall, he cut out the Treasure with a large knife while his wife packed the finds into her shawl, must cause head-shaking today. Yet he did cut systematically down through the *tell*, keep all his finds, record where he had found them and have them drawn or photographed. He tried to apply the principles of stratification, although at first he hardly knew how to do so. Moreover, very unlike Layard and most of the Mesopotamian diggers, he seems to have insisted on constant personal supervision. "I had three capital foremen," he wrote, "and my wife and myself were present at the work from sunrise to sunset."

His principal fault was his faith that everything that glittered must be Homeric, for it led him to misdate his sites and fail to reconstruct their true history. But it is vain to censure this faith, for it was entirely his long-repressed passion for Homer that impelled his feats of discovery and made him great. What he in fact accomplished in archaeological terms was almost the same as that being simultaneously accomplished by the successors of Layard and Botta. While they pushed back beyond the Assyrians to reveal the unknown Bronze Age civilization of Mesopotamia, Schliemann went behind the classical Greeks to their equally unknown Bronze Age predecessors of the second and third millennia B.C.

Yet how much poorer the time would have been if this inspired excavator had not been able to proclaim the finding of the men, women and cities of Europe's greatest epic. It is the old issue between science and imagination. Blegen's forty-six building periods at Hissarlik are as nearly as possible accurate and "true," but could he write anything about them which could lift up the heart or rouse the imagination? His three admirable volumes are found only on scientific and scholastic shelves.

In 1890 Heinrich Schliemann caught an illness in Naples, and died there on Christmas Day. He left a small part of his fortune for the continuance of the work at Hissarlik, and Dörpfeld directed several useful seasons there. Two years before his death, Schliemann had travelled in Crete, had recognized the site of Knossos and even done a little unsuccessful digging. Ten years after his death, Arthur Evans (who had been greatly excited by his visit to the excavations at Mycenae) began large-scale exploration at Knossos.

Arthur Evans was the son of the antiquary John Evans (p. 33, I), and inherited comfortable means from his family business. He accepted the Greek tradition of the early importance of Crete, and his interest was further roused by the few specimens of script that came his way (p. 132, II). Having himself played a courageous part against the tottering Turkish Empire in Yugoslavia (he was briefly imprisoned), he rejoiced when in 1898 Crete declared her independence of Turkey. Indeed he already saw Crete as the cradle of European civilization, and he told the British Association, "Crete stands forth again today as the champion of the European spirit against the yoke of Asia." It was the very next year (1899) that he was at Knossos starting his excavations.

They were immediately successful, and as early as 1901 he was able to create a sensation by the publication of his discovery of a large palace and of an entirely new Bronze Age civilization with a lovely and original art. To him it seemed clear that he had found the main root of the mainland civilization which Schliemann had revealed at Mycenae. In 1904 he announced his intention of calling this new civilization Minoan, after the legendary Cretan law-giver Minos.

Evans worked at Knossos for a quarter of a century, digging, classifying and restoring. The results, with his own lively interpretations, appeared between 1921 and 1935 in the four volumes of *The Palace of Minos* (p. 84 ff., II).

Even while Schliemann was still at work (unknown to himself) in finding the remains of early Bronze Age Anatolians at Hissarlik, progress was being made in the recovery of a powerful, semi-historic people of Anatolia: the Hittites. Although they are several times mentioned in the Old Testament and in Egyptian inscriptions, they had become the merest ghosts in the historical scene.

During the first half of the nineteenth century many traces of the Hittites had in fact been detected. The first was a curiously sculptured and inscribed stone noticed in 1812 by that most extraordinary Swiss, John Burckhardt, when he was walking in the bazaar of Hama in northern Syria. He spoke of "signs which appear to be a kind of hieroglyphic writing, though it does not resemble Egyptian." Then, in 1839, Texier came upon the walls and sculptured gateways of a large ruined city near the village of Boghazköy, east of Ankara. He was impressed by "the grandeur and peculiar nature of the ruins," and decided they could not be those of Celtic Tavium for which he was searching. In this he was wiser than Sir William Hamilton, who was there a few years later and rashly attributed the city to the Celts. In 1860 the French art historian Georges Perrot went to Boghazköy, where his trained sensibilities at once recognized a new art.

Yet it was not until over a decade later that the scattered evidence began to be drawn together, one reason for the slow progress being the complication of Hittite history.

The original Armenoid people of Anatolia, the Hatti, with their high, almost conical heads and big noses, were overrun in the late third millennium B.C. by Indo-European invaders who mixed freely with them. In the outcome of this fusion, while the racial type of the older population was dominant, the language of the Indo-Europeans prevailed. On the other hand, the old name (Hebrew *Hittim,* Egyptian *Kheta* and perhaps Homeric *Keteioi*) was maintained, while their ancient capital at Boghazköy was continued with the name of Hattusas.

The compound Hittites proved a most potent people, able, early in the second millennium, to conquer Babylonia. They borrowed the Babylonian cuneiform for their writing, though it never seems to have been much used except in and around the capital. They continued to employ it until about 1200 B.C., but meanwhile developed an altogether new hieroglyphic script of their own. The Hittites had enjoyed their period of greatest power during their New Empire of the two centuries before 1200 B.C. At about that date they were broken by the so-called Sea People, and their centre of gravity shifted from Hattusas and Anatolia to northern Syria. There a number of small states arose, Carchemish the greatest among them. A very large part of the known hieroglyphic inscriptions date from this time after the age of Hittite ascendancy was at an end.

The picture which the scholars and archaeologists had to reassemble was therefore a complex one. In about 1870 the American Consul General, Augustus Johnson, and a missionary friend called Jessup, rediscovered the Hama stone, and learnt that others existed nearby. But when they tried to transcribe it, the bazaar crowd became hostile. A little later, much the same difficulty defeated members of the American Palestine Exploration Society, and also Richard Burton, the traveller. (It was found that there were four stones, and that one of them effected miracle cures for rheumatism.)

In 1872 a more enlightened Turkish governor of Syria invited the British Consul General at Damascus and William Wright, a missionary, to visit Hama with him. With a ruthlessness that now seems embarrassing, the governor used his troops to quell the angry citizens while the sculptured and inscribed stones were extracted. Wright took casts and dispatched them to London, while the booty itself went to Constantinople. A few years afterwards more relics of the later Hittites came to light when George Smith, during his last fatal journey, went to the large mound of Jerablus on the Euphrates and identified it at once as the site of Carchemish. As a result the British Museum sent an expedition which dug into the *tell* and brought quantities of sculptures and texts to London.

Speculation and dispute concerning the scripts and the people responsible for them were now active on both sides of the Atlantic. William Wright, who as a theologian was mainly interested in identifying the people with the biblical Hittites, published his *Empire of the Hittites*, a useful summary of the evidence then available. But the great advance was made by a Welshman, A. H. Sayce, a leading Assyriologist at Oxford. Gladstone called him "high priest of the Hittites."

With sudden insight Sayce recognized that there was a common element in scattered sculpture and inscriptions which had been found throughout Anatolia and northern Syria. He had already assigned the Hama stone to the Hittites, and seeing the parallels at Carchemish, Boghazköy, Ivriz and many other sites, he realized the probable range and power of the Hittite empire. In his *Reminiscences*, Sayce describes how he was talking to a friend about the Hama type of script when "a sudden inspiration came to me. I asked for a copy of Rawlinson's *Herodotus*, and then pointed out that a picture of a monument in the Pass of Karabel near

Smyrna, which Herodotus believed to have been a memorial of
the Egyptian Pharaoh Sesostris, presented us with a figure in
precisely the same style of art as that of the monuments of Ivriz
and Carchemish, and accompanied by badly copied hieroglyphs
which would probably turn out to be those I called Hittite." The
two friends then excitedly looked up other material from Boghazköy
and elsewhere and found the same association of art and script.
"It was clear that in pre-Hellenic days a powerful empire must have
existed in Asia Minor which extended from the Aegean to the Halys
and southward into Syria to Carchemish and Hamath, and possessed its own script. And so the story of the Hittite empire was
introduced to the world." He performed that introduction more
thoroughly when in 1888 he published *The Hittites: the Story of a
Forgotten Empire* (p. 37, II).

Sayce's interpretation was not accepted all at once, but more
and more evidence came to support it, in particular the royal correspondence from Tell el Amarna (p. 45, II). Letters from Syrian and
Palestinian rulers complained of Hittite attacks, and there were
two from Hittite kings, including that of Suppiluliumas congratu-
lating the young Amenophis IV (Akhenaten) on his accession.
Among this correspondence, much of which was in the usual diplomatic language of the time, Akkadian, and could therefore be
read, there were two tablets written in cuneiform but in an unknown language. Then tablets in the same tongue began to come
out of central Anatolia—and it proved that peasants were grubbing
them up at Boghazköy. In 1902, prematurely but as it proved
correctly, C. A. Knudtzon, a Norwegian working on the el Amarna
letters, declared that in his opinion they were in an early Indo-
European tongue.

A great interest in the Hittites had now been aroused, and
archaeologists were eager to find the imperial capital. The evidence
pointed more and more clearly to Boghazköy. For a long time
Sayce had been trying to arrange an expedition there—he had
even approached Schliemann as a possible excavator. At last he
induced the University of Liverpool to send a party under John
Garstang, but while they were on the way they learnt that the
Turkish authorities had withdrawn their permits in favour of a
German expedition led by the philologist Hugo Winckler. The
disconsolate British had to be content with digging at Carchemish.

Winckler was an indoor not an outdoor archaeologist, and his
excavations were atrociously conducted. When he decided to tackle
the lofty citadel of the place, for some reason he drove his trench
uphill and the men worked in constant danger of being crushed
by "overhanging masses of earth and rock." However, he was fortunate, and quite soon struck a series of store chambers containing

archives of some ten thousand cuneiform tablets. The great majority were in Hittite and could not be read, but a proportion were in Akkadian. Among these Winckler was greatly moved to find the text of the famous treaty between Ramses II and the Hittite king Hattusilis—the Egyptian version of which is inscribed at Karnak. He was also able to translate a treaty between the Hittites and Mitanni in which the gods of the two peoples were invoked. This document proved of exceptional significance for the history of religion, as the deities included Indra, Mithra and Varuna, Indo-European deities worshipped also by the Persians and Indians. Moreover, Winckler was able to prove beyond dispute that he was indeed on the site of the royal city of Hattusas.

The appearance of so many new tablets was a great challenge, and epigraphists of many nations responded. After the usual limited successes that precede a decipherment, the final break was achieved by a Bohemian, Friedrich Hrozny, who published a sketch for a Hittite grammar as early as 1915. The language proved to be, as Knudtzon had somehow divined, predominantly Indo-European, although with plentiful survivals from the original Hattic tongue (p. 46, II).

So the Hittite cuneiform had been read, but the hieroglyphic script still held out, although again a great international effort at decipherment was maintained. In fact, advances in understanding the grammar and script had already been made in the 1930's, but the most spectacular achievement came with the German Helmuth Bossert's discovery of Karatepe in 1945. The story of how Bossert heard of this Black Mound that existed somewhere in wild hill country above the Cilician plain and was said to have a lion stone covered with inscriptions, and of how he found it with the help of the local schoolmaster, is so picturesque that perhaps its importance as a contribution to the decipherment of Hittite hieroglyphs has been a little exaggerated. However, important it was, for the king who built this city in the eighth century B.C. embellished the entrance gates not only with crude sculptures, of extraordinary interest for showing such things as a sea battle, various sports and an orchestra, but also with lengthy inscriptions in two languages—Phoenician on the left as one went in, Hittite hieroglyphs on the right. This extensive "bilingual" has vastly extended the known Hittite vocabulary, and so made easier the full reading of the innumerable texts that have come to light since the first discovery at Hama. The Hittites, once hardly more than a word in the Bible, have now been restored to history.

By the end of the nineteenth century, then, archaeologists had recovered many Old World civilizations that had either fallen into total oblivion or had been only very dimly remembered. These

were the Sumerian, Babylonian, the Mycenaean and Hittite. The
Minoan civilization was just on the verge of discovery. Then there
were the other civilizations which had kept a place in history but
which were really only brought to life and significance by excavation—those of the Egyptians, Assyrians and Etruscans. In the Old
World, only central and eastern Asia had not as yet been deeply
enough probed by inquisitive European minds and spades to expose their earliest achievements. Meanwhile some progress had
been made to recover the late but in many ways brilliant civilizations of the New World. If there was a certain delay, it was because the Spanish and Portuguese had not the curiosity, the North
Americans had not the time. Most of them were too busy building a
new civilization to give much thought to old ones. And of those
who did, the majority were still close to their European cultural
roots and were more inclined to help to explore round the Mediterranean and in south-west Asia than to turn back to pre-Columbian
America.

The circumstances of the Central and South American monuments and remains were different in several ways from those of
the Old World. Most obviously they were different because the
Spaniards and other Europeans had broken in upon the Incas,
Aztecs and Maya when they were living at a cultural stage similar
to that of the Egyptian and Asian Bronze Age theocracies, except
that they were technically more backward. Some of the surviving
monuments, and especially those of the Incas of Peru, had actually
been seen in occupation and had even been directly incorporated
in the conquerors' buildings. Others, though unknown outside their
own region until travellers discovered them, were more recent than
many European buildings still in normal use. (When Hiram Bingham came upon Machu Picchu, for example (p. 673, II), it was
rather as though someone had returned to a place deserted through
plague—or biological warfare. It was just a little old town with all
the roofs fallen in.)

In much of the mountain and jungle country of Guatemala and
Honduras, the Maya ruins really were virtually unknown to anyone, so tragically had the whole region been depopulated. These
marvellous architectural achievements were just as effectively
overwhelmed by vegetation as others in the Old World by sand or
soil. But in most parts of Central and South America the monuments were known to the natives and often to the Spaniards. They
could only be "discovered" in the sense that Avebury was "discovered" by Aubrey—that is to say, by being made known to the
learned world.

These factors, together of course with the survival of Indian
cultures in North America, have meant that in the Americas

INTRODUCTION 66

archaeology and anthropology (in the sense of the study of living "primitive" peoples) have always been far closer together than in the Old World. This close association has persisted even after the uncovering of many far more ancient cultures, and has on the whole been of advantage to both disciplines.

The first serious survey of Central American monuments was initiated by Charles IV of Spain, who sent a Frenchman, Captain Guillaume Dupaix, together with a Spanish draughtsman, Castenada, to report on Mexican ruins. They made three expeditions from 1805-7, and brought back valuable records of many sites that were to become famous, among them Cholula, Quilapa and Palenque. Owing, presumably, to the Napoleonic turmoil, very little notice was taken of their discoveries and these remained unpublished for many years. When they did at last get into print it was in an unlucky context—so much so that their work has seldom been sufficiently recognized.

This context was provided by an admirable young man, Edward King, Viscount Kingsborough, son and heir of an Irish peer, the Earl of Kingston. The sources of historical information about the pre-Columbian civilizations—those documents that had been written after the conquest together with some religious texts in Maya script—had by now become widely scattered in European libraries. While still at Oxford young Kingsborough saw some Mexican manuscripts in the Bodleian, and so greatly did they fascinate him that he determined to devote his life to a study of ancient Mexico. Gradually he gave up public life, resigning his seat in Parliament to a younger brother. In 1831 he published seven magnificent volumes in imperial folio at a price of £210. (Two more volumes and part of a tenth were to appear after Kingsborough's death.) The nearly full title of his work was *Antiquities of Mexico, comprising facsimiles of Ancient Mexican Paintings and Hieroglyphics preserved in . . . Various Libraries, together with the Monuments of New Spain by M. Dupaix, with . . . accompanying Descriptions.* A special edition of four was printed on vellum with hand-painted illustrations. The whole venture cost £132,000, which was more than even a nobleman could command. Thrown into a filthy Dublin prison for debt, Kingsborough caught typhus and was dead at forty-two. Only a year or so later he would have inherited the earldom together with £40,000 a year. Moreover, this unlucky scholar had devoted his text to trying to prove that American civilization had been created by the ten lost tribes of Israel.

Here is one of the saddest stories in the eccentrics' section of archaeological biography. It is a little comforting to be able to record that Kingsborough was respected by the next outstanding explorer of Mexican ruins—who was also eccentric but far from unfortunate. This was the Comte de Waldeck, of a German family which had emigrated to France. Waldeck had gone to Egypt with Napoleon, had stayed behind after the defeat and soon after had taken part in an effort to cross the Sahara on which every one of his companions died. He himself was to live to be one hundred and nine. He first visited Guatemala in 1821 and next year illustrated an account of the Palenque ruins published by the Spaniard, del Rio. He went to London, met Kingsborough and had fierce arguments with him, for whereas the Viscount attributed the Mexican ruins to the children of Israel, M. le Comte had a natural preference for the Egyptians. However, they became friends and Kingsborough added to his own difficulties by financing Waldeck on further expeditions. As a mark of esteem and gratitude, Waldeck named the finest of the Uxmal pyramid temples after the Irishman. "Because," as he wrote, "it seemed to me, of all the buildings in Yucatan, the worthiest of immortalizing the memory of that noblest of all great gentlemen, to whom the world of scholarship is indebted for that redoubtable book about Mexico."

William Prescott, too, paid a tribute to Kingsborough in his *Conquest of Mexico* (p. 664, II). He speaks of the immense erudition put into the arguments in favour of an Israelite colonization. "For this hieroglyphs are unriddled, manuscripts compared and monuments delineated. . . . By this munificent undertaking, which no government, probably, would have, and few individuals could have executed, he has entitled himself to the lasting gratitude of every friend of science." It was handsome—but perhaps hardly fair to "science." Prescott's two famous books, which played an immense part in rousing public interest in ancient Mexico and Peru, are derived almost entirely from the historical sources. In spite of his knowledge of Dupaix's work, the half-blind historian evidently had little interest in the archaeological approach to his subject.

Yet it was just after he had started research for *The Conquest of Mexico* that a substantial advance was made in the recovery of pre-Columbian history by archaeological means. The new adventurers were John Stephens of Shrewsbury, New Jersey, and the Englishman Frederick Catherwood. Stephens had already crossed the Atlantic, visited many famous sites in Europe and the Near East and published two books describing his travels. Catherwood, who has already been noticed (p. 49, I) at work as a skilled draughtsman recording the monuments of Egypt, became his friend and illustrator.

Lured by the rumours of ruined cities hidden in the jungles and wastes of Guatemala and Mexico, Stephens secured himself an appointment as United States Special Confidential Agent in Central America, and together with Catherwood embarked for Belize

in October 1839. Thereafter he journeyed, always at least pro-
fessedly in search of a government to which he could accredit
himself, through much of Guatemala to Costa Rica and San Sal-
vador, then back by way of Guatemala to the Yucatan peninsula
of Mexico. Altogether, as he states in his famous classic *Incidents
of Travel in Central America, Chiapas and Yucatan* (p. 500 ff., II),
he visited and recorded at least something of forty-four ruins, among
which those of Copan and Palenque were the most important.
Occasionally he cleared buildings and even attempted small
excavations; nearly always he drew adequate plans. Meanwhile
Frederick Catherwood shared most of his adventurous travels, but
sometimes stayed behind to work on his drawings of the profoundly strange sculptures, the hieroglyphs and richly ornamented
façades that they found in profusion. His early difficulties over
rendering the spirit of an art entirely alien to his experience are
well known (p. 520, II), yet he mastered them, and his engravings
are among the most satisfactory archaeological illustrations of the
prephotographic age.

In the autumn of 1841, the two friends returned to Yucatan and
made a more thorough study of its extraordinary monuments, particularly those of Uxmal and Chichen Itza. Later they published
their findings (always well spiced with true adventure stories) in
Incidents of Travel in Yucatan (p. 592 ff., II).

As an archaeologist, John Stephens was working very much in
the dark, and it was impossible for him to make any serious estimate as to the age and cultural background of the Maya civilization he was revealing to the world. But in general his opinions
were sensible ones—far more sensible, indeed, than the wild speculation involving the settlement of Central and South America by
Phoenicians or "white men" which have persisted into the present
century. Stephens believed, incredible as it might seem now that
the Indians had been decimated, humbled and impoverished, that
the great ceremonial cities and distinguished architecture he had
visited were the work of their ancestors of no very remote date.
Some of the ruins he saw were in fact more ancient than he supposed, and he was not particularly lucky in his guesses as to their
chronological sequence, yet his interpretation was on the right lines
and was the best that could possibly have been made at that date.

John Stephens had the same adventurous spirit as the young
Henry Layard and wrote of his hardships, dangers and comical
mishaps with equal spirit. But much of the lasting charm of his
books is due to a lighthearted attitude, a refusal to take himself
too seriously, more often found in such women travellers as Amelia
Edwards than among European males. The fantastic vicissitudes
of the civil war in which he found himself did not in the least

distress him; perhaps indeed they gave him more time (in spite
of very real dangers) to pursue the ancient Maya. He is always
amusing and never solemn concerning his vain pursuit of "any
government" to receive this unusual Confidential Agent.

In spite of the popularity of Stephens's and Catherwood's books,
little was done immediately to follow up the study of the Maya
or other neighbouring peoples. Between 1857 and 1882 Desiré
Charnay, on a mission for the French Minister of Public Instruction, made extensive explorations in Central America and published
the results in a work that appeared in English as *The Ancient Cities
of the New World*. But it is fair to say that the first substantial
foundations at least for Mayan archaeology were laid by Sir Alfred
Maudslay, who visited the Central American forests merely as a
curious traveller, but was so enthralled by "the sight of the truly
wonderful monuments which it was my good fortune to behold"
that he stayed for fourteen years (1881-94) of systematic work.
His report in five volumes, which has been called "the first scientific account of Central American archaeology," included an ap-
pendix on archaic Maya hieroglyphs.

After Maudslay's time, Central America began to become more
easily accessible and gradually scientific study increased, led by
the first of many expeditions from the Peabody Museum in Harvard,
which was dispatched in 1888.

Although, as for the Aztecs and Maya, there were literary sources
for the history of the Incas, and Prescott's *Conquest of Peru* was
no less popular than his Mexican volume, Peru was remote for the
men of enquiring mind in the north, and its desert coasts and
lofty mountain valleys were cruelly inhospitable. One of the first
men to travel the country with antiquarian interests was the geographer Sir Clement Markham, who was in the Andes between 1852
and 1854. He recorded something of the monuments in his *Cuzco
and Lima* and *Travels in Peru and India,* and he studied the
Quechua language, but his *History of the Incas*, like Prescott's
work, is drawn from the written sources.

Something of the cultural achievements of the pre-Inca peoples
of the coast of Peru began to be known through the loot from the
marvellously preserved burials (p. 683, II): lovely or extraordinary
pottery, textiles, and works of art and craft in stone, wood, copper
and gold reached the hands of dealers and were to be seen here
and there in museums. But it was not until the 1890's that serious
archaeological investigation began. The pioneer was a German,
Max Uhle, who conducted excavations for many years—at first for
the University of Pennsylvania, then for the University of California and finally for the Peruvian government. Unfortunately,
Uhle did not himself succeed in publishing much of his work, but

his notes and collections were mostly ably edited and written up by A. L. Kroeber. In this way something was learnt of such early coastal cultures as the Mochica and Nazca. Overlapping with the later of Uhle's excavations was the work of Julio Tello, who from 1913 onwards explored most of Peru, making his way into many wild and inaccessible places. The two men long disputed the origin of the Peruvian cultures, Uhle wishing to derive them from Central America, while Tello held that they were the native creation of the peoples of the Andes. This argument is not fully resolved even yet, although it now appears certain that there was at least some influence on the Andes from Central America.

Probably the last event in this still essentially nineteenth century investigation of pre-Columbian civilizations which succeeded in arousing great public interest was the discovery of Machu Picchu. It was found in July 1911 by Hiram Bingham, the leader of an expedition from Yale University. Climbing towards the spike of a precipitous mountain above the Urubamba gorge in the heart of jagged ranges and snow-covered peaks, this small town has the most extraordinary natural setting of any ancient monument known to the writer. It is hardly at all ruined, and its small but beautifully masoned houses, palaces and temples, its stepped alleys and bright conduits of mountain water, the gnomon at the summit for marking the movements of the divine sun, even its poor but brilliantly-clad Indian custodians, seem to retain the atmosphere of the past. Bingham was inclined to think that Machu Picchu might be the place of origin of the Incas, but it has proved in fact to belong to the last phase of their history.

While something was being done to study the monuments left by those Indian peoples who had attained civilization, the humbler remains of the North American Indians were not entirely neglected. About the middle of the nineteenth century there was a spate of sound studies on the subject. Squier and Davis's *Ancient Monuments of the Mississippi Valley* appeared in 1848, and Squier's *Ancient Monuments of New York* in the next year; Lapham's *Antiquities of Wisconsin* dates from 1853, and Samuel Haven summarized "The progress of information and opinion respecting vestiges of antiquity in the United States" in his *Archaeology of the U.S.* published in 1855.

Scientific Prehistory and the Evolution of Man

After the great events of 1859 (p. 34, I), the road was clear for a rapid advance in the investigation of man's origins and earliest history. The prehistorians now had all the time they wanted for his gradual cultural development, while the palaeontologists were allowed to assume that the human body and brain had also been changing and developing during those vast stretches of time. It remained to find the material evidence.

The very name of "prehistory" was a new one, having apparently first been coined by a Scottish ancient historian in 1851. It quickly caught on, and may be said to have been given the final stamp of respectability when it was used by Mr. Gladstone in 1878. The whole question of classification and nomenclature was, indeed, one of the main preoccupations of the "scientific" archaeologists of the second half of the nineteenth century. The original Danish Three Age System still held firm as a basis, but every decade saw it further sub-divided and elaborated.

The French were probably the first to recognize that the Stone Age must be split into two further large divisions, the periods of "chipped stones" and of "polished stones," and roughly this same division was recognized by John Evans in the great debates of 1859 when he said "there is for the most part a marked difference between the worked flints of the Drift and those of the ordinary stone period." By the Drift was meant such deposits as the Somme and Thames gravels with their hand-axes and other very early artifacts. Sir John Lubbock (afterwards Lord Avebury) performed a very useful service when in his *Prehistoric Times* of 1865 (p. 158, I) he firmly accepted the two parts of the Stone Age and named them the Palaeolithic (Old Stone Age) and Neolithic (New Stone Age). He explained them by saying that the first age was "that of the Drift, when men shared the possession of Europe with the Mammoth, the Cave Bear, the Woolly-haired Rhinoceros, and other extinct animals," while the second was "the later or polished stone age; a period characterised by beautiful weapons and instruments of flint and other kinds of stone, in which, however, we find no trace of any metal excepting gold. . . ." Soon, too, it began to be accepted that the Palaeolithic phase of human history coincided with the Pleistocene Ice Age of geology, while the Neolithic phase belonged to post-glacial times, well after the final retreat of the ice.

Knowledge of Neolithic man in Europe was increasing rapidly. Not only were the Danes pressing on with their study of their Stone Age antiquities (which they now recognized as dating very largely from the Neolithic period), but an altogether new type of settlement was being recognized in many of the lakes of Switzerland. Amazingly well preserved in marshy deposits below water level in the Lakes of Geneva, Zurich, Neuchâtel, Bienne and others, the remains of wooden houses were exposed together with those of the householders' clothes and other stuffs, their cereals and fruit and bread, their simple but efficient domestic equipment in wood, bone, basketry and matting. At the time, and for long after, these famous Swiss Lake Dwellings were believed to have been built on high piles well out into the lake. It is now known that they usually in fact rested directly on the muddy verge of the lakes, but this in no way detracts from the unique interest of these sites, where for the first time the everyday life of some of the earliest farming communities in western Europe could be reconstructed in detail.

The Lake Dwellings not only had a humanizing influence on prehistoric studies, making people think of flesh and blood men and women and family life instead of the classification of stones and bones, but simultaneously they made a contribution to scientific method. It soon began to appear that the lakeside settlements were not all of one age, but that while some were Neolithic, others could be assigned to the Bronze and Iron Ages. This encouraged very careful digging and the use of stratification for establishing the succession of one period of construction by another. Digging on these lines was being meticulously carried out in the mud of the Swiss lake beds and Danish bogs, considerably before it began to be adopted on the great dusty excavations in Mesopotamia and Egypt.

As excavation became a conscientious search for historical evidence in place of treasure hunting, it also inevitably became slower and more exacting. Partly for that reason it was no longer so liable to be dominated by single dashing individuals, but became more a matter of collaboration among many patient toilers. This was already beginning to be true of the exploration of the Lake Dwellings, but, if a leading figure is to be picked out, it is that of Ferdinand Keller, a schoolmaster who did the pioneer work on the Lake of Zurich (p. 268, I) and published his findings in five influential Memoirs that appeared between 1854 and 1863. Many other publications on the subject appeared during the sixties and later, all to be well summarized eventually by Robert Munro in his *Lake Dwellings of Europe*.

While the Neolithic Age and the later periods were being illumined in Switzerland and elsewhere, the more remote Palaeolithic was very far from being left in the dark. The excavation of the accumulated litter left in caves by Stone Age hunters had already contributed to the recognition of "Antediluvian Man" (p. 29, I), but now it was continued with greater understanding. The main centre of activity was in France, where inhabited caves are far more numerous than in Britain.

Many archaeologists were at work, but outstanding among them was Edouard Lartet, a magistrate who had forsaken law in favour of palaeontology and prehistory. He was far ahead of his time in recognizing the antiquity of man and the reality of his evolution—

indeed already in the 1830's and '40's he was unearthing very early fossil apes and declaring that fossil ancestors of man might turn up in the same deposits. Now he turned from animal to human remains. In 1852 a roadmender at work near Aurignac in the French Pyrenees opened a cave containing some seventeen human skeletons, together with flint and ivory implements and the remains of extinct animals. The skeletons were given Christian burial, and nothing more was done for several years, when Lartet, who lived in the neighbourhood, heard of the discovery and re-examined the cave. At first he could not decide whether the remains were of Palaeolithic or Neolithic age, but he rightly came to the conclusion that although the skeletons might be later (this is now never likely to be known), the tools and other finds were certainly Palaeolithic. In a paper published in 1860 and received with much more enthusiasm in Switzerland and England than in France (p. 29, I), he described the Aurignac cavern, and at the same time put forward a suggestion that the Stone Age from the Drift period onwards should be classified according to the great animals dominant in each epoch—the Great Cave Bear, the Elephant and Rhinoceros, and so on. The general idea of such systematisation was an advance in itself, and the "dominant animal" scheme had some currency. Although in the end it was superseded by the system of naming cultures after sites where they were found, the end of the Palaeolithic period is still sometimes called the Reindeer Age.

In the same year in which he published his important paper, Lartet dug another Pyrenean cave, at Massat, where he found not only new tool forms, including barbed antler harpoon-heads, but also an engraving on bone of a bear. With his usual quickness of perception, he linked this with a much earlier find of a bone engraved with deer, and claimed, against much opposition, that Palaeolithic man was not only a skilled hunter, but also an artist.

While he was still working in the Pyrenees, Lartet learnt that flints could be found in many of the caves that honeycombed the limestone hills of the Dordogne region of France. There then came about one of those happy associations between an intelligent man of wealth and a brilliant specialist. An English banker named Henry Christy, who was interested in the prehistoric past, provided funds for excavations in the Dordogne, particularly in the caves that open on to the beautiful valley of the Vézère round Les Éyzies. It proved as happy a hunting ground for Christy and Lartet as it had been for Palaeolithic man. Several of the caves where they dug—La Madeleine, Le Moustier (as well as the original Aurignac) —have given their names to cultures and today are taught to students throughout the world; nearly all are famous in the annals of archaeology. In 1864 at La Madeleine, Lartet found the piece of ivory engraved with the hairy outline of a mammoth that convinced many doubters of the antiquity of man (p. 34, I).

As for the actual manufacturers and creators of these implements and works of art, the remains of some of them came to light in 1868, when railway engineers blasted away some rock near Les Éyzies and exposed flints and fossil bones. By now Edouard Lartet was aging, and his son Louis was entrusted with the exploration of this Cro-Magnon rock shelter. He found the skeletons of an old man, two young adult men, a woman and a foetus, associated with pierced shells and other ornaments, and apparently formally buried. Here was the first recognized find of the Cro-Magnon race of men—tall, powerfully built, long-headed, large-brained and acquiline of nose. At the time of the discovery many savants refused to believe that the Palaeolithic cave dwellers could be men of modern type, whose like they might encounter any day in the Dordogne, still less that they could have practised careful interment of their dead. Many anthropologists, however, were in no doubt, and today it is recognized that the Cro-Magnons were widespread and among the most successful creators of late Palaeolithic culture.

What in fact Lartet, assisted by Christy, achieved during the third quarter of the nineteenth century, was to discover the existence of the high hunting cultures that had been created by *Homo sapiens* after the disappearance of the more ape-like Neanderthal men, and which lasted until the final retreat of the ice and the end of the Palaeolithic Age. This was the period, now known as the Upper Palaeolithic, which saw the first great acceleration in human cultural advance—the elaboration of implements, the invention of spear-thrower and bow and arrow, and, above all, the development of the visual arts.

In many parts of the world in the period after this Upper Palaeolithic Age, men had to adapt their way of life to meet the sharp climatic changes that followed the retreat of the ice sheets of the last glaciation. Everywhere, except in the very earliest farming centres (p. 251, I), they remained hunters and food gatherers, but often had to take to fishing, fowling and hunting smaller prey as forest spread and the great game herds disappeared. Prehistorians had extraordinary difficulty in interpreting the cultures which were in fact developed to meet this situation, and a curious idea arose that there was a sharp break, a gap, in human history at this point. The French systematizers named it the *ancien hiatus*.

Although the remains of many cultures which in fact filled the gap were distinguished during the latter part of the nineteenth century, they were either tacked on to the end of Palaeolithic times

or considered to be early Neolithic. It was not until the present
century that the *ancien hiatus* was recognized as a period in its
own right and called the Mesolithic Age.

All circumstances encouraged a ferment of interest in prehistoric research in Western Europe, and especially in France. New
learned journals, societies and museums were brought into being
(the French national museum of antiquities was founded in 1867),
and the work of the archaeologists was recognized by a fine display of prehistoric material in the great Paris Exhibition of this
same year of 1867. Lartet presided over the arrangement of the
collections in the *Galerie de l'Histoire du Travail*, but it was his
pupil, Gabriel de Mortillet, who wrote the much-admired hand-
book, *Promenades préhistoriques à l'Exposition Universelle*. In it
he proclaimed the triumph of the new science, and wound up his
"tour" by declaring that it was now impossible to doubt the great
law of human progress. Across the Channel Darwin and Huxley
were triumphing too—it was a great time for the doctrine of onward and upward. Three years later the Germans were in Paris—
something of a jolt to complacency. Indeed Lartet died in the course
of the Franco-Prussian war, a saddened and lately frustrated old
man.

The last quarter of the century saw many more caves dug, but
the first concern of the prehistorians, among whom de Mortillet
was pre-eminent, was now with classification. All kinds of alternative systems were devised, and learned society meeting rooms all
over Europe rang with the names suggested for subdivisions of the
Palaeolithic Age, from de Mortillet's Chellean, Mousterian, Solu-
trean and Magdalenian to Piette's painful Amygdalithic, Niphetic
and Glyptic. Valiant attempts were also made at dating, some of
them, including de Mortillet's estimate of about 240,000 years for
the beginning of the Chellean, being not altogether wide of the
mark.

Later prehistory, too, became involved in the scholarly enthusiasm for classification. The Neolithic, Bronze and Iron Ages were
all subject to it, though increasing difficulty was experienced in
finding schemes that would have meaning beyond a limited territory. De Mortillet had a Bronze Age system, but the strong man
who did most to put later prehistory into a strait jacket was Oscar
Montelius, a Swede who fully maintained the Scandinavian gift
for putting-in-order already manifest in the original Three Age
System. Montelius travelled Europe and the Mediterranean examining and comparing types of antiquities, especially of Bronze
Age antiquities such as swords, spears, axes, ornaments and pottery, until he had forged a mighty chronological framework for the
European Bronze Age, with periods austerely and scientifically la-

beled I, II, III and so on. After publishing his *Bronze Age Chronology in Europe* in 1889, Petrie's dating of Mycenaean pottery (p. 52, I) enabled him to introduce absolute dates into his chronology. He also devised a useful scheme for the Neolithic Age in his own northern lands.

Montelius might be called the Linnaeus of archaeology. It is always tempting for the imaginative to make fun of systematizers, and the great Swedish dramatist August Strindberg made fun of his fellow countryman. "There was once a man," he wrote, "who collected buttons. Determined to follow scientific principles, he did not classify his collection by the natural system of trouser buttons, coat buttons, shirt buttons and the like. Instead he arranged them according to a new and epoch-making system: buttons with one hole, buttons with two holes, and so on." Certainly there are weaknesses and even absurdities in the typological method, but when it is remembered how helpless the old antiquaries felt groping in the fog of ignorance, the achievement of Oscar Montelius and his like can be appreciated.

The laborious, necessary, and yet in many ways sterile effort to get historical control of the Stone Age by breaking it down and classifying, was continued by the next generation under the leadership of yet another great French prehistorian, the Abbé Breuil —and indeed still continues to the present day. Even in the 1960's, Hallam Movius of Harvard is struggling with the results of a large-scale and immensely thorough-going excavation back in the heart of the Christy-Lartet country—at Les Éyzies itself. It seems to upset the previously accepted system for a large part of the Upper Palaeolithic without making it very clear what should be substituted. One constant factor in all this has been ever-increasing elaboration—as in every branch of science and learning, the closer the scrutiny, the greater the complexity revealed.

There has also been one important change in approach. While Lartet, de Mortillet, Montelius and others of that time saw their divisions, by whatever name they were known, as representing strictly successive periods of time identical with the geological ages, it has since become more and more apparent that they really represent cultural groupings—the creations of particular societies, in particular areas. To use the names otherwise might lead to mistakes as absurd as trying to find an "Anglo-Saxon period" in China or Peru. Yet some of the larger subdivisions first established in France were sufficiently long-lasting and widespread to have some real chronological meaning, and moreover a very extensive validity. Now that the study of the emergence and development of mankind during the Pleistocene period has become a world-wide subject, the retention of these parts of the old classification can be used to prevent the total Balkanisation, as it were, of archaeological terms: a very real danger when names of newly discovered regional cultures are multiplying like rabbits.

The work of trying to chart the vast stretches—for much of them one might justifiably say wastes—of the Palaeolithic Age has been and remains very much for specialists, with only a limited interest for the public. Yet the results are of immense general interest, for it is this branch of archaeology that has enabled us to set human history in its proper planetary setting. It has enabled us to substitute for that symbolic creation on the sixth day in the year 4004 B.C. a slow but equally wonderful creation through the course of a million years.

One aspect of Stone Age studies that was anything but arid was the discovery of Palaeolithic art. It must have seemed so nearly incredible that these cave-dwelling "savages," whose very existence at so remote a time had only just been reluctantly conceded, were gifted artists able to carve, model, engrave, draw and paint, that one can hardly blame the many savants who maintained a stubborn scepticism.

What makes the reluctance to accept the antiquity or genuineness of the art found on cave walls a little hard to understand is that engravings on fragments of bone, antler and ivory had already won acceptance in the learned world. Lartet's very first finds (p. 73, I), it is true, aroused doubts, but the La Madeleine engraving of a mammoth on a piece of mammoth tusk clinched the question for most people. For one thing the lines were clean-cut and had therefore plainly been made while the tusk was fresh; for another no palaeontologist, let alone an amateur forger, would have been able to achieve this lively portrait of a beast long extinct. Anyone with an understanding of artistic creation, it might have been thought, would have known that the men who could sketch so brilliantly on a small scale could also be masters of more ambitious works. Nor were Lartet's the only early finds of what is now rather horribly named "mobiliary art"—that is to say small pieces usually found among the occupation litter on cave floors. In the same decade of the sixties, several others were found, supreme among them a spear-thrower carved in deep relief with two reindeer following one another, from the Bruniquel cave in the department of the Tarn-et-Garonne. This sculpture is vigorous, catches exactly the essential character of the reindeer, and is miraculously adapted to the shape and function of the antler spear-thrower: compared with this, work on a cave wall would be child's play.

Many other examples of mobiliary art were brought to light before 1879, when the Marquis de Sautuola and his small daughter found the famous paintings of Altamira near Santander. The story of this discovery is one of the favourites in the more romantic annals of archaeology (p. 199, I). Almost everyone knows how the Spanish nobleman was excavating a trench in the cavern floor when his daughter, her eyes by now adapted to the gloom, looked up to the low roof and recognized the marvellous cluster of bison painted in polychrome. Almost everyone, too, knows how she called out to her father "*Papá, mira toros pintados.*" Perhaps it is not quite so widely known that the two painted caves which easily eclipse all the rest in the quantity and quality of their art, Altamira and Lascaux, were first detected not through human will and perseverance but by the nosiness and enterprise of dogs.

When de Sautuola published his findings the next year, few authorities believed him. While some of the sceptics thought he had been duped, others went so far as to accuse him of having himself used a French artist, whom he was befriending, to fake the painted ceiling. His good sense, or honour, had still not been vindicated when he died in 1888. Then a few years later a farmer in the Vézère valley, clearing out a small rock shelter for use as a tool shed, not only noticed flints and bones in the soil he was shovelling but also broke through into a cave. Inquisitive boys went in to investigate and after crawling and wriggling along for about a hundred yards, reported animals engraved on the roof and walls. By now farmers round Les Éyzies understood the importance of Palaeolithic Man, and Émile Rivière—who had unearthed Palaeolithic skeletons at Mentone—was sent for. His careful digging of this cave of La Mouthe not only confirmed the engravings and discovered a decorated stone lamp that had been used by the hunter-artists, but also demonstrated that the mouth of the cave had become completely blocked with earth and rubbish *before the end of Palaeolithic times*.

This convinced many doubters, but it was not until the beginning of this century that belief in cave art became wholly respectable. In 1901 the Abbé Breuil and others of impeccable scientific reputation found very many more engravings and paintings in caves (Combarelles and Font-de-Gaume) in the classic Dordogne region, and in the following year the *Association Française pour l'Avancement des Sciences* made a solemn visit to the Dordogne caves and put their seal upon the authenticity of the artists of 12,000 years and more in the past. Émile Cartailhac, who had been one of the most determined and influential disbelievers, very honestly appeared in sackcloth, publishing an article on Altamira which he sub-titled the "*Mea culpa d'un sceptique.*" "I am a party to a mistake of twenty years' standing," he wrote, "to an injustice which must be frankly admitted and put right." But the Marquis de Sautuola was dead.

After the excursion of the *Association*, the elderly Cartailhac and the youthful Breuil suddenly decided to cross the Pyrenees and visit Altamira. They had intended to stay only a few days, but became so absorbed in copying the paintings that they remained for nearly a month. Breuil worked at his tracings day after day, while it rained mercilessly outside, lying on his back on straw-filled sacks and with candles as his only source of light.

No one can think of Palaeolithic art without thinking also of the Abbé Breuil. Not only did he discover great numbers of works of art in all the three main centres—the Dordogne region, the central French Pyrenees and the Cantabrian mountains of northwest Spain—but he toiled with almost superhuman endurance at copying them. He was a skilled draughtsman, and in the days before colour photography most of the world came to appreciate the genius of the cave painters through his great folios. Some people thought that he improved upon the originals, and perhaps there was a smoothness and bloom not to be found on a cave wall. Yet there were losses as well, and certainly the colour camera has done nothing to diminish the reputation of the first artists.

These artists often liked to create their works of art in most inaccessible places, and sometimes the pursuit of them has needed tremendous courage. There was, for instance, the penetration to the inner cave at Montespan (Haute Garonne) when Norbert Casteret had to plunge blindly in a cave flooded to the roof, swim some distance under water and negotiate a siphon before coming up safely in the chamber. There he found roughly modelled animals (a bear and probably a lion) which had evidently been used for the same hunting magic that was also undoubtedly enacted in connection with many of the murals.

Other outstanding finds have been of the fine paintings half a mile into the rock in the huge cave of Niaux, the male and female bison modelled in clay in high relief at the Tuc d'Audubert, the splendid sculptured frieze of horses at Cap Blanc and the reliefs of voluptuously fat women, undoubtedly connected with fertility cults, at Laussel and Angles-sur-l'Anglin. A few minor examples of cave art have now been detected outside the famous French and Spanish centres—most notably in Italy, where a cave on Monte Pelegrino near Palermo contains some of the best engravings of human figures (graceful and full of movement) in all Palaeolithic art.

But there has been only one recent discovery extraordinary enough to rouse public enthusiasm: the cave of Lascaux which has brought fame and prosperity to the little neighbouring town of Montignac-sur-Vézère. There again the Abbé Breuil was quickly on the scene, once the cavern had been discovered by young Ravidat's dog, by young Ravidat and his three friends and by Laval, their schoolmaster. This was in the autumn of 1940, and the writer well remembers how the Abbé, who had been bravely sending cards to English friends trying to tell them of the whereabouts of German military installations under a thin disguise of archaeological news, now sent word of this very real discovery. The information was bound to be scrappy, and some of us at any rate got the impression that the painting at Lascaux consisted exclusively of one gigantic black bull. It was delightful in those days to have news of any subject other than military disaster, and after the war it was exciting to be free at last to visit what is the most imaginatively stirring of all the painted caves.

The study of man's bodily evolution from fossil remains is, of course, a subject distinct from archaeology, the study of his cultural remains, yet in the field the two have overlapped so much that something must be said about the finding of the men behind the tools and the art. The Neanderthal skull itself, the unearthing of which chimed in so well with the events of 1859, had been accidentally discovered by workmen digging in the small Feldhofer cave in the Neanderthal ravine near Düsseldorf. Although some experts shared Huxley's perceptiveness in immediately accepting the skull cap, with its low vault and projecting browridges, as that of the most primitive known type of man, many others, especially anti-evolutionists, put up a barrage of foolish suggestions: the skull was that of an idiot, of a sufferer from hypertrophic osteitis, of a modern Irishman and of a Cossack killed during the Napoleonic wars. No one is more prejudiced than a prejudiced man of science.

In fact another specimen of Neanderthaler had been found some years before in a fissure on the Rock of Gibraltar; it was brought out and demonstrated at a meeting of the British Association in 1864, but in the baffling manner in which these "dead spots" sometimes occur, very little notice was, or ever has been, taken of it. Unhappily, too, just before this, Boucher de Perthes, who had fought so long for the acceptance of his perfectly genuine finds, was tricked by his workmen into publishing a faked human jawbone—a trick which was soon exposed but inevitably gave ammunition to the opponents of evolution.

However, they could not hold out indefinitely, and by 1887 refusal to recognize the existence of Neanderthal or other primitive types of men had become virtually impossible. In that year two skeletons were found in a cave at Spy in the Namur province of Belgium. Not only were they embedded in a deposit known to date from the Pleistocene Ice Age, but they were almost identical with the original Neanderthal man. That there should be *three* finds of skeletons of congenital idiots or errant Irishmen or Cossacks was too much to swallow. Since that time a surprisingly large number of Neanderthal or Neanderthal-like remains have been found, and have proved that this breed, which was in the ascendancy during the beginning of the last glaciation, had a very wide range—all round the Mediterranean, throughout Europe and eastward as far as Uzbekistan. In this last region Soviet archaeologists excavated the burial of a Neanderthal boy from the cave of Teshik-Tash—the small body appears to have been deliberately surrounded by horns of mountain goats.

The discovery of the old man of Cro-Magnon had been followed by several others either of the same race or of others equally of modern type, so that it soon became overwhelmingly certain that *Homo sapiens,* the creator of the Upper Palaeolithic cultures, had succeeded Neanderthal Man towards the end of the Ice Age. But what kind of being had preceded him?

There was perhaps a tendency at the time to think along the lines of "the missing link," that is to say of a species half way between modern man and modern ape, rather than to envisage a very generalized creature ancestral to both. Many scientists were eager for the appearance of such an ape-man, but one among them was not content to "wait to see what would turn up." Eugene Dubois, a young lecturer in anatomy at Amsterdam, took an enthusiastic interest in human fossils, and became wholly seized of the idea that he, Dubois, would find the ape-man. It has already been seen in the case of Schliemann and others what concentrated will can do, even in the rather intractable field of archaeology.

Dubois's plans were based on a simple premise. The modern large anthropoid apes lived in only two regions: in Central Africa and the East Indies. Therefore these were the most likely places to find the early ancestor—and of the two he, as a Dutch citizen, naturally chose the East Indies. Neither his colleagues nor anyone else in Amsterdam seems to have had much sympathy with his ambition, and in the end Dubois had to make his way to Sumatra as a military doctor. He arrived in 1887, the year in which the Neanderthal men were discovered at Spy. At first he had little time to spare for digging, but gradually various clues led him to focus his efforts on central Java, and in particular on the deposits, largely volcanic, brought down by the Solo river, which were immensely rich in animal fossils.

During 1891 and '92 his unswerving determination was rewarded. From among the welter of fossil bones of elephants, rhinoceroses, hippopotamuses, tapirs, antelopes and monkeys contained in the Solo beds he was able to extricate two teeth, a skull cap and femur of a large primate (the order to which apes and men belong) with a brain capacity very much greater than that of the anthropoid apes but smaller than that of modern men. In 1894 he published a monograph on his find, claiming that this *Pithecanthropus erectus* was indeed an "intermediate form between the Apes and Man." A little later Dubois returned to Europe and addressed the International Zoological Congress then meeting at Leyden. There was hot dispute as to whether or not the new fossil species should be allowed to rank as human, but there was at least a general recognition of the extreme interest of the find. Before long this being gained popular recognition as Java Man.

Although *Pithecanthropus* was given the specific name of *erectus* because the femur suggested an upright carriage, there was nevertheless a failure to learn from Dubois's discovery that the early species of humans had evolved a body and carriage very much like our own long *before* the skull and the brain within approached those of *Homo sapiens*. This failure may have been due partly to a false conviction that the evolution of the brain must, as it were, lead the way in human evolution, partly to a very exaggerated idea which had been formed of the ape-like stance and gait of the later Neanderthal men. It is only since the realization that even the very ancient Australopithecines already walked upright nearly a million years ago that it has been fully realized that it was in fact the body which led the evolutionary way.

No history of archaeology can omit the tragicomedy of the Piltdown affair. It was in 1908 that Charles Dawson, a country solicitor with a good reputation as an amateur palaeontologist, was going along a country road in Sussex when he noticed that the road had been repaired with an iron-stained gravel unusual for the neighbourhood. He learnt that this had come from a small surface gravel pit nearby, and before long workers gave him a fragment of iron-stained bone from the pit and told him that previously they had broken up "a sort of large coconut"—which of course, sounded very much like a complete human skull.

An odd part of the story is that nothing more happened until 1911, when Dawson himself found another skull fragment in the Piltdown gravels. He at once got into touch with Professor Smith Woodward, and the next year they organized a considerable excavation in the gravel pit. They came upon some teeth, a lower jaw and enough cranial fragments to make possible a reconstruction of the brain case.

The cranium was quickly recognized as being close to that of *Homo sapiens* (although various subtle differences were laboriously noted), while the jaw was just as clearly ape-like (again, it was said, with significant differences). From the first some experts insisted that the brain case and jaw could not have belonged to the same individual, but others, and particularly the English, were only too eager to accept such a blend of ape and human in our early ancestors.

An enormous amount of analytical study was devoted to the Piltdown remains, and hundreds of thousands of words written about them. Sir Arthur Keith alone must have lavished precious years on these supposed fossils. That was the real tragedy of this forgery—the exposure of which is so amusingly described by Dr. Weiner (p. 213, I). The public naturally found it highly comic that so many experts should have been fooled for so long. Indeed, so it was, and their ability to detect many special features in what proved to be a fairly recent cranium and a quite modern ape's jaw warns us of the amount of subjectivity in the most "scientific" observations.

Yet it must also be allowed that science was vindicated in the end. By 1953 knowledge of human evolution had made so much progress that palaeontologists were able to see that something *must* be wrong with the anomalous Piltdown Man. That is why tests were started.

It was as early as 1903 that the first hint of the existence of primitive human fossils in China was made known. This took the form of an upper molar purchased from one of those Chinese apothecaries who used to deal in "dragon's tooth" medicines. The German palaeontologist who published the fossil pointed out that it appeared to be extremely ancient and yet had well-marked human features. The next step was taken in 1920 when a Swedish geologist, Gunnar Andersson, observing that the deposits in limestone caves at Chou-k'ou-tien were rich in fossil bones, persuaded his rich compatriot, Ivar Kreuger, to finance excavations.

Two more teeth with a human appearance had come to light when, in 1925, Dr. Davidson Black, a Canadian, appeared on the scene. It seems that, like Dubois, he had purposely taken a foreign post (at Peking) in the hope of finding human fossils. He was impressed by the possibilities of Chou-k'ou-tien, and won a substantial Rockefeller grant to carry out more systematic digging. He was, indeed, a remarkably bold and decisive man, for when, in 1927, another molar in unusually good condition was found, Black claimed it as representing a new genus of man which he named *Sinanthropus pekinensis*.

During the following season the field direction of this most international excavation passed to the Chinese Dr. W. C. Pei, and the party was also joined by the American Young and the now famous French Jesuit, Père Teilhard de Chardin. The Rockefeller Foundation continued to pour out money, and as much as 12,000 cubic metres of cave earth was shifted in three years.

Further human fragments were found, but the first real excitement was not until 1929, when Pei came upon a well-preserved skull cap rather like that of Java Man but with an appreciably higher vault. A little later he announced what was in some ways an even more important discovery: unmistakable evidence that inhabitants of the caves, and presumably *Sinanthropus*, had maintained large fires and chipped very rough stone implements. No implements had been identified with Java Man, so that the proof that culture had already started in the hands of these very primitive beings (now known to be over a quarter of a million years old) was of great significance. The ability to *manufacture* has in fact become accepted as the only sound criterion for distinguishing the first human beings.

Work continued right up to the outbreak of the war. By 1939 it was claimed that remains representing as many as thirty-eight individuals had been found. An unduly large proportion of the fossils were of head bones. This led a few people to say that the tool- and fire-maker had been an altogther more advanced type of man who had hunted *Sinanthropus* and kept the heads as trophies. This is a not-quite-impossible, yet far-fetched, argument that has been used frequently since to confuse the interpretation of cave deposits. Most people today believe that *Sinanthropus* (like Neanderthal Man and *Homo sapiens* after him) both killed and ate his fellows.

One change has been made since the years when digging was in progress at Chou-k'ou-tien. Peking Man has been judged to belong to the same genus as Java Man, and given the specific name of *Pithecanthropus pekinensis*. The true fossils of the thirty-eight individuals from Chou-k'ou-tien are never likely to be seen again. In one of those moments when his inheritance from the primitive past took possession of *Homo sapiens*, they were destroyed. The story of what happened varies. One version tells that on the outbreak of war the sixty-three cases containing the bones were put in the American medical college in Peking under the eye of Teilhard de Chardin, who was a prisoner of the Japanese. At the end of hostilities the Japanese wished to evacuate the fossil men with their own, but an American torpedo sent the ship carrying them to the bottom of the China Sea. After a quarter of a million years of oblivion underground, the Peking bones were quickly returned to oblivion below water. Happily, casts had already been taken.

Modern Archaeology

The age of modern archaeology can best be taken as beginning after the First World War. All such divisions are, of course, largely arbitrary—and indeed several topics have already been carried through well beyond 1918, where there was an obvious continuity of development. In the same way it may occasionally be necesary

85 *Modern Archaeology*

to look back behind 1914 to see the beginnings of some trends in modern archaeology.

Yet the great disaster which ended an age could not fail to change archaeology as it changed everything else. Most conspicuously, the subject became increasingly professional. In all European countries, and to a lesser extent in the United States, wealthy individuals, whether patrician or, like Schliemann and Evans, men with fortunes made in trade and industry, who had excavated to please themselves and at their own expense, became extremely rare and finally extinct. Instead, more and more expeditions were financed by institutions, often with state aid, while the directors and their staffs were full-time archaeologists from universities or museums or government departments. More and more such posts were created, and although no archaeologist was likely to grow rich, it became increasingly possible to be sure of earning a living —and of enjoying life—within the archaeological fold. During the period between the two wars, numbers of outstandingly able young people were in fact attracted to what was plainly an exciting and rapidly-growing subject, and universities responded by instituting degree and post-graduate courses.

Thus archaeology became a profession, if always a small one, and inevitably instituted professional standards. Standards of excavation which had already been raised towards the end of the nineteenth century now reached an altogether new level, and, what is more, were often strictly enforced. Not only was there much stringent criticism between colleagues, but, in a number of countries, official inspectors of monuments and excavations were introduced. Many special techniques of a simple but effective kind became established alike for excavation and preservation, while the need for every major dig to be directed according to a carefully planned strategy was generally accepted. Indeed, as knowledge increased and the picture of the past became more nearly complete, it was sometimes possible to adopt a wider strategy and undertake excavations to solve particular problems in national prehistory.

Such wider planning could on occasion be open to abuse. In general the strong nationalism that followed the "self determination" of Versailles encouraged archaeological research in a perfectly healthy way. Young or newly-independent countries wanted to root themselves by rediscovering their past. On the other hand, there might sometimes be an excessive concentration on nationalistic schemes—in Czechoslovakia, for example, a disproportionate amount of effort went in pursuit of Slav origins. Far worse, in Germany, attempts were made in various directions to distort archaeological evidence to support doctrines of blood and soil and

Aryan superiority. This also had its negative effects; for example, a professor was dismissed when he announced a course of lectures, *Mediterranean Influences on Ancient Germany*—all influence had to go the other way.

It would be false to suggest that the new high standards of excavation became universal during the interwar years. In particular, where armies of raw peasants had to be employed on *tells* and other sites demanding the shifting of great masses of soil, procedure was sometimes less far removed from that of Layard and Mariette than it should have been. Mortimer Wheeler, whose own digging is directed with para-military precision, made famous a photograph which had been taken as late as 1935. He called it *Chaos in the East*. It shows a large, roughly rectangular hole, swarming with turbanned workmen, some just finding elbow room to use long-handled shovels and baskets, but all apparently quite undirected. Even today many of us have seen eastern excavations that were, to put it generously, slightly dishevelled.

Some of the new methods in archaeology were involved with changing aims. Already in the nineteenth century the old notion of extracting works of art or individual monuments had been giving way to a determination to examine whole cities from the point of view of the way of life of their inhabitants (p. 46, I). This ideal became clearer and more coherent and began to be applied to new kinds of site. It received tremendous encouragement from the growing prestige of social and economic history at the expense of military, political and "great man" history. From the nature of its evidence, archaeology was perfectly suited to throw light on early economics, on the growth of technology and the history of the common man.

In all this a powerful influence was exerted by Professor Gordon Childe, perhaps the most original and distinguished prehistorian the subject has as yet produced. An Australian who early came to England, Childe was a theoretical Marxist. Yet only for a very brief period did he allow this philosophy to warp the evidence—when he realized that this might be happening he became a partial "deviationist." What he did, and brilliantly, was to use archaeology to show man as a self-sufficient organism specializing in brain who has pulled himself up by the bootstraps of technology. The very title of his best-known book, *What Happened in History* (1936), is deliberately cocking a snook at the traditional values of history. Here, he is saying, in the progress of technology is what was really important in human affairs going on almost unnoticed below the din of dynastic struggles, and the rise and fall of faiths and empires. Whether one was for or against it, his clear, vigorously-expressed philosophy gave archaeology a fresh impetus.

Childe, like several of the pioneers of his subject, was a good linguist, and this gave him command of a wide literature. (His ear was always bad: it was unkindly said that he was unintelligible in twelve languages.) He used this ability to make himself a link between the extensive researches going on in eastern Europe and the U.S.S.R., and those of the West. Such a go-between and interpreter is badly needed today.

The effect of the new interest in the economic and social life of past communities on archaeological method was to encourage the excavation of complete prehistoric sites. In the past, while the most urgent need was to establish a chronological framework for prehistory and to trace the movements of peoples and the spread of cultures, there had been a tendency to sample sites by cutting a few trenches or sinking pits. This might reveal much of the age and history of, say, a village or farmstead, but very little of its economic foundations or social structure. Unfortunately the exposure of a whole settlement is an immensely more expensive business than sampling, and, in countries where archaeological research is always short of funds, has only occasionally been accomplished.

This is the place to honour a man who seems now to be widely accepted as "the father of modern excavation" (though undoubtedly some of the German classicists could claim to be its grandfather). This is General Augustus Henry Lane-Fox Pitt-Rivers, who belongs by the calendar to the nineteenth century and yet through his methods to modern times. Working on the huge estate in the south of England, rich in antiquities, that he inherited rather unexpectedly in 1880, he excavated a number of prehistoric and Roman sites. Believing in the need for continuous supervision, he trained assistants—even, it is recorded, putting them into his colours and allowing them to ride behind his own dog-cart on highwheeled, penny-farthing bicycles. Not only did he record every find, whether or not it appeared to have any significance, both in plan and section (he was aware that his successors would understand things which he could not), but probably alone among his European contemporaries he uncovered complete villages, making it possible to count the houses and store pits, estimate the number of inhabitants, the amount of their food and so on. One of his reports on a Romano-British village was so full and exact that it proved possible in recent years to use it for an altogether new interpretation of the economic history of the region in Romano-British times.

The General died at the turn of the century, having published his discoveries in the handsome blue-and-gold volumes of *Cranborne Chase* (p. 330, II). Few if any of his immediate followers had the combined authority, patience, skill and wealth to maintain his extraordinary standards. Yet his influence certainly endured, and in a sense came into its own in the interwar years when the policy of total excavation had been formulated. In carrying out this expensive policy the Scandinavians and Germans, with generous state endowment, were well to the fore. The complete opening up of the Neolithic village of Köln-Lindenthal, near Cologne, accomplished in the early 1930's, was a notable instance of what could be done. From it an immense amount was learnt about the very early farming communities which pushed westward into Europe along the line 'of the Danube and beyond: how the colonists had moved into the village, cleared the land, prospered, and moved on again when the soil was exhausted.

In Britain (where money was short) the most nearly comparable achievement of this period was the total excavation of a third century B.C. Celtic farmstead at Little Woodbury near Salisbury. The dig was directed by a German, Dr. Gerhard Bersu, and by uncovering the whole of the massive circular farm building, the many storage pits, the granaries, seed stores, corn drying frames and winnowing floors, he was not only able to present a complete and vivid picture of life in an early Celtic establishment of this kind, but also to reckon the approximate size of the kindred who would have owned the farm, the acreage and cropping system, the amount of pasture and arable land. Little Woodbury carried "economic archaeology" a step further, but in the end total excavation was overtaken by total war. Dr. and Frau Bersu were among those who presently found themselves interned in the Isle of Man.

In spite of nationalism and the temporary fissures of war, the general trend of recent archaeology has inevitably been towards a more unified world prehistory. The huge gap in our knowledge for long presented by Africa-outside-Egypt has been largely filled, and its immense importance in the early history of humanity recognized. The American hemisphere with its relatively short human past, has been fitted into its place in the story of the great expansion of our species. For parts of central and eastern Asia and of the lands and islands of the Pacific, knowledge is still less exact and coherent, and still not fully integrated with that of the rest of the world. But it is catching up. The Russian, Indian and Pakistani archaeologists are tackling the huge tasks confronting them, and the Chinese are making some progress in the discovery of their prehistoric origins. In Australia and New Zealand, where for so long anthropologists were content to study the native populations without much thought for the time dimension of their history, archaeological appointments are now at last being made and stratified sites discovered. Even the Australian aborigine has a past.

As archaeology has become increasingly world-wide and coherent, and as it has revealed the larger movements in human history underlying the development of different races and cultures, it must surely have contributed to our appreciation of the very real bonds uniting mankind—just as its recovery of so many brilliant civilizations must have helped to reduce the arrogant intolerance of existing peoples who have claimed unique virtue and truth for their own habits and beliefs.

Modern Excavations and Discoveries

Both the professionalization of archaeology and its growth into a world-wide discipline have encouraged a complexity and abundance of research that make it impossible any longer to attempt to describe all its main undertakings and discoveries. Since the First World War there have been thousands of excavations, and the literature both in books and learned journals has become as swollen and unmanageable as that of most other subjects. It is only feasible to select a few finds that were particularly dramatic or significant or aroused exceptional public interest, and to try to relate them to one or two big changes in our interpretation of the past.

Exploration in Mesopotamia was restarted after the war with almost indecent speed. Even before the 1918 armistice was signed, a British Museum expedition to Ur and Eridu had begun excavations that were to lead to discoveries that reached the headlines (by now much enlarged) and stirred the popular imagination just as those of Evans and Schliemann had done. This happened after the British Museum had joined forces with the University of Pennsylvania, and the direction of the work had been entrusted to Leonard Woolley. Woolley was an experienced excavator, sharp-eyed, intuitive and skilled at technical improvisations. Above all he had the imagination to be an excellent writer, well able to rouse public enthusiasm—and therefore the disapproval of the more high-and-dry type of academic scholar.

Woolley did much to reveal the character of an early Sumerian city (p. 343 ff., I) and of its great temple mound or *ziggurat* (p. 345, I)—so closely comparable in function and idea with the temple pyramids of central America—but the great excitement of his excavations at Ur was the discovery of the Royal Tombs, particularly the graves of one A-bar-gi and his queen Shub-ad who seem to have ruled about 3000 B.C., a few centuries before the First Dynasty of Ur. The splendid vessels, ornaments and weapons in gold and *lapis lazuli* from these tombs, as well as humbler grave goods from the burials of the commoners that surround them, gave an altogether new understanding of the arts, craftsmanship and riches of what we now know to have been the first high civilization ever created by man.

Historically of almost equal interest were the discoveries made by Woolley and his predecessors concerning the Neolithic and Chalcolithic communities of the district which had flourished there before the coming of the Sumerians. At al 'Ubaid, a few miles from Ur, they found remains of a settlement of this kind, and it gave its name to a culture now dated back to 4000 B.C. One of Leonard Woolley's greatest intuitive feats was when, sinking a trial pit into the oldest deposits at Ur, he reached an horizon containing remains of the same 'Ubaid culture and then, below it, a bed of absolutely sterile clay. Almost any other excavator would have stopped at this point, convinced he had reached the natural ground level, but Woolley accepted a hunch, dug down and down and presently came upon another deposit of rubbish left by 'Ubaid villagers. The clay had undoubtedly been laid down by a heavy and prolonged flood, and it was everywhere hailed as being that of the biblical Deluge. If this is no longer accepted in quite these terms, it must certainly represent flooding of the kind recorded in Genesis—and we can be grateful to that bed of clay for helping to raise money for the excavation from all those whose purses are most readily opened to prove the truth of the Bible.

In pushing back the history of Mesopotamia to 4000 B.C., Woolley was continuing the process which had already led from the Assyrians back through the Akkadians and Babylonians to the Sumerians themselves. The further prolonging of the Neolithic period, that is to say of the time when men had already become farmers but were still dependent on stone implements, was to be one of the main features of the archaeology of the following decades. Already before the First World War, two sites in central and northern Mesopotamia had yielded traces of a people still essentially Neolithic though using a little copper, who could be recognized by their beautiful painted pottery. After the war expeditions from America, Britain and Germany, and presently, too, those of the Iraq Department of Antiquities newly created by Gertrude Bell and her friends, began to find settlements of these people, often underlying later cities, and then pushed back earlier still.

An English party under Campbell Thompson, which had returned to the famous Kuyunjik mound of Nineveh, sank a shaft from the Assyrian level to a depth of seventy feet, where they reached virgin soil. There at the base they found remains of a simple Neolithic community, which can now be dated well back into the fifth millennium B.C. How surprised Layard and Botta would have been, when they were driving their rival trenches through the Assyrian temples and palaces, to know that far below their feet lay the relics of a village which had fallen into oblivion three thousand years before the power of Assyria had been heard of.

Meanwhile the range of these Neolithic cultures was also being

extended in space. A great French expedition had long been working at Susa in Persia, south of the Zagros mountains, and now its
discovery of an early settlement by people making painted pottery
of extraordinary beauty and artistic inspiration (to be seen in the
Louvre) could be better understood and fitted into the emerging
chronological scheme of this historically vital area of south-west
Asia. Neolithic peoples were then traced further north in Persia
to the area between the Caspian Sea and the Zagros range. In
particular the mounds of Tepe Siyalk when excavated during the
thirties produced a great depth of deposits representing millennia
of village life—the earliest communities being contemporary with
the earliest at Kuyunjik and other Mesopotamian sites.

The remains of peoples of Neolithic culture were also being
traced westward, particularly into Anatolia. The important expedition from the Oriental Institute of Chicago University, which started
work there in 1926, not only did much to fill out and shape our
knowledge of Hittite history, but also, at Alishar, east of Ankara,
it cut down to much earlier settlements. Then, at Mersin in Cilicia
at the north east corner of the Mediterranean, the Neilsen expedition under the Englishman, John Garstang, found a site which led
them back and back into the remains of early Neolithic villages
where farming communities were living in the sixth millennium
B.C. or even before.

In Egypt excavations were greatly expanding and complicating
the history of the predynastic peoples of the Nile delta and valley.
Many of these were peasants of pure Neolithic culture, yet it was
gradually proved beyond all doubt that their settlements were less
ancient than the oldest coming to light in Iraq and Iran.

By now it was in fact abundantly clear that man had made the
all-important advance from the hunting life to one based on a farming economy, somewhere in south-west Asia. Excavations along
the northern shores of the Mediterranean and throughout Europe
were also revealing just how the new farming economy had spread
into these regions, as Neolithic colonists sought virgin lands for
crops and pasture. It was found that one thoroughfare of this
expansion had lain along the valley of the Danube—which in the
end led peasant cultivators into the extreme west of Europe. This
story, together with the succeeding Bronze Age developments, was
given coherence by Gordon Childe in his massive *Danube in Prehistory* (1929). The other line of expansion had been from Asia
and Egypt along the shores of the Mediterranean, and could be
detected in Italy, Spain and Portugal and on into France and
Switzerland; while a side route had taken seafarers up the Atlantic
coasts to Britain and Scandinavia (p. 275, I). The megalithic architecture of western Europe, including the great tombs which had

always attracted the attention of the early antiquaries, was now recognized as the creation of a late phase of this westward expansion of Neolithic peoples.

During the whole of this time when knowledge of the early farming peoples was being won by innumerable excavations in Asia, Egypt, Anatolia and Europe, it was assumed that their Neolithic cultures had from the first been characterized not only by the development of farming techniques, but also of domestic crafts such as weaving and pot-making. During the decade of the 1950's all this was changed—and the beginning of what Childe called the "Neolithic Revolution" (the first domestication of plants and animals) pushed even further back into the past. Two expeditions beyond all others were responsible for this startling change in archaeological thought—those of Professor and Mrs. Robert Braidwood of Chicago at Jarmo in the hills of northern Iraq, and of Dr. Kathleen Kenyon of the British Palestine Exploration Fund at Jericho in the Jordan valley. The Braidwoods dug a modest village site on a small promontory. Below the houses of a community of the accepted early Neolithic kind, they exposed the superimposed ruins of earlier villages whose inhabitants had raised animals and a somewhat primitive type of wheat, but who had been altogether without the craft of pot-making. By the time of these excavations, the Carbon-14 method of dating (p. 135, I) had come into use, and although the results for Jarmo proved somewhat erratic, it is now accepted that a farming settlement had been established there as long ago as the seventh millennium B.C.

The findings at Jericho were even more astonishing—they may indeed be said to be the most significant contribution to the history of *Homo sapiens* made since the last war (our species is named in order to exclude the all-important discoveries concerning human origins, p. 102, I). In the *tell* beside the oasis at Jericho, Kathleen Kenyon explored far below Joshua's city, far below the earlier Bronze Age town and then below the ordinary pottery-using Neolithic settlement which had already been recognized on the site. She struck down into many metres of deposits left by inhabitants who, like those at Jarmo, had been cultivators but had no pottery of any kind. They had lived in roundish houses of sun-dried brick, and—here is the greatest surprise of all—had enclosed their settlement with a free-standing stone wall (surviving to a height of thirty feet) and built inside it a lofty round tower with a flight of stone steps leading to the summit. A walled and towered settlement of ten acres can hardly be denied the title of a town, and yet Carbon-14 dating has assigned its first foundation to about 7000 B.C. Though the general public was not greatly interested, the whole archaeological world hummed at this revelation. Everywhere textbook

writers and lecturers had to push back their dates for the beginning
of the Neolithic Age and recognize that cultivation began well before pot-making. They also had to recognize that where local conditions were exceptionally favourable, as they were at the Jericho
oasis, our ancestors were able to form what were at least partially
urbanized communities as much as 9,000 years ago.

But this was not the end of the historical importance of the
Jericho excavations. About twenty years before, another famous
Palestinian dig conducted by a woman—that of Professor Dorothy
Garrod on the south-west slopes of Mount Carmel—had found not
only the tools and skeletons of Neanderthal men but also, at another
cave, abundant remains of a late Mesolithic people who had come
to be known to archaeology as Natufians. These people had depended very largely on hunting, but had used stone sickles to reap
some crop—generally assumed to have been of wild grasses. Professor Garrod at once recognized them as a group living on the
borderline between the hunting and the farming economy—
although their flint implements belonged entirely to the earlier
(Mesolithic) tradition.

Now below the oldest mudbrick houses at Jericho, Kathleen
Kenyon found considerable evidence to show that people with a
Mesolithic cultural tradition very much like that of the Natufians
had visited the oasis from time to time, evidently as nomadic
hunters, and had even established a shrine there. The similarity
of the flint implements, and the absence of any break between the
latest Mesolithic and the lowest Neolithic horizons, seemed to prove
that the hunting Natufians had settled down at Jericho, and,
blessed with a permanent water supply and fertile soil, had quite
rapidly adopted a settled and then urbanized way of life. The
continuity of two "Ages" had been proved.

Jericho symbolizes the conclusion of another happy union—this
time within the subject of archaeology. Earlier in this introduction
some emphasis was put upon the division between the "scientific"
branch of archaeology which had been linked with geology and the
evolution of man and was mainly therefore concerned with the
Palaeolithic hunters of Pleistocene times, and the "humanist"
branch of the scholars, linguists and art collectors, typified by the
work of such men as Rawlinson and Layard among the ruins of
high civilizations. In the excavations at Jericho the two branches,
already linked by the acceptance of many common aims and
methods, may be said to celebrate their final coming together. Even
the two ladies most concerned illustrate the same theme, for
Dorothy Garrod was a student of the Palaeolithic period under
Breuil who, with her discovery of the Natufians, had strayed into
a slightly later age, while Kathleen Kenyon was a humanist and

classicist, who was led back in time by the depth of the deposits at Jericho.

In spite of the great significance of Jarmo and Jericho, it must not of course be assumed that farming necessarily began in their areas alone. Indeed, as so often happens when once a new phenomenon has been recognized, other examples soon came to light. Several "pre-pottery" Neolithic settlements have now been recognized, including a large village of domed huts (not unlike those at Jericho) in Cyprus. Claims for the beginning of farming in the southern Caspian region have also been advanced by Professor Carleton Coon as a result of his remarkable discoveries in caves of that region (p. 253, I).

While these explorations fundamental to our understanding of a crucial phase of human advance were being made, many other expeditions from many lands were in the field in south-west Asia and Anatolia, consolidating our knowledge of these areas and particularly of their rich Bronze Age civilizations. Indeed in the prosperous twenties some American expeditions, such as that of the Oriental Institute of Chicago at Mediddo, went to work in a really big way, ensuring that their archaeologists should be neither hurried nor uncomfortable. Substantial houses for the members of the expedition were built, and even tennis courts laid down. A far cry from the fleeting encampments of Layard and the other pioneers.

One excavation among so many proved to be of such unique interest that it demands special mention. This was Ras Shamra on the north Syrian coast, site of the Canaanite and Phoenician city of Ugarit. It has been called the "Shanghai of the mid-second millennium B.C." because it was a port where traders and official and ordinary travellers drawn from most of the ancient world—from the land of the Hittites, from Crete and other Mediterranean lands, from Egypt, Palestine and above all from Mesopotamia—met and mingled. All their languages were current in the city. Texts in Sumerian, Akkadian, Hurrian, Egyptian and Hittite have been recovered by the French expedition under Professor Claude Schaeffer which has dug there for an unprecedented number of years—starting in 1929 and still in progress. Most illuminating of all were texts in the native Canaanite, proto-Phoenician tongue, written in a cuneiform which proved to be not syllabic but alphabetic—in fact the earliest alphabet known in the world. Moreover, the texts themselves showed how close the Hebrews had been to the Canaanites in the days before Moses. The godhead of El or Elohim appears in this Canaanite literature, much of the moral teaching and ideal of justice of the Hebrew prophets is foreshadowed, and there are parallels to biblical psalms and possibly also prototypes of Adam and Eve. As well as religious texts, Ugarit yielded diplomatic dispatches comparable in interest with those of el Amarna. Indeed, Schaeffer's patient work at this cosmopolitan city has revealed with extraordinary clarity the degree of the cultural borrowing and commercial and political interchange that helped to unite the many and often warring peoples of the ancient world.

In Egypt the archaeological picture was much the same as in Mesopotamia. There was a great consolidation of the knowledge won by the pioneers—most of all, exploration round Memphis and Sakkara threw light on the formative years of the Old Kingdom and on the original unification of the kingdom. The Americans were late on the scene in Egypt, but when they came their contribution to Egyptology was very great. The Metropolitan Museum of New York published magnificent records of the art of the Theban tombs, while the devoted labours of J. H. Breasted prepared the way for the Chicago Oriental Institute's meticulous recording of the Theban temples. In Egypt the extraordinary amount of art and architecture surviving above ground has meant that the tedious, unspectacular and only mildly rewarding task of making exact records has always been of equal importance with excavation. Nor has modern photography displaced the taking of squeezes and rubbings and careful copying by eye and hand—for complete accuracy, all are needed to reinforce and correct one another. The dedicated workers of the Oriental Institute spend long hours day after day, year after year, slung like window cleaners on the vast, sun-grilled walls of such temples as that of Medinet Habu, checking every detail of the seemingly endless reliefs and inscriptions.

There could hardly be a sharper contrast than between this selfless toil and the excitement of the discovery which was Egypt's counterpart to that of the Royal Tombs of Ur. Indeed there was something belonging to a past age in the whole setting of the opening of Tutankhamen's tomb in 1923 (p. 495 ff., I). There was the expert, Howard Carter, working for the nobleman, Lord Carnarvon, his long vain search, and then the urgent message sent to summon his patron when at last an unopened tomb was found. Afterwards, too, there was the widespread belief that the curse of Pharaoh had killed Lord Carnarvon and (after an interval, admittedly) Howard Carter himself. All in all, it is probably true to say that no archaeological event ever has, or ever will, rouse such enormous interest. The writer can remember not only the bulging folder of press cuttings she was able to amass with the limited resources of a young schoolgirl, but also how the centrepiece of the Armistice Day rag at Cambridge that year consisted in the solemn disentombment of an undergraduate mummiform body from the public lavatory in the market place. All the world was involved with this young and obscure Pharaoh.

Unlike the Royal Tombs of Ur, the grave chambers of Tutankhamen did not add greatly to knowledge or the history of art. Nevertheless their crowded abundance, like the store rooms of some great and sumptuous emporium, did bring to modern man an authentic picture of the riches of the royal household and the charm and elegance of the best of its possessions. Moreover, the gold-encrusted splendour of the actual mummy and its many containers, which now dazzles visitors to the Cairo Museum, was far beyond anything previously imaginable. It gave an idea of the divine honours heaped upon even the least eminent of Pharaohs.

Another major excavation, far less spectacular but of greater historical significance, was that of the city of Akhetaten at el Amarna. This was the place where the "heretic" Pharaoh Akhenaten had come to found a new city where he and his court could live in the light of the one true god, the divine sun-disk or Aten. His glorious, impossible venture had lasted less than twenty years before the powers of tradition triumphed and Akhenaten's successor was brought back to Thebes. There is an extraordinary interest in a place inhabited for such a short time, and the excavations first of the Germans, then after 1914-18 of the British, brought to light the most intimate details of the life of Akhenaten and Nefertiti, of their revolutionary artists, of the courtiers and workmen who built the town. They also recovered many exquisite art treasures, including the famous sculptured head of Nefertiti, which has probably been more reproduced than any other Egyptian masterpiece.

The same decade that saw the brilliant discoveries of Woolley and Howard Carter also witnessed the recovery of one more great civilization which had been as completely forgotten as those of the Sumerians, Minoans and Mycenaeans. It seems probable that it is the last time that archaeology will know such an achievement. Between 1922 and 1927 Sir John Marshall excavated at Mohenjo-Daro and Harappa in the Punjab, and was able to announce to the world (p. 234, II) the existence of an Indus civilization which had flourished and created great cities a thousand years before the coming of the Indo-European invaders in about 1500 B.C.—hitherto the first recorded event in Indian history. Since the last war, Sir Mortimer Wheeler (p. 241, II) and the Indian Antiquities Service that he did so much to establish have further explored these two cities, as regularly planned as Manhattan, and corrected some of Marshall's findings—notably his belief that there were no defensive walls. This civilization did not produce a very notable school of art, yet the excavations have added a few very distinctive little pieces to our human store.

Still further into Asia, the same Swedish geologist, Gunnar Andersson, who took part in extracting the bones of *Pithecanthropus* from the caves at Chou-k'ou-tien, turned his attention to the

Neolithic Age (p. 253 ff., II). At various sites in the Yellow River area
of China he excavated villages and burials of pig-keeping peasants
who made noble jars and bowls painted in a style which irresistibly
recalls the wares of far-away Mesopotamia and eastern Europe. It
appears that the *idea* of farming must have spread to China from
further west, but that there was a more direct relationship between
the two ceramic traditions is unlikely—although not impossible.
Many other sites of Neolithic and Bronze Age date have since been
excavated by the Chinese, but the character of this Yang Shao
culture seems to remain the most substantial and well defined.

In the Americas the progress of archaeological research acceler-
ated after 1918, as citizens of the United States woke to the interest
of Central and South American civilizations as well as to the history
of their own Indian tribes. The Mayan civilization continued to be
particularly well served. As early as 1915 the Carnegie Institute
of Washington followed the Peabody Museum (p. 69, I) into the
field, and since then has made a great range of investigations
including major digs at Uaxactun in the Peten region of Guatemala,
at the marvellous Chichen Itza ruins in Yucatan and at Kaminaljuyu
on the outskirts of Guatemala City. The University of Pennsylvania
is conducting large-scale excavations at Tikal. Sylvanus Morley
was not only active out of doors, but did much to draw existing knowledge together in his excellent *Ancient Maya* (p. 620, II),
published in 1946 and recently revised. Morley made himself an
expert on Mayan hieroglyphic writing, the only real script evolved
in the New World (the Aztecs had glyphs but depended mainly on
picture writing). So, too, did Eric Thompson (p. 636, II), but in spite
of all efforts at decipherment most Maya glyphs still cannot be
read. Only those concerned with the enormously elaborate Maya
calendar and related calculations can usually be understood, and
have proved invaluable in setting absolute dates to the ruins of
Classic Mayan times (about the third to the tenth centuries A.D.).
The decipherment which a Russian student recently obtained with
the help of an electronic computer does not seem to have gained
much support.

The discovery of quite important Maya ruins, particularly in the
forests of Guatemala and Honduras, is still far from complete even
today. Chicle gatherers, working in the cause of compulsive chew-
ing, have reported many new sites, and so, too, of recent years have
engineers and geologists surveying the huge oil concessions for
Shell and other companies.

Three discoveries in the Maya area have especial dramatic
appeal. One was altogether macabre—that of the sacrificial victims
and precious offerings in the sacred *cenote* at Chichen Itza (p.
641, II). The second was made in 1946, when an American film

unit working for the United Fruit Company penetrated deep into the wild forests of Chiapas. One of their number, Giles Healy, made such good friends with the local descendants of the Maya that they took him to see one of their holy places. There at Bonampak he was astounded at the sight of a well-preserved building with the walls and sloping roof almost entirely covered with magnificent paintings. Not only were these executed with exceptional naturalism, power and technical accomplishment, but they included a rare variety of scenes—of war, human sacrifice and everyday life. Later expeditions to Bonampak have brought back full-size copies which can be seen in the Peabody Museum at Harvard as well as in the National Museum of Mexico.

The third, and perhaps the most remarkable, discovery was of the noble's tomb which in 1949 Ruz found below the Temple of the Inscriptions at Palenque. This find, which was totally unexpected, must have compared in dramatic excitement with the most famous of the Old World. It was not only richly furnished and decorated with paintings, but was of importance because it confounded the long-held view that Mayan and Aztec temple pyramids were never used as tombs (p. 629, II).

In South America, although research continued into Inca monuments and history, more progress was made in disinterring the stories of all the earlier peoples of the coast as well as of the Andes, whose fate it was eventually to submit to the Inca conquerors. Cultures of these peoples, such as the Chavin in the mountains, the Nazca, Mochica and Chimu of the coasts, with their architecture and often beautiful ceramics, were defined and fitted into a time scheme by the efforts of Kroeber, Lothrop, Wendell Bennett, Duncan Strong and many others who were following up the work of Uhle and Tello. The big coastal site of Pachacamac with its temple and burials of Virgins of the Sun threw light on coastal history, while the cultures of the Andes were better understood after Wendell Bennett's digging at the fascinating Tiahuanaco on Lake Titicaca.

But most of all, here and elsewhere in the Americas, the new archaeology was successful in pushing our knowledge further and further back into the past. It was the New World counterpart of the process that has already been seen at work in the Old. Rafael Larco Hoyle and his family explored their estates in the Chicama valley of the north coast of Peru, and learnt much about farming communities going back to the beginning of the first millennium B.C., while immediately after the last war the Viru Valley project was launched by a combination of North American with Peruvian institutions. The plan was to make a complete and intensive survey of a limited area, covering all human history "from the earliest times to the present day." Largely as a result of this work it proved possible to extend the earliest farming in the region back into the third millennium B.C., and the mastery of potting to about 1000 B.C.

In all this research the newly-perfected Carbon-14 method proved invaluable in establishing a reliable chronology—indeed the very first American Carbon-14 date, announced by Libby in 1949, was for a Chavin site on the Peruvian coast. The method was, of course, particularly indispensable in the continent of its invention because of the lack of any absolute dates (except for slightly doubtful Maya calendars) before the Spanish Conquest.

Meanwhile in North America, too, the beginning of cultivation, at least in the Southwest, was proved to be much earlier than anyone had guessed. Excavations undertaken by Harvard University in 1952 at Bat Cave, New Mexico, exposed a series of occupations of which the earliest may go back to as much as 2000 B.C. It was of extraordinary interest, because the first cave dwellers had grown maize of a most primitive kind with tiny pods not an inch long. At Danger Cave on the edge of the Bonneville Salt Flats in Utah, the evidence suggests (if the Carbon-14 dates are reliable) that basketry may have been practised in North America as early as 8000 B.C.—well before it is certainly known in the Old World.

Recent years, then, have seen a remarkable increase in our knowledge of the first steps in crafts and in agriculture and of the sources of the high civilizations of Central and South America. What has been done to answer the even more pressing questions concerning the first arrival of man in America and his peopling of the two sub-continents? When it is remembered that as early as the seventeenth century an intelligent observer (p. 25, I) could say that the American Indians probably originated among the Mongolian peoples of Asia (or, as he put it, the Northern Tartars) and had entered America by way of some narrow straits, it is surprising to learn what fantastic theories have been put forward in quite recent times. Perhaps because it appears remote from the normal historical disciplines of the Old World, this subject has attracted rash speculation, crankiness and even fantasy. Poor Lord Kingsborough's faith in the tribes of Israel as the original colonists has never been quite without support; others have looked to Atlantis, to the Egyptians, the Phoenicians and to Africa, or have postulated large-scale immigration from Asia within historical times. Fanatical diffusionists such as P. J. Perry and Eliot Smith were naturally particularly attracted to such ideas, and the latter's fancy that he could recognize elephants in some Maya sculpture at Palenque and elsewhere led to a well-known controversy. It can be pursued by those fascinated by such oddities in Eliot Smith's *Elephants and Ethnologists*.

Modern anthropologists have had little doubt that American

Indians are predominantly of mongoloid stock and that they came to the continent in the north, probably mainly by way of the Bering Straits. Archaeologists have not been able finally to clinch this by pointing to close cultural parallels between Siberia and North America, but they have won much information about the earliest settlement, and have been able to put an end to extreme speculations as to when it took place.

The first important find was made as early as 1925, when a Negro cowboy, George McJunkin, riding along an arroyo near Folsom in the Guadalupe Mountains of New Mexico, spotted some large bones in the cut. Embedded with them he found flint points, or spearheads, quite different from any of the later Indian weapons with which he was familiar. After this had been reported to J. D. Figgins of the Denver Museum, excavations were made and it was proved that this strange type of spearhead was definitely associated with the bones of a breed of bison known to be long extinct. Since then many similar flints have been found, particularly in the High Plains area along the east side of the Rocky Mountains.

In 1936 a student from the University of New Mexico was exploring a long, tunnel-like cave in the Sandia Mountains near Aubuquerque when he saw that the deposits appeared to contain interesting remains, including artifacts and the bones of extinct ground sloths. His Professor, Dr. Frank C. Hibben, then undertook several seasons of excavation. Dr. Hibben claimed that the cave deposits were stratified, and that in a layer below that which contained Folsom points, there were spearheads of a new type, as well as a hearth and the remains of extinct forms of horse, bison, camel, mastodon, and mammoth. The new flints, which at that site at least appeared to be definitely older than the Folsom, were given the name of Sandia points. Most archaeologists still believe these points to represent the oldest hunting cultures in America, but subsequent discoveries in the United States and Mexico have led others (p. 691, II) to think that there may be yet earlier cultures dating from a time before projectile points of any kind had been developed.

These two important discoveries silenced those who had said that men failed to reach America until quite recent times. Since they were made, much has been learnt about these early hunters who pursued bison and mammoth and other big game in the millennia after the last glaciation. It appears that while these hunting traditions were developed in the more easterly parts of North America, the West and Southwest supported peoples who depended rather more on the collection of wild plants—seed, roots and fruit.

Questions of absolute age remain a little uncertain in spite of Carbon-14 dating, but it seems that the Folsom culture was flourishing about 8000 B.C., while that of Sandia may be everywhere appreciably earlier. Several very much more ancient Carbon-14 readings have been recorded, but none of them is as yet considered to be reliable. As for the spread southward, Junius Bird has found traces of settlement in Patagonia suggesting that men had reached the extreme tip of South America by 6000 B.C.

While the recovery of the civilizations of Maya, Aztecs and Inca has been more spectacular, this gradual piecing together of the earliest history of man in America has been a great archaeological feat. Where before absolutely nothing was known and the wildest guesses therefore had to be tolerated, there is now a clear picture of events and the prehistory of the New World falls into place with that of the Old.

Recent years have seen an extraordinarily swift development in the discovery and interpretation of human fossils, and hence in our knowledge of the evolution of our kind. While human palaeontology is now a highly specialized subject of its own, its findings have always been related with those of archaeology, just as they were in the days of Darwin and Huxley and the struggle over human evolution.

It was in 1925 that Professor Raymond Dart first announced the discovery at Taungs, eighty miles north of Kimberley, South Africa, of the fossil skull of a young primate. He named it *Australopithecus africanus,* and claimed that far more clearly than *Pithecanthropus* it represented the much-sought intermediate form between the great apes and man. Although Arthur Keith recognized that in relation to his size this new being had a brain capacity larger than that of the apes, and moreover that its teeth had certain human features, most palaeontologists preferred to see this as an early ape. However, a whole series of further finds spread over the next quarter of a century supported Dart's claims for the Taungs skull. From Sterkfontein near Johannesburg, then from nearby Kromdraai, from Swartkrans and finally from Makapansgat, 120 miles north of Pretoria, came more and more fossils of creatures evidently belonging to the same genus as *Australopithecus,* though of several species, some of them larger and more heavily built than the original little ape-man.

The apparent association of teeth of *Australopithecus* with roughly-shaped stone tools, which was observed at Sterkfontein, suggests that not only had this South African creature a larger brain than that of the apes, but that he used it to become a tool-maker. If so, he can be recognized as a true human being. Meanwhile, up in the Olduvai Gorge in Tanganyika, Mary and Louis Leakey unearthed several fossils from different levels in the magnificent series of deposits through which the Gorge is cut. The first to come to light (after Mary Leakey had spotted a small projecting fragment) was a being with a massive jaw and a great bony crest on his head like a gorilla. Leakey called him *Zinjanthropus boisii* —but the popular name is Nutcracker Man. It is generally agreed that he in fact belongs to the same general grouping as the Australopithecines.

What is most significant about the Nutcracker Man is that he appears to have been the maker of the very roughly shaped pebble tools which Leakey and others had already established as being the oldest recognizable human artifacts, dating back towards the beginning of the Pleistocene Age—something like 750,000 years ago. All these finds, both of fossil men and of stone implements, help to confirm the view that mankind originated in Africa.

In the Olduvai Gorge the earliest pebble tools can be seen to have developed into types of handaxe (known as Chellean and Acheulian from the long-ago discoveries of Boucher de Perthes and his friends in the Somme gravels) as the skill of the knappers increased—infinitely slowly and yet persistently. For a long time it had been a burning question as to what sort of man had been the maker of handaxes, and there was a tendency, due to wishful thinking, to suppose that it had been direct ancestors of *Homo sapiens* who had early split off from such simian types as *pithecanthropus*. This opinion seemed to be confirmed when in 1935 an amateur palaeontologist (a dentist by profession), who for many years had been scrutinizing the gravel pits along the lower Thames, was at last rewarded by finding fragments of a fossilized skull in a stratum which also yielded handaxes. Although the lower forehead is missing, this Swanscombe Man has quite a high vault to his head and appears certainly to be nearer to *Homo sapiens* than are any of the *Pithecanthropi* of much the same age.

After the war, however, jaw bones of Pithecanthropic type were found with handaxes in North Africa, and then Louis Leakey, a year or two after the discovery of Nutcracker Man, found an almost complete human skull in the early handaxe level in the Olduvai Gorge. It belongs once again to the Pithecanthropic (Java and Peking Man) breed, and so finally destroys any hopes of attributing to precocious representatives of our own kind the creation of the most progressive of the early Palaeolithic cultures—the Chellean and Acheulian.

As a result it is now usual to see the Australopithecines, the Pithecanthropians and *Homo sapiens* as representing the three main stages of human evolution which followed one another during the course of Pleistocene times. Yet Swanscombe Man and other analagous fossils still suggest that the line leading to *Homo sapiens* began to diverge quite early (Swanscombe Man is about a quarter of a million years old), and must have evolved for a long period side by side with that of *Pithecanthropus*. When we come back to Neanderthal Man, whose skull was so useful to the Darwinians, there is no doubt at all that this breed, with its large brain but strongly marked simian features, co-existed with *Homo sapiens* before its final extinction. Indeed the ape-like features actually increased in this last representative of the more ancient types of man, perhaps as a result of the harsh conditions of the final glaciation.

Thus all subsequent discovery has substantiated Darwin's theoretical claim for a common ancestry for apes and men. But whether this amazing evolution, which has led from the near-ape *Australopithecus* to Socrates, Shakespeare and Einstein, has been due wholly and exclusively to the workings of natural selection is an altogether different question which every man must judge for himself.

One development which may be thought to be most characteristic of the recent history of archaeology has been left until the last. The relegation has been deliberate, as the subject appears to the writer to involve a moral with which it would be right and proper to end a history of archaeology. This is the sudden enormous increase in the scientific techniques made available to the archaeologist.

Roughly speaking, it can be said to have begun before the last war with the invention of pollen analysis. By taking counts of the microscopically small pollen grains preserved in certain soils, it proved possible to make an exact picture of the vegetation and climate of the period, which could then be fitted into the known climatic phases of post-glacial times. This was of particular value in western and northern Europe, where it helped to date many key finds in boggy and moorland country.

Then American archaeologists devised the method of building a calendar on tree-rings, which has made it possible to assign many Indian remains to an exact date. This method has been used with outstanding success in the American Southwest, where timbers can be large and well preserved.

Immediately after the war, and as a result of wartime atomic research, came the most important technique of all: that of Carbon-14 analysis (p. 135, I). With it a thing that had always seemed totally impossible suddenly came to pass—the ability to give absolute dates to the dim events of prehistory reaching back as far as fifty thousand years. The writer happened to be in the United States during the year when Libby's discovery was first being rumoured, and an archaeologist who was something of an *enfant terrible* declared that his colleagues would soon be "climbing up trees" when their datings were subjected to this scientific check. His unkind prophecy has not in fact been fulfilled. There have been a few small surprises—the Neolithic Age in western Europe has been pushed back by about half a millennium, and some Palaeolithic periods have been brought down—but in general Carbon-14 has confirmed dates arrived at by historical argument. Indeed, the method is still sufficiently unreliable for counts that will not fit into the broad historical picture to be discreetly dropped.

While Carbon-14 depends on the rate of loss of atomic particles from once living substances, certain other techniques use the rate of absorption of chemical particles, particularly of fluorine. This type of analysis is far less accurate than Carbon-14, but can reach even further back into the past. It was first successfully employed for the exposure of the Piltdown fraud (p. 221, I).

All these techniques and many more have been devised to help with the chronology of the prehistoric past or with the reconstruction of the natural environment. There are others of indescribable ingenuity which have provided labour-saving devices for the excavator. The nuclear-magnetometer, for example, provides an eye which can, as it were, look through the ground and tell the archaeologist something at least of what lies concealed. (It is true that on one of the first occasions it was tried out in England it found only not-so-old iron bedsteads, but it has had its triumphs since.)

Then again, the method of neutron activation has made the analysis of metals and other minerals infinitely more subtle, enabling the source of ores used by different peoples at different times to be more surely traced. So it goes on: technique after technique is pressed into the archaeologists' hands by botanists, chemists, physicists. They are wonderful, they are useful—but they may also be dangerous. Archaeology can use scientific aids, but it has to use them in the service of an art—the writing of history. One danger is loss of quality in historical thinking from the sheer weight of technology. In our world of communications it is well known that the more marvellous the technique of transmission, the poorer the quality of the thing transmitted is likely to be. If this is not to happen with archaeology, the historical thinker must remain in control, firm control, of the technician's aids. The second and even more serious danger is that archaeologists will be tempted to neglect art and religion and all those aspects of life that are most fully human, in favour of elements which can be measured and estimated and subjected to scientific laws. If, in the future, they were to allow this to happen, then Schliemann scrabbling after "Priam's Treasure," Layard seeking works of art in his dim tunnels, would be superior to them—better men and better archaeologists.

JACQUETTA HAWKES

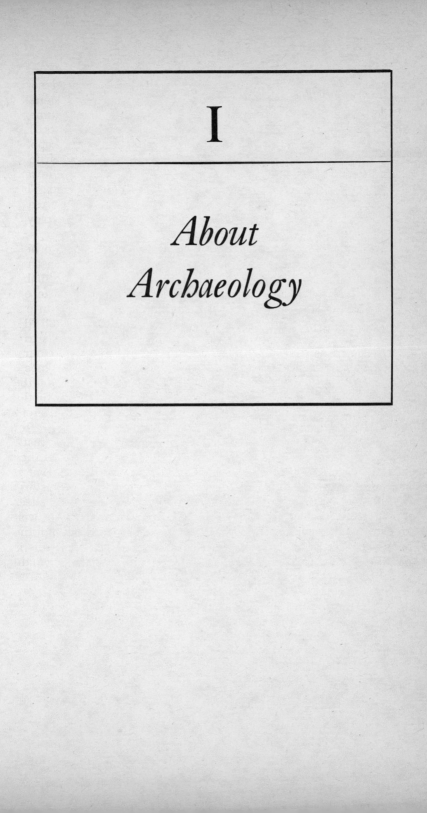

I

About Archaeology

NOTE

THE editor's notes that precede many se-
lections are identified by the use of Italic
capitals for the first word or words. The
typographic ornament shown here separates it from the selection.

THE text of the selection invariably starts
with the first word or words in capital and
small capitals.

INTRODUCTORY

UNTIL archaeology became a distinct discipline using its own techniques and with a huge store of specialized knowledge to draw upon, antiquaries and others interested in the tangible remains of the past seldom thought of theorizing about their studies. It was assumed that cultivated men and women were interested in works of art and architecture and their history, while less elegant remains, deriving from uncivilized peoples both ancient and modern, could also be allowed to interest them as "curiosities" or as various evidence of the ways of the Creator.

More recently, however, while many skilled and successful field workers never find it necessary to formulate any general aims or philosophical basis for their work, most of those archaeologists who are primarily interested in the interpretation of finds are almost certain to do so.

In this more theoretical approach to the subject, there is still some faint division surviving between what in my Introduction I have distinguished as the scientific and humanist wings of the archaeological advance. To open the anthology I have chosen a representative from each side. Professor Grahame Clark of Cambridge University is essentially scientific in his approach, and has appropriately concentrated on some of the remoter fields of prehistory. He is, as he says, interested in archaeology as a way of revealing the life of the past, but he would put the emphasis on the economic and social aspects of that life. Sir Leonard Woolley, on the other hand, came to the subject by way of the humanities, and was always most interested in the purely historical approach and in the lives of individuals—whether great men or obscure.

As well as their theories, archaeologists have their successes and failures, their personal problems and their adventures. Indeed of the last, their habit of penetrating into the wildest regions and behaving in strange ways while at close quarters with the native inhabitants, has given them more than their fair share.

The extracts in the following section reveal something of these aspects of archaeology and of archaeologists. The same themes will, of course, be substantially reinforced during the course of the anthology, but it is often considered good to begin with a well mixed *hors d'oeuvre*.

GRAHAME CLARK

The Purpose of Archaeology*

ARCHAEOLOGY is often defined as the study of antiquities. A better definition would be that it is the study of how men lived in the past. It is true that your archaeologist is compelled by circumstances to rely upon the material remains surviving from the people he is studying to arrive at any idea of their daily life; yet, however much he may appear to be preoccupied with things, often in themselves unattractive, he is really interested all the time in people. In this and many other ways he resembles the criminologist. He has to rely upon circumstantial evidence and much of his time is taken up with details which may appear to be trivial, although as clues to human actions they can be of absorbing interest.

LEONARD WOOLLEY

The Ideal Archaeologist†

THE prime duty of the field archaeologist is to collect and set in order material with not all of which he can himself deal at first hand. In no case will the last word be with him; and just because

* From *Archaeology and Society*. London: Methuen & Co. Ltd.; 1947 (1st ed., 1939), p. 1. Reprinted by permission of Methuen & Co. Ltd.
† From *Digging up the Past*. New York: Thomas Y. Crowell Company; 1954 and London: Ernest Benn Limited; 1954 (1st ed., 1930), pp. 120-2. Reprinted by permission of Thomas Y. Crowell Company and Ernest Benn Ltd.

that is so his publication of the material must be minutely detailed, so that from it others may draw not only corroboration of his views but fresh conclusions and more light. Should he not then stop at this? It might be urged that the man who is admirably equipped to observe and record does not necessarily possess the powers of synthesis and interpretation, the creative spirit and the literary gift which will make of him a historian. But no record can ever be exhaustive. As his work in the field goes on, the excavator is constantly subject to impressions too subjective and too intangible to be communicated, and out of these, by no exact logical process, there arise theories which he can state, can perhaps support, but cannot prove: their truth will depend ultimately on his own calibre, but, in any case, they have their value as summing up experiences which no student of his objects and his notes can ever share. Granted that the excavator is adequate to his task, the conclusions which he draws from his own work ought to carry weight, and he is bound to put them forward; if they are palpably wrong then his observations also may justly be held suspect. Between archaeology and history there is no fenced frontier, and the digger who will best observe and record his discoveries is precisely he who sees them as historical material and rightly appraises them: if he has not the power of synthesis and interpretation he has mistaken his calling. It is true that he may not possess any literary gifts, and that, therefore, the formal presentation of results to the public may be better made by others; but it is the field archaeologist who, directly or indirectly, has opened up for the general reader new chapters in the history of civilized man; and by recovering from the earth such documented relics of the past as strike the imagination through the eye, he makes real and modern what otherwise might seem a far-off tale.

THUCYDIDES

The First
Archaeological Deduction*

THE Islanders were Carians and Phoenicians by whom most of the islands were colonised, as was proved by the following fact. During the purification of Delos by Athens in this war all the graves in the island were taken up, and it was found that half their inmates were Carians: they were identified by the fashion of the arms buried with them, and by the method of interment which was the same as the Carians still follow.

STANLEY CASSON

Some Early
Archaeological Howlers†

BUT with this one preliminary attempt at archaeological research [see above], the ancient world abandoned the method of inquiry and ceased to trouble itself about the history of human inventions and manufactures. Curiosity, it is true, was aroused from time to

* From *The History of the Peloponnesian War*, 5th century B.C.
† From *The Discovery of Man*. London: Hamish Hamilton Ltd.; 1939, pp. 71-3. Reprinted by permission of Hamish Hamilton, Ltd.

time in the unexpected discovery of the relics of past ages. In late Greek times a tomb was opened by chance at Haliartus in Central Greece, and its discoverers were astonished to find inside it a bronze tablet on which were engraved signs which no Greek could transliterate or recognize. The local wiseacres, who believed the tomb to be that of Alcmena, mother of Hercules, sent the tablet to Egypt for a report upon its origin and meaning. For Egypt, throughout Greek history, was looked upon as the repository of all antique lore and all knowledge of human origins. The supposedly wise priests of the temples of Egypt had impressed the Greeks with their learning, as we can see from the pages of Herodotus where he describes his visit to Egypt and his conversations with priests. How mistaken the Greeks were in the case of this bronze tablet can be seen from their reply. The "Society of Antiquaries" of Egypt sent its report. They replied in the words of Plutarch, in whose work entitled *The Genius of Socrates* the story is preserved, that the writing belonged to the time of King Proteus and contained a general exhortation to the Greeks to found a contest in honour of the Muses and "Setting arms aside, to devote themselves to the peaceful rivalry of letters and philosophy."

Intelligent commentators can infer from the reply that the priest who composed it knew less than nothing about the tablet and was quite unable to decipher the inscribed signs. But, like all members of learned unions who are faced with a problem which they are unable to solve, he burked the issue and hid his ignorance. Knowing what we do to-day of the archaeology of this region, it seems likely that the tomb and the tablet were Minoan and that the writing was the as yet undeciphered script of Crete. Neither Egyptian nor Greek in this age knew anything about Cretans of the prehistoric age and their culture, so that the evasion of the Egyptian priest, if unpardonable, is comprehensible to those who have a tendency to compromise.

Another similar archaeological discovery is recorded in Roman times. Peasants and shepherds guarding their sheep on the site of Knossos, found one day the remains of a tomb, gaping open as the result of an earthquake. In it were tablets which the finders described as being of "grey birch bark" bearing inscriptions in an unknown writing. Again the pundits were summoned. Again they refused to admit ignorance. They maintained that the writing was Phoenician and that the tablets contained the work of a lost writer, known as Dictys of Crete, who was reputed to have composed a work on the Trojan war. The Phoenician text was translated into Greek and presented to the Emperor Nero at Rome.

Here was more humbug and more chicanery. The tablets of "grey birch bark" seem to resemble most clearly the grey clay tablets found at Knossos by Sir Arthur Evans in the great Palace. Modern archaeological discovery seems to have been anticipated once again, but without results comparable to the importance of the discoveries. For many apples fell on many heads before that which fell on the head of Newton!

GRAHAME CLARK

Another Howler

PREMONITIONS of the impending revolution in thought had been felt for some years before the publication of *The Origin of Species.* As long ago as 1797, John Frere, F.R.S., claimed in his communication to the Society of Antiquaries that certain flints "fabricated and used by a people who had not the use of metals" had been obtained from a brick-earth in which "were found some extraordinary bones, particularly a jaw-bone of enormous size, of some unknown animal, with the teeth remaining in it." His conclusion that "the situation in which these weapons were found may tempt us to refer them to a very remote period indeed; even beyond that of the present world" was prophetic, but attracted little attention at the time. As the years passed other discoveries were made, but these also were either ignored or quietly suppressed, not because the leading scientists of the day were dishonest, but simply because their preconceptions were too strong for them. It is worth noting that it was the amateurs like Frere and MacEnery, the discoverer of flint implements associated with the bones of extinct animals in Kent's Cavern, who most clearly perceived the meaning of what they had seen, while the professional geologists, of whom Dean Buckland was outstanding, proved themselves the most conservative and obtuse.

The case of Dean Buckland (1784-1856) is instructive. The first Reader in Geology at Oxford and perhaps the most eminent geologist of his day, he contrived at the same time to hold a Studentship at

From *Archaeology and Society*, pp. 8-10.

Christchurch and the Deanery of Westminster. The dedication of his most important book, published in 1823, was fulsome in the best tradition of the previous century and significantly enough was addressed to the Honourable and Right Reverend Shute Barrington, LL.D., Lord Bishop of Durham. Its full title—*Reliquiae Diluvianae; or Observations on the organic remains contained in Caves, Fissures, and Diluvial Gravel and on other Geological Phenomena attesting the action of an Universal Deluge*—gives some foretaste of the author's general attitude of mind. Entirely typical was his treatment of one of his own discoveries, the so-called "Red Lady" of Paviland, actually a male skeleton covered in ochre and accompanied by ivory rods and bracelets. To-day the "Red Lady" is recognized as the first ceremonial burial of Upper Palaeolithic Age to be discovered, but to Dean Buckland she was "*clearly* not coeval with the antediluvian bones of the extinct species" with which her remains were found. To dissociate the skeleton from inconvenient surroundings the Dean decided to connect it with "the remains of a British camp existing on the hill immediately above (the) cave." As he thoughtfully pointed out: "whatever may have been her occupation, the vicinity of a camp would afford a motive for residence, as well as means of subsistence in what is now so exposed and uninviting a solitude." His conclusion that the date of the "Red Lady" "is coeval with that of the military occupation of the adjacent summits, and anterior to, or coeval with, the Roman invasion of this country" followed quite simply. By such sophistry was the "Red Lady" of Paviland rejuvenated by some 20,000 years.

REVEREND CHARLES WOOLS

Respect for the Dead

THE real Antiquary will always respect the Skeletons, Ashes, and Bones of the dead, which he may discover in his subterranean excavations. With hallowed feelings sanctified by the knowledge

From *The Barrow Diggers*. Blanford: Whittaker & Co.; 1839, p. 78.

that the dry bones shall live, he will do unto them as he would wish
should be done unto his own remains when he has passed away
and has been forgotten; for in opening Barrows it is not the
Antiquary's object to violate the receptacles of the Dead, but from
the relics which may be found in them, to trace the manners and
the customs of the Early Britons, as the spade is almost their only
historian. When the Antiquary meets with Skeletons near the
surface of the earth he will bury them deeper than they were before
they were denuded. When he opens a cist he will not disturb its
contents unnecessarily. The Ashes and Bones of the Dead he will
collect together with reverential awe, and he will never fail to
restore those circling mounds of earth over them, which pointed
out to him as they will point out to future Antiquaries, if not
destroyed, the Tumuli of the Ancient Britons.

J. P. DROOP

Propriety on Excavations

BY WAY of epilogue I may perhaps venture a short word on the
question much discussed in certain quarters, whether in the work
of excavation it is a good thing to have cooperation between men
and women. I have no intention of discussing whether or no woman
possesses the qualities best suited for such work: opinions, I believe,
vary on the point, but I have never seen a trained lady excavator
at work, so that my view if expressed would be valueless. Of a mixed
dig, however, I have seen something, and it is an experiment that
I would be reluctant to try again. I would grant if need be that
women are admirably fitted for the work, yet I would uphold
that they should undertake it by themselves.

My reasons are twofold. . . . In the first place there are the pro-
prieties . . . not only of those that rule in England or America, but

From *Archaeological Excavation*. Cambridge: Cambridge University Press; 1915,
p. 27.

those of the lands where it is proposed to dig . . . the work of an
excavator on the dig and off it lays on those who share in it a bond
of closer daily intercourse than is conceivable . . . between men and
women, except in chance cases, I do not believe that such close and
unavoidable companionship can ever be other than a source of
irritation; at any rate I believe that however it may affect women,
the ordinary male at least cannot stand it . . . mixed digging I think
means loss of easiness in the atmosphere and consequent loss of
efficiency. A minor . . . objection lies in one particular form of
constraint . . . moments will occur on the best regulated dig when
you want to say just what you think without translation, which before the ladies, whatever their feelings about it, cannot be done.

LEONARD WOOLLEY

The Birth
of an Archaeologist

I HAVE seldom been more surprised than I was when—it is nearly
fifty years ago now—the Warden of New College told me that he
had decided that I should be an archaeologist. It is true that I had
taken a course in Greek sculpture for my degree, but so had lots of
other undergraduates. Because of their bearing on Homer I had
read Schliemann's romantic account of his discoveries, the Treasure
of Priam at Troy and the Tomb of Agamemnon at Mycenae, and like
everyone else I was rather vaguely aware that Flinders Petrie was,
year after year, making history in Egypt and that Arthur Evans was
unearthing the Palace of Minos in Crete; but all this was at best only
background knowledge and the idea of making a life study of it
had never occurred to me. And I must confess that when the

From *Spadework*. London: Lutterworth Press; 1953, pp. 11-12. Reprinted by permission of Lutterworth Press.

prospect did present itself, not as a mere idea to be played with (for one did not lightly play with the Warden's decisions) but as something definite and settled, I was not altogether happy about it. For me, and I think for the Warden too, archaeology meant a life spent inside a museum, whereas I preferred the open air and was more interested in my fellow men than in dead-and-gone things; I could never have guessed that after a short—and invaluable— apprenticeship in the Ashmolean Museum at Oxford, all my work was to be out of doors and, for the most part, out of England; and I had yet to learn that the real end of archaeology is, through the dead-and-gone things, to get at the history and the minds of dead-and-gone men.

LEONARD WOOLLEY

Lawrence of Arabia as an Archaeologist

In 1911 the British Museum invited me to take charge of the excavations at Carchemish. Hogarth had done one season's work, to test the site, and now the Museum was prepared (thanks to a generous benefactor) to embark upon the biggest excavation it had yet attempted. Naturally I was delighted to agree to the offer. Hogarth had had T. E. Lawrence on his staff and suggested that I might like to continue the arrangement. I had known Lawrence since my time in the Ashmolean Museum when as a shy schoolboy, with a friend even more tongue-tied than himself, he used to bring me bits of medieval pottery found by workmen digging house foundations in Oxford, and I was very glad to have him now as my sole assistant. Of course the expedition was, by modern standards,

From *Spadework*, pp. 60, 63-4.

most inadequately staffed. There were only the two of us, myself
not nearly as experienced as I liked to think, Lawrence virtually
new to the job.

Our Carchemish house (planned for a ten-years' dig) was of
rough stone collected from the site, and mud-brick, one story
high with a flat roof made native fashion of earth spread over
poles and matting. It was built round a courtyard and contained,
apart from little bedrooms, a bathroom and the kitchen and servants' quarters, a museum storeroom (which could be expanded
indefinitely), photographic darkroom, mapping office, and a large
living-room where we could eat, read and entertain guests. The
last was a source of pride to us. There was a good open fireplace,
a bookcase recess for our small library, we hung rugs (our personal property) on the walls, and when the railway employees
digging the foundations of the station found a large and very fine
Roman mosaic we lifted it, glueing canvas on to the *tesserae* and
undercutting and then rolling the whole thing up on a pole, like
a sheet of linoleum, and relaid it in new cement in our sitting-room,
and so could boast of a floor-covering which was a real museum
exhibit. One piece of decoration however was less genuine. The
lintel over the entrance door was made of a single big block of
soft limestone, and Lawrence amused himself by carving on it the
winged sun-disk which was the emblem of Hittite god-head. Only
a month or so ago a distinguished archaeologist sent me a photograph of the doorway anxiously inquiring what had happened to
this fine and unpublished monument of Hittite sculpture! Lawrence
would have enjoyed the joke immensely. Altogether ours was a very
nice house, and since the total cost of it to the expedition was only
£140 we could scarcely be accused of extravagance.

LEONARD WOOLLEY

Bandits and Excavations

THE following adventure happened during the early days of
Woolley's excavations at Ur.

❦

THAT NIGHT, or rather in the early hours of the next morning, I
was awakened by shots and found that bullets were coming through
the canvas of the tent. I went out and saw half a dozen men shooting at us from a slope thirty yards away; after emptying their
magazines they rushed into the camp shouting "Rob, rob!" and
disappeared into the tents, from which everybody had now
emerged. We had only two revolvers in the camp and my main
concern was to prevent anyone shooting, since we were no match
for six men with rifles. I was standing beside the (unarmed) head
of the new guard when one of the robbers coming from my own
tent passed close to us, carrying my suitcase; the guard rashly
called out "I have seen you, I know you!", upon which the other
turned and shot him through the stomach, killing him almost immediately. Then they all vanished with their loot.

The sequel was interesting. The thieves belonged to a sub-tribe
of Munshid's Muntafiks and the dead man was his cousin; the
murder meant a blood-feud, and in this the entire tribe was involved; the murderers therefore had no chance, and after three
days they surrendered and threw themselves on Munshid's mercy.
Tribal law was still allowed by the Government in cases between
tribesmen, so the sheikh held his court and assessed the blood-
money, which was promptly paid by the relatives of the guilty men,
and, having thus secured his own interests, he handed the prisoners
over to the State police, explaining in answer to their indignant
protests that while the murder charge had been properly disposed
of they had, unfortunately, also been guilty of armed robbery of

From *Spadework*, pp. 91-2.

Englishmen, and for that must be tried by the Government courts;
so tried they were and sentenced to two year's imprisonment. Two
years later four men turned up at my house and demanded to be
enrolled on the dig, claiming that they were old hands. They were;
they had worked for me for one day and then shot me up! Sheikh
Munshid's brother was at that time the head of my guard so I
asked him whether he had any objection to my enrolling the men
who had shot his cousin; he said, of course not; they had paid
blood-money and he had nothing against them; crime was absolved
by punishment. I agreed with his virtuous sentiments and the four
men were at work the next morning.

O. G. S. CRAWFORD

Flints as Contraband

In 1932 I used the whole of my annual leave on a trip to the USSR
in company with a friend whom I had met at Oxford when I was a
Junior Demonstrator. We saw much that was both new and old,
and I was greatly impressed and for a time fooled by the imposing
façade of the structure; that phase passed, I am thankful to say,
largely through the influence of Harold W. Edwards, whom I met
for the first time on the boat going from London to Leningrad. On
looking back now I regard that meeting as much the most valuable
result of the trip. The Sidney Webbs were also on the boat, the
Smolny; Bernard Shaw came to see them off, and I was greatly
tempted to ask leave to take a photograph of them all, and regret
now that my courage failed me. One day there was a public discussion on the deck of the *Smolny* opened by the captain, a quiet-
mannered, pleasant, intelligent man. Mrs. Webb asked him many
questions.

On arrival at Leningrad the Webbs were whisked off at once in

From *Said and Done*. London: Phoenix House Ltd.; 1955, p. 231. Reprinted by
permission of Phoenix House Ltd.

a special conveyancc, but the rest of us had to undergo a long, confused, and searching ordeal at the Customs. I had brought with me a few palaeolithic stone axes, which I thought would smooth the way for me in some of the museums; but they merely aroused the suspicions of the searchers and were confiscated.

─────────

LEONARD WOOLLEY

How the Past Is Buried

TREASURE-HUNTING is almost as old as Man; scientific archaeology is a modern development, but in its short life of about seventy years it has done marvels. Thanks to excavation, thousands of years of human history are now familiar which a hundred years ago were a total blank, but this is not all, perhaps not even the most important part. The old histories, resting principally on written documents, were largely confined to those events which at every age writers thought most fit to record—wars, political happenings, the chronicles of kings—with such side-lights as could be gleaned from the literature of the time. The digger may produce more written records, but he also brings to light a mass of objects illustrating the arts and handicrafts of the past, the temples in which men worshipped, the houses in which they lived, the setting in which their lives were spent; he supplies the material for a social history of a sort that could never have been undertaken before. Until Schliemann dug at Mycenae, and Sir Arthur Evans in Crete, no one guessed that there had been a Minoan civilization. Not a single written word has been found to tell of it, yet we can trace the rise and fall of the ancient Minoan power, can see again the splendours of the Palace of Minos, and imagine how life was lived alike there and in the crowded houses of the humbler folk. The whole history of Egypt has been recovered by archaeological work, and that in astonishing detail; I suppose we know more about ordinary life in Egypt in the

‿‿‿‿‿‿‿‿‿‿‿‿‿‿
From *Digging up the Past*, pp. 10-16, 120-2.

fourteenth century before Christ than we do about that of England in the fourteenth century A.D. To the spade we owe our knowledge of the Sumerians and the Hittites, great empires whose very existence had been forgotten, and in the case of other ancient peoples, the Babylonians and the Assyrians, the dry bones of previously known fact have had life breathed into them by the excavation of buried sites. It is a fine list of achievements, and it might be greatly expanded; all over Europe, in Central America, in China and in Turkestan excavation is supplementing our knowledge, and adding new vistas to our outlook over man's past; and to what is it all due? Not to the mere fact that antique objects have been dug out of the ground, but to their having been dug out scientifically.

But before I describe methods there is another point arising out of that first question "Why does anyone dig?" People sometimes put the accent in a different place, and ask "Why does anyone *dig*? Why do they have to use the spade to achieve these admirable results? How does it come about that things get buried and have to be dug up?"

Clearly, in the case of graves, which yield many of the archaeologist's treasures, the question does not arise, for the things were put underground deliberately and have remained there; but how do houses and cities sink below the earth's surface? They do not: the earth rises above them, and though people do not recognize the fact, it is happening all around them every day. Go no further than London. How many steps does one have to go down to enter the Temple Church? Yet it stood originally at ground level. The mosaic pavements of Roman Londinium lie twenty-five to thirty feet below the streets of the modern City. Wherever a place has been continuously occupied the same thing has happened. In old times municipal scavenging did not amount to much, the street was the natural receptacle for refuse and the street level gradually rose with accumulated filth; if it was re-paved the new cobbles were laid over the old dirt, at a higher level, and you stepped down into the houses on either side. When a house was pulled down and rebuilt the site would be partly filled in, and the new ground floor set at or above street level; the foundations of the older building would remain undisturbed below ground. The process would be repeated time after time so that when foundations are made for the huge buildings of to-day which go down nearly as far into the earth as they rise into the air, the excavating gangs cut through layer after layer or wall stumps and artificial filling of which each represents a stage in the city's growth. In the Near East the rate of rise is faster. The commonest building material is mud brick, and mud brick walls have to be thick; when they collapse the amount of debris is very great and fills the rooms to a considerable height, and as you cannot use mud bricks twice over, and the carting away of rubbish is expensive, the simplest course is to level the surface of the ruins and build on the top of them—which has the further advantage that it raises your new mud-brick building out of reach of the damp. In Syria and in Iraq every village stands on a mound of its own making, and the ruins of an ancient city may rise a hundred feet above the plain, the whole of that hundred feet being composed of superimposed remains of houses, each represented by the foot or so of standing wall which the collapse of the upper part buried and protected from destruction.

But what happens when a site is no longer inhabited? A Roman camp, for instance, occupied by the legionaries and abandoned after a few years—how does that get buried? Here we have Nature to thank. I remember how, when the London County Council cleared the slum area where Bush House stands to-day, the heaps of broken brickwork and loose mortar were in the following year entirely hidden by a mass of purple willow-herb, and people used to take 'bus rides down the Strand just for the pleasure of looking over the high hoarding at this miracle of wild flowers. That happened in the space of a few months; had the "island site" been left undisturbed for as many years, coarse turf would have covered the mounds and the ruins of Booksellers' Row would have been buried like those of Silchester. And if this can happen in the heart of London, how much more so in the country where Nature fights at close range?

I have not mentioned one way in which buildings may be buried, because it is so lamentably rare; that is by volcanic action. If the field archaeologist had his will, every ancient capital would have been overwhelmed by the ashes of a conveniently adjacent volcano. It is with a green jealousy that the worker on other sites visits Pompeii and sees the marvellous preservation of its buildings, the houses standing up to the second floor, the frescoes on the walls, and all the furniture and household objects still in their places as the owners left them when they fled from the disaster. Failing a volcano, the best thing that can happen to a city, archaeologically speaking, is that it should be sacked and very thoroughly burnt by an enemy. The owners are not in a position to carry anything away and the plunderers are only out after objects intrinsically valuable, the fire will destroy much, but by no means everything, and will bring down on the top of what does remain so much in the way of ashes and broken brickwork that the survivors, if there are any, will not trouble to dig down into the ruins; a burnt site is generally a site undisturbed. It is where cities have decayed slowly that least is to be found in their ruins; the impoverished inhabitants will have pulled down the older buildings to re-use the material in their own hovels, they will make nothing good of their own and they will certainly leave nothing behind them when at last they desert the place; the top levels of such a site generally produce therefore few objects, and not much history except the melancholy history of decadence.

LEONARD WOOLLEY

Archaeological Ingenuities

ON the cement foundation the limestone blocks for wall and floor had been bedded in mortar [in a temple at el Amarna]; when they were pulled up for removal it generally happened that the mortar was left adhering to the cement and bore on its upper surface the impression of the stone; we could count the stones which were not there, and even see the toolmarks on them; looking at them carefully I thought it might be possible to distinguish between the blocks which had been set in lines for the walls and those which had been the pavement of the rooms, so I told the workmen to sweep the whole surface clean with brooms. As Mr. Newton, the architect of the party, and myself were examining the site, trying to decide whether it was worth while making a plan of the position of the blocks, we saw a peculiar thing.

Sometimes the mortar had come away with the stone, leaving the face of the cement clean, and here and there on the clean face there were faint red marks which carried on the lines of the mortar-impressions of what we supposed to be wall blocks. The explanation was obvious. When the cement foundation was dry the builders had worked out on it the architect's plan; a cord dipped in red paint had been stretched taut along the line of each proposed wall, the middle of it lifted and allowed to come slap down again on the cement with the result that a red streak was left as straight as if ruled with a ruler; between two such lines the builder laid his wall-stones. We

From *Digging up the Past*, pp. 58-9, 94-5, 97-8.

had no need to exercise our imagination, we had before us the actual plan drawn out by the Egyptian architect. Having transferred this to paper we could proceed to the next part of our task—to find out what the building was really like.

One of our richest graves at Ur, that which contained the famous golden helmet, was located by the discovery of a copper spear-head sticking point upwards in the earth. The soil was cleared from round it, and there came to light a length of thin gold tube which adorned the top of the shaft; below this there was a hole in the ground left by the wooden shaft itself when it turned to dust. We followed the hole downwards, and it led us to the grave, against the corner of which it had been leaning when the earth was thrown back into the pit; with this forewarning we were able to trace the entire outline of the grave before we started to lay bare its contents, and so could record in order all the offerings heaped and crowded round the coffin. In another case, a simple hole in the ground was found, and then a second; something unusual about their shape seemed to call for special treatment, and accordingly plaster-of-paris was poured in to fill up the void which decaying wood had left: the result was a complete plaster cast of a harp whose substance had long since vanished (except for the copper bull's head and the shell plaque which decorated the front end of it and were later found sticking to the ‚plaster.), and thus the first hint that we had of a grave's presence also enabled us to preserve the best object in it before we knew what it was—in fact, before we really knew that the grave was there.

A fine example of the patience which goes to the salving of an antiquity is given by the tomb of Queen Hetep-heres, found by Dr. Reisner close to the Great Pyramid at Gizeh. In a walled-up recess behind the rock-cut chamber in which stood the empty stone coffin of the mother of King Khephren [Chephren], the pyramid builder, there lay a mass of decayed and powdered wood and bits of gold plate, and scattered over the floor were tiny figures cut in gold, hieroglyphs which had been inlaid in the wood and had fallen out as that crumbled to dust. Had these just been gathered up they would have been a pretty illustration of the elaborate fashion in which the royal furniture of Egyptian kings five thousand years ago was adorned, and that would have been all. As it was, the excavators cleared the chamber laboriously square inch by square inch, recording the exact position of every tiny fragment: they spent 280 days working there, took hundreds of pages of notes and more than a thousand photographs. From three bits of wooden frame and one panel, shrunk to a sixth of their original size, but preserving traces of the joints, tenons and mortices, they were able to reconstruct a unique object, the carrying-chair of the queen; the gold hieroglyphs, assembled according to the position in which they lay on the floor, formed groups which could be arranged so as to give sense, proper texts which decorated the upright panels of the chair; and the chair which was built up with new wood and the ancient gold was an exact replica of the vanished original. From the other remains of gold and wood the same painful methods recovered an elaborate arm-chair, a jewel-box and a bed; but after all had been removed from the tomb the work of reconstruction took Dr. Reisner's men two whole years.

H. J. PLENDERLEITH

Restoration: an Ivory Is Saved

DURING an excavation at Nimrûd in 1952, Professor Mallowan recovered a number of magnificent ivories from the bottom of a well, dating from the period of Assur-nasir-pal II (883–859 B.C.) and, by drying them slowly and uniformly, he was able to preserve their shape and prevent serious cracking. It may be of interest to describe the subsequent treatment that was applied to one of them—a masterpiece of exquisite carving, embellished with gold and incrusted with lapis lazuli and carnelian.

When this reached the British Museum Laboratory it was covered with fine clay, and an X-ray examination showed the presence of deep cracks which were widest at the back, or external side, of the tusk, but, fortunately, scarcely apparent on the decorated side. The clay was carefully scraped from the back and, as this revealed a surface without decoration, it was rigidly secured (as a first-aid precaution to prevent any further opening of the cracks) by backing it with layers of broad adhesive tape, the equivalent of surgical strapping. The front was then dealt with, working under a binocular at a magnification of 10 diameters. First the upper layers of clay were removed with needles to expose the sculpture. Many fragments of gold leaf were recovered from the clay; these were

From *The Conservation of Antiquities and Works of Art*. London: Oxford University Press; 1956, pp. 153-5. By permission of Oxford University Press.

washed with 1 per cent nitric acid and then with water, and set aside for subsequent replacement. The ivory was further cleaned with pellets of blotting-paper held between pointed forceps and moistened with detergents in order to peptize and release the clay with the minimum of strain, and later the surface was washed and polished by the same technique, doing small areas at a time. The final stage in the restoration was the replacement of the loose fragments of gold leaf in their correct positions on the cleaned ivory, using Durofix as the adhesive.

The background of this superb object—thought to be part of a throne—is decorated with an all-over floral pattern consisting of alternating flowers and seed capsules, the stems and sepals being covered with fine gold. The forms are deeply carved and the thin walls that outline the flowers are also gilt so that they appear like metal cloisons framing the lapis lazuli inlays of the petals. The seeds (or buds?) are represented by polished carnelians of dome shape, serrated at the base to engage with the gilt ivory calyces. This rich background forms a canopy for the main carving below, a scene in high relief depicting a lioness in the act of killing a Nubian. The ivory body of the animal is unadorned, and powerfully modelled. It stands out in sharp contrast to the relaxed human victim with his gleaming golden loin-cloth, and spikelets of crisp curly hair, an effect obtained by fixing gilt-topped pegs into the head which was stained black beforehand. In spite of the loss of much of the gold overlay and the blue and red incrustation, this ivory carving still gives the effect of a faceted polychrome jewel.

The following technical points relating to the construction of the ivory were noted during the cleaning and are of special interest. The lapis lazuli inlays are of varying thickness, but the recesses in the ivory are of uniform depth. Consequently, it was found necessary to bed the inlays in a cement so that their polished surfaces would be level with the cloisons. This is the only case known to the author where a blue cement has been used for inlaying lapis lazuli. It is composed of lime putty coloured to match the lapis lazuli by the addition of copper frit and where inlays are missing the ivory is often stained by a residue of this frit cement. Another interesting observation was made on examining the *back* of fragments of gold leaf from the ivory. Traces of a brownish film were clearly visible on the gold under the microscope. This material which was of organic origin and swelled in water, becoming very sticky, appeared to be the original adhesive employed in laying the gold leaf. It is difficult to believe that a reversible colloid could have survived in such circumstances but apparently this was the case, and it was due no doubt to the protection from air and moisture afforded by the coherent film of gold.

WILLIAM CAMDEN

Crop Marks: an Early Record

THE following description refers to the Roman port of Rutupiae at Richborough in Kent. It is probably the first recorded instance of the use of crop marks, caused by the differential growth and ripening of corn, for the detection of ancient structures. This method could only become of real importance with the development of air-photography.

※

BUT now age has eras'd the very tracks of it; and to teach us that Cities dye as well as men, it is at this day a corn-field, wherein when the corn is grown up, one may observe the draughts of streets crossing one another, (for where they have gone the corn is thinner) and such *crossings* they commonly call *S. Augustine's cross*. Nothing now remains, but some ruinous walls of a tower, of a square form, and cemented with a sort of sand extremely binding. One would imagine this had been the *Acropolis*, it looks down from so great a height upon the wet plains in *Thanet*, which the Ocean, withdrawing itself by little and little, has quite left. But the plot of the City, now plow'd, has often cast up the marks of it's Antiquity, gold and silver coyns of the Romans.

From *Britannia*. Gibson Edition, 1695 (1st ed. 1586).

O. G. S. CRAWFORD

Archaeology from the Air

LONG before aeroplanes were invented it was confidently hoped that vertical photographs would some day be taken, and it was felt certain that, if so, they would greatly assist archaeology. Major Elsdale was the pioneer of air-photography in the British Army. Between about 1880 and 1887 he carried out many experiments from free balloons, and also invented a method of sending up small balloons just large enough to carry a camera, which exposed a certain number of plates automatically; then the balloon emptied itself of some of its gas and came down. Some of the results were quite good considering the difficulties. In 1891 Lieutenant C. F. Close (now Colonel Sir Charles Close) suggested to the Surveyor-General of India that the India Office should be asked to send out similar apparatus to photograph from the air the ancient ruined cities round Agra with the view of constructing a map from the air-photographs. The scheme was approved and the apparatus was sent to India, but official difficulties of the usual type supervened. The result was that Agra was cut out of the scheme, and a few photographs were taken over Calcutta at an unfavourable season of the year, and the opportunity was lost. After Major Elsdale left the Balloon Establishment in 1888 little or nothing was done at home in this matter: and after 1892 the Survey of India took no more interest in balloon photography. Major Elsdale spent much of his own money on the experiments in question, but ballooning was not much in favour in the 'eighties, although some progress was made, and he received little or no official support in his balloon-photography experiments.

In 1906 Lieutenant P. H. Sharpe took a vertical and an oblique photograph of Stonehenge from a war-balloon; these were published in *Archaeologia* (vol. lx) by Colonel Capper. During several years immediately preceding the War, Mr. Henry S. Wellcome successfully used large box-kites with specially devised automatic con-

From *Wessex from the Air*. Oxford: The Clarendon Press; 1928, pp. 3-7. By permission of The Clarendon Press, Oxford.

trol cameras for photographing his archaeological sites and excavations in the Upper Nile regions of the Anglo-Egyptian Sudan.

During the War, when aeroplane photographs first became common, it might have been expected that archaeological features would have been observed, but in the British sector in France none were seen, so far as I know. The photographs were often taken at a great height, over country which is archaeologically barren, or which was too rankly overgrown to show results. Moreover, the interpretation of air-photographs for military purposes was a new art and in itself sufficiently fascinating to oust academic interests for a time. On other fronts time was found for archaeology. Pioneer work in the air was carried out by the Germans in Northern Sinai. Dr. Theodor Wiegand was appointed to a special Commission (Denkmalschutzkommando) which was sent out with the German forces operating in Southern Palestine and Sinai. One cannot but admire the scientific enthusiasm of a country which could remember archaeology in the midst of a world war. The results were published by Dr. Wiegand, and his monograph is the first publication containing direct reproductions of archaeological photographs taken from an aeroplane (1920). The first thirty-five pages contain an account of the military operations, written by General Kress von Kressenstein; the remaining hundred and ten pages are by Dr. Wiegand, and contain a valuable description of the wonderful air-photographs obtained. There are eight well-reproduced collotype plates, each containing two air-photographs, and in the text are five half-tone reproductions of air-photographs of ancient sites. In addition, much archaeological material of the ordinary kind is described and illustrated.

The principal air-photographs are of El Arish, Ruhebe (Rehoboth), Umm el Keisume, Mishrefe, Sbeita, and Hafir el Aujsha. The results are most remarkable. The plan of each of these now deserted cities can be seen at a glance with astonishing clearness. Streets, churches, courtyards, gardens, and fields are evident, and orderly rows of cairns (for vine-growing, it is stated) are a prominent feature. Most certainly there is a vast and almost unexplored field for archaeology from the air in Arabia.

About the time that the fortunes of war brought German interest in Sinai to an end, Colonel Beazeley, R.E., was discovering ancient sites in Mesopotamia. Others no doubt had observed the streets and public gardens of Eski Baghdad from the air, but Colonel Beazeley was the first to publish an account of them (1919), and indeed his article appeared a year before the German report on Sinai. If, as has been said, the date of an archaeological discovery is the date of its publication, to Colonel Beazeley belongs the credit of being the pioneer of archaeology from an aeroplane. His article

in the *Geographical Journal* is illustrated, however, not by actual
reproductions of air-photographs, but by plans of ancient cities and
irrigation-works which, to the ground-observer, appear formless.
Most remarkable perhaps are the four huge circles tangential to
each other, with a fine pavilion in the centre.

The air-photographs were taken, of course, for military purposes,
and it was in the course of this work that the ancient city was
discovered. "It was," says Colonel Beazeley, "some 20 miles long
and anything up to 2½ miles in width. . . . [It was] well planned,
with wide main streets or boulevards, from which wide roads
branched off. . . . Had I not been in possession of these air-photographs the city would probably have been merely shown [on the
map] by meaningless low mounds scattered here and there, for
much of the detail was not recognizable on the ground, but was
well shown up in the photographs, as the slight difference in the
colour of the soil came out with marked effect on the sensitive film,
and the larger properties of the nobles and rich merchants could
be plainly made out along the banks of the Tigris." Colonel Beazeley
continues: "When riding as a passenger in an aeroplane *en route*
for survey over enemy territory, I could clearly see on the desert
area the outline of a series of detached forts shaped as in Fig. 3
[of his article], whereas when walking over them on the ground
no trace was visible. Another interesting thing I could plainly see
in my flights was the outline of an ancient scientific irrigation system, such as has been introduced in the Punjab only in comparatively recent years. Unfortunately I was shot down and captured
before being able to make a detailed survey of the system during a
lull in the military operations."

On the 29th December 1922 Professor R. A. MacLean, of Roches-
ter University, read a paper before the Archaeological Institute of
America on "The Aeroplane and Archaeology"; an abstract was
published in 1923. Professor MacLean had flown in Transjordania,
and also recorded some results obtained—he does not state by
whom—in Mesopotamia.

An air-photograph of the town and fortress of Dura (Salihiyeh)
on the Euphrates, 250 miles above Baghdad, was taken, apparently
in December 1922, by the French Air Force at the suggestion of
Professor J. H. Breasted. It is reproduced, not very successfully, on
p. 93 of Professor Breasted's book.

Arabia and the countries bordering it have played a leading role
in the history of this new method of research. Circumstances are
largely responsible for this. The ancient sites there are so plain that
no special training or interest is required to detect them. In England
the ancient sites are sometimes plain enough, but the remains
themselves are seldom self-explanatory. Any one can recognize an

ancient city, but even the best-preserved prehistoric earthwork is
something of a mystery, at any rate to those unfamiliar with primitive culture. Those, however, whose main interests lay at home
had long hoped for that instrument of discovery which the invention of the aeroplane provided. The War, while it promoted the
development of flying, delayed its archaeological exploitation. My
own interest dates from the time, before flying became at all common, when I used to discuss with Dr. J. P. Williams-Freeman the
possibilities of an overhead view. We knew that the low banks and
mounds of prehistoric fields, villages, and barrows were plainly
revealed at sunset, even to an observer on the ground, for the long
shadows then cast made visible even the slightest undulation on
the surface of the downs. We knew also that the course of prehistoric boundary-ditches could often be seen in the corn when the
observer could view them from a distance, on a hill or on the opposite slopes of a valley. We longed for overhead views of Wessex
before the first air-photograph had been taken. After the War I
made one or two attempts to follow up the subject. In March 1919
I made a suggestion to the Earthworks Committee (of the Congress
of Archaeological Societies) that they should get in touch with the
Royal Air Force, but it was not taken up and an opportunity was
thus lost. On the 22nd October 1922 an air-photograph was taken
of Old Winchester Hill by the R.A.F. School of Photography at Farnborough, at the suggestion of Mr. C. J. P. Cave. On the hill is a
prehistoric hill-fort and several barrows; one more barrow was
revealed by the air-photograph, but it is also plainly visible on the
ground. The site is about two miles east of Meon Stoke in Hampshire.

The birth of the new study in England may be said to date from
1922 when Air-Commodore Clark Hall observed certain curious
marks on R.A.F. air-photos taken in Hampshire. With him must be
mentioned Flight-Lieutenant Haslam, who took a number of photographs near Winchester showing what turned out to be Celtic fields.
Air-Commodore Clark Hall showed these photographs to Dr.
Williams-Freeman, who took me to see them. Dr. Williams-
Freeman and I had always been hoping for air-photographs of
English soil, and looking at these we saw that our expectations
were fulfilled, and even surpassed, by what was revealed. It was
possible from these photographs to make a map of the Celtic field-
system near Winchester, which was published in the *Geographical
Journal* for May 1923, and reprinted in *Air Survey and Archaeology*,
1924 (Ordnance Survey Professional Paper, New Series, No. 7).
Many archaeological air-photographs have been taken by the School
of Army Co-operation at Old Sarum, and by officers of the R.A.F.
stations at Farnborough, Calshot, Lee-on-Solent, and Gosport.

Recently the Air Ministry has sanctioned the transfer to the Ordnance Survey Office of all air-photographs containing archaeological information, which are not required for service purposes. Thus the connexion between air-photography and the Royal Engineers, begun about 1880 by Major Elsdale and continued by Colonel Beazeley, has been maintained. Needless to point out, air-photographs are of great use, when checked and supplemented by field work, in revising the archaeological information on the ordnance maps.

Popular interest was first aroused by the discovery of negatives showing, for the first time, the complete course of the Stonehenge Avenue. The history of this has been told before, and I do not propose to repeat it here. Full details will be found in my monograph on *Air Survey and Archaeology*. The photographs of the Avenue were taken in the dry year of 1921 by the Old Sarum squadron, but their archaeological importance was not recognized until two years later, in 1923, when I unearthed them at Old Sarum. At the present moment the problem before us is to devise a system by which the pictures may become generally accessible to archaeologists for purposes of study.

It is usually imagined that the camera, when fixed in an aeroplane, records marks on the ground which are invisible to the eye of an observer. That is not so. The observer can see these marks more plainly than the camera, for he sees them in colour. The most remarkable discoveries which have been made are due to plants, which are sensitive to slight differences of soil and moisture. For example, if a ditch has been dug on a chalk down and the down has afterwards been ploughed flat and sown with corn, for ever afterwards the subsoil filling (or silt) of that ditch differs from the adjacent never-disturbed soil. Nothing can ever restore chalk once dug to its former state of compactness. Archaeologists have long known this, for one of the principal needs in excavation is to distinguish between disturbed and undisturbed soil. But one cannot dig up a whole field or several fields to find a ditch which after all may not exist. Here it is that a vertical view helps; for the effect of this moister silt upon a crop of corn is to promote its growth and deepen its colour. Thus from above one sees and can photograph, a belt of darker green corn following the line of the vanished ditch. These lines are sometimes visible on the ground, from across a valley, or at even closer quarters. Sometimes (as in parts of the Stonehenge Avenue) they are quite invisible. But always, when more than a single ditch is concerned, the *distant* view is necessary to convert chaos into order. The reason for this necessity can best be explained by means of a comparison. If one looks through a magnifying-glass at a half-tone illustration made through a coarse screen, it ceases to be seen as a picture and becomes a meaningless maze of blurred dots. If one holds it some distance off and looks at it with the naked eye it becomes a picture again. The observer on the ground is like the user of the magnifying-glass; the observer (or camera) in the air is like him who looks at the half-tone picture from a distance.

Now the majority of our prehistoric sites, and many later ones, were seamed with ditches and pits, dug for drainage, storage, habitation, defence, or boundary purposes. Many exist to-day on the downs, undisturbed and turf covered; many more have been flattened by cultivation. All of the latter can be rediscovered by air-photography, provided only that the arable has not been allowed to revert to grass. Even then traces of the ditches are sometimes visible, especially on poor soils and in dry summers, by a belt of darker green. Air observation, however, is most fruitful when young crops are growing; then discovery is easy and rapid, and every flight is productive, Such sites may afterwards be seen to exist by an observer on the ground, but few of them could ever have been *discovered* except from the air. Chalk is not the only soil that produces these streak-sites; they have been observed on oolitic limestone near Bath and plateau gravel near Exbury.

A few words only are necessary to describe the other factors which enable air-photography to record ancient sites. Prehistoric cultivation-banks—what I have called lynchets of Celtic type—are revealed because either they throw slight shadows or when ploughed appear as belts of lighter soil, from the chalk grains mixed with them. From photographs the Celtic field-system of a district can be accurately mapped. Again, rabbits work in the looser silt of filled-up ditches (as well as in the soil of the lynchets), and if there are many rabbits a white line, or row of white patches, is visible from the air. Daisies and poppies grow for choice above these ditches, and barrows and hill-top camps have thus been revealed by white and scarlet circles.

Lastly, the low shadows at sunrise and sunset etch the outline of low banks in deep black. That is the time to photograph lynchets. On a June morning before breakfast the greater part of Salisbury Plain is seen to be covered with the banks of abandoned Celtic fields, but afterwards they "fade into the common light of day." The great ramparts of hill-top camps are strong enough to throw a shadow even at midday, but even they are best photographed when the sun is low, for then not only do the ramparts stand out best, but also the banks and pits of the habitations.

GEOFFREY BIBBY

Dating by Radio-Active Carbon

CARBON is the basic ingredient of all organic matter, the major constituent of animal and vegetable life, and at the same time, in the form of carbon dioxide, one of the principal ingredients of the air. Carbon is absorbed from the carbon dioxide of the air by plants, which release the surplus oxygen; and this assimilated carbon in the plants is in turn consumed by animals and by man. Both in plants and in animals the carbon is partly used to replace structural wastage and to build up new structure, the process we call growth. There is a constant influx of new carbon to any living growing organism, and a constant, though lesser, outflow of the old.

Now, carbon is not the simple element that it was believed in pre-atomic times to be. It consists of three isotopes, three distinct substances which are chemically indistinguishable but which have different physical characteristics, the most obvious being a difference in atomic weight, 12, 13 and 14. Ordinary everyday carbon is of atomic weight 12. But C-12 is mixed with one part to several million of C-13 and C-14. These tiny proportions of the heavier carbon are manufactured in the upper levels of the atmosphere. There the carbon dioxide of the air is exposed to bombardment by cosmic rays, the unexplained streams of ionized particles which shower down upon the earth from outer space. When such a particle strikes an atom of carbon in the carbon dioxide of the atmosphere, sufficient of the energy, or matter, of the particle is absorbed to convert the C-12 into C-13 or C-14.

This "heavy carbon" is, like ordinary carbon, absorbed from the atmosphere, at first or second hand, by every living thing.

This process would be of only academic interest, were it not for a very important fact. Carbon-14 is radioactive.

From *The Testimony of the Spade* by Geoffrey Bibby, by permission of Alfred A. Knopf, Inc., New York. Copyright © 1956 by Geoffrey Bibby. Permission also granted by William Collins & Sons, Ltd., London.

Now, radioactive materials do two things. They emit particles, the rate of emission of which can be measured on a Geiger counter, and in the process they break down into other, normally non-radioactive, substances. They break down at a fixed rate for each radioactive substance, so that it is possible to state that after a definite length of time the amount of radioactivity in a quantity of material will be reduced to half, and after the same period again to a quarter, and so on. This fixed period is known as the "half-life" of the substance.

Libby, a gangling six-foot atomic chemist, first became interested in Carbon-14 in 1946, after an exciting four years on the Manhattan Project. And he reasoned out that, since the proportion of C-14 in the carbon of the atmosphere is kept constant by the continual streams of cosmic rays, and since every living creature keeps renewing its C-14 by absorption of the atmospheric carbon, then every living creature is radioactive, and to exactly the same degree.

This rather disturbing thought was still not of immediate concern to the prehistorian interested in determination of chronology. But in 1947 Libby took his reasoning a step further. When an organism dies, it ceases to absorb new carbon from the air. From that point the natural breakdown of its C-14 is not counterbalanced by new intake. Therefore its proportion of C-14 to C-12 will slowly drop—*and drop at a fixed rate*. The half-life of Carbon-14 was found to be 5,568 years, to an accuracy of 0.54 per cent. So that a tree cut down 5,568 years ago would produce only half as many clicks on a Geiger counter as a tree cut down yesterday.

Now the prehistorians woke up. For the reverse was also true. If a piece of wood gave only half the number of clicks given by a modern piece, then that piece of wood was 5,568 years old. And any other proportion of clicks could likewise be converted into a date, as far back as the limits of accuracy of the machine. A method of dating any prehistoric material containing carbon had suddenly appeared out of the blue.

And so it proved. A committee of four archaeologists was set up by the American Anthropological Association in February of 1948 and proceeded to submit samples of every conceivable type of prehistoric material containing carbon to Libby and his battery of Geigers. The first samples were objects of known date—wood from the graves of Egyptian Pharaohs and from Hittite palaces, ashes from Roman encampments, and cloth from the Dead Sea scrolls. In every case Libby came up with a date conforming to within ten per cent with the date already known. The new method had proved itself.

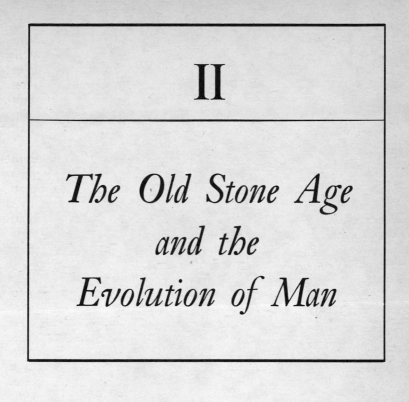

II

The Old Stone Age and the Evolution of Man

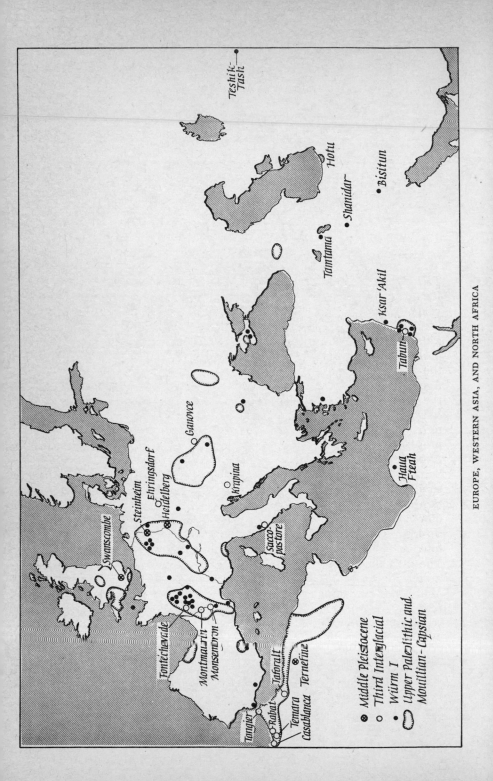

Teshik-Tash

Hotu

Bisitun

Shanidar

Tamtama

Ksar 'Akil

Tabun

Haua Fteah

Ganovce

Steinheim

Ehringsdorf

Heidelberg

Krapina

Swanscombe

Sacco pastore

Fontéchevade

Montmaurin

Monsempron

Taforalt

Ternefine

Tanger

Rabat

Temara

Casablanca

⊗ Middle Pleistocene
○ Third Interglacial
● Würm I
◖ Upper Paleolithic and.
   Mouillian - Capsian

EUROPE, WESTERN ASIA, AND NORTH AFRICA

INTRODUCTORY

THE Old Stone, or Palaeolithic, Age coincides with the Pleistocene Ice Age of the geologists. That is to say it ended about ten thousand years ago, having lasted for something like a million years. It is usually divided into three phases, the Lower, Middle and Upper Palaeolithic periods, of which the first is by far the longest— probably lasting until about one hundred thousand years ago. For the whole of the Palaeolithic Age and the relatively brief Mesolithic Age which succeeded it, men depended entirely upon hunting and the collection of wild foodstuffs.

During this vast stretch of our earliest history, progress in material culture was almost unbelievably slow. For example, the most progressive of the Lower Palaeolithic cultures, those known as the Abbevillian and Acheulian after the famous discoveries in the Somme valley (p. 30, I), had a span of some three hundred thousand years, yet achieved nothing more spectacular than the perfection of the hand-axe that was their most characteristic tool. The dominant types of men of this period were variants of *Pithecanthropus,* such as Peking Man, but breeds evolving more rapidly toward our own species probably began to emerge before its end. The best known of the Middle Palaeolithic cultures is that known as the Mousterian, which is commonly attributed to Neanderthal Man. This physically regressive breed, with its several simian features, certainly co-existed for a time with *Homo sapiens,* but seems to have been finally superseded by our species between thirty and forty thousand years ago, during the course of the last glaciation.

This was the beginning of the Upper Palaeolithic period, which saw not only a great improvement in tools and weapons and the beginning of mechanical invention in the spear-thrower and the bow, but also the sudden flowering of the visual arts. That hunters living so long ago and struggling against the rigours of a glacial climate should have been able to create the superb animal art of the French and Spanish caves appears miraculous. This also was the time during which the first men entered America from Asia and began their gradual settlement of the whole continent.

By the beginning of the tenth millennium B.C., the final glaciation was coming to an end—and with it the Palaeolithic Age. In some parts of the world the hunters and food-gatherers of the succeeding Mesolithic Age maintained themselves for thousands of years, but in South-west Asia they soon began the experiments that were to lead to farming and the great economic and social revolution which it brought about.

A century and a half ago none of this was known—nor could it have been believed. The following extracts are mainly concerned with the first tentative hints of the great antiquity of man, and with the revolution in thought which accompanied its recognition. Lyell, Darwin, Huxley and other leaders of this revolution are represented, together with some of the lesser men who contributed to it—or opposed it. Finally there are a few records of modern researches on Palaeolithic and Mesolithic sites, and, as an amusing corrective to possible scientific arrogance, a full account of the fraudulent affair of Piltdown Man.

JOHN BAGFORD

The First Discoveries:
An Implement and an Elephant
from Gray's Inn, London

THESE two finds, made well before the great antiquity of man had been recognized, were both of hand-axes dating from Lower Palaeolithic times. Conyers found the hand-axe at Gray's Inn as early as 1690; the complete incomprehension of its age and significance is made plain by the identification of an associated fossil elephant with the beasts brought to England by the Roman Emperor Claudius. In contrast, John Frere showed great perspicacity in assigning his specimens to "a very remote period."

AND HERE I cannot forget to mention the honest Industry of my old Friend Mr. John Conyers, an Apothecary formerly living in Fleet-street, who made it his chief Business to make curious Observations, and to collect such Antiquities as were daily found in and about London. His character is very well known, and therefore I will not attempt it. Yet this I must note, that he was at great Expence in prosecuting his Discoveries, and that he is remembered with respect by most of our Antiquaries that are now living. 'Tis this very Gentleman that discovered the Body of an Elephant, as he was digging for Gravel in a Field near to the Sign of Sir John

From John Leland's *Collectanea*, Hearne's Edition, 1770.

Old-Castle in the Fields, not far from Battlebridge, and near to the River of Wells, which tho' now dryed up, was a considerable River in the time of the Romans.

How this Elephant came there? is the Question. I know some will have it to have lain there ever since the Universal Deluge. For my own part, I take it to have been brought over with many others by the Romans in the time of Claudius, and conjecture . . . that it was killed in some Fight by a Britain. For not far from the Place where it was found, a British Weapon made of a Flint Lance like unto the Head of a Spear . . . was also dug up, they having not at that time the use of Iron or Brass, as the Romans had. . . . This conjecture, perhaps, may seem odd to some; but I am satisfied myself, having often viewed this Flint Weapon. . . .

JOHN FRERE

Flint Implements Discovered at Hoxne, in Suffolk

THEY are, I think, evidently weapons of war, fabricated and used by a people who had not the use of metals. They lay in great numbers at the depth of about twelve feet, in a stratified soil, which was dug into for the purpose of raising clay for bricks. . . .

The situation in which these weapons were found may tempt us to refer them to a very remote period indeed, even beyond that of the present world; but whatever our conjectures on that hand may be, it will be difficult to account for the stratum in which they lie being covered with another stratum which, on that supposition, may be conjectured to have been once the bottom, or at least the

From *Archaeologia*, XIII, 1800. Read to the Society of Antiquaries, June, 1797.

shore, of the sea. The manner in which they lie would lead to the
persuasion that it was a place of their manufacture and not of
their accidental deposit. . . .

W. BOYD DAWKINS

Cave Hunting in Germany

THE rest of this chapter must be devoted to an outline of the
history of cave-exploration during the last two centuries. The dread
of the supernatural, which preserved the European caves from
disturbance, was destroyed in the sixteenth and seventeenth centuries by the search after "ebur fossile," or unicorn's horn, which
ranked high in the materia medica of those days as a specific for
many diseases, and which was obtained, in great abundance, in the
caverns of the Hartz, and in those of Hungary and Franconia. As
the true nature of the drug gradually revealed itself, the German
caves became famous for the remains of the lions, hyaenas, fossil
elephants, and other strange animals, which had been used for
medicine. We owe the first philosophical discussion on the point
to Dr. Gesner, who, although he maintained that the fossil unicorn consisted, in some cases, of elephant's teeth and tusks, and
in others of its fossil bones, did not altogether give up the idea of
its medicinal value. It is a singular fact, that fossil remains of a
similar kind are, at the present time, used by the Chinese for the
same purpose, and sold in their druggists' shops. The cave which
was most famous at the end of the seventeenth century was that
of Bauman's Hole, in the Hartz, in the district of Blankenbourg.
It is noticed in the Philosophical Transactions for the year 1662,
and was subsequently described by Dr. Behrens, Leibnitz, De Luc,
and Cuvier, along with others in the neighbourhood. Those of
Hungary come next in point of discovery, the first notice of them

From *Cave Hunting*. London: Macmillan & Co., Ltd.; 1874, pp. 11-22.

being due to Patterson Hayne in 1672. They penetrate the southern slopes of the Carpathian ranges, and are known by the name of dragons' caves, because the bones which they contain had been considered from time immemorial to belong to those animals by the country people. These remains were identified by Baron Cuvier as belonging to the cave-bear.

It was not, however, until the close of the eighteenth century that the exploring of caves was carried on systematically, or their contents examined with any scientific precision. The caves of Franconia, in the neighbourhood of Muggendorf, were described by Esper in 1774, by Rosenmuller in 1804, and six years later by Dr. Goldfuss. The most important was that of Gailenreuth, both from the vast quantity of remains which it was proved to contain, and the investigations to which it led. The bones of the hyaena, lion, wolf, fox, glutton, and red deer were identified by Baron Cuvier; while some of the skulls which Dr. Goldfuss obtained have been recently proved, by Professor Busk, to belong to the grizzly bear. They were associated with the bones of the reindeer, horse and bison. Rosenmuller was of opinion that the cave had been inhabited by bears for a long series of generations; and he thus realized that these remains proved that the animals found in the cave had once lived in that district, and had not been swept from the tropics by the deluge. The interest in these discoveries was at its height in the year 1816, when Dr. Buckland visited the cave, and acquired that knowledge of cave-exploring which he was subsequently to use with such good effect in this country. From this time down to the present day, no new fact of importance has been added to our knowledge of caves by explorations in Germany.

J. MacENERY, S.J.

An Early Cave Digger: MacEnery at Kent's Cavern

To the following incident I am indebted for first directing my steps towards the Cavern.

Having one morning in the summer of 1825 chanced to hear my friend Captain Welby express his intention to join an exploring party there, I was induced to accompany him. We found his relation Mr. Northmore, of whom mention has already been made, at its entrance, surrounded by about a dozen persons, among whom were remarked the Commander of the Coast Guard and his men, all busy in equipping themselves for their expedition under ground.

The passage being too narrow to admit more than one person at a time, and that only in a stooping posture, the company entered in files, each bearing a light in one hand and a pick-axe in the other, headed by a guide carrying a lantern before the chief of the party. I made the last of the train, for I could not divest myself of certain undefinable sensations, it being my first visit to a scene of this nature. As soon as the party was assembled in the vestibule Mr. Northmore ascended a rock, from which he delivered instructions to the group around him, respecting the plan to be pursued in their operations during the day. He next distributed the Coast Guard through the several chambers, and employed himself in passing to and fro superintending their proceedings; notwithstanding which there was little or nothing added, on that occasion, to what was already known of the Cavern; indeed no individual, with his single arm, could do more than pierce the crust superficially. If instead of these desultory proceedings all hands had been brought to bear on any particular point, they must necessarily have reached the bones, for there is no part where they may not be found below the stalagmite.

The party were, however, somewhat consoled for their disap-

From *Cavern Researchers*. London: Simpkin Marshall; 1859, pp. 2-3.

pointment by the discovery, in the black mould, of certain rudely shaped pieces of oak, one of which was immediately shewn me by Mr. Braham, the finder; it was about the length and form of the human foot, and hollowed in the centre, not unlike a sandal. I accordingly gave it the name which it has since borne of the "Druid's sandal." The designation, although applied only in allusion to the lecture we have just heard, was too good not to be caught up and adopted, as it seemed to countenance certain fanciful doctrines then promulgated with all the authority of an oracle.

Perceiving that it was in vain to look for the fossils without first piercing the crust, which stood between them and the mould underfoot, I betook myself alone, to a spot which had the appearance of being disturbed. It was one of those perforations in the floor which further observation enabled us to trace to burrowing animals, situated half way down the vestibule, or sloping chamber, in a cove on the right against the wall. The mouth was partially choked up with soil, of which a heap was thrown up round its margin, it was slightly glazed over with the droppings, the earth was of a reddish brown, unctuous to the touch, and from the presence of a profusion of recent bones, bore evident marks of frequent disturbance. On tumbling it over, the lustre of the enamel soon betrayed its contents; they were the first fossil teeth I had ever seen, and as I laid my hand on these relicts of distinct races, and witnesses of an order of things which passed away with them, I shrunk back involuntarily; though not insensible to the excitement attending new discoveries, I am not ashamed to own, that, in the presence of these remains, I felt more of awe than joy; but whatever may have been the impressions or speculations that rushed into my mind, this is not the place to indulge them; my present business is with facts.

I pursued my search in silence, and kept my good fortune a secret, fearing that amidst the press and avidity of the party to possess some fossil memorial of the day, my discoveries would be damaged, or perhaps share the fate of those abstracted from Mr. Northmore's basket [on an earlier visit Mr. Northmore had filled a basket with fossils, but on return to his lodging "found they were gone"] I was anxious to send them in a state in which they were found to Oxford.

In addition to the specimens of the five species figured in Mr. W. C. Trevilyan's plate, there appeared several new ones, belonging to horse, deer, hare, rabbit, &c., head of field rat, (campagnol) and a small feline or cat, with the bones of two species of birds. But the most remarkable discovery of all, was of the upper jaw of a hyena, the bone of which was eaten away close to the roots of the teeth, and even the upper portion, or gum, bore impressions of gnawing. The whole was accompanied by bones belonging, principally, to the small quadrupeds, some of which were fractured at their extremities as if by the bite of a dog, and their barrels loaded with mud; along with the above was sent a lump of the soil through which were disseminated small splinters of bone, and teeth of the campagnol, the whole was immediately drawn on stone in a superior style, by the lady who executed Mr. Trevilyan's plate; this may be regarded as the first gleam of light that was thrown on the condition of the contents of the Cavern. My communication was followed by an answer which urged me to follow up my good fortune.

JOHN EVANS

A Momentous Visit to the Somme

THIS visit of John Evans and the geologist Prestwich to Boucher de Perthes at Abbeville, made in the same year as the publication of the *Origin of Species*, was of great importance. The Englishmen were at last convinced of the great antiquity of the implements the Frenchman was finding (which we now know to date from the Lower Palaeolithic period), and on their return to England easily persuaded their colleagues to accept their verdict.

MAY 1st, 1859. I crossed from Folkestone to Boulogne and had as rough a passage as the strongest stomach could desire. . . . I had about an hour and a half in Boulogne and at 9 took the train to

From the Diary of John Evans, 1859. Quoted by Joan Evans in *Time and Chance*. London: Longmans, Green & Co.; 1943, pp. 101-5. By permission of Longmans, Green & Co. and Joan Evans.

Abbeville, where I found Prestwich waiting for me at the Station, and very glad to see me, as of all the party he had asked to meet him there, I was the only one who came. We went straight to bed and soon after 7 the next morning M. Boucher de Perthes, the first discoverer of the stone axes we were in pursuit of, came to take us to some of the gravel pits from whence his collection had been derived. A M. Marotte, the Curator of the Museum, accompanied us but we did not succeed in finding anything. We then adjourned to the house of M. de Perthes which is a complete museum from top to bottom, full of paintings, old carvings, pottery etc. and with a wonderful collection of flint axes and implements found among the beds of gravel and evidently deposited at the same time with them—in fact the remains of a race of men who existed at the time when the deluge or whatever was the origin of these gravel beds took place. One of the most remarkable features of the case is that nearly all if not quite all of the animals whose bones are found in the same beds as the axes are extinct. There is the mammoth, the rhinoceros, the Urus—a tiger, etc. etc. After the examination of his museum, M. de Perthes gave us a most sumptuous *déjeuner à la fourchette* and we then set off for Amiens. Of course our object was if possible to ascertain that these axes had been actually deposited with the gravel, and not subsequently introduced; and we had received intelligence from Amiens that in one of the gravel pits there an axe was to be seen in its original position, which made us set off at once. At Amiens we were met by the President of their Society of Antiquaries and the public Librarian, MM. Dufour and Garnier, and with them a M. Pinsard, an architect. We proceeded to the pit where sure enough the edge of an axe was visible in an entirely undisturbed bed of gravel and eleven feet from the surface. We had a photographer with us to take a view of it so as to corroborate our testimony and had only time to get that done and collect some 12 or 15 axes from the workmen in the Pit when we were forced to take the train again to Abbeville. The early part of Friday we spent in and about Abbeville and returned to London in the afternoon reaching home or rather the Euston Hotel about midnight. Altogether I enjoyed the trip very much, and am now only troubled to find time to write an account of our investigations for the Antiquaries, as Prestwich is going to do for the Royal Society.

CHARLES LYELL

Men in the Ice Age: the First Proofs

SIR CHARLES LYELL was the greatest geologist of his day, and his clear summary of the evidence for the antiquity of man carried great weight. His discussion of the religious and philosophical implications of the doctrine of human evolution are of considerable interest.

❧

THROUGHOUT a large part of Europe we find at moderate elevations above the present river-channels, usually at a height of less than forty feet but sometimes much higher, beds of gravel, sand, and loam containing bones of the elephant, rhinoceros, horse, ox, and other quadrupeds, some of extinct, others of living, species, belonging for the most part to the fauna already alluded to in the last chapter as characteristic of the interior of caverns. The greater part of these deposits contain fluviatile shells, and have undoubtedly been accumulated in ancient river-beds. These old channels have long since been dry, the streams which once flowed in them having shifted their position, deepening the valleys, and often widening them on one side.

It has naturally been asked, if man coexisted with the extinct species of the caves, why were his remains and the works of his hands never embedded outside the caves in ancient river-gravel containing the same fossil fauna? Why should it be necessary for the geologist to resort for evidence of the antiquity of our race to the dark recesses of underground vaults and tunnels, which may have served as places of refuge or sepulture to a succession of human beings and wild animals, and where floods may have confounded together in one breccia the memorials of the fauna of

From *Geological Evidences of the Antiquity of Man*. London: John Murray; 1863, pp. 93-105, 504-6.

more than one epoch? Why do we not meet with a similar assemblage of the relics of man, and of living and extinct quadrupeds, in places where the strata can be thoroughly scrutinised in the light of day?

Recent researches have at length demonstrated that such memorials, so long sought for in vain, do in fact exist, and their recognition is the chief cause of the more favourable reception now given to the conclusions which MM. Tournal, Christol, Schmerling, and others, arrived at thirty years ago respecting the fossil contents of caverns.

The first great step in this new direction was made thirteen years after the publication of Schmerling's "Researches," by M. Boucher de Perthes, who found in ancient alluvium at Abbeville, in Picardy, some flint implements, the relative antiquity of which was attested by their geological position. The antiquarian knowledge of their discoverer enabled him to recognise in their rude and peculiar type a character distinct from that of the polished stone weapons of a later period, usually called "celts." In the first volume of his "Antiquités Celtiques," published in 1847, M. Boucher de Perthes styled these older tools "antediluvian," because they came from the lowest beds of a series of ancient alluvial strata bordering the valley of the Somme, which geologists had termed "diluvium." He had begun to collect these implements in 1841, from which time they had been dug out of the drift or deposits of gravel and sand whenever excavations were made in repairing the fortifications of Abbeville; or annually, as often as flints were wanted for the roads, or loam for making bricks. Fine sections, therefore, were laid open, from twenty to thirty-five feet in depth, and the bones of quadrupeds of the genera elephant, rhinoceros, bear, hyaena, stag, ox, horse, and others, were found, and had been sent from time to time to Paris to be examined and named by Cuvier, who described them in his "Ossements Fossiles." A correct account of the associated flint tools and of their position was given in 1847 by M. Boucher de Perthes in his work above cited, and they were stated to occur at various depths, often twenty or thirty feet from the surface, in sand and gravel, especially in those strata which were nearly in contact with the subjacent white chalk. But the scientific world had no faith in the statement that works of art, however rude, had been met with in undisturbed beds of such antiquity. Few geologists visited Abbeville in winter, when the sand-pits were open, and when they might have opportunities of verifying the sections, and judging whether the instruments had really been embedded by natural causes in the same strata with the bones of the mammoth, rhinoceros, and other extinct mammalia. Some of the tools figured in the "Antiquités Celtiques" were so rudely shaped, that many imagined them to have owed their peculiar forms to accidental fracture in a river's bed; others suspected frauds on the part of the workmen, who might have fabricated them for sale, or that the gravel had been disturbed, and that the worked flints had got mingled with the bones of the mammoth long after that animal and its associates had disappeared from the earth.

No one was more sceptical than the late eminent physician of Amiens, Dr. Rigollot, who had long before (in the year 1819) written a memoir on the fossil mammalia of the valley of the Somme. He was at length induced to visit Abbeville, and, having inspected the collection of M. Boucher de Perthes, returned home resolved to look for himself for flint tools in the gravel-pits near Amiens. There, accordingly, at a distance of about forty miles from Abbeville, he immediately found abundance of similar flint implements, precisely the same in the rudeness of their make, and the same in their geological position; some of them in gravel nearly on a level with the Somme, others in similar deposits resting on chalk at a height of about ninety feet above the river.

Dr. Rigollot having in the course of four years obtained several hundred specimens of these tools, most of them from St. Acheul in the south-east suburbs of Amiens, lost no time in communicating an account of them to the scientific world, in a memoir illustrated by good figures of the worked flints and careful sections of the beds. These sections were executed by M. Buteux, an engineer well qualified for the task, who had written a good description of the geology of Picardy. Dr. Rigollot, in this memoir, pointed out most clearly that it was not in the vegetable soil, nor in the brick-earth with land and fresh-water shells next below, but in the lower beds of coarse flint-gravel, usually twelve, twenty, or twenty-five feet below the surface, that the implements were met with, just as they had been previously stated by M. Boucher de Perthes to occur at Abbeville. The conclusion, therefore, which was legitimately deduced from all the facts, was that the flint tools and their fabricators were coeval with the extinct mammalia embedded in the same strata.

Brixham Cave, near Torquay, Devonshire

Four years after the appearance of Dr. Rigollot's paper, a sudden change of opinion was brought about in England respecting the probable coexistence, at a former period, of man and many extinct mammalia, in consequence of the results obtained from a careful exploration of a cave at Brixham, near Torquay, in Devonshire. As the new views very generally adopted by English geologists had no small influence on the subsequent progress of opinion in France, I shall interrupt my account of the researches made in the Valley of the Somme, by a brief notice of those which were carried on in

1858 in Devonshire with more than usual care and scientific method. Dr. Buckland, in his celebrated work, entitled "Reliquiae Diluvianae," published in 1823, in which he treated of the organic remains contained in caves, fissures, and "diluvial gravel" in England, had given a clear statement of the results of his own original observations, and had declared that none of the human bones or stone implements met with by him in any of the caverns could be considered to be as old as the mammoth and other extinct quadrupeds. Opinions in harmony with this conclusion continued until very lately to be generally in vogue in England; although about the time that Schmerling was exploring the Liége caves, the Rev. Mr. MacEnery, a Roman Catholic priest, residing near Torquay, had found in a cave one mile east of that town, called "Kent's Hole," in red loam covered with stalagmite, not only bones of the mammoth, tichorhine rhinoceros, cave-bear, and other mammalia, but several remarkable flint tools, some of which he supposed to be of great antiquity, while there were also remains of man in the same cave of a later date.

About ten years afterwards, in a "Memoir on the Geology of South Devon," published in 1842 by the Geological Society of London, an able geologist, Mr. Godwin-Austen, declared that he had obtained in the same cave (Kent's Hole) works of man from undisturbed loam or clay, under stalagmite, mingled with the remains of extinct animals, and that all these must have been introduced "before the stalagmite flooring had been formed." He maintained that such facts could not be explained away by the hypothesis of sepulture, as in Dr. Buckland's well-known case of the human skeleton of Paviland, because in the Devon cave the flint implements were widely distributed through the loam, and lay beneath the stalagmite.

As the osseous and other contents of Kent's Hole had, by repeated diggings, been thrown into much confusion, it was thought desirable in 1858, when the entrance of a new and intact bone-cave was discovered at Brixham, three or four miles west of Torquay, to have a thorough and systematic examination made of it. The Royal Society made two grants towards defraying the expenses, and a committee of geologists was charged with the investigations, among whom Mr. Prestwich and Dr. Falconer took an active part, visiting Torquay while the excavations were in progress under the superintendence of Mr. Pengelly. The last-mentioned geologist had the kindness to conduct me through the subterranean galleries after they had been cleared out in 1859; and I saw, in company with Dr. Falconer, the numerous fossils which had been taken from the subterranean fissures and tunnels, all labelled and numbered, with references to a journal kept during the progress of the work, and in which the geological position of every specimen was recorded with scrupulous care.

The discovery of the existence of this suite of caverns near the sea at Brixham was made accidentally by the roof of one of them falling in. None of the five external openings now exposed to view in steep cliffs or the sloping side of a valley were visible before the breccia and earthy matter which blocked them up were removed during the late exploration. According to a ground-plan drawn up by Professor Ramsay, it appears that some of the passages which run nearly north and south are fissures connected with the vertical dislocation of the rocks, while another set, running nearly east and west, are tunnels, which have the appearance of having been to a great extent hollowed out by the action of running water. The central or main entrance, leading to what is called the "reindeer gallery," because a perfect antler of that animal was found sticking in the stalagmatic floor, is ninety-five feet above the level of the sea, being also about sixty above the bottom of the adjoining valley. The united length of five galleries which were cleared out amounted to several hundred feet. Their width never exceeded eight feet. They were sometimes filled up to the roof with gravel, bones, and mud, but occasionally there was a considerable space between the roof and floor. The latter, in the case of the fissure-caves, was covered with stalagmite, but in the tunnels it was usually free from any such incrustation. The following was the general succession of the deposits forming the contents of the underground passages and channels: —

1st. At the top, a layer of stalagmite varying in thickness from one to fifteen inches, which sometimes contained bones, such as the reindeer's horn, already mentioned, and an entire humerus of the cave-bear.

2ndly. Next below, loam or bone-earth, of an ochreous red colour, from one foot to fifteen feet in thickness.

3rdly. At the bottom of all, gravel with many rounded pebbles in it, probed in some places to the depth of twenty feet without its being pierced through, and as it was barren of fossils, left for the most part unremoved.

The mammalia obtained from the bone-earth consisted of *Elephas primigenius*, or mammoth; *Rhinoceros tichorhinus; Ursus spelaeus; Hyaena spelaea; Felis spelaea*, or the cave-lion; *Cervus Tarandus*, or the reindeer; a species of horse, ox, and several rodents, and others not yet determined.

No human bones were obtained anywhere during these excavations, but many flint knives, chiefly from the lowest part of the bone-earth; and one of the most perfect lay at the depth of thirteen feet from the surface, and was covered with bone-earth of that thickness. From a similar position was taken one of those siliceous nuclei, or cores, from which flint flakes had been struck off on every side. Neglecting the less perfect specimens, some of which were met with even in the lowest gravel, about fifteen knives, recognised as artificially formed by the most experienced antiquaries, were taken from the bone-earth, and usually from near the bottom. Such knives, considered apart from the associated mammalia, afford in themselves no safe criterion of antiquity, as they might belong to any part of the age of stone, similar tools being sometimes met with in tumuli posterior in date to the era of the introduction of bronze. But the anteriority of those at Brixham to the extinct animals is demonstrated not only by the occurrence at one point in overlying stalagmite of the bone of a cave-bear, but also by the discovery at the same level in the bone-earth, and in close proximity to a very perfect flint tool, of the entire left hind-leg of a cave-bear. This specimen, which was shown me by Dr. Falconer and Mr. Pengelly, was exhumed from the earthy deposit in the reindeer gallery, near its junction with the flint-knife gallery, at the distance of about sixty-five feet from the main entrance. The mass of earth containing it was removed entire, and the matrix cleared away carefully by Dr. Falconer in the presence of Mr. Pengelly. Every bone was in its natural place, the femur, tibia, fibula, ankle-bone, or astragalus, all in juxtaposition. Even the patella or detached bone of the knee-pan was searched for, and not in vain. Here, therefore, we have evidence of an entire limb not having been washed in a fossil state out of an older alluvium, and then swept afterwards into a cave, so as to be mingled with flint implements, but having been introduced when clothed with its flesh, or at least when it had the separate bones bound together by their natural ligaments, and in that state buried in mud.

If they were not all of contemporary date, it is clear from this case, and from the humerus of the *Ursus spelaeus*, before cited, as found in a floor of stalagmite, that the bear lived after the flint tools were manufactured, or in other words, that man in this district preceded the cave-bear. . . .

Dr. Falconer, after aiding in the investigations above alluded to near Torquay, stopped at Abbeville on his way to Sicily, in the autumn of 1858, and saw there the collection of M. Boucher de Perthes. Being at once satisfied that the flints called hatchets had really been fashioned by the hand of man, he urged Mr. Prestwich, by letter, thoroughly to explore the geology of the Valley of the Somme. This he accordingly accomplished, in company with Mr. John Evans, of the Society of Antiquaries, and, before his return that same year, succeeded in dissipating all doubts from the minds of his geological friends by extracting, with his own hands, from a bed of undisturbed gravel, at St. Acheul, a well-shaped flint hatchet. This implement was buried in the gravel at a depth of seventeen feet from the surface, and was lying on its flat side. There were no signs of vertical rents in the enveloping matrix, nor in the overlying beds of sand and loam, in which were many land and fresh-water shells; so that it was impossible to imagine that the tool had gradually worked its way downwards, as some had suggested, through the incumbent soil, into an older formation.

There was no one in England whose authority deserved to have more weight in overcoming incredulity in regard to the antiquity of the implements in question than that of Mr. Prestwich, since, besides having published a series of important memoirs on the tertiary formations of Europe, he had devoted many years specially to the study of the drift and its organic remains. His report, therefore, to the Royal Society, accompanied by a photograph showing the position of the flint tool *in situ* before it was removed from its matrix, not only satisfied many inquirers, but induced others to visit Abbeville and Amiens; and one of these, Mr. Flower, who accompanied Mr. Prestwich on his second excursion to St. Acheul, in June 1859, succeeded, by digging into the bank of gravel, in disinterring, at the depth of twenty-two feet from the surface, a fine, symmetrically shaped weapon of an oval form, lying in and beneath strata which were observed by many witnesses to be perfectly undisturbed.

Shortly afterwards, in the year 1859, I visited the same pits, and obtained seventy flint tools, one of which was taken out while I was present, though I did not see it before it had fallen from the matrix. I expressed my opinion in favour of the antiquity of the flint tools to the meeting of the British Association at Aberdeen, in the same year. On my way through Rouen, I stated my convictions on this subject to Mr. George Pouchet, who immediately betook himself to St. Acheul, commissioned by the municipality of Rouen, and did not quit the pits till he had seen one of the hatchets extracted from gravel in its natural position.

M. Gaudry also gave the following account of his researches in the same year to the Royal Academy of Sciences at Paris. "The great point was not to leave the workmen for a single instant, and to satisfy oneself by actual inspection, whether the hatchets were found *in situ*. I caused a deep excavation to be made, and found nine hatchets, most distinctly *in situ* in the diluvium, associated with teeth of *Equus fossilis* and a species of Bos, different from any now living, and similar to that of the diluvium and of caverns. In 1859, M. Hébert, an original observer of the highest authority, declared to the Geological Society of France that he had, in 1854, or four years before Mr. Prestwich's visit to St. Acheul, seen the sections at

Abbeville and Amiens, and had come to the opinion that the hatchets were imbedded in the "lower diluvium," and that their origin was as ancient as that of the mammoth and the rhinoceros. M. Desnoyers also made excavations after M. Gaudry, at St. Acheul, in 1859, with the same results.

After a lively discussion on the subject in England and France, it was remembered, not only that there were numerous recorded cases leading to similar conclusions in regard to cavern deposits, but, also, that Mr. Frere had, so long ago as 1797, found flint weapons, of the same type as those of Amiens, in a fresh-water formation in Suffolk, in conjunction with elephant remains; and nearly a hundred years earlier (1715), another tool of the same kind had been exhumed from the gravel of London, together with bones of an elephant; to all which examples I shall allude more fully in the sequel.

I may conclude this chapter by quoting a saying of Professor Agassiz, "that whenever a new and startling fact is brought to light in science, people first say, 'it is not true,' then that 'it is contrary to religion,' and lastly, 'that everybody knew it before.' "

The inventors of useful arts, the poets and prophets of the early stages of a nation's growth, the promulgators of new systems of religion, ethics, and philosophy, or of new codes of laws, have often been looked upon as messengers from Heaven, and after their death have had divine honours paid to them, while fabulous tales have been told of the prodigies which accompanied their birth. Nor can we wonder that such notions have prevailed when we consider what important revolutions in the moral and intellectual world such leading spirits have brought about; and when we reflect that mental as well as physical attributes are transmissible by inheritance, so that we may possibly discern in such leaps the origin of the superiority of certain races of mankind. In our own time the occasional appearance of such extraordinary mental powers may be attributed to atavism; but there must have been a beginning to the series of such rare and anomalous events. If, in conformity with the theory of progression, we believe mankind to have risen slowly from a rude and humble starting point, such leaps may have successively introduced not only higher and higher forms and grades of intellect, but at a much remoter period may have cleared at one bound the space which separated the highest stage of the unprogressive intelligence of the inferior animals from the first and lowest form of improvable reason manifested by man.

To say that such leaps constitute no interruption to the ordinary course of nature, is more than we are warranted in affirming. In the case of the occasional birth of an individual of superior genius, there is certainly no break in the regular genealogical succession;

and when all the mists of mythological fiction are dispelled by historical criticism, when it is acknowledged that the earth did not tremble at the nativity of the gifted infant, and that the face of heaven was not full of fiery shapes, still a mighty mystery remains unexplained, and it is the *order* of the phenomena, and not their *cause*, which we are able to refer to the usual course of nature.

Dr. Asa Gray, in the excellent essay already cited, has pointed out that there is no tendency in the doctrine of Variation and Natural Selection to weaken the foundations of Natural Theology; for, consistently with the derivative hypothesis of species, we may hold any of the popular views respecting the manner in which the changes of the natural world are brought about. We may imagine "that events and operations in general go on in virtue simply of forces communicated at the first, and without any subsequent interference, or we may hold that now and then, and only now and then, there is a direct interposition of the Deity; or, lastly, we may suppose that all the changes are carried on by the immediate orderly and constant, however infinitely diversified, action of the intelligent, efficient Cause." They who maintain that the origin of an individual, as well as the origin of a species or a genus, can be explained only by the direct action of the creative cause, may retain their favourite theory compatibly with the doctrine of transmutation.

Professor Agassiz, having observed that "while human thought is consecutive, divine thought is simultaneous," Dr. Asa Gray has replied that, "if divine thought is simultaneous, we have no right to affirm the same of divine action."

The whole course of nature may be the material embodiment of a preconcerted arrangement; and if the succession of events be explained by transmutation, the perpetual adaptation of the organic world to new conditions leaves the argument in favour of design, and therefore of a designer, as valid as ever; "for to do any work by an instrument must require, and therefore presuppose, the exertion rather of more than of less power, than to do it directly."

As to the charge of materialism brought against all forms of the development theory, Dr. Gray has done well to remind us that "of the two great minds of the seventeenth century, Newton and Leibnitz, both profoundly religious as well as philosophical, one produced the theory of gravitation, the other objected to that theory, that it was subversive of natural religion."

It may be said that, so far from having a materialistic tendency, the supposed introduction into the earth at successive geological periods of life, sensation, instinct, the intelligence of the higher mammalia bordering on reason, and lastly the improvable reason of Man himself, presents us with a picture of the ever-increasing dominion of mind over matter.

JOHN LUBBOCK (LORD AVEBURY)

The Evidence of the Tools

Nor have these discoveries been confined to France. There has long been in the British Museum a rude stone weapon, described as follows:—"No. 246. A British weapon, *found with elephant's tooth,* opposite to black Mary's, near Grayes inn lane. Conyers. It is a large black flint, shaped into the figure of a spear's point." Mr. Evans tells us, moreover, "that a rude engraving of it illustrates a letter on the Antiquities of London, by Mr. Bagford, dated 1715, printed in Hearne's edition of Leland's Collectanea. From his account it seems to have been found with a *skeleton* of an elephant in the presence of Mr. Conyers." This most interesting weapon agrees exactly with some of those found in the valley of the Somme.

Mr. Evans, on his return from Abbeville, observed in the museum belonging to the Society of Antiquaries, some specimens exactly like those in the collection of M. Boucher de Perthes. On examination, it proved that they had been presented by Mr. Frere, who found them with bones of extinct animals in a gravel pit at Hoxne in Suffolk, and had well described and figured them in the Archaeologia for the year 1800. This communication is of so much interest that I have thought it desirable to reproduce his figures, reduced one-half.

Some of the Hampshire specimens also have been found *in situ,* in a mass of drift gravel which covers the Tertiary beds, and is intersected by all the streams which now run into the Southampton water. This mass of drift gravel, moreover is not confined to the mainland but caps also the Foreland Cliffs on the East of the Isle of Wight, where an oval flint implement has recently been discovered by Mr. T. Codrington. As Mr. Evans has pointed out, we seem, in this discovery, to have clear evidence that man existed in this country before the Southampton Water was formed, or the Isle of Wight was separated from the mainland, and we may therefore regard these implements as among the most striking proofs of Man's Antiquity, which they carry back to a period far more ancient than that which had previously been assigned to him.

From *Prehistoric Times*. London: Williams and Norgate Ltd.; 1869, pp. 335, 340-4.

We cannot therefore wonder that the statement by Mr. Frere has been distrusted for more than half a century; that the weapon found by Mr. Conyers has lain unnoticed for more than double that time; that the discoveries by M. Boucher de Perthes have been ignored for fifteen years; that the numerous cases in which caves have contained the remains of men together with those of extinct animals have been suppressed or explained away: these facts show how deeply rooted was the conviction that man belonged altogether to a more recent order of things; and, whatever other accusation may be brought against them, geologists can at least not be said to have hastily accepted the theory of the coexistence of the human race with the now extinct Pachydermata of Western Europe.

Still, it might be supposed that they were forgeries, made by ingenious workmen to entrap unwary geologists. They have, however, been found by Messrs. Boucher de Perthes, Henslow, Christy, Flower, Wyatt, Evans, myself, and others. One seen, though not found by himself *in situ*, is thus described by Mr. Prestwich: "It was lying flat in the gravel at a depth of seventeen feet from the original surface, and six and a half from the chalk. One side slightly projected. The gravel around was undisturbed, and presented its usual perpendicular face. I carefully examined the specimen, and saw no reason to doubt that it was in its natural position, for the gravel is generally so loose, that a blow with a pick disturbs and brings it down for some way around; and the matrix is too little adhesive to admit of its being built up again as before with the same materials. . . . I found also afterwards, on taking out the flint, that it was the thinnest side which projected, the other side being less finished and much thicker." But evidence of this nature, though interesting, is unnecessary; *the flints speak for themselves.* Many of them are more or less rolled or worn at the edges. Those which have lain in siliceous or chalky sands are more or less polished and have a beautiful glossiness of surface, very unlike that of a newly-broken flint. In ochreous sand, "especially if argillaceous, they are stained yellow, whilst in ferruginous sands and clays they assume a brown colour," and in some beds they become white and porcellaneous. In many cases, moreover, they have incrustations of carbonate of lime and small dendritic markings. The freshly-broken chalk flints, on the contrary, are of a dull black or leaden color; they vary a little in darkness but not in color, and do not present white or yellow faces; moreover, the new surfaces are dead, and want the glossiness of those which have been long exposed. It is almost unnecesary to say, that they have no dendritic markings, nor are they incrusted by carbonate of lime.

W. BOYD DAWKINS

A Doubting Thomas

THE fact that caves were largely used as sepulchres in the Neolithic age renders it necessary to use extreme caution in assigning any interments to the Palaeolithic dwellers in caves without unmistakable evidence. This seems to me to be wanting in most of the examples generally accepted, which I have classified under the head of doubtful in my work on *Cave-Hunting*. For the reasons there given the antiquity of the Neanderthal skull is doubtful, while the interments in Cro-Magnon are seen to be later than the Palæolithic accumulation below. The so-called "fossil man of Mentone" may be referred to the same date as the polished stone axe of the Neolithic age found in the cave, and now preserved in the museum at St. Germain. The pottery found in the caves of Engis and Trou de Frontal in Belgium, and in those of Aurignac, Bruniquel, and Bize, is identical with the Neolithic pottery, and may therefore be taken to indicate the date of the interments.

Those experienced in digging caves know how very difficult it is to separate the contents of deposits of two different ages lying together in the same place, and frequently mingled together by previous diggers, as well as by the burrowing animals. There seems to me no case on record up to the present time which establishes the fact that the Cave-men were in the habit of burying their dead so securely as to keep out the hyænas. The fragmentary remains of the human frame left in the refuse-heaps may reasonably be taken to imply that disregard for the bodies of the dead which is so conspicuous among the modern Eskimos.

From *Early Man in Britain*, pp. 229-30.

THOMAS H. HUXLEY

Huxley on Apes and Men

THE question of questions for mankind—the problem which under-
lies all others, and is more deeply interesting than any other—is
the ascertainment of the place which man occupies in nature and
of his relations to the universe of things. Whence our race has
come; what are the limits of our power over nature, and of nature's
power over us; to what goal we are tending; are the problems which
present themselves anew and with undiminished interest to every
man born into the world. Most of us, shrinking from the difficulties
and dangers which beset the seeker after original answers to these
riddles, are contented to ignore them altogether, or to smother the
investigating spirit under the featherbed of respected and respect-
able tradition. But, in every age, one or two restless spirits, blessed
with that constructive genius, which can only build on a secure
foundation, or cursed with the spirit of mere scepticism, are unable
to follow in the well-worn and comfortable track of their forefathers and contemporaries, and unmindful of thorns and stum-
bling-blocks, strike out into paths of their own. The sceptics end in
the infidelity which asserts the problem to be insoluble, or in the
atheism which denies the existence of any orderly progress and gov-
ernance of things: the men of genius propound solutions which
grow into systems of Theology or of Philosophy, or veiled in musical
language which suggests more than it asserts, take the shape of the
Poetry of an epoch.

Each such answer to the great question, invariably asserted by
the followers of its propounder, if not by himself, to be complete
and final, remains in high authority and esteem, it may be for one
century, or it may be for twenty: but, as invariably, Time proves
each reply to have been a mere approximation to the truth—toler-
able chiefly on account of the ignorance of those by whom it was
accepted, and wholly intolerable when tested by the larger knowledge of their successors.

From *Man's Place in Nature*. London: Williams and Norgate Ltd.; 1864, pp. 57-60,
69-70, 105-6, 110-11.

In a well-worn metaphor, a parallel is drawn between the life of man and the metamorphosis of the caterpillar into the butterfly; but the comparison may be more just as well as more novel, if for its former term we take the mental progress of the race. History shows that the human mind, fed by constant accessions of knowledge, periodically grows too large for its theoretic coverings, and bursts them asunder to appear in new habiliments, as the feeding and growing grub, at intervals, casts its too narrow skin and assumes another, itself but temporary. Truly the imago state of Man seems to be terribly distant, but every moult is a step gained, and of such there have been many.

Since the revival of learning, whereby the Western races of Europe were enabled to enter upon that progress towards true knowledge, which was commenced by the philosophers of Greece, but was almost arrested in subsequent long ages of intellectual stagnation, or, at most, gyration, the human larva has been feeding vigorously, and moulting in proportion. A skin of some dimension was cast in the 16th century, and another towards the end of the 18th, while, within the last fifty years, the extraordinary growth of every department of physical science has spread among us mental food of so nutritious and stimulating a character that a new ecdysis seems imminent. But this is a process not unusually accompanied by many throes and some sickness and debility, or, it may be, by graver disturbances; so that every good citizen must feel bound to facilitate the process, and even if he have nothing but a scalpel to work withal, to ease the cracking integument to the best of his ability.

In this duty lies my excuse for the publication of these essays. For it will be admitted that some knowledge of man's position in the animate world is an indispensable preliminary to the proper understanding of his relations to the universe—and this again resolves itself, in the long run, into an inquiry into the nature and the closeness of the ties which connect him with those singular creatures whose history has been sketched in the preceeding pages.

The importance of such an inquiry is indeed intuitively manifest. Brought face to face with these blurred copies of himself, the least thoughtful of men is conscious of a certain shock, due perhaps, not so much to disgust at the aspect of what looks like an insulting caricature, as to the awakening of a sudden and profound mistrust of time honoured theories and strongly-rooted prejudices regarding his own position in nature, and his relations to the under-world of life; while that which remains a dim suspicion for the unthinking, becomes a vast argument, fraught with the deepest consequences, for all who are acquainted with the recent progress of the anatomical and physiological sciences.

I now propose briefly to unfold that argument, and to set forth, in a form intelligible to those who possess no special acquaintance with anatomical science, the chief facts upon which all conclusions respecting the nature and extent of the bonds which connect man with the brute world must be based: I shall then indicate the one immediate conclusion which, in my judgment, is justified by those facts, and I shall finally discuss the bearing of that conclusion upon the hypotheses which have been entertained respecting the Origin of Man.

Let us endeavour for a moment to disconnect our thinking selves from the mask of humanity; let us imagine ourselves scientific Saturnians, if you will, fairly acquainted with such animals as now inhabit the Earth, and employed in discussing the relations they bear to a new and singular "erect and featherless biped," which some enterprising traveller, overcoming the difficulties of space and gravitation, has brought from that distant planet for our inspection, well preserved, may be, in a cask of rum. We should, all at once, agree upon placing him among the mammalian vertebrates; and his lower jaw, his molars, and his brain, would leave no room for doubting the systematic position of the new genus among those mammals, whose young are nourished during gestation by means of a placenta, or what are called the "placental mammals."

Further, the most superficial study would at once convince us that, among the orders of placental mammals, neither the Whales, nor the hoofed creatures, nor the Sloths and Anteaters, nor the carnivorous Cats, Dogs, and Bears, still less the Rodent Rats and Rabbits, or the Insectivorous Moles and Hedgehogs, or the Bats, could claim our *"Homo"* as one of themselves.

There would remain then but one order for comparison, that of the Apes (using that word in its broadest sense), and the question for discussion would narrow itself to this—is Man so different from any of these Apes that he must form an order by himself? Or does he differ less from them than they differ from one another, and hence must take his place in the same order with them?

Being happily free from all real, or imaginary, personal interest in the results of the inquiry thus set afoot, we should proceed to weigh the arguments on one side and on the other, with as much judicial calmness as if the question related to a new Opossum. We should endeavour to ascertain, without seeking either to magnify or diminish them, all the characters by which our new Mammal differed from the Apes; and if we found that these were of less structural value than those which distinguish certain members of the Ape order from others universally admitted to be of the same order, we should undoubtedly place the newly discovered tellurian genus with them.

But if Man be separated by no greater structural barrier from the brutes than they are from one another—then it seems to follow that if any process of physical causation can be discovered by which the genera and families of ordinary animals have been produced, that process of causation is amply sufficient to account for the origin of Man. In other words, if it could be shown that the Marmosets, for example, have arisen by gradual modification of the ordinary Platyrhini, or that both Marmosets and Platyrhini are modified ramifications of a primitive stock—then, there would be no rational ground for doubting that man might have originated, in the one case, by the gradual modification of a man-like ape; or, in the other case, as a ramification of the same primitive stock as those apes.

At the present moment, but one such process of physical causation has any evidence in its favour; or, in other words, there is but one hypothesis regarding the origin of species of animals in general which has any scientific existence—that propounded by Mr. Darwin. For Lamarck, sagacious as many of his views were, mingled them with so much that was crude and even absurd, as to neutralize the benefit which his originality might have effected, had he been a more sober and cautious thinker; and though I have heard of the announcement of a formula touching "the ordained continuous becoming of organic forms," it is obvious that it is the first duty of a hypothesis to be intelligible, and that a qua-quâ-versal proposition of this kind, which may be read backwards, or forwards, or sideways, with exactly the same amount of signification, does not really exist, though it may seem to do so. . . . No one is more strongly convinced than I am of the vastness of the gulf between civilized man and the brutes; or is more certain that whether *from* them or not, he is assuredly not *of* them. No one is less disposed to think lightly of the present dignity, or despairingly of the future hopes, of the only consciously intelligent denizen of this world.

We are indeed told by those who assume authority in these matters that the two sets of opinions are incompatible, and that the belief in the unity of origin of man and brutes involves the brutalization and degradation of the former. But is this really so? Could not a sensible child confute, by obvious arguments, the shallow rhetoricians who would force this conclusion upon us? Is it, indeed, true, that the Poet, or the Philosopher, or the Artist whose genius is the glory of his age, is degraded from his high estate by the undoubted historical probability, not to say certainty, that he is the direct descendant of some naked and bestial savage, whose intelligence was just sufficient to make him a little more cunning than the Fox, and by so much more dangerous than the Tiger? Or is he bound to howl and grovel on all fours because of the wholly unquestionable fact, that he was once an egg, which no ordinary power of discrimination could distinguish from that of a Dog? Or is the philanthropist

or the saint to give up his endeavours to lead a noble life, because
the simplest study of man's nature reveals, at its foundations, all
the selfish passions and fierce appetites of the merest quadruped?
Is mother-love vile because a hen shows it, or fidelity base because
dogs possess it?

The common sense of the mass of mankind will answer these
questions without a moment's hesitation. Healthy humanity, finding itself hard pressed to escape from real sin and degradation,
will leave the brooding over speculative pollution to the cynics and
the "righteous overmuch" who, disagreeing in everything else, unite
in blind insensibility to the nobleness of the visible world, and in inability to appreciate the grandeur of the place Man occupies therein.

Nay more, thoughtful men, once escaped from the blinding influences of traditional prejudice, will find in the lowly stock whence
man has sprung, the best evidence of the splendour of his capa-
cities; and will discern in his long progress through the past, a reasonable ground of faith in his attainment of a nobler Future.

They will remember that in comparing civilized man with the
animal world, one is as the Alpine traveller, who sees the mountains
soaring into the sky and can hardly discern where the deep shadowed crags and roseate peaks end, and where the clouds of heaven
begin. Surely the awe-struck voyager may be excused if, at first,
he refuses to believe the geologist, who tells him that these glorious masses are, after all, the hardened mud of primeval seas, or
the cooled slag of subterranean furnaces—of one substance with the
dullest clay, but raised by inward forces to that place of proud and
seemingly inaccessible glory.

But the geologist is right; and due reflection on his teachings,
instead of diminishing our reverence and our wonder, adds all the
force of intellectual sublimity, to the mere æsthetic intuition of the
uninstructed beholder.

CHARLES LYELL

The Neanderthal Discovery

BEFORE I speak more particularly of the opinions which anatomists have expressed respecting the osteological characters of the human skull from Engis, near Liége, mentioned in the last chapter and described by Dr. Schmerling, it will be desirable to say something of the geological position of another skull, or rather skeleton, which, on account of its peculiar conformation, has excited no small sensation in the last few years. I allude to the skull found in 1857, in a cave situated in that part of the valley of the Düssel, near Düsseldorf, which is called the Neanderthal. The spot is a deep and narrow ravine about seventy English miles north-east of the region of the Liége caverns treated of in the last chapter, and close to the village and railway station of Hochdal between Düsseldorf and Elberfeld. The cave occurs in the precipitous southern or left side of the winding ravine, about sixty feet above the stream, and a hundred feet below the top of the cliff. The accompanying section will give the reader an idea of its position.

When Dr. Fuhlrott of Elberfeld first examined the cave, he found it to be high enough to allow a man to enter. The width was seven or eight feet, and the length or depth fifteen. I visited the spot in 1860, in company with Dr. Fuhlrott, who had the kindness to come expressly from Elberfeld to be my guide, and who brought with him the original fossil skull, and a cast of the same, which he presented to me. In the interval of three years, between 1857 and 1860, the ledge of rock on which the cave opened, and which was originally twenty feet wide, had been almost entirely quarried away, and, at the rate at which the work of dilapidation was proceeding, its complete destruction seemed near at hand.

In the limestone are many fissures, one of which, still partially filled with mud and stones, is continuous from the cave to the upper surface of the country. Through this passage the loam, and possibly the human body to which the bones belonged, may have been

From *Geological Evidences of the Antiquity of Man*, pp. 75-9.

washed into the cave below. The loam, which covered the uneven
bottom of the cave, was sparingly mixed with rounded fragments of
chert, and was very similar in composition to that covering the
general surface of that region.

There was no crust of stalagmite overlying the mud in which the
human skeleton was found, and no bones of other animals in the
mud with the skeleton; but just before our visit in 1860 the tusk of a
bear had been met with in some mud in a lateral embranchment of
the cave, on a level corresponding with that of the human skeleton.
This tusk, shown us by the proprietor of the cave, was two and a
half inches long and quite perfect; but whether it was referable
to a recent or extinct species of bear, I could not determine.

From a printed letter of Dr. Fuhlrott we learn that on removing
the loam, which was five feet thick, from the cave, the human skull
was first noticed near the entrance, and, further in, the other
bones lying in the same horizontal plane. It is supposed that the
skeleton was complete, but the workmen, ignorant of its value,
scattered and lost most of the bones, preserving only the larger ones.

The cranium, which Dr. Fuhlrott showed me, was covered both
on its outer and inner surface, and especially on the latter, with a
profusion of dendritical crystallisations, and some other bones of
the skeleton were ornamented in the same way. These markings, as
Dr. Hermann von Meyer observes, afford no sure criterion of
antiquity, for they have been observed on Roman bones. Nevertheless, they are more common in bones that have been long embedded
in the earth. The skull and bones, moreover, of the Neanderthal
skeleton had lost so much of their animal matter as to adhere
strongly to the tongue, agreeing in this respect with the ordinary
condition of fossil remains of the post-Pliocene period. On the
whole, I think it probable that this fossil may be of about the same
age as those found by Schmerling in the Liége caverns; but, as no
other animal remains were found with it, there is no proof that it
may not be never. Its position lends no countenance whatever to
the supposition of its being more ancient.

When the skull and other parts of the skeleton were first exhibited at a German scientific meeting at Bonn, in 1857, some
doubts were expressed by several naturalists, whether it was truly
human. Professor Schaaffhausen, who, with the other experienced
zoologists, did not share these doubts, observed that the cranium,
which included the frontal bone, both parietals, part of the
squamous, and the upper third of the occipital, was of unusual size
and thickness, the forehead narrow and very low, and the projection
of the supra-orbital ridges enormously great. He also stated that
the absolute and relative length of the thigh bone, humerus, radius,
and ulna, agreed well with the dimensions of a European individual

of like stature at the present day; but that the thickness of the bones was very extraordinary, and the elevation and depression for the attachment of muscles were developed in an unusual degree. Some of the ribs, also, were of a singularly rounded shape and abrupt curvature, which was supposed to indicate great power in the thoracic muscles.

In the same memoir, the Prussian anatomist remarks that the depression of the forehead is not due to any artificial flattening, such as is practised in various modes by barbarous nations in the Old and New World, the skull being quite symmetrical, and showing no indication of counter-pressure at the occiput; whereas, according to Morton, in the Flat-heads of the Columbia, the frontal and parietal bones are always unsymmetrical. On the whole, Professor Schaaffhausen concluded that the individual to whom the Neanderthal skull belonged must have been distinguished by small cerebral development, and uncommon strength of corporeal frame.

When on my return to England I showed the cast of the cranium to Professor Huxley, he remarked at once that it was the most ape-like skull he had ever beheld. Mr. Busk, after giving a translation of Professor Schaaffhausen's memoir in the Natural History Review, added some valuable comments of his own on the characters in which this skull approached that of the gorilla and chimpanzee.

Professor Huxley afterwards studied the cast with the object of assisting me to give illustrations of it in this work, and in doing so discovered what had not previously been observed, that it was quite as abnormal in the shape of its occipital as in that of its frontal or superciliary region.

CHARLES DARWIN

Darwin on Man's Lowly Origin

THE nature of the following work will be best understood by a brief account of how it came to be written. During many years I collected notes on the origin or descent of man, without any intention of publishing on the subject, but rather with the determination not to publish, as I thought that I should thus only add to the prejudices against my views. It seemed to me sufficient to indicate, in the first edition of my "Origin of Species," that by this work "light would be thrown on the origin of man and his history;" and this implies that man must be included with other organic beings in any general conclusion respecting his manner of appearance on this earth. Now the case wears a wholly different aspect. When a naturalist like Carl Vogt ventures to say in his address as President of the National Institution of Geneva (1869), "personne, en Europe au moins, n'ose plus soutenir la création indépendante et de toutes pièces, des espèces," it is manifest that at least a large number of naturalists must admit that species are the modified descendants of other species; and this especially holds good with the younger and rising naturalists. The greater number accept the agency of natural selection; though some urge, whether with justice the future must decide, that I have greatly overrated its importance. Of the older and honoured chiefs in natural science, many unfortunately are still opposed to evolution in every form.

In consequence of the views now adopted by most naturalists, and which will ultimately, as in every other case, be followed by other men, I have been led to put together my notes, so as to see how far the general conclusions arrived at in my former works were applicable to man. This seemed all the more desirable as I had never deliberately applied these views to a species taken singly. When we confine our attention to any one form, we are deprived of the weighty arguments derived from the nature of the affinities which

From *The Descent of Man*. London: John Murray; 1871, pp. 1-3, 32-3, 404-5.

connect together whole groups of organisms—their geographical distribution in past and present times, and their geological succession. The homological structure, embryological development, and rudimentary organs of a species, whether it be man or any other animal, to which our attention may be directed, remain to be considered; but these great classes of facts afford, as it appears to me, ample and conclusive evidence in favour of the principle of gradual evolution. The strong support derived from the other arguments should, however, always be kept before the mind.

The sole object of this work is to consider, firstly, whether man, like every other species, is descended from some pre-existing form; secondly, the manner of his development; and thirdly, the value of the differences between the so-called races of man. As I shall confine myself to these points, it will not be necessary to describe in detail the differences between the several races—an enormous subject which has been fully discussed in many valuable works. The high antiquity of man has recently been demonstrated by the labours of a host of eminent men, beginning with M. Boucher de Perthes; and this is the indispensable basis for understanding his origin. I shall, therefore, take this conclusion for granted, and may refer my readers to the admirable treatises of Sir Charles Lyell, Sir John Lubbock, and others. Nor shall I have occasion to do more than to allude to the amount of difference between man and the anthropomorphous apes; for Prof. Huxley, in the opinion of most competent judges, has conclusively shewn that in every single visible character man differs less from the higher apes than these do from the lower members of the same order of Primates.

Thus we can understand how it has come to pass that man and all other vertebrate animals have been constructed on the same general model, why they pass through the same early stages of development, and why they retain certain rudiments in common. Consequently we ought frankly to admit their community of descent: to take any other view, is to admit that our own structure and that of all the animals around us, is a mere snare laid to entrap our judgment. This conclusion is greatly strengthened, if we look to the members of the whole animal series, and consider the evidence derived from their affinities or classification, their geographical distribution and geological succession. It is only our natural prejudice, and that arrogance which made our forefathers declare that they were descended from demi-gods, which leads us to demur to this conclusion. But the time will before long come when it will be thought wonderful, that naturalists, who were well acquainted with the comparative structure and development of man and other mammals, should have believed that each was the work of a separate act of creation.

The beginnings of religious art are represented by this carving, probably of a Mother Goddess, on a limestone block. Upper Palaeolithic, c. 20,000 B.C. From Laussel, Dordogne, France.

I

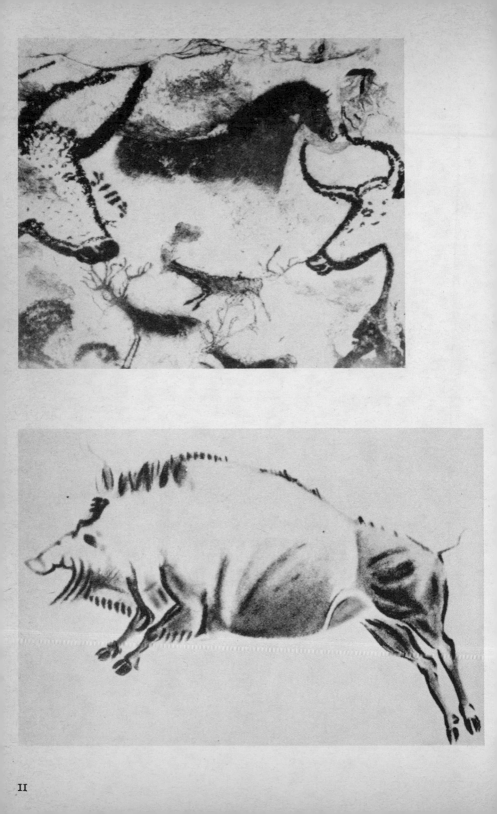

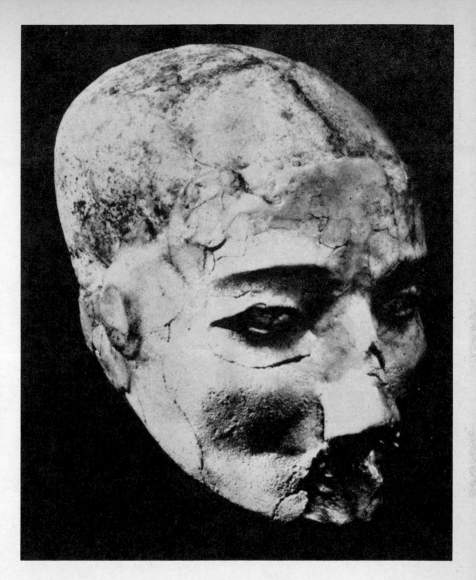

Probably the head of an ancestor, but possibly a war trophy. A skull with features finely modelled in plaster and cowrie shell eyes from the second Neolithic settlement at Jericho, Palestine, c. 6000 B.C.

Upper Left: The Old Stone Age hunters' feeling for game animals is expressed in cave paintings of stags (in red), oxen (in black) and horses (in brown). Upper Palaeolithic, probably c. 15,000 B.C. From Lascaux, Dordogne, France.

Lower Left: A painting (in black with touches of red) of a wild boar in full career, representing the last phase of Old Stone Age art. Late Upper Palaeolithic, c. 12,000 B.C. Altamira, Santander, Spain.

Domestic comfort in a remote village of Late Neolithic times. A stone-built hut with dresser, bed,
shellfish store and central hearth in the village of
Skara Brae, Orkneys, c. 2000 B.C.

A queen's golden drinking cup. From the tomb of
Queen Shub-ad in the Royal Cemetery at Ur, c.
2600 B.C.

A prototype of the Tower of Babel—the Ziggurat of Ur during excavation. The three ramps supported stairways leading up the staged, brick-built tower to a temple of the Moon God on the summit. Built predominantly c. 2100 B.C.

Upper Right: The stiff and staring convention of this statuette of the God Abu is typical of many Sumerian sculptures found in a shrine at Tell Asmar near Baghdad. C. 2500 B.C.

Lower Right: A King of Lagash. One of several black diorite statues of Gudea with a cuneiform Sumerian inscription. C. 2300 B.C.

One of the famous Assyrian ivories from Nimrûd.
A divine figure, dressed in an elaborately embroidered
tunic, is grasping the Tree of Life, c. ninth century B.C.

. . . The main conclusion arrived at in this work, namely that man is descended from some lowly-organised form, will, I regret to think, be highly distasteful to many persons. But there can hardly be a doubt that we are descended from barbarians. The astonishment which I felt on first seeing a party of Fuegians on a wild and broken shore will never be forgotten by me, for the reflection at once rushed into my mind—such were our ancestors. These men were absolutely naked and bedaubed with paint, their long hair was tangled, their mouths frothed with excitement, and their expression was wild, startled, and distrustful. They possessed hardly any arts, and like wild animals lived on what they could catch; they had no government, and were merciless to every one not of their own small tribe. He who has seen a savage in his native land will not feel much shame, if forced to acknowledge that the blood of some more humble creature flows in his veins. For my own part I would as soon be descended from that heroic little monkey, who braved his dreaded enemy in order to save the life of his keeper; or from that old baboon, who, descending from the mountains, carried away in triumph his young comrade from a crowd of astonished dogs—as from a savage who delights to torture his enemies, offers up bloody sacrifices, practises infanticide without remorse, treats his wives like slaves, knows no decency, and is haunted by the grossest superstitions.

Man may be excused for feeling some pride at having risen, though not through his own exertions, to the very summit of the organic scale; and the fact of his having thus risen, instead of having been aboriginally placed there, may give him hopes for a still higher destiny in the distant future. But we are not here concerned with hopes or fears, only with the truth as far as our reason allows us to discover it. I have given the evidence to the best of my ability; and we must acknowledge, as it seems to me, that man with all his noble qualities, with sympathy which feels for the most debased, with benevolence which extends not only to other men but to the humblest living creature, with his god-like intellect which has penetrated into the movements and constitution of the solar system—with all these exalted powers—Man still bears in his bodily frame the indelible stamp of his lowly origin.

REVEREND SAMUEL LYSONS

A Fundamentalist Opponent

LYSONS came of an able Gloucestershire family. Both his father, Daniel, and his uncle, Samuel, were distinguished topographers and antiquaries. He himself was a parson with enlightened social views but an absolute faith in the historical reliability of the Bible. He was prepared to agree that the "six days of creation" might have represented "epochs of thousands of years' duration" in human terms, but he insisted on the descent of all men from Adam and Noah. He accepted the view that Celts and other Europeans were descended from Japhet, and thought that the "special aptitude for colonization of the British" fulfilled Noah's prophecy that God would "enlarge Japhet." He was also inclined to believe the mediaeval legend (p. 14, I) that the British kingdom was founded by the Trojan Brutus.

❧

IT has been said by one of our poets that the most "proper study for mankind is man." Man, under whatever form he is presented to us, historically, morally, physically, or religiously, must claim our attention beyond every other study.

To know our future destiny as we should do, it requires to know something of the past; the two conditions seem to be intimately connected in that book which alone gives us the history of our origin, and unfolds to us our future hopes.

I confess I have no sympathy with those who would trace our origin to the gorilla or the ape, and still less with those who give us the far less intelligent or intelligible origin of the oyster.

The Bible tells us that "of one blood hath God made all nations of men for to dwell on all the face of the earth, and hath determined the times before appointed, and the bounds of their habitation." It also tells us that "all flesh is not the same flesh, but there is one

From *Our British Ancestors*. London: Henry & Parker; 1865, pp. i-ii.

kind of flesh of men, another flesh of beasts, another of fishes, and another of birds."

We have therefore the highest guarantee—if the Bible is to be accepted, and if not accepted, what are we?—that we all proceed from one common stock, and that stock far, far beyond the lower order of animals, however intelligent some of them may appear to be, and that the lines of demarcation are so strong as cannot by any possibility be overpassed. God is the God of order and not of confusion.

JAMES GEIKIE

England Under Ice

JAMES GEIKIE was an able Scottish geologist specializing in problems of the Pleistocene Ice Age. This extract from his chief book, in spite of uncertainties and mistakes (for example the association of reindeer with the Neolithic Age) shows what rapid progress was made in the understanding of Palaeolithic men and their natural environment once the general principle of the antiquity of man had been accepted.

A FASCINATION attaches to the early history of every people. We long to penetrate that mystery which the lapse of ages has drawn like a thick curtain round the cradle of our race. How eagerly do we scan the oldest written records that have any reference to our country and its people; and how assiduously do we try to shape a coherent story out of those vague myths, legends, and traditions which have come down to us from the long-forgotten past. But there are memorials of man in this, as in other countries, which

From *The Great Ice Age*. London: Edward Stanford; 1877, pp. 493-4, 561-5. (1st ed., 1874).

date back to so remote a period that even the oldest traditions have nothing whatever to say about them. The English historian begins his narrative with the Roman invasion, and the archaeologist until recent years could hardly trace the story farther back; but now he can tell us of a time infinitely far beyond the first dim beginnings of history and tradition, when races of savage men and tribes of wild animals, some of which have long been extinct, were denizens of Britain. Hitherto we had been taught to look upon Stonehenge and the so-called Druid-circles as the oldest memorials of man in this country—mysterious monuments belonging to the shadowy past, about whose age and uses only vague conjectures could be offered. If older races than the builders of Stonehenge ever lived in Britain, we knew nothing, and could hardly hope to know anything, about them. The past was apparently separated from us by a gulf which it was vain to think that any ingenuity would succeed in bridging over.

Now all this is changed. The massive monoliths of Stonehenge, however venerable their antiquity, seem but as structures of yesterday; the standing-stones of Avebury, of Callernish, and Stennis, the so-called vitrified forts, the round towers of Ireland, and all those remains of ancient camps, dwellings, and burial-places so abundantly met with throughout the British Islands, are of im- measurably more recent date than certain rude stone implements which our cave-deposits and ancient river-gravels have yielded. Since Stonehenge rose upon Salisbury plains no great change in the physical geography of Britain has taken place. The destruction of ancient forests and the cultivation of the soil have doubtless in some measure altered the aspect of the land, and influenced the character of the climate. Our hills and valleys, however, we are sure have remained the same, and even the coast-line has experi- enced probably little change. Changes undoubtedly there have been, yet none so considerable as to invalidate the truth of the statement, that since the days of the builders of Stonehenge no great geological revolution has taken place in Britain. But the rude stone implements to which I have referred date back to a period when the appearance presented by our country differed greatly from that which obtains now; and for so vast a time did the old tribes who used these rude implements occupy the British area, that the slowly-acting forces of Nature were enabled, during that time, to bring about many geological changes, each of which required long ages for its evolution.

. . . Upwards of 200,000 years ago the earth, as we know from the calculations of astronomers, was so placed in regard to the sun that a series of physical changes was induced, which eventually resulted in conferring upon our hemisphere a most intensely severe climate. All northern Europe and northern America disappeared beneath a thick crust of ice and snow, and the glaciers of such regions as Switzerland assumed gigantic proportions. This great sheet of land-ice levelled up the valleys of Britain, and stretched across our mountains and hills down to low latitudes in England. Being only one connected or confluent series of mighty glaciers, the ice crept ever downwards and outwards from the mountains, following the direction of the principal valleys, and pushing far out to sea, where it terminated at last in deep water, many miles away from what now forms the coast-line of our country. This sea of ice was of such extent that the glaciers of Scandinavia coalesced with those of Scotland, and the north-eastern districts of England, upon what is now the floor of the shallow North Sea, while a mighty stream of ice flowing outwards from the western seaboard obliterated the Hebrides, and sent its icebergs adrift in the deep waters of the Atlantic. In like manner massive glaciers, born in the Welsh and Cumbrian mountains, swept over the low grounds of England, and united with the Scotch and Irish ice upon the bottom of the Irish sea. At the same period the Scandinavian mountains shed vast ice-bergs into the northern ocean, and sent southward a sheet of ice that not only filled up the basin of the Baltic but overflowed Finland, and advanced upon the plains of northern Germany; while from every mountain-region in Europe great glaciers descended, some-times for almost inconceivable distances, into the low countries be-yond.

Ere long this wonderful scene of arctic sterility passed away. Gradually the snow and ice melted and drew back to the mountains, and plants and animals appeared as the climate ameliorated. The mammoth and the woolly-coated rhinoceros roamed in our valleys, the great bear haunted our caves, and pine-trees grew in the south of England; but the seasons were still well marked. In winter-time frost often covered the rivers with a thick coat of ice, which the summer again tore away, when the rivers, swollen with the tribute of such receding glaciers as still lingered in our deeper glens, rushed along the valleys and spread devastation far and wide. By slow degrees, however, the cold of winter abated, while the heat of summer increased. As the warmth of summer waxed, the arctic mammalia gradually disappeared from our valleys, and sought out northern and more congenial homes. Step by step the climate con-tinued to grow milder, and the difference between the seasons to be less distinctly marked, until eventually something like perpetual summer reigned in Britain. Then it was that the hippopotamus wallowed in our rivers, and the elephant crashed through our forests; then, too, the lion, the tiger, and the hyaena became denizens of the English caves.

Such scenes as these continued for a long time; but again the climate began to change. The summers grew less genial the winters more severe. Gradually the southern mammalia disappeared, and were succeeded by arctic animals. Even these, however, as the temperature became too severe, migrated southward, until all life deserted Britain, and snow and ice were left in undisputed possession. Once more the confluent glaciers overflowed the land, and desolation and sterility were everywhere.

During these oscillations of climate there would seem to have been not infrequent mutations of land and sea, but such vicissitudes, although doubtless producing local effects, certainly do not seem to have been the causes of the chief climatic changes. It is much more likely that the mild interglacial periods were induced by eccentricity of the earth's orbit, combined with precession of the equinoxes.

We cannot yet say how often such alternations of cold and warm periods were repeated; nor can we be sure that palaeolithic man lived in Britain during the earlier warm intervals of the glacial epoch. But since his implements are met with at the bottom of the very oldest palaeolithic deposits, and since we know that the animals with which he was certainly contemporaneous did occupy Britain in early interglacial ages, and even in times anterior to the glacial epoch itself, it is in the highest degree likely that man arrived here as early at least as the mammoth and the hippopotamus.

Be this, however, as it may, the evidence appears to be decisive as to the presence of man in Britain during the last mild interglacial period. And this being so, it is startling to recall in imagination those grand geological revolutions of which he must have been a witness.

During the last interglacial period he entered Britain at a time when our country was joined to Europe across the bed of the German Ocean; at a time when the winters were still severe enough to freeze over the rivers in the south of England; at a time when glaciers nestled in our upland-and mountain-valleys, and the arctic mammalia occupied the land. He lived here long enough to witness a complete change of climate—to see the arctic mammalia vanish from England, and the hippopotamus and its congeners take their place. At a later date, and while a mild and genial climate still continued, he beheld the sea slowly gain upon the land, until little by little, step by step, a large portion of our country was submerged —a submergence which, as we know, reached in Wales to the extent of some 1,300 ft. or thereabout.

Once more, however, the land re-emerged, and glaciers yet again thickened in our mountain-valleys, and advanced to coalesce upon the low grounds. Gradually the confluent ice-streams continued to increase, until eventually the British and Scandinavian *mers de glace* became confluent for the last time. All Scotland, save the higher mountain-tops, lay buried, and one and the same overwhelming mantle of ice wrapped the northern part of England, Wales, and Ireland in its folds. The sea between Scotland and the Hebrides was filled up, the Irish Sea was in like manner obliterated, while the united Scandinavian and British *mer de glace* flowed south in our island as far as middle Lincolnshire at least, and perhaps to a yet more southerly latitude in Germany. It is not improbable, indeed, that at this time a considerable part of the low grounds of northern Prussia were covered by the sea, and that ice-rafts and bergs floated over the drowned districts; while we know that in Switzerland the Alpine glaciers crept out upon the low grounds and overwhelmed the forest-lands of Zurich and Constance.

A similar succession of changes characterized North America. After a great continental ice-sheet had retired, wide inland seas of fresh water appeared, and a luxuriant forest-growth overspread the land, which became the resort of a prolific mammalian fauna— mastodons, elephants, buffaloes, peccaries, and other animals. By-and-by, however, the last cold period ensued, and another great ice-sheet streamed over the continent, ploughing up the old forest- land, or burying it under heaps of rubbish and erratic blocks.

During this latest cold period of the glacial epoch, palaeolithic man, for aught that we can say, may have occupied the south of Europe; but it is in the highest degree unlikely that he lived so far north as the unsubmerged and nonglaciated areas of southern England.

Another great change now ensued. The climate again became less arctic, and great floods descending from the melting ice spread devastation far and wide over the low grounds to which the ice itself had not extended. Step by step the glaciers retired, and were followed by the sea, until the area of land was reduced to somewhat less than its present dimensions. Eventually the ice retired to the deep mountain dales and glens, and then Britain for the last time became continental. The treeless land was now invaded by the reindeer, the moose-deer, the arctic fox, the lemming, and the marmot, and neolithic man likewise entered upon the scene: his palaeolithic predecessor had, as far as Britain and northern Europe are concerned, vanished for ever.

Thus the palaeolithic and neolithic ages are separated by a vast lapse of time—by a time sufficient for the submergence and re- elevation of a large part of our country, and the slow growth and decay of a great ice-sheet.

JOHN EVANS

Britain Before the Channel

THERE is yet another means at our command for forming, at all events, an approximate idea of the time that has elapsed since the deposit of the beds containing the remains of the old Quaternary fauna, inasmuch as at the time of their introduction into this country, if not for a lengthened period afterwards, Britain had apparently not become an island, but was still connected by an isthmus of greater or less width with the Continent. To estimate the time, however, that would be required for cutting through this isthmus and widening the Channel to its present dimensions, is a work from which the mind almost recoils. Even the wearing away of that tract of land to the south of the present Hampshire coast, which must almost of necessity have existed at the time when the Bournemouth flint implement-bearing gravels were deposited, taking the present rapid inroad of the sea on the unusually soft cliffs at Hordwell as a guide, would seem to involve a period of not less than 10,000 years; but inasmuch as the cliffs during a considerable portion of the time must have been of chalk instead of sand and clay, and as a chalk cliff 500 feet high, instead of being worn away at the rate of a yard each year, is said only to recede at the rate of an inch in a century, the actual period necessary for the removal of this tract must probably have been many times 10,000 years, and can with certainty be regarded as having been immensely in excess of such a lapse of time.

On the whole, it would seem that for the present, at least, we must judge of the antiquity of these deposits rather from the general effect produced upon our minds by the vastness of the changes which have taken place, both in the external configuration of the country and its extent seaward, since the time of their formation, than by any actual admeasurement of years or of centuries. To realize the full meaning of these changes almost transcends the powers of the imagination. Who, for instance, standing on the edge of the lofty

From *Ancient Stone Implements of Great Britain*. London: Longmans, Green & Co.; 1897, pp. 707-9.

cliff at Bournemouth, and gazing over the wide expanse of waters between the present shore and a line connecting the Needles on the one hand, and the Ballard Down Foreland on the other, can fully comprehend how immensely remote was the epoch, when what is now that vast bay was high and dry land, and a long range of chalk downs, 600 feet above the sea, bounded the horizon on the south? And yet this must have been the sight that met the eyes of those primeval men who frequented the banks of that ancient river which buried their handiworks in gravels that now cap the cliffs, and of the course of which so strange but indubitable a memorial subsists in what has now become the Solent Sea.

Or again, taking our stand at Ealing, or Acton, or Highbury, and looking over a broad valley fully four miles in width, with the river flowing through it at a depth of 100 feet below its former bed, in which, beneath our feet, are relics of human art deposited at the same time as the gravels; which of us can picture to himself the lapse of time represented by the excavation of a valley on such a scale, by a river larger, it may be, in volume than the Thames, but still draining only the same tract of country? But when to this long period we mentally add that during which the old fauna, with the mammoth and rhinoceros, and other to us strange and unaccustomed forms, was becoming extinct, so far as Britain was concerned; and also that other, we know not how lengthened period, when our barbarous predecessors sometimes polished their stone implements, but were still unacquainted with metallic tools; and then beyond this, add the many centuries when bronze was in use for cutting purposes; and after all this, further remember that the ancient and mighty city now extending across the valley does not, with all its historical associations, carry us back to the times even of the bronze-using people, the mind is almost lost in amazement at the vista displayed.

So fully must this be felt, that we are half inclined to sympathize with those who, from sheer inability to carry their vision so far back into the dim past, and from unconsciousness of the cogency of other and distinct evidence as to the remoteness of the origin of the human race, are unwilling to believe in so vast an antiquity for man as must of necessity be conceded by those, who however feebly they may make their thoughts known to others, have fully and fairly weighed the facts which modern discoveries have unrolled before their eyes.

W. BOYD DAWKINS

Reindeer at Windsor

THE discovery of numerous fossil bones, teeth, and antlers in a bed of gravel by Captain Luard, R.E., in digging the foundations for the new cavalry barracks at Windsor, in 1867, affords us the means of forming a striking picture of the valley of the Thames in the late Pleistocene age. On visiting the spot with him, I found that more than one half of the remains belonged to the reindeer, the rest to bisons, horses, wolves, and bears. They had evidently been swept down by the current from some point higher up the stream. In illustration of this accumulation a parallel case may be quoted from the observations of Admiral von Wrangel, in Siberia. "The migrating body of reindeer," he writes, "consists of many thousands, and though they are divided into herds of two or three hundred each, yet the herds keep so near together, as to form only one immense mass, which is sometimes from fifty to a hundred versts, or thirty to sixty miles, in breadth. They always follow the same route, and in crossing the river Anyuj, near Plobishtshe, they choose a place where a dry valley leads down to a stream on one side, and a flat sandy shore facilitates their landing on another. As each separate herd approaches the river, the deer draw more closely together, and the largest and strongest takes the lead. He advances, closely followed by a few of the others, with head erect, and apparently intent on examining the locality. When he has satisfied himself he enters the river, the rest of the herd crowd after him, and in a few minutes the surface is covered with them." Wolves, bears, and foxes hang upon the flanks and rear of these great migratory bodies, and prey upon the stragglers; and invariably many casualties occur at the fords, where the weak or wounded animal is swept away by the current. From these facts we may infer that a Palaeolithic hunter, standing on one of the hills commanding a view of the district above Windsor in the winter time, would have seen vast herds of reindeer crossing the stream, and in the summer herds of horses and bisons availing themselves of the same fords, with

From *Early Man in Britain*, pp. 155-6.

wolves and bears in their train. We shall see, in the next chapter, that reindeer and bisons occupied the same districts of Derbyshire in different seasons of the year; and we may therefore conclude that the same thing happened in the valley of the Thames.

In other fluviatile deposits in the Thames valley the reindeer has been found in considerable abundance—at Kew, for example, in association with the bison, and in London with the lion, Irish elk, bison, urus, horse, woolly rhinoceros, mammoth, straight-tusked elephant, and hippopotamus.

ARTHUR KEITH

The Old Man of Cro-Magnon

SIR ARTHUR KEITH was an eminent anatomist and human palae-ontologist who in style and outlook seems to be a Victorian rather than a twentieth century scientist. He was unlucky in backing a number of bad horses (particularly Piltdown Man, p. 210, I), and as the end of the present extract shows, his more philosophical observations were sometimes unfortunate.

IN tracing the various kinds of men who lived in the Neolithic period, the open country, the river valleys, and the submerged land surfaces served us very well. When, however, we try to follow man beyond the bounds of the Neolithic period—when the Thames was depositing the deepest layers of ballast gravel in her ancient bed—we must seek sequestered nooks where the earth keeps a more orderly register of events than in the turmoil of flooded valleys. The ideal place we seek is a cave, particularly a limestone cave, for the

From *The Antiquity of Man*. London: Williams and Norgate Ltd.; 1915, pp. 46-55. Reprinted by permission of Ernest Benn Ltd.

drip from the roof, laden with lime salts, seals up with a covering of stalagmite any bones which chance to lie on the floor. The floor of such a cave is always having additions made to it. If men make their hearths on it, human debris accumulates. Chips and dust are always falling from the roof; the mud washed in by rain or flood is added to other accumulations. In course of time the floor may grow until it actually reaches the roof, thus obliterating the cave. If no living thing has visited the cave as it became filled up, then the strata of the floor are "sterile"; but if men have used the cave as a habitation or as a passing shelter, or if they chance to die there, then the earth-buried stratum of the floor becomes a page of history. It has taken us nearly a century to understand that caves may contain historical documents of the most precious kind. By a study of cave records, we have come by a knowledge of the races who preceded the men of the Neolithic period—the races of the Palaeolithic period. In 1825, in one of the wooded dales lying behind the picturesque town of Torquay, on the south coast of Devonshire, Mr. MacEnery began to explore that great rambling subterranean series of chambers known as Kent's Cavern. In the dense layer of stalagmite, covering the floor of the cave, he found implements in stone and in bone, shaped by the hand of man, mingled with the bones of the same extinct animals as Dean Buckland had found at Paviland. The priest had the courage to draw a just conclusion from these observations in Kent's Cavern, and to face the opposition of the Dean and of the opinion of his time. Mr. MacEnery was convinced that man had lived in England as a contemporary of the mammoth, the rhinoceros, the cave-bear, and all those animals which we now know were native to Europe before our present climatic conditions dawned with the advent of Neolithic man. Mr. MacEnery did not dare to even publish his records; they were discovered and published by the Torquay Natural History Society many years after his death. It was thus a priest who first broke into the world of Palaeolithic man—at least in England.

How slowly a belief in man's antiquity made headway will be realised if we follow Sir Charles Lyell in his journey abroad in 1833. He, the great geologist, was preparing a third edition of his *Principles*, and, as was his habit, visited every site in Europe where any discovery of note had been made. In 1833 his way lay through Belgium, and he stopped at Liége to see one of the Professors at the University—Dr. Schmerling. The banks of the Meuse, before that river reaches Liége, are flanked by steep limestone cliffs, often 200 feet in height. On their vertical face open many rambling caves. Dr. Schmerling had been caught in the vortex of cave exploration, and was able to place before the English geologist in 1833 the results gained by four years of severe toil in over forty caves. The collection represented those extinct forms of animals which Dean Buckland discovered in the Welsh cave, but Dr. Schmerling had found them in greater abundance and in greater variety. The same evidences of man's presence were found mingled with the fossil remains of animals—worked flint implements, weapons and ornaments in ivory and in bone. In one of the caves— that of Engis—Dr. Schmerling found a human skull, besides other fragments in the same cemented stratum of stalagmite as contained the fossil bones. "The cranium," says Dr. Schmerling, "was met with at a depth of a metre and a half (nearly 5 feet), hidden under an osseous breccia, composed of the remains of small animals, and containing one rhinoceros tusk. . . . The earth which contained this human skull exhibited no trace of disturbance; teeth of rhinoceros, horse, hyena, bear, surrounded it on all sides." Dr. Schmerling had thus advanced our knowledge of man's antiquity a point beyond that reached by the Rev. Mr. MacEnery at Kent's Cavern. Not only had he found proof of man's existence with animals now extinct— animals which had disappeared from the face of Europe before the Neolithic age dawned—but he had actually discovered Palæo-lithic man himself. Sir Charles Lyell was a true scientist, with an open and just mind, but he turned away from Dr. Schmerling's discovery—still sceptical. Thirty years after the date just mentioned (1833), Sir Charles published a work which convinced thinking minds that man's antiquity was infinitely greater than usually believed. It took the scientific world thirty years to assimilate Schmerling's discovery. The discovery of the remains of a human being as the contemporary of extinct animals was more than even the open, well-balanced mind of Sir Charles Lyell could admit in 1833. Schmerling's work, like that of other pioneers, had to wait for a new generation.

We shall examine presently the facts which afterwards convinced Sir Charles Lyell that Dr. Schmerling had made a great discovery. Meantime, let us see what kind of man he discovered— the man who lived when the mammoth and woolly rhinoceros had a home in Belgium. When an exact drawing of the Engis skull is placed within the standard frame, the one we have employed in the case of Neolithic skulls, we see that in shape and size it is merely a variant of the river-bed type. It is longer, higher, and rather narrower; it is very similar to the skull of the Neolithic man found at Sennen, in Cornwall. The skull is that of a man of middle age. The maximum length is 198 mm.; the width, 140 mm., is 70.7 per cent of the length. The height of the vault above the ear-holes is 121 mm.; the calculated brain capacity 1500 c.c.—a little above the modern average. There is not a single feature that marks this skull off from men of the Neolithic or modern times. No doubt, if the face and the jaws had been found we should recognise certain points of difference in them, but, unfortunately, these parts were not recovered. If we believe that the human frame must change during the lapse of a long period, then we shall be inclined to regard the evidence of the Engis cave with scepticism. If, how ever, we regard Dr. Schmerling as a competent and truthful observer—and I think the time has come when belated justice must be done to him—then we must conclude that a human type can be reproduced for many generations and over a very long period of time, and still remain almost unchanged. The man who lived in Belgium with the extinct animals of the Pleistocene period was reproduced in the Neolithic period, and still abounds in modern times. When Professor Boyd Dawkins wrote his classical work on *Cave Hunting,* he was not convinced on the evidence produced by Schmerling that the skull was contemporaneous with the fossil animals. Lately, my friend, Dr. Rutot, has again, in company with Professor Fraipont, examined the Engis skull, and he, too, is inclined to place it in the list of doubtful specimens. It is true, as we shall see presently, that people of the Neolithic period did use caves as sepulchres, but there is no instance of Neolithic man having dug a hole in the hard breccia of a cave floor and buried his dead at a depth of 5 feet: Schmerling has placed it on record that the breccia was intact, and therefore we must admit that the river-bed type of skull was already evolved in the Palæolithic period.

The discovery which cleared away all doubts as to the great antiquity of man—which carried home the conviction that he was contemporary with extinct animals—takes us to the year 1860. The discoverer was Edouard Lartet, then aged fifty-nine. He had, in his early years, forsaken law for geology, and latterly had been caught in the passion for cave exploration. The year 1860 found him visiting the caves of Southern France, particularly those situated in the departments lying among the northern spurs of the Pyrenees. We have to deal with two of these particular departments of France—Haute Garonne and Ariége, drained by rapid-running tributaries of the Garonne. Lartet's excursion took him to the village of Aurignac, in Haute Garonne. Near by the town is a little hill; on the side of the hill a cave had been discovered, buried beneath a mass of debris, which had fallen from the face of a cliff. Apparently in ancient times the cave had opened on the face of the cliff. When the debris which hid the cave was removed, the opening was found to be closed by a great vertical slab of stone. Before Lartet's arrival, the human skeletons seen piled up within the cave had been given a Christian burial by order of the Mayor. We now know, although Lartet was not then aware of the fact, that the pile of skeletons—representing at least seventeen individuals of various

ages—were in reality the remains of Neolithic people. It was the
Neolithic men who set up the slab at the entrance and used the
cave as a sepulchre, a custom of the period. But when Lartet came
to explore the floor of the cave—2 to 3 feet in thickness—he found
it to abound in evidences of human habitation, and to contain the
remains of extinct animals, which were charred, cut, and artificially
broken, showing that man not only lived at the same time as extinct animals, but actually used them as sources of his food supply.
He found remains of the cave-bear, the cave-lion, the cave-hyena,
the mammoth, the woolly rhinoceros, the wild pig, the Irish elk,
the bison; and also remains of animals which live in our time. He
found, further, as will be seen from his drawing, that the strata
of the floor extended out to cover the little terrace in front of the
cave. Under the floor of the terrace he found abundance of charcoal and remains of hearths. Embedded in the debris of the floor
he found implements and ornaments of that form of human culture
which is now known as Aurignacian—the same culture as was exposed at Paviland and at Engis. The flint implements of all three
caves were worked in the same style—in all there were the same
carvings in ivory, the same ornaments, necklaces of shells and
perforated teeth, the same kind of barbed implements in bone,
antlers of reindeer, and in ivory. When we consider that the culture of the people on the South Welsh coast was the same as that
at the northern foot of the Pyrenees, we begin to realise that already in the Pleistocene period—when animals now extinct
abounded in Europe—interchange and intercommunication had
already made Europeans sharers in a common culture. Lartet also
found amongst the undisturbed debris in the floor of the cave,
fragments of human bones—not enough to tell us what kind of
men these ancient Aurignacians were, but sufficient to indicate
their bodily presence. It was the discovery at Aurignac that convinced Sir Charles Lyell that man went beyond the Neolithic
horizon, and with his conversion, the new conception of man's
antiquity made rapid progress.

    Eight years later, in 1868, M. Louis Lartet discovered the actual
men of the Aurignacian culture. The scene of the discovery is not
in the region of the Garonne, but in the watershed of a companion
river, the Dordogne, which, rising in southern central France,
joins the Garonne at Bordeaux. The Vézère is a northern tributary
of the Dordogne. The caves and rock-shelters in the cliffs which
border the Vézère have yielded some of the most important and
most complete records of ancient man. In 1868, when a railway
was being made along the lower part of the valley of the Vézère
to unite the town of Perigueux with the main line along the
Dordogne valley, an old rock-shelter was opened at Cro-Magnon, a

little above the picturesque cliff-set village of Les Éyzies. The strata on the floor of the shelter or cave were marked by hearths and the culture of the Aurignacian period. In the upper strata were found the remains of four skeletons. They were tall people; the men were about 5 feet 11 inches in height—tall, lanky fellows, more like, so far as bodily physique is concerned, the tall Sikhs of the Punjab than any race now living. The proportion of their limbs was somewhat peculiar; their tibiæ or leg bones were relatively long, their humeri or upper arm bones, short. Individuals with similar limb proportions still occur amongst negroid races, but no modern European Race can show the negroid limb proportions of the Cro-Magnon race—men of the Aurignacian period. The skeleton which Dean Buckland had found in the Paviland cave, regarded by him as that of a woman buried in Neolithic times, but which we now know, as proved by Professor Sollas, to be of Aurignacian age, was also a tall, slender man—about 5 feet 10 inches in stature. The skull of the Paviland man is not known, but we do know the form of head which characterised the Cro-Magnon men. Their skulls cannot be classed in the river-bed groups; they are too large and too much flattened on the vault to be assigned to that type. They differ from the Aurignacian man of Engis, who, we have seen, had a skull of the river-bed type. At Cro-Magnon, then, we meet with another race of men. They had massive skulls, large in all dimensions, much too large for the conventional modern frame. The maximum length is 203 mm., half an inch beyond the modern or Neolithic mean; the width, 150 mm., 10 mm. beyond; the height of the vault, 125 mm., also 10 mm. above the modern mean for British men. It will be observed, however, that although the actual dimensions are greater, in the relative proportions of the diameters the Cro-Magnon skulls are not unlike those of the river-bed type. The width is very nearly 74 per cent of the length, just as in skulls of the river-bed type. The brain capacity is much greater—roughly 1660 c.c., being 180 c.c. above the modern average. We have to remember that a certain amount— a small amount—of that is due simply to a big body; a big body needs a bigger brain for its animal administration. We have come across, in those large heads, a puzzling and unexpected fact; we are naturally astonished to find that men who have preceded us so long ago—men of a former geological epoch—should so far outstrip their successors of to-day who regard themselves as "the survival of the fittest," and believe the fittest to be the race with the biggest brains. We cannot quarrel with the facts, but how are we to explain them? The conclusion to be drawn is, not that brain mass, on the average, is to be rejected as an index of brain power, but that there are other virtues or characters which go to ensure success of a human race in the struggle of life—other than brain power. A philosopher may be miserable or die childless, when a brainless savage or an industrious labouring man may be happy and leave a large family.

CARLETON S. COON

Stag Hunters of Behistun

PROFESSOR COON is better known as a physical anthropologist than as an archaeologist, and at the time of his work at Behistun (Bisitun) he had little experience of excavation. On his first visit in 1948 he was led to identify another cave as the one which George Cameron had seen while working on the famous Darius inscriptions (see also p. 382, I), but on returning the next year was able to correct this mistake. The Mousterian tools he found, evidently as usual the handiwork of men of Neanderthal type, consisted predominantly of well-worked triangular points and double-edged knives.

MY second venture into the world of caves was as accidental as the first. In the autumn of 1948 the University Museum of the University of Pennsylvania and the Oriental Institute of the University of Chicago sent a joint expedition to Iraq to resume excavation at the vast, ancient city mound of Nippur, the fabled seat of Enlil, paramount god of the Sumerians. Fifty years earlier the powdered

From *Seven Caves*. New York: Alfred A. Knopf; 1957, pp. 93-94, 99-107, 111-13, 124-5. By permission of Alfred A. Knopf, Inc. and Jonathan Cape Ltd. © 1956 by Carleton S. Coon.

debris of this long-dead metropolis had yielded to the current crop
of Pennsylvania excavators the major part of the world's collection
of Sumerian tablets, over which cuneiform scholars have been
straining their eyes ever since. My job on the expedition, representing Pennsylvania, was to study whatever skeletons might be unearthed.

In the middle of our five weeks' stay there, our expedition house
was visited by the Director of the Oriental Institute, Dr. Thorkild
Jacobsen. Knowing of my interest in fossil men, he advised me to
visit Iran, a country completely unexplored from that point of view.
A little later he was followed by Dr. George Cameron, then of the
same institution, who had just finished making a latex squeeze of
the famous trilingual cuneiform inscription of Behistun, first
copied in 1837 and again in 1843 by Sir Henry Rawlinson. This
inscription, carved shortly before 500 B.C., commemorates the military successes of the Emperor Darius I, in three languages: Old
Persian, Elamitic, and Assyrian. It was carved on a twelve-by-thirty-
foot smooth space on the face of a seventeen-hundred-foot mountain, some two hundred and fifty feet above the level of the road
below, by sculptors who cut away their stone steps as they climbed
down, thus preserving the monument from future vandals. Besides
the trilingual inscription, the sculptors carved bas-reliefs of Darius
himself with henchmen behind him, and of nine captive chiefs or
kings facing him and bound with cords around their necks. Overhead they placed the figure of Darius's god, Ahuramazda.

This monument was more than an imperial signboard or even the
product of aerial daring and skill. It was a cuneiform equivalent
to the Rosetta stone, giving Rawlinson and others the means to
break the riddle of cuneiform writing, and thus to unlock the
treasure house of Sumerian, Babylonian, Assyrian, and early
Persian literature. While Sir Henry had managed to reach the
inscription itself by ropes from above, he had lacked the equipment
provided by later scientific inventions to make an exact copy, and
in 1948 certain errors and uncertainties still remained, which Dr.
Cameron wished to clear up. So he made an actual facsimile impression of the inscription in latex, working from the planks of a
painter's ladder perilously dangling and swinging in the breeze,
about forty times his own height above the bleak and stony ground.
As he recounted this experience to us in the expedition house of
Nippur, Dr. Cameron still seemed to tremble.

Neither the inscription itself, nor the impressive conquests of
the mighty Darius I which it recorded, nor George's daring aerial
feat impressed me so much as his revelation that while teetering
on his giddy ladder he had seen, at ground level below the inscription, a small cave, its floor apparently undisturbed by either the

inscription-carvers or the myriads of travellers who had passed that way. I was eager to see that cave. . . .

Six months later, on June 30, 1949, we returned to Bisitun [Behistun]—this time from the east, for we had left the jeep on blocks at the National Museum in Tehran [Teheran]. Our party now consisted of six persons: Lisa and myself; my son Charles, who was now eighteen; David Elder, aged fifteen, the son of the Reverend John Elder, of the Presbyterian Mission in Tehran; Mr. Habibollah Samadie; and Asadullah, the Lion of God. David was the interpreter. He had been born in Iran and spoke Persian as well as English; his only problem was how to translate my blunt Anglo-Saxon monosyllables into polite Persian. Sometimes he just said nothing, which was probably the best course of all.

Mr. Samadie was an official of the Iranian Government sent with us as official representative of the Department of Antiquities. We spoke French together, and here again our vocabularies did not exactly match, for his French was exceedingly polite while mine had been learned in Morocco talking principally with Foreign Legion and Arab soldiers. I am afraid that I taught him a few words that he might not ordinarily need. Asadullah was an exceptionally handsome young Persian from Hamadan, the son of the cook of one of the missionaries. A convert to Christianity, he had attended the High School at Hamadan and was trying to earn money to put himself through the University of Tehran. He had joined the expedition as cook, temporarily following his father's profession.

During my first few days with Mr. Samadie he seemed extraordinarily incompetent at pronouncing my name. Instead of saying Coon in the regular way, he would stammer a little and come out with Cowan, or Co-own, or even call me Mr. Carleton, using my first name. As these attempts seemed to embarrass him, I asked the missionaries at Hamadan what was the trouble, and before long learned that in Persian *Coon* means *rectum,* a word that Mr. Samadie could not bring himself to pronounce. I also learned that the name *Payne* means *excrement.* Once when Mr. Coon in Hamadan telephoned Mr. Payne, the executive officer of the Mission in Tehran, all circuits were connected at once. The operators all along the line were prostrated with laughter, while Mr. Payne and I conversed on a clear line.

By the time we got to Bisitun, however, this misunderstanding between Mr. Samadie and me had been overcome and I had resigned myself to the need of disguising my name, a subterfuge that, in time to come, alternately gave us trouble with permits and let us through security barriers on the strength of sheer embarrassment. I can never make fun of a person's name, nor can I fail to understand the Persian requirement of a little clean deception in such matters to grease the social machine.

The Department of Antiquities in Iran, as in most Middle Eastern countries, is a branch of the Ministry of Education. Therefore Sammy (as we came to call Mr. Samadie) had brought with him a letter from Tehran to the head of the Department of Education at Kermanshah, and he in turn assigned us the schoolhouse to live in. Because the schoolchildren were having summer vacation, it was comparatively empty. I say comparatively because one front room was inhabited by the schoolmaster, a tall, thin, sensitive man, who was delighted to have Sammy and Asadullah to talk with; the other front room was occupied by the school janitor, a very old man with a magnificent hawk-like nose and long white moustache, and by his wife, who had suffered a psychic trauma when someone told her, as a joke, that her husband had taken a second wife. Since that time she had been unable to speak, and she communicated by gestures alone. The woman whom the joker had named in this tragic jest inhabited the corridor. A tall, thin, stately, and once beautiful Kurdish widow named Khavar, she looked about fifty. She wore a russet-coloured nightgown-like dress, full of holes, through one of which the attenuated tip of a pendulous breast occasionally protruded. She was the janitor's assistant. When not otherwise occupied, she spent her time spinning wool.

Asadullah set up the kitchen in one classroom, Lisa and I took over a second with our camp cots, and Charles and David requisitioned a third, while Sammy moved into a front room with his new friend, the schoolmaster. As soon as we had established ourselves I set out eagerly to revisit the cave. Outside the schoolhouse we passed a stand where a young man sold cucumbers and played his short-wave radio; he was listening to the Voice of America as we passed, and saluted us smartly. Next came the house where we had eaten shish kebabs with the Watsons in the winter; this had now moved out of doors, and guests lounged comfortably on settees perched over a babbling brook, part of the irrigation system of the village. Beyond this bubbled the famous spring, from which the maidens of Bisitun were filling their shapely jars, mushroom-like copper vessels, and ugly oil tins. Some of them had started to walk home with these containers perched on their heads, and as I looked at the top of an oil tin, over it I saw an opening in the rock.

Running up to it, I found myself in a second cave. This must be Cameron's grotto, for it could easily be seen from the face of the inscription, while the one that John Watson had showed me lay around a corner and much higher up. This, the Cameron cave, had been filled with snow last winter. I placed myself in the role of a Palæolithic hunter and followed the well-known law of least effort in my thinking about the cave. Why in the world should I run up and down that seven-hundred-foot slope of limestone blocks every time I wanted a drink of water, and make my wife or wives and children do the same, when I could live on the ground floor and get my drink by a minimum of exertion? How would I like to drag the carcass of a horse, stag, or other animal up that slope? No, I would not like any of these things. Unless the terrain were infested with hideous enemies from whose presence I had to conceal myself, I would live in the lower cave, and if such enemies did exist, the upper cave, exposed as it was and permitting movement only downward, was strategically untenable.

POSSIBLE STONE AGE MIGRATION ROUTES IN THE MIDDLE EAST. DURING UPPER PALAEOLITHIC AND MESOLITHIC TIMES, SIMILAR BLADE TOOLS WERE MADE ON BOTH SIDES OF THE EAST-WEST MOUNTAIN BARRIER IN WESTERN ASIA. SOME OF THE IMPLEMENTS FOUND TO THE SOUTH, AT MOUNT CARMEL, KSAR AQUIL, THE HEIFER'S OUTWASH, HAZER MERD, ZARZI, AND SHANIDAR, MATCH OTHERS FROM THE NORTH, EXCAVATED AT BELT, HOTU, AND KARA KAMAR. BLADE-USING HUNTERS MAY HAVE CROSSED THE HIGHLANDS OVER A ROUTE STILL IN USE: UP THE GREAT ZAB AND DOWN THE VALLEY OF THE SEFID RUD TO THE CASPIAN SHORE. OR THEY MAY HAVE WALKED AROUND TURKEY AND OVER THE LOW TRANSCASPIAN TROUGH.

People have often asked me how I select caves for excavation. The answer is very simple, I merely imagine myself a primitive man, which is not very difficult, and look for caves that are better than others in respect to size, shape, exposure, protection from the elements, view of pastures on which game could have grazed, and source of water. In many parts of the world such first-class caves are still occupied by human beings, who have to be ejected by some legal means before excavation can begin. In all respects save one the lower cave of Bisitun filled the bill. That respect was that it was small, being no more than twenty feet long or wide, and small caves are usually shallow. However, not knowing so much about caves then as I do now, I took a chance and decided to dig at once.

The next morning, July 1, I hired four men and began laying out Trench A, an area eight metres by two metres (twenty-four feet by six feet), on the right side of the floor, which ran into a crevice to the rear. This crevice was, of course, the solution cavity through which a stream of water, comparable to the existing springs, had once flowed. After the water had been diverted elsewhere, people had (as I supposed) begun to live in the crevice, and its floor had risen until its roof was now only two feet high. That people had also lived out front in the sunshine was evident from the presence of a fan of earth and stones, known to geologists as a *talus slope*, strewn with sherds and flints. The foot of the talus reached the road right opposite the bus stop on the Baghdad-Tehran route. As work went on, the bus passengers soon discovered our presence and we had a visitor problem. Crowding one another on the lip of the dig, they kicked dirt and small stones on to the workmen below, and before the excavation was over I had to take drastic steps to keep them at a safe distance from the edge.

The trouble with digging caves in different countries or parts of a country is that new men must be trained each time, and as soon as a good crew has been got together the job is finished. The city-mound archæologists in Egypt and Iraq employ workmen whose ancestors have been archæological excavators for as many as four generations, and who move about from site to site with different expeditions. Compared with the surfaces of city sites, the area of a cave floor is small and the amount of material per square metre of earth great. The stratification of a cave is laid down on a smaller scale, the light is often poor, and quarters are crowded. Despite ladders, pulleys, and other devices, the problem of soil-removal may become a bottleneck when disposal fails to keep pace with the digging. Under these conditions one needs good men of even temper who will not quarrel, for a blow with a pick or even a harsh word suddenly spoken may cause a man to fall into a deep trench, and it is easy for an angry man to kick stones of various sizes down on to a rival's head. The morale of a submarine crew is needed in a cave.

How to find such men in a particularly poverty-stricken village without knowing more than a few words of Persian—actually, the men of Bisitun spoke Kurdish, and Persian was only a second language to them—was a problem. One of the men, Ali Akbar, had worked for George Cameron. While ladderflitting was no training for digging, it did give him an excuse to make himself appear superior to his fellows. He was a trouble-maker whom I eventually had to fire. Then there was a father-and-son combination: Qasem, a one-eyed man from another village, and his son Abbas, who was clearly too young to do strenuous work. I kept him on, however, when Qasem told me that the boy's stepmother was cruel and he did not dare leave the two in the house together. The presence of this boy created a disturbance because the other men complained that he was being paid disproportionately on half-wages. The fourth worker was a boy of about seventeen named Abdul Ali, a bright-eyed lad with an aquiline nose and a marvellous memory for poetry. Although illiterate, he used to entertain us by reciting Persian classics, dozens of lines at a time, including Hafiz and Firdusi. It was his oft-stated ambition to marry Rita Hayworth and tour Europe with her in a jeep.

On the first day the school janitor squatted at the edge of the trench joining in the conversation. He told us a tale of a dervish who had kidnapped a woman from her husband and brought her to this very cave, where he abused her constantly until one night, when he was exhausted, she asked his permission to go outside to relieve herself. Being too tired to go with her, he tied a long string to her wrist and held the end. Once outside she tied her end of the cord to a bush and escaped to rejoin her husband, who ran back to the cave and engaged in mortal combat with the dervish. I never heard the outcome of this tale, either because it was considered too immoral for my ears or simply because the narrative was interrupted by the arrival of Asadullah, who announced that the kitchen roof had fallen in on his Primus stove. I halted the work, arranged for the repairs with an itinerant Assyrian carpenter whom I found on the road, and was back again in a few minutes. Too late for the punch line.

Stimulated by his success as a teller of tales, the janitor volunteered to serve as night watchman at the cave, and I hired him. He failed, however, to keep this job for more than a single night, owing to his many-faceted ability as entrepreneur. At noon the next day Asadullah suggested that we eat lunch in the cool, shady garden in back of the schoolhouse, where a small tile-lined pool of running water produced a pleasant atmosphere. As we rounded the bushes into this shady nook we surprised three couples busily engaged in an active phase of love-making. They had brought a complete *Rubá'iyát* equipment of rugs, blankets, food, and drink out from Kermanshah in a taxi, paying the old janitor for the use of the premises. As the highest ranking representative of the

Ministry of Education present, Mr. Samadie dispersed this fun-loving group and reprimanded the janitor sharply. His feelings ruffled, the old man resigned his post as night watchman immediately and retired in sullen hostility to the passive company of his speechless spouse.

I took on in his place a short, thick-set man who smoked opium, and added to the digging staff two muscular Kurdish brothers, one of whom looked Irish and the other like a Scots Guard, as well as a fat man with a round face and bulging eyes, whom we called Banjo Eyes. These four were excellent workmen. This second day did not, however, end without further incident. When I got back to the schoolhouse to relax by the pool in the late afternoon sun, a blood-red jeep stopped at the front door and two large, sinister-looking men dressed in good European clothes walked through the corridor, stepping over the pallet of Khavar, the janitor's assistant, and confronted me. They were licensed opium-distributors, whose business it was to provide addicts with their rations. They had come to Bisitun to sell opium, and, according to them, the Kermanshah representative of the Ministry of Education had told them that they could live in the schoolhouse: we must get out, or share our quarters with them. Mr. Samadie valiantly defied them, but to no avail. I therefore stood up and stretched myself to an inch or two beyond my full height, so that I looked down on the tops of their heads. Clenching and unclenching my fists, I said, with an attempt at dignified belligerence: "If you do not leave quietly, I will throw you out."

As no one was willing to translate this, I repeated it in as many languages as I could think of, with appropriate gestures. Somehow or other they understood, and left. Soon we heard the jeep engine start and the tyres grip the road bed. The two men drove about fifty yards down the road to the teahouse, in which they took up residence, and from which they later cast evil glances at me as I passed to and from my work at the cave. As if the day had not been full enough, as soon as dark had fallen a busload of Kurdish Jews stopped in front of the schoolhouse to disgorge its occupants, male and female, dressed in Western garb, who sang loudly to the music of guitars and accordions as they danced wildly in rings, holding hands, in the middle of the road, in the glow of the head-lights. I fell asleep before they had finished.

Despite the interruptions of the first two days, I was still able to keep the work moving at the cave, and I was keenly interested in what we found in it. I was apprehensive lest we should find it filled with the angular rubble produced by stonecutters' picks, for there had been quarrying here as well as inscription-carving. At Tangier, Hugh Hencken had excavated a small cave down to the

floor only to find it completely filled with this debris. I had no
wish to repeat his experience. Scraps of this kind there were in
the top twenty centimetres, along with old bricks, a G.I. trouser
button, and pieces of a brown bottle in the base of which was
stamped: "NOT TO BE REFILLED." In the second level no more bricks,
bottles, or buttons appeared, their place being taken by a few sherds
of black-burnished pottery, a tiny flint core used in post-glacial
times for the production of miniature implements called microliths,
several scraps of ordinary flint, and some bones of sheep or goat. I
was happy to see no more stonecutters' chips. This meant that at
the time of Darius I, about 500 B.C., the surface of the cave stood
at only twenty centimetres below its present height. What lay under
it had to be older than 500 B.C.

By the end of the second day, we had cleared out sixty centimetres of this upper, or black layer. Its contents included some
coarse pottery of the kind made from the time of Darius to the
present for carrying water or storing liquids; two sherds of
burnished ware with red stripes, which I later learned was Assyrian
(a few centuries older than the Darius period); and a few dozen
worked flints. The flints were of two kinds: microliths matching
the tiny core, which could have been post-glacial; and flakes of the
kind made by Neanderthal man in Europe and similar to the industry of Red No. 2 in Tangier.

All of this material had been disturbed at one time or another
between the end of the glacial age and the arrival of the inscription-carvers, as well as by an occasional overnight guest symbolized
by the story of the amorous dervish. The presence of the flake
implements, which could have been left behind when an older
floor had been eroded, cheered me greatly. Here was the handiwork
of Neanderthal man, comparable to the implements found by
Dorothy Garrod in 1928 one hundred and twenty miles to the
north-west in the same mountain range, in the cave of Iraqi
Kurdistan known as Hazer Merd. As far as I knew then, Bisitun
was the eastern-most stratified site of this kind yet found. Russian
reports on the cave of Teshik Tash in Soviet Uzbekistan, which
contained the skeleton of a Neanderthal child, were not published
until 1949. When we were at Bisitun I had not seen it.

It was also interesting to see that no Upper Palæolithic blade
tools were to be found in the level over the rich deposit of flakes.
Reputable archæologists, at a loss to find the cradle of European
Upper Palæolithic culture, had postulated that it might lie in the
archæological void of Iran. Bisitun, the first Ice Age cave dug in
that country, failed to confirm these hopes.

    . . . I began work . . . and had the pleasure of excavating some
beautiful flints from the reddish earth in which we were digging.

Flint is technically an inaccurate word to describe the material from which these implements had been flaked. Mineralogists prefer *chert* as a general term, but some of the Bisitun pieces were not exactly that. They were chalcedony, of many colours: red, white, green, blue, and in some cases milky and translucent. One piece that we found was chalcedony on one side and chert on the other, with a transitional zone between. So handsome were these pieces that they were almost jewellery. The thrill of discovering something of high æsthetic quality, not as individuals but as a small group of initiated cave-diggers, gave the workmen as well as me a deep feeling for these pieces. In the face of this feeling, snake-bites, fallen roofs, and quarrels over who kept the fast and who did not were soon forgotten.

Sometimes One-Eyed Qasem was in the pit. As he handed each piece up to me he cleaned the sleek dirt off its shiny side, his single orb also sparkling. At other times he was relieved by Ali Shah, the Irish-looking one of the two brothers, who placed the flints, like a clutch of peacock eggs, on his cloth cap to hand them up to me, his big teeth bared in a grin. When his brother, the one who looked like a Scots Guardsman, followed him below, he too used his cap, and finally One-Eyed Qasem did likewise. These caps became symbols of their new profession of flint-finding, and at the end of the dig I bought them all new headpieces so that they could preserve their flint-cushion caps as family treasures to show their posterity.

As we dug downward, the sides of the cave expanded until I came to believe that we were uncovering the opening of a lower cave, as in the jinn's office of Tangier. In that case the amount of earth to be moved might be increased immeasurably. As I have since found, this is Illusion Number One in cave-digging: every concavity in the rock wall is a potential secret cavity. Most of them flatten themselves out, as this one did.

As far as stratification was concerned, two possibilities faced us: either the deposit in the Bisitun cave was all of one piece, or we would be obliged to deal with several cultural layers possibly culminating in hand axes. I gave the men long lectures on the subject of changes of soil, but we found none of a dramatic nature. Gradually the coarse red turned into a sleek brown, as it had in the High Cave, and in the brown the implements were commoner than before. In fact, they were stuffed like plums in a pudding, and the men ceased all work with the pick and excavated with trowels, pack-saddle needles, and their fingers. What they were now finding was a series of caches where someone had tucked away whole tool-kits of perfect implements. Not a piece was broken.

Along with the flints we removed thousands of splinters of bone

which rang like cymbals when struck with the blade of a knife.
Very few of these bones were articulating ends, and teeth and horn
cores were also rare. Most of them were plain splinters shattered
by some hungry people to extract the marrow. About two-thirds of
the ungulate bones were those of the red deer, or stag, the Asiatic
equivalent of our wapiti or elk. About one-third were those of
horses. It would seem, therefore, that before axe-wielding people
had cut down the forests in this neighbourhood the hunters of
Bisitun had their choice of two hunting-grounds: the forest behind
them, teeming with stag, or the plain in front, grazed by herds of
horses. From the standpoint of protein intake, their standard of
living must have been as high as that of the average American, and
well above that of the modern occupant of the village of Bisitun.
In a nutritional sense, therefore, one might say that the civilization of Bisitun has deteriorated since the end of the Ice Age.

I think that the men in the cave felt this, for they were villagers
by force of circumstance rather than by heredity or inclination.
As they saw all these bones come out they could see what they
were, for every Kurd is a zoologist in this respect, and they realized
how much better off had been their predecessors, who, as far as
they were aware, were also their ancestors. Some readers may
doubt that these illiterate workmen understood what they were
excavating, and may think that their work with me was as vacant
of intellectual stimulus as sewer-digging. I am sure, however, that
these cave-diggers were just as receptive of new ideas as the rest
of us, and that I succeeded, with little effort, in communicating
to them the feeling, if not the exact knowledge, of what we were
doing.

We continued digging until Sunday, July 17, when at a depth
of 6.5 metres (about 22.5 feet) Qasem finally struck bottom. For
the last two days he had been excavating with a spoon, as the
crevice had narrowed itself down to a slit. The stratigraphy of
Bisitun Cave held no complications. The soil changes were gradual,
and the flints were more or less the same all the way down. What
changes could be found from metre to metre could most readily
be explained on the basis of a gradual evolution, over a continuous
time span, of tool-making in the hands of a single and skilful
people who perfected an art that they had brought to Bisitun without further invention. Later I measured the butts of the spear
points and found that the hunters had recognized an optimum
thickness for hafting. If the butt was too thin the point would
break easily, and if too thick it would make a clumsy joint, im-
peding penetration into the animal's body. Furthermore, from strip
to strip I found a constant ratio between the number of single-
edged and double-edged knives. These tools must have had separate

uses, and the hunters were methodical people who knew what they needed and made it. They were no fools.

Although we cannot be sure, exactly, who these hunters were, we did find two small pieces of human material which give us a clue. One was an upper median incisor tooth, the other a section of the ulna, the longer of the two bones in the forearm. Both were characteristically Neanderthaloid. These hardy people were, therefore, men of a different race from our own, one which can no longer be seen in unaltered form anywhere in the world.

. . . they existed at some part of the last glacial sequence, but more than that it is impossible to say. There was not a trace of fire in the cave, but we did not excavate far enough forward to be sure that no hearths had existed. No Carbon-14 dating was possible. Judging entirely from the excellence of their craftsmanship, which improved as one went upward level by level, the hunters of Bisitun were able to perfect their tool-making skill gradually without outside interruption and without the stimulus of new ideas produced by meeting people of other races and cultural backgrounds. The achievement of perfection takes time. As the blade-users of Europe were already making tools more varied and advanced than these in a technical sense during the first cool interval of the last glaciation, this could not be their place of origin. Even if the entire Bisitun sequence were squeezed into the time span of the first ice advance, still the virtual absence of burins and the low proportion of blades to flakes would put this region out of the running. What we needed was a cave with blades and burins in the time of the first advance of the fourth ice sheet. Bisitun appeared to have been off the main line of history.

PAOLO GRAZIOSI

Cave Art:
Altamira Discovered

THE circumstances that surrounded the finding of the Altamira paintings have been related in many treatises and textbooks on prehistory; nevertheless we shall repeat them briefly here, for they concern an important event in the history of great discoveries, whose purely historical connotations should not be overlooked.

About ten years prior to the discovery a sportsman, while searching the thickets on the gentle slopes on which Santillana del Mar is built, noticed that his dog, who was pursuing a fox, had disappeared among the bushes, and that the sound of its barking seemed to be coming from a great way away. He immediately realized that the animal had crawled into a hole in the earth, and searched the scrub until he found a narrow opening. That was how the Altamira cave was discovered. It is a very large cave, burrowing for hundreds of metres into the bowels of the hill. Seventy years later a dog once more touched off a discovery of the same kind—equally sensational: the Lascaux cave in France.

Nothing of particular interest was found at the time in the Altamira cave, and it was forgotten until six years later when Marcelino de Sautuola, who used to spend the summer months on his property near Altamira, was told by a labourer of the discovery of the cave; he decided to excavate the deposits that had accumulated in several parts of it, as he was interested in prehistory.

His research continued intermittently for four years, and finally one day in the summer of 1879, while rummaging in the blackish earth of a large trench the sensational discovery was made. On that day, as on many others, de Sautuola had taken his little daughter Maria with him; suddenly the child, who had wandered off into the cave to where light filtered in, raised her eyes to the ceiling and exclaimed: "Papá, mira toros pintados!" Her father

From *Palaeolithic Art*. London: Faber and Faber Ltd.; 1960, pp. 16-17. Reprinted by permission of Faber and Faber Ltd. and McGraw Hill Book Company, Inc.

rushed in, shone his lamp to where the child was pointing and in the uncertain glimmer saw the outline of a great bison, vigorously painted on the uneven rock surface; then he saw another, and yet another, all painted in vivid colour, fresh and clear as though they had been finished that very day.

After initial doubts de Sautuola recognized that the painted figures represented animals that had long been extinct in those regions, but had lived there in the remote ages which were the object of his studies and research in the same cave; they also showed analogies in style with the small sculptures fashioned out of reindeer antler and engravings on fragments of bone or stone that the Palaeolithic caves of France were yielding in increasing numbers. Furthermore, who could have executed those great paintings, requiring such hard work as well as exceptional skill and artistry, when the cave, until a few years before, was inaccessible to man and completely unknown to the local population? De Sautuola's conviction that the Altamira paintings were the work of Palaeolithic troglodytes was quite unshakable, and Villanova, another Spanish scholar, to whom Don Marcelino appealed for advice and collaboration, was equally certain. In 1880 de Sautuola published a monograph describing the discovery of the paintings and establishing their origin and age.

GEOFFREY BIBBY

Lascaux Discovered

The afternoon of Friday, September 12, (1940) was warm and sunny, and on such a day even the recent defeat of France and the occupation of half their country could not weigh heavily on the spirits of four fifteen-year-old boys who, that afternoon, were out combing the woods of Lascaux on the estate of the Countess de La Rochefoucauld not far from Montignac in the Dordogne. Their terrier, Robot, was even more infected with high spirits and dashed

From *The Testimony of the Spade*, pp. 88-92.

hither and yon through the scrub oak, investigating every sound and scent. Suddenly it disappeared into a cranny among a tumbled mass of stones, and did not return.

The situation was exactly the same as at Altamira seventy-two years before. But seventy-two years can make a difference, even in the outlook of teen-age boys. Montignac lies only fourteen miles from Les Éyzies, and the boys were familiar with the possibilities latent in undiscovered caves. Their former schoolmaster, Léon Laval, was himself an enthusiastic archaeologist and had frequently impressed upon his pupils that they should be on the lookout for cave entrances in their wanderings over the limestone hills. It was for this reason that their equipment on this occasion included an electric torch.

The acknowledged leader of the four boys and the owner of Robot, Ravidat, determined to follow the dog, undeterred by the hollow sound of dislodged stones rolling and falling a considerable distance. He subsequently wrote an account of the afternoon's events for his former schoolmaster, the schoolboy phraseology of which gives a vivid account of the thrill of discovery.

I succeeded in penetrating five or six metres, vertically, head first. . . . At that point I lit my torch and looked around; but I had scarcely taken a step when I lost my balance and rolled to the bottom. I picked myself up, bruised and battered, and relit the torch, which I had had the presence of mind to keep my grip on.

Seeing that the descent was not too dangerous I called my three pals to come down, advising them to take great care.

Once reunited we started exploring the cavern, looking to right and to left. We made slow progress as the torch was not working very well. In this way we crossed a large hall and, meeting no obstacle on our way, reached a passage, narrow but quite high. It was there that, lifting the torch high, we saw by its trembling light many traces of different colours.

Intrigued by these designs we began to inspect the walls carefully and to our great surprise discovered there many figures of animals of a respectable size. It was then that the notion struck us that we had discovered a cave with prehistoric paintings. Encouraged by this success we went through the whole cave, making discovery after discovery.

Our excitement was indescribable. A band of savages dancing a war dance could not have expressed themselves more vividly. Thereupon we made a solemn promise not to tell anyone of our discovery for the moment, and to return on the next day with more powerful torches.

The next day, laden with equipment, the four boys left Montignac at ten-minute intervals, so as not to excite suspicion, and again penetrated to the cave.

The wonders that met their eyes under the powerful light of four torches beggar description. Along the snow-white limestone walls animal succeeded animal as far as the eye could reach. The blacks and reds and yellows of the paintings stood out as though they had been completed the day before. Horses, stags, bison, wild cattle were portrayed in endless series. Across the domed ceiling sprawled four colossal bulls in jet black, three times life size, their curved horns almost meeting at the highest point of the dome. To one side of the main cavern a succession of stags' heads clearly portrayed a herd swimming over a lake; on the other side a file of shaggy ponies cantered along the wall. Two wild goats were on the point of meeting in head-on collision. One of the largest beasts portrayed on the cavern wall defied identification. It was a large ruminant with a humped neck, with large black spots on its white body, and with two extremely long straight forward-pointing horns springing from its forehead.

From the main cavern two galleries ran off, their walls and ceilings similarly covered with scores of painted animals. At a bend in one of the galleries the boys found the first action picture in all the Palaeolithic, a drawing of a man falling beneath the charge of a wounded bison. Beside this scene was an outline portrait of a two-horned rhinoceros.

Confident now that the newly discovered cave was not merely a true prehistoric site but one that surpassed in richness every other site in the Périgord, the four boys returned to their homes, still determined to preserve their secret from the damage that might be caused by unregulated hordes of sensation-hunters. The next day being Sunday, they took no action, but on Monday morning Marsal, another of the four, called on M. Laval and told him of the discovery. The middle-aged schoolmaster was accustomed to youthful exaggeration and not disposed to embark on a hazardous and exhausting excursion for what might well, as he says, have been nothing more than some curiously shaped natural stone formations. He proposed that another of his ex-pupils, an art student, should accompany the youths and make some drawings of the figures.

These drawings left no doubt in Léon Laval's mind. Here was something of the first importance. He set off at once for the cave. On arrival he had some qualms at the prospect of crawling into the entrance hole, which was scarcely more than two feet wide. But, he tells us, shamed by a farmer's wife who had followed them up and who expressed the firm intention of "going down to have a look," he wriggled in and slid down among the stalagtites. A glance was sufficient. Here was a discovery that could not, should not, be investigated by an amateur, however experienced. Instructing the boys to establish a twenty-four-hour guard at the entrance and to let no one descend, Laval hurried back to Montignac and sent a telegram to the Abbé Breuil.

ABBÉ HENRI BREUIL

Discovery of the Caves of Les Trois Frères and Le Tuc d'Audoubert

FEW discoveries have more of the flavour of romantic fiction than these. I only wish the Comte H. Begouen could tell the story himself.

The Comte was a friend of the prehistorian Emile Cartailhac, and was himself of wide intellectual interests, having given very many years of his life to travel and to political and historical writing. He had given up his affairs in Toulouse and retired to his small estate of Montesquieu-Avantés—at least for so long as the Ariège sun tempered the chill of the Pyrenean foothills. His three young sons, Max, Jacques and Louis, came there for their holidays and enjoyed themselves in the company of a father they adored—and one who understood them and knew how to guide them in their first adventures among ideas.

The whole family was very much aware of cave prehistory, for the Mas d'Azil, with its gigantic vault, like an earthfast cathedral, and its labyrinth of dim passages, was only a few kilometres away, while at no great distance there were the deep caverns of Niaux, Bédeilhac, Portel and Gargas, already famous for their prehistoric paintings and engravings.

From *Les Cavernes du Volp*. Paris: Arts et Métiers Graphiques; 1958. Translated by Jacquetta Hawkes. By permission of Arts et Métiers Graphiques.

At that time the river Volp offered the strongest lure to exploration. It flowed not far from Arise and Salat before joining the
Garonne at Cazères. A little way from Montesquieu-Avantés it had
cut deep tunnels between the point where it went underground at
Enlène and le Tuc d'Audoubert, where the limestone hill disgorged
it. Two systems of underground galleries, one dry and the other
flooded, honeycombed the slopes where the manors of Pujol and
Espas stood—and near them the ruins of a mediaeval building.

Long ago those seasoned diggers, the Abbé Cau-Durban and
Félix Regnault, had partially removed the Neolithic deposits from
the Enlène entry; nearby Comte Begouen had found a piece of
sculpture, a reindeer antler carved in full relief in the best Magdalenian IV style. In 1912 his three boys decided to use a frail craft
which they had made out of packing cases and petrol cans to explore beyond the deep lake where the Volp emerged after its two
kilometres underground.

On July 12th, without too much difficulty, they reached some
huge, half-flooded galleries with a small annex containing engravings, and made their way underground to another lake at the con-
fluence of the stream of Touréou and the Volp. An 18th Century
inscription soon proved to them that they were not the first to penetrate so far.

An ascending passage led the boys into a narrow upper gallery
where there were a few engravings. It was there that on the morning of October 12th, 1912, Max Begouen had an intuition that certain hanging folds of stalactite concealed a further corridor. He
broke them off and pushed on into a vast gallery—knowing that
he was the first human being to tread there since the Reindeer
Age. In the afternoon he and his brothers and the faithful Francis
explored the gallery, penetrating to the last chamber. There, leaning against a rock, they saw the forms of two bison, marvellously
modelled in clay. The very same evening their father was taken to
see their great discovery.

Four days later Émile Cartailhac and I arrived from Toulouse
and Paris. We, too, made our way into the chamber and were confronted by the bison.

Two years later, on July 21st, 1914, the three Begouen brothers
and Francis Camel and Marcellin Bermon all determined to go
down a shaft which a peasant working a nearby field declared to
be always very draughty and to cause the snow to melt in winter-
time. Comte Begouen stationed himself at the entrance to wait for
their return.

Several hours dragged by and the sentinel was beginning to suffer from fatherly anxiety, when suddenly he saw his sons above
ground, and capering towards him. They had dropped through a

hole pierced in the roof of a narrow passage, then entered another, one end of which, so cramped and low that they had to crawl, had led them into the dry cave of Enlène. The other end, however, took them up to a maze of galleries, all quite unknown, which were decorated with many groups of splendid engravings and a few little paintings. The now famous cave of Les Trois Frères had been discovered. Since that day it has been thoroughly explored.

ABBÉ HENRI BREUIL

Copying Cave Art

IN presenting this collection of sketches of our ancestors in the Old Stone Age to the public, I feel that I should explain how they came to be made, since they are so far removed from my usually much more serious work.

From my early childhood the study of Nature had an unconquerable attraction for me and I turned instinctively towards it. A taste for keen observation and a searching curiosity led me first towards the study of Insects (Entomology). From my earliest years my father, whom I accompanied on his walks, amused himself by collecting Coleoptera. The trunk of an old rotten willow tree, inside which we found two specimens of *Elater sanguineus,* the most beautiful of our click-beetles; the capture on the trunk of a poplar of a ground beetle (*Calosoma inquisitor*); on an oak tree which had been felled, of a whole tribe of biting *Rhagium* and of *Clytia,* coloured like wasps; or on the flexible twigs of an osier of the beautiful *Aromia moschata* (musk-beetle) with its long goat horns, are my chief recollections of moments of strong, exciting emotion. Then I extended my interest to butterflies, catching my first Swallow-tail (*Papilio machaon*) in a field of lucerne; the discovery of a poplar "Dead Leaf" on the cornice of an old wall; the care of strange, beautiful caterpillars—of that of the Puss moth, or the Privet Hawk

From Abbé Henri Breuil: *Beyond the Bounds of History.* London: Hawthorn Books; 1949, pp. 11-16. Translated by Mary Boyle. By permission of T. V. Boardman & Co. Ltd.

moth—what marvellous childhood thrills of pure joy these names bring back to me!

My father, except for his collection of insects, was nothing of a naturalist. It was a very humble schoolmaster, Monsieur Paul André, the son-in-law of my grandfather's gamekeeper, who first spoke to me of geology during his and my holidays in Soissonais, showing me moulds of the interior of giant Cerithiums preserved in the coarse Eocene limestone. In those days these were dated from the time of the Flood, but they gave me a deep, though no doubt vague impresssion, of a past so very far away that I could hardly imagine it.

In Prehistory I had already been struck by two things. The worthy schoolmaster at Clermont, Monsieur Devimeux, who was the first person to whom I announced my election to the Collège de France in later years, taught me the rudiments of knowledge in his private lessons, from the time I was seven to ten years old. One day he gave me to read aloud the description of the discovery of a Neolithic burial and the site of Aurignac. I did not properly understand what this meant till much later, but the fact that I remember it shows that I was not deaf to the call of those mysterious Stone Ages. I already knew of their existence, for on wet days in the Soissonais country, where my mother's parents lived, my grandmother allowed me to open her showcase, into which I often gazed, and gently handle some polished axes—Pressigny knives and one Levallois flake (the latter not much esteemed), that the plough had turned up in the clay of the neighbouring fields. Naturally, all these objects were to her and to me, Celtic or Gaulish. But Humanity's long past opened before me and I began to dream. There was no one near me to teach me more.

The month of August spent in Picardy often brought me to the Château of Bouillancourt-en-Sery where, under the roof, there was an attic in which I was often allowed to rummage, and it was there I discovered a small collection of rocks and fossils. I was instinctively fascinated and began to ask many questions of a distinguished geologist from Abbeville, d'Ault de Mesnil, a family friend. More than once he went to the attic with me and, amused by my curiosity, answered me as well as he could. Although I understood very little, it gave me a new world, with an ocean peopled by Ichthyosaurus, Plesiosaurus, Ammonites and Belemnites.

I began to collect strange stones myself, silicified cerithiums from soft chalk beds, shark teeth from the Lutetian level; a mammoth tooth from the Saint Médard gravels was for long the finest ornament of my small collection. Again, instinctively, I added to these a series of skulls of vermin, trapped by my grandfather's gamekeeper, and these, I own, gave me my first and very valuable introduction to comparative osteology.

When I had passed my school certificate, d'Ault, whom I met every summer, sent me to collect fossils in the green chalk at Nesle near Blangy; he also showed me some deerhorn picks found near

LETTER FROM THE AUTHOR TO HIS FATHER,
DATED 3RD JANUARY, 1897;
THE DECORATIONS SHOWS AN EARLY INTEREST
IN BOTANY AND ENTOMOLOGY

Bouillancourt in a pit from which the Neolithic people extracted flint. I began to realize more fully the long past of geological and prehistoric times, but insects were always my first love and the blue wings of a Morpho in the Desmonville Museum at Abbeville held for me ever the same magic.

I must confess that my artistic education was never the outcome of study in a well-known studio. The ten to sixteen-year-old schoolboy that I was learnt to sharpen his pencils or charcoal and laboriously to blacken a sheet of paper, copying some print or cast. He much preferred sketching according to his fancy, hens, ducks, dogs and cows at harvest time on his aunt's farm in Picardy, where she made butter and delicious cakes which were washed down with cider. The gaining of his "bachot" (school certificate) earned the longed-for shooting license, and his pencil recorded the movements of rabbits, hares, partridges and pheasants living on his maternal grandfather's property near Soissons. His grandmother had been a good pupil of Justin Louvrié, and sometimes gave him a few hints. A keen entomologist, sometimes a botanist, the young student often drew with a certain facility, butterflies, coleoptera and wild flowers; but he was never more than a mediocre water-colourist.

Somewhat later, it must be admitted that he devoted his energies to drawing uncharitable portraits of the inspiring profiles of some of his professors, or to illustrating satirically the archaic descriptions in the pious biographies which lulled him during his meals in the refectory. Certain professors of ethics, who made quick eloquent gestures, involuntarily taught him to sketch characteristic attitudes rapidly.

Then towards 1900—and ever since—the neophyte prehistorian began the unending work which during several months every year led him to decipher and copy the engravings and frescoes in the Reindeer Age caves. The teachings of this hard school lasted for nearly fifty years, during which the schoolboy of 1890, the seminarist of 1895-1900, had to learn all alone, and with makeshift materials, techniques and ways of working inspired by his models, familiarize himself with the "feeling" of these old masters—the hunters of reindeer, mammoth and bison. These were, in fact, his only Masters, nearly all of them purely animal painters. But after 1908 the enthusiastic student spent many months looking at the Art of the Eastern Spanish caves where there were rock frescoes of frenzied hunting and war scenes in which gesticulation played an important part.

Visits to many of the most celebrated museums of Europe, where the public can study the finest work of ancient sculptors and classic painters, awoke in this pupil of the great Masters of the Stone Age a fervent but very eclectic interest in all creations of human art throughout the ages. And thus, little by little, the background was formed which was to produce the drawings in this book.

From Fossil Man I had learnt to sketch animals and people from memory, without correction; often during banquets at scientific congresses I decorated my neighbours' menu cards with bison in silhouette, or other prehistoric beasts, and sometimes there was great competition for these.

The last world war drove me into exile, first at Lisbon, then in South Africa, and I was so warmly welcomed in both these places that I was able to continue my researches on fresh ground. Having no other means of showing my gratitude to kind foreign colleagues or hospitable friends, it sometimes happened that I tried to draw some scene recalling an episode of those far-off times to the study of which I had devoted my life. Occasionally I felt that I was successful.

In December, 1944, the South African summer induced us to wait till the sun was less strong before setting off for the bushveld sites and dongas, and our work was reduced to the daily study of the material we had gathered in the preceding months. Tired by the excessive altitude of the Rand, my faithful fellow-worker, Miss M. E. Boyle, who had accompanied me to these southern limits of the Old World, went for some weeks' rest to the orange orchards on a lower level at Rustenburg. Meanwhile my own work at the Archæological Survey left me free in the early morning and after supper. It was then that the idea occurred to me to amuse myself by again trying to make sketches of prehistoric life. At week-ends, when I always went to see Dr. Grasset and his family who were to us like our own family, I showed these efforts to entertain my hosts, whose manifest interest encouraged me.

A drawing of a bison hunt, done for Mrs. Diana Dent in gratitude for a small service, was framed and hung in her drawing-room, where, if I may say so, it looked rather well. One day two children visiting the house climbed up on the sofa so as to see the picture better.

"This is drawn by a great artist, isn't it? The bison is so frightened, I can see it in his eyes," said the boy. He had re-acted to the violent atmosphere that I had tried to give to the struggle between the hunter and his quarry. This sincere homage from unprejudiced children impressed me greatly. Instead of sketching, as I had been doing, on no matter what piece of white paper, I had now, in obedience to my friends, to use more costly sheets which they made an effort to find for me. I then set out in my early mornings and evenings to draw a series of small pictures showing the stages of development of Fossil Man and his civilizations. Begun at Christmas, 1944, this work was interrupted in the beginning of February by a fresh departure for the south coast where I studied the ancient sea levels and their relation to the different chipped stone industries. Since then I have had neither the leisure nor peace of mind to return to my drawings.

To the children, to the adolescents, I dedicate these. Perhaps, judging by what I have seen, some grown-up people may also take pleasure in them? We certainly owe that much to the children. Was it not the little five year-old girl of Marcelino de Sautuola who, in 1879, whilst her father was digging in the floor of the cave of Altamira (Santander, Spain), was the first to see the great and magnificent frescoes on the roof, greeting them with a cry of "Bulls! Bulls! (Toros! Toros!)? Although it is true that she now remembers nothing about it!

Was it not the band of lads at Montignac (Dordogne), led by Ravidat and Marsal, who slipped through a narrow shaft into the Hall of the Great Bulls, on the 12th September, 1940, and thus were the first to see and understand the incredible frescoes of Lascaux (though their first emotion was fear)?

Was it not the three young sons of Count Begouen who, whilst exploring wide dark corridors in 1912-14, had the incomparable luck of finding one after the other the clay bisons of the Tuc d'Audoubert (Ariège) and the neighbouring sanctuary of the Trois Frères, with its horned God looking down on hundreds of admirable engravings?

It is, therefore, to the children and adolescents and those older people who have known how to preserve their freshness of soul and imagination that I dedicate these modest efforts. May they inspire some among them to become explorers or prehistorians! Without the teaching of schoolmaster Laval, Marsal and Ravidat would certainly not have understood what a marvel of art was Lascaux.

ARTHUR KEITH

Faith in Piltdown Man

WHEN he had fitted the fragments of the skull into their approximate position, Dr. Smith Woodward was able to obtain a cast of the cavity which held the brain. So closely does that organ fill its

From *The Antiquity of Man*, pp. 335-6, 397-9.

space that such a cast reveals not only the size and form of the brain, but also many of the finer markings which give the anatomist a clue to the actual anatomy of the brain. The brain cast was entrusted to Professor Elliot Smith for examination. No one is so well qualified as he to interpret the significance of its features. His verdict, pronounced after his first preliminary examination, was that, "taking all its features into consideration, we must regard this as being the most primitive and most simian human brain so far recorded."

When we sum up all the characters which Dr. Smith Woodward has portrayed in this new form of being—the anthropoid characters of the mouth, teeth, and face, the massive and ill-filled skull, the simian characters of the brain and its primitive and pre-human general appearance—one feels convinced that he was absolutely justified in creating a new genus of the family Hominidæ for its reception. This new genus he named *Eoanthropus*. Ever since Darwin impressed the truth of his theory of man's origin on his fellow-scientists we have expected to encounter man's progenitors, but no one, so far as I know, ever anticipated the discovery of one showing the remarkable mixture of simian and human characters—such a one as Mr. Dawson brought to light at Piltdown. . . . In the previous chapters I have thrust the tedious and technical details relating to the reconstruction of the Piltdown skull before the reader, but our real objective is to see what sort of brain was enclosed within it. The cranial wall is moulded to fit the brain. Hence when the skull is rightly reconstructed—but not until then—it provides us with a means of telling the size and shape of the brain. So exactly does the brain fill its cavity that the impress of its various parts—of its lobes and convolutions—are preserved. When a cast is taken of the interior of the cranial cavity, we see before us a rough image of the organ which guides mankind through the intricacies of life and reveals the world in which men live. In the case of the Piltdown skull, considerable parts of the cranial walls are missing, but enough are preserved to show us not only the general form and size, but also to give us definite information relating to the mental capacity of its original owner.

We all agree that a man with a big head or a large brain is not necessarily an exceptionally clever man. Those, however, who have studied the brain as experts are firmly convinced that unless a man has a certain size of brain he cannot think and act as ordinary men do. Professor Elliot Smith is of opinion that a brain must reach a weight of 950 grammes (or about 1000 c.c. in volume) before it can serve the ordinary needs of a human existence—before it can become the seat of even a low form of human intelligence. If we accept this definition, and most of us are content to accept the

Professor of Anatomy in the University of Manchester as our leading authority on this matter, then it is certain that Pithecanthropus
—that peculiar fossil form of man from Java—falls rather below
the human limit. His discoverer, Dr. Eugene Dubois, has estimated
that the brain was about 855 c.c.; for certain reasons I regard this
as rather an underestimate—900 c.c. will probably prove to be
nearer the truth. The anthropoid apes fall far below the human
level. A gorilla has been found to have a brain capacity of 610 c.c.;
in an exceptional chimpanzee it was as low as 290 c.c.. In the
majority of great anthropoids—orangs, chimpanzees, and gorillas—
the capacity fluctuates between 400 and 500 c.c. Amongst modern
human races the brain is found to vary in size; it may be as low as
950 c.c. or as high as 1900 c.c. The late Sir William Flower divided
human skulls into three sizes—small or microcephalic, medium or
mesocephalic, and large or macrocephalic. In this manner of classifying skulls an individual with a brain space of less than 1350 c.c.
falls into the microcephalic group; if above 1450, into the macrocephalic group. Thus, including all the races of mankind in our
survey, we are prepared to regard those with a brain measuring between 1350 c.c. and 1450 c.c. as having reached the standard brain
size of modern human races. Suppose, then, the Piltdown man, who
lies thirty or fifty thousand generations behind us, were to reappear
among us in the flesh, to what group would he be attached? If we
take Dr. Smith Woodward's estimate of 1070 c.c., then he is microcephalic and falls almost to the limit which lies between the lowest
human and the highest prehuman brain capacity. Dr. Smith Woodward had a brain cast made from the Piltdown skull. When that
cast is measured, it is found to displace 1195 c.c. of water; in round
numbers, then, the size of the brain, even when the cranial fragments overlap their normal positions, measures 1200 c.c.—thus
reaching a middle place in the small-headed group. As I write, another official reconstruction of the skull has been exhibited at a
meeting of the Geological Society, held on the 17th of December
1913, exactly a year after the famous one mentioned in a former
chapter. In the new official reconstruction the hinder end of the
skull has been opened out to a very considerable extent. As amended,
the cranial capacity cannot fall much short of 1300 c.c. Thus we
see the brain capacity of this very ancient man, even in official
hands, steadily climbing from the bottom to the top of the microcephalic group of humanity.

The reader will now begin to see why I have taken so much care
to verify and prove every step taken in the reconstruction of the
Piltdown skull. If my methods are right, if the laws which hold good
for skulls in general are applicable at Piltdown, then we must promote this early Pleistocene or late Pliocene man to a still higher

group. In the previous chapter we found from the measurements of the skull that the brain capacity should be about 1400 c.c. The original reconstruction assigns the Piltdown individual, as regards mere size of brain, to the small-headed group; my own gives him or her a good place in the medium-headed group. In either case, the important fact remains that so long ago as the beginning of a former geological period a form of mankind had come well within the human standard of brain size. We could have no better assurance that the antiquity of man is very great.

J. S. WEINER

The Piltdown Affair

The Story of the Discovery

ON 18 December 1912 Arthur Smith Woodward and Charles Dawson announced to a great and expectant scientific audience the epoch-making discovery of a remote ancestral form of man—The Dawn Man of Piltdown. The news had been made public by the *Manchester Guardian* about three weeks before, and the lecture room of the Geological Society at Burlington House was crowded as it has never been before or since. There was great excitement and enthusiasm which is still remembered by those who were there; for, in Piltdown man, here in England, was at last tangible, well-nigh incontrovertible proof of Man's ape-like ancestry; here was evidence, in a form long predicted, of a creature which could be regarded as a veritable confirmation of evolutionary theory.

Twenty years had elapsed since Dubois had found the fragmentary remains of the Java ape-man, but by now in 1912 its exact evolutionary significance had come to be invested with some uncertainty and the recent attempt to find more material by the expensive and elaborate expedition under Mme. Selenka had proved entirely

From *The Piltdown Forgery*. London: Oxford University Press; 1955, pp. 1-16, 19-22, 26-33, 35-8, 41-2, 51, 53, 203-5. By permission of Oxford University Press.

unsuccessful. Piltdown man provided a far more complete and certain story. The man from Java, whose geological age was unclear, was represented by a skull cap, two teeth, and a disputed femur. Anatomically there was a good deal of the Piltdown skull and, though the face was missing, there was most of one side of the lower jaw. The stratigraphical evidence was quite sufficient to attest the antiquity of the remains; and to support this antiquity there were the animals which had lived in the remote time of Piltdown man; there was even evidence of the tool-making abilities of Piltdown man. In every way Piltdown man provided a fuller picture of the stage of ancestry which man had reached perhaps some 500,-000 years ago.

Dawson began by explaining how it came about that he had lighted on the existence of the extremely ancient gravels of the Sussex Ouse:

I was walking along a farm-road close to Piltdown Common, Fletching (Sussex), when I noticed that the road had been mended with some peculiar brown flints not usual in the district. On inquiry I was astonished to learn that they were dug from a gravel-bed on the farm, and shortly afterwards I visited the place, where two labourers were at work digging the gravel for small repairs to the roads. As this excavation was situated about four miles north of the limit where the occurrence of flints overlying the Wealden strata is recorded, I was much interested, and made a close examination of the bed. I asked the workmen if they had found bones or other fossils there. As they did not appear to have noticed anything of the sort, I urged them to preserve anything that they might find. Upon one of my subsequent visits to the pit, one of the men handed to me a small portion of an unusually thick human parietal bone. I immediately made a search, but could find nothing more, nor had the men noticed anything else. The bed is full of tabular pieces of iron-stone closely resembling this piece of skull in colour and thickness; and, although I made many subsequent searches, I could not hear of any further find nor discover anything—in fact, the bed seemed to be quite unfossiliferous. It was not until some years later, in the autumn of 1911, on a visit to the spot, that I picked up, among the rain-washed spoil-heaps of the gravel-pit, another and larger piece . . .

As geologist, Dawson described the formation of these gravels, none of which had been mapped or previously recorded, giving a detailed account of the different strata from which the fossil remains of man and fauna and the tools must have come. He dealt with the question of the chronological age of the gravels and whether all the bones were of the same age, concluding that Piltdown man and some of the mammals were of the Early Ice Age, while others were probably older. They represented the remains from an earlier

time (the Late Pliocene) which had been washed into the gravels.
The gravel itself was composed of layers corresponding to these
different ages.

As archaeologist, Dawson gave an account of the salient features
of the flint implements. Of these there were two sorts, the "paleo-
liths" which were patently of human manufacture, of an early
technique reminiscent of the "Pre-Chellean" style and technically
in accordance with the geological date of the human remains. The
other flints, much more abundant, were of doubtful manufacture:
they belonged to the class of "eoliths," flints so crude that archaeologists were acutely divided on the question of their human authorship.

Then Arthur Smith Woodward presented the anatomical description of the animal and human material. Nearly all the animals were
represented by fragments of teeth, and these Woodward identified,
giving his reasons in detail. Contemporaneous with Piltdown man
he concluded were hippopotamus, deer, beaver, and horse. More
ancient than the Piltdown man were the remains of elephant, mastodon, and rhinoceros. The Piltdown skull came in for a very detailed
examination. Woodward dealt with each cranial piece in turn, and
explained how they had been fitted together to give the reconstruction of the complete cranium which was there on view. It had been
built up from the nine pieces of cranium and the piece of mandible
already unearthed. The striking feature of the cranium was its
unusual thickness.

The fragment of lower jaw with the first and second molar teeth
still in place obtained, as it deserved, the most careful and systematic description. The shape and size, the markings and ridges
for the muscle attachments, the curvature and construction of the
specimen, all these, feature by feature, came under scrutiny and
led Woodward to his main conclusion: "While the skull is essentially human . . . the mandible appears to be that of an ape, with
nothing human except the molar teeth." Woodward emphasized in
particular those features which served to link the jaw and cranium
together in a skull of a single individual. The cranium, for all its
human resemblances, exhibited a few simian features—and in this
he found support from other distinguished anatomists, while the
jaw, ape-like though it was, displayed in the wear of the molars "a
marked regular flattening such as has never been observed
among apes, though it is occasionally met with in low types of
men." This unique fossil represented by apish jaw and human
brain-case, he was satisfied, merited its own place in the zoological
scheme. He therefore proposed its allocation to a new genus and
species of man, named "in honour of its discoverer, *Eoanthropus
dawsoni*."

At this long-remembered meeting of the Geological Society there was acclaim for Dawson for his part in noticing the gravel pit, for recognizing its great antiquity, and for keeping a constant watch for fossils for many years. There were some who thought that the date which he, as the geologist and archaeologist of the team, had assigned erred on the side of modernity. They urged that a still older date as far back as the Pliocene was indicated, but Dawson gave good reasons for his conservative estimate. Of the extreme antiquity of Piltdown man there was no doubt in anyone's mind. The early Ice Age seemed an entirely reasonable date of emergence for this very early ancestral form, a "paradox of man and ape" as the creature from Piltdown undoubtedly appeared to be. That his brain had advanced more rapidly than his face and jaw was precisely in accord with current ideas. It was all just as many in the audience had expected. Many there had heard and been convinced by the fervent lectures of Thomas Henry Huxley on the ape-like affinities of man, and Darwin himself in *The Descent of Man* had painted a picture of the earliest human ancestor, the males with "great canine teeth, which served them as formidable weapons." "That we should discover such a race as Piltdown, sooner or later, has been an article of faith in the anthropologist's creed ever since Darwin's time," wrote Keith. "On the anatomical side," declared another authority, "the Piltdown skull realized largely the anticipation of students of human evolution." The palaeontologist Sollas certainly expressed the prevailing view when he wrote: "In *Eoanthropus dawsoni* we seem to have realized a creature which had already attained to human intelligence but had not yet wholly lost its ancestral jaw and fighting teeth." It was "a combination which had indeed long been previously anticipated as an almost necessary stage in the course of human development." And finally, Elliott Smith declared the brain of *Eoanthropus,* as judged by the endocranial cast, to be the most primitive and most ape-like human brain yet discovered.

Yet there were a few, at that first meeting, who could not agree with Woodward and Dawson. David Waterston, Professor of Anatomy at King's College, one of the six privileged speakers in the general discussion, found it hard to conceive of a functional association between a jaw so similar to that of a chimpanzee and a cranium in all essentials human. He found it difficult to believe that the two specimens came from the same individual. He and a few others took the view that two distinct fossil creatures had been found together in the gravel. Indeed, those who could not believe that the jaw bone belonged to the skull agreed that the jaw, like the "Pliocene" group of mammalian fossils—mastodon, elephant and rhinoceros—had been washed into the Piltdown gravel from an earlier geological deposit, whereas the braincase belonged to the later group of Pleistocene fossils like beaver and red deer.

But Woodward's case was coherent and convincing. The creature did fulfil evolutionary expectations in his form, in his age, his tools, and in the character of the animals of the time. Woodward pointed out that the remains had been found very close together, how similar they were in colour and apparently in mineralization, how complementary they were to one another, and how they were functionally connected, as testified above all by the inescapable fact that in this jaw the teeth were essentially human. Their flat wear had never been seen in the molars of apes. It was the sort of wear to be expected from a jaw which was articulated on to a human cranium. That two different individuals were present, a fossil man, represented by a cranium without a jaw, and a fossil ape, represented by a jaw without a cranium, within a few feet of each other and so similar in colour and preservation, would be a coincidence, amazing beyond belief.

Arthur Keith, Conservator of the Hunterian Museum of the Royal College of Surgeons, admitted the strength and logic of Smith Woodward's interpretation. In subsequent years he submitted the Piltdown remains to the most searching examination, adjudicating between the two camps which had formed at the very first meeting. His own criticisms at the time concerned mainly the reconstruction of the cranium and to a lesser extent of the jaw, and these reconstructions were to occupy him in protracted controversy for many years.

Keith drew attention to a crucial point: there was no eyetooth in the jaw, for most of the chin region had been broken away. What sort of canine would such a creature possess? On this point he did not agree with Smith Woodward's opinion. But Smith Woodward was quite definite. If his interpretation was correct, the tooth when found would certainly be somewhat like that of the chimpanzee, but not projecting sensibly above the level of the other teeth, and its mode of wear would also be utterly different from that of an ape. Like the wear on the molars, the canine tooth would be worn down in a way expected from a freely moving jaw such as the Piltdown man must clearly have possessed in view of its association with so human a cranium. The sort of canine he expected could be discerned in the plaster cast which was before the meeting.

It was very clear to those present how much the missing canine would help to decide the issue of the incipient humanity of the jaw.

Throughout that next long season of digging and sieving of 1913, the oft-discussed canine remained the principal objective. Little indeed came to light that season, but on Saturday, 30 August, at the end of a day which again had so far proved fruitless, the young priest, Teilhard de Chardin, found the canine, "close to the spot whence the lower jaw itself had been disinterred." There was jubilation. The Kenwards, tenants of Barkham Manor (Dawson was the Steward) who had followed the fortunes of the search with unfailing enthusiasm, were appraised of the triumph. It was indeed a triumph. The eye-tooth was just what they had hoped for and closely fulfilled Smith Woodward's prediction of its shape, size, and above all of the nature of its wear. As Dawson wrote in 1915, "the tooth is almost identical in form with that shown in the restored cast." Dr. Underwood in 1913 also pointed out this remarkable resemblance, in an article in which, for the first time, X-rays of all the teeth were provided. "The tooth," wrote Dr. A. S. Underwood, "is absolutely as modelled at the British Museum."

The new facts further strengthened Woodward's position. Piltdown man could now be said with confidence to possess a dentition in a number of different respects human rather than ape-like, and in the X-ray appearance Keith discovered that the roots of the molar tooth were inserted in the bone in the human and not the ape manner.

The next year's excavation at Barkham Manor yielded what Keith called "the most amazing of all the Piltdown revelations." Digging a few feet from the place where the Piltdown skull had first been found, the workman with Woodward and Dawson exposed a fossil slab of elephant bone which had been artificially shaped to form a club-like implement. It was found in two pieces "about a foot below the surface, in dark vegetable soil beneath the hedge which bounds the gravel pit." The clay encrusting the object enabled Woodward to settle its contemporaneity with Piltdown man, to whose kit of stone tools there was added this, the earliest known bone implement.

The finding of the canine convinced many of the sceptics of the rightness of Woodward's interpretation, but not Waterston, whose opinion remain unchanged till his death in 1921. The two camps persisted. Like Waterston, Gerrit Miller, Curator of Mammals at the United States National Museum, preferred to believe that two fossil creatures were really represented in the Piltdown remains and introduced the new name *Pan vetus* for what seemed to him a new fossil form of chimpanzee. His arguments were met by the zoologists of the British Museum, but Miller continued in his disbelief. At this period Woodward's case was very strong and it had the benefit of Keith's powerful advocacy, presented in masterly fashion in the *Antiquity of Man*.

In 1915 the last, and in its way the most conclusive, of the Piltdown discoveries was announced, for Dawson found the remains of yet another individual two miles away. To those who had been prepared to accept the theory (however far-fetched it might appear) that at Barkham Manor somehow two different creatures had become commingled, this new discovery came as a devastating refutation, for it was hard to conceive of so astonishing a coincidence happening yet again. At the second site at Sheffield Park there were, as before, parts of the brain-case and a molar tooth quite like those previously found. From that site came also another tooth of rhinoceros of, at least, lower Pleistocene age and perhaps older.

The news of the second Piltdown man spread rather slowly and was not fully appreciated until the First World War was over. The foremost French anthropologist, Marcellin Boule, changed his views on learning of this new development. Among the Americans, who for the most part had supported the sceptical attitude of Waterston and Miller, there was a process of general conversion to Woodward's belief. A leader of American anthropological opinion, Fairfield Osborn, had stood out against Woodward with great resolution; his change of mind assumed the nature of a religious conversion. He tells in *Man Rises to Parnassus* how he visited the British Museum after World War I in a mood of the greatest thankfulness that the bombs of the Zeppelins had spared the treasure-house of the Natural History Museum and in particular the priceless Piltdown remains. He tells of the hours he spent that Sunday morning with Woodward going over and over the material and all the arguments, and how at last, in the words of the Opening Prayer of his Yale college song, he felt he had to admit: "Paradoxical as it may appear, O Lord, it is nevertheless true." Direct handling of the material convinced him that he had been too dogmatic in his two-creatures belief. Woodward had, after all, been right, and like Keith, Osborn was happy to find himself on common ground and reconciled with Arthur Smith Woodward.

There had been a period of coolness, and indeed, hostility, between Keith and Woodward. Keith admitted the fault lay partly in himself and arose from a feeling of resentment that the unique fossils had not come to him, an established human anatomist, a recognized authority on the skeleton of man and apes, and the Conservator of John Hunter's great anatomical museum at the Royal College of Surgeons. Woodward had treated him with coldness, had kept the new discovery secret from him until a bare fortnight before its public announcement, and then had allowed him only a short twenty-minute visit to South Kensington to view the finds from the Piltdown gravel. Keith's differences with Smith Woodward and Elliot Smith were aroused by the (faulty) reconstruction of the brain-case which Woodward exhibited at the Geological Society meeting. This rather painful argument about the cranium probably did something to distract Keith's attention from the problem of the jaw, for he spent much time and ingenuity and made many searching tests in an endeavour to arrive at a really accurate reconstruction of the cranium, so as to get at its real shape and size. To the whole problem of Piltdown man Keith devoted much painstaking and indeed brilliant anatomical analysis, in the course of which he studied with the greatest thoroughness, to the permanent benefit of other workers, all the relics of ancient man available to him. Though intellectually convinced by Woodward's arguments and the evidence, Keith from the first felt some uneasiness. Many times he assessed the strength and weakness of the case and concluded in favour of *Eoanthropus dawsoni*. But puzzled he remained and his ambivalent attitude to Piltdown man coloured all his pronouncements. In his work he used the plaster casts made by Mr. Barlow of the British Museum, and distributed in April and May of 1913 to the scientific men principally interested—to Elliot Smith, who was working on the brain of Piltdown man as revealed by the cast of the inside of the skull, to Duckworth at Cambridge, and through Teilhard de Chardin to Boule in Paris. Dawson received one and was able to show it to the many inquirers who now flocked to Piltdown and Uckfield, as Mr. Eade, the present chief clerk at the firm of Dawson and Hart, recollects. There it was seen at this time by Captain Guy St. Barbe, a client of the firm, and by another informant.

By 1915 the British anatomists and palaeontologists were generally of one mind and had accepted Woodward's views—though Waterston still stood out. A Royal Academy portrait in oils of 1915 shows us the group of men concerned with the evolutionary study of Piltdown man, who now passed into the general histories and encyclopaedias as easily the best-known of the primal ancestors of the human species. In the centre, holding the reconstructed skull, is Keith, as if to symbolize the newly won harmony of view, with Woodward on one side and Elliot Smith on the other. Woodward's assistants, the zoologist Pycraft (he had been concerned in some interesting study of the jaw and refutation of Gerrit Miller) and Barlow, the skilful maker of the casts, are also of the group. The others depicted are Charles Dawson, Ray Lankester, who had been somewhat sceptical over the implements, and Dr. Underwood, who had advised on dental matters.

The season of excavation of 1916 proved completely unsuccessful. There were many helpers, but nothing was found, either human or animal. Dawson had fallen ill towards the end of 1915, and took no part, though Woodward kept in touch with him. His anaemia however led to septicaemia and his condition became steadily worse. He died on 10 September 1916.

In 1917, after correspondence with Mrs. Dawson, Smith Woodward obtained from Dawson's home, before the auctioneers' sale, the fragments known as the Barcombe Mills skull, and these he deposited in the British Museum.

During the next few years Smith Woodward opened up a number of pits in the vicinity of the original excavation. He also watched closely the digging of some foundations near the farmhouse at Barkham Manor. Except for a flint which he took to be a "pot-boiler" at the latter site and miscellaneous bone fragments of recent animals, nothing came to light. After his retirement Woodward went to live at Hayward's Heath, near Piltdown, in order to search the original site and the fields of Site II at Sheffield Park, but with no success whatever. He occasionally employed one of the local labourers to do a little digging in these excursions. One such expedition, as late as 1931, yielded only a sheep's tooth.

The site of the first excavations was cleared under the auspices of the Nature Conservancy in 1950 and a large new section of the gravel terrace opened up. Everything was carefully sieved and examined, but the many tons of soil and gravel yielded nothing. This re-excavation made possible the exhibition of a demonstration section of the famous strata protected by a glass window. The cleared area was scheduled as a national monument.

Piltdown Exposed

AS long as very few human fossils had come to light, Piltdown Man remained credible as an early hominid.

THE picture changed as discoveries accumulated from China, Java, and Africa. About 1936 a whole series of new finds of Java man were made. One of these was almost a duplicate of Dubois' first specimen, and thoroughly vindicated the original claims. *Pithecan-thropus* was an undeniable primitive hominid; his skeletal features were settled beyond any doubt. And by that time a closely allied creature from Peking, probably a slightly more advanced hominid, was known from the remains of a score or more individuals—cave-dwelling, fire-making, and tool-using primitive men. By 1948, when Keith wrote his worried Foreword to Woodward's posthumous book, a still earlier pre-human stage in man's ancestry had been recognized by Dart and Broom in the caves of the Transvaal. These were the Australopithecinae, very ape-looking, but with many marks of an incipient humanity.

From all this there emerged a picture of human evolution quite different from that which had been worked out from the interpretation of the Piltdown material. Contrary to the beliefs of the Piltdown supporters, all these other fossils agreed in showing Man as having obtained his large brain only slowly, whereas many features of jaws and teeth became human very early on. These early forms had a chin region, teeth, and a general shape of jaw which like that of modern man differed basically from those of the ape or Piltdown. Where Piltdown had an extremely modern forehead and an ape's jaw, Java and Peking man possessed the combination in reverse—a simian looking forehead and an unapelike jaw.

It had now to be concluded, and Woodward himself did so in 1944, that two quite separate evolutionary lines existed. Along one went the South African, Java, Peking, Neanderthal sequence— an overlapping series of transformations; alone on the other was Piltdown man. The two lines were irreconcilable. No common ancestor for the two lines was in sight, and now much argument was heard as to which line had given rise to *Homo sapiens*. Many, including Woodward and Keith, still favoured the Dawn Man.

This was a rather complex state of affairs, but by no means an impossible one—though, of course, it was made still more complicated by those who still believed in the existence of two fossil Piltdown creatures, fossil man and fossil ape; but they, however, could add no conclusive evidence on this point nor demolish Woodward's case.

Complete confusion succeeded when the geologists decided that the early date of *Eoanthropus* could not possibly be correct. The result of the fluorine dating test announced by Dr. Kenneth Oakley in 1949 brought about this decisive change of outlook. . . .

There was here no question of a vast antiquity for Piltdown man; in fact, the fluorine accumulation was so small that the bones could be given a dating hardly later than the Upper Pleistocene, i.e. the last part of the Ice Age, "probably at least 50,000 years old." . . .

Towards the end of July 1953 a congress of palaeontologists was held in London under the auspices of the Wenner-Gren Foundation. The problems of fossil man were the subject of its deliberations. Java man, Neanderthal man, Rhodesian man, the South African prehumans—all these were given close attention. But Piltdown man was not discussed. Not surprisingly. He had lost his place in polite society. What more could one usefully say about him? Yet, unofficially, the Dawn Man did manage an appearance. Most of

those present had not seen the original fossil specimens, so on a
tour of the Natural History Museum these were shown along with
others housed there. The sight of the actual fragments provoked
the familiar tail-chasing discussion. As always there were those
who could not feel that the famous jaw really harmonized with the
rest, but there were others who took the opposite view. The enigma
remained.

At the dinner that night Dr. Oakley remarked casually to Professor Washburn of Chicago and myself that owing to Dawson's early
death in 1916 the Museum had no record of the exact spot where
the remains of the second Piltdown had been found. They knew
the place—Sheffield Park—but the actual spot or even the field had
never been marked on a map. "The fact is," said Oakley, "that all we
know about site II is on a postcard sent in July 1915 by Dawson to
Woodward, and an earlier letter in that year, from neither of
which one can identify the position of Piltdown II." This was surprising. . . .

This small puzzle turned my thoughts to the larger Piltdown
conundrum. My own conclusion when reviewing the matter in 1950,
like that of others, was that Woodward's *Eoanthropus* had become
a complete anomaly, that the only course was to wait till more
material was dug up, and that it was really profitless to spend much
time on choosing between possibilities, none of which was suscepti-
ble of final proof. Thinking it all over again, I realized with
astonishment that while there were in fact only the two possible
"natural" theories, i.e., that Piltdown man was in fact the composite
man-ape of Woodward's interpretation, or that two distinct
creatures, fossil man and fossil ape, had been found side by side,
neither of the "natural" explanations was at all satisfactory. If the
two "natural" explanations failed in some way or another, what
other possible explanation could there be? Was there any other way
of resolving the whole disorder of fragments, dates, chronology?
On evolutionary grounds alone a late Dawn Man stood out as an
obvious incongruity. The riddle might be approached more simply
(I argued) by accepting at once the extraordinary difficulties of
regarding the fossil as an organically single individual and by
concentrating entirely on the perplexities of the two-creature
hypothesis. What were feasible alternative explanations of the
coincidence of two distinct individuals? If the jaw and cranium had
not come together by nature or by blind accident then could they
have got there by human agency? This would mean that someone
by mischance or error had dropped a fossil jaw in the pit (perhaps
used as a rubbish dump) dug in gravel which happened to contain
other fossil remnants.

But surely this could hardly have been repeated at the second site? Perhaps site II was after all of exaggerated significance or had been mistakenly interpreted. As Hrdlicka and others had been saying all along, perhaps the single molar might not really be ape or have any affinity whatever with the first teeth, so that the Sheffield Park fragments, despite their other similarities to those at Piltdown, would simply be a quite ordinary set of human remains. Or we could dispose of Piltdown II by supposing that the bits had actually come from the Barkham Manor site two miles away, in gravel brought across for some reason or other. Even if one were prepared to accept them, this elaboration of ancillary hypotheses still avoided the main issue. For even if the jaw had been thrown on to the gravel, to meet with the cranium, it was still a *fossil* jaw and we had not in fact escaped the original dilemma: what fossil ape could it possibly be? Still, the idea of an accidental deposit or loss of a jaw could be pursued a stage further (still disregarding site II) if we postulated that the jaw was not a fossil, but really that of a *modern* ape. We might then accept the accidental coincidence. But could the jaw possibly be modern? Immediately strong objections loomed up. To say the jaw was modern implied that the fluorine analysis had been inaccurate or that the published results must be in some way compatible with modern bone recently buried. In effect this would imply that the most reasonable interpretation of the results had been in error. That difficulty was dwarfed at once by a far more serious objection. The teeth were almost unanimously acknowledged to possess features quite unprecedented in modern apes—the flat wear of the molars and the curious type of wear of the canine had never been matched in an ape's mandible.

A *modern jaw with flat worn molars and uniquely worn-down eye tooth*? That would mean only one thing: deliberately ground-down teeth. Immediately this summoned up a devastating corollary —the equally deliberate placing of the jaw in the pit. Even as a mere hypothesis this inference could at once dispose of two of the most intransigent Piltdown posers: how the jaw and teeth had ever got there and how the teeth had come by their remarkable wear. But the hypothesis of a deliberate "salting" of the Piltdown gravels clearly carried much wider implications, and the idea was repellent indeed. Could one not find a fatal flaw at once, and quickly dimiss this as a solution of the Piltdown mystery? There would be no need to consider the idea any further or even to examine the specimens (or rather the casts) in the laboratory next day. (For this cogitation had occupied the small hours on my return to Oxford after the Wenner-Gren dinner.) . . .

This *a priori* case obtained added support from discussions with Professor Le Gros Clark and our examinations of the Piltdown casts in the Department of Anatomy at Oxford. Perhaps the most

telling argument which could be marshalled at this stage lay in
an extraordinary fact revealed by the anatomical reconsideration
of the remains. It appeared to me that, despite the many claims
advanced from time to time for the existence of a whole variety of
human features in the jaw and of ape-like features in the cranium,
the only completely acceptable and undoubted characteristic of a
human kind in the jaw turned out to be the flat wear. Nothing
else could unequivocally be said to be human. How strange, then,
that this one feature should be present to link jaw and cranium
and yet these were supposed to form a harmonious combination in
a live animal. Surely a few other modifications should have been
apparent in the jaw. Yet, as Woodward himself had often pointed
out, such functional features of the jaw as its muscle attachments
were entirely ape-like. The moment one attributed this flat wear
to a deliberate abrasion of the teeth it became understandable.

It now appeared from our discussion that the canine was not
merely peculiar in its mode of dental wear, but that it was itself
paradoxical in that the wear was so heavy as to be quite out of
keeping with the immaturity of the tooth. This was a fact first
pointed out in 1916 by the dentist Mr. (C. W.) Lyne, and never
properly explained. Lyne's cogent arguments had been brushed
aside by Woodward and Underwood.

Then we examined the plaster casts. These revealed features
quite understandable as the outcome of artificial abrasion of the
dental crowns. In particular we were struck by the extraordinary
flatness of the second molar and the lack of a smooth continuity of
biting surface from the one molar to the next. Next, a chimpanzee's
molar, of about the same size as the Piltdown, was experimentally
filed down. This proved easy enough to do and, even without any
polishing of the surface, by staining with permanganate an appearance very like the Piltdown molars was obtained, as far as
could be judged from the casts and from photographs.

Yet another piece of positive information emerged when one
re-read Dr. Oakley's fluorine paper. During the course of drilling to
obtain his sample of dentine, Dr. Oakley had made an observation
which now assumed a special significance: "Below the extremely
thin ferruginous surface stain," he had written, "the dentine was
pure white, apparently no more altered than the dentine of recent
teeth from the soil." Re-reading of Dawson's and Woodward's
papers further made it clear that they themselves had missed a
chance of making what might have been a decisive comparison of
jaw and cranium. It appeared that only on the cranium had chemical
tests for organic matter and other constituents been made, and the
cranium had been found to contain no organic matter. If the jaw

was modern, its organic context would be high, but the analysis had not been done. . . .

The tests we had in mind at this stage turned simply on the issue of the modernity or otherwise of the jaw and teeth, but it was obvious that the implications extended to every aspect of the Piltdown discoveries.

At this time awaiting the outcome of our "predictions" and repeatedly arguing and reviewing our case, and seeing no other possible solution to the problem, we could well appreciate Holmes's sage advice to Watson:

"How often have I said to you that when you have eliminated the impossible, whatever remains, *however improbable,* must be the truth.". . .

On the basis of our preliminary arguments and our anatomical re-examination of the fragments, Mr. W. N. Edwards, the Keeper of Geology of the Natural History Museum, felt justified in allowing the specimens of mandible, cranium, and teeth to be drilled for much larger samples than could ever have been sanctioned hitherto. These larger samples and the use of improved chemical methods guaranteed a high degree of analytical reliability.

The drilling itself gave us an encouraging start. As the drilling proceeded, Dr. Oakley and his assistant perceived a distinct smell of "burning horn" when the jaw was sampled, but they noticed nothing of the sort with any of the cranial borings. This subjective indication of some distinct difference between the constitution of jaw and cranium soon gained objective confirmation. The drilled sample from the jaw proved to be utterly unlike those from the cranium. In keeping with the belief in its fossil or semi-fossilized character, the latter produced a fine particulate granular powder, whereas the jaw yielded little shavings of bone, just as did a fresh bone sampled as a control. Here was the beginning of the series of findings which progressively widened the gulf between jaw and cranium.

Very soon Dr. Oakley obtained clear chemical evidence to justify fully the strong suspicion of the modernity of the jaw and of the totally distinct origin of the cranium. An improved technique for estimating small quantities of fluorine produced this decisive result. The cranial fragments of site I were found to contain fluorine in a concentration of 0.1 per cent., a value somewhat similar to that of specimens of known Late Ice Age. The jaw and the three teeth on the contrary gave much lower figures, at levels below 0.03 per cent., values well within the range of known modern and fresh specimens. Indeed, these values are on the borderline of the sensitivity of the method. The fluorine test gave its verdict twice over. For the two cranial fragments from the second Piltdown site contained a

fluorine concentration of 0.1 per cent. and the isolated molar which
went with these fragments contained less than 0.01 per cent. These
fluorine results alone go far to settle the main issue. As the
reader will recall, the method serves essentially to compare the
dates of material from any one deposit, and the Piltdown fluorine
values prove not only that the jaw and teeth do not belong to the
crania but that they are of younger date, and the test shows this
to be true at both Barkham Manor and Sheffield Park.

With this Dr. Oakley and his associates now launched a whole
battery of chemical and physical tests at the fragments, bringing
to bear on the Piltdown problem an array of new techniques in the
last few months of 1953 exceeding all endeavours of this kind in
the whole history of palaeontology. In succession they tested and
compared the fragments for iron, nitrogen, collagen, organic carbon,
organic water, radio-activity and crystal structure. This list is an
epitome of the resources which the chemist and physicist have in
recent years put in the hands of the archaeologist and palaeontologist, and in the Piltdown problem these methods obtained a
thorough trial. . . .

Of deliberate staining we obtained a striking proof when the
canine came to be examined. The tooth has a darkish brown outer
coat, always taken to be an ordinary iron-stain, and it was under
this "ferruginous" layer that Dr. Oakley, it will be recalled, remarked with surprise the whiteness and freshness of the dentine.
But there proved to be only minimal quantities of iron (oxide) in
this stain, the nature of which eluded identification for some time.
The layer was found to be a paint-like substance forming a flexible
film. The possibility that it was a dried-out layer of Chatterton's
compound was ruled out, amongst other things, by its low solubility
in organic solvents, but like this compound it contained bitumen.
Finally, it turned out to be a bitumen earth containing iron oxide,
in all probability the well-known paint—Vandyke brown. It might
have been argued that bituminous earth could produce a natural
incrustation were it not known that bituminous matter is entirely
out of place in a highly oxidized gravel. Its artificiality is established
beyond doubt by the finding by Dr. Claringbull of a minute spherule
of an iron alloy embedded in the coating on the outer (labial) surface of the crown. The reddish brown stain on the occlusal or chew-
ing surface (like that on the molars) is probably also a ferruginous
earth pigment applied as an oil paint (e.g. red sienna). . . .

The completeness of the coherence between anatomical and
chemical evidence can be easily illustrated. The independent evidence of the chemical tests is such that the extraordinary nature of
the wear of the teeth cannot be other than fraudulent, since in a

modern ape such characters cannot be matched; conversely, the independent anatomical evidence of the maltreatment of the teeth leads one to predict in detail (as we did) the very results of the chemical tests. When the reader recalls, in addition, that evolutionary and chronological considerations make the real existence of *Eoanthropus dawsoni* in the highest degree incredible, then the exact correspondence between the anatomical and the other tests is altogether comprehensible. The Man of Piltdown was an artifact. . . .

The creation of the composite man-ape, Piltdown man, was evidently an elaborate affair; much thought and work had gone into the preparation of the fraudulent jaw and in the provision of the other items of the deception. We can discern in this elaboration the whole history of the successive discoveries, each new find adding to the whole case for the fossil man. Thus we see the discovery of an ancient gravel formation followed by the finding of a thick fossilized cranium, and this by the remarkable simian mandible, then comes the equally remarkable eye tooth and in due course the fragments of a second composite creature. And as if this was not persuasion enough, there is still the weighty ballast of the animal bones and the implements. As we are now aware beyond doubt of the spurious nature of some of these elements in the discovery, we naturally wonder about them all. . . .

It remains now only to attempt briefly a final evaluation of the Piltdown affair—its authorship and its scientific significance.

We have seen how strangely difficult it is to dissociate Charles Dawson from the suspicious episodes of the Piltdown history. We have tried to provide exculpatory interpretations of his entanglements in these events. What emerges, however, is that it is not possible to maintain that Dawson could not have been the actual perpetrator; he had the ability, the experience, and, whatever we surmise may have been the motive, he was at all material times in a position to pursue the deception throughout its various phases. For anyone else to have played this complicated role is to raise a veritable Hyde to Dawson's Jekyll. Complementary, also, to the difficulty of excluding Dawson from the authorship—there is nothing that will serve to do this—is the difficulty of accepting his known activities as compatible with a complete unawareness of the real state of affairs.

Yet to condemn Dawson on considerations of this sort is to base the case ultimately on arguments by exclusion. It is true that of the evidence which throws so much suspicion on him, part is derived from his own papers and letters, and that most of the information which has come to us indirectly has not gone uncorroborated, but none of it furnishes the positive and final proof of his responsibility.

So long as the weight of circumstantial evidence is insufficient to prove beyond all reasonable doubt that it was Dawson himself who set the deception going by "planting" the pieces of brain-case, our verdict as to the authorship must rest on suspicion and not proof. In the circumstances, can we withhold from Dawson the one alternative possibility, remote though it seems, but which we cannot altogether disprove: that he might, after all, have been implicated in a "joke," perhaps not even his own, which went too far? Would it not be fairer to one who cannot speak for himself to let it go at that?

The end of Piltdown man is the end of the most troubled chapter in human palaeontology. From the first moment of the introduction of *Eoanthropus dawsoni* to the scientific world, the complexities and contradictions of the "enigma," as Keith continued to call him, took up quite unduly and unnecessarily the energies of students of Man's evolution. This ill-begotten form of primitive man in the several hundred papers devoted to him received nearly as much attention as all the legitimate specimens in the fossil record put together.

The removal of *Eoanthropus dawsoni* does nothing to weaken that record. It provides a clearer picture of the succession of fossil forms in Man's genealogy. When Darwin wrote *The Descent of Man* he had available hardly a single fossil on which to base his arguments, and he relied on a mass of anatomical, physiological, and embryological evidence to illuminate his extraordinarily skilful comparisons between man and other living animals. For Darwin and Huxley the links were still missing, but for us the discoveries of the last thirty years have gone far to provide the fossil fulfilments of Darwin's predictions; but amongst these there is no place for anything like a Piltdown man. Though today we are still far from an understanding of many matters concerning Man's origins, we are in no doubt about the reality of the transformation which has brought Man from a simian status to his *sapiens* form and capability.

GRAHAME CLARK

Hunter-Fishers of Yorkshire

OUR object in digging at Star Carr was to learn more about the daily life of the hunter-fishers who inhabited eastern England in early Mesolithic times, shortly after the end of the Ice Age, but before Britain had been finally separated from the Continent. Research over the past thirty years had already told us something of the various groups occupying different parts of Britain during the Mesolithic period, which began around 8,000 B.C. with the onset of a more genial climate and the retreat of the ice-sheets, and was brought to an end by the arrival of Neolithic farmers round about 2,500 B.C. Our knowledge of the Mesolithic hunter-fishers was still very slight before we started digging, because it was based in the main on stray finds, mostly of worked flints, and on comparisons made between these and material from settlements excavated on the Continent, more particularly in Denmark. It was known, for instance, that low-lying areas of eastern England had been occupied during the boreal climatic phase (c. 6,800-5,000 B.C.), before the temperature had reached its post-glacial peak, by folk whose equipment resembled that of the "Maglemosian" hunter-fishers identified from widely separated points of the north European plain from Flanders to the Ural Mountains. Indeed, in 1932 the trawler *Colinda* had actually brought up a Maglemosian spearhead of stag antler from a depth of 19-20 fathoms between the Leman and Ower Banks, some 25 miles from the Norfolk coast.

As the war drew to an end and archaeologists began to plan a resumption of their normal activities, the discovery and excavation of a Maglemosian settlement on British soil was accepted as a main objective of prehistoric research. In order to obtain the fullest information it was essential to find a site where organic materials, such as antler and bone and the remains of wood and former vegetation, were most likely to survive, since it was only by ex-

From *Recent Archaeological Excavations in England* (ed. by Rupert Bruce-Mitford). London: Routledge & Kegan Paul Ltd.; 1956, pp. 1-20. By permission of Routledge & Kegan Paul Ltd.

amining such that we could hope to reconstruct in detail the physical environment of the hunter-fishers and to discover precisely how they utilized it to secure food and raw materials for daily life. The best chance of finding such conditions seemed to be to locate a settlement on the shore of one of the numerous lakes which originated from the melting of the Pleistocene ice-sheets and in the course of post-glacial times became converted more or less completely into bogs or marshland, since the evidence we needed would be most likely to survive in waterlogged deposits. In the case of the Maglemosians, the prospects were particularly good, since these people favoured lakeside settlement, and the most famous sites explored in Denmark and elsewhere had in fact been situated in bogs. The very name Maglemosian, indeed, is taken from the locality Maglemose (Danish *magle mose* or great bog), near Mullerup, on Zealand, where the culture was recognized for the first time.

When looking for such a site the first and most obvious clue is the presence of worked flints, since these alone are likely to survive when exposed on the surface of the ground. It was Mr. John Moore's discovery of flint implements of recognizably Maglemosian type in the peaty carrlands of Flixton and Seamer, near Scarborough, in 1948, that first drew attention to the Vale of Pickering as a likely area for Mesolithic research. What made Mr. Moore's flints all the more interesting was that by examining the sections exposed in field ditches he was able to trace them to an organic mud deposit underlying the peat. When samples of this mud were examined in the laboratories of the Sub-Department of Quaternary Research at Cambridge, it was found that they belonged to an early phase of the post-glacial period. The next task was to pick the site where organic materials were likely to be most fully preserved. The thing to look for was the presence of antler or bone in one of the field ditches, and this Mr. Moore found at Star Carr. The specimens he obtained were badly decayed, black in colour and quite soft in texture, but they held out the possibility that better preserved material might be forthcoming in the immediate neighbourhood. Testing by means of a borer showed, indeed, that the shore of the lake shelved comparatively deeply at this point, so the odds were that the archaeological level would be found to extend down to or even into the zone of waterlogging. Trial excavations undertaken during the summer of 1949 by a party from Cambridge proved that this was, in fact, the case; and in the two following seasons we uncovered what proved to be the site of a Mesolithic hunters' camp.

Before describing the excavations it may be emphasized that archaeological research as it is conducted to-day depends to an important degree on co-operation with specialists in other branches of knowledge, and in the case of prehistoric sites more particularly with natural scientists. Much of the success obtained at Star Carr was due to assistance both in the field and during the subsequent task of interpretation from Dr. Harry Godwin, F.R.S., and Dr. Donald Walker of the Sub-Department of Quaternary Research at Cambridge, and to members of the staff of the British Museum, Natural History, particularly to Dr. F. C. Fraser and Miss J. E. King of the Department of Zoology. When seeking to reconstruct the lives of relatively primitive hunter-fishers one of the first necessities is to gain a clear idea of the ecological setting—of the climate, topography, vegetation, and wild animal life—among which they gained a livelihood. Further, one needs to know precisely which and how much of the available resources were utilized for food and handicrafts. The archaeologist needs this information before he can begin to reconstruct the way of life of the people he is studying, but he can only obtain it through the active help of geologists, botanists, zoologists, and other natural scientists.

In the case of Star Carr it was necessary to examine the sequence of deposits over an extensive area by means of borings, in order to discover the history of the lake by which prehistoric man camped. Examination of the actual deposits which accumulated in the basin and by the shores of the old lake, and analysis of the fossil pollen-grains incorporated in them, showed that in late-glacial times the basin was occupied by an open-water lake, and that the surrounding land supported an open herb vegetation, modified during a brief warm phase by the spread of tree birches. With the final onset of temperate conditions marking the post-glacial period, reed swamps began to develop; at first only on the margins of the lake, but later, as the bed silted up, spreading over the whole surface and converting the basin into a fen or carr. During the pre-boreal phase of post-glacial times, forests replaced the predominantly open vegetation of the final late-glacial stage. At first the climate was too cold for any but birch and willow trees, but towards the end of this phase pine began to establish itself. It was at this time, late in Zone IV of the forest sequence, established for this part of the world by means of pollen-analysis—before the pine began to predominate over the birch and before the growth of great hazel thickets and the first tentative spread of deciduous trees marking the full boreal phase (Zones V-VI)—that Mesolithic man established himself at Star Carr. This gave us a preliminary idea of the date of the Star Carr settlement, because the pre-boreal period (Zone IV) has been assigned to c. 8,000-6,800 B.C. by reference to Baron de Geer's geochronology (based on counts of annual layers of sediment or varves deposited in the melt-waters of the Scandinavian ice-sheet as this withdrew from south Sweden). In order to obtain an independent check, samples of birch-wood obtained during the excavations were sent to

the Institute of Nuclear Physics at Chicago University and there
subjected to radio-carbon tests by Dr. W. F. Libby. The average of
two counts gave a date of 9,488 ± 350 years before the date of the
tests, or 7,538 ± 350 years B.C. We can say with some assurance,
therefore, that our site was occupied at some time during, and
almost certainly near the end of, the eighth millennium B.C.

During the first season our task was to cut an exploratory trench
from what had once been dry land on the north shore southwards
into the lake basin. The section originally discovered in the field
ditch on the north showed that the archaeological level was at its
shallowest some 3½ feet below the surface, and we had every
reason to think that as we followed it southwards towards the
middle of the former lake it would get deeper. As we had to depend
entirely on our own labour we limited the width of the trench to
3 yards, enough to expose the nature of the site but not so wide
that we could not dispose of the soil by throwing out on either side.
One of our chief problems in digging a waterlogged site was obviously to dispose of the water, a task which was not rendered
easier by the fact that the drainage cuts were situated on the higher
northern side. We had to resort to prolonged use of pumps, and
found it a wise insurance to have a hand-operated machine to
supplement and when necessary replace the petrol-driven one—
pumps being notoriously temperamental. Our tactics in opening
up the site were to begin at the dry northern end to see how it
worked, and then as soon as we came to the waterlogged zone to
cut a deep sump well away to the south, and so attempt to drain
off water from the critical intervening area in which we hoped to
make our most important finds.

When we removed the overlying organic mud from the archaeological layer at the northern end of the section we found little else
apart from quantities of waste flints, some glacial pebbles and some
scraps of badly decayed bone and antler. It was only as we worked
down into the waterlogged area that we began to find animal remains in a better state of preservation and, what was even more
interesting, traces of birch brushwood with the bark intact. The
wood proved to be so soft that in order to expose it we had to lie
on planks erected over the deposit, hanging down and using our
hands to remove the mud. What we uncovered appeared as a rough
platform of birch brushwood, thrown down on the reed-swamp
bordering the lake and consolidated by glacial stones and wads of
clay. Intermingled with the brushwood were the discarded remains
of wild animals slaughtered for food, implements and weapons
made from flint, antler and bone, together with the debris of their
manufacture, a few beads and a number of tightly-wound rolls
of birch bark. Although we had examined only a small proportion

of the site, we recovered from this single cutting about ten times as many artifacts of Mesolithic age made from materials other than flint as had previously been obtained from the rest of England and Wales, proof if one were needed of the wisdom of digging sites where conditions for the survival of organic materials are most favourable. The bulkiest organic traces, apart from the actual platform, were the discarded animal bones, antlers and teeth. These were extremely precious for the light they might be expected to throw on the food and technology of the Star Carr hunters, as well as constituting the only closely dated assemblage of mammalian fauna of early post-glacial age from the country. The skeletal material from the waterlogged parts of the site contrasted markedly with those from the drier marginal area, being firm and pale chest-nut-brown in colour as they were removed from the mud, instead of soft and black. Unhappily these conditions proved to be ephemeral; soon after exposure to the air they changed to a dark brown colour, and if allowed to dry for any length of time began to crack and ultimately to disintegrate. We therefore packed them in sodden newspaper and sent them in a damp condition to the Natural History Museum, where they were kept in alcohol while a decision was reached as to the best method of preserving them. It was decided that the only adequate treatment was to replace the water in the antler and bone by a more stable substance, polyvinyl acetate, which could be made to impregnate the specimens deeply under vacuum conditions. The bones were washed, drained overnight and immersed in a tank of the plastic emulsion, which was then placed in a metal-plated chamber with an observation panel. The air was then pumped out of the chamber until air-bubbles had ceased to appear on the surface of the emulsion. The specimens could then be taken out, sponged free of surplus emulsion and allowed to dry. When trial tests were made it was found that the preservative had, in fact, permeated the substance of the bone and antler. During the following seasons all the larger specimens were treated on or near the scene of operations by Mr. P. E. Purves of the Natural History Museum. Spear-heads and other delicately shaped objects on the other hand we placed individually in bottles of water, for treatment under museum conditions.

When we began our second season we had a better idea of what we were after and larger resources with which to operate. We began by opening trenches on either side of the original one, leaving balks a yard wide to prevent the refill of the original trench from slipping back into the new working areas. Both cuttings produced their share of small finds, and the eastern one revealed particularly clearly the lakeward margin of the brushwood platform. Immediately con-tiguous with and at right-angles to this we found two recumbent birch trees and other birch wood. It was evident that the birch trees had been placed there, possibly as a primitive landing-stage, during the period of the occupation, because barbed spear-heads of antler were found under the larger one, and in one instance wedged between branches of the two. What was particularly interesting about the trees is that the lower ends of their trunks showed clear traces of their having been felled. It had long been appreciated by prehistorians that the flint axe and adze-blades found in the equipment of the Maglemosian hunter-fishers of northern Europe represented an adaptation to forest conditions. Here at Star Carr we had actual evidence of the ability of their pre-boreal forerunners to fell trees. The larger of the two birches—and incidentally the oldest specimen of a felled tree yet discovered anywhere— had a maximum diameter of some 14 inches. The base of the trunk was pointed rather like a pencil. This is most interesting, because recent experiments in felling trees by means of ancient flint-axes, carried out by members of the National Museum of Denmark, have shown that the most convenient method was to alternate between cutting notches into the trunk at right-angles and removing long splinters by oblique strokes delivered from higher up the trunk, a method that results in the lower extremities being pointed like those from Star Carr. Considering that only small chipped blades were available to the Star Carr people, instead of the heavy polished axe-blades used in the Danish experiments, the Mesolithic lumbermen made a remarkably neat job.

Before closing down for the second season, trial trenches were cut to define, or at least reduce within limits, the lateral extent of the site. At the same time numerous borings were made, and these showed that the camping place had evidently been sited on a gravel promontory on the north shore of the lake and that the limits were likely to have been determined on the east by a transition in the sub-soil from gravel to a stiff clay on the west by a marked inlet of the lake. The objective in the third and final season was as far as possible to complete the uncovering of the entire site, so as to establish its limits for certain and recover a complete assemblage of finds. An extensive area was opened up on the west and smaller ones were explored on the east, amounting in the aggregate to substantially more than the total excavated during the first two seasons. To round off the job the balks left between the earlier cuttings were removed as far as this proved possible.

What then did the excavations tell us about the settlement itself? It may first be emphasized that the whole superstructure has disappeared. We were, in fact, exploring no more than what the inhabitants had trampled into the waterlogged swamp, notably the brushwood platform thrown down to consolidate its surface and rubbish discarded in the course of their daily life. Yet, if we could find out nothing about the huts or shelters in which they lived, at least we could gain definite information about the scale of the settlement: by keeping a careful record of the exact number of worked flints found in each square yard, we were able to plot the precise density of these imperishable clues to Stone Age activity and, since it was possible to correlate this density with the actual extent of the brushwood platform on the lakeward half of the site, we were able to gain a sufficiently accurate notion of the area occupied. On any count the site was extremely restricted, occupying hardly more than 220–240 square yards. While this is much smaller than the villages even of Neolithic farmers, as known to us from the Continent, it falls well within the range of Mesolithic settlements, whether in the open air or at the entrances to caves. Despite the preponderance of evidence for male activities, such as hunting and tool-making, Star Carr yielded abundant traces of skin-working, an activity which among such people as the Eskimo is predominantly the women's job, and it seems probable that we have to do with an actual settlement, even if only a temporary one. There can hardly have been room for more than three or four primary families, and it would seem that the social unit must have resembled that prevalent among such simple hunting-groups as the aboriginal Tasmanians. Clear evidence was found during the excavations that the site was periodically abandoned, and analysis of the animal remains suggests that occupation was confined to the winter and early spring. How frequently the site was reoccupied cannot be certainly determined, but it is suggestive that the amount of meat indicated by the skeletal material would have been sufficient of itself to feed a community of the size indicated for an aggregate period of around six years. There are, indeed, hints that the site was reoccupied over some period of time: for instance, it was possible to observe a considerable difference in the types of spearhead found at successive levels on the lakeward margin of the site. Here, again, there are plenty of analogies from the observation of modern "primitive" peoples, who commonly return to occupy favourite spots during the course of seasonal migrations.

It can be assumed that the main energies of the Star Carr people were concentrated more or less directly on securing food, for which they had to depend entirely on what they could wrest from wild nature. We cannot say for certain how far they utilized wild plants for this purpose, but among the woodland, herbaceous and swamp species identified from the archaeological layer were many whose leaves, fruits, seeds or rhizomes, as the case may be, are known to have been consumed during later prehistoric and in several instances during recent historic times. As regards meat the evidence is quite

definite, because in the case of the larger herbivores at any rate we
can assume that individuals whose bones are found on the site
were brought there by man primarily for his sustenance; and
further, in almost every instance the tubular bones—and in the case
of elk and red deer the jaw bones—had been broken open for the
extraction of marrow. By identifying the number of individuals of
each species, and calculating the weight of meat likely to have been
carried by each carcase, indeed, we were able to discover more or
less exactly how this important part of their menu was composed.
We found that red deer easily headed the list, contributing more
than one and a half times as much as the other leading food
animals put together; wild ox or urus (*Bos primigenius*) came
easily second, and elk third; roe deer, although killed in large numbers, contributed only to a minor degree by weight; and wild pig,
which was probably still scarce during pre-boreal times, was quite
unimportant. Other sources of animal protein were relatively insignificant: doubtless some at least of the carnivores and rodents,
killed primarily in some instances for their skins, were eaten, but
only comparatively small numbers were taken, except in the case
of beaver; again, if nine species of birds, nearly all water-birds,
were represented among the bones, in no case was more than one
individual indicated; and finally there was no evidence that fishing
had been carried on at all, though we have to remember that fish
bones are highly perishable.

Owing to the relatively good conditions and to the completeness
of the excavation a wealth of material was obtained bearing on
the technology of the Star Carr hunters. It was not merely that we
recovered a much greater range of material equipment than would
be provided by an ordinary dry-land site, but by collecting all the
waste as well as finished implements we were able to reconstruct
the processes by which many of them were manufactured. The
basic craft was that of flint-knapping, since it was ultimately by
means of flint tools and weapons that our hunters were able to
gain a living from their surroundings: with flint axes and adzes
they felled trees and lopped the brushwood needed for their living
platform; with flint microliths they barbed and tipped the arrows
with which to shoot their game; with flint scrapers they dressed the
animal skins needed for clothing and, perhaps, for shelter; with
flint burins and flakes they worked antler and bone into tools and
weapons; and with flint awls they perforated beads for their personal
adornment, as well as implements. The bulk of the raw flint, together with a few pieces of chert and the quartzites and similar
stones used for hammers and rubbers, came from the local drift, but
blocks of grey flint were almost certainly obtained from the chalk
Wolds on the south shore of the lake. The quantities of waste,

amounting to at least 85% of all the flints, quite apart from tiny chips, shows that the knapping was at least mainly done on the site. Study of the waste material, and particularly of half-made implements discarded in the making, told us much of the actual methods of manufacture. Again, signs of wear and indications of resharpening threw light on the way in which they were used: for instance, signs of polishing at the extremities of some of the narrow flake awls suggest, in conjunction with the nature of the perforation through the stone beads from the site, that drills, whether rotated by hand or by means of a bow, were used; and again, the quantity of transversely struck flakes in relation to the small number of axes and adzes reminds us how often unpolished tools of this kind had to be re-sharpened when subjected to heavy use. The recovery of a microlith with its resin mounting still largely intact was a tantalizing reminder of the wooden shafts we failed to find, but as we shall see, it helped to solve another problem.

Second only to flint as a raw material for implements and weapons was antler, first and foremost of red deer, but also of elk. Red deer antler was chiefly important for making the barbed spear-heads, which mounted on wooden handles were one of the leading items in the equipment of the Star Carr hunters. The raw material was detached from the beam and occasionally also from the brow tine of the antler in the form of narrow splinters formed by cutting deep parallel grooves through the hard outer surface and levering these out by means of wedges. The leading tool used in this process was the flint burin, and this was the commonest type of implement found. Much of the work on antler and bone, such as cutting the notches and shaping the barbs of spear-heads, was carried out by means of simple flint flakes, and it is significant that the edges of rather more than one in every eleven of these showed signs of wear. Elk antler provided the raw material for two kinds of mattock-head which might have been used for such purposes as grubbing up roots or digging pit-falls: in both, the greater part of the palmated area of the antler was cut away and discarded and the thicker lower part utilized; but, whereas in the case of shed specimens the whole object was fashioned out of antler, in those broken out of the skull the blade was formed from the adhering pedicle bone, so ensuring that the working-edge was made from the tougher material. It was particularly evident on the blades of these objects how important was the role of polishing in the finish of antler tools, a process which had clearly been applied in their final stage to the spear-heads already described. Presumably this was carried out by means of the quartzite rubbing-stones found fairly commonly on the site. Perforation for the insertion of a handle was made in both types close to where the antler began to palmate, but below the point at which it diminished sharply in thickness, and was so contrived that the angle formed by the handle and the main axis of the head was substantially less than a right-angle. In one instance we found the forepart of the wooden handle still in position, due to the fact that it had been hardened in the fire and so become carbonized.

One of the things we noticed about the equipment of the Star Carr people was that they made very little use of bone, in spite of the fact that it was available in even larger quantities than antler. No implements whatever were found of red deer bone. The metacarpal and metatarsal bones of elk were very occasionally cut up into splinters for making spear-heads, and rather more commonly the lateral metacarpal bones were made slightly more pointed for use possibly as bodkins or awls. The only bones used at all commonly were the metacarpals and metatarsals of the urus (aurochs), which, together sometimes with portions from the femur of the same animal, were used to make skin-working tools.

Study of waste products and unfinished specimens showed that in the former case the rough-out for working was obtained by detaching the distal end by means of a deep V-sectioned groove made by a sharp-edged flake and then splitting the remainder from end to end; the pieces of femur on the other hand seem to have been broken out of the wall of the bone. The rough-outs were then trimmed into shape by flaking, just as in flint or stone. In the final stage the working-edge, which because of the shape of the bone was slightly hollowed, was ground and polished, producing a smooth concave edge like that of the tools used among the Central Eskimos for working caribou skins. It is most interesting that the trimming technique used on these bones should have been derived from flint or stone-working—just as the polishing also found on these tools and proper to antler and bone should later have been applied to stone and flint: it shows how easily among people with little or no specialization in the manufacture of tools techniques could be transferred from one craft to another, and illustrates the need to study as broad a range as possible of the material equipment of prehistoric man, organic as well as inorganic.

Even under the relatively favourable conditions at Star Carr one could hardly expect to find more than a comparatively limited proportion of the industrial products of the original inhabitants. Inevitably the picture has to be filled out by inference from what survives. For instance, no trace of leather was found, although the bone scrapers just described and the numerous flint scrapers— scrapers were second only to burins among the flint implements— show clearly enough that the Star Carr people by no means neglected the skins of the animals they took for food. The climate of pre-boreal Britain was still only in the early stages of warming up after the passing of the Ice Age, and even by the end of the period it is unlikely that the July temperature rose to more than 12° Centigrade: clothing must have been one of the first necessities, particularly during the winter months. For hunters, ignorant of weaving, animal skins would have been the obvious material for garments. Although we have no direct knowledge, it may be inferred that the skin clothes worn by Star Carr man resembled those used in the extensive circumpolar regions to-day. For personal adornment he wore necklaces made up of discs of lias stone about the size of a finger-nail, deer teeth and lumps of amber.

Although successful in uncovering the brushwood forming the basis of the living area, our haul of wooden objects was disappointingly small. We failed to find any recognizable portion of bow, or arrow- or spear-shaft, although these must have been common enough; and in the case of the forepart of one of the mattock-handles this only survived because it was partly carbonized. How is this apparent anomaly to be explained? The probability is that the great majority of wooden objects of daily use perished on the surface—and here we must recall that the brushwood we found represented only what had been trodden into the waterlogged mud. Further, all the wood was in extremely soft condition, but, whereas the brushwood was protected by its comparatively tough bark and so could be isolated without great difficulty, wooden artifacts by their very nature were deprived of this covering. By way of illustration the one notable wooden object, the middle portion of a paddle —incidentally the oldest piece of navigational gear yet found anywhere in the world—was almost as soft as the mud in which it lay. Apart from some flattening of the handle, the form of this precious object has survived these nine or ten thousand years quite remarkably, even though grown through with reeds. We had to remove it with the greatest care, and got it back to Cambridge in a container of water, bound to splints in bandages of sodden newspaper.

One of the surprises of the excavation was the discovery of numerous rolls of birch-bark in relatively good condition. They varied in size from the equivalent of the stump of a cigar to a roll consisting of a strip 8 inches wide and 30 long, and the most likely explanation is that they represent the original spools wound off the trees and stored for use. Despite a careful watch, no traces of bark with stitch-marks or other indications of utilization came to light, and the suggestion is that the substance was collected as a source of birch-pitch—a dark resinous material known to have been used in later prehistoric times for mounting arrow-heads on the shafts and similar purposes. We had some confirmation of this from the occurrence of thin cakes resulting from the spilling, while still viscous, of this or a closely allied substance and, again, in the adhesion of more of the same material to a flint microlith of the type that served as the tip of an arrow. Slight traces of what appeared to be birch-pitch were also found on the tangs of two of the antler spear-heads. There seems little doubt that the Star Carr hunters secured the heads of their most important weapons by means of the pitch obtained from the bark of the principal tree flourishing in their territory during pre-boreal times.

Another unexpected feature was the presence of numerous specimens of the bracket fungus *Fomes fomentarius*. Although some of these may have been brought to the site while still adhering to the birch stems on which they commonly grow, their numbers were too great to be explained on any other theory than that they had been gathered by man. The interesting thing is that the outer skin of this particular fungus is well known in European folk-usage as amadou or German tinder, and that several of the Star Carr specimens have in fact been stripped. The conclusion is irresistible that the Star Carr hunters—or more likely their wives—gathered these fungi for tinder. The vital spark could well have been obtained by striking flint with iron pyrites, several abraded lumps of which were found on the site.

It will be apparent that the excavations at Star Carr have told us a good deal about the economic aspects of life in pre-boreal Britain, but little or nothing about its spiritual side. The beads of different substances reflect, indeed, some concern with personal adornment, but no traces of art were found, unless in some undecipherable scratchings on a smooth stone pebble. Of religious belief or practice we found no sign. The only group of finds, other than the beads, which cannot certainly be interpreted in narrowly economic terms, is the group of twenty or more stag frontlets, which had apparently been prepared for wearing as a kind of mask. Although they had all been damaged to a greater or less degree, the frontlets had originally carried their antlers in place but reduced in girth by some two-thirds and hollowed by excavation of the inner core. In their original condition, therefore, they would have retained the profile of the antlers more or less complete, while very greatly reducing their weight. It is difficult to think of any other explanation than that they were intended to be worn on the head. This interpretation is supported by the fact that in every instance where the parietal bones behind the antlers were intact they had been artificially perforated as though for attachment and by the further detail that in a number of cases sharp irregularities could be seen to have been cut away from the rim and inner surface of the brain case. For horned masks of this kind there are many analogies from ethnographic literature, as well as from the archaeological record.

From what we know of their use among recent communities, two main motives suggest themselves: either the frontlets were intended for stalking or even decoying deer, so bringing them within range of the hunter, or they may have been worn in some ritual dance or mime connected with ensuring the fertility of deer (and possibly of man) and with serving to enhance the confidence and solidarity of the hunters. The general character of the site suggests that the first alternative is more likely to be correct in this case; but whether directly functional or whether magical in intent, the masks reflect the overriding preoccupation of the Star Carr people with hunting and in particular with red deer.

Archaeological excavation is, or should be, experimental in character, and though we can choose our site to answer a definite problem, it does not always follow that we find precisely what we anticipate. At Star Carr we certainly recovered sufficient evidence to reconstruct more fully than hitherto the daily life of a group of Mesolithic people in eastern England. On the other hand we proved to be exploring something a good deal more interesting than a version on British soil of the Maglemosian sites known in detail from Danish excavations. In point of fact we had hit on a settlement of what can best be described as proto-Maglemosians. The Star Carr people were not just an English version of the continental Maglemosians: they were much more in the nature of forebears.

There are two reasons for thinking this: for one thing the Star Carr site, being of late pre-boreal age and belonging to a late phase of Zone IV in the forest sequence, is geologically older than the sites of the "classical" Maglemosian, which belong to the full boreal phase of the post-glacial period; and, secondly, detailed study of the material from Star Carr, and more particularly of the antler and bonework, shows that it differs markedly from that known from such sites as Mullerup and Svaerdborg in Denmark and reflects in certain respects a more archaic tradition. The flint industry itself, which gave the original clue to the site, is indeed Maglemosian in general aspect, though even here the narrow flake awls from the Yorkshire site stand out as distinctive. Yet, though absent from the "classical" Maglemosian, these objects are as a matter of fact characteristic of the flint industry recovered from another Danish locality, that of Klosterlund in central Jutland, which dates from approximately the same period as Star Carr. The essential difference between Star Carr and Klosterlund is that at the latter site artifacts of antler and bone had failed to survive. One of the most significant features of the Star Carr industry is that much greater reliance was placed on antler for making spear-heads than on bone. This is a situation exactly the reverse of that found in the classical Maglemosian, but on the contrary carries on an old Upper

Palaeolithic tradition. Moreover, the "groove and splinter" technique employed in the working of antler by the Star Carr people was in widespread use among the Upper Palaeolithic inhabitants of western Europe and was applied to mammoth tusk over extensive tracts of Soviet Russia.

Our excavations at Star Carr have thus proved doubly fruitful. They have in the first place enabled us to study a limited group winning their livelihood some nine or ten thousand years ago amid the rigours of pre-boreal climate, living at what by modern urban values would be termed a squalid standard, yet betraying a remarkably exact knowledge of the resources available in their surroundings of lake, swamp and birch forest. From the wider perspective of European prehistory, on the other hand, they have helped to fill in what had previously been a gap in the evolution of the widespread Maglemosian culture.

III

The New Stone Age
and the
Beginnings of Farming

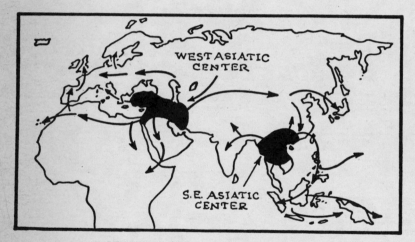

NEOLITHIC ORIGINS AND EXPANSIONS

INTRODUCTORY

THE New Stone, or Neolithic, Age of each region can be said to be the period when people had adopted farming as the basis of their economy, but were still entirely dependent on stone, wood and bone for their tools and weapons. This stage of cultural development did not, of course, exist everywhere at the same time. For example, the Neolithic way of life had been followed in Asia for about four thousand years, and had already come to an end, before it was introduced into Britain. In many parts of the world it persisted until recent times. On the other hand there is an underlying unity in the main Neolithic cultures of the Old World in the sense that the new economy certainly originated in a nuclear area in western Asia, Asia Minor and Iran (p. 249, I), where the wild species of animals and plants were available for domestication, and from there spread to Egypt, through Europe and into central Asia and India. Sometimes this spread was effected by cultural borrowing, but in many areas it was brought about by the gradual advance of farming peoples seeking to find new lands and carrying with them their livestock and seed grain.

In most of this wide area, although there were occasional herding societies that had not adopted agriculture (p. 261, I), the Neolithic economy was based on mixed farming with wheat, barley, cattle, sheep and often pigs. After its very earliest stages it usually led to the adoption of a more or less settled life in villages and farmsteads. Although we now know that in the nuclear area and probably elsewhere a considerable time passed before the invention of ceramics, later Neolithic cultures are characterized by the development of potting, spinning, weaving and other home crafts.

In China the Neolithic way of life appeared relatively late, and millet and pigs were at first the staples of diet. For this reason it has been suggested that farming may have developed independently there, but it seems almost inevitable that at least the idea of agriculture and stock-raising must have percolated through from the west. The same problem arises again in America, where agriculture depended on squash and beans and, a little later, maize, and where domestic animals were never of great importance. An agriculture so completely different from that of the Old World may well have been an independent creation.

The dating of Neolithic cultures has fluctuated widely—one might almost say wildly—during the history of archaeological studies. It has now, one hopes, been stabilized by Carbon-14 and other scientific dating methods. Developing in the nuclear area some nine thousand years ago, it radiated out from it during the next three or four thousand years, reaching Britain on the one hand and western India on the other during the fourth millennium B.C.

The following section first illustrates our present knowledge of farming origins in western Asia, then follows its spread westward into Europe and then into Britain and so to a late-surviving Neolithic society in the Orkneys. It ends with a comparison of the origins of the two most ancient civilizations, those of Mesopotamia and Egypt, which were built on the foundations laid in the Neolithic Age.

GRAHAME CLARK

The Beginning of Farming: Jericho and Jarmo

THE possibility of advancing towards civilization depended in the first instance on a new relationship between man and the animals and plants on which he depended for food. So long as he had to subsist on the game animals, birds and fish he could catch and trap, the insects and eggs he could collect and the foliage, roots, fruits and seeds he could gather, he was limited in the kind of social life he could develop; as a rule he could only live in small groups, which gave small scope for specialization and the sub-division of labour, and in the course of a year he would have to move over extensive tracts of country, shifting his habitation so that he could tap the natural resources of successive areas. It is hardly to be wondered at that among communities whose energies were almost entirely absorbed by the mere business of keeping alive, technology remained at a low ebb. It is true that peoples like the Kwakiutl and Nootka tribes of British Columbia, who were able to win a basic supply of food by catching and storing the salmon that came up their rivers at the spawning season, could maintain permanent settlements, build massive timber houses and support elaborate social institutions involving the ceremonial destruction of wealth. Yet the fact remains that no such peoples, other than the pioneers of farming, were able by their own efforts to emerge from the Stone Age. It was only through the control of breeding of animals and plants that early man was able to ensure himself a reliable and readily expandable source of food and thereby estab-lish a secure basis for cultural advance. The invention of farming was indeed revolutionary in the sense that it alone made possible the rise of literate civilizations, though one does well to remember

From *World Prehistory*. Cambridge: Cambridge University Press; 1961, pp. 76-84. By permission of the Cambridge University Press.

that the new economy was established so gradually and its effects upon other aspects of culture were at first so imperceptible as to be hardly discernible in the archaeological record.

The historic civilizations of the Near East were centered on great rivers: the Euphrates and Tigris, the Nile and, somewhat later, the Indus; but archaeology, supported by radio-carbon dating, makes it clear that the antecedent stages, which witnessed the genesis of farming, metallurgy, urban settlement and a complex social hierarchy, were passed through elsewhere. The birth of farming and the origins of settled life in the Near East occurred somewhere in the zone extending from Palestine, Syria and Cilicia, and thence across the piedmont or foot-hill zone of Turkey and northern Iraq to Iran, the Caspian shore and Turkestan. Whereas the alluvial lands had an arid climate and needed irrigation to render them fertile, the upland territories have a rainfall to-day exceeding 16 inches a year and even at the driest phase of neothermal time must have been relatively more favourable to primitive farmers. Moreover, it was precisely in these latter territories that the prototypes of the relevant crops and livestock flourished in the wild state. At least it is the case that *Triticum dicoccoides* and *Hordeum spontaneum,* progenitors respectively of emmer wheat and barley, the two cereals that dominated agriculture in this zone, are both found wild in just these regions to-day; there is no evidence that either was available in Egypt before being introduced by man; and the only cereal growing wild in Europe, *Triticum aegilopoides,* known from Albania, Yugoslavia and northern Greece, is unlikely to have played a significant part, since *Einkorn, T. monococcum,* to which it gave rise, seems never to have been cultivated as a separate crop and, having as a rule only one grain on a spikelet, was not much use for breeding purposes. Again, though wild prototypes of oxen and swine were rather widely distributed in the temperate zone during neothermal times, wild sheep were much more narrowly confined, the Mouflon variety to a zone from Syria and southern Turkey to Iraq, the Urial to one from the Caspian across Iran to Afghanistan and northern Pakistan, and the Argali to the region from Turkestan to the Uzbek republic. Equally it was the piedmont and mountain zone that held metal ores and so offered conditions favourable to technological advance among societies whose economies long remained on a subsistence basis. It was not until social development was comparatively advanced that occupation of the alluvial territories, involving irrigation of the soil and wholesale importation of basic raw materials, first became feasible.

If the original focus of farming is to be located somewhere within the territory just defined, it is among the advanced hunter-fishers and food-gatherers occupying the area at or near the beginning of neothermal times that we have to seek the innovators, who in a sense were responsible for the whole future of civilization in the Old World. Insufficient is yet known about the Mesolithic peoples of western Asia to allow any firm conclusions to be drawn about those most likely to have been responsible. The possibility has to be allowed that in reality several different groups rose to the same challenge—the desiccation that marked the onset of neothermal times in this area. In any case, even if some one group was in fact ahead of the others, conditions were such that people were more receptive than usual to new ways of easing the burden of subsistence, so that the picture would soon be blurred by diffusion. It would seem therefore that we must await a more exact definition of the Mesolithic groups occupying the region, and above all a network of radio-carbon dates sufficiently close to make it possible to trace the areas where the new form of economy first emerged.

Meanwhile excavations in the Tell es-Sultan, the site of the ancient Jericho, in Jordan and at the mound of Jarmo in the Kurdish foothills of northern Iraq have thrown some welcome light on an early stage in the history of farming. The base of the tell at Jericho yielded traces of the Natufian hunter-fishers, whose remains, previously known from rock-shelters and open stations, mainly in Palestine, are the most complete for any Mesolithic group in western Asia. According to radio-carbon dates they were camping around the spring at Jericho about 7800 B.C. and to judge from the constricted space they occupied it would seem that they formed only a small group, probably a few primary families such as might have lived in the mouth of a large cave. Like their relatives at Mount Carmel they lived mainly by hunting gazelle, and supplemented their diet by harvesting grain by means of reaping knives inset with flint blades. Whether this grain was wild or in any sense domesticated has been much discussed, but it is worth pointing out that wild, self-grown cereals grow in the immediate neighbourhood at the present day and there is no evidence that the Natufians had any special arrangements for storing their grain or that they had developed any true querns or milling-stones, though they certainly used stone rubbers of the type employed in many parts of the world for preparing wild plant foods. Until specimens of the grain harvested by the Natufians have been examined by a competent botanist, one can hardly be sure about its precise status. What is certain is that the Natufians had hardly gained enough control over cereals to affect in any noticeable way their mode of life.

By contrast the forty-five feet or so of archaeological deposits overlying the Natufian layer, though they still yielded no real pottery, gave clear indications of greatly enlarged social groups and of more permanent settlement, and it seems reasonable to

expect that when the plant remains have been reported upon they
will show that definite progress had been made in the domestication of cereals; already comparison of the horn cores of the numerous goats from the site with those of wild ones has given some
evidence for domestication. Two distinct stages have been distinguished in the proto-Neolithic deposits. The earlier one, which
yielded a flint industry in the Natufian tradition, though lacking
certain types and supplemented by ground stone axes, was characterized by well-constructed round huts with sunken floors and
beehive walls made from long oval bricks with flat bases and curved
or hog-backed upper surfaces. In the course of this earlier or "hog's-
back" stage of the proto-Neolithic, which to judge from the flints
was an outgrowth from the Natufian, the settlement, which by now
extended over the whole area of the tell, was defended by a ditch
cut in the solid rock to a depth of 3 metres and a width across the
top of 9 metres, backed by a massive stone wall with great round
towers set at intervals and incorporating inner stairways for man-
ning the defences.

The fact that such primitive people found it necessary to erect
defences on such a scale suggests the presence of rivals at an
analogous stage of development and it seems likely that these are
represented in the upper proto-Neolithic layer that began to form
around 6000 B.C. This need not of course imply that the transition
to a more settled form of life based on incipient farming, added to
the hunting of plentiful game, was made by more than one Mesolithic stock in the region. More likely it reflects the possibility that
the attainment of a more settled way of life favoured the development from the same basic Natufian stock of locally differentiated
communities, and it is noteworthy that the lithic industry in the
upper Jericho level, with its pressure-flaked tanged arrowheads
and heavy, serrated reaping-knife blades compares closely with
that of the Tahunian, previously recognized in the Judaean cave
of El-khiam overlying successive stages of the younger Natufian.
A feature of the upper proto-Neolithic of Jericho is the appearance
of a specialized type of quern, wedge-shaped with a grinding hollow
running out at the broader end, another sign that the use of grain
for food was already long-established. The houses at this level
consisted of rectangular rooms grouped round courtyards in which
the cooking was done: the walls were built of sun-dried bricks on a
stone foundation course and the floors were characteristically made
of clay coated by burnished lime-plaster and covered by rush mats.
Indications of what may have been family shrines were found in
the houses, but the most telling evidence for spiritual development
is to be found in the treatment of the dead. Already in the lower
level the custom of severing the heads from the trunks and burying

them in separate nests seems to have been established, a practice paralleled in a Mesolithic context in South Germany at Ofnet and Kaufertsberg near Nordlingen. A notable feature of the rite as practised by the plaster-floor people at Jericho was the way in which the skulls were filled with clay, the eyes inlaid with shell and the faces finely modelled in clay, the expressions of which are so personal as to suggest veritable portraits. Burial had been accorded to the dead since early in Late Pleistocene times and among Advanced Palaeolithic peoples it had become customary to inter them clothed and with their ornaments in place; but though burial had become formalized as a means of separating the dead from the living and though some differentiation in the objects placed with the dead might be made according to sex, there is no indication that individuals were memorialized as such in those early times. The modelled faces from Jericho on the other hand point the way to the funerary masks and portraits of later and more sophisticated cultures from Pharaonic Egypt to Stuart England. More vividly than anything else, unless it be the scale of the settlement and its defences, they emphasize the significance of the change initiated by hunter-fishers and carried forward during the seventh millennium B.C. by men who added to a plentiful supply of gazelle meat the increment of domesticated cereals and herds of goats, citizens of no mean community who were yet ignorant of pottery, for long regarded as a symbol of settled life.

CARLETON S. COON

Belt Cave and the
First Domestic Animals

BELT CAVE is situated in the foothills of the Elburz mountains in Iran, overlooking the south-east corner of the Caspian plain. Professor Coon was excavating there in the autumn of 1949.

From *Seven Caves*, pp. 141-2, 145-53, 165-7.

❧

THANKS to the local doctor, the next morning I was up early and
back at the wheel, convinced that the caves we sought were ten
miles west of Behshahr, and so they were. For the first time we
passed the limestone outcrop in full daylight, and then rode past a
stream, arriving at some tobacco fields.

A village stood two hundred yards inland from the road; facing
the village and the stream, on the sunny side of the outcrop, was a
beautiful arched sea cave. Both jeeps were immediately abandoned,
as everyone raced across the fields to the cave. There we surprised
two families of dervishes from Sultanabad who had come to the
shore for the winter season. One man was coughing with tubercu-
losis, one woman was nursing a baby, two dogs began barking at
us, and two donkeys, tethered in the back of the chamber, were
craning their necks to see what all the rumpus was about. Although
the dervishes had spread some straw about, and scuffed the surface
making hearths, they had not damaged the deposit. There it stood,
a perfect floor, fifteen feet above the stream bed outside. Before
the sun had set, the dervishes had been lured out—donkeys, dogs,
babies, and all—to take up more sumptuous residence in a tobacco
shed at the expedition's expense. The villagers would not take
them into their houses for fear of fleas.

That day I hired five men from the village, which was named
Turujan. As the dervishes went back and forth removing their few
possessions, my new employees cleaned off the floor, down to the
top of the more permanent part of the usual layer of sheep manure,
the bedded compost in which individual pellets have lost their
identity and been merged into a springy carpet. The cave was
named Ghar-i-Kamarband, or "Belt Cave"—why I did not discover.
In references to this cave which have since appeared in archaeological literature the shorter, translated version, has been used.

During the delay caused by the gradual evacuation of the
dervishes we spent our time studying the position and dimensions
of the cave. Facing north-west, it overlooks a broad expanse of the
Caspian plain. Immediately to the west of it runs a small, intermittent stream, which has built a raised fan of gravel out on to
the plain. The point where the road crosses this fan, about two
hundred yards north of the cave, is the most elevated part of the
roadbed in that neighbourhood. The level of the cave floor above
the Caspian Sea turned out to be sixteen metres, or about fifty-three
feet.

Between the road and the sea we could see two ancient mounds of the village type, the bases of which could hardly have been more than twenty feet above present sea-level. As these mounds might well have been begun as early as 3000 B.C. (a conservative estimate), it was clear that the floor of Belt Cave had been above sea-level since that date at the latest. The ancient beach lying to the north of the road represented an earlier high-water level of unknown age. At the time of its formation Belt Cave would still have been dry. Although I knew little about the history of the Caspian sea-levels, it was obvious that only the highest of them could have disturbed this site.

I laid out a trench on the sunny side of the cave, long enough to give us working room and wide enough to permit passage along the southern side to the rear. In the back we would have a good face; in front we would leave the best material, which is always found in that position, until we had finished Trench A and thoroughly familiarized ourselves with the stratigraphy. Parviz and Abbas immediately demonstrated their skill as excavators. They are the two best pick men I have ever employed except for Murat, another Schmidt alumnus, who joined us a few days later, and who was their peer. As they were good companions as well as intelligent men, I tried to take advantage of their presence by talking with them. This they made easy for me by using simple words and speaking slowly. I was now beginning to understand rudimentary Persian, a very different thing from carrying on polite conversation with educated people, which was unnecessary anyhow because most educated Persians speak either French or English. It was with the class in between, the minor officials, that I really needed the services of an interpreter.

As these men took out the first twenty-centimetre strip, I realized that we faced a complicated problem in stratigraphy, because this thin layer showed a variety of earths from one end of the trench to the other. At the front end, black soil that had drifted in from a bank outside encroached some twenty centimetres over our excavating area. Moving backward, we found this to be followed by a metre, more or less, of yellowish soil, which turned out to be a *lens*—a thin, discontinuous layer of intrusive material. Beyond this we came upon a fine, greyish soil, composed of a mixture of brown earth and wood ash. In it the blackened remains of many hearths were visible. In the back half of the trench, some five to ten centimetres of peated manure still overlay this grey earth.

The grey earth was pay dirt. It contained a wealth of flint, bone, and pottery, including twenty-three flint blades of the finest and most delicate quality, and of Neolithic type. The potsherds seemed to represent various periods from what could have been Neolithic to modern wares, and the bones were those of domestic animals, particularly sheep, goats, and cattle. By the time we had finished this first level, which in most caves is unproductive, we were aware of our good fortune. We had found Neolithic remains right at the very top of the deposit, and would not have to remove metres of more recent materials, such as Islamic, Achaemenian (First Persian Empire), or Bronze Age, to get at the implements, pottery, and animal bones that we needed for the solution of an important problem. That was: what part had the Caspian shore region, in which so many early European-type cultural survivals were to be seen, played in the origin of the Neolithic of Europe?

In the second twenty-centimetre strip, now all in grey earth, we found two Neolithic *celts*—small, jewel-like axe-heads of polished stone, one of them of jade. Not a single trace of metal appeared here or at any point farther down. In the second level a few sherds of more modern type still appeared in the front of the trench, but in level No. 3 all of them were of a single type, a coarse, thick, mealy, ill-fired ware, made by hand without the potter's wheel, rubbed with ochre, and burnished with pebbles. It did not resemble in any way the usual Neolithic pottery of the Fertile Crescent and Iranian plateau, which is thinner and harder and either solid grey or painted with geometric or animal designs. Mr. Samadie, who had studied pottery in the Tehran Museum and on other digs, had never seen anything like it. It appeared to be a true early Neolithic ware.

We excavated five levels on that first day. The next day was Friday, normally a day of rest, but the men wanted to work and we had no objection. In level No. 6 it was soon apparent that we were moving below the pottery horizon: only eight pieces came out, and those in the very front, where the strata sloped downward and outward a little under the dune. In No. 7 Parviz found near the front of the trench a perfect limestone globe, about six inches in diameter, pierced with a hole drilled conically from both ends, presumably with a stone drill, and lipped at both openings. A second pierced stone of inferior workmanship soon followed it. Much speculation ensued as to the purpose of these objects. Some said they were loom weights, others net-sinkers, still others anchors for boats. I did not find the answer until many months later, when Dr. Robert Braidwood, of Chicago, who had done much digging in Neolithic sites in Iraq, visited the University Museum. They were, he said, digging-stick weights. When one was hafted on a pointed stick, a foot or eighteen inches above its tip, an early root-digger or farmer could press the point into the soil by treading with his bare foot on the globe's upper surface. We examined the globes with this in view, and, sure enough, the surfaces were polished from such use.

Level No. 8 was entirely without pottery, and we found no more in this trench except one spook in level No. 10. A *spook* is a potsherd or other specimen that is found in an apparently undisturbed level in which it does not rightfully belong. Its presence can be explained in several ways: by the action of roots—and roots went down four metres in this cave; by falling down the hole of a prehistoric burrowing animal such as a mole vole or small rodent; or by slipping down along the rock wall of the side of the cave, where air spaces sometimes occur, probably owing to water action. At any rate, the presence of spooks is interpreted statistically. One or two may be forgiven for being in the wrong place, but if too many turn up, then either they indicate a disturbance, as where someone has dug a grave through several levels, or else they really belong in the place in which they are found and must be interpreted as trade objects or part of the local toolkit of that period.

In levels No. 8 to No. 10 we not only lost the pottery, but also most of the fine flint blades, particularly the ones that show polish on the cutting edge when turned about in the light. This polish is an overlay of silica granules deposited on the surfaces of flint blades used as reaping-knives. Silica is found in the stems of all grasses, including cereals. Millions of years before, the teeth of the horse family had become adapted to the rapid wear that a diet of silica-bearing stalks imposes, and in Neolithic times the flint blades that early farmers used for cutting these stalks were polished in the process. Whenever these polished blades turn up, one may be reasonably sure that the people who made them were farmers. Food-gatherers who collect wild-grass seeds have no time for reaping and threshing, for wild grasses spill or eject their seeds the moment they are ripe, and people must be present with sticks and baskets to gather as many as they can at that moment. Cultivated grains hold their seeds in the glumes or pods until they have been reaped. In levels No. 8 to No. 10 we had no certain indication of agriculture, but plenty of evidence of animal-husbandry, for the bones of the four standard barnyard animals, ox, pig, sheep, and goat, continued down, with ox, and pig at the top and only sheep and goat at the bottom.

In two days we had found in Trench A an early Neolithic industry that had pottery, following, without soil change or interruption, a still earlier Neolithic that lacked it. Whereas the ceramic Neolithic people had reaped grain and herded cows and pigs as well as sheep and goats, the pre-ceramic Neolithic people, who can have been their immediate ancestors, had been simple herdsmen, pasturing only sheep and goats. This was the first time to my knowledge that this cultural transition had been recorded. I did not believe then, however, nor do I now, that these folk were the inventors of pottery, for what they used, though crude by later standards, was too stylized and too good to have been invented on the spot at the time this deposit was laid down. The technique must have evolved elsewhere. Neither can I believe that these people were the Old World's first farmers or first herdsmen. Finding a "first" is an exciting thing, and it is easy to delude oneself into believing that one has done so. On a simple statistical basis, if one site and one site only is dug in an area thousands of miles in extent in which some trait or combination of traits may have been discovered, it is too much to ask of the law of chance that the first archæologist who digs a hole in the ground should locate the exact site where the invention took place.

The floor of level No. 10 was also the bottom of the Neolithic soil. Although the colour of the earth did not perceptibly change, its consistency did, as Parviz immediately noticed. Whereas the upper soil had been soft and loose, and had contained a few large stones, this new earth was harder to excavate, owing to the presence of many small chips of limestone. In this respect it resembled the Palaeolithic-bearing soil of equal depth at Bisitun. There was also a change in the soil's contents. The flint yield of the previous afternoon had been mostly scrap pieces, but now we began to remove implements that belonged to a new and distinct industry. Exotic honey-coloured flint pieces came out in the forms of retouched blades, backed blades, and snub-nosed scrapers of the type used for cleaning the flesh from the insides of skins. This was not a Neolithic assemblage at all. It had to be either Palaeolithic or Mesolithic—at the time I could not tell which. Later we found that it was Mesolithic, which is a term covering the various industries used by hunters between the end of the last glaciation and the beginning of agriculture, roughly from 9000 to 5400 B.C., the dates varying in different places.

Most conspicuous among the animal remains were the horn cores of an animal then unknown to us. Later on, in America and in England, it took me much time and consultation with zoologists to identify it. It turned out to be *Gazella subgutturosa Güldenstädt*, the goitred gazelle, described as follows by Mochi and Carter: "General colour pale sandy with indistinct side band. In winter the colour paler and the coat much thicker. Female either lacking or with poorly developed horns. Derives its name from the swelling of the larynx in the male during the breeding season. From northwest Iran and Asia Minor east to the southern Gobi Desert."

Although no goitred gazelles graze, as far as I know, in the neighbourhood of Belt Cave today, the presence of their bones in level No. 11 and below does not indicate a climate radically different from that of today. It might have been a little colder then than now, and it was certainly drier, for the nearest border of the grasslands on which the goitred gazelle could have grazed is now at least forty miles to the north-east of the cave, on the Turkoman steppe east of the Caspian Sea. It is conceivable but hardly likely that the principal food animal of these Mesolithic people would have been carried over forty miles for every feast. The border of the steppe must have been much closer at that time than it is now.

All the horn cores were abraded at the tips, indicating some use. As the cores were shaped exactly like the picks that Parviz and Murat were using, and as the Persian word for pick, *kolang*, is a cognate of the old Indo-European root for *horn*, as in Latin *cornus*, I concocted the theory which I can neither substantiate nor disprove, that these people used the horns of the goitred gazelle for digging, just as Bushmen and their women in the Kalahari dig with oryx horns today. The Mesolithic people ate the rest of the animal, as was evident from the great quantity of their bones.

In the Neolithic levels the bones of sheep and goats bore a high ratio of immature specimens: twenty-five per cent in the pre-ceramic and fifty per cent in the ceramic. This meant that the animals were domesticated, because hunters rarely kill the young. The gazelle bones were nearly all those of mature animals. Furthermore, the domestic animal bones were white, fatty-feeling, soft, and light, whereas the gazelle bones and those of the other wild animals were brown, hard, glossy, and heavy.

The reason is that wild animals always arrive at a state of natural balance with the other elements in their environment over periods of thousands of years, through nature's version of the trial-and-error process. By a rigid process of natural selection, the plants that wild animals eat have acquired their present sizes, shapes, leaf colours, and ways of flowering. They have thus become perfectly suited to the local variations in temperature, rainfall, wind velocity, and other meteorological features, to the local soil composition, and to the activities of animal species, including the bees that fertilize them and the hoofed creatures that derive sustenance from their stems and leaves. During the same period the local animals have been just as rigidly selected by nature as the plants, and adapted especially to the nutritional qualities of their plant foods. The relationship between animals and plants is like that of an eland with the bird that sits on his back, removing insect pests. Wild grasses are never over-grazed and the wild animals that live on them are sleek and in good flesh, as anyone who has visited an African game park knows.

When man began breeding animals he started with a poor lot

anyhow, the ones that he was able to catch and tame. As time went on he began selecting them for qualities which had nothing to do with the balance of nature, but which suited his own needs. Thus, he bred animals that yielded exaggerated quantities of wool, milk, and fat; animals with thick fleeces, pendulous udders, and chubby bodies, caricatures of their wild cousins that still browsed the forests or leaped from crag to crag in the mountains. These unnatural beasts had developed nutritional requirements different from those of their free-ranging ancestors, and as they were also confined by herdsmen to smaller pastures than before, they upset the delicate balance between plants and animals which had hitherto obtained. Overgrazing led to soil-erosion, and in some parts of the world with less rainfall than the Caspian shore, man-made deserts came into being.

Meanwhile, the meat that the herdsmen ate came to differ from the hunter's fare. Animals living under domestication tend to have slender bones, tender flesh, and much fat. The body type that they have achieved under human interference with natural laws is exactly the one that in man himself is most prone to degenerative diseases, particularly coronary attacks, linked to high cholesterol content, and in this sense the Neolithic farmers ate food inferior to that of hunters. This change in body type was reflected in the special appearance and texture of the bones of Neolithic animals, which I soon learned to distinguish from the Mesolithic bones of wild animals by a simple sense of touch, as anyone could. The Neolithic bones feel greasy and light, and the Mesolithic ones polished and heavy.

The Mesolithic hunters apparently used bows and arrows. We knew this because we found many beautiful small backed blades of flint which could be gummed to the tips of arrows as barbs. Along with their staple diet of goitred-gazelle meat these hunters ate quantities of swan, goose, bustard, and grouse, and hunted with the domestic dog. The possession of the bow and the dog gave Mesolithic man a great advantage over his Palaeolithic predecessors, who had to hunt in groups in which some men would do the dog's work of driving and flushing game toward the killers. The hunter's task was made immeasurably easier by substituting the bow for the spear. A bow, in fact, is superior to a muzzle-loading gun in that it can be loaded much more quickly and makes no noise to frighten the game. The men who lived in Belt Cave during the period represented by levels No. 11 to No. 21 must have been prosperous and well-fed by any standards.

During the second season we therefore collected large charcoal samples from hearths at all levels, placing them in glass bottles purchased at the pharmacy next door to the hotel. These bottles bore the label MALE FERN EXTRACT, a substance whose use baffled me until I discovered later, after much inquiry and many evasive answers, that it was worm medicine. Abbas and Murat in particular became ardent charcoal-collectors, picking it up in tongs and placing it in tinfoil to avoid contaminating it, and the sieve men saved every fleck of it. We got much more than we needed, so that several runs could be made, in more than one laboratory, if warranted. Later it was analysed in our own laboratory in Philadelphia, where the following dates were obtained:

CERAMIC NEOLITHIC
   (3 *samples*)   7,280±260 B.P.=   5330 B.C.

PRE-CERAMIC NEOLITHIC
   (2 *samples*)   7,790±330 B.P.=   5840 B.C.

GAZELLE MESOLITHIC
   (2 *samples*)   8,570±380 B.P.=   6620 B.C.

INTERVENING YELLOW SOIL
   (1 *sample*)   12,275±380 B.P.=10,325 B.C.

SEAL MESOLITHIC
   (2 *samples*)   11,480±550 B.P.=   9530 B.C.

   [B.P.=Before Present]

These dates made sense both internally and when compared to those from other Neolithic and Mesolithic sites. Our ceramic Neolithic was still the oldest so far found in the world, though how long it will hold that title is questionable. Its date, more than two millennia older than the oldest Neolithic of Europe, clearly indicates that the Caspian shore may indeed have been a Neolithic breeding-ground from which some of our ancestors moved westward into northern Europe. At least, it may have been part of such a breeding-ground. The date for the pre-ceramic Neolithic falls earlier, as it should. Although the probable errors of the two samples overlap by some eighty years, the order of dates is that of the stratigraphy, and there can be no question that herding was earlier in this area than pottery, and probably also earlier than agriculture. The Gazelle Mesolithic is separated from the Neolithic by a clean gap in time, as the condition and slope of the floor between them indicated, and the Seal Mesolithic is also similarly isolated. The only inconsistency in this series is the date of the yellow soil found in the front of the cave between the two Mesolithic layers. Although older than that of the Seal Mesolithic, it falls inside the latter's range of probability.

If I might venture to interpret this series, I would say that the varved clay at the bottom of Belt Cave, which is as old as 10,000 B.C., was laid down at a time when the high level of the Caspian, possibly as high as eighty-five feet above its present surface, had fallen off and the mouth of Belt Cave was open to the air. By 9500 B.C. the cave had become dry enough for habitation, and it was occupied by hunters who mainly killed seals, on or near the shore, and who had already acquired two of the principal assets of Mesolithic life: the bow and arrow, and the dog. For some reason they departed, and after about three thousand years other Mesolithic hunters, pursuers of the goitred gazelle, occupied the cave, which was now situated in a much drier countryside, one in which the grassland of the Turkoman steppe came within a few miles of their door. Then again the cave was abandoned and herdsmen moved in, eventually to become farmers.

JOHN EVANS

The Polished Stone Axe

JOHN EVANS was writing when the existence of a Neolithic period characterized by polished stone tools had recently been established. He distinguishes it from the Stone Age of the Caverns (usually to be identified with the Upper Palaeolithic) and of the Drift (the Lower Palaeolithic).

To COME nearer home, it is not to be expected that in this country, the earliest written history of which (if we except the slight account derived from merchants trading hither), comes from the pen of foreign conquerors, we should have any records of the Stone Age. In Caesar's time, the tribes with which he came in contact were already acquainted with the use of iron, and were, indeed, for the most part immigrants from Gaul, a country whose inhabitants had, by war and commerce, been long brought into close relation with the more civilized inhabitants of Italy and Greece. I have elsewhere shown that the degree of civilization which must be conceded to

From *Ancient Stone Implements of Great Britain*, pp. 10-13, 56-8.

those maritime tribes far exceeds what is accorded by popular belief. The older occupants of Britain, who had retreated before the Belgic invaders, and occupied the western and northern parts of the island, were no doubt in a more barbarous condition; but in no case in which they came in contact with their Roman invaders do they seem to have been unacquainted with the use of iron. Even the Caledonians, in the time of Severus, who tattooed themselves with the figures of animals, and went nearly naked, carried a shield, a spear, and a sword, and wore iron collars and girdles; they however deemed these latter ornamental and an evidence of wealth, in the same way as other barbarians esteemed gold.

But though immediately before and after the Christian era the knowledge of the use of iron may have been general throughout Britain, and though probably an acquaintance with bronze, at all events in the southern part of the island, may probably date many centuries farther back, it by no means follows, as I cannot too often repeat, that the use of stone for various purposes to which it had previously been applied should suddenly have ceased on a superior material, in the shape of metal, becoming known. On the contrary, we know that the use of certain stone weapons was contemporary with the use of bronze daggers, and the probability is that in the poorer and more inaccessible parts of the country, stone continued in use for many ordinary purposes long after bronze, and possibly even iron, was known in the richer and more civilized districts.

Sir William Wilde informs us that in Ireland "stone hammers, and not unfrequently stone anvils, have been employed by country smiths and tinkers in some of the remote country districts until a comparatively recent period." The same use of stone hammers and anvils for forging iron prevails among the Kaffirs of the present day. In Iceland also, perforated stone hammers are still in use for pounding dried fish, driving in stakes, for forging and other purposes; "knockin'-stones" for making pot-barley, have till recently been in use in Scotland, if not still employed; and I have seen fruit-hawkers in the streets of London cracking Brazil nuts between two stones.

With some exceptions it is, therefore, nearly impossible to say whether an ancient object made of stone can be assigned with absolute certainty to the Stone Period or no. Much will depend upon the circumstances of the discovery, and in some instances the form may be a guide.

The remarks I have just made apply most particularly to the weapons, tools, and implements belonging to the period more immediately antecedent to the Bronze Age, and extending backwards in time through an unknown number of centuries. For besides the

objects belonging to what was originally known by the Danish antiquaries as the Stone Period, which are usually found upon or near
the surface of the soil, in encampments, on the site of ancient
habitations, and in tumuli, there are others which occur in caverns
beneath thick layers of stalagmite, and in ancient alluvia, in both
cases usually associated with the remains of animals either locally
or entirely extinct. In no case do we find any trace of metallic tools
or weapons in true association with the stone implements of the old
ossiferous caverns, or with those of the beds of gravel, sand, and
clay deposited by the ancient rivers; and, unlike the implements
found upon the surface and in graves, which in many instances are
ground or polished, those from the caves, and from what are termed
by geologists the Quaternary gravels, are, so far as at present
known, invariably chipped only, and not ground, besides as a rule
differing in form.

This difference in the character of the implements of the two
periods, and the vast interval of time between the two, I pointed out
in 1859, at the time when the discoveries of M. Boucher de Perthes,
in the Valley of the Somme, first attracted the attention of English
geologists and antiquaries. Since then, the necessity of subdividing
what had until then been regarded as the Stone Age into two distinct stages, an earlier and a later, has been universally recognized;
and Sir John Lubbock has proposed to call them the Palæolithic and
the Neolithic Periods respectively, terms which have met with almost general acceptance, and of which I shall avail myself in the
course of this work. In speaking of the polished and other implements belonging to the time when the general surface of the country had already received its present configuration, I may, however,
also occasionally make use of the synonymous term Surface Period
for the Neolithic, and shall also find it convenient to treat the Palæolithic Period under two subdivisions—those of the River-gravels and
of the Caves, the fauna and implements of which are not in all cases
identical.

In passing the different kinds of implements, weapons, and ornaments formed of stone under review, I propose to commence with
an examination of the antiquities of the Neolithic Period, then to
proceed to the stone implements of human manufacture discovered
imbedded with ancient mammalian remains in Caverns, and to
conclude with an account of the discoveries of flint implements in
the Drift or River-gravels in various parts of England. But before
describing their forms and characters, it will be well to consider the
method of manufacture by which the various forms were produced.

The general form of stone celts is well known, being usually that
of blades, approaching an oval in section, with the sides more or
less straight, and one end broader and also sharper than the other.

In length they vary from about two inches to as much as sixteen inches. I do not, however, propose to enter at once into any description of the varieties in their form and character, but to pass in review some of the opinions that have been held concerning their nature and origin.

One of the most universal of these is a belief, which may almost be described as having been held "*semper, ubique et ab omnibus,*" in their having been thunderbolts.

"The country folks of the West of England still hold that the 'thunder-axes' they find, once fell from the sky." In Cornwall they still have medical virtues assigned to them; the water in which "a thunderbolt," or celt, has been boiled being a specific for rheumatism. In the North of England, and in parts of Scotland, they are known as thunderbolts, and, like flint arrowheads, are supposed to have preservative virtues, especially against diseases of cattle. In Ireland the same superstition prevails, and I have myself known an instance where, on account of its healing powers, a stone celt was lent among neighbours to place in the troughs from which cattle drank.

In the British Museum is a thin highly polished celt of jadeite, reputed to be from Scotland, mounted in a silver frame, and with a hole bored through it at either end. It is said to have been attached to a belt and worn round the waist as a cure for renal affections, against which the material nephrite was a sovereign remedy.

In most parts of France, and in the Channel Islands, the stone celt is known by no other name than "*Coin de foudre,*" or "*Pierre de tonnerre*"; and Mr. F. C. Lukis gives an instance of a flint celt having been found near the spot where a signal-staff had been struck by lightning, which was proved to have been the bolt by its peculiar smell when broken. M. Ed. Jacquard has written an interesting paper on "Céraunies ou pierres de tonnerre."

In Brittany a stone celt is frequently thrown into the well for purifying the water or securing a continued supply; and in Savoy it is not rare to find one of these instruments rolled up in the wool of the sheep, or the hair of the goat, for good luck, or for the prevention of the rot or putrid decay.

In Sweden they are preserved as a protection against lightning, being regarded as the stone-bolts that have fallen during thunderstorms.

In Norway they are known as Tonderkiler, and in Denmark the old name for a celt was Torden-steen. The test of their being really thunderbolts was to tie a thread round them, and place them on hot coals, when, if genuine, the thread was not burnt, but rather rendered moist. Such celts promote sleep.

In Germany both celts and perforated stone axes are regarded

as thunderbolts (*Donnerkeile* or *Thorskeile*); and, on account of
their valuable properties, are sometimes preserved in families for
hundreds of years. I possess a specimen from North Germany, on
which is inscribed the date 1571, being probably the year in which
it was discovered. The curious perforated axe or hammer found
early in the last century, now preserved in the Museum of Antiquities at Upsala, seems to have been a family treasure of the same
kind. It bears upon it, in early Runes, an inscription thus interpreted
by Professor Stephens—"Owns Oltha this Axe." Another, with four
Runic characters upon it, was found in Denmark, and it has been
suggested that the letters on it represent the names of Loki, Thor,
Odin, and Belgthor. The appearance of the American inscribed axe
from Pemberton, New Jersey, described by my namesake, Dr. J. C.
Evans, and published by Sir Daniel Wilson, is not calculated to inspire confidence in its authenticity.

The German belief is much the same as the Irish. Stone celts are
held to preserve from lightning the house in which they are kept.
They perspire when a storm is approaching; they are good for diseases of man and beast; they increase the milk of cows; they assist
the birth of children; and powder scraped from them may be taken
with advantage for various childish disorders. It is usually nine
days after their fall before they are found on the surface.

GEOFFREY BIBBY

The Swiss Lake Dwellings

THE excavation of the Lake Dwellings provided the first full picture
of a Neolithic culture in Europe. It has recently become apparent
that these villages did not stand on piles well out into the lake, but
above the mud of the shore. The earliest are now known to date
back to about 4000 B.C.

From *The Testimony of the Spade*, pp. 201-13.

THE WINTER of 1853 was the dryest and coldest within living memory. All winter little snow fell and such snow as there was was locked up until late into the spring on the high mountains that form the backcloth to the Lake of Zurich. All over Switzerland the rivers ran low, and the levels of the lakes dropped. The level of Lake Zurich was the lowest that the oldest inhabitant could remember. Wide expanses of stony beach were exposed where normally the clear glacier waters of the lake extended. On the stone at Stäfa, where for centuries unusually high and unusually low water levels had been recorded, the watermark of 1674 had always been considered the lowest known in Swiss history. But in the spring of 1854 the water lay a full foot below this mark. On the Rhone, the Aare, and the Limmat, remains of Roman construction which had been hidden for centuries came to light with the dropping of the waters.

The unusual situation was put to good use by the land-hungry farmers along the lake shores. Land-reclamation projects were started everywhere where the lake shores exposed stretches of dry land. The system was simple and effective. Massive stone and earth walls were built out from the normal shore line and along the edge of the receded waters. The area thus enclosed was then filled up with rich alluvial mud dredged up from the shallow waters beyond the walls. Thereby the new lake shore was made permanent and a new field won.

At Obermeilen, on the north side of Lake Zurich some six miles from the city of Zurich at the foot of the lake, the local inhabitants set to work to reclaim two fields in this way from the wide and shallow bay on which their village lay. But when they came to dredge up the mud from beyond the new walls they found an unexpected hindrance. Just below the surface of the mud they met with a whole forest of piles, stout pointed balks of timber, seven to twelve feet long, which had been driven into the soft mud a foot or so apart. On investigating further to try to find a place where they could dredge without hindrance, they discovered that the piles stretched the whole length of the bay in a broad belt four hundred yards wide and commencing about three hundred paces offshore. . . .

It was soon noted that the mud being dredged up contained a variety of unusual objects. The large number of bones and pieces of flint and fragments of worked wood which first turned up were disregarded and tipped without further thought into the reclaimed area. But the first bronze axes and bracelets to come up on the grabs gave the workmen pause. Here was something that could not be ignored. Wiser heads were needed, they thought, to explain such strange objects, and one evening a deputation of the farmers went up to the house of the village schoolmaster, Johannes Aeppli, with a representative collection of the objects they were finding.

Johannes Aeppli immediately saw that here was a site of un-paralleled historical importance. He instructed the workmen to put to one side everything of human workmanship, and himself spent several days with the dredgers, picking out bronzes, flint knives, and axes of deer antler. When he was sure of his facts he wrote a letter to the Zurich Antiquarian Society in which he said: "In the neighbourhood of my home, in the lake bed left uncovered by the water, there are found relics of the work of man's hands which, it would seem, might throw light on the earliest inhabitants of our land." The letter was delivered to the president of the Antiquarian Society, Professor Ferdinand Keller.

Ferdinand Keller was at that time fifty-three years old and, after twenty years as president of the Zurich Antiquarian Society, was recognized as one of the foremost archaeologists in Switzerland. He was not, however, professor af archaeology, but of English! . . .

A working party moved out to Obermeilen and began combing the site. It was an investigation that would make a modern archae-ologist shudder. All the objects lay buried in the peaty mud below the shallow waters of the lake. There was no possibility of systematic digging or accurate recording. Half the party investigated the soil dredged up by the land-reclaimers, breaking up the clods and pick-ing up any objects found in them. The others coasted over the sunken piles in shallow-draft boats, examining the lake bed and picking up with grabs any objects showing there. It was a respect-able pile of miscellaneous objects which they had assembled by the time the rise of the water with the summer thaw put an end to their work. There was a considerable quantity of bronzes—flat axes with rudimentary flanges along the sides, and more massive axes with a hole for the shaft. A variety of flint implements gave a picture of an incredibly advanced technique. There were axes, too, of flint, with helves formed of stag antler in a hole in which the flint blade was mounted. Chisels formed of finely struck flint blades were neatly mounted in antler handles, while other blades were mounted lengthwise, for use as knives, in semicircular wooden grips. The finding of wood was the greatest surprise. This was the first major discovery in waterlogged soil, and it had not previously been realized that water could preserve a whole variety of objects which decay completely away when exposed to the air. But it was not only wood that was preserved. Fragments of basketry and mat-ting, scraps of cloth and of netting were also found. And among the debris were thousands of bones, identified by the Zurich zoologists as those of deer and fox, goat and pig, cattle and sheep and dogs.

The examination of the forest of piles went on simultaneously with the dredging for treasure trove. It became obvious that the piles had been driven in in rough rows, and in some places cross-beams could still be distinguished connecting the piles, and traces of flooring could be made out above the beams. . . .

It was in that year [1858] that excavation commenced on the most famous site of them all, that of Robenhausen, by the little lake of Pfäffikon, a scant score of miles from Zurich. The lake of Pfäffikon acts as a natural reservoir, banking up the waters from the surrounding hills until they can run out by way of the River Aa. The Aa cuts through the terminal moraine blocking the lake end and was used during the last century to supply power to a spinnery at the little village of Robenhausen. In the course of time the banked-up waters had deposited quantities of silt and vegetable refuse at the foot of the lake, forming a thick layer of peat, and across the peat the Aa meandered toward its outlet through the moraine.

In the winter of 1857 the work of straightening and deepening the course of the Aa through the peat morass was set in hand, in order to ensure a constant water supply to the spinning-mill. And in February of 1858 the workmen making a new cut for the river to short-circuit a bend came upon in the peat the now familiar phenomenon of rows of wooden piles. The same evening they went up to the house of a farm labourer in the village and told him that they had found him the pile village for which he had been looking.

Jakob Messikommer was no ordinary farm labourer. He was twenty-nine years old, a lean, wiry, rawboned man, accustomed to working from dawn to dusk in all weathers and prepared to turn his hand to any of the multifarious jobs that country life demands. But he had at the same time a sharp eye, a disciplined imagination and a taste for learning. Compelled at the age of fifteen, through the death of his father and the necessity of supporting his mother and his three younger brothers and sisters, to leave secondary school after only a year and a half's attendance, he made up for it by reading anything on which he could lay his hands. . . .

Messikommer at once reported his discovery to Keller, in time for it to be included in the second pile-dwelling report, and thereafter spent all the time he could spare working at the diggings and collecting the objects that came up. When the cut was completed he could not bear to think of abandoning the site and going back to his humdrum work on the land. He scraped together all his savings and bought the land on either side of the cut. Fortunately, its value was not great; it was useless for grazing or agriculture and was used only as a source of peat fuel.

For the next fifty years and more, until well into the eighties, Jakob Messikommer dug regularly on his site, methodically staking out small plots and excavating them one after the other. His son has left us a detailed description of the course of a typical excavation and of the technique that mounting years of experience recommended. Only a small section could be dug at any one time, perhaps six yards by three, as otherwise the quantity of water draining into the site could not be kept under control by the wooden buckets and hand pumps that were the only means available.

First Messikommer and his helpers would remove the first foot or so of earth, which never contained artifacts. From then on they took greater care, as at this level the tops of the piles might well be found and the wood was so waterlogged that it could be cut through by the spade like cheese. Every spadeful of soil had to be broken up by hand and examined, for small objects might well be encountered already. In the course of the first day the workmen would reach a depth of three to four feet, and already it would be necessary to dig a drainage sump at one end of the excavation and set one man to the task of hauling up the accumulated water by bucket. The next day, work would proceed until the level corresponding to the surface of the lake was reached, and now it would be necessary, if it was desired to go deeper, to sink a cage in the sump hole and to use a hand pump continuously to keep the water down. By now the piles would be standing clear in serried ranks, and it would be seen that their tops stood at two, and sometimes at three, different levels. For it was one of the most important features of Robenhausen that there had been three different phases of occupation. Twice the village that had stood here had been burned down, and twice rebuilt, before, after a third conflagration, it had been abandoned. The layers of burned wood and wattle marking the three burnings could be clearly seen in the sides of the pit, and they allowed the objects recovered from the successive stages of the occupation to be kept separate from one another.

A single excavation did not give many objects, a fact that disappointed the frequent visitors to the site, who normally came with the expectation of seeing every spadeful uncover something exciting. A typical list from one pit comprised two pottery vessels, three stone implements and two pieces of worked bone, a saddle quern, a number of bones, and a store of hazelnuts.

But as section after section was opened up, the collection of objects reached impressive dimensions. Axes of stone and flint set in antler sleeves, knives of flint in antler and wooden handles, chisels of flint and bone, awls and needles of bone and antler slivers, harpoons and spearheads of antler, arrowheads of flint, weaving-weights of stone and spinners of wood, net weights and

floats, wooden knives and daggers, wooden cups and ladles, pottery
of diverse shapes and sizes all gave a many-sided picture of life
in this most primitive of all villages. Even more important were
the more perishable objects that had been preserved by the slightly
acid water of the peat bog: balls and skeins of flaxen thread, tassels
and plaited beltwork, fragments of fishing-nets and ropes, of woven
cloth and piled matting, wickerwork baskets and raffia-worked mats.
And among it all lay the evidence for the diet of the inhabitants:
bones of domestic and game animals, stores of grain and whole
ears of barley, emmer and flax, heaps of hazelnuts and the scorched
remains of apples and fir cones. Unlike the settlement of Obermeilen, Robenhausen gave practically no bronze, only two metal
objects being ever found there—one a simple flat ax blade of copper, and the other, found at some distance from the actual site, a
bronze ax blade with rudimentary flanges, exactly of the Obermeilen
type . . .

The vanished world of the pile villages had become very real
to the people of Europe during the thirty years in which Ferdinand
Keller had been leading and interpreting its investigation. The
diversified nature of the remains had enabled a many-sided picture
of the life of the lake peoples to be built up, and many of the Swiss
museums had been able to construct accurate scale models of
actual villages which brought the prehistoric inhabitants of Switzerland very close. With such a wealth of material it was not difficult
for visitors to see in their mind's eye a vivid sequence of pictures
from the past.

JACQUETTA HAWKES

First Farmers in Britain

THIS SPREAD of the deciduous trees [after the Ice Age] was probably hastened by another event—the junction of the North
Sea with the Channel and the ensuing isolation of Britain. To us

From *A Land*. London: The Cresset Press Ltd.; 1951, pp. 153-9. By permission of The
Cresset Press Ltd.

now, islanders of such long standing, this seems a dramatic and significant happening, but for the scattered groups of food gatherers it can have meant very little. They were familiar with stretches of coast, but can hardly have comprehended islands and continents, for neither interest nor knowledge stretched much beyond their own hunting grounds. Even those communities that lived in the southeast cannot have been much affected, for the channel widened only gradually, and boats were now an effective part of man's equipment. The conditions in northern Britain had so far improved that Mesolithic hunters and fishermen were able to push up the west coast of Scotland, while even the exposed Pennines were much visited as summer hunting grounds. But the population remained small, and although some tribes, particularly those living in southeast and eastern England, had heavy flint axes capable of felling and shaping timber, the mark they could make on the face of Britain must have been slight indeed. A few trees cut—extending here and there to a small clearing; boats moving on the rivers and along the shore; some huddles of low-roofed huts, sometimes on platforms raised above the marsh, sometimes with floors sunk into the ground for greater warmth and shelter. On winter nights their fires might throw a ring of light, marking out a diminutive and weakly held human world, but a world lit by the sound of voices, by the faint flickering of mind.

Turning away from these islands to see the ancient world as a whole, it is plain that these small encampments were already backward, their way of life no longer the only way known to men. In late Palaeolithic times Europe had been supreme, the work of her artists the greatest achievement the world had known, but now the continent was stagnant, choked and deadened by interminable forests. While European savages were still using their cunning to live off their lands without changing them or imposing themselves, many Eastern societies had long abandoned this passive habit. This is not the place to repeat the familiar, though still astonishing, history of the sudden rise of civilization in the Middle East, where within a few thousand years city life had grown from its roots in primitive agriculture and stock raising. Nor is it my purpose to trace in detail the story of the slow, indirect and partial impact of this revolution on life in Britain, of the three thousand years that it took for the elementary ideas of a farming economy to spread so far among the western mists, storms and forests. They did come, even while the yet more difficult idea that in the place of his ring of firelight man could create his own world within city walls was delayed in the Mediterranean for another two thousand years. When about 2500 B. C. Neolithic peoples began to reach Britain across the still narrow sleeve of the Channel, they brought, with their livestock and seed wheat and barley, a promise of deep-seated change. Peering through time, it is easy to ignore the solidity of the past, to see abstractedly "the Introduction of Farming." I want only to remember that there was a day, as real as to-day when the hens are cackling in my neighbours' back garden and Mr. Bevin is flying back from another United Nations conference, when the first of these boats groped along our coasts looking for a good landing place or a river that promised an entry to the interior. That there was a moment when the first domestic cattle and sheep, lowing and bleating indignantly, were driven ashore and when men and women disembarked to choose a camping ground for their first night in our island.

At this period the formations of Jurassic and Cretaceous Ages began to exert their strongest influence on human affairs. The farming peoples might occasionally occupy gravel terraces in river valleys when these were open and well drained, but for the most part they spread over the English uplands, the chalk downs of Sussex and Wessex and their extensions into Norfolk, Lincolnshire and Yorkshire, and on the limestone hills of the Jurassic belt.

Meanwhile those more ancient parts of Britain, the stretches of mountain and moorland which events of so many millions of years ago had raised and which now formed our Atlantic coasts, were not left unclaimed. The historic role of these antique highlands has been to offer resistance to new peoples and new practices when these have swept across the narrow seas and lowland England, but to allow something of the new element to penetrate, altered and moulded to suit traditional forms. They were usually, in fact, the rocky fortresses of conservatism that they still are to-day when they hold at bay the main tide of the Industrial Revolution. But at this time a connection with the Mediterranean thoroughfare of civilization gave them a more positive, a more active part. Adventurers sailing from Spain, Portugal and Brittany came to our western coast, and from Cornwall to the Orkneys fitted themselves into its fretted line, settling on coastal plains, round sea inlets and estuaries, rarely penetrating far from the sea. While the peoples living on the English uplands must have been accustomed to look down from their safer eminence into the tangled forests of the plains and valleys, these other tribes instead would look upwards at the stark and hostile country of the mountain crests. Their coming, and the establishment of this Atlantic coast route to the Mediterranean, meant that for many centuries the highlands would have their own contribution to make to the development of human life in this country.

The occupation of Britain by Neolithic peoples could not fail to have a profound effect on the character of the islands. The Mes-

olithic hunters had studied the habits of their fellow creatures—
the routes of the deer, the coming of salmon to our rivers, the movements of mackerel and herring shoals, the spring and autumn
flights of geese. With simple craft they devised their snares and
fish traps, their nets, hooks, harpoons, bows and arrows to enable
them to claim their tithe of this natural harvest. The Neolithic
farmers were humble enough, they could not forsee how their
successors would destroy the forests and subjugate the whole land,
but they came with an additional equipment of conscious purpose
and of will. Working where the conditions were manageable on
the relatively open hills and round the fringes of the mountains,
they set themselves to begin the domestication of the land. They
felled trees, and burnt undergrowth to improve the pasture for their
flocks and herds and free the soil for the cultivation of their wheat.
They embanked and fenced hilltops as cattle corrals and built
themselves huts which were perhaps not very substantial but whose
rectangular forms must have been conspicuous in their wild
surroundings.

This same will, this refusal merely to accept, led the Neolithic
peoples to success in another most remarkable enterprise. Not
content with surface flints, they went in pursuit of the larger, more
readily worked nodules bedded in the chalk. With antler picks taken
from the foreheads of deer, and shovels from the shoulders of oxen,
they sank pits and followed the seams of flint with a network of
galleries. They were the first men to cut down through the accumulations of time to reach hidden resources which would then be used
to transform the land itself.

Their mining has left its mark on the countryside in the grass-
grown pits and spoil heaps that pock the turf in many places on
the Sussex Downs, in Wiltshire, and most conspicuously of all at
Grimes Graves, in Suffolk. Here flint is still being worked to-day.
The Snares were for generations the leading knappers, and I
remember going to see the Snare family in their Thetford workshop.
The cabin was deep in silica dust and flakes, and a neat-wristed man
in a leather apron sat knacking gun flints and tossing them into
a large barrel, already half full of the glistening black squares.
They were to go, I was told, to Africa. Others now bring us dollars
by their sale to those curiously atavistic organizations, the flint-lock
gun clubs of the United States.

The mined flint was used mainly for making heavy axes suitable
for tree-felling; other axes, equally effective, were made from the
tough igneous rocks of the highlands and, like the flint variety, were
widely traded throughout the country. The products of sponges and
of volcanoes, both long extinct, were being turned by human will
against the domination of the forests.

The Neolithic peoples showed the new spirit of mastery in another small but significant accomplishment; they were the first to use our local clays to make pottery. They knew how to take and prepare it, and, by firing, deliberately to change its chemical nature to produce the jars and pots now needed for dairy produce and many other domestic employments unknown to the old hunters. Before the introduction of metallurgy, this was the only activity by which men took hold of the raw material of their land and changed not only its form but its substance.

It was not, however, for directly material ends that these farming communities put out their greatest energies or made their deepest mark on the countryside. They had brought with them from the Mediterranean the worship in some form of that variously named divinity the Great Goddess or Earth Mother and the attendant male god who is her son or lover. It may well be that throughout the ancient world there were in fact only two high gods, the Earth Mother and that opposite principle represented by Zeus, Jehovah, the Sky Father—all lesser divinities representing no more than special attributes of these great ones.

Several rough effigies have been found in Britain, sometimes carved in chalk, a substance which must at all times have recalled the flesh of the White Goddess. At the bottom of one of the mine shafts of Grimes Graves a figure of the goddess was discovered enthroned above a pile of antlers on which rested a chalk-carved phallus. This shrine had been set up in one of the few pits that by chance had failed to strike the flint bed, and Our Lady of the Flint Mines, it seems, was being asked to cure such sterility. It is worth meditating on this story, for it perfectly represents the unity of life these people enjoyed. They were confident that by carving the symbols of a woman and a phallus and rendering the appropriate ritual words, movements, and offerings, they could ensure an increase of flint just as readily as their fellows could multiply their calves and lambs.

The spirit of the Great Goddess must also have presided over the religious observances centred on the megalithic tombs. These tombs, our earliest stone architecture and an extraordinary manifestation of the energy and purpose of the Neolithic peoples, still survive in numbers along our Atlantic seaboard. There are no images or symbols of the goddess in our megaliths comparable to those found in France; her symbolism, nevertheless, is implicit in the whole structure, in the earthfast chamber carefully hidden, made cave-like, below a huge mound of earth or stones. These massive communal vaults were not intended simply for a backward-looking cult of the dead or the appeasement of ancestors; they were to suggest a return to the Earth Mother for rebirth, the association of death with fecundity which inspires all the myths of the goddess and the dying god. In this sense they represented the timeless unity of the tribe, of its members, dead, living and unborn all enclosed within their common matrix, the rock and the earth.

V. GORDON CHILDE

An Orkney Village

SKARA BRAE consisted of a small cluster of huts connected by carefully roofed passages. The villagers depended mainly on sheep, cattle and the collection of shellfish. At the time of the publication of this book, Professor Childe still thought that although this was essentially a Neolithic type of culture, it might have been quite late in absolute age. It was later established, however, that Skara Brae can be assigned to the "secondary Neolithic" of Britain, and that it was flourishing at the beginning of the second millennium B.C., when bronze was coming into use further south.

OF PREHISTORIC man's habitations only exiguous and insignificant traces usually survive north of the Alps. The dwellings of his dead are indeed often impressive and always instructive; circles of stone provoke speculations as to his religious ideas; and elaborate defensive works remind us forcibly of the constant perils of that age and its continuous feuds. But of everyday dwelling-places the foundations alone have come down to us, and these are generally poorly furnished. Owing mainly to this defect in the archaeological record a reconstruction of commonplace scenes of prehistoric life is for the most part a work of pure imagination assisted by none too

From *Skara Brae*. London: Routledge & Kegan Paul Ltd.; 1931, pp. 1, 39-41. By permission of Routledge & Kegan Paul Ltd.

reliable analogies from among modern barbarians or savages. Skara Brae in Orkney fills an unique role in supplementing this defect. Here a gigantic sand dune has embalmed a whole complex of huts and lanes, preserving even their walls to a height of eight or nine feet; lack of timber had obliged their builders to translate into stone, and thus perpetuate, articles of furniture usually constructed of perishable wood; finally the inhabitants, deserting their dwellings in precipitate haste, have left them exactly as they were during their occupation with implements, ornaments and vessels all in place.

The culture thus revealed, whatever its absolute date, is extremely archaic, indeed literally a Neolithic culture. And so Skara Brae unfolds a picture of Stone Age life in the British Isles that can be matched nowhere else. The actual occupation of the village may certainly be comparatively recent, perhaps indeed post-Roman, in date. But that in no way detracts from the value of such an illustration of how men lived in Neolithic fashion, isolated from all commerce with the outside world and forced to use exclusively home-made implements of stone and bone.

Hut 7 was discovered exactly as it had been left when its occupants beat a hasty retreat. The observations made during its excavation accordingly afford a graphic and reliable picture of a Stone Age interior. The first impression produced was one of indescribable filth and disorder. Scraps of bones and shells were lying scattered promiscuously all over the floor, sometimes masked by broken slates laid down like stepping stones over the morass. Even the beds were no cleaner; the complete skull of a calf lay in the left hand bed, and the green matter usually associated with drains was observed on its floor. The disposition of actual relics was less haphazard.

A very fine tusk pendant, several pins and beads, a Skail knife and a broken pot with its slate lid probably belonged to the occupants of the left hand bed where they were discovered.

Other beads, pins and sherds lay in the right hand bed as did a bone shovel. Between the beds and the hearth seven flint flakes, two pairs of bone adzes, a stone axe-head (celt) and a carved stone ball came to light. A large pot had stood just to the left of the hearth, but had been crushed by the fall of the pillar. A broken whalebone basin was found close to the bed on the opposite side of the fireplace. The enclosed dais on the right of the door was furnished with a basin of cetaceous bone, a stone mortar and two large cooking pots that had contained animal bones. In the left hand corner a small whale-bone dish full of red pigment stood embedded in the floor. Two large mortars were set in the floor of the left hand rear corner and, close by, two bone adzes and a shovel, evidently a single group lay against the head slab of the bed. A pot and a small hoard of beads and pendants had been secreted in the adjacent cell, and a couple of fine pendants were collected just in front of its door. A large pot had stood under the left hand shelf of the dresser and another between the limpet boxes in the right hand rear corner.

Most of the foregoing objects may be regarded as lying in the positions where they had been used or placed before the hut's abrupt desertion. Definite evidence of a hasty flight is, however, afforded by a trail of beads picked up in the doorway and along passage C to the left. Most lay between the actual jambs. All had fallen from a necklace broken as its wearer squeezed hurriedly through the narrow gap where she lost most beads while the rest continued to fall from her as she scampered up the passage.

HANS FRANKFORT

The Form of Civilization

PROFESSOR FRANKFORT is trying to seize upon the essential character of each civilization, which he calls its "form." He insists that each must be judged according to its own "form," and not according to extraneous values. Arnold Toynbee had likened civilizations to motor cars on one-way streets; and again, primitive societies to people lying torpid on a ledge on a precipice, and civilizations to people beginning to climb the cliff face. These images, Frankfort says, betray the mental processes of a western progressive.

From *The Birth of Civilization in the Near East*. London: Williams and Norgate Ltd.; 1951, pp. 16, 24-5, 30-1. By permission of Ernest Benn Ltd.

OUR problem is pre-eminently a historical one, and it has, accordingiy, two aspects: that of *identity* and that of *change*. What constitutes the individuality of a civilization, its recognizable character, its identity which is maintained throughout the successive stages of its existence? What, on the other hand, are the changes differentiating one stage from the next? We are not, of course, looking for a formula; the character of a civilization is far too elusive to be reduced to a catchword. We recognize it in a certain coherence among its various manifestations, a certain consistency in its orientation, a certain cultural "style" which shapes its political and its judicial institutions, its art as well as its literature, its religion as well as its morals. I propose to call this elusive identity of a civilization its "form." It is this "form" which is never destroyed although it changes in the course of time. And it changes partly as a result of inherent factors—development—partly as a result of external forces—historical incidents. I propose to call the total of these changes the "dynamics" of a civilization.

The interplay of form and dynamics constitutes the history of a civilization and raises the question—which lies outside our present inquiry—to what extent the form of a civilization may determine its destiny. . . .

Toynbee's images betray an evolutionistic as well as a moral bias which interferes with the historian's supreme duty of doing justice to each civilization on its own terms. Why should we characterize civilizations which have achieved a deep and lasting harmony (like those of the Zuni or of certain Polynesians) as "arrested civilizations" where "no energy is left over for reconnoitring the course of the road ahead, or the face of the cliff above them, with a view to a further advance?" Where is this road or this cliff? Why should these chimaeras and a feverish desire for "advancement" disturb the satisfaction of people who have attained the double integration of individual and society and of society and nature? Toynbee merely projects postulates which fulfil an emotional need in the West into human groups whose values lie elsewhere. In our own terms: Toynbee declares the "dynamism" of western civilization to be universally valid; and he can do that only by ignoring the "form" of non-western civilizations. But understanding is thereby precluded.

Toynbee is not the first historian to introduce the notion of "progress" in his work, and the fallacy of this procedure has been well demonstrated by Collingwood. Of his arguments we can quote only two passages. He maintains that a historian comparing two historical periods or ways of life must be able to "understand (them) historically, that is with enough sympathy and insight to reconstruct their experience for himself." But that means that he has already accepted them as things to be judged by their own standards. Each is for the historian "a form of life having its own problems, to be judged by its success in solving those problems and no others. Nor is he assuming that the two different ways of life were attempts to do one and the same thing and asking whether the second did it better than the first. Bach was not trying to write like Beethoven and failing; Athens was not a relatively unsuccessful attempt to produce Rome." . . .

Our criticism does not proceed from a positivistic belief in a so-called "scientific" historiography which is supposed first to assemble objective facts which are subsequently interpreted. Our objection here is not against Toynbee's procedure, but against a terminology which obscures what is the starting-point, and what the outcome, of his procedure. And we make the further criticism that he does not actually evolve from each particular historical situation the notion of a particular challenge to which it can be construed as a response; he applies the formula, as I have said, from the outside, and it is therefore doomed to irrelevance. For example: Toynbee considers the descent of the prehistoric Egyptians into the marshy Nile valley as their response to the challenge of the desiccation of North Africa. In their new homeland they faced, in due course, as a further challenge, "the internal articulation of the new-born Egyptiac society" and failed. The truth is that the Egyptians flourished exceedingly for two thousand years after the Pyramid Age; but Toynbee thinks they failed because he cannot conceive of a "response" in Egyptian terms, but only in those with which he is familiar: secular government, democracy, and the Poor Law. But since neither the rich nor the poor Egyptians took this view of their state, Toynbee's conclusion is irrelevant. It is true that he quotes the tales which dragomans told to late Greek travellers about the oppressive rule of the builders of the pyramids. But the actual folk-tales of Pharaonic Egypt show us that the people took as great a delight in tales of royalty as the public of the Arabian Nights took in the doings of the despot Harun al Rashid. Snefru, whom Toynbee names, is known as one of the most popular rulers in legend. The fact of the matter is that Toynbee should have started from an analysis of the "response." This would not have shown, as Toynbee has it, that "Death laid its icy hand on the life of the growing civilization at the moment when the challenge that was the stimulus of its growth was transferred from the external to the internal field (from the subjugation of nature to the organization of society, H. F.) because in this new situation, the shepherds of the people betrayed their trust." Studied without preconceived ideas the "response" of the Egyptians stands revealed as a vastly different achievement. The ideal of a marvellously integrated society had been formed long before the pyramids were built; it was as nearly realized, when they were built, as any ideal social form can be translated into actuality; and it remained continuously before the eyes of rulers and people alike during subsequent centuries. It was an ideal which ought to thrill a western historian by its novelty, for it falls entirely outside the experience of Greek or Roman or Modern Man, although it survives, in an attenuated form, in Africa. It represents a harmony between man and the divine which is beyond our boldest dreams, since it was maintained by divine power which had taken charge of the affairs of man in the person of Pharaoh. Society moved in unison with nature. Justice, which was the social aspect of the cosmic order, pervaded the commonwealth. The "trust" which the people put in their "shepherds" was by no means what Toynbee imagines; their trust was that Pharaoh should wield to the full the absolute power to which his divinity entitled him, and which enabled him—as nothing else could—to ensure the well-being of the whole community.

HANS FRANKFORT

The Birth of Civilization: Egypt and Mesopotamia Compared

FRANKFORT pursues the contrasting "forms" of Mesopotamian and Egyptian civilization as they develop from the late Neolithic cultures of their river valleys. His conclusion is that while the isolation and unity of the Nile valley, and the dependable regularity of the seasons there, led to the formation of a single kingdom under a divine ruler with unchanging order as its ideal, the erratic and

From *The Birth of Civilization in the Near East*, pp. 40-8.

often catastrophic nature of the seasonal flooding of the Tigris-Euphrates valley and its lack of unity and openness to invasion, encouraged the formation of separate city states and a belief in men as the helpless slaves of the gods.

MODERN Egypt, even if we disregard the aridity of its climate, differs entirely from the land with which we are here concerned. Nowadays the whole of the country is so intensively cultivated that it does not possess sufficient grazing for its cattle, and one sees cows, buffaloes and asses tethered at the desert edge and fed on cultivated crops such as clover. The river is thoroughly controlled. The desert valleys—wadis—are devoid of vegetation except for bushes of camelthorn. But in prehistorc, as well as in Pharaonic times, Egypt was a land of marshes in which papyrus, sedge, and rushes grew to more than man's height. The wadis, too, teemed with life; they are best described as park land where as late as the New Kingdom (1400 B.C.) man could hunt Barbary sheep, wild oxen, and asses, and a wide variety of antelopes with their attendant carnivores. It has been pointed out that the methods of hunting prove that different types of landscape could be found here. Sometimes rows of beaters are shown driving the game towards the hunter or into nets, a method possible only in areas which are somewhat thickly wooded. At other times lassos are used, which presuppose pampa-like open spaces with low shrub.

In the valley, the annual flood of the Nile continuously changed the lay of the land. When the water overflowed the river banks the silt, previously kept in suspension by the speed of the swollen current, precipitated. Some of this precipitation raised the river bed, the remainder covered the banks and the area closest to them; towards the edges of the valley there was comparatively little deposit. Thus banks of considerable height were formed, and after some years the weight of water broke through these natural dikes to seek a new course in low-lying parts, some distance away. The old bed turned into swamp, but its banks remained as ridges and hillocks whose height and area were increased by wind-blown dust and silt caught at their edges. Trees took root, and man settled there, sowing his crops and grazing his beasts in the adjoining lowlands, to retire with them to the high ground of the old banks when the river overflowed. During the inundation, fish, wild boar, hippopotamus, and huge flocks of water birds invaded the surrounding fields and supplied an abundance of food throughout the summer.

All traces of these settlements in the valley proper have long since disappeared; they have been not merely silted over but washed away by the changes in the river's course. This explains why we find traceś of early settlements only at the edge of the valley, on the spurs of detritus at the foot of the high cliffs. We must imagine the valley, not flat and featureless as it is to-day, but dotted with hamlets perched on the high banks of former watercourses and surrounded by an ever-changing maze of channels, marsh, and meadow. Even as late as the First Intermediate period, just before 2000 B.C., the populace of a province in Middle Egypt left their homes and hid in swamps in the valley to escape the dangers of civil war and marauding soldiers. And the early predynastic settlements at the valley's edge were built in groves; among the remains of huts and shelters, tree roots of considerable size have been found.

The prehistoric, "predynastic," period of Egypt clearly falls into two parts or stages. The earliest of these is known in three successive phases called Tasian, Badarian, and Amratian, each a modified development of its predecessor. Together they represent the African substratum of Pharaonic civilization, the material counterpart of the affinities between ancient Egyptian and modern Hamitic languages; of the physical resemblances between the ancient Egyptians and the modern Hamites; and of the remarkable similarities in mentality between these two groups which make it possible to understand ancient Egyptian customs and beliefs by reference to modern Hamitic analogies. The second stage of predynastic culture—called Gerzean—is in many ways a continuation of Amratian; in other words, the preponderantly African character remained. But new elements were added, and these point to fairly close relations with the East, with Sinai, and with Palestine. Foreign pottery was imported from that quarter. A new type of Egyptian pottery, implying a change in ceramic technique, was derived from a class of wavy-handled vases which were at home in Palestine. Several new kinds of stone used for vases may have come from Sinai, and the increase in the use of copper points certainly to closer relations with that peninsula. Although flint remained in use and flint-work achieved an unrivalled beauty and refinement, copper was no longer an odd substance used for luxuries but appeared in the form of highly practical objects: harpoons, daggers, axes (one of which weighs 3½ pounds). The language of the country may also have been affected.

The innovations of Gerzean can best be explained as the effect of a permeation of Upper Egypt by people who had affinities with their Asiatic neighbours and derived from them certain features of their culture. We know that in historical times a similar gradual but continuous drift of people from Lower Egypt into Upper Egypt can be observed. During the Gerzean period the country seems to have become more densely populated; and it has been suggested that the reclamation of the marshland was begun. Such work presupposes co-operation between neighbouring groups and organization of men in some numbers. We may assume that this took place, but on a strictly limited scale. For there are no signs of large political units. There are no ruins of great size, no monuments of an exceptional nature; and if it is objected that these may have existed but may not have been discovered yet, we must insist on the significant fact that among the many thousands of predynastic graves which have been found, there is not a single one which by its size or equipment suggests the burial of a great chief. The Gerzean innovation did not change the general character of the country's culture; the remains suggest a prosperous homogeneous population, fully exploiting its rich environment and loosely organized in villages and rural districts. It was in this setting that the efflorescence of Pharaonic civilization occurred.

In Mesopotamia the corresponding change took place in the extreme south, in the marshy plain between the head of the Persian Gulf and the higher ground which stretches north from Samarra and Hit. The older diluvial part of the country had been farmed already for many centuries before the south was inhabited. The northern farmers had passed through three phases which can be distinguished by their material equipment. When the third was predominant in the north, men from the Persian plateau entered the southern marshes. Under present conditions it would be inconceivable that highlanders would elect to do so, or even that they would be able to survive there. But in the fifth and fourth millennia B.C. the Iranian plateau had not yet become a salt desert. Many rivers, descending from the surrounding mountains, ended in upland seas without an outlet and ringed by swamps. Even to-day, in eastern Iran, marsh dwellers are found on the shores of the great lake of the river Hamun. Like the Marsh Arabs of southern Iraq, they build boats and huts of reeds, fish and keep water buffaloes and cattle. Similar conditions must have prevailed over much of Persia in the period we are discussing, and immigrants from such regions would be well prepared to face life in the delta of the Euphrates and Tigris.

The pottery made by the earliest settlers of South Mesopotamia shows that they came from Persia. At first they retained the tightly interwoven geometric designs used in their homeland; but left to themselves they soon adopted an easier flowing, careless decoration (called al 'Ubaid) which remained in use for many centuries and represents the Persian tradition in only a very debased form. In many places it is found on virgin soil, which shows that the settlers spread farther through the country of which they had at first occupied only certain localities. At Ur, for instance, detailed observations were made which reveal the conditions in which men lived when the site was first inhabited. The relevant layers show:

a stratum of irregular thickness composed of refuse resulting from human occupation—ashes, disintegrated mud brick, potsherds, etc. This went down almost to sea-level; below it was a belt about one metre thick of mud, grey in colour above, and darkening to black below, much of which was clearly due to the decay of vegetation. In it were potsherds, sporadic above but becoming more numerous lower down and massed thickly at the bottom, all the fragments lying horizontally; they had the appearance of having sunk by their own weight through water into soft mud. At a metre below sea-level came stiff, green clay pierced by sinuous brown stains resulting from the decay of roots; with this all trace of human activity ceased. Evidently this was the bottom of Mesopotamia.

Southern Mesopotamia resembled the Egyptian Delta, rather than the Nile Valley where cliffs constrain the meanderings of the river, and old banks and spurs provide high ground. In Mesopotamia the lowest course of Euphrates and Tigris presents, even to-day, a wilderness of reed forests where the Marsh Arabs lead an amphibious existence. All traffic is by narrow bituminous skiffs; the people fish and keep some cattle, living in reed huts built on mattresses of bent and trodden-down reed stems. Their dwellings are described as follows:

at one end is a low and narrow aperture which serves as a doorway, window and chimney combined; on the rush-strewn and miry floor sleep men and women, children and buffaloes, in warm proximity . . . the ground of the hut often oozing water at every step.

The chiefs' reed tents are more impressive; they are large tunnels of matting covering a framework of reed bundles which form semi-circular arches. Doors and windows are arranged in the mats closing either end. We know that such structures were also used in the fourth millennium B.C., for they are represented, with all the necessary detail, in the earliest renderings of sacred buildings, notably the byres and folds of temple animals.

But modern savages are but diminished shadows of the true primitives, and the ancient people of the al 'Ubaid period exercised a mastery over the marsh to which the modern inhabitants never as much as aspire. Moreover, the people of the al 'Ubaid period belonged to the most advanced group of the prehistoric farmers. Copper was used in their homeland for axes and adzes and even for mirrors. Bricks were known there, too; and brick buildings and the waterproofing of reeds with bitumen are certified for the period.

It is likely that some reclamation and drainage of marshland was undertaken. In any case, the men of the al 'Ubaid period appear from the first as cultivators, and we are free to imagine their fields as shallow islands in the marsh or as reclaimed and diked-in land.

The vitality and power of these earliest settlers is astonishing. Their influence can be traced upstream, where their pottery replaced the Tell Halaf wares completely, even occurring in appreciable quantities in North Syria. Since it has nothing to recommend it as an article of export, we must assume that its makers came with it and settled widely throughout the upper reaches of Tigris and Euphrates. Nevertheless, the al 'Ubaid people were simple cultivators like their contemporaries in Egypt and their predecessors in northern Iraq and Syria. This is most clearly shown by their inability to organize trade in order to obtain the copper which they had been accustomed to use in their country of origin. Once settled in Mesopotamia and removed from the sources of the metal, they used a substitute material that was locally available, making axes, choppers, and sickles of clay which they fired at so high a temperature that it almost vitrified and thus obtained a useful cutting edge. These implements were, of course, very brittle and were broken by the hundreds. But they could be easily replaced; and the isolated settlements achieved that autarchy which is characteristic of early peasant cultures.

And yet the al 'Ubaid period has left us some remains which suggest that certain centres began to be of outstanding importance and that a change in the rural character of the settlements was taking place. At Abu Shahrein in the south, and at Tepe Gawra in the north, temples were erected. And these not only testify to a co-ordinated effort on a larger scale than we would expect within the scope of a village culture, but show also a number of features which continue in historical times—for instance: the simple oblong shape of the sanctuary, with its altar and offering table; the platforms on which the temples were set; the strengthening buttresses (which developed into a system of piers and recesses, rhythmically articulating the walls). Moreover, it is likely that at Eridu there was continuity, not only of architectural development, but of worship. In the absence of inscriptions this contention cannot be proved. But the god worshipped there in historical times was called Enki— lord of the earth, but also god of the sweet waters. He is depicted surrounded by waters (for he "had founded his chamber in the deep") and fishes sport in the streams which spring from his shoulders. Now an observation made during the excavation of the al 'Ubaid temples suggests that the same god was adored in them. At one stage the offering table and sanctuary were covered with a layer of fish bones six inches deep, remains, no doubt, of an offering to the god of whom it was said:

> *When Enki rose, the fishes rose and adored him.*
> *He stood, a marvel unto the Apsu (Deep),*
> *Brought joy to the Engur (Deep).*
> *To the sea it seemed that awe was upon him,*
> *To the Great River it seemed that terror hovered around*
>   *him*
> *While at the same time the south wind stirred the depths*
>   *of the Euphrates.*

The importance which one attaches to these signs of a possible continuity remains a matter of personal judgment. But, in any case, the al 'Ubaid culture which we have described was the first to have occupied Mesopotamia as a whole. It seems to have spread along the rivers from the south. And it was in the south that, after an interval, the profound change was brought about which made first Sumer, and then Babylon, the cultural centre of Western Asia for three thousand years.

IV

Mesopotamia and Palestine

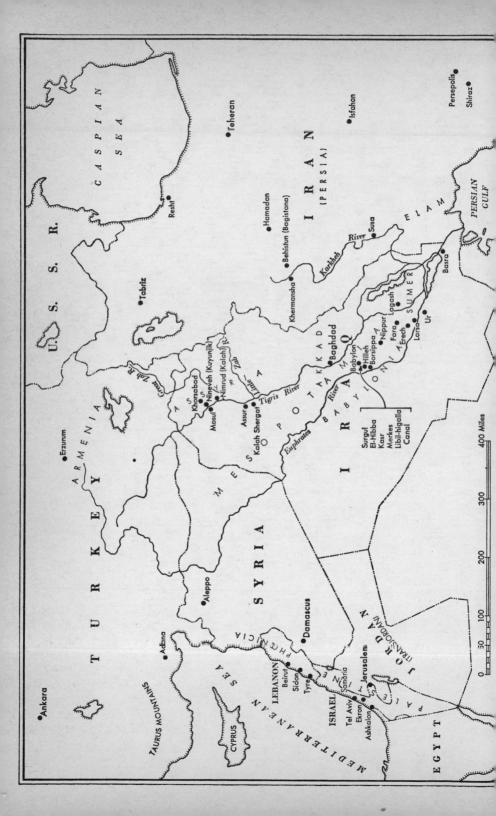

INTRODUCTORY

EARLY Neolithic cultures had developed, mostly in upland country, on three sides of the enormous "Valley of the Two Rivers"—the Tigris and Euphrates. As the silt of the valley bottom, if properly worked, irrigated and drained, was immensely fertile, it is not surprising that it became the cradle of urban civilization. Flourishing agricultural villages grew up in the more northern parts of the valley, and spread southward by the middle of the sixth millennium B.C. (p. 251, I). During the next millennium the working of copper and bronze reached them and there was a striking development in architecture, particularly for religious buildings. By 4000 B.C., new settlers had moved into the lower part of the valley, possibly from southern Iran, and there developed what is known to archaeologists as the 'Ubaid culture (p. 411, I). At some places, as at Eridu (p. 286, I), temples built by 'Ubaid villagers had a continuous history with those of historic Sumerian times. Meanwhile, however, in the middle of the fourth millennium a further influx of vigorous peoples, now thought to have come from eastern Iran, galvanized the life of the valley and created the Uruk culture. It was from this blending of the newcomers with the earlier population that the first civilization of our world—the Sumerian—came into being in southern Mesopotamia. At Uruk itself (the biblical Erech), Eridu, Ur and many other places, true cities dominated by great temples and temple mounds (*ziggurats*) grew up under the rule of kings who were agents of the gods. Architecture became monumental, metallurgy perfected and other arts and crafts more and more refined: Sumerian civilization had established its "form." Already by 3000 B.C. the practice of writing with reeds on clay, soon to develop into the true cuneiform script, was well under way.

There was constant bitter rivalry between the cities, first one and then another establishing some degree of power over the rest. For many centuries the true Sumerians, speaking a non-Semitic language, were supreme, their cultural influence and probably their political dominance extending as far north as Ashur, later to become the first capital of the Assyrians. But, in about 2370 B.C., Sargon of Agade (an unknown site, probably near Babylon) conquered the valley, and for the first time a Semitic language, Akkadian, was spoken by the dominant political power. From that time Mesopotamia was often referred to as the land of Sumer and Akkad.

There was a temporary revival of Sumerian hegemony, then the centre of political power shifted decisively north, and by 2000 B.C. another Semitic-speaking dynasty, that of Babylon, was in command. Changes in political control, however, did nothing to lessen the complete dominance of the old Sumerian culture. From the time of Hammurabi of Babylon onwards, the city grew in might and splendour, and for long was the most influential city of the ancient world.

Meanwhile in the northern part of the valley the predominantly Semitic people later to be called the Assyrians were building up their strength and founding dynasties. By the 14th century B.C., they were giving trouble to the Babylonians, and before the end of the millennium their first great conquering monarch, Tiglath Pileser I, had marched southward and captured Babylon.

After this triumph Assyria had a period of weakness, but by the 9th century rose once again as a cruel and ruthless militaristic empire. From their successive capitals of Ashur, Nimrûd (the Biblical Calah), Nineveh and Dur Sharrukin (Khorsabad), its monarchs led armies out to ravage and conquer neighbouring lands —including Babylonia. It was in the palaces and temples of these warlike and plunder-laden kings that the first great archaeological discoveries in Mesopotamia were to be made.

I. *Assyria*

HENRY A. LAYARD

Layard's First Sight of Nineveh and Nimrûd

DURING the autumn of 1839 and winter of 1840, I had been wandering through Asia Minor and Syria, scarcely leaving untrod one spot hallowed by tradition, or unvisited one ruin consecrated by history. I was accompanied by one no less curious and enthusiastic than myself [Edward Mitford]. We were both equally careless of comfort and unmindful of danger. We rode alone; our arms were our only protection; a valise behind our saddles was our wardrobe, and we tended our own horses, except when relieved from the duty by the hospitable inhabitants of a Turcoman village or an Arab tent. Thus unembarrassed by needless luxuries, and uninfluenced by the opinions and prejudices of others, we mixed amongst the people, acquired without effort their manners, and enjoyed without alloy those emotions which scenes so novel, and spots so rich in varied association, cannot fail to produce.

I look back with feelings of grateful delight to those happy days when, free and unheeded, we left at dawn the humble cottage or cheerful tent, and lingering as we listed, unconscious of distance and of the hour, found ourselves, as the sun went down, under some hoary ruin tenanted by the wandering Arab, or in some crumbling village still bearing a well-known name. No experienced dragcman measured our distances and appointed our stations. We were honoured with no conversations by pashas, nor did we seek any civilities from governors. We neither drew tears nor curses from villagers by seizing their horses, or searching their houses for provisions: their welcome was sincere; their scanty fare was placed before us; we came and ate, and went in peace.

From *Nineveh and Its Remains*. London: John Murray; 1867, pp. 1-3 (1st ed., 1849).

I had traversed Asia Minor and Syria, visiting the ancient seats of civilisation, and the spots which religion has made holy. I now felt an irresistible desire to penetrate to the regions beyond the Euphrates, to which history and tradition point as the birthplace of the wisdom of the West. Most travellers, after a journey through the usually frequented parts of the East, have the same longing to cross the great river, and to explore those lands which are separated on the map from the confines of Syria by a vast blank stretching from Aleppo to the banks of the Tigris. A deep mystery hangs over Assyria, Babylonia, and Chaldaea. With these names are linked great nations and great cities dimly shadowed forth in history; mighty ruins, in the midst of deserts, defying, by their very desolation and lack of definite form, the description of the traveller; the remnants of mighty races still roving over the land; the fulfilling and fulfilment of prophecies; the plains to which the Jew and the Gentile alike look as the cradle of their race. After a journey in Syria the thoughts naturally turn eastward; and without treading on the remains of Nineveh and Babylon our pilgrimage is incomplete.

I left Aleppo, with my companion, on the 18th of March. We still travelled as we had been accustomed—without guide or servants. The road across the desert is at all times impracticable, except to a numerous and well-armed caravan, and offers no object of interest. We preferred that through Bir and Orfa. From the latter city we traversed the low country at the foot of the Kurdish hills, a country little known and abounding in curious remains. The Egyptian frontier, at that time, extended to the east of Orfa, and the war between the Sultan and Mohammed Ali Pasha being still unfinished, the tribes took advantage of the confusion, and were plundering on all sides. With our usual good fortune, we succeeded in reaching Nisibin unmolested, although we ran daily risks, and more than once found ourselves in the midst of foraging parties, and of tents which, an hour before, had been pillaged by the wandering bands of Arabs. We entered Mosul on the 10th of April.

During a short stay in this town we visited the great ruins on the east bank of the river, which have been generally believed to be the remains of Nineveh. We rode also into the desert, and explored the mound of Kalah Sherghat, a vast ruin on the Tigris, about fifty miles below its junction with the Zab. As we journeyed thither we rested for the night at the small Arab village of Hammum Ali, around which are still the vestiges of an ancient city. From the summit of an artificial eminence we looked down upon a broad plain separated from us by the river. A line of lofty mounds bounded it to the east, and one of a pyramidical form rose high above the rest. Beyond it could be faintly traced the waters of the Zab. Its position rendered its identification easy. This was the pyramid which Xenophon had described, and near which the ten thousand had encamped: the ruins around it were those which the Greek general saw twenty-two centuries before, and which were even then the remains of an *ancient* city. Although Xenophon had confounded a name, spoken by a strange race, with one familiar to a Greek ear, and had called the place Larissa, tradition still points to the origin of the city, and, by attributing its foundation to Nimrod, whose name the ruins now bear, connects it with one of the first settlements of the human race.

HENRY A. LAYARD

Nimrûd: Discovery and Removal of the Man-Headed Beasts

DURING his first season of 1845-6 Layard excavated along the west side of the platform of the acropolis at Nimrûd. He began with a building known as the south-west palace, but finding it much damaged by fire he shifted to the north-west palace, afterwards proved to be that of Ashur-nasir-pal (883-59 B.C.). It was here that the huge man-headed lions, standing on each side of the gate into the great hall, were found in the spring of 1846. They were so colossal that they were not transported until January 1850, during Layard's second season (p. 41, I); the lion and the bull that were moved with such difficulty in May, 1847, were of a smaller size. The bas reliefs described in the next account lined rooms in the same north-west palace.

From *Nineveh and its Remains*, pp. 49-51, 308-15.

On the morning following these discoveries, I had ridden to the encampment of Sheikh Abd-ur-Rahman, and was returning to the mound, when I saw two Arabs of his tribe coming towards me and urging their mares to the top of their speed. On reaching me they stopped. "Hasten, O Bey," exclaimed one of them—"hasten to the diggers, for they have found Nimrod himself. Wallah! it is wonderful but it is true! we have seen him with our eyes. There is no God but God;" and both joining in this pious exclamation, they galloped off, without further words, in the direction of their tents.

On reaching the ruins I descended into the newly opened trench, and found the workmen, who had already seen me, as I approached, standing near a heap of baskets and cloaks. Whilst Awad advanced and asked for a present to celebrate the occasion, the Arabs withdrew the screen they had hastily constructed, and disclosed an enormous human head sculptured in full out of the alabaster of the country. They had uncovered the upper part of a figure, the remainder of which was still buried in the earth. I saw at once that the head must belong to a winged lion or bull, similar to those of Khorsabad and Persepolis. It was in admirable preservation. The expression was calm, yet majestic, and the outline of the features showed a freedom and knowledge of art, scarcely to be looked for in works of so remote a period. The cap had three horns, and, unlike that of the human-headed bulls hitherto found in Assyria, was rounded and without ornament at the top.

I was not surprised that the Arabs had been amazed and terrified at this apparition. It required no stretch of imagination to conjure up the most strange fancies. This gigantic head, blanched with age, thus rising from the bowels of the earth, might well have belonged to one of those fearful beings which are described in the traditions of the country as appearing to mortals, slowly ascending from the regions below. One of the workmen, on catching the first glimpse of the monster, had thrown down his basket and had run off towards Mosul as fast as his legs could carry him. I learnt this with regret, as I anticipated the consequences.

Whilst I was superintending the removal of the earth, which still clung to the sculpture, and giving directions for the continuation of the work, the noise of horsemen was heard, and presently Abd-ur-Rahman, followed by half his tribe, appeared on the edge of the trench. As soon as the two Arabs I had met had reached their tents, and published the wonders they had seen, every one mounted his mare and rode to the mound to satisfy himself of the truth of these inconceivable reports. When they beheld the head they all cried together, "There is no God but God, and Mohammed is his Prophet!" It was some time before the Sheikh could be prevailed upon to descend into the pit, and convince himself that the image he saw was of stone. "This is not the work of men's hands," exclaimed he, "but of those infidel giants of whom the Prophet, peace be with him! has said, that they were higher than the tallest date tree; this is one of the idols which Noah, peace be with him! cursed before the flood." In this opinion, the result of a careful examination, all the bystanders concurred.

I now ordered a trench to be dug due south from the head, in the expectation of finding a corresponding figure, and before night-fall reached the object of my search about twelve feet distant. Engaging two or three men to sleep near the sculptures, I returned to the village, and celebrated the day's discovery by a slaughter of sheep, of which all the Arabs near partook. As some wandering musicians chanced to be at Selamiyah, I sent for them, and dances were kept up during the greater part of the night. On the following morning Arabs from the other side of the Tigris, and the inhabitants of the surrounding villages, congregated on the mound. Even the women could not repress their curiosity, and came in crowds, with their children, from afar. My Cawass was stationed during the day in the trench, into which I would not allow the multitude to descend.

I formed various plans for lowering the smaller lion and bull, dragging them to the river, and placing them upon rafts. Each step had its difficulties, and a variety of original suggestions were made by my workmen, and by the good people of Mosul. At last I resolved upon constructing a cart sufficiently strong to bear the sculptures. As no wood but poplar could be procured in the town, a carpenter was sent to the mountains with directions to fell the largest mulberry tree, or any tree of equally compact grain, he could find; and to bring back with him beams of it, and thick slices from the trunk.

By the month of March this wood was ready. I purchased from the dragoman of the French Consulate a pair of strong iron axles, which had been used by M. Botta in moving sculptures from Khorsabad. Each wheel was formed of three solid pieces of wood, nearly a foot thick, bound together by iron hoops. Across the axles were laid three beams, and above them several cross-beams. A pole was fixed to one axle, to which were also attached iron rings for ropes, to enable men, as well as buffaloes, to draw the cart. The wheels were provided with hooks for the same purpose.

Simple and rude as this cart was, it became an object of wonder in the town, as carts are unknown in this part of Turkey. Crowds came to look at it, as it stood in the yard of the Vice-consul's khan;

and the Pasha's topjis, or artillery-men, who, from their acquaintance with the mysteries of gun carriages, were looked up to as
authorities on such matters, daily declaimed on the properties and
use of this vehicle, and of carts in general, to a large circle of
curious and attentive listeners. As long as the cart was in Mosul, it
was examined by every stranger who visited the town. But when the
news spread that it was about to leave the gates, and to be drawn
over the bridge, the business of the place was completely suspended.
The secretaries and scribes of the Pasha left their divans; the guards
their posts; the bazaars were deserted; and half the population assembled on the banks of the river to witness the manoeuvres of
the cart, which was forced over the rotten bridge of boats by a pair
of buffaloes, and a crowd of Chaldaeans and shouting Arabs.

To lessen the weight of the lion and bull, without in any way
interfering with the sculpture, I reduced the thickness and considerably diminished the bulk of the slabs, by cutting away as much
as possible from the back, which, being placed against a wall of
sun-dried bricks, was never meant to be seen. As, in order to move
these sculptures at all, I had to choose between this plan and that
of sawing them into several pieces, I did not hesitate to adopt it.

To enable me to move the bull from the ruins, and to place
it on the cart in the plain below, a trench or road nearly two hundred
feet long, about fifteen feet wide, and, in some places, twenty feet
deep, was cut from the entrance, in which stood the sculpture, to the
edge of the mound. As I had not sufficient mechanical power at
command to raise the bull out of the trenches, like the smaller
bas-reliefs, this road was necessary. It was a tedious undertaking, as
a very large accumulation of earth had to be removed. About fifty
Arabs and Nestorians were employed in the work.

On digging this trench it was found that a chamber had once
existed to the west of the great hall. The sculptured slabs had been
destroyed or carried away; but part of the walls of unbaked bricks
could still be traced. The only bas-relief discovered was lying flat on
the pavement, where it had evidently been left when the adjoining
slabs were removed. It was the small relief of the lion-hunt now
in the British Museum, and remarkable for its finish, the elegance
of the ornaments, and the spirit of the design. It resembles, in its
style and details, the battle-scene first discovered in the South-west
palace, and I am inclined to believe that they both belonged to this
ruined chamber; in which, perhaps, the bas-reliefs were more
elaborate and more highly finished than in any other part of the
building. The work of different artists may be plainly traced in the
Assyrian sculptures. Frequently when the outline is spirited and
correct, and the ornaments designed with considerable taste, the
execution is defective or coarse; evidently showing, that, whilst

The fierce energy of the militaristic Assyrians is expressed by this lion from Nimrud—the biblical Calah. It dates from the reign of Assurnasirpal, 883-858 B.C.

Man-headed and winged bull from Dur-Sharrukin (Khorsabad). This characteristic Assyrian form comes from one of the gates of the Palace of Sargon II, 722-705 B.C.

A noble example of late Assyrian bas-relief sculpture from Nineveh. A slab from a gallery in the palace of King Sennacherib, 705-681 B.C.

Left: The powerful Semitic face of a royal attendant from the same Palace of Sargon II at Dur-Sharrukin.

XI

A fabulous beast in glazed brick from the Ishtar Gate at Babylon, as reconstructed in the Berlin Museum. Seventh to sixth centuries B.C.

The Great Sphinx of Gizeh with the head of the Sun God
and the body of a lion. It was cut from the rock in the
reign of the Pharaoh Chephren about 2620 B.C. The
tablet was set up by Tuthmosis IV (1450-1405 B.C.) to
commemorate a dream he had when sleeping in the
shadow of the Sphinx before he came to the throne.

XIV

Left: The Pharaoh's Burial Chamber in the heart of the great Pyramid of Cheops. The sarcophagus is of highly polished red granite. C. 2650 B.C.

Bas-relief of a cowherd and calves from the tomb of Ti at Sakkara, near Cairo. A fine example of Egyptian art of the Old Kingdom. Ti held many offices, including Controller of the Palace, under a pharaoh of the Vth Dynasty. C. 2500 B.C.

The hippopotamus in blue faience from a tomb of Middle Kingdom times displays artistic naturalism, and even humour. It is decorated with lotus and other appropriate marsh plants. C. 2000 B.C.

the subject was designed by a master, the carving of the stone had been entrusted to an inferior hand. In many bas-reliefs some parts are more highly finished than others, as if they had been retouched by a more experienced sculptor. The figures of the enemy are generally rudely executed and left unfinished, to show probably that, being those of the conquered or captive race, they were unworthy of the care of the artist. It is rare to find an entire bas-relief equally well executed and finished in all its parts. The most perfect hitherto discovered in Assyria, are probably the lion hunt from the principal chamber, the lion-hunt just described, and the large group of the king sitting on his throne, in the midst of his attendants and winged figures, all now placed in the British Museum.

Whilst making this trench, I also discovered, about three feet beneath the pavement, a drain, which appeared to communicate with others previously opened in different parts of the building. It was probably the main sewer, through which all the minor watercourses were discharged. It was built of baked bricks, and covered in with large slabs and tiles.

As the bull was to be lowered, so that the unsculptured side of the slab should be placed on rollers, I removed the walls behind it to form a clear space large enough to receive it when prostrate, and to leave room for the workmen to pass on all sides of it. The principal difficulty was of course to lower it; when once on the ground, or on rollers, it could be dragged forwards by the united force of a number of men; but, during its descent, it could only be sustained by ropes. If these ropes, not strong enough to bear the weight, chanced to give way, the sculpture would be precipitated to the ground, and would, probably, be broken in the fall. The few ropes I possessed had been sent to me, across the desert, from Aleppo; but they were small and weak. From Baghdad I had obtained a thick hawser, made of the fibers of the palm. In addition I had been furnished with two pairs of blocks, and a pair of jackscrews belonging to the steamers of the Euphrates expedition. These were all the means at my command for moving the bull and lion. The sculptures were wrapped in mats and felts, to preserve them, as far as possible, from injury in case of a fall, and to prevent the ropes chipping or rubbing them.

The bull was ready to be moved by the 18th of March. It had been completely isolated, and was now only supported by beams resting against the opposite wall of earth. Amongst the wood obtained from the mountains were several thick rollers. These were placed upon sleepers, formed of the trunks of poplar trees, well greased and laid on the ground parallel to the sculpture. The bull was to be lowered upon these rollers. A deep trench had been cut behind the second bull, completely across the wall, and, consequently, extending from chamber to chamber. Ropes coiled round this mass of earth served to hold two blocks, two others being attached to ropes wound round the bull to be moved. The ropes, by which the sculpture was to be lowered, were passed through these blocks; the ends, or falls of the tackle, as they are technically called, being held by the Arabs. The cable which was first passed through the trench, and then round the sculpture, was to be gradually slackened by two bodies of men, one at each end. Several of the strongest Chaldaeans placed thick beams against the back of the bull, and were directed to use them in checking it in its descent.

My own people were reinforced by a large number of the Abou-Salman. I had invited Sheikh Abd-ur-Rahman to be present, and he came attended by a body of horsemen. The inhabitants of Naifa and Nimrûd, having volunteered to assist on the occasion, were placed amongst my Arabs. The workmen, except the Chaldaeans who supported the beams, were divided into four parties, two in front of the bull, to hold the ropes, and two at the ends of the cable. They were directed to slack off gradually as the sculpture descended.

The men being ready, and all my preparations complete, I stationed myself on the top of the high bank of earth over the second bull, and ordered the wedges to be struck out from under the sculpture to be moved. Still, however, it remained firmly in its place. A rope having been passed round it, six or seven men easily tilted it over. The thick, ill-made cable stretched with the strain, and almost buried itself in the earth round which it was coiled. The ropes held well. The bull descended gradually, the Chaldaeans propping it up with the beams. It was a moment of great anxiety. The drums and shrill pipes of the Kurdish musicians increased the din and confusion caused by the war-cry of the Arabs, who were half frantic with excitement. They had thrown off nearly all their garments; their long hair floated in the wind; and they indulged in the wildest postures and gesticulations as they clung to the ropes. The women had congregated on the sides of the trenches, and by their incessant screams, and by the ear-piercing tahlehl, added to the enthusiasm of the men. The bull once in motion, it was no longer possible to obtain a hearing. The loudest cries I could produce were lost in the crash of discordant sounds. Neither the hippopotamus hide whips of the Cawasses, nor the bricks and clods of earth with which I endeavoured to draw attention from some of the most noisy of the group, were of any avail. Away went the bull, steady enough as long as supported by the props behind; but as it came nearer to the rollers, the beams could no longer be used. The cable and ropes stretched more and more. Dry from the climate, as they felt the strain, they creaked and threw out dust. Water was thrown over them, but in vain, for they all broke together when the sculpture

was within four or five feet of the rollers. The bull fell to the
ground. Those who held the ropes, thus suddenly released, followed
its example, and were rolling one over the other, in the dust. A
sudden silence succeeded to the clamour. I rushed into the trenches,
prepared to find the bull in many pieces. It would be difficult to
describe my satisfaction, when I saw it lying precisely where I had
wished to place it, and unbroken! The Arabs no sooner got on their
legs again, than, seeing that the sculpture was uninjured and safely
placed on the rollers, they darted out of the trenches, and, seizing
by the hands the women who were looking on, formed a large circle,
and, yelling their war-cry with redoubled energy, commenced a
most mad dance. The musicians exerted themselves to the utmost;
but their music was drowned by the cries of the dancers. Even Abd-
ur-Rahman shared in the excitement, and, throwing his cloak to one
of his attendants, insisted upon leading off the *debké*. It would
have been useless to endeavour to put any check upon these
proceedings. I preferred allowing the men to wear themselves out—
a result which, in consequence of the amount of exertion and energy
displayed by limbs and throat, was not long in taking place.

I now prepared, with the aid of Behnan, the Bairakdar, and the
Nestorians, to move the bull into the long trench which led to the
edge of the mound. The rollers were in good order; and as soon as
the excitement of the Arabs had sufficiently abated to enable them
to resume work, the sculpture was dragged out of its place by ropes.
Sleepers were laid to the end of the trench, and fresh rollers
were placed under the bull as it was pulled forwards by cables, to
which were fixed the tackles held by logs buried in the earth, on
the edge of the mound. The sun was going down as these preparations were completed. I deferred any further labour to the morrow.
The Arabs dressed themselves; and, placing the musicians at their
head, marched towards the village, singing their war-songs, occasionally raising a wild yell, throwing their lances into the air,
and flourishing their swords and shields over their heads.

I rode back with Abd-ur-Rahman. Schloss and his horsemen
galloped round us, playing the jerrid, and bringing the ends of
their lances into a proximity with my head and body which was far
from comfortable; for it was evident enough that had the mares
refused to fall almost instantaneously back on their haunches, or
had they stumbled, I should have been transfixed on the spot. As
the exhibition, however, was meant as a compliment, and enabled
the young warriors to exhibit their prowess, and the admirable
training of their horses, I declared myself highly delighted, and
bestowed equal commendations on all parties.

The Arab sheikh, his excitement once cooled down, gave way to
moral reflections. "Wonderful! wonderful! There is surely no God

but God, and Mohammed is his Prophet," exclaimed he, after a long pause. "In the name of the Most High, tell me, O Bey, what you are going to do with those stones. So many thousands of purses spent upon such things! Can it be, as you say, that your people learn wisdom from them; or is it, as his reverence the Cadi declares, that they are to go to the palace of your Queen, who, with the rest of the unbelievers, worships these idols? As for wisdom, these figures will not teach you to make any better knives, or scissors, or chintzes; and it is in the making of those things that the English show their wisdom. But God is great! God is great! Here are stones which have been buried ever since the time of the holy Noah —peace be with him! Perhaps they were under ground before the Deluge. I have lived on these lands for years. My father, and the father of my father, pitched their tents here before me; but they never heard of these figures. For twelve hundred years have the true believers (and, praise be to God! all true wisdom is with them alone) been settled in this country, and none of them ever heard of a palace under ground. Neither did they who went before them. But lo! here comes a Frank from many days' journey off, and he walks up to the very place, and he takes a stick (illustrating the description at the same time with the point of his spear), and makes a line here, and makes a line there. Here, says he, is the palace; there, says he, is the gate; and he shows us what has been all our lives beneath our feet, without our having known anything about it. Wonderful! wonderful! Is it by books, is it by magic, is it by your prophets, that you have learnt these things? Speak, O Bey; tell me the secret of wisdom."

HENRY A. LAYARD

Nimrûd: "Idols and Eunuchs"— the Bas-Reliefs

THE figures in these fine bas-reliefs were about eight feet high. They were in an extraordinary state of preservation, and seemed as if they had just come from the hands of the sculptor, the most delicate chasings being still distinct, and the outline retaining all its original sharpness. On the other slabs forming the walls of this chamber were alternate groups, representing the king holding his bow in one hand and two arrows in the other, standing between winged figures; and the king also erect, raising the sacred cup, and attended by eunuchs. The details in these sculptures were similar in character to those already described. They furnished, however, many new and interesting groups; such as the combats of winged figures with monsters of various kinds, scenes of the chase, goats and bulls kneeling before the sacred tree, and the king performing religious ceremonies.

The king represented in these finely preserved and elaborate sculptures was undoubtedly the builder of the palace or temple which I was exploring; and his name had been found in every inscription hitherto discovered amongst its ruins. It was the same image, too, which occurred in other bas-reliefs, in the same edifice. The Assyrian form of this name, according to some interpretations of the cuneiform characters in which it is written, appears to approach so nearly to that of the monarch, whose name has been handed down to us by the Greeks, that I shall call him "Sardanapalus." A name very similar to it appears, however, to have been borne by a later Assyrian king, and it may therefore be doubtful to which of the two the traditionary history recorded by the Greeks may apply.

The Arabs marvelled at these strange figures. As each head was uncovered they showed their amazement by extravagant gestures,

From *Nineveh and Its Remains*, pp. 102-5.

or exclamations of surprise. If it were a bearded man, they concluded at once that it was an idol or an evil spirit, and cursed or spat upon it. If an eunuch, they declared that it was the likeness of a beautiful girl, and kissed or patted the cheek. They soon felt as much interest as I did in the discoveries, and worked with renewed ardour when their curiosity was excited by the appearance of a fresh sculpture. On such occasions, stripping themselves almost naked, throwing the kerchief from their heads, and letting their matted hair stream in the wind, they would rush like madmen into the trenches to carry off the baskets of earth, shouting, at the same time, the war-cry of their tribe.

HENRY A. LAYARD

Nimrûd: Misadventure of the Winged Lions

By the 28th of January, the colossal lions forming the portal to the great hall in the north-west palace of Nimrûd were ready to be dragged to the river-bank. The walls and their sculptured panelling had been removed from both sides of them, and they stood isolated in the midst of the ruins. We rode one calm cloudless night to the mound, to look on them for the last time before they were taken from their old resting-places. The moon was at her full, and as we drew nigh to the edge of the deep wall of earth rising around them, her soft light was creeping over the stern features of the human heads, and driving before it the dark shadows which still clothed the lion forms. One by one the limbs of the gigantic sphinxes emerged from the gloom, until the monsters were unveiled before

From *Discoveries in the Ruins of Nineveh and Babylon*. London: John Murray; 1853, pp. 201-5.

us. I shall never forget that night, or the emotions which those venerable figures caused within me. A few hours more and they were to stand no longer where they had stood unscathed amidst the wreck of man and his works for ages. It seemed almost sacrilege to tear them from their old haunts to make them a mere wonder-stock to the busy crowd of a new world. They were better suited to the desolation around them; for they had guarded the palace in its glory, and it was for them to watch over it in its ruin. Sheikh Abd-ur-Rahman, who had ridden with us to the mound, was troubled with no such reflections. He gazed listlessly at the grim images, wondered at the folly of the Franks, thought the night cold, and turned his mare towards his tents. We scarcely heeded his going, but stood speechless in the deserted portal, until the shadows again began to creep over its hoary guardians.

Beyond the ruined palaces a scene scarcely less solemn awaited us. I had sent a party of Jebours to the bitumen springs, outside the walls to the east of the inclosure. The Arabs having lighted a small fire with brushwood awaited our coming to throw the burning sticks upon the pitchy pools. A thick heavy smoke, such as rose from the jar on the seashore when the fisherman had broken the seal of Solomon, rolled upwards in curling volumes, hiding the light of the moon, and spreading wide over the sky. Tongues of flame and jets of gas, driven from the burning pit, shot through the murky canopy. As the first brightened, a thousand fantastic forms of light played amidst the smoke. To break the cindered crust, and to bring fresh slime to the surface, the Arabs threw large stones into the springs; a new volume of fire then burst forth, throwing a deep red glare upon the figures and upon the landscape. The Jebours danced round the burning pools, like demons in some midnight orgie, shouting their war-cry and brandishing their glittering arms. In an hour the bitumen was exhausted for the time, the dense smoke gradually died away, and the pale light of the moon again shone over the black slime pits.

The colossal lions were moved by still simpler and ruder means than those adopted on my first expedition. They were tilted over upon loose earth heaped behind them, their too rapid descent being checked by a hawser, which was afterwards replaced by props of wood and stone. They were then lowered, by levers and jack-screws, upon the cart brought under them. A road paved with flat stones had been made to the edge of the mound, and the sculpture was, without difficulty, dragged from the trenches.

Beneath the lions, embedded in earth and bitumen, were a few bones, which, on exposure to the air, fell to dust before I could ascertain whether they were human or not. The sculptures rested simply upon the platform of sun-dried bricks without any other sub-structure, a mere layer of bitumen, about an inch thick, having been placed under the plinth.

Owing to recent heavy rains, which had left in many places deep swamps, we experienced much difficulty in dragging the cart over the plain to the river side. Three days were spent in transporting each lion. The men of Naifa and Nimrûd again came to our help, and the Abou-Salman horsemen, with Sheikh Abd-ur-Rahman at their head, encouraged us by their presence. The unwieldy mass was propelled from behind by enormous levers of poplar wood; and in the costumes of those who worked, as well as in the means adopted to move the colossal sculptures, except that we used a wheeled cart instead of a sledge, the procession closely resembled that which in days of yore transported the same great figures, and which we see so graphically represented on the walls of Kuyunjik. As they had been brought so were they taken away.

It was necessary to humor and excite the Arabs to induce them to persevere in the arduous work of dragging the cart through the deep soft soil into which it continually sank. At one time, after many vain efforts to move the buried wheels, it was unanimously declared that Mr. Cooper, the artist, brought ill luck, and no one would work until he retired. The cumbrous machine crept on-wards for a few more yards, but again all exertions were fruitless. Then the Frank lady would bring good fortune if she sat on the sculpture. The wheels rolled heavily along, but were soon clogged once more in the yielding soil. An evil eye surely lurked among the workmen or the bystanders. Search was quickly made, and one having been detected upon whom this curse had alighted, he was ignominiously driven away with shouts and execrations. This impediment having been removed, the cart drew nearer to the village, but soon again came to a standstill. All the sheikhs were now summarily degraded from their rank and honors, and a weak ragged boy having been dressed up in tawdry kerchiefs, and invested with a cloak, was pronounced by Hormuzd to be the only fit chief for such puny men. The cart moved forwards, until the ropes gave way, under the new excitement caused by this reflection upon the character of the Arabs. When that had subsided, and the presence of the youthful sheikh no longer encouraged his subjects, he was as summarily deposed as he had been elected, and a greybeard of ninety was raised to the dignity in his stead. He had his turn; then the most unpopular of the sheikhs were compelled to lie down on the ground, that the groaning wheels might pass over them, like the car of Juggernaut over its votaries. With yells, shrieks, and wild antics the cart was drawn within a few inches of the prostrate men. As a last resource I seized a rope myself, and with shouts of defiance between the different tribes, who were divided into separate parties and pulled against each other, and amidst the deafening *tahlehl* of the women, the lion was at length fairly brought to the water's edge.

The winter rains had not yet swelled the waters of the river so as to enable a raft bearing a very heavy cargo to float with safety to Baghdad. It was not until the month of April, after I had left Mosul on my journey to the Khabour, that the floods, from the melting of the snows in the higher mountains of Kurdistan, swept down the valley of the Tigris. I was consequently obliged to confide the task of embarking the sculptures to Behnan, my principal over-seer, a Mosulean stonecutter of considerable skill and experience, Mr. Vice-consul Rassam kindly undertaking to superintend the operation. Owing to extraordinary storms in the hills, the river rose suddenly and with unexampled rapidity. Mr. and Mrs. Rassam were at the time at Nimrûd, and the raftmen had prepared the rafts to receive the lions. It was with difficulty that they escaped before the flood, from my house in the village to the top of the ruins. The Jaif was one vast sea, and a furious wind drove the waves against the foot of the mound. The Arabs had never seen a similar inundation, and before they could escape to the high land many persons were overwhelmed in the waters.

When the flood had subsided, the lions on the river bank, though covered with mud and silt, were found uninjured. They were speedily placed on the rafts prepared for them, but unfortunately during the operation one of them, which had previously been cracked nearly across, separated into two parts. Both sculptures were doomed to misfortune. Some person, uncovering the other during the night, broke the nose. I was unable to discover the author of this wanton mischief. He was probably a stranger, who had some feud with the Arabs working in the excavations.

The rafts reached Baghdad in safety. After receiving the neces-sary repairs they floated onwards to Busrah. The waters of the Tigris throughout its course had risen far above their usual level. The embankments, long neglected by the Turkish government, had given way, and the river, bursting from its bed, spread itself over the surrounding country in vast lakes and marshes. One of the rafts was dragged into a vortex which swept through a sluice newly opened in the crumbling bank. Notwithstanding the exertions of the raftmen, aided by the crew of a boat that accompanied them; it was carried far into the interior, and left in the middle of a swamp, about a mile from the stream. The other raft fortunately escaped, and reached Busrah [Basra] without accident.

For some time the stranded raft was given up for lost. Fortu-nately it bore the broken lion, or its recovery had probably been impossible. Captain Jones, with his usual skill and intrepidity, took his steamer over the ruined embankment, and into the unexplored morass. After great exertion, under a burning sun in the midst of summer, he succeeded in placing the two parts of the sculpture on large boats, provided for the purpose, and in conveying them to their destination.

HENRY A. LAYARD

Nineveh:
How Not to Excavate

THE mound of Kuyunjik is part of the ruins of Nineveh, across the Tigris from Mosul.

❦

THE sculptured remains hitherto discovered in the mound of Kuyunjik had been reached by digging down to them from the surface, and then removing the rubbish. After the departure of Mr. Ross, the accumulation of earth above the ruins had become so considerable, frequently exceeding thirty feet, that the workmen, to avoid the labor of clearing it away, began to tunnel along the walls, sinking shafts at intervals to admit light and air. The hardness of the soil, mixed with pottery, bricks, and remains of buildings raised at various times over the buried ruins of the Assyrian palace, rendered this process easy and safe with ordinary care and precaution. The subterraneous passages were narrow, and were propped up when necessary either by leaving columns of earth, as in mines, or by wooden beams. These long galleries, dimly lighted, lined with the remains of ancient art, broken urns projecting from the crumbling sides, and the wild Arab and hardy Nestorian wandering through their intricacies, or working in their dark recesses, were singularly picturesque.

From *Discoveries in the Ruins of Nineveh and Babylon*, p. 69.

HENRY A. LAYARD

Nineveh: a Visit from Rawlinson

As I ascended the mound next morning I perceived a group of travellers on its summit, their horses picketted in the stubble. Ere I could learn what strangers had thus wandered to this remote region, my hand was seized by the faithful Bairakdar. Beneath, in an excavated chamber, wrapped in his travelling cloak, was Rawlinson deep in sleep, wearied by a long and harassing night's ride. For the first time we met in the Assyrian ruins, and besides the greetings of old friendship there was much to be seen together, and much to be talked over. The fatigues of the journey had, however, brought on fever, and we were soon compelled, after visiting the principal excavations, to take refuge from the heat of the sun in the mud huts of the village. The attack increasing in the evening, it was deemed prudent to ride into Mosul at once, and we mounted our horses in the middle of the night.

During two days Colonel Rawlinson was too ill to visit the excavations at Kuyunjik. On the third we rode together to the mound. After a hasty survey of the ruins we parted, and he continued his journey to Constantinople and to England, to reap the laurels of a well-earned fame.

Ibid., p. 100.

HENRY A. LAYARD

Layard Goes to Petra

THESE adventures befell Layard in 1840, during his early travels.

❦

AFTER toiling up a very steep and stony track for about two hours, the camels, unaccustomed to such mountain ascents, appeared to be much fatigued. Leaving them to rest for a while under the care of Antonio, I ascended on foot, with Awad and Musa, a high peak in the neighbourhood. The day being cloudless, I anticipated a fine prospect from it, and was not disappointed. The scene was wonderful, and magnificent from its savage desolation. Range after range of barren, naked hills of the most varied and fantastic shapes, like the waves of a sea which had been suddenly arrested when breaking and curling, stretched before me. Beneath me lay the inhospitable valley of the Ghor. In the extreme distance, to the north, could just be distinguished the Dead Sea.

We continued, during the afternoon, the ascent of the remarkable and picturesque range of mountains we had entered in the morning. They were of standstone, and had been worn into the most fantastic shapes, such as domes, pinnacles, and pyramids, which looked as if they had been the work of human hands.

We then entered a long, narrow gorge, formed on either side by lofty cliffs. Through it ran the bed of a torrent, then dry and filled with trees and shrubs. I was desirous of pitching my tent, as I saw many excavations in the rocks which I wished to examine; but my guards declared the place to be specially dangerous from robbers, and hurried me through it as fast as the camels could go.

I pitched my tent for the night under a huge projecting rock, by which we were completely concealed. As I sat by it in the calm evening, large red-legged partridges swarmed around me, loudly

From *Early Adventures in Persia, Susiana and Babylonia*. London: John Murray; 1894, pp. 13-19 (1st ed. 1887).

cackling and crowing. They offered tempting materials for an excellent supper, after the privations of the previous days, when my
only food had been boiled rice and cakes of unleavened bread baked
in the ashes; but my Arab guards implored me not to use my gun,
as they were still haunted by the fear of robbers, and its report
would disclose our hiding-place.

On the following morning we entered the Wadi Musa, or Valley
of Moses, and in an hour and a half I found myself amid the ruins
of Petra. Everywhere around me were remains of ancient buildings of all descriptions, whilst in the high rocks which formed the
boundaries of the valley were innumerable excavated dwellings and
tombs. As I had intended to visit the ruins leisurely, I did not stop
to examine them, but, passing through them on my camel, ascended
to a spacious rock-cut tomb, in front of which was a small platform covered with grass. There I made up my mind to pitch my
tent.

I dismounted and spread my carpet. I had scarcely done so when
a swarm of half-clad Arabs, with dishevelled locks and savage looks,
issued from the excavated chambers and gathered round me. I
asked for some bread and milk, which were brought to me, and
Antonio prepared my breakfast, the Arabs watching all our movements. Their appearance was far from reassuring, and my guides
were evidently anxious as to their intentions. They were known to
be treacherous and bloodthirsty, and a traveller had rarely, if ever,
ventured among them without the protection of some powerful
chief or without a sufficient guard.

They remained standing round me in silence, until they perceived that I was about to rise from my carpet with the object of
visiting the ruins in the valley. Then one of them advanced and
demanded of me in the name of the tribe a considerable sum of
money, which, he said, was due to it from all travellers who entered its territory. I refused to submit to the exaction, alleging that
I was under the protection of Sheikh Abu-Dhaouk. I was ready, I
added, to pay for any provisions that might be furnished to me, or
for any service of which I might be in need.

This answer gave rise to loud outcries on the part of the assembled Arabs. They began by abusing my two guides, whom they
accused of having conducted me to Wadi Musa without having
first obtained the permission of their sheikh. A violent altercation
ensued, which nearly led to bloodshed, as swords were drawn on
both sides. An attempt was made to seize my effects, and I was
told that I should not be allowed to leave the place until I had
paid the sum demanded of me. As I still absolutely refused to do
so, one, more bold and insolent than the rest, advanced towards
me with his drawn sword, which he flourished in my face. I raised

my gun, determined to sell my life dearly if there was an intention to murder me. Another Arab suddenly possessed himself of Mausa's gun, which he had imprudently laid on the ground whilst unloading the camels.

I directed Antonio to inform the crowd, which was now increasing in numbers, as men and women issued from the rock-cut tombs like rabbits from a warren, that I was under the protection of Sheikh Abu-Dhaouk, who had made himself personally responsible to the Governor of Hebron, and consequently to Ibrahim Pasha, for my safety. If any violence were offered to me he would lose his head, unless his tribe took full vengeance upon those who had committed it, and the Egyptian Government would not be satisfied until they were exterminated.

The tribe inhabiting the Wadi Musa had not long before been at war with that of Sheikh Abu-Dhaouk, who had inflicted considerable losses upon it, killing some of its best warriors and carrying off a large number of its sheep and camels. It had reason, therefore, to fear that an outrage upon a traveller who was under his protection might lead to serious consequences. A consultation took place among those who appeared to have some authority over the crowd, which ended by my being informed that if I agreed to pay about half the sum at first demanded I should be allowed to remain as long as I liked in the valley, and to visit the ruins without molestation. What they asked, they declared, was far less than had been paid by other travellers, and it was only out of consideration for a guest and friend of Abu-Dhaouk that they would be satisfied with so small a sum.

I still refused. In the first place, I thought it right to resist this attempt to blackmail a traveller; and, in the second, had I been even disposed to yield, I had not enough money with me to give what was asked. I therefore directed Musa and Awad to reload the camels and to prepare to accompany me. Seeing that I was determined to carry out my intention of visiting the ruins without their permission, the Arabs formed a circle round me, threatening to prevent me from doing so by force, gesticulating and screeching at the top of their voices. With their ferocious countenances, their flashing eyes and white teeth set in faces blackened by sun and dirt, and their naked limbs exposed by their short shirts and tattered Arab cloaks, they had the appearance of desperate cut-throats ready for any deed of violence.

In this juncture, and when an affray which might have led to fatal results seemed imminent, the sheikh of Wadi Musa, who had been absent from the valley, made his appearance. Having somewhat calmed his excited tribesmen and obtained silence, he inquired into the cause of the disturbance. Having been told it, he announced that he had a right, as chief of the tribe in whose territory the ruins were situated, to the sum originally demanded, and that unless I paid it he would not permit me to visit them. He was a truculent and insolent fellow, tall, and with a very savage countenance; rather better dressed than his followers, and armed with a long gun and pistols, whilst they only carried swords and spears.

I repeated my resolution not to submit to this imposition, and warned him that if any injury befell me he would be held personally responsible by Ibrahim Pasha, who had given ample proof that he could punish those who defied his authority. Abu-Dhaouk, moreover, I said, was a hostage for my safety. I then rose from my carpet and, directing Awad and Musa to follow me with the camels, which they were loading, prepared to begin my examination of the ruins.

The sheikh, seeing that I was not to be intimidated, and fearing the consequences should any violence be offered to me or to my guides which might lead to a blood-feud between his tribe and that of Abu-Dhaouk, ordered his men to stand back, and I went on my way without further interference. As I descended into the valley he called out to me by way of benediction, "As a dog you came, as a dog you go away." I gave him the usual Arab salutation in return, and threw him a piece of money in payment for the bread and milk which had been brought to me on my arrival. This return for hospitality would have been resented as an insult by a true Bedouin, but he picked up the silver coin, and as I left I saw him crouching down on his hams surrounded by his Arabs, evidently discussing the manner in which I ought to be dealt with.

Awad and Musa were a good deal alarmed at my reception, and feared that the sheikh and his followers would find some means of avenging themselves upon me for having defied them. They urged me, therefore, to leave the valley as soon as possible. But I was convinced that, notwithstanding the chief's threats, he would not venture to rob or injure me. The name of Ibrahim Pasha was at that time feared throughout Syria, and the sheikh could not but be well persuaded that Abu-Dhaouk, to save his own head, would execute summary vengeance upon those who had plundered or murdered a traveller under his protection. I was determined, as I had come so far to visit the ruins of Petra, to examine its principal monuments leisurely, and I spent the whole day in doing so. I was not molested, but I observed Arabs watching all my movements.

I had sufficient time to visit the principal ruins—the great amphitheatre carved out of the rock, the various temples and public edifices, and many of the tombs sculptured in the precipitous cliffs forming the sides of the valley. These tombs, some of which were elaborately ornamented with pediments, friezes, and columns, were mostly used as habitations by Arab families, and their spacious chambers were filled with smoke and dirt.

The scenery of Petra made a deep impression upon me, from its extreme desolation and its savage character. The rocks of friable limestone, worn by the weather into forms of endless variety, some of which could scarcely be distinguished from the remains of ancient buildings; the solitary columns rising here and there amidst the shapeless heaps of masonry; the gigantic flights of steps, cut in the rocks, leading to the tombs; the absence of all vegetation to relieve the solemn monotony of the brown barren soil; the mountains rising abruptly on all sides; the silence and solitude, scarcely disturbed by the wild Arab lurking among the fragments of pediments, fallen cornices, and architraves which encumber the narrow valley, render the ruins of Petra unlike those of any other ancient city in the world.

The most striking feature at Petra is the immense number of excavations in the mountain-sides. It is astonishing that a people should, with infinite labour, have carved the living rock into temples, theatres, public and private buildings, and tombs, and have thus constructed a city on the borders of the desert, in a waterless, inhospitable region, destitute of all that is necessary for the sustenance of man—a fit dwelling-place for the wild and savage robber tribes that now seek shelter in its remains.

Towards evening, yielding to the urgent entreaties of Awad and Musa, who declared that it would not be safe for me to pass the night among the ruins, I left them by the valley through which we had arrived. We encamped some time after nightfall in a narrow wadi. But we had little sleep, as we had to keep watch, fearing that the Arabs of Wadi Musa might have followed us with evil intent.

HENRY A. LAYARD

An Arab Dentist

SHEIKH Abu-Dhaouk arrived in the night. He came to me early in the morning, and apologised for not having been at his tents to receive me. He had been detained, he said, at Hebron, by the governor, who had demanded a much larger sum as tribute from the tribe than the Government was entitled to, and had threatened to throw him into prison unless it were forthcoming. I had slept little, as I was suffering greatly from toothache. The sheikh declared that there was a skilful dentist in the encampment, and as the pain was almost unbearable, I made up my mind to put myself in his hands rather than endure it any longer. He was accordingly sent for. He was a tall, muscular Arab. His instruments consisted of a short knife or razor, and a kind of iron awl. He bade me sit on the ground, and then took my head firmly between his knees. After cutting away at the gums he applied the awl to the roots of the tooth, and, striking the other end of it with all his might, expected to see the tooth fly into the air. The awl slipped and made a severe wound in my palate. He insisted upon a second trial, declaring that he could not but succeed. But the only result was that he broke off a large piece of the tooth, and I had suffered sufficient agony to decline a third experiment.

After I had undergone this very disagreeable and unsuccessful operation, the sheikh, whilst expressing his sympathy for me, suggested that the sum he was to receive for the hire of his camels and for his protection was not sufficient, and that the agreement which he had made with me had been extorted from him by Colonel Yusuf Effendi. I ought therefore to make a voluntary addition to it by way of bakshish. I refused to do so, and as he began to make difficulties about finding camels and a man who was willing to run the risk of accompanying me, I threatened to return at once to Hebron and to refer the matter to the colonel. Finding that I was resolute and was preparing my baggage, he gave way somewhat sulkily. But it was already ten o'clock before the two camels were

Ibid., pp. 7-8.

forthcoming. Instead of sending his brother with me, as he had promised to do, he brought two Arabs on foot, armed with long guns, who, he said, would accompany me as guards as well as guides, the country being very unsafe. I was under the necessity of yielding, and at length, after many delays and much squabbling, I left his encampment.

C. J. GADD

Nineveh After Its Fall

IN all the twenty-four centuries which intervened between the burial and the re-appearance of the buildings of Assyria it is impossible to say what monuments scattered throughout the former Assyrian empire were seen by human eyes. Few and seldom, beyond doubt, for they were emblems of conquest and the fall of Nineveh set free half a world of stuttering Nahums besides all the monkey-paws that are ever itching to mar and smash. Whence had Daniel his vision of the first beast that was "like a lion and had eagle's wings," if his book was not written until the late century to which critics assign it? Some carved stones even then were perhaps visible in the old land of Assyria, for there were Greeks of the following of Alexander who had to tell of a "tomb of Sardanapallos" at "Ninos," which, they agreed, bore an epitaph of that prince of profligates who "proceeded to such a degree of Voluptuousness and sordid Uncleanness that he compos'd Verses for his Epitaph, with a Command to his Successors to have them inscrib'd upon his Tomb after his Death; which was thus Translated by a Grecian out of the Barbarian Language

> What once I gorg'd I now injoy
> And wanton Lusts me still imploy
> All other things by Mortals priz'd
> Are left as Dirt by me despis'd."

From *The Stones of Assyria*. London: Chatto and Windus Ltd.; 1936, pp. 2-3. Reprinted by permission of C. J. Gadd.

This was the more elaborate version of the epitaph, as it was known to Aristotle perhaps from reports of Alexander's companions. He thought it more suitable to the grave of an ox than of a king.

P. E. BOTTA

Botta and the Palace of Sargon

THE French excavator, Paul Botta, had shifted his activities to Khorsabad in March, 1843, after his unsuccessful soundings at Nineveh. It was the site of Dur Sharrukin, founded by King Sargon II, at the end of the 8th century B.C., as a new capital for the Assyrian Empire. The monarch had his palace built on a huge artificial platform, and it was here that Botta commenced his digging.

Mosul, May 2nd, 1843.

SIR,

I return from Khorsabad more astonished than ever at my discovery. Notwithstanding some interruptions, my workmen have restored to light a vast number of bas-reliefs and inscriptions, without any clue being yet afforded me by which to ascertain the design, or even to form an idea respecting the general arrangement of this monument; consequently, in order to understand my explanation, you will necessarily be obliged to follow the plan I now send you, and which is very nearly correct. I have numbered the prominent parts with Roman cyphers; they will help me to describe them. . . .

From *Letters of M. Botta on the Discoveries of Nineveh.* London: John Murray; 1850, pp. 31, 42-5, 55-8.

As those who are better informed than myself will probably undertake to determine the age of this monument, I shall avoid all discussion on the subject, but solely point out a few particulars that may prove useful in the inquiry.

Although the hair, beards, and even clothes show a resemblance to Sassanian models, I have, nevertheless, discovered no vestige of an inscription in any other writing than that of which I send you specimens. It is exactly like what is observed upon the bricks found at Nineveh. The bricks themselves are the same as those last named, and are equally cemented with bitumen. I have also found at Nineveh fragments of sculptures in a style precisely similar. It is likewise remarkable, that up to the present moment, all the mythological emblems are Babylonian, and quite the same as those so frequently seen on seals and cylinders. Finally, not a trace has yet been discerned of any iron employed in this monument, whilst numerous remains of copper objects have been found; nails, rings, bands, and even part of a small wheel with a slender felloe, about 50 centimetres in diameter. These facts argue favorably for the antiquity of the monument, but, on the other hand, I have discovered that the stones with which it is built belonged to a still older edifice. Indeed, some of the gypsum slabs bear traces of cuneiform inscriptions, evidently destroyed by time. The writing, too, entirely resembles the inscriptions of the actual monument. The specimen I now send will enable you to judge for yourself.

I sincerely regret being the only person on the spot to describe these ruins. I am no artist, and the sketches I transmit to you are not merely unworthy copies of the originals, but, further, they engross much of my time. Besides, I feel myself incompetent, through want of requisite learning, to appreciate the historic value of several details which, perhaps, might set others on the track to make interesting discoveries.

In my opinion, it would be worthy of the munificence of the French government to send here some one capable of assisting me in the excavations and who can draw well. The field is large, for, I repeat, this monument extends through the whole interior of the mound; and, in proportion as we advance towards its centre, the sculptures are better preserved. Almost all the bas-reliefs are historical; the inscriptions are very numerous, and, if they can be read, will probably throw great light upon certain facts and unfold many new ones. Above all, it would be necessary to copy everything from those walls which at once decay when exposed to the air; or, pushed by the earth, immediately fall to pieces. Already, notwithstanding my props, part of what I have seen and drawn remains no longer. I hope those persons who prize archæological researches will unite with you in endeavouring to obtain from our government the means of rescuing as much as possible, and of carefully copying whatever cannot be saved.

E. BOTTA.

Mosul, July 24th, 1843

The construction of this edifice is invariably the same; always large and small gypsum slabs set upright against the earth of the mound. I cannot believe such walls have ever supported a stone roof, and this is one reason for my suspecting it was of wood. Nevertheless, I have acquired no certain knowledge on this subject; the charcoal, very abundant in some places, is not seen in others where, however, the walls offer an equally calcined appearance. I therefore remain undecided. I shall merely observe that the dimensions of the bull are so enormous, it is impossible to suppose it could have been conveyed to its place through narrow passages excavated in the mound. Perhaps it was stationed outside one of the portals. In this case, the wall must have formed the exterior part of this monument, and, consequently, the state of preservation in which both the sculptures and stone itself are found is fully explained. It would not have suffered by the falling in of the burning roof. But the time has not yet come for entering upon these discussions; when everything is disinterred we may probably understand all that at present seems doubtful. By making enquiries I have endeavoured, but in vain, to learn whether this village had not anciently some other name of more Chaldaean sound than Khorsabad, or Khestéabad (for so it is still written): there is no local tradition on the subject, and even the inhabitants themselves were ignorant of the archæological treasures lying buried under their feet, and which chance enabled me to discover; my researches shall continue, notwithstanding. With regard to the future direction of the works, I have, Sir, the satisfaction of informing you that, in all probability, I shall encounter no further obstacles. His Excellency the Minister of the Interior having kindly assisted my labours, I am able to act more freely, and have succeeded in persuading the Chief of the village to vacate his house, which barred our passage; he will take up his abode in the plain, and the rest of the people will follow him; the entire mound will thus be left at my disposal, and nothing shall escape my scrutiny. I am, however, compelled to stop the excavations for some time; the air of Khorsabad is particularly unhealthy, as I not only myself experienced, but likewise all those who accompanied me. Already, I have frequently been obliged to change the workmen; and their head, who served me with intelligence, is now dangerously ill. For this reason I cannot return to Khorsabad before the heats are over, and were the works to proceed at this moment, such is the condition of the sculptures, they would be lost before I could go and draw them; I have therefore suspended my labours for a short period, and re-interred those parts which I had not time to copy. As for the others, I regret to say they will soon fall to atoms. Being no longer supported, the walls yield to the swelling of the ground;* the action of the sun reduces the surface to powder, and even now a considerable portion has disappeared. This is truly grievous, but I can devise no remedy, unless the whole, as I draw it, should be again filled up, and thus preserved for future investigation; this is my present purpose, since, everything considered, it will always be possible to make a fresh clearing, whilst, by leaving the walls uncovered, in three months not a vestige of them would remain.

E. BOTTA.

* Monsieur BOTTA was careful, from the commencement, to support the uncovered sculptures by props; but during the long interruption to his excavations imposed upon him by the cupidity and malevolence of the last Pasha of Mosul, the props were stolen by the country people, and thus several bas-reliefs fell to pieces. The obstacles with which M. BOTTA has had to contend were infinitely greater and more numerous than could be imagined, judging merely from the letters I have published; at each step he has had to struggle against the cunning and spite of the Pasha, who on some occasions prohibited and on others allowed him to proceed, while secretly forbidding the inhabitants of the village to sell him their houses; at one time imprisoning and wishing to torture the workmen, in order to wring from them information regarding the treasures found (as he declared) by M. BOTTA; then writing complaints to Constantinople, asserting that M. BOTTA caused trenches to be made in the hill with design to erect a fortress, &c.

2. *Babylon*

HERODOTUS

Babylon and Babylonia According to Herodotus

HAVING subdued the rest of the continent, he [Cyrus of Persia] turned his attention to Assyria, a country remarkable for the number of great cities it contained, and especially for the most powerful and renowned of them all—Babylon, to which the seat of government was transferred after the fall of Nineveh. Babylon lies in a wide plain, a vast city in the form of a square with sides nearly fourteen miles long and a circuit of some fifty-six miles, and in addition to its enormous size it surpasses in splendour any city of the known world. It is surrounded by a broad deep moat full of water, and within the moat there is a wall fifty royal cubits wide and two hundred high (the royal cubit is two inches longer than the ordinary cubit). And now I must describe how the soil dug out to make the moat was used, and the method of building the wall. While the digging was going on, the earth that was shovelled out was formed into bricks, which were baked in ovens as soon as a sufficient number were made; then using hot bitumen for mortar the workmen began by building parapets along each side of the moat, and then went on to erect the actual wall. In both cases they laid rush-mats between every thirty courses of brick. On the top of the wall they constructed, along each edge, a row of one-roomed buildings facing inwards with enough space between for a four-horse chariot to turn. There are a hundred gates in the circuit of the wall, all of bronze with bronze uprights and lintels.

Eight days' journey from Babylon there is a city called Is on a smallish river of the same name, a tributary of the Euphrates, and

From *The Histories*, Book I, 5th century B.C. Translated by Aubrey de Sélincourt. London: Martin Secker & Warburg Ltd.; 1954, pp. 85-7, 91-3. By permission of David Higham Associates Ltd.

in this river lumps of bitumen are found in great quantity. This was the source of supply for the bitumen used in building the wall of Babylon. The Euphrates, a broad, deep, swift river which rises in Armenia and flows into the Persian Gulf, runs through the middle of the city and divides it in two. The wall is brought right down to the water on both sides, and at an angle to it there is another wall on each bank, built of baked bricks without mortar, running through the town. There are a great many houses of three and four stories. The main streets and the side streets which lead to the river are all dead straight, and for every one of the side streets or alleys there was a bronze gate in the river wall by which the water could be reached.

The great wall I have described is, so to speak, the breastplate or chief defence of the city; but there is a second one within it, not so thick but hardly less strong. There is a fortress in the middle of each half of the city: in one the royal palace surrounded by a wall of great strength, in the other the temple of Bel, the Babylonian Zeus. The temple is a square building, two furlongs each way, with bronze gates, and was still in existence in my time; it has a solid central tower, one furlong square, with a second erected on top of it and then a third, and so on up to eight. All eight towers can be climbed by a spiral way running round the outside, and about half way up there are seats for those who make the ascent to rest on. On the summit of the topmost tower stands a great temple with a fine large couch in it, richly covered, and a golden table beside it. The shrine contains no image, and no one spends the night there except (if we may believe the Chaldaeans who are the priests of Bel) one Assyrian woman, all alone, whoever it may be that the god has chosen. The Chaldaeans also say—though I do not believe them—that the god enters the temple in person and takes his rest upon the bed. There is a similar story told by the Egyptians at Thebes, where a woman always passes the night in the temple of the Theban Zeus and is forbidden, so they say, like the woman in the temple at Babylon, to have any intercourse with men; and there is yet another instance in the Lycian town of Patara, where the priestess who delivers the oracles when required (for there is not always an oracle there) is shut up in the temple during the night.

In the temple of Babylon there is a second shrine lower down, in which is a great sitting figure of Bel, all of gold on a golden throne, supported on a base of gold, with a golden table standing beside it. I was told by the Chaldaeans that, to make all this, more than twenty-two tons of gold were used. Outside the temple is a golden altar, and there is another one, not of gold, but of great size, on which sheep are sacrificed. The golden altar is reserved for the sacrifice of sucklings only. Again, on the larger altar the Chaldaeans offer something like two and a half tons of frankincense every year at the festival of Bel. In the time of Cyrus there was also in this sacred building a solid golden statue of a man some fifteen feet high—I have this on the authority of the Chaldaeans, though I never saw it myself. Darius the son of Hystaspes had designs upon it, but he never carried it off because his courage failed him; Xerxes, however, did take it and killed the priest who tried to prevent the sacrilege. In addition to the adornments I have described there are also many private offerings in the temple. . . .

The rainfall of Assyria is slight and provides enough moisture only to burst the seed and start the root growing, but to swell the grain and bring it to maturity artificial irrigation is used, not, as in Egypt, by the natural flooding of the river, but by labourers working hand-pumps. Like Egypt, the whole country is intersected by dykes; the largest of them has to be crossed in boats and runs in a south-easterly direction from the Euphrates until it joins another river, the Tigris, on which Nineveh was built. As a grain-bearing country Assyria is the richest in the world. No attempt is made there to grow figs, grapes, or olives or any other fruit trees, but so great is the fertility of the grain fields that they normally produce crops of two-hundredfold, and in an exceptional year as much as three-hundredfold. The blades of wheat and barley are at least three inches wide. As for millet and sesame, I will not say to what an astonishing size they grow, though I know well enough; but I also know that people who have not been to Babylonia have refused to believe even what I have said already about its fertility. The only oil these people use is made from sesame; date-palms grow everywhere, mostly of the fruit-bearing kind, and the fruit supplies them with food, wine, and honey. The method of cultivation is the same as for figs, particularly in regard to the practice of taking the fruit of what the Greeks call the "male" palm and trying it into the "female" or date-bearing tree, to allow the gall-fly to enter the fruit and ripen it and prevent it from dropping off. For it is a fact that the male palms have the gall-fly in their fruit, like wild figs.

I will next describe the thing which surprised me most of all in this country, after Babylon itself: I mean the boats which ply down the Euphrates to the city. These boats are circular in shape and made of hide; they build them in Armenia to the northward of Assyria, where they cut withies to make the frames and then stretch skins taut on the under side for the body of the craft; they are not fined-off or tapered in any way at bow or stern, but quite round like a shield. The men fill them with straw, put the cargo on board— mostly wine in palm-wood casks—and let the current take them downstream. They are controlled by two men; each has a paddle which he works standing up, one in front drawing his paddle towards him, the other behind giving it a backward thrust. The boats vary a great deal in size; some are very big, the biggest of all having a capacity of some fourteen tons. Every boat carries a live donkey—the larger ones several—and when they reach Babylon and the cargoes have been offered for sale, the boats are broken up, the frames and straw disposed of and the hides loaded on the donkeys' backs for the return journey overland to Armenia. It is quite impossible to paddle the boats upstream because of the strength of the current, and that is why they are constructed of hide instead of wood. Back in Armenia with their donkeys, the men build another lot of boats to the same design.

The dress of the Babylonians consists of a linen tunic reaching to the feet with a woollen one over it, and a short white cloak on top; they have their own fashion in shoes, which resemble the slippers one sees in Boeotia. They grow their hair long, wear turbans, and perfume themselves all over; everyone owns a seal and a walking-stick specially made for him, with a device carved on the top of it, an apple or rose or lily or eagle or something of the sort; for it is not the custom to have a stick without some such ornament.

CLAUDIUS RICH

Ruins of Babylon:
the First Survey

CLAUDIUS RICH made his survey of Babylon and Birs Nimrûd in 1811. Many early travellers believed the tower at Birs with its mass of vitrified bricks to be the ruins of the Tower of Babel. Rawlinson was to prove it to be in fact the site of the city of Borsippa.

From *Memoir on the Ruins of Babylon*. London: Longman, Hurst etc. and John Murray; 1815, pp. 191-4, 20-7, 34-7.

THE site of Babylon having never been either thoroughly explored, or accurately described, I beg leave to offer to the associates of the *Mines de l'Orient* an account of my observations on that celebrated spot, the completion of which has been retarded by frequent interruptions from indisposition and official occupation.

I have frequently had occasion to remark the inadequacy of general descriptions to convey an accurate idea of persons or places. I found this particularly exemplified in the present instance. From the accounts of modern travellers, I had expected to have found on the site of Babylon more, and less, than I actually did. Less, because I could have formed no conception of the prodigious extent of the whole ruins, or of the size, solidity, and perfect state, of some of the parts of them; and more, because I thought that I should have distinguished some traces, however imperfect, of many of the principal structures of Babylon. I imagined, I should have said: "Here were the walls, and such must have been the extent of the area. There stood the palace, and this most assuredly was the tower of Belus."—I was completely deceived: instead of a few insulated mounds, I found the whole face of the country covered with vestiges of building, in some places consisting of brick walls surprisingly fresh, in others merely of a vast succession of mounds of rubbish of such indeterminate figures, variety, and extent, as to involve the person who should have formed any theory in inextricable confusion.—This, together with the impossibility, in such a remote situation, of referring to all the authorities I should have consulted, will cause my account of the remains of Babylon to appear very meagre and unsatisfactory. I announce no discovery, I advance no interesting hypothesis; I am sensible that to form any thing like a correct judgment, much study and consideration, and frequent visits to the same place, are requisite. As probably more weight may be attached to my opinions from my residence on the spot, and advantages of observation, than they would otherwise be entitled to, I would rather incur the imputation of being an ignorant and superficial observer, than mislead by forming rash decisions upon subjects so difficult to be properly discussed; and I shall therefore confine myself, in the present memoir, to a plain, minute, and accurate statement of what I actually saw, avoiding all conjectures except where they may tend to throw light on the description, or be the means of exciting others to inquiry and consideration. I have added a few sketches illustrative of the principal objects, for which I claim no other merit than that of scrupulous fidelity, having been solicitous to render them accurate representations rather than good drawings. For the sake of greater intelligibility in my descriptions, I have added a general sketch of the ground, for the measurements of which I am indebted to a gentleman who accompanied me (Mr. Lockett), who superintended that operation whilst I was employed in drawing and exploring. I project other excursions to the same spot to confirm and prosecute my researches; and preparatory to them I solicit the communications and queries of the learned, for my guidance and information.

An inquiry concerning the foundation of Babylon, and the position of its remains, does not enter into my present plan; the latter subject has been already so ably treated by Major Rennel, in his *Geography of Herodotus* (a work to which I have often been under obligations, which I take this opportunity of acknowledging), that I shall consider the site of Babylon as established in the environs of Hellah [Hilla], and commence my description with an account of the country about that place.

Before entering into a minute description of the ruins, to avoid repetition, it is necessary to state that they consist of mounds of earth, formed by the decomposition of building, channelled and furrowed by the weather, and the surface of them strewed with pieces of brick, bitumen, and pottery.

On taking a view of the ruins from south to north, the first object that attracts attention is the low mound connected with the embankment; on it are two little parallel walls close together, and only a few feet in height and breadth, which bear indisputable marks of having formed part of a Mohammedan oratory or *Koubbè*. This ruin is called *Jumjuma* (Calvary) and gives its name to a village a little to the left of it. The Turkish Geographer says, "To the north of Hellah on the river is Jumjuma, which is the burial place of a Sultan." To this succeeds the first grand mass of ruins, which is one thousand one hundred yards in length, and eight hundred in greatest breadth, its figure nearly resembling that of a quadrant: its height is irregular; but the most elevated part may be about fifty or sixty feet above the level of the plain, and it has been dug into for the purpose of procuring bricks. Just below the highest part of it is a small dome in an oblong inclosure, which, it is pretended, contains the body of a son of Ali, named Amran, together with those of seven of his companions, all slain at the battle of Hellah. Unfortunately for the credit of the tradition, however, it is proved on better authority to be a fraud not uncommon in these parts, Ali having had no son of this description. From the most remarkable object on it I shall distinguish this mound by the name of Amran.

On the north is a valley of five hundred and fifty yards in length, the area of which is covered with tussocks of rank grass, and crossed by a line of ruins of very little elevation. To this succeeds the second

grand heap of ruins, the shape of which is nearly a square, of
seven hundred yards length and breadth, and its south-west angle
is connected with the north-west angle of the mounds of Amran,
by a ridge of considerable height, and nearly one hundred yards in
breadth. This is the place where Beauchamp made his observations,
and it is certainly the most interesting part of the ruins of Babylon:
every vestige discoverable in it declares it to have been composed
of buildings far superior to all the rest which have left traces in
the eastern quarter: the bricks are of the finest description; and
notwithstanding this is the grand storehouse of them, and that the
greatest supplies have been and are now constantly drawn from it,
they appear still to be abundant. But the operation of extracting
the bricks has caused great confusion, and contributed much to
increase the difficulty of deciphering the original design of this
mound, as in search of them the workmen pierce into it in every
direction, hollowing out deep ravines and pits, and throwing up
the rubbish in heaps on the surface. In some places they have bored
into the solid mass, forming winding caverns and subterranean
passages, which, from their being left without adequate support,
frequently bury the workmen in the rubbish. In all these excavations walls of burnt brick laid in lime mortar of a very good quality
are seen; and in addition to the substances generally strewed on
the surfaces of all these mounds we here find fragments of alabaster
vessels, fine earthen ware, marble, and great quantities of varnished
tiles, the glazing and colouring of which are surprisingly fresh. In
a hollow near the southern part I found a sepulchral urn of earthen
ware, which had been broken in digging, and near it lay some
human bones which pulverized with the touch.

To be more particular in my description of this mound, not
more than two hundred yards from its northern extremity is a
ravine hollowed out by those who dig for bricks, in length near a
hundred yards, and thirty feet wide by forty or fifty deep. On one
side of it a few yards of wall remain standing, the face of which
is very clean and perfect, and it appears to have been the front
of some building. The opposite side is so confused a mass of rubbish, that it should seem the ravine had been worked through a
solid building. Under the foundations at the southern end an opening is made, which discovers a subterranean passage floored and
walled with large bricks laid in bitumen, and covered over with
pieces of sand stone, a yard thick and several yards long, on which
the whole being so great as to have given a considerable degree of
obliquity to the side walls of the passage. It is half full of brackish
water (probably rain water impregnated with nitre, in filtering
through the ruins which are all very productive of it,) and the
workmen say that some way on it is high enough for a horseman

to pass upright: as much as I saw of it, it was near seven feet in height, and its course to the south. This is described by Beauchamp, who most unaccountably imagines it must have been part of the city wall. The superstructure over the passage is cemented with bitumen, other parts of the ravine with mortar, and the bricks have all writing on them. The northern end of the ravine appears to have been crossed by an extremely thick wall of yellowish brick cemented with a brilliant white mortar, which has been broken through in hollowing it out; and a little to the north of it I discovered what Beauchamp saw imperfectly, and understood from the natives to be an idol. I was told the same thing, and that it was discovered by an old Arab in digging, but that not knowing what to do with it, he covered it up again. On sending for the old man, who pointed out the spot, I set a number of men to work, who after a day's hard labour laid open enough of the statue to show that it was a lion of colossal dimensions, standing on a pedestal, of a coarse kind of gray granite and of rude workmanship; in the mouth was a circular aperture into which a man might introduce his fist.

A little to the west of the ravine is the next remarkable object, called by the natives the Kasr, or palace, by which appellation I shall designate the whole mass. It is a very remarkable ruin, which being uncovered and in part detached from the rubbish, is visible from a considerable distance, but so surprisingly fresh in its appearance, that it was only after a minute inspection I was satisfied of its being in reality a Babylonian remain. It consists of several walls and piers (which face the cardinal points) eight feet in thickness, in some places ornamented with niches, and in others strengthened by pilasters and buttresses, built of fine burnt brick, (still perfectly clean and sharp,) laid in lime-cement of such tenacity, that those whose business it is have given up working, on account of the extreme difficulty of extracting them whole. The tops of these walls are broken, and may have been much higher. On the outside they have in some places been cleared nearly to the foundations, but the internal spaces formed by them are yet filled with rubbish in some parts almost to their summit. One part of the wall has been split into three parts and overthrown as if by an earthquake; some detached walls of the same kind, standing at different distances, show what remains to have been only a small part of the original fabric; indeed it appears that the passage in the ravine, together with the wall which crosses its upper end, were connected with it. There are some hollows underneath, in which several persons have lost their lives; so that no one will now venture into them, and their entrances have now become choked up with rubbish. Near this ruin is a heap of rubbish, the sides of which

are curiously streaked by the alternation of its materials, the chief
part of which, it is probable, was unburnt brick, of which I found
a small quantity in the neighbourhood, but no reeds were discoverable in the interstices. There are two paths near this ruin, made
by the workmen who carry down their bricks to the river side,
whence they are transported by boats to Hellah; and a little to the
north-north-east of it is the famous tree which the natives call
Athelè, and maintain to have been flourishing in ancient Babylon,
from the destruction of which they say God purposely preserved
it, that it might afford Ali a convenient place to tie up his horse
after the battle of Hellah! It stands on a kind of ridge, and nothing
more than one side of its trunk remains (by which it appears to
have been of considerable girth); yet the branches at the top are
still perfectly verdant, and gently waving in the wind produce a
melancholy rustling sound. It is an evergreen, something resembling the *lignum vitæ,* and of a kind, I believe, not common in this
part of the country, though I am told there is a tree of the same
description at Bassora [Basra].

All the people of the country assert that it is extremely dangerous
to approach this mound after night-fall, on account of the multitude
of evil spirits by which it is haunted.

But although there are no ruins in the immediate vicinity of the
river, by far the most stupendous and surprising mass of all
the remains of Babylon is situated in this desert about six miles to
the south-west of Hellah. It is called by the Arabs *Birs Nemroud,*
by the Jews *Nebuchadnezzar's Prison,* and has been described both
by Père Emanuel and Niebuhr (who was prevented from inspecting
it closely by fear of the Arabs), but I believe it has not been noticed
by any other traveller. Rennel, on the authority of D'Anville, admits
Père Emanuel's ruin into the limits of Babylon, but excludes Niebuhr's, which he says cannot be supposed to have been less than
two or three miles from the south-west angle of the city. No one
who had not actually examined the spot could ever imagine them in
fact to be one and the same ruin.

I visited the Birs under circumstances peculiarly favourable to
the grandeur of its effect. The morning was at first stormy, and
threatened a severe fall of rain; but as we approached the object
of our journey, the heavy clouds separating discovered the Birs
frowning over the plain, and presenting the appearance of a circular hill crowned by a tower with a high ridge extending along the
foot of it. Its being entirely concealed from our view during the
first part of our ride, prevented our acquiring the gradual idea, in
general so prejudicial to effect, and so particularly lamented by
those who visit the Pyramids. Just as we were within the proper
distance, it burst at once upon our sight in the midst of rolling

masses of thick black clouds, partially obscured by that kind of haze whose indistinctness is one great cause of sublimity, whilst a few strong catches of stormy light, thrown upon the desert in the back ground, served to give some idea of the immense extent, and dreary solitude, of the wastes in which this venerable ruin stands.

The Birs Nemroud [Nimrûd] is a mound of an oblong figure, the total circumference of which is seven hundred and sixty-two yards. At the eastern side it is cloven by a deep furrow, and is not more than fifty or sixty feet high; but at the western it rises in a conical figure to the elevation of one hundred and ninety-eight feet, and on its summit is a solid pile of brick thirty-seven feet high by twenty-eight in breadth, diminishing in thickness to the top, which is broken and irregular, and rent by a large fissure extending through a third of its height. It is perforated by small square holes disposed in rhomboids. The fine burnt bricks of which it is built have inscriptions on them; and so admirable is the cement, which appears to be lime-mortar, that, though the layers are so close together that it is difficult to discern what substance is between them, it is nearly impossible to extract one of the bricks whole. The other parts of the summit of this hill are occupied by immense fragments of brick-work of no determinate figure, tumbled together and converted into solid vitrified masses, as if they had undergone the action of the fiercest fire, or been blown up with gunpowder, the layers of the bricks being perfectly discernible,—a curious fact, and one for which I am utterly incapable of accounting. These, incredible as it may seem, are actually the ruins spoken of by Père Emanuel, who takes no sort of notice of the prodigious mound on which they are elevated.

It is almost needless to observe that the whole of this mound is itself a ruin, channelled by the weather and strewed with the usual fragments and with pieces of black stone, sand-stone, and marble. In the eastern part layers of unburnt brick are plainly to be seen, but no reeds were discernible in any part: possibly the absence of them here, when they are so generally seen under similar circumstances, may be an argument of the superior antiquity of the ruin.

ROBERT KOLDEWEY

German Excavations
at Babylon

THE ascent was from the north in the north-east corner. All uncertainty on this point has been removed by our recent excavations.
Here we had to uncover walls of great extent and deeply buried,
and discover their connection with each other. To do this, almost
the whole of our men were set to work on the site. We regularly
employ from 200 to 250 men, divided into gangs. The leader breaks
up the ground with a pickaxe, and 16 men carry away the earth
in baskets which are filled by 3 men with broad axes. This is the
usual method, which is necessarily varied according to circumstances. The leader receives 5 piastres daily, the basket-fillers 4,
and the carriers 3, as wages. At the diggings we adopt various
methods according to the nature of the site and the object aimed at.

Here the workmen descend abreast in a broad line down a slanting incline to the prescribed verge. Having reached it, they draw
back to a distance of 5 metres and recommence work. In this way
sloping layers of earth are successively peeled off and the walls
gradually emerge. By means of a field railway the earth is removed
some distance to a site which provisionally we decide to be unimportant. When one of these slopes reaches the lowest level, which
is generally the water-level, the workmen face in the opposite direction and remove the remainder in a similar fashion, only leaving
a portion of the slope on the edge of each excavation available for
transport.

At this point the ends of two parallel walls came to light running
south, which we shall describe later with the fortification walls. Between them is a broad street or roadway, which leads direct to the
Ishtar Gate, made by Nebuchadnezzar as a processional road for
the God Marduk, to whose temple of Esagila it eventually leads. It

From *The Excavations at Babylon*. Translated by Agnes S. John. London: Macmillan & Co. Ltd.; 1914, pp. 24-30. By permission of Macmillan & Co. Ltd.

still possesses the brick pavement covered with asphalt which formed a substratum for the immense flagged pavement. The central part was laid with mighty flags of limestone measuring 1.05 metres each way, and the sides with slabs of red breccia veined with white, 66 centimetres square. The bevelled edges of the joints were filled in with asphalt. On the edges of each slab, which, of course, were not visible, was an inscription, "Nebuchadnezzar, King of Babylon, son of Nabopolassar, King of Babylon, am I. The Babel Street I paved with blocks of shadu stone for the procession of the great Lord Marduk. Marduk, Lord, grant eternal life." On the flags of breccia the word *turminabanda,* breccia, has been substituted for *shadu,* mountain. The fine hard limestone may have been brought from the neighbourhood of Hit or Anah, where a similar stone is quarried, and transport by river would present little difficulty; of the provenance of the turminabanda I have not been able to acquire any knowledge. The great white paving-stones give the impression of being intended for wheeled traffic, but those that are still *in situ* do not show the slightest traces of being used for any such purpose, they are merely polished and slippery with use.

The Kasr roadway lies high, 12.5 metres above zero, and slopes gently upwards from the north to the Ishtar Gateway. A later restoration, possibly of the Persian (?) period in brick, rendered it horizontal. Before the time of Nebuchadnezzar it was considerably lower, but as he placed the entire palace on a level higher than that of its predecessor, he was forced also to raise the roadway. In consequence of this we can to-day enjoy the glorious view over the whole city as far as the outer walls. It is clearly of this work of his that Nebuchadnezzar speaks in his great *Steinplatten* inscription: "From Dulazag, the place of the decider of fates, the Chamber of Fate, as far as Aibur-shabu, the road of Babylon, opposite the gateway of Beltis, he (Nabopolassar) had adorned the way of the procession of the great lord Marduk with turminabanda stones. Aibur-shabu, the roadway of Babylon, I filled up with a high filling for the procession of the great lord Marduk, and with turminabanda stone and with shadu stone I made Aibur-shabu, from the Illu Gate to the Ishtar-sakipat-tebisha, fit for the procession of his godhead. I connected it together with the portions that my father had built and made the road glorious" (translated by H. Winckler). Ishtar-sakipat-tebisha is the Ishtar Gate, and from this we find that the inscription does not refer to the whole of the Kasr Street, but only to part of it, either that which adjoined the Ishtar Gate on the north or on the south.

The fine view now obtainable from the street of Kasr was certainly not visible in antiquity, for the roadway was bordered on both sides with high defensive walls. They were 7 metres thick and formed the junction between the northern advanced outworks and the earlier defences, of which the Ishtar Gateway is part. They guarded the approach to the gate. Manned by the defenders, the road was a real pathway of death to the foe who should attempt it. The impression of peril and horror was heightened for the enemy, and also for peaceful travellers, by the impressive decoration of long rows of lions advancing one behind the other with which the walls were adorned in low relief and with brilliant enamels.

The discovery of these enamelled bricks formed one of the motives for choosing Babylon as a site for excavation. As early as June 1887 I came across brightly coloured fragments lying on the ground on the east side of the Kasr. In December 1897 I collected some of these and brought them to Berlin, where the then Director of the Royal Museums, Richard Schöne, recognised their significance. The digging commenced on March 26, 1899, with a transverse cut through the east front of the Kasr. The finely coloured fragments made their appearance in great numbers, soon followed by the discovery of the eastern of the two parallel walls, the pavement of the processional roadway, and the western wall, which supplied us with the necessary orientation for further excavations.

The tiles represented lions advancing to right or to left according to whether they were on the eastern or the western wall. Some of them were white with yellow manes, and others yellow with red manes, of which the red has now changed to green owing to decomposition. The ground is either light or dark blue, the faces whether seen from the left or the right, are all alike, as they have been cast in a mould. None have been found *in situ*. The walls were plundered for brick, but they were not so completely destroyed as to prevent our observing that they were provided with towers that projected slightly and were obviously placed at distances apart equal to their breadth. Black and white lines in flat enamel on the edges of the towers divided the face of the two walls into panels, defining the divisions made by the towers in the two long friezes of 180 metres, the plinth was decorated with rows of broad-leaved rosettes. As the lions are about 2 metres long, it is possible that each division contained two lions. That would give 60 lions at each side, a total of 120 that agrees well with the number of fragments found.

We must now consider the reliefs and their colouring. For the reliefs a working model must first have been obtained of which the several parts could be used for making the mould. The most natural method would be to build a temporary wall the size of one of these lions with bricks of a plastic clay, and with a strong mortar compounded with sand, on which the relief could be modelled. The jointing was carefully considered, for it is so arranged as not to cut through the figures too obviously, and each brick bears a considerable share of the relief. The joints serve an actual purpose in regulating the proportions, and take the place of the squaring lines with which Egyptian artists prepared their work.

With the help of these models, moulds could be made for each separate brick. They were probably of burnt pottery similar to the moulds made for the abundant terracottas of Babylonia. The mould would form one side of the frame in which the brick was struck, and, according to the regular method of bonding, a course of whole bricks (33 x 33 centimetres) would be followed by a course of half bricks (33 x 16½). Thus the ground of the reliefs and the wall surface were actually identical, and there is not even a projecting base on which the paws of the great beasts might appear to rest, as would be the case with stone reliefs. This is art in clay, a specialised art, distinguished from all other kinds of relief. The edges of the figures do not project more or less squarely as they do in Assyrian alabaster reliefs, but in an obtuse angle. Also there are no even upper surfaces as there are on Assyrian stone carvings. Both peculiarities would considerably facilitate the withdrawal of the tile from the mould.

The same conception of art influenced the marvellous, highly developed, glyptic art of Babylonia. The style of the gem reliefs during the time of Hammurabi was also transferred to stone, while the older Babylonian stone reliefs distinctly show their direct derivation from the previous flat bas-reliefs, to which Assyrian art of the later period still adhered. Previous to our excavations no example of the plastic art of the time of Nebuchadnezzar was known.

The brick when moulded and before it was enamelled was burnt like any ordinary brick; the contours were then drawn on it with black lines of a readily fusible vitreous composition, leaving clearly marked fields. These were filled with liquid coloured enamels, the whole dried and then fused, this time apparently in a gentler fire. As the black lines had the same fusing-point as the coloured portions they often mixed with the colours themselves, thus giving the work that marvellous and harmonious brilliancy and life which we admire to-day. With the Persian enamels which we shall meet with in connection with the Persian buildings these black lines have a higher melting-point and therefore remain distinct and project above the coloured enamels after the firing.

The bricks had then to be arranged according to the design. In order to facilitate this and to ensure an accurate distribution of them on the building site, the bricks were marked on the upper side in rough glaze with a series of simple signs and numerals. The sign on the side of a brick and on that which was to be placed next it are identical. We shall learn more of the system in the Southern Citadel, where it was employed in the enamelled decorations of the great court.

L. W. KING

The Hanging Gardens?

THE actual site of Babylon was never lost in popular tradition. In spite of the total disappearance of the city, which followed its gradual decay under Seleucid and Parthian rule, its ancient fame sufficed to keep it in continual remembrance. The old Semitic name Bâb-ilî, "the Gate of the Gods," lingered on about the site, and under the form Bâbil is still the local designation for the most northerly of the city-mounds. Tradition, too, never ceased to connect the exposed brickwork of Nebuchadnezzar's main citadel and palace with his name. Kasr, the Arab name for the chief palace-mound and citadel of Babylon, means "palace" or "castle," and when in the twelfth century Benjamin of Tudela visited Baghdad, the Jews of that city told him that in the neighbouring ruins, near Hilla, the traveller might still behold Nebuchadnezzar's palace beside the fiery furnace into which Hananiah, Mishael and Azariah had been thrown. It does not seem that this adventurous rabbi actually visited the site, though it is unlikely that he was deterred by fear of the serpents and scorpions with which, his informants said, the ruins were infested.

In the sixteenth century an English merchant traveller, John Eldred, made three voyages to "New Babylon," as he calls Baghdad, journeying from Aleppo down the Euphrates. On the last occasion, after describing his landing at Falûja, and how he secured a hundred asses for lack of camels to carry his goods to Baghdad, he tells us that "in this place which we crossed over stood the olde mightie citie of Babylon, many olde ruines whereof are easilie to be seene by daylight, which I, John Eldred, have often behelde at my goode leisure having made three voyages between the New Citie of Babylon and Aleppo over this desert." But it would seem probable from his further description that "the olde tower of Babell," which he visited "sundry times," was really the ruin of 'Akarkûf, which he would have passed on his way to Baghdad. Benjamin of Tudela, on

From *A History of Babylon.* London: Chatto and Windus Ltd.; 1915, pp. 14-21, 46-9. By permission of Chatto and Windus Ltd.

the other hand, had taken Birs-Nimrûd for the Tower of Babel, and had noted how the ruins of the streets of Babylon still extend for thirty miles. In fact, it was natural that several of the early travellers should have regarded the whole complex of ruins, which they saw still standing along their road to Baghdad, as parts of the ancient city; and it is not surprising that some of the earlier excavators should have fallen under a similar illusion so far as the area between Bâbil and El-Birs is concerned. The famous description of Herodotus, and the accounts other classical writers have left us of the city's size, tended to foster this conviction; and, although the centre of Babylon was identified correctly enough, the size of the city's area was greatly exaggerated. Babylon had cast her spell upon mankind, and it has taken sixteen years of patient and continuous excavation to undermine that stubborn belief. But in the process of shrinkage, and as accurate knowledge has gradually given place to conjecture, the old spell has reappeared unchanged. It may be worth while to examine in some detail the results of recent work upon the site, and note to what extent the city's remains have thrown light upon its history while leaving some problems still unsolved. . . .

In view of the revolution in our knowledge of Babylonian topography, which has been one of the most striking results of recent work, no practical purpose would be served by tracing out the earlier but very partial examinations of the site which were undertaken successively by Rich in 1811, by Layard in 1850, by Oppert as the head of a French expedition in the years 1852–54, and by Hormuzd Rassam, between 1878 and 1889, when he was employed on excavations for the British Museum. During the last of these periods the British Museum obtained a valuable series of tablets from Babylon, some of the texts proving of great literary and scientific interest. In 1887, and again after a lapse of ten years, Dr. Robert Koldewey visited the site of Babylon and picked up fragments of enamelled bricks on the east side of the Kasr. On the latter occasion he sent some of them to Berlin, and Dr. Richard Schöne, at that time Director of the Royal Museums, recognized their artistic and archaeological interest. Thus it was with the hope of making speedy and startling discoveries that the German Oriental Society began work upon the site at the end of March in the year 1899; and it is the more to the credit of the excavators that they have not allowed any difficulties or disappointments to curtail and bring to a premature close the steady progress of their research.

The extent of ground covered by the remains of the ancient city, and the great accumulation of *débris* over some of the principal buildings rendered the work more arduous than was anticipated, and consequently the publication of results has been delayed. It is true that, from the very beginning of operations, the expert has been kept informed of the general progress of the digging by means of letters and reports distributed to its subscribers every few months by the society. But it was only in 1911, after twelve years of uninterrupted digging, that the first instalment was issued of the scientific publication. This was confined to the temples of the city, and for the first time placed the study of Babylonian religious architecture upon a scientific basis. In the following year Dr. Koldewey, the director of the excavations, supplemented his first volume with a second, in which, under pressure from the society, he forestalled to some extent the future issues of the detailed account by summarizing the results obtained to date upon all sections of the site. It has thus been rendered possible to form a connected idea of the remains of the ancient city, so far as they have been recovered.

In their work at Babylon the excavators have, of course, employed modern methods, which differ considerably from those of the age when Layard and Botta brought the winged bulls of Assyria to the British Museum and to the Louvre. The extraordinary success which attended those earlier excavators has, indeed, never been surpassed. But it is now realized that only by minuteness of search and by careful classification of strata can the remains of the past be made to reveal in full their secrets. The fine museum specimen retains its importance; but it gains immensely in significance when it ceases to be an isolated product and takes its place in a detailed history of its period.

In order to grasp the character of the new evidence, and the methods by which it has been obtained at Babylon, it is advisable to bear in mind some of the general characteristics of Babylonian architecture and the manner in which the art of building was influenced by the natural conditions of the country. One important point to realize is that the builders of all periods were on the defensive, and not solely against human foes, for in that aspect they resembled other builders of antiquity. The foe they most dreaded was flood. Security against flood conditioned the architect's ideal: he aimed solely at height and mass. When a king built a palace for himself or a temple for his god, he did not consciously aim at making it graceful or beautiful. What he always boasts of having done is that he has made it "like a mountain." He delighted to raise the level of his artificial mound or building-platform, and the modern excavator owes much to this continual filling in of the remains of earlier structures. The material at his disposal was also not without its influence in the production of buildings "like mountains," designed to escape the floods of the plain.

The alluvial origin of the Babylonian soil deprived the inhabitants of an important factor in the development of the builder's art: it produced for them no stone. But it supplied a very effective building-material in its place, a strongly adhesive clay. Throughout their whole history the Babylonian architects built in crude and in kiln-burnt brick. In the Neo-Babylonian period we find them making interesting technical experiments in this material, here a first attempt to roof in a wide area with vaulting, elsewhere counteracting the effects of settlement by a sort of expansion-joint. We shall see, too, that it was in this same medium that they attained to real beauty of design.

Brick continued to be the main building-material in Assyria too, for that country derived its culture from the lower Euphrates valley. But in the north soft limestone quarries were accessible. So in Assyria they lined their mud-brick walls with slabs of limestone, carved in low relief and brightly coloured; and they set up huge stone colossi to flank their palace entrances. This use of stone, both as a wall-lining and in wall-foundations, constitutes the main difference between Babylonian and Assyrian architectural design. Incidentally it explains how the earlier excavators were so much more successful in Assyria than in Babylonia; for in both countries they drove their tunnels and trenches into most of the larger mounds. They could tunnel with perfect certainty when they had these stone linings of the walls to guide them. But to follow out the ground-plan of a building constructed only of unburnt brick, with mud or clay for mortar, necessitates a slower and more systematic process of examination. For unburnt brick becomes welded into a solid mass, scarcely to be distinguished from the surrounding soil, and the lines of a building in this material can only be recovered by complete excavation.

An idea of the labour this sometimes entails may be gained from the work which preceded the identification of Esagila, the great temple of Marduk, the city-god of Babylon. The temple lies at a depth of no less than twenty-one metres below the upper level of the hill of *débris;* and portions of two of its massive mud-brick walls, together with the neighbouring pavements, were uncovered by bodily removing the great depth of soil truck by truck. But here even German patience and thoroughness have been beaten, and tunnelling was eventually adopted to establish the outer limits of the ground-plan, much of the interior of which still remains unexplored.

One other building within the palace deserves mention, as it has been suggested that it may represent the remains of the famous Hanging Gardens of Babylon. It is reached from the north-east corner of the Central Court along a broad passage-way, from which a branch passage turns off at right angles; and on the left side of this narrower passage are its two entrances. It must be confessed that at first sight the ground-plan of this building does not suggest a garden of any sort, least of all one that became famous as a wonder of the ancient world. It will be seen that the central part, or core, of the building is surrounded by a strong wall and within are fourteen narrow cells or chambers, seven on each side of a central gangway. The cells were roofed in with semicircular arches, forming a barrel vault over each; and the whole is encircled by a narrow corridor, flanked on the north and east sides by the outer palace-wall. This part of the building, both the vaulted chambers and the surrounding corridor, lies completely below the level of the rest of the palace. The small chambers, some of them long and narrow like the vaults, which enclose the central core upon the west and south, are on the palace level; and the subterranean portion is reached by a stairway in one of the rooms on the south side.

There are two main reasons which suggested the identification of this building with the Hanging Gardens. The first is that hewn stone was used in its construction, which is attested by the numerous broken fragments discovered among its ruins. With the exception of the Sacred Road and the bridge over the Euphrates, there is only one other place on the whole site of Babylon where hewn stone is used in bulk for building purposes, and that is the northern wall of the Kasr. Now, in all the literature referring to Babylon, stone is only recorded to have been used for buildings in two places, and those are the north wall of the Citadel and in the Hanging Gardens, a lower layer in the latter's roofing, below the layer of earth, being described as made of stone. These facts certainly point to the identification of the Vaulted Building with the Hanging Gardens. Moreover, Berossus definitely places them within the buildings by which Nebuchadnezzar enlarged his father's palace; but this reference would apply equally to the later Central Citadel constructed by Nebuchadnezzar immediately to the north of his main palace. The size of the building is also far greater in Strabo and Diodorus than that of the Vaulted Building, the side of the quadrangle, according to these writers, measuring about four times the latter's length. But discrepancy in figures of this sort, as we have already seen in the case of the outer walls of the city, is easily explicable and need not be reckoned as a serious objection.

The second reason which pointed to the identification is that, in one of the small chambers near the southwest corner of the outer fringe of rooms on those two sides, there is a very remarkable well. It consists of three adjoining shafts, a square one in the centre flanked by two of oblong shape. This arrangement, unique so far as the remains of ancient Babylon are concerned, may be most satisfactorily explained on the assumption that we here have the water-supply for a hydraulic machine, constructed on the principle of a chain-pump. The buckets, attached to an endless chain, would have passed up one of the outside wells, over a great wheel fixed

above them, and, after emptying their water into a trough as they
passed, would have descended the other outside well for refilling.
The square well in the centre obviously served as an inspection-
chamber, down which an engineer could descend to clean the well
out, or to remove any obstruction. In the modern contrivances of
this sort, sometimes employed to-day in Babylonia to raise a continuous flow of water to the irrigation-trenches, the motive-power
for turning the winch is supplied by horses or other animals moving
around in a circle. In the Vaulted Building there would have been
scarcely room for such an arrangement, and it is probable that
gangs of slaves were employed to work a couple of heavy hand-
winches. The discovery of the well undoubtedly serves to strengthen
the case for identification.

Two alternative schemes are put forward to reconstitute the upper
structure of this building. Its massive walls suggest in any case that
they were intended to support a considerable weight, and it may be
that the core of the building, constructed over the subterranean
vaults, towered high above its surrounding chambers which are on
the palace-level. This would have been in accordance with the
current conception of a hanging garden; and, since on two sides
it was bounded by the palace-wall, its trees and vegetation would
have been visible from outside the citadel. Seen thus from the lower
level of the town, the height of the garden would have been reinforced by the whole height of the citadel-mound on which the
palace stands, and imagination once kindled might have played
freely with its actual measurements.

3. Ur and the Sumerians

LEONARD WOOLLEY

Ur, Its Life and Times

In the year 1854 Mr. J. E. Taylor, British consul at Basra, was commissioned by the Trustees of the British Museum to investigate some of the ruined sites of southern Mesopotamia. Amongst the places he visited was one called by the Arabs *al Muqayyar*, the Mound of Bitumen, lying about eleven miles west of the Euphrates, a tangled mass of low sandy mounds dominated by one great pile where above the debris rose walls of red kiln-fired bricks set in the bitumen mortar which earned the place its name: the obvious importance of the building attracted Taylor, and he determined to excavate it.

In the upper part of the mound he found a rectangular structure whose walls, tolerably preserved, were of baked bricks enclosing a core of light red bricks of sun-dried clay. He drove a great shaft into the heart of the mass and proved that it was solid throughout; then he dug down into the corners, demolishing the brickwork, and discovered in each of them, hidden away in little boxes contrived in the courses of the bricks, cylinders of baked clay covered with cuneiform inscriptions. The discovery was of first-rate importance, for the cylinders commemorated the rebuilding by Nabonidus, the last native ruler of Babylon, of the Moon-god's ziggurat at Ur: "Nabonidus king of Babylon," the text reads, "the upholder of Esagila and Ezida, the reverent worshipper of the great gods am I. E-lugal-malga-sidi, the ziggurat of E-gish-shir-gal in Ur, which Ur-Nammu, a king before me, had built but not completed, did Dungi his son finish. On the inscription of Ur-Nammu and of his son Dungi saw I that Ur-Nammu had built but not completed that ziggurat and that Dungi his son had finished the work. Now was that ziggurat old. Upon the ancient foundations whereon Ur-Nammu and his son Dungi had built I made good the structure of that ziggurat, as in old times,

From *Abraham*. London: Faber and Faber Ltd.; 1936, pp. 61-71. By permission of the Executors of the Estate of the late Sir Leonard Woolley.

with mortar and burnt brick. . . ." and he dedicates the restored building anew to Nannar, Lord of the gods of heaven and earth, and ends with prayers for the life of himself and of Belshazzar his son. Here was proof that the hitherto nameless ruins of *al Muqayyar* were those of the city which alike in Nabonidus' day, 555-539 B.C., and in the time of Ur-Nammu, *circa* 2300 B.C., was known as Ur. This city, famous as the capital of the great empire of Ur-Nammu, was the only city that was called by that name. It was, at the time when the Old Testament was written, a Chaldaean town, Ur of the Chaldees. It is true that to-day its ruins lie outside Mesopotamia proper, west of the confines of the Mesopotamian "island" enclosed between the Euphrates and the Tigris, but that is only because the Euphrates has changed its course: air photographs clearly shew the old river-bed running from al 'Ubaid past the foot of the western wall of Ur towards the ancient city of Eridu in the south, whence it turns sharply eastward to empty into the great marshes that extend to Kurna; in ancient times the city did indeed lie "beyond the River." Here then was the Ur of the Old Testament, the birth-place of Abraham.

The Old Testament phrase "Ur of the Chaldees" as applied to the city of Abraham is an anachronism. In the twentieth century before Christ, Ur was a Sumerian town subject to the Elamite dynasty of Larsa, and the "Chaldaeans" had not yet emerged into the light of history. It was only towards 1100 B.C., when the Tigris valley was being overrun by Aramæan invaders, that a kindred people, the Šutû, invaded the south country; and with the Šutû, or after them, came a tribe called the Khaldu who, securing the mastership, founded a dynasty of kings and gave to southern Mesopotamia their own name, Chaldaea. The writers of the sacred books of the Hebrews naturally applied to the city of Abraham's birth the name by which it was known in their own time; it is just as if a modern historian wrote that Julius Caesar, having landed on the south coast of Britain, marched north and crossing the Thames fell upon London from the west—the form of the names would be an anachronism, but the truth of the narrative would not be impaired thereby; but in the Old Testament the gloss "of the Chaldees" is of positive value because it definitely locates the Ur of Abraham in that south Mesopotamian area which alone was Chaldaea. To Taylor then belongs the credit of having discovered the site of Ur.

But in spite of the importance of his discovery the work was not continued, for that chanced to be the time when in the northern part of the country Layard was unearthing the palaces of Assyrian kings and bringing to light the colossal man-headed bulls and the rows of bas-reliefs which are to-day one of the chief treasures of the British Museum, and compared with them the brick buildings and the clay tablets of the lower valley seemed a poor reward for the labour and cost of excavation. It was only when the tablets had been deciphered and the site identified that the scientific world could realise its interest, and then it appealed rather as the ancient capital of the empire than as the birth-place of Abraham; but in the meanwhile Taylor's work had been shut down and the mounds of *al Muqayyar* were to know sixty years of neglect before the British Museum again took up the task it had begun. Then the war gave archaeology its chance in Mesopotamia; after two seasons of preliminary work the Joint Expedition of the British Museum and of the Museum of the University of Pennsylvania was formed, and from 1922 until 1934 excavations were conducted regularly. After that, field work had to stop in order that the publication of the vast amount of historical material brought to light might be pushed forward; and how necessary it was is shewn by the fact that whereas in King's *History of Sumer and Akkad,* issued in 1916, the discussion of the site and monuments of Ur could be dismissed in a page, to-day the description of them requires many volumes. Much of the old city remains still untouched, but the Sacred Area with its temples and various sites within the town walls have been cleared and the work carried down through layer after layer of historical remains, in some cases to virgin soil; the buildings and the graves which we have found represent successive stages in a life-history of not less than four thousand years. Most of that long record does not concern us here; this book deals with but a brief interlude of a few generations. Since Abraham is the subject, the preceding ages of struggle and progress which made his city what it was must be taken for granted and only that described which he may have known; but chance has ordained that of all the periods of Sumerian history this of Abraham is most fully represented by monuments of every sort, by the ruins of houses and of temples and by written texts. Therefore we can picture with surprising detail the scene and the society wherein Abraham is said to have spent his youth, and that without invoking the powers of imagination; for every statement made we have the concrete evidence which archaeology affords.

Only to those who have seen the Mesopotamian desert will this evocation of the ancient world seem well-nigh incredible, so complete is the contrast between past and present. The transformation of a great city into a tangle of shapeless mounds shrouded in drift-sand or littered with broken pottery and brick is not easy to understand, but it is yet more difficult to realize that that blank waste ever blossomed and bore fruit for the sustenance of a busy world of men. Why, if Ur was an empire's capital, if Sumer was one vast granary, has the population dwindled to nothing, the very soil lost its virtue? The witness of the buried walls is indeed irrefragable, but how comes it of Ur and her sister realms that they are to-day "a desolation, a dry land, and a wilderness, a land wherein no man dwelleth, neither doth any son of man pass thereby"!

It is the change in the Euphrates' course that accounts for the desolation of Ur. Lower Mesopotamia, the Sumer of Abraham's day, the Chaldaea of the time of the Old Testament writers, was a reclaimed marsh. That wide delta had once been a waste of reeds and brackish water; gradually the silt brought down by the current from the upper reaches and dropped here where the stream ran more sluggishly formed islands, the richness of whose soil attracted immigrants to the valley. The first task of the inhabitants was the drainage of the land, the second was the making of high-level canals for its irrigation, and in time the whole country was covered by a network of channels, great and small, which brought water to the thirsty fields or drained the water-logged ploughlands: the upkeep of this elaborate system was one of the main concerns of the government. The nature of the country made the problem a difficult one. In the time of Abraham the distance from Ur to the sea was at least a hundred miles, and to-day, with the delta's edge encroaching annually on the Gulf, it is a hundred and fifty miles, yet the plain is only fourteen feet above sea level, and in antiquity it certainly was less; drainage therefore was not easy. For the same reason the Euphrates had to be restrained between high artificial banks; its bed, like the beds of all the irrigation-canals, was sensibly higher than the surface of the surrounding plain, so that any breach would mean disastrous floods and had to be guarded against by all conceivable precautions; on such depended the well-being of the country whose fertility astonished Herodotus when he visited it in the fifth century before Christ. We do not know exactly when the change came, but it was not so very long after that visit, perhaps about the end of the reign of Alexander the Great, towards 300 B.C. Then the river Euphrates burst its banks and, flowing across the open plain, made a new bed for itself more or less where it runs now, eleven miles to the east; and with that change the entire system of water-supply was broken up. The old irrigation-canals that had tapped the river further up were left high and dry; the new river-course, not yet confined between artificial banks, was a wide lake whose waters, level with the plain, blocked the ends of the drainage-channels so that these became stagnant back-waters: the surface of the plain was scorched by the tropic sun, the sub-soil was saturated, and the constant process of evaporation left in the earth such quantities of salt that to-day irrigation brings to the surface a white crust like heavy hoar-frost which blights all vegetation at birth.

To make good the disaster required a co-ordinated effort which the country then was too poor or too ill-organised to attempt. In the course of centuries efforts have indeed been made, but on a small scale. The river now, as of old, runs between high-piled banks and is fringed by a narrow belt of cultivation which widens out for some miles round the modern capital of the province, Nasiriyah, and in good years puts out tentative feelers almost as far afield as the suburbs of Ur: looking eastwards from Ur one sees the thin, feathery palm-belt that marks the river's course, the darker mass of the gardens of Nasiriyeh, and closer at hand some sparse green of the barley-fields. But to north and west and south the scene is one of absolute desolation; grey and yellow, the dried alluvial mud and the wind-blown sand stretch monotonously as far as the eye can see. The flat line of the horizon is accentuated rather than relieved by a low ridge of sand-dunes on the south, from behind which shews the weathered peak of the brick-built ziggurat of Eridu shimmering in the mirage; to the north-west the little mound of al 'Ubaid, four and a half miles away, is scarcely visible, withdrawn into the flatness; westwards indeed there are gravel beaches shelving to the upper desert, the vast plateau of Arabia, but they are beyond the range of eyesight; all that one sees is the barren stretch which once was fields and palm-groves and is now more dead even than the brick-strewn mounds that hide the city's ruins.

———————

LEONARD WOOLLEY

The Ziggurat of Ur

FROM the excavations at Ur one can get some idea of what the capital of the empire was like in the palmy days of the Third Dynasty. Of the temples erected by Ur-Nammu and his descendants some survive to the present day; others were rebuilt by later

From *The Sumerians*. Oxford: The Clarendon Press; 1928, pp. 12-16, 140-5. By permission of The Clarendon Press, Oxford.

kings, but in that case the ground-plan of the original was so faithfully followed—often indeed the foundations were the same—that
the new work may be taken as a replica of the old and can be used
indifferently to complete the picture.

The outstanding feature of the city was the ziggurat or staged
tower. Every great town in the land possessed a building of this
type, which seems to have been a peculiarly Sumerian invention.
One of the facts from which it is deduced that the Sumerians were
by origin a hill-people is that their gods are often represented as
standing upon mountains; it would naturally follow that in their
first home they worshipped their gods "on high places and on every
high hill." Coming into the alluvial plain of southern Mesopotamia,
those hill-folk were confronted with the difficulty that here were
no hills on which their rites could decently be practised. But the
swampy character of the soil and the recurrent floods had from
the outset taught the earliest settlers that their mud buildings must
be raised on platforms, natural or artificial; a combination of this
necessary precaution and of the traditional idea of a hill-temple
resulted in the ziggurat, an artificial mountain. In so far as it was
the base on which stood a shrine, the ziggurat was only the platform
of the king's palace writ large, just as that in its turn was a more
ambitious version of the platform of the commoner's house: in
so far as it was a hill,—and the ziggurat would have a name such
as "the Mountain of God," or "the Hill of Heaven,"—it possessed
a sanctity of its own and was elaborately planned so that every
part and every line should have significance and symbolize the
creed which it subserved. The most famous ziggurat was that of
Babylon, the "tower of Babel" of Hebrew legend, now utterly
destroyed; the ziggurat of Ur, which in plan closely resembled that
of Babylon, is the best preserved in Mesopotamia.

Ur-Nammu's building, which occupied the site of an older and
smaller ziggurat, is a rectangle measuring a little more than two
hundred feet in length by a hundred and fifty feet in breadth and
its original height was about seventy feet; the angles are orientated
to the cardinal points of the compass. The whole is a solid mass of
brickwork, the core of crude mud bricks, the face covered with a
skin, eight feet thick, of burnt bricks set in bitumen; at regular intervals in the face there are "weeper"-holes for draining the interior
and so preventing the mud brick from swelling and bursting the
outer walls. The walls, relieved by broad shallow buttresses, lean
inwards with a pronounced batter which gives a fine impression of
strength, and it is noteworthy that on the ground-plan the base of
each wall is not a straight line but convex, from which again an
idea of strength results—it is the same principle as was observed
by the builders of the Parthenon. The upper terraces were curiously

irregular; narrow along the long sides, they were broader at the
ends of the building, so that the top stage approximated rather to
the square; and at the south-east end the bottom terrace was lower
than at the north-west; from it a central flight of stairs led to the
shrine on the top stage. The approach was on the north-east face.
Three stairways, each of a hundred steps, converged before a
monumental gateway on the level of the lowest terrace, the two
side staircases leant against the wall of the ziggurat, the central
flight running out boldly at right angles from the building; the two
angles between the staircases were filled by buttresses with sides of
panelled brickwork. It is probable that both the tops of these buttresses and the terraces of the ziggurat itself were planted with
trees in closer imitation of the wooded hills of the Sumerian homeland. As an architectural feat the ziggurat is remarkable. Limited
by his material, the architect has dispensed with ornament and
relied on mass and line. The design might easily have been both
primitive and ugly, a mere superposition of cubes; as it is, while
bulk predominates, all the lines, those of the sloped outer walls
and the sharper slant of the stairways, lead the eye inwards and
upwards to the temple which was the religious as well as the artistic crown of the whole structure. This ethical idea was emphasized
by the horizontal division of the terraces which contrast with but do
not interrupt the upward-converging lines; in the late period at
least, when the tower was restored by Nabonidus of Babylon, but
probably in Ur-Nammu's day also, the stages symbolized the
divisions of the universe, the underworld, the earth, the firmament
of heaven; and the approach to the House of God passes through
them all.

The ziggurat stood on a high raised terrace called E-temen-ni-il,
surrounded by a double wall. Partly on this terrace and partly at
its feet, below the north-east face of the ziggurat, lay the great
temple of Nannar. The shrine on the ziggurat's summit was the
holiest place of all, but it was too small to be the sole temple of
so great a god and the main building had perforce to be elsewhere.
The sanctuary of this lower temple stood against the north-west
side of the tower, and on the lower stage stretched its wide outer
court surrounded by store-chambers and offices. Since to every temple there were attached lands more or less extensive, the produce
of which either belonged to the god or paid tithe to him, and since
offerings in kind were brought by tenants and by worshippers alike,
plenty of store space was essential and the affairs of the god had to
be run on business lines. The temple officials duplicated in title and
in function those of the king's palace; besides the priests proper
there were ministers of the Harem, of War, of Agriculture, of
Transport, of Finance, and a host of secretaries and accountants

responsible for the revenues and the outgoings of the temple. To the Ga-makh, the Great Storehouse, perhaps this courtyard below the ziggurat, the countrymen would bring their cattle, sheep and goats, their sacks of barley and rounds of cheese, clay pots of clarified butter and bales of wool, all would be checked and weighed and the scribes would give for everything a receipt made out on a clay tablet and would file a duplicate in the temple archives, while the porters would store the goods in the magazines which opened off the court.

LEONARD WOOLLEY

Ur: a Crucial Inscription

WHAT really gave us a firm basis for archaeological dating was the excavation of Tell al 'Ubaid [Less than five miles from Ur]. There we were continuing the work which Dr. Hall had begun, and to his remarkable discoveries we added a great deal more— copper statues and reliefs, mosaics in limestone and in shell, all of a kind new to Mesopotamian archaeology—and then had the crowning luck of finding an inscription which dated the building and all the objects connected with it. I can remember few occasions more exciting than that on which the workman handed to me the little foundation-tablet of grey soapstone covered with what even I could see was very archaic writing; I passed it on to C. J. Gadd, who was standing beside me, for his verdict, and that usually staid epigraphist executed a *pas seul* of triumph before he could so much as tell me what he was triumphing about. The text might not seem to have warranted such enthusiasm—"A-anni-padda, King of Ur, son of Mes-anni-padda, King of Ur, has built this for Ninkhursag, his Lady"; that was all. But Mes-anni-padda was recorded as the first king of that First Dynasty of Ur which scholars had rejected

From *Spadework*. London: Lutterworth Press; 1953, pp. 91-3. By permission of Lutterworth Press.

as a mythological invention, and here was his name and that of his son on a contemporary document to prove that the supposed myth was sober history; we had rescued a whole period from oblivion and carried back the history of Ur by many hundreds of years. Our inscription would have done that much if it had been an isolated discovery, but as the foundation-tablet of a building so rich in objects of art it did much more; it enabled us to put those objects in their right place in the historical sequence and make the First Dynasty of Ur the starting point for the systematic archaeology of the Euphrates valley.

What the field worker wants to establish is a sequence so that he may arrange all his material in correct order to illustrate the progress of culture, and with that done his immediate task is finished. But if the cultures of different countries have to be compared, a mere sequence is not enough; for such comparison the time relation is all-important, and therefore you want not only to define your periods but also to date them in terms of years. You cannot do that on the basis of pottery types or what-not; exact dates must depend on literary evidence, and therefore the establishment of a fixed chronology is the task not of the field worker as such but of the historian. The task is not an easy one, nor is the first solution necessarily correct. In 1924 it was thought that the First Dynasty of Ur must have started about 3100 B.C. and my publication both of *Tell al 'Ubaid* and of the *Royal Cemetery at Ur* proceeded on that assumption. Now it is agreed that the date 3100 B.C. was too early by two centuries at least and my chronology— for which I was not responsible—must be revised accordingly; that is a common experience, but the change of date ought not to affect at all the truth of the sequence which the archaeologist has evolved from the material which is properly his own.

LEONARD WOOLLEY

Discovery of the Royal Tombs

Ur lies about half-way between Baghdad and the head of the Persian Gulf, some ten miles west of the present course of the Euphrates. A mile and a half to the east of the ruins runs the single line of railway which joins Basra to the capital of Iraq, and between the rail and the river there is sparse cultivation and little villages of mud huts or reed-mat shelters are dotted here and there; but westwards of the line is desert blank and unredeemed. Out of this waste rise the mounds which were Ur, called by the Arabs after the highest of them all, the ziggurat hill, "Tell al Muqayyar," the Mound of Pitch.

Standing on the summit of this mound one can distinguish along the eastern skyline the dark tasselled fringe of the palm-gardens on the river's bank, but to north and west and south as far as the eye can see stretches a waste of unprofitable sand. To the south-west the flat line of the horizon is broken by a grey upstanding pinnacle, the ruins of the staged tower of the sacred city of Eridu which the Sumerians believed to be the oldest city upon earth, and to the north-west a shadow thrown by the low sun may tell the whereabouts of the low mound of al 'Ubaid; but otherwise nothing relieves the monotony of the vast plain over which the shimmering heat-waves dance and the mirage spreads its mockery of placid waters. It seems incredible that such a wilderness should ever have been habitable for man, and yet the weathered hillocks at one's feet cover the temples and houses of a very great city . . .

The greater part of three seasons' work has been devoted to the clearing of the great cemetery which lay outside the walls of the old town and occupied the rubbish heaps piled up between them and the water-channel, and the treasures which have been un-

From Ur of the Chaldees. London: Ernest Benn Ltd.; 1929, pp. 13-14, 83-9. By permission of Ernest Benn Ltd.

earthed from the graves during that time have revolutionised our ideas of the early civilisation of the world.

The cemetery (there are really two cemeteries, one above the other, but I am speaking now only of the lower and older) consists of burials of two sorts, the graves of commoners and the tombs of kings. Because the latter have yielded the richest works of art one is inclined to think of them alone, but the graves of the common folk, as well as being a hundred-fold as many in number, have also produced very fine objects, and have afforded precious evidence for the dating of the cemetery.

The tombs of the kings appear to be on the whole earlier in date than the graves of their subjects, and this is not so much because they lie at a deeper level, for that might be explained as a natural precaution, the larger and richer graves being dug deeper as a protection against robbers, but because of their relative positions. It is a common sight to see in a Moslem graveyard the tomb of some local saint surrounded by its little domed chapel and the other graves crowded round this as close as may be, as if the occupants sought the protection of the holy man. So it is with the royal tombs at Ur. The older private graves are clustered around them; later it seems as if the visible monuments of the dead kings vanished and their memory faded, leaving only a vague tradition of this being holy ground, and we find the newer graves invading the shafts of the royal tombs and dug right down into them.

The private graves are found at very varying levels, partly perhaps because there was no regular standard of depth, partly because the ground surface of the cemetery was far from uniform; but, generally speaking, the higher graves are the later, and this is due to the rise in the ground-level, which went on steadily throughout the time that the graveyard was in use. The result of this rise obliterating the position of the older graves was that a new grave might be placed directly above an old but, being started from a higher level, would not go quite so far down, and we may find as many as half a dozen graves superimposed one above the other. When this is so, the position in the ground necessarily corresponds to the order in time, and from these superimposed graves we get most valuable evidence for chronology.

Judging from the character of their contents, pottery, etc., the later graves seem to come just before the beginning of the First Dynasty of Ur, which we date to about 2700 B.C., and a few are actually contemporary with that dynasty; for the cemetery age as a whole, I think that we must allow a period of at least 200 years. The first of the royal tombs then, may be dated soon after 3000 B.C., and by 2700 B.C. the graveyard was falling out of use. There is not space here to go into all the arguments, but everyone, I think, will

agree that some time must have elapsed before the kings, buried
as they were with such ghastly pomp, could be forgotten and the
sanctity of the tomb-shafts be invaded by the common dead; and if
we find above them six or more superimposed burials, between each
of which there must have been a decent lapse of time, and the
topmost of these dates before 2700 B.C., then the chronology which
I suggest will not seem exaggeratedly long . . .

The first of the royal tombs proved a disappointment. At the
very end of the season 1926-7 two important discoveries were made.
At the bottom of an earth shaft, amongst masses of copper weapons,
there was found the famous gold dagger of Ur, a wonderful weapon
whose blade was gold, its hilt of lapis lazuli decorated with gold
studs, and its sheath of gold beautifully worked with an openwork
pattern derived from plaited grass; with it was another object
scarcely less remarkable, a cone-shaped reticule of gold ornaments
with a spiral pattern and containing a set of little toilet instruments,
tweezers, lancet, and pencil, also of gold. Nothing like these things
had ever before come from the soil of Mesopotamia; they revealed
an art hitherto unsuspected and they gave promise of future
discoveries outstripping all our hopes.

The other discovery was less sensational. Digging down in another
part of the cemetery we found what at first appeared to be walls of
terre pisée, i.e. of earth not moulded into bricks but used as concrete
is used for building. As the sun dried the soil and brought out the
colours of its stratification, it became evident that these were not
built walls but the clean-cut sides of a pit sunk in the rubbish; the
looser filling of the pit had fallen away as we worked and had left
the original face exactly as the first diggers had made it. As the
excavation continued we came on slabs and blocks of rough limestone which seemed to form a paving over the pit's base. This was
an astonishing thing, because there is no stone in the Euphrates
delta, not so much as a pebble in its alluvium, and to obtain blocks
of limestone such as these it is necessary to go some thirty miles
away into the higher desert. The cost of transport would be considerable, and the result is that stone is scarcely ever found in
buildings at Ur: a stone pavement underground would therefore
be an unheard of extravagance. As the season was just at its end
we could no more than clear the surface of the "pavement" and
leave its fuller examination for the next autumn.

Thinking the matter over during the summer, we came to the
conclusion that the stones might be not the floor of a building but
its roof, and that we might have discovered a royal grave. It was
with high hopes that we resumed work in the following autumn
and very soon we could assure ourselves that our forecast was correct: we had found a stone-built underground structure which had

indeed been the tomb of a king, but a rubbish-filled tunnel led from near the surface to the broken roof, robbers had been there before us, and except for a few scattered fragments of a gold diadem and some decayed copper pots there was nothing left for us to find.

But in spite of that disappointment the discovery was most important. We had laid bare the ruins of a two-chambered structure built of stone throughout with one long and narrow chamber vaulted with stone and a square room which had certainly once been covered with a stone dome, though the collapse of the roof made it difficult to establish the exact method of construction. A doorway, blocked with rubble masonry, afforded entrance to the tomb and was approached by a slanting ramp cut down from the ground surface in the hard soil. Nothing of the sort had ever been found before, and the light thrown on the architectural knowledge of this remote period might well atone for the loss of the tomb's contents; moreover, there was no reason to suppose this was an isolated tomb, and we could hope for others to which the plunderers had not made their way.

During that season (1927-8) and in the course of last winter more royal tombs came to light, and it is curious to find that never more than two of them are alike. Two large tombs, both plundered, consist of a four-roomed building occupying the whole area of the excavated shaft at the bottom of which they lie; walls and roofs alike are of limestone rubble, and in each case there are two long outer chambers which are vaulted and two smaller central chambers crowned with domes; a ramp leads to the arched door in the outer wall, and arched doors give communication between the rooms. Two graves, those of Queen Shub-ad and her supposed husband, consist of a pit open to the sky and approached by a sloped ramp, at one end of which is a single-chamber tomb with limestone walls and a roof constructed of burnt brick, vaulted and with apsidal ends; the chamber was destined to receive the royal body, the open pit was for offerings and subsidiary burials, and was simply filled in with earth. In another case the pit was found, but the tomb chamber did not lie inside it, but seems to have been close by on a different level. A small grave found last winter consists of a single stone-built domed chamber with a little front court at the bottom of the shaft and, higher up in the shaft, mud-brick buildings for the subsidiary burials and offerings, the whole being covered with earth; another has the same general arrangement, but instead of the domed stone chamber there was a vaulted chamber of mud brick.

There is variety enough therefore in the actual structures, but underlying all there was a common ritual for which different generations provided in different ways; what that ritual was can best be explained by describing the excavation of the graves.

In 1927-8, soon after our disappointment with the plundered stone tomb, we found, in another part of the field, five bodies lying side by side in a shallow sloping trench; except for the copper daggers at their waists and one or two small clay cups, they had none of the normal furniture of a grave, and the mere fact of there being a number thus together was unusual. Then, below them, a layer of matting was found, and tracing this along we came to another group of bodies, those of ten women carefully arranged in two rows; they wore head-dresses of gold, lapis lazuli, and carnelian, and elaborate bead necklaces, but they too possessed no regular tomb furnishings. At the end of the row lay the remains of a wonderful harp, the wood of it decayed but its decoration intact, making its reconstruction only a matter of care; the upright wooden beam was capped with gold, and in it were fastened the gold-headed nails which secured the strings; the sounding-box was edged with a mosaic in red stone, lapis lazuli and white shell, and from the front of it projected a splendid head of a bull wrought in gold with eyes and beard of lapis lazuli; across the ruins of the harp lay the bones of the gold-crowned harpist.

By this time we had found the earth sides of the pit in which the women's bodies lay and could see that the bodies of the five men were on the ramp which led down to it. Following the pit along, we came upon more bones which at first puzzled us by being other than human, but the meaning of them soon became clear. A little way inside the entrance to the pit stood a wooden sledge chariot decorated with red, white and blue mosaic along the edges of the framework and with golden heads of lions having manes of lapis lazuli and shell on its side panels; along the top rail were smaller gold heads of lions and bulls, silver lionesses' heads adorned the front, and the position of the vanished swingle-tree was shown by a band of blue and white inlay and two smaller heads of lionesses in silver. In front of the chariot lay the crushed skeletons of two asses with the bodies of the grooms by their heads, and on the top of the bones was the double ring, once attached to the pole, through which the reins had passed; it was of silver, and standing on it was a gold "mascot" in the form of a donkey most beautifully and realistically modelled.

Close to the chariot were an inlaid gaming-board and a collection of tools and weapons, including a set of chisels and a saw made of gold, big bowls of gray soapstone, copper vessels, a long tube of gold and lapis which was a drinking tube for sucking up liquor from the bowls, more human bodies, and then the wreckage of a large wooden chest adorned with a figured mosaic in lapis lazuli and shell which was found empty but had perhaps contained such perishable things as clothes. Behind this box were more offerings, masses of vessels in copper, silver, stone (including exquisite examples of volcanic glass, lapis lazuli, alabaster, and marble), and gold; one set of silver vessels seemed to be in the nature of a communion-service, for there was a shallow tray or platter, a jug with tall neck and long spout such as we know from carved stone reliefs to have been used in religious rites, and tall slender silver tumblers nested one inside another; a bowl, a chalice, and a plain oval bowl of gold lay piled together, and two magnificent lions' heads in silver, perhaps the ornaments of a throne, were amongst the treasures in the crowded pit. The perplexing thing was with all this wealth of objects we had found no body so far distinguished from the rest as to be that of the person to whom all were dedicated; logically our discovery, however great, was incomplete.

The objects were removed and we started to clear away the remains of the wooden box, a chest some 6 feet long and 3 feet across, when under it we found burnt bricks. They were fallen, but at one end some were still in place and formed the ring-vault of a stone chamber. The first and natural supposition was that here we had the tomb to which all the offerings belonged, but further search proved that the chamber was plundered, the roof had not fallen from decay but had been broken through, and the wooden box had been placed over the hole as if deliberately to hide it. Then, digging round the outside of the chamber, we found just such another pit as that 6 feet above. At the foot of the ramp lay six soldiers, orderly in two ranks, with copper spears by their sides and copper helmets crushed flat on the broken skulls; just inside, having evidently been backed down the slope, were two wooden four-wheeled waggons each drawn by three oxen—one of the latter so well preserved that we were able to lift the skeleton entire; the waggons were plain, but the reins were decorated with long beads of lapis and silver and passed through silver rings surmounted with mascots in the form of bulls; the grooms lay at the oxen's heads and the drivers in the bodies of the cars; of the cars themselves only the impression of the decayed wood remained in the soil, but so clear was this that a photograph showed the grain of the solid wooden wheel and the grey-white circle which had been the leather tyre.

Against the end wall of the stone chamber lay the bodies of nine women wearing the gala head-dress of lapis and carnelian beads from which hung golden pendants in the forms of beech leaves, great lunate earrings of gold, silver "combs" like the palm of a hand with three fingers tipped with flowers whose petals are inlaid with lapis, gold, and shell, and necklaces of lapis and gold; their heads were leaned against the masonry, their bodies extended

on to the floor of the pit, and the whole space between them and
the waggons was crowded with other dead, women and men, while
the passage which led along the side of the chamber to its arched
door was lined with soldiers carrying daggers, and with women.
Of the soldiers in the central space one had a bundle of four spears,
and by another there was a remarkable relief in copper with a
design of two lions trampling on the bodies of two fallen men
which may have been the decoration of a shield.

On the top of the bodies of the "court ladies" against the chamber
wall had been placed a wooden harp, of which there survived only
the copper head of a bull and the shell plaques which had adorned
the sounding-box; by the side wall of the pit, also set on the top of
the bodies, was a second harp with a wonderful bull's head in gold,
its eyes, beard, and horn-tips of lapis, and a set of engraved shell
plaques not less wonderful; there are four of them with grotesque
scenes of animals playing the parts of men, and while the most
striking feature about them is that sense of humour which is so
rare in ancient art, the grace and balance of the design and the
fineness of the drawing make of these plaques one of the most
instructive documents that we possess for the appreciation of the
art of early Sumer.

Inside the tomb the robbers had left enough to show that it
had contained bodies of several minor people as well as that of
the chief person, whose name, if we can trust the inscription on a
cylinder seal, was A-bar-gi; overlooked against the wall we found
two more model boats, one of copper now hopelessly decayed, the
other of silver wonderfully well preserved; some 2 feet long, it has
a high stern and prow, five seats, and amidships an arched support
for the awning which would protect the passenger, and the leaf-
bladed oars are still set in the thwarts; it is a testimony to the
conservatism of the East that a boat of identical type is in use to-
day on the marshes of the Lower Euphrates, some 50 miles from Ur.

The king's tomb-chamber lay at the far end of his open pit; continuing our search behind it we found a second stone chamber
built up against it either at the same time or, more probably, at a
later period. This chamber, roofed like the king's with a vault of
ring arches in burnt brick, was the tomb of the queen to whom
belonged the upper pit with its ass chariot and other offerings: her
name, Shub-ad, was given us by a fine cylinder seal of lapis lazuli
which was found in the filling of the shaft a little above the roof
of the chamber and had probably been thrown into the pit at the
moment when the earth was being put back into it. The vault of
the chamber had fallen in, but luckily this was due to the weight of
earth above, not to the violence of tomb-robbers; the tomb itself was
intact.

At one end, on the remains of a wooden bier, lay the body of the queen, a gold cup near her hand; the upper part of the body was entirely hidden by a mass of beads of gold, silver, lapis lazuli, carnelian, agate, and chalcedony, long strings of which, hanging from a collar, had formed a cloak reaching to the waist and bordered below with a broad band of tubular beads of lapis, carnelian, and gold: against the right arm were three long gold pins of lapis heads and three amulets in the form of fish, two of gold and one of lapis, and a fourth in the form of two seated gazelles, also of gold.

The head-dress whose remains covered the crushed skull was a more elaborate edition of that worn by the court ladies: its basis was a broad gold ribbon festooned in loops round the hair—and the measurement of the curves showed that this was not the natural hair but a wig padded out to an almost grotesque size; over this came three wreaths, the lowest hanging down over the forehead, of plain gold ring pendants, the second of beech leaves, the third of long willow leaves in sets of three with gold flowers whose petals were of blue and white inlay; all these were strung on triple chains of lapis and carnelian beads. Fixed into the back of the hair was a golden "Spanish comb" with five points ending in lapis-centred gold flowers. Heavy spiral rings of gold wire were twisted into the side curls of the wig, huge lunate earrings of gold hung down to the shoulders, and apparently from the hair also hung on each side a string of large square stone beads with, at the end of each, a lapis amulet, one shaped as a seated bull and the other as a calf. Complicated as the head-dress was, its different parts lay in such good order that it was possible to reconstruct the whole and exhibit the likeness of the queen with all her original finery in place.

For the purposes of exhibition a plaster cast was made from a well-preserved female skull of the period (the queen's own skull was too fragmentary to be used), and over this my wife modelled the features in wax, making this as thin as possible so as not to obliterate the bone structure; the face was passed by Sir Arthur Keith, who has made a special study of the Ur and al 'Ubaid skulls, as reproducing faithfully the character of the early Sumerians. On this head was put a wig of the correct dimensions dressed in the fashion illustrated by terra-cotta figures which, though later in date, probably represent an old tradition. The gold hair-ribbon had been lifted from the tomb without disturbing the arrangement of the strands, these having been first fixed in position by strips of glued paper threaded in and out between them and by wires twisted round the gold; when the wig had been fitted on the head, the hair-ribbon was balanced on the top and the wires and paper bands were cut, and the ribbon fell naturally into place and required no further arranging. The wreaths were re-strung and tied on in the order noted at the time of excavation. Though the face is not an actual portrait of the queen, it gives at least the type to which she must have conformed, and the whole reconstructed head presents us with the most accurate picture we are likely ever to possess of what she looked like in her lifetime.

By the side of the body lay a second head-dress of a novel sort. On to a diadem made apparently of a strip of soft white leather had been sewn thousands of minute lapis lazuli beads, and against this background of solid blue were set a row of exquisitely fashioned gold animals, stags, gazelles, bulls, and goats, with between them clusters of pomegranates, three fruits hanging together shielded by their leaves, and branches of some other tree with golden stems and fruit or pods of gold and carnelian, while gold rosettes were sewn on at intervals, and from the lower border of the diadem hung palmettes of twisted gold wire.

The bodies of two women attendants were crouched against the bier, one at its head and one at its foot, and all about the chamber lay strewn offerings of all sorts, another gold bowl, vessels of silver and copper, stone bowls, and clay jars for food, the head of a cow in silver, two silver tables for offerings, silver lamps, and a number of large cockle-shells containing green paint; such shells are nearly always found in women's graves, and the paint in them, presumably used as a cosmetic, may be white, black or red, but the normal colour is green. Queen Shub-ad's shells were abnormally big, and with them were found two pairs of imitation shells, one in silver and one in gold, each with its green paint.

The discovery was now complete and our earlier difficulty was explained: King A-bar-gi's grave and Queen Shub-ad's were exactly alike, but whereas the former was all on one plane, the queen's tomb-chamber had been sunk below the general level of her grave-pit. Probably they were husband and wife: the king had died first and been buried, and it had been the queen's wish to lie as close to him as might be; for this end the grave-diggers had reopened the king's shaft, going down in it until the top of the chamber vault appeared; then they had stopped work in the main shaft but had dug down at the back of the chamber's pit in which the queen's stone tomb could be built. But the treasures known to lie in the king's grave were too great a temptation for the workmen; the outer pit where the bodies of the court ladies lay was protected by 6 feet of earth which they could not disturb without being detected, but the richer plunder in the royal chamber itself was separated from them only by the bricks of the vault; they broke through the arch, carried off their spoil, and placed the great clothes-chest of the queen over the hole to hide their sacrilege.

Nothing else would account for the plundered vault lying im-

mediately below the untouched grave of the queen, and the connecting of Shub-ad's stone chamber with the upper "death-pit," as
we came to call these open shafts in which the subsidiary bodies
lay, made an exact parallel to the king's grave and, in a lesser
degree, to the other royal tombs. Clearly, when a royal person died,
he or she was accompanied to the grave by all the members of the
court: the king had at least three people with him in his chamber
and sixty-two in the death-pit; where there was a larger stone
building with two or four rooms, then one of these was for the royal
body and the rest for the followers sacrificed in precisely the same
way; the ritual was identical, only the accommodation for the
victims differed in different cases.

On the subject of human sacrifice more light was thrown by the
discovery of a great death-pit excavated last winter. At about 26 feet
below the surface we came upon a mass of mud brick not truly laid
but rammed together and forming, as we guessed, not a floor but
the stopping, as it were, of a shaft. Immediately below this we were
able to distinguish the clean-cut earth sides of a pit, sloping inwards and smoothly plastered with mud; following these down, we
found the largest death-pit that the cemetery has yet produced. The
pit was roughly rectangular and measured 37 feet by 24 at the bottom, and was approached as usual by a sloped ramp. In it lay the
bodies of six men-servants and sixty-eight women; the men lay
along the side by the door, the bodies of the women were disposed in
regular rows across the floor, every one lying on her side with legs
slightly bent and hands brought up near the face, so close together
that the heads of those in one row rested on the legs of those in the
row above. Here was to be observed even more clearly what had been
fairly obvious in the graves of Shub-ad and her husband, the neat-
ness with which the bodies were laid out, the entire absence of any
signs of violence or terror.

We have often been asked how the victims in the royal graves
met their death, and it is impossible to give a decisive answer. The
bones are too crushed and too decayed to show any cause of death,
supposing that violence had been used, but the general condition of
the bodies does supply a strong argument. Very many of these
women wear head-dresses which are delicate in themselves and
would easily be disarranged, yet such are always found in good
order, undisturbed except by the pressure of the earth; this would be
impossible if the wearers had been knocked on the head, improbable
if they had fallen to the ground after being stabbed, and it is equally
unlikely that they could have been killed outside the grave and
carried down the ramp and laid in their places with all their
ornaments intact; certainly the animals must have been alive when
they dragged the chariots down the ramp, and if so, the grooms who

led them and the drivers in the cars must have been alive also; it is safe to assume that those who were to be sacrificed went down alive into the pit.

That they were dead, or at least unconscious, when the earth was flung in and trampled down on top of them is an equally safe assumption, for in any other case there must have been some struggle which would have left its traces in the attitude of the bodies, but these are always decently composed; indeed, they are in such good order and alignment that we are driven to suppose that after they were lying unconscious someone entered the pit and gave the final touches to their arrangement—and the circumstances that in A-bar-gi's grave, the harps were placed on the top of the bodies, proves that someone did enter the grave at the end. It is most probable that the victims walked to their places, took some kind of drug—opium or hashish would serve—and lay down in order; after the drug had worked, whether it produced sleep or death, the last touches were given to their bodies and the pit was filled in. There does not seem to have been anything brutal in the manner of their deaths.

None the less, the sight of the remains of the victims is gruesome enough with the gold leaves and the coloured beads lying thick on the crushed and broken skulls, but in excavating a great death-pit such as that of last winter we do not see it as a whole, but have to clear it a little at a time. The soil was removed until the bodies were almost exposed, covered only by the few inches of broken brick which had been the first of the filling thrown over the dead; here and there a pick driven too deep might bring to view a piece of gold ribbon or a golden beech leaf, showing that everywhere there were bodies richly adorned, but these would be quickly covered up again and left until more methodical work should reveal them in due course. Starting in one corner of the pit, we marked out squares such as might contain from five to six bodies, and all these were cleared, noted, and the objects belonging to them collected and removed before the next square was taken in hand.

It was slow work, and especially so in those cases where we decided to remove the entire skull with all its ornaments in position on it. The wreaths and chains and necklaces re-strung and arranged in a glass case may look very well, but it is more interesting to see them as they were actually found, and therefore a few heads on which the original order of the beads and gold-work was best preserved were laboriously cleaned with small knives and brushes, the dirt being removed without disturbing any of the ornaments—a difficult matter as they are loose in the soil—and then boiling paraffin wax was poured over them, solidifying them in one mass. The lump of wax, earth, bone and gold was then strengthened by waxed cloth pressed carefully over it, so that it could be lifted from the ground by undercutting. Mounted in plaster, with the super-fluous wax cleaned off, these heads form an exhibit which is not only of interest in itself but proves the accuracy of the restorations which we have made of others.

Of the sixty-eight women in the pit, twenty-eight wore hair-ribbons of gold. At first sight it looked as if the others had nothing of the kind, but closer examination showed that many, if not all, had originally worn exactly similar ribbons of silver. Unfortunately silver is a metal which ill resists the action of the acids in the soil, and where it was but a thin strip and, being worn on the head, was directly affected by the corruption of the flesh, it generally disap-pears altogether, and at most there may be detected on the bone of the skull slight traces of a purplish colour which is silver chloride in a minutely powdered state: we could be certain that the ribbons were worn, but we could not produce material evidence of them.

But in one case we had better luck. The great gold earrings were in place, but not a sign of discoloration betrayed the existence of any silver head-dress, and this negative evidence was duly noted: then, as the body was cleared, there was found against it, about on the level of the waist, a flat disk a little more than 3 inches across of a grey substance which was certainly silver; it might have been a small circular box. Only when I was cleaning it in the house that evening, hoping to find something which would enable me to catalogue it more in detail, did its real nature come to light: it was the silver hair-ribbon, but it had never been worn—carried ap-parently in the woman's pocket, it was just as she had taken it from her room, done up in a tight coil with the ends brought over to prevent its coming undone; and since it formed thus a comparatively solid mass of metal and had been protected by the cloth of her dress, it was very well preserved and even the delicate edges of the ribbon were sharply distinct. Why the owner had not put it on one could not say; perhaps she was late for the ceremony and had no time to dress properly, but her haste has in any case afforded us the only example of a silver hair-ribbon which we are likely ever to find.

Another thing that perishes utterly in the earth is cloth, but oc-casionally on lifting a stone bowl which has lain inverted over a bit of stuff and has protected it from the soil one sees traces which, although only of fine dust, keep the texture of the material, or a copper vessel may by its corrosion preserve some fragment which was in contact with it. By such evidence we were able to prove that the women in the death-pit wore garments of bright red woollen stuff; and as many of them had at the wrists one or two cuffs made of beads which had been sewn on to cloth, it was tolerably certain that these were sleeved coats rather than cloaks. It must have been a very gaily dressed crowd that assembled in the open mat-lined pit for the royal obsequies, a blaze of colour with the crimson coats, the silver, and the gold; clearly these people were not wretched slaves killed as oxen might be killed, but persons held in honour, wearing their robes of office, and coming, one hopes, voluntarily to a rite which would in their belief be but a passing from one world to another, from the service of a god on earth to that of the same god in another sphere.

This much I think we can safely assume. Human sacrifice was confined exclusively to the funerals of royal persons, and in the graves of commoners, however rich, there is no sign of anything of the sort, not even such substitutes, clay figurines, etc., as are so common in Egyptian tombs and appear there to be reminiscent of an ancient and more bloody rite. In much later times Sumerian kings were deified in their lifetime and honoured as gods after their death: the prehistoric kings of Ur were in their obsequies so distinguished from their subjects because they too were looked upon as super-human, earthly deities; and when the chroniclers wrote in the annals of Sumer that "after the Flood kingship again descended from the gods," they meant no less than this. If the king, then, was a god, he did not die as men die, but was translated; and it might therefore be not a hardship but a privilege for those of his court to accompany their master and continue in his service . . .

This is the story of the excavations at Ur, not a history of the Sumerian people, but something must be said here to show how important those excavations have been for our knowledge of early civilisations. The contents of the tombs illustrate a very highly developed state of society of an urban type, a society in which the architect was familiar with all the basic principles of construction known to us to-day. The artist, capable at times of a most vivid realism, followed for the most part standards and conventions whose excellence had been approved by many generations working before him; the craftsman in metal possessed a knowledge of metallurgy and a technical skill which few ancient peoples ever rivalled; the merchant carried on a far-flung trade and recorded his transactions in writing; the army was well organised and victorious, agriculture prospered, and great wealth gave scope to luxury. Our tombs date, as has already been said, between 2900 and 2700 B.C., and, as the nature of the civilisation would lead one to expect, and as has been demonstrated by the discoveries in the rubbish below the tombs . . . by 2900 B.C. this civilisation was already many centuries old.

Until recently it was thought that the Egyptian civilisation was the oldest in the world and that it was the fountain-head wherefrom the latter civilisations of other Western countries drew at any rate the inspiration which informed them. But up to 3400 B.C. Egypt was still barbarous, divided into petty kingdoms not yet united by "Menes," the founder of the First Dynasty, into a single state. Egypt and Sumer therefore are more or less contemporary in origin and when Egypt makes a real start forward under Menes the beginnings of a new age are marked by the introduction of models and ideas which derive from that older civilisation which, as we know now, had long been developing and flourishing in the Euphrates valley; and to the Sumerians we can trace also much that is at the root of Babylonian, Assyrian, Hebrew, and Phoenician art and thought, and so see that the Greeks too were in debt to this ancient and for long forgotten people, the pioneers of the progress of Western man. It is this that makes excavation in the oldest levels at Ur of such absorbing interest, the knowledge that almost every object found is not merely an illustration of the achievement of a particular race at a particular time, but also a new document helping to fill up the picture of those beginnings from which is derived our modern world.

LEONARD WOOLLEY

The Queen's Tomb:
Further Details

AT the south-west end of the shaft there lay a harp and the bodies of ten women. The harp stood against the pit wall and one woman lay right against it with the bones of her hands actually in the place of the strings; she must have been the harpist and was playing almost to the last. The other nine women were ranged in two rows facing each other, three in one and six in the other; all wore the rich head-dress of the court.

In the middle of the pit just in front of the *dromos* down which

From *Ur Excavations*, Vol. II, pp. 74, 265. Published for the British Museum and the Museum of the University of Pennsylvania, 1934. Reprinted by courtesy of the British Museum and the Museum of the University of Pennsylvania.

it had been driven was the sledge-chariot of the queen drawn by two asses: mixed up with the bones of the animals were those of four grooms, and a fifth human skeleton lay just clear of the asses' hoofs against the corner of the entrance. In front of the stone-paved recess were large vessels of copper and silver and then, close to the chariot and occupying the middle of the north-east part of the pit, was a great wooden chest measuring 2.25 m. by 1.10 m.; it was empty, presumably not because it had always been so but because its contents were of a nature to decay and leave no trace; we may fairly safely assume that they were stuffs and that the chest was the wardrobe of the queen. It had itself been an object of art, for along its south-east side ran a band of mosaic in shell and lapis-lazuli with a design of human and animal figures in the same technique as the "Standard" but unfortunately in very bad condition; against its south-west end lay the body of a man who may have been the Keeper of the Wardrobe, and another skeleton was found near its north corner and one at the north-east end. All round the chest was an amazing wealth of offerings, vessels of gold, silver, copper, clay, and of such stones as white calcite, steatite, obsidian, and lapis-lazuli; silver heads of lionesses from a piece of furniture, gold drinking-tubes, gold saws and chisels, an inlaid gaming-board, &c.; the richness of the death-pit attached to the "King's Tomb" was nothing compared to this. . . .

The Goat Statuettes

FROM the shoulder of each animal rises a gold tube which was the sheathing of a wooden upright; the figures therefore are not complete in themselves but are supports for something that has disappeared. What that was it is impossible to tell, but it must have been of some perishable substance such as wood; possibly it was no more than a little table-top on which might be stood a lamp or a pot of incense—nothing of any sort was found, but one suspects something small, because of the size of the stand, light, yet large enough to require that the flowers and leaves and the tips of the goat's horns should be approximately at the same level, and a circular table-top would seem a not unreasonable suggestion. The only importance of this is that it warns us not to regard the goat figures as independent works of art; they are applied art, the decoration of a piece of furniture, and must be judged as such, judged, that is, by a different and a somewhat lower standard than would be applied to a work of art created for its own sake; thus a certain stiffness of the body and the undoubted clumsiness of the shoulders is explained when the figure is looked upon as a support. But it would be difficult to overrate the technical qualities of the

work and the extraordinarily skilful use of colour and the real sense
of design. These are by far the finest examples yet found of that
curious and refined Sumerian art of the goldsmith and lapidary
which loved to combine in one object the richest materials and the
strongest contrasts of colour and texture, to design in bold lines
and to complicate that design with an almost morbid elaboration
of detail, the sort of art that arises sometimes when inspiration has
passed its zenith and invention loses itself in the baroque. At first
sight these polychrome—one might almost say chryselephantine—
statuettes seem strangely alien to the prehistoric world of the Near
East; they would be more at home in Italy of the sixteenth century:
but in fact they are perhaps of all the objects found in the Royal
Cemetery the most characteristic of the civilization that produced
them.

C. J. GADD

Ur: Sumerian Self-Portraits

DEEP beneath one of the least conspicuous parts of the city's area
have been found the tombs and the funeral appurtenances of the
population which succeeded the painted-pottery makers. The contrast of these with the poor villagers of the al 'Ubaid, whose only
luxury was their gaily decorated earthenware, is astonishing. If
those were the humble ministrants of a rustic shrine, these were
the great of a city-kingdom, recipients of a wealth only to be acquired from the revenues of a lucrative trade which their citizens
carried on, for scarce any of the rich commodities in which they
abounded is to be found in their own land. Gold is the material of
their possessions and the symbol of their superfluity. In their
flourishing days and at their lavish court, the arts of manufacture
rose to a perfection and beauty in their products which was never
seen again. The articles made were, indeed, of much the same

From *History and Monuments of Ur*. London: Chatto and Windus Ltd.; 1929, pp.
28-33. By permission of C. J. Gadd.

kind as those of later ages, but they were, at this very early period, marked by a richness and splendour rather of Egyptian sumptuosity than of the supposed sobriety of the River-lands. These deposits amaze by their riot of gold; silver also is there in great profusion, evidently "nothing accounted of," and there are actually fragments of iron, doubtless the earliest historical examples of that metal.

What makes this earliest passage of the city's history rise before us with a life more vivid than any later age is not merely the unmatchable richness and beauty of its craftsmen's work, but two monuments in particular which preserve the actual personality and appearance of the people, and display them in several of their most important activities. . . . Of the two monuments already mentioned by far the most interesting is the pictorial "standard" (so-called, though its real purpose is very doubtful) found in a stone-built, three-chambered tomb which must have contained funerary offerings of great magnificence before it was plundered by ancient robbers. This most fascinating of all the antiquities of Ur is at once the oldest and the fullest series of pictures from anywhere in the ancient world; the famous "Stele of the Vultures" itself is not only, it may be presumed, rather later in date, but shows nothing like the wealth of details of Sumerian life in war and peace, not to mention the crude but strangely pleasing blend of bright colours, which are found upon the "standard." . . . the scenes depicted are made by inlaying shell figures in a background of lapis-lazuli, the whole mounted with a bitumen backing on boards, these colours (white and blue) being diversified by red and black fillings which emphasize the details of the shell figures. One side of the standard reveals the king at war, almost in the manner of a primitive cinematograph. The king himself, tallest of all the figures, attended by his principal officers or perhaps his sons, receives a line of prisoners haled before him; his chariot, with driver and boygroom, awaits him behind. The two lower registers show all arms of his troops in action—the skirmishers, the heavy phalanx, and the splendid chariotry, with their four-abreast teams of asses and four-wheeled cars. They move in single file to the right, the first is already at full gallop, the next two are less extended, the fourth has just begun to move; it is not yet in touch with the enemy, who fall under, or are bowled over by, the charging van. On the other side of the standard are the celebrations after victory. The king and his officers sit on chairs at a feast drinking wine to the sound of harping and song. Below, the booty captured from the enemy is led or carried in by servants and porters, the cattle to furnish the banquet, the teams and gear to be divided among the chiefs. A dozen details reveal themselves to more careful examination: the shape of the harp and of the cups, of the rein-rings on the chariots, of the weapons carried, the various head-coverings and dressings, the mode of carrying burdens by a band around the forehead, the goats and even the fish brought in for the meal, the animals so faithfully observed, the utensils all exactly portrayed, as the surviving originals are there to prove.

The second of these monuments is a small rectangular plaque of limestone, made to be affixed to a wall or chest, sculptured on the front in low relief. The upper part of this being almost wholly broken away, only a part of the lower register survives. It is occupied by a man standing behind, and seemingly about to mount, a chariot drawn by four asses harnessed abreast. His right hand holds a stick, his left is raised and grasps the thick cord reins, the slack end of which is fastened to the front of the car; before reaching the animals' heads they pass through a double ring on the high-arched pole. The chariot itself has a wooden frame with a covering of wickerwork or matting, a leopard's fell thrown over the whole. A deep quiver contains the warrior's weapons, his axes with heads like a reversed ϵ, and his arrows, point downwards. The wheels are of a curious fashion which discovers alike the ingenuity of the workman and the practical experience of many years. But the highest interest is in the driver himself. He is naked except for an unusually short skirt of sheepskin, rendered in the invariable though rather unnatural convention of the Sumerian artists. Short as it is, this skirt nevertheless displays a triangular patch in the middle of its front, which can hardly be other than a sort of cod-piece, and the same garment is worn by the two attendants who are also to be seen before and behind the equipage. The driver's head-dress is elaborate and seems to be a wig though not necessarily so; it falls down over each shoulder in a broad band, with horizontal marks to indicate rows of curls or waves. The beard is worn full, but apparently without moustache. Two more human figures appeared in this scene, one standing behind the driver, bearing on a stick over his left shoulder some oddly-shaped bag or vessel, the other in front of, and no doubt holding, the animals' heads, but the upper parts of both are now missing, though their dress can still be seen, identical with the driver's. That the chariot, both two and four-wheeled, was already in common use is remarkable enough when it is considered that it did not appear in Egypt until introduced by the Hyksos conquerors, but since Eannatum of Lagash led his army so mounted at a time which cannot, in any case, have been very much later, the existence of chariots in the earliest days of Ur is not so much to be wondered at, and the skill of the wheelwright shows that it was even then no new thing in the land. . . .

C. J. GADD

The Last Days of Ur

. . . THIS writer of the second century B.C. definitely implies that the city of Ur was known to him, or at least that it was known to Berossus, his source, whose own work was written at the beginning of the third century, and that it was at that time the abode of Arabs who called it Kamarina, "moon-city" by a word (ḳamar) peculiar to their own language. Thus the tradition at least of its old worship still endured, but of the worship and even of the city itself perhaps little or nothing. Under the successors of Alexander there was fostered some little revival of Babylonian culture, but it was confined to a very few places, and no reason exists to believe that Ur had any share in it. While Erech, for example, was still populous, fairly flourishing, and supporting a famous school of astronomers, Ur was already, so we may suppose, unwatered, almost depopulated, and fast declining into the desert. When the last permanent houses disappeared and the temples were long since buried in the dust of their own ruin the solid bulk of the ziggurat still rose up as a mark and centre for the encampment of nomads, who soon lost even a far-off remembrance of the works of the old infidels, and knew their haunt only by the name of the bitumen which Ur-Nammu had laid between its bricks those thousands of years before.

From *History and Monuments of Ur*, pp. 255-6.

SETON LLOYD

Sumerian Sculpture

. . . WE should now perhaps consider Sumerian art from a purely
critical point of view, when dissociated from its historical connec-
nection, and here is a subject which one approaches with a certain
diffidence. Contacts between archaeologist and art critic almost
inevitably produce friction. Yet it has been interesting in recent
years to notice the sometimes successful intrusion of the one upon
the sphere of the other. It begins to be a little puzzling to know
why the study of a subject which is, after all, mainly concerned
with the history of art and culture generally, should exclude a
scholar from interesting himself in the process of abstract reasoning which constitutes art criticism, or from assimilating the main
bases of criticism which would enable him to make an intelligent
appraisement of any work of art, ancient or modern. Here, however,
is the view of an art critic, Mr. R. H. Wilenski, expressed in a recent
book on modern sculpture:

"Archaeologists are people whose business it is to examine objects of the past and documents relating thereto with real care and
thoroughness and to record *without omissions and without comment* the knowledge thus obtained.

"When they stick to their business, as they occasionally do, they
are useful to historians and critics.

"But they usually divulge in art criticism for which they are not
equipped by their studies. . . ."

Thus we find Sir Leonard Woolley prefacing his newest book on
Sumerian Art with a modest disclaimer. "This is not intended,"
he says, "to be a critical appreciation of Sumerian art—for such a
task I do not hold myself competent and should prefer to leave
it to experts; my whole aim has been to show what were its sources
and to trace its development as influenced by accidents of history.
Some such introduction will, I believe, help towards the understanding of an art whose ideals and conventions are necessarily un-

From *Mesopotamia*. London: Lovat Dickson; 1936, pp. 172-84. Reprinted by courtesy
of Seton Lloyd, C.B.E.

familiar and may prepare the way for the critic's more considered
judgments."

Again one finds the same note in M. Zervos' introduction to his
new "Cahier d'Art" volume with its magnificent photographs of
Sumerian sculpture. "On ne trouvera dans ce volume, pas plus que
dans le précédent, des appréciations scientifiques sur l'art étudié.
Des savants de haute érudition, tant en France qu'en Angleterre, en
Allemagne et ailleurs, ont parlé de l'art de Basse Mésopotamie dans
d'importants ouvrages qui apportent des connaissances étendues en
même temps qu'ils procurent un trés vif plaisir."

Yet where one can find *importants ouvrages* on this subject other
than purely technical archaeological publications? One can only return to Sir Leonard Woolley's book and observe those passages
where he has overstepped his own self-imposed limitations and
embarked upon what is quite frankly abstract criticism. Here one
is immediately faced with a succession of apposite and concisely-
worded comments which, *qua* criticism, are surely irreproachable.
There is, for instance, the gold and lapis lazuli head of a bull from
a lyre found in one of the "royal tombs" of which he remarks:
"Very few people, looking at it, have noticed the absurdity of a
bull having a beard, and a blue beard at that; the only impression
they have got is of strength and dignity—precisely the impression
which the artist wanted to convey." In contrast to this, consider
his reaction to the Gudea statues in the Louvre and British Museum:

"Certain conventions, artistic as well as technical, survive; the
clumsy block behind the feet still supports the weight of the standing figure, the elbows are grotesquely pointed, the head as a rule
disproportionately large, the shoulders unduly broad and square
with the head on its short neck sunk between them; there is little
or no undercutting of the stone, nothing to mitigate the rigid pose of
the figure still so little regarded as such that it can be treated as
a mere field for inscriptions. On the other hand, the modelling of
the exposed parts of the body is admirable, and the polished surface of the stone, by the interplay of lights on its contrasted curves
produces, as in the British Museum fragment, an astonishing illusion of flesh." And later: "They are portraits up to a certain extent, so that Gudea the young man has a freshness and a vigour
very different from the serenity of his middle life or the drawn
severity of his old age; yet it is difficult to see quite wherein that
difference lies, for there is no realism in them at all." Here he would
almost certainly fall foul of Mr. Wilenski. Let us hear that "critic's
more considered judgment" on the subject of these very statues:
"Modern sculptors," he admits, "have been much impressed by
Sumerian sculpture. They set aside, of course, the archaeologists'
prattle which describes these (presumably Gudea) figures as por-

traits. The Sumerian sculptors were obviously not attempting to convert the stones into the likeness of Gudea or anyone else. These statues are no more portraits than the statues of the Pharaohs or the Assyrian Kings are portraits. They are not particularized representations of individuals. If the sculptors had wanted to make life-like likenesses they would have of course done so . . . but the sculptor who had done this in ancient Egypt, Assyria or Sumeria (*sic*) would have been headless in ten minutes. The sculptor did what he was required to do, which was to collaborate with a block of hard stone and to convert it to a form which would suggest in a symbolic way certain qualities in the prince and his office, which would make men revere and respect him. . . ." Finally he concludes that "the formal meaning of Sumerian sculpture is the meaning of the mutual play of angular and curved forms which constitute a formal architecture peculiar to themselves. The cubic form of the clasped hands in the British Museum statue is continued in the flatness of the front of the arms and the sharply defined angles of the side planes. The gesture is given permanent meaning by the form."

This seems fairly coherent, except that his "formal architecture" and "cubic form" can easily be attributed to the technical limitations of the material, and one need not credit the sculptor with the conscious intention of giving meaning to the gesture. Meanwhile Mr. Wilenski aligns the British Museum piece with a modern work by Henry Moore called "Mother and Child." He proposes to judge both by the same standards, or rather to treat them as mutually explanatory. But he writes of Mr. Moore: "He believes that permanent shapes in permanent materials must symbolize universal and permanent ideas. . . . He admits no meaning resulting from particularization; all local and topical experience is excluded from his work. His concept of truth in sculpture is the organization of stone form as a symbol of life."

Surely this is the comment of an intellectually rather musclebound littérateur, and is concerned with an art in the last stages of what another critic calls "self-consciousness, inbreeding and exhaustion."

Most Sumerian sculpture, on the other hand, is not the work of artists, far less of intellectuals. Like the ornaments of Gothic cathedrals, it is the work of good craftsmen, carving to the best of their ability because they are afraid to do less, but also carving in a manner strictly prescribed by tradition; a manner evolved for them by many generations of predecessors, influenced now by the technical possibilities of new materials, now by the ever-changing standards of, let us say, human appearance. Any fine abstract quality which a modern critic may detect in their work is due to the accumulated technical experience of a whole race, rather than to the artistic conception of individuals. Perhaps it is the study of this very process of evolution which is pre-eminently the concern of archaeologists, on account of their knowledge of its cultural background. And it is not altogether surprising if this study occasionally leads them to the wider issues involved in the process of pure abstract criticism.

When the group of statuary discovered at Tell Asmar and Khafaje in the spring of 1934 began to assume such unexpected proportions, it became clear that it constituted an important new phase in the early history of sculpture. Dr. Frankfort therefore determined to pass the whole group in review and endeavour, by applying some sort of formal criticism, to dissociate the various styles which are represented, to attribute to each a motive and assign it to its appropriate place in the evolution of contemporary art. This he did with considerable thoroughness in a recent article in the *Burlington Magazine*. He begins by pointing out the importance of Sumerian sculpture, generally as representing a new aspect of the pre-Greek art which has up to now been almost exclusively thought of as connoting Egyptian art, simply because no other early civilization had till recently produced anything like the wealth of achievement discovered in Egypt. He recalls the preoccupation of the pre-Greek artist with nonorganic forms and his tendency to approximate the spatial arrangement of a statue to some familiar geometric shape, and accordingly contrasts the universal tendency among Egyptian sculptors to treat the cube or rectangular block as their predominating unity, with the Sumero-Babylonian preference for cylindrical or conical shapes. This will explain the fact that a seated figure is such a popular motive with the Egyptians, since the bending of knees and elbows can so conveniently be stylized to stress the cubic quality and the seat simplified into a pure cubic form, providing a contrast with the more complicated shaping of the human form which it supports. In Sumerian sculpture a seated figure seldom occurs. When it does, the legs are usually out of proportion and the bend of the knees awkwardly managed. Generally speaking, the artist is out of his element and the result unsatisfactory. Yet the typical standing figure, with its symmetrical cloak or kilt and arms bent at the elbow, is easily adapted to a geometrical shape based on a cylinder or a cone.

The question immediately arises to what extent these distinctive abstract qualities, which, to our eyes, constitute the principal characteristics of the two national styles, were the effect of self-conscious aesthetic considerations. Dr. Frankfort admits that the part played by individual genius in their evolution cannot be estimated, and attributes the preference for one geometric formula rather than another to a "collective aesthetic predisposition." Nevertheless, it is essential to bear in mind the great contrasting conditions under which sculptors worked in these two countries. In Egypt an unlimited quantity of first-rate stone or marble was easily obtainable, and a sculptor's pupil or the sculptor himself was at liberty to spoil any number of blocks while experimenting or designing in a tentative way. In Babylonia good stone for carving was as rare as metal. Little experimenting could be done, and the "trial-pieces" which are such common finds on most Egyptian sites scarcely ever appear in Mesopotamia. It must have been essential for the sculptor to go to almost any length to avoid a slip of the tool which would spoil the statue; and this in itself may have been responsible for a certain lack of modelling in cases where any further attempt at realism would tend to increase that risk. Conditions such as these are not a fair test of a sculptor's capacity for design, and it is fairly obvious that they are the direct cause of any obvious shortcomings in the very early Sumerian statues.

Similarly one may safely assume that the form in which stone was obtainable must have been the most important factor in determining any geometrical convention such as we have discussed above. In Egypt stone was the normal building material and it was quarried in rectangular blocks. When one of these earliest sculptors was faced with the problem of carving a statue or a group which would, after all, most likely be incorporated in the architectural scheme of some building, it seems highly improbable that he would select a block of stone to work upon of a notably different shape from those normally used for constructional purposes. All Egyptian architectual elements are cubic or very slightly pyramidal, and there was nothing to divert the sculptor's attention from the motive behind these. In Babylonia, on the other hand, stone had to be imported from neighbouring countries in lumps, as evidenced by the fact that none of these early statues which we are discussing is more than thirty inches high, and the majority much less. The type of lump likely to be selected by a stone-merchant as most suitable for a statue would probably be a rather shapeless oblong, so that it is not improbable that the main formal quality of these statues is dictated by an ignorant merchant's conception of the general shape of a man and therefore of a statue. The exigencies of economy in stone would thus influence the sculptor's ideas of design. We know, for instance, that at the time of Gudea diorite was quarried in Elam and imported into Mesopotamia in the form of boulders. Taking a boulder to imply a less attenuated shape, we may perhaps assume that the introduction at this later period of seated figures and squat, truncated shapes generally was due not so much to a new aesthetic predisposition amongst sculptors as to a fortuitous change of the form in which their material was available.

To return to Dr. Frankfort's article, he goes on to distinguish between two distinctive styles which apparently belong to two different subdivisions of the Early Dynastic period. Both are actuated by the same primary impulse towards a single geometric unity; yet the earlier style, which is represented by the *câche* in the square temple at Tell Asmar, is characterized by a general stylization of organic forms, including the exposed parts of the body, and to this he attaches great significance. In contrast to this the later group, which can be attributed to a period contemporary with the "royal tombs" at Ur, suggests that the sculptor had become preoccupied with the physical nature of his model, and consequently relapsed into a not always very competent attempt at naturalism.

The first explanation which offers itself of this transition from one style to another is almost disconcertingly simple. For if one attributes the so-called formal stylization of the earlier group merely to the timidity of a sculptor whose craft was still in its infancy and whose material was in any case too valuable to risk any attempt at virtuosity, yet crediting him with an instinctive eye for a visually satisfactory shape, one may examine every detail of these statues and at once apprehend the mental and technical process which brought it about.

If we are to follow this argument to its conclusion, we must attribute the naturalism of the later style to increased confidence and technical accomplishment, rather than to a lapse of aesthetic feeling for stylization. It should, incidentally, be remembered that by the time of Gudea the experience of something over fifty intervening generations had contributed to the maturity of sculpture generally.

=====

LEONARD WOOLLEY

The Sumerian Legacy

THREE generations ago the existence of the Sumerians was un-known to the scientific world; to-day their history can be written and their art illustrated more fully than that of many ancient peoples. It is the history and the art of a race which died out nearly four thousand years ago, whose very name had been forgotten be-fore the beginning of our era, and it might well be asked whether the knowledge recently acquired is not merely a matter of curiosity, whether the Sumerians at all deserve this literary resurrection. It is true that a novel discovery is liable to upset our perspective and an individual or a nation may from an accident of discovery or from the intrinsic excellence of their products assume an import-ance altogether out of proportion to the role they have filled in history: the records of man's activities, the works of his hands, are never without interest, but those activities may end in a blind alley, the works be isolated examples of art doing no more than illustrate how the human mind reacts to certain stimuli; the real criterion of value is, how far have these people contributed to human progress? what part had they in forming that culture which is the heritage of the living world? and it is by this standard that we must estimate the importance of the civilization now rescued from oblivion. . . .

Sumerian genius evolved a civilization which persisted for nearly fifteen hundred years after its authors had vanished, and Babylon and Nineveh did not keep this heritage to themselves; they also were imperial peoples, and their dominion over or their intercourse with the west fostered in those lands the seed which earlier Sumerian conquerors had planted. The Hittites of Asia Minor adopted the cuneiform script which was one of the greatest of the Sumerian inventions; Babylonian became the diplomatic language of the courts of Syria and even of Egypt; the cylinder seals of Syria and Cappadocia are both in form and in style derived from Mesopotamia; the sculptures of Carchemish trace their descent

From *The Sumerians*, pp. 183-4, 189-93.

through Assyria to Sumer; the eclectic art of the Phoenicians in so far as it drew from Oriental models was in the same indirect way an offshoot of the Sumerian. This is not to say that these countries were slavish copyists of a civilization which had as a matter of fact passed clean out of their ken; in each of them the arts developed in a normal way and received a more or less distinctive stamp of their nationality. But on each of them the Sumerian tradition has had a profound influence, stronger, naturally, in the home lands of the lower river valleys where it is indeed the direct begetter of all that is to follow, more subtle in the outlying provinces where it is a collateral rather than a source; and through these later peoples of the Near East it has influenced the material civilization of the modern world.

Such a claim is not easy to establish by concrete example, partly because we can seldom, if ever, know all the links in so long a chain, partly because the arts are not static and the inspiration which originates also modifies and transmutes so that its first and its final manifestation may seem to have nothing at all in common. But an instance of plain indebtedness may illustrate a wider truth. The arch in building was unknown in Europe until the conquests of Alexander, when Greek architects fastened eagerly on this, to them, novel feature and they, and later the Romans, introduced to the western world what was to be the distinguishing element in architecture. Now the arch was a commonplace of Babylonian construction—Nebuchadnezzar employed it freely in the Babylon which he rebuilt in 600 B.C.; at Ur there is still standing an arch in a temple of Kuri-Galzu, king of Babylon about 1400 B.C.; in private houses of the Sumerian citizens of Ur in 2000 B.C. the doorways were arched with bricks set in true voussoir fashion; an arched drain at Nippur must date to about 3000 B.C.; true arches roofing the royal tombs at Ur now carry back the knowledge of the principle another four or five hundred years. Here is a clear line of descent to the modern world from the dawn of Sumerian history. What is true of the arch is true also of the dome and the vault. Here, where the principle once invented is fixed for all time and only minor changes in form can be introduced, the sequence is easier to follow than in the more fluid arts of design: the influence of Sumer on the plastic art of later peoples is perhaps just as real, but it can be apprehended rather than demonstrated. But it is in the more abstract realm of ideas that the Sumerians have most obviously and most directly contributed to the development of western civilization, through the Hebrew people. Not only did the Semites adopt ready-made those stories of the Creation and the Flood which viewed as history or as parable have affected the Christian even more than the Jewish Church; the Jewish religion, as it owed not a little of its origin to the Sumerian, so also was throughout the period of the Kings and the Captivity brought into close contact with the Babylonian worship which was taken over from Sumer, and partly by its precept and partly in opposition to it attained to higher growth. The laws of Moses were largely based on Sumerian codes, those same codes which lay at the bottom of the great Code of Hammurabi, and so from the Sumerians the Hebrews derived the ideals of social life and justice which informed all their history and have by Christian races been regarded in theory if not in practice as criteria for their own customs and enactments. The difficulty lies not in recognizing the fact but in estimating the importance of the debt which the modern world owes to this race so recently rescued from complete oblivion. If human effort is to be judged merely by its attainment, then the Sumerians, with due allowance made for date and circumstance, must be accorded a very honourable though not a pre-eminent place; if by its effect on human history, they merit higher rank. Their civilization, lighting up a world still plunged in primitive barbarism, was in the nature of a first cause. We have outgrown the phase when all the arts were traced to Greece and Greece was thought to have sprung, like Pallas, full-grown from the brain of the Olympian Zeus; we have learnt how that flower of genius drew its sap from Lydians and Hittites, from Phoenicia and Crete, from Babylon and Egypt. But the roots go farther back: behind all these lies Sumer. The military conquests of the Sumerians, the arts and crafts which they raised to so high a level, their social organization and their conceptions of morality, even of religion, are not an isolated phenomenon, an archaeological curiosity; it is as part of our own substance that they claim our study, and in so far as they win our admiration we praise our spiritual forebears.

4. Cuneiform: History and Texts

THE earliest known writing is inscribed on a limestone tablet found at Kish. It dates from about 3500 B.C. and is entirely pictographic. The oldest considerable collections of clay tablets are a few centuries later and come from Uruk (the biblical Erech). Of these the most ancient are still wholly pictographic, but those of slightly later date already show the beginning of a transition to both phonetic and ideographic script. Meanwhile the pictures themselves were being simplified and conventionalized. About 3200 B.C. Sumerian scribes took to writing in such a way that the completed symbols appeared on the tablet lying on their backs—the position in which they were finally to be rendered in cuneiform. This last transition came about when the scribes saw that the symbols could be more effectively written if instead of being *incised* they were *impressed*. The instrument first used for the purpose seems to have been a section of reed; later, however, the stylus might be shaped in bone, wood or metal.

S. N. KRAMER

The Early History
of Cuneiform

. . . TODAY the Sumerians are one of the best-known peoples of
the ancient Near East. We know what they looked like from their
own statues and steles scattered throughout several of the more
important museums in this country and abroad. Here, too, will be
found an excellent representative cross section of their material
culture—the columns and bricks with which they built their
temples and palaces, their tools and weapons, pots and vases, harps
and lyres, jewels and ornaments. Moreover, Sumerian clay tablets
by the tens of thousands (literally), inscribed with their business,
legal, and administrative documents, crowd the collections of these
same museums, giving us much information about the social structure and administrative organization of the ancient Sumerians.
Indeed—and this is where archaeology, because of its mute and
static character, is usually least productive—we can even penetrate
to a certain extent into their hearts and souls. We actually have a
large number of Sumerian clay documents on which are inscribed
the literary creations revealing Sumerian religion, ethics, and philosophy. And all this because the Sumerians were one of the very
few peoples who not only probably invented a system of writing,
but also developed it into a vital and effective instrument of communication.

It was probably toward the end of the *fourth* millennium B.C.,
about five thousand years ago, that the Sumerians, as a result of
their economic and administrative needs, came upon the idea of
writing on clay. Their first attempts were crude and pictographic;
they could be used only for the simplest administrative notations.
But in the centuries that followed, the Sumerian scribes and

From *History Begins at Sumer*. London: Thames and Hudson Ltd.; 1956, pp.
18-20. Published at Indian Hills, Colorado, by The Falcon's Wing Press, as
From the Tablets of Sumer. Reprinted by permission of Thames and Hudson and
The Falcon's Wing Press.

teachers gradually so modified and molded their system of writing that it completely lost its pictographic character and became a highly conventionalized and purely phonetic system of writing. In the second half of the third millennium B.C., the Sumerian writing technique had become sufficiently plastic and flexible to express without difficulty the most complicated historical and literary compositions. There is little doubt that sometime before the end of the third millennium B.C. the Sumerian men of letters actually wrote down—on clay tablets, prisms, and cylinders—many of their literary creations which until then had been current in oral form only. However, owing to archaeological accident, only a few literary documents from this earlier period have as yet been excavated, although this same period has yielded tens of thousands of economic and administrative tablets and hundreds of votive inscriptions.

It is not until we come to the first half of the *second* millennium B.C. that we find a group of several thousand tablets and fragments inscribed with the Sumerian literary works. The great majority of these were excavated between 1889 and 1900 at Nippur, an ancient Sumerian site not much more than a hundred miles from modern Baghdad. They are now located primarily in the University Museum of Philadelphia and the Museum of the Ancient Orient at Istanbul. Most of the other tablets and fragments were obtained from dealers rather than through excavations, and are now largely in the collections of the British Museum, the Louvre, the Berlin Museum, and Yale University. The documents range in size from large twelve-column tablets, inscribed with hundreds of compactly written lines of text, to tiny fragments containing no more than a few broken lines.

SETON LLOYD

The Decipherment
of Cuneiform

RICH, on his last, fatal journey to Shiraz, like many previous European travellers, had seen and endeavoured to copy some of these inscriptions, particularly those in the vicinity of Persepolis—Takht-i-Jamshîd, Murghâb (the Tomb of Cyrus) and Naqsh-i-Rajab. But the even more important inscription on the great rock at Behistun, twenty miles from Kermanshah, he had only heard of from Bellino who had visited it shortly before his death. Almost all the other inscriptions had been copied with greater or lesser accuracy by Karsten Niebuhr late in the previous century. Like the Behistun inscription, they were trilingual; that is, the same cuneiform text was repeated in three different languages, which we now know to be Old Persian, Elamite and Babylonian. In Egypt, some years before, Napoleon's soldiers had discovered the famous Rosetta Stone with its parallel inscriptions in Greek and Egyptian hieroglyphs, fulfil something of the same function in deciphering cuneiform. pictographs. Now these trilingual inscriptions in Persia were to which served as a clue for the decipherment of the Pharaonic

As early as 1802, working mainly on Niebuhr's copyings, a young German college-lecturer, called Grotefend, succeeded first of all in establishing that, on the basis of the smaller number of signs used, one of the three languages was probably alphabetical rather than syllabic. He therefore selected this version for further study. Grotefend recollected that in the later Pehlevi inscriptions the Persian kings were usually given the title "Great King, King of Kings," so taking two short alphabetical cuneiform texts copied by Niebuhr from above the heads of royal figures carved in relief, he proceeded to do a lot of logical thinking. In each case the groups of signs at the beginning and end of the text were different, so he

From *Foundations in the Dust*. Harmondsworth: Penguin Books Ltd.; 1953, pp. 176-8. By permission of Oxford University Press, London.

took each text to refer to a different king. But in the middle of each text the same group occurred twice and then a third time with certain additions. He at once realized that these additions could be taken to signify the genitive case, and that if the repeating group spelt the word "king," here was the familiar formula of the Pehlevi. Next he noticed that the final group of each text also ended with genitive signs. So why should each not read: "So-and-So, the Great King, King of Kings, son of So-and-So." This, as it proved, fitted perfectly, and by a little judicious guessing he was even able to identify the two kings as "Darius, son of Hystaspes" and "Xerxes, son of Darius."

Progressing ingeniously from the known to the unknown, Grotefend eventually succeeded in reconstructing a complete alphabet and in attributing the correct phonetic value to twelve of its letters. Yet, on account of the academic snobbery of contemporary German scientists, his discovery was refused publication by the Göttingen Academy and was not actually vindicated until ninety years later. Meanwhile others, working independently, had arrived at much the same results. Foremost among these was Henry Creswicke Rawlinson whom we have last seen leaving India for Persia as part of a military mission to the court of the Shah.

Lieutenant Rawlinson's little detachment arrived at Bushire [Basra] by ship in the autumn of 1833, but were unable to cross the mountain passes to Teheran until the following spring. He was then able to make a preliminary examination of the Persepolis inscriptions on the way and was immensely intrigued by their possibilities. In March 1835 he found himself posted to Kermanshah in the capacity of military adviser to the Shah's brother, the governor of Kurdistan, and therefore within easy reach of the Rock of Behistun.

Actually the rock lies twenty-two miles to the east of Kermanshah, but it is only necessary to recollect Rawlinson's equestrian exploits as a subaltern in India in order to realize how inconsiderable such a distance would seem. Budge, in fact, mentions that "on one occasion, when it was necessary to warn the British Ambassador at Teheran of the arrival of the Russian agent at Herât, Rawlinson rode 750 miles in 150 consecutive hours." In any case, he at once began a series of regular visits to the rock, and between 1835 and 1837 set himself the task of making exact copies of the inscriptions. The process required every bit of skill which he possessed as an expert climber and involved the continual and repeated risk of his life.

Let us now examine a much more recent visitor's account of the rock itself. Mr. Filmer, in a travel book published in 1937, says: "To obtain a sight of the great inscription and the sculpture surmounting it I had to descend from my automobile opposite a

Persian tea house at the point of the rock by the road and then clamber over the strewn boulders at the foot of the mountain as far as it was possible conveniently to climb. From a corner of the rock thus gained, a view, although still somewhat indistinct, may be had of the smooth-faced ledges [*sic*] bearing in three languages a record of Darius' rule." The sculptured panel, which is actually about 400 feet from the ground, represents Darius himself, standing in judgment upon nine rebel chiefs, including, at the end of the row, a strange-looking individual called "Skunka" wearing a sort of dunce's cap. Also, the king is treading underfoot a figure representing the usurper, Smerdis, while the group is completed by two attendants, standing behind, and the god Ahuramazda in his winged disk.

The early visitors to the rock could by no means be expected to know all this, and owing partly to the preference of Western travellers for Biblical associations, their conclusions were often sufficiently remarkable. Ker Porter, for instance, who examined the sculptures through a telescope, identified the minor figures as "representatives of the Ten Tribes" standing before a "King of Assyria and of the Medes," and surmised that Skunka's dunce-cap was probably "the mitre worn by the sacerdotal tribe of Levi."

During the process of copying, Rawlinson naturally made a minute examination of the rock-face. He consequently made certain discoveries which are not generally known. In the first place the whole prepared area—about twelve hundred square feet of it— had been carefully smoothed and the unsound portions of the stone replaced with better material embedded in lead. After this the whole face had received a high polish, "which could only have been accomplished by mechanical means." After the sculpture and inscriptions had been carved, it had been given a thick coat of hard, siliceous varnish to protect it. The varnish was plainly harder than the actual stone, for in certain places where moisture had broken out from the face of the rock it had pushed away great flakes of the varnish, which Rawlinson found fallen on the ledge beneath, sometimes still bearing the clear impression of the lettering which they had covered.

During his early visits to the rock in 1835, Rawlinson began his copying of the Persian and Elamite inscriptions without the help of ladders or ropes, simply climbing down to the ledge beneath the panel. But the intentionally inaccessible location chosen by Darius for the sculptures made the area to be reached in this way very small, and during his return visits, in later years, ropes and ladders had to be used to read the remoter panels. Even so, the Babylonian inscription remained inaccessible until 1847, when a chance circumstance enabled Rawlinson to obtain "squeezes." He says:

At length, however, a wild Kurdish boy, who had come from a distance, volunteered to make the attempt, and I promised him a considerable award if he succeeded. The mass of rock in question is scarped, . . . so that it cannot be approached by any of the ordinary means of climbing. The boy's first move was to squeeze himself up a cleft in the rock a short distance to the left of the projecting mass. When he had ascended some distance above it, he drove a wooden peg firmly into the cleft, fastened a rope to this, and then endeavoured to swing himself across to another cleft at some distance on the other side; but in this he failed owing to the projection of the rock. It then only remained for him to cross over the cleft by hanging on by his toes and fingers to the slight inequalities on the bare face of the precipice, and in this he succeeded, passing over a distance of twenty feet of almost smooth perpendicular rock in a manner which to a looker-on appeared quite miraculous. When he reached the second cleft, the real difficulties were over. He had brought a rope with him attached to the first peg, and now, driving in a second, he was able to swing himself right over the projecting mass of rock. Here with a short ladder he formed a swinging seat, like a painter's cradle, and, fixed upon this seat, he took under my direction the paper cast of the Babylonian translation of the records of Darius.

Fifty years later, after much exhibition, these same "squeezes" were partly eaten by mice in the British Museum, but they had by then fulfilled their function and the record had been fully deciphered.

Rawlinson's first clue to the decipherment of the Persian version, though he was probably unaware of it, was almost the same phrases as had so much helped Grotefend over thirty years earlier—"Darius, the King, son of Hystaspes," and "Xerxes, the King, son of Darius." The identification of these phrases gave him enough phonetic values to identify many of the other proper names mentioned in the inscription, and by comparing them with possible Greek equivalents to compose an alphabet. By the end of 1837 he had succeeded in making a translation of the entire first two paragraphs of the inscription, which he sent in the form of a paper to the Royal Asiatic Society. It was on this paper and on a subsequent one written in 1839 that Rawlinson's claim to be the "Father of Cuneiform" rests.

GEORGE SMITH

George Smith and
the Flood Tablet

IN 1872 George Smith had announced his discovery of a part of
the story of the Deluge among the tablets from Nineveh in thc
British Museum (p. 44, I). The *Daily Telegraph* offered £1,000 for
Smith to go to Nineveh to seek the missing portion of the text. He
left for Mosul in January of 1873, but owing to a delay in getting
an excavation permit, he did not start work until May.

ON the 14th of May my friend, Mr. Charles Kerr, whom I had
left at Aleppo, visited me at Mosul, and as I rode into the khan
where I was staying, I met him. After mutual congratulations, I
sat down to examine the store of fragments of cuneiform inscriptions from the day's digging, taking out and brushing off the earth
from the fragments to read their contents. On cleaning one of
them I found to my surprise and gratification that it contained the
greater portion of seventeen lines of inscription belonging to the
first column of the Chaldaean account of the Deluge, and fitting
into the only place where there was a serious blank in the story.
When I had first published the account of this tablet I had conjectured that there were about fifteen lines wanting in this part of
the story, and now with this portion I was enabled to make it nearly
complete.

I have said I telegraphed to the proprietors of the "Daily Telegraph" my success in finding the missing portion of the Deluge
tablet. This they published in the paper on the 21st of May, 1873;
but from some error unknown to me, the telegram as published
differs materially from the one I sent. In particular, in the pub-

From *Assyrian Discoveries*. London: Sampson Low, Marston Ltd.; 1875, pp. 97,
100-2.

lished copy occurs the words "as the season is closing," which led to the inference that I considered that the proper season for excavating was coming to an end. My own feeling was the contrary of this, and I did not send this. I was at the time awaiting instructions, and hoped that as good results were being obtained, the excavations would be continued. The proprietors of the "Daily Telegraph," however, considered that the discovery of the missing fragment of the Deluge text accomplished the object they had in view, and they declined to prosecute the excavations further, retaining, however, an interest in the work, and desiring to see it carried on by the nation. I was disappointed myself at this, as my excavations were so recently commenced; but I felt I could not object to this opinion, and therefore prepared to finish my excavations and return. I continued the Kuyunjik excavations until I had completed my preparations for returning to England, and in the north palace, near the place where I found the tablet with warnings to kings, I disinterred a fragment of a curious syllabary, divided into four perpendicular columns. In the first column were given the phonetic values of the cuneiform characters, and the characters themselves were written in the second column, the third column contained the names and meanings of the signs, while the fourth column gave the words and ideas which it represented.

I searched all round for other fragments of this remarkable tablet, pushing my trench further through the mass of stones and rubbish, the remains of the fallen basement wall of the palace. Large blocks of stone, with carving and inscriptions, fragments of ornamental pavement, painted bricks, and decorations, were scattered in all directions, showing how complete was the ruin of this portion of the palace. Fixed between these fragments were found, from time to time, fragments of terra-cotta tablets; and one day a workman struck with his pick an overlying mass of mortar, revealing the edge of a tablet, which was jammed between two blocks of stone. We at once cleared away the rubbish, and then, bringing a crow bar to bear, lifted the upper stone block, and extracted the fragment of tablet, which proved to be part of the syllabary, and joined the fragment already found. The greater part of the rest of this tablet was found at a considerable distance in a branch trench to the right. It was adhering to the roof of the trench, and easily detached, leaving the impression of all the characters in the roof.

L. W. KING

The Sack of Lagash

THE city of Lagash was at Tello, the site excavated by the French under de Sarzec. Its neighbour and constant rival was Umma. Both cities were on the same branch of the Euphrates, and most of their disputes arose over the sharing of the water supply.

THE document from which we learn details of the sack of Lagash is a strange one. It closely resembles in shape and writing the tablets of household accounts from the archive of the patesis, which date from the reigns of Urukagina and his immediate predecessors; but the text inscribed upon it consists of an indictment of the men of Umma, drawn up in a series of short sentences, which recapitulate the deeds of sacrilege committed by them. It is not a royal nor an official inscription, and, so far as one can judge from its position when discovered by Commandant Cros, it does not seem to have been stored in any regular archive or depository. For it was unearthed, at a depth of about two metres below the surface of the soil, to the north of the mound which covered the most ancient constructions at Tello, and no other tablets were found near it. Both from its form and contents the document would appear to have been the work of some priest, or scribe, who had formerly been in Urukagina's service; and we may picture him, after the sack of the city, giving vent to his feelings by enumerating the sacred buildings which had been profaned by the men of Umma, and laying the weight of the great sin committed upon the head of the goddess whom they and their patesi served. That the composition was written shortly after the fall of Lagash may be held to explain the absence of any historical setting or introduction; the city's destruction and the profanation of her shrines have so

From *A History of Sumer and Akkad*. London: Chatto and Windus Ltd.; 1910, pp. 188-91. By permission of Chatto and Windus Ltd.

recently taken place that the writer has no need to explain the circumstances. He plunges at once into his accusations against the men of Umma, and the very abruptness of his style and the absence of literary ornament render their delivery more striking. The repetition of phrases and the recurrent use of the same formulae serve only to heighten the cummulative effect of the charges he brings against the destroyers of his city.

"The men of Umma," he exclaims, "have set fire to the Eki[kala]; they have set fire to the Antasurra; they have carried away the silver and the precious stones! They have shed blood in the palace of Tirash; they have shed blood in the Abzu-banda; they have shed blood in the shrine of Enlil and in the shrine of the Sun-god; they have shed blood in the Akhush; they have carried away the silver and the precious stones! They have shed blood in E-babbar; they have carried away the silver and the precious stones! They have shed blood in the Gikana of the goddess Ninmakh of the Sacred Grove; they have carried away the silver and the precious stones! They have shed blood in the Baga; they have carried away the silver and the precious stones! They have set fire to the Dugru; they have carried away the silver and the precious stones! They have shed blood in Abzu-ega; they have set fire to the temple of Gatumdug; they have carried away the silver and the precious stones, and have destroyed the statue! They have set fire to the . . . of the temple E-anna of the goddess Ninni; they have carried away the silver and the precious stones, and have destroyed the statue! They have shed blood in the Shagpada; they have carried away the silver and the precious stones! In the Khenda . . . ; they have shed blood in Kiab, the temple of Nindar; they have carried away the silver and the precious stones! They have set fire to Kinunir, the temple of Dumuzi-abzu; they have carried away the silver and the precious stones! They have set fire to the temple of Lugal-uru; they have carried away the silver and the precious stones! They have shed blood in the temple E-engur, of the goddess Ninâ; they have carried away the silver and the precious stones! They have shed blood in the Sag . . . , the temple of Amageshtin; the silver and precious stones of Amageshtin have they carried away! They have removed the grain from Ginarbaniru, from the field of Ningirsu, all of it that was under cultivation! The men of Umma, by the despoiling of Lagash, have committed a sin against the god Ningirsu! The power that is come unto them, from them shall be taken away! Of sin on the part of Urukagina, king of Girsu, there is none. But as for Lugal-zaggisi, patesi of Umma, may his goddess Nidaba bear this sin upon her head!"

It will be noticed that, in addition to the temples in the list, the writer mentions several buildings of a more secular character, but

the majority of these were attached to the great temples and were
used in connection with the produce from the sacred lands. Thus
the Antasurra, the palace of Tirash, the Akhush, the Baga, and the
Dugru were all dedicated to the service of Ningirsu, the Abzu-
banda and the Shagpada to the goddess Ninâ, and the Abzu-ega
to Gatumdug. The text does not record the destruction of the king's
palace, or of private dwellings, but there can be little doubt that
the whole city was sacked, and the greater part of it destroyed by
fire. The writer of the tablet is mainly concerned with the sacrilege
committed in the temples of the gods, and with the magnitude of
the offence against Ningirsu. He can find no reason for the wrongs
the city has suffered in any transgression on the part of Urukagina,
its king; for Ningirsu has had no cause to be angry with his
representative. All he can do is to protest his belief that the city-god
will one day be avenged upon the men of Umma and their goddess
Nidaba. Meanwhile Lagash lay desolate, and Umma inherited the
position she had held among the cities of Southern Babylonia. We
know that in course of time the city rose again from her ruins, and
that the temples, which had been laid waste and desecrated, were
rebuilt in even greater splendour. But, as a state, Lagash appears
never to have recovered from the blow dealt her by Lugal-zaggisi.
At any rate, she never again enjoyed the authority which she
wielded under the rule of her great patesis.

L. W. KING

Gudea Builds a Temple at Lagash

GUDEA was the seventh and best-known governor of Lagash, and
did much rebuilding there. Many standardized statues of him were
among the wealth of Sumerian sculpture discovered during the
excavations at Lagash.

THE detailed account of the building of this temple [for the city-god, Ningirsu], which Gudea has left us, affords a very vivid picture of the religious life of the Sumerians at this epoch, and of the elaborate ritual with which they clothed the cult and worship of their gods. The record is given upon two huge cylinders of clay, one of which was inscribed while the work of building was still in progress, and the other after the building and decoration of the temple had been completed, and Ningirsu had been installed within his shrine. They were afterwards buried as foundation-records in the structure of the temple itself, and so have survived in a wonderfully well-preserved condition, and were recovered during the French excavations at Tello. From the first of the cylinders we learn that Gudea decided to rebuild the temple of the city-god in consequence of a prolonged drought, which was naturally ascribed to the anger of the gods. The water in the rivers and canals had fallen, the crops had suffered, and the land was threatened with famine, when one night the patesi had a vision, by means of which the gods communicated their orders to him.

Gudea tells us that he was troubled because he could not interpret the meaning of the dream, and it was only after he had sought and received encouragement from Ningirsu and Gatumdug that he betook himself to the temple of Ninâ, the goddess who divines the secrets of the gods. From her he learnt that the deities who had appeared to him in his vision had been Ningirsu, the god of his city, Ningishzida, his patron deity, his sister Nidaba, and Nindub, and that certain words he had heard uttered were an order that he should build E-ninnû. He had beheld Nindub drawing a plan upon a tablet of lapis lazuli, and this Ninâ explained was the plan of the temple he should build. Ninâ added instructions of her own as to the gifts and offerings the patesi was to make to Ningirsu, whose assistance she promised him in the carrying out of the work. Gudea then describes in detail how he obtained from Ningirsu himself a sign that it was truly the will of the gods that he should build the temple, and how, having consulted the omens and found them favourable, he proceeded to purify the city by special rites. In the course of this work of preparation he drove out the wizards and sorcerers from Lagash, and kindled a fire of cedar and other aromatic woods to make a sweet savour for the gods; and, after completing the purification of the city, he consecrated the sur-

Ibid., pp. 265-8.

rounding districts, the sacred cedar-groves, and the herds and cattle belonging to the temple. He then tells us how he fetched the materials for the temple from distant lands, and inaugurated the manufacture of the bricks with solemn rites and ceremonies.

We are not here concerned with Gudea's elaborate description of the new temple, and of the sumptuous furniture, the sacred emblems, and the votive objects with which he enriched its numerous courts and shrines. A large part of the first cylinder is devoted to this subject, and the second cylinder gives an equally elaborate account of the removal of the god Ningirsu from his old shrine and his installation in the new one that had been prepared for him. This event took place on a duly appointed day in the new year, after the city and its inhabitants had undergone a second course of purification. Upon his transfer to his new abode Ningirsu was accompanied by his wife Bau, his sons, and his seven virgin daughters, and the numerous attendant deities who formed the members of his household. These included Galalim, his son, whose special duty it was to guard the throne and place the sceptre in the hands of the reigning patesi; Dunshagga, Ningirsu's waterbearer; Lugal-kurdub, his leader in battle; Lugal-sisa, his counsellor and chamberlain; Shakanshabar, his grand vizir; Uri-zi, the keeper of his harîm (harem); Ensignun, who tended his asses and drove his chariot; and Enlulim, the shepherd of his kids. Other deities who accompanied Ningirsu were his musician and fluteplayer, his singer, the cultivator of his lands, who looked after the machines for irrigation, the guardian of the sacred fish-ponds, the inspector of his birds and cattle, and the god who superintended the construction of houses within the city and fortresses upon the city-wall. All these deities were installed in special shrines within E-ninnû, that they might be near Ningirsu and ready at any moment to carry out his orders.

S. N. KRAMER

A Love Song

WHILE working in the Istanbul Museum of the Ancient Orient as Fulbright Research Professor—it was toward the end of 1951—I came upon a little tablet with the museum number 2461. For weeks I had been studying, more or less cursorily, drawerful after drawerful of still uncopied and unpublished Sumerian literary tablets, in order to identify each piece and, if possible, assign it to the composition to which it belonged. All this was spadework preparatory to the selection, for copying, of those pieces which were most significant—since it was clear that there would be no time that year to copy all of them. The little tablet numbered 2461 was lying in one of the drawers, surrounded by a number of other pieces.

When I first laid eyes on it, its most attractive feature was its state of preservation. I soon realized that I was reading a poem, divided into a number of stanzas, which celebrated beauty and love, a joyous bride and a king named Shu-Sin (who ruled over the land of Sumer close to four thousand years ago). As I read it again and yet again, there was no mistaking its content. What I held in my hand was one of the oldest love songs written down by the hand of man.

It soon became clear that this was not a secular poem, not a song of love between just "a man and a maid." It involved a king and his selected bride, and was no doubt intended to be recited in the course of the most hallowed of ancient rites, the rite of the "sacred marriage." Once a year, according to Sumerian belief, it was the sacred duty of the ruler to marry a priestess and votary of Inanna, the goddess of love and procreation, in order to ensure fertility to the soil and fecundity to the womb. The time-honored ceremony was celebrated on New Year's day and was preceded by feasts and banquets accompanied by music, song, and dance. The poem inscribed on the little Istanbul clay tablet was in all probability recited by the chosen bride of King Shu-Sin in the course of one of these New Year celebrations.

From *History Begins at Sumer*, pp. 285-7.

Bridegroom, dear to my heart,
Goodly is your beauty, honeysweet,
Lion, dear to my heart,
Goodly is your beauty, honeysweet.

You have captivated me, let me stand tremblingly before you,
Bridegroom, I would be taken by you to the bedchamber,
You have captivated me, let me stand tremblingly before you,
Lion, I would be taken by you to the bedchamber.

Bridegroom, let me caress you,
My precious caress is more savory than honey,
In the bedchamber, honey filled,
Let us enjoy your goodly beauty,
Lion, let me caress you,
My precious caress is more savory than honey.

Bridegroom, you have taken your pleasure of me,
Tell my mother, she will give you delicacies,
My father, he will give you gifts.

Your spirit, I know where to cheer your spirit,
Bridegroom, sleep in our house until dawn,
Your heart, I know where to gladden your heart,
Lion, sleep in our house until dawn.

You, because you love me,
Give me, pray, of your caresses,
My lord god, my lord protector,
My Shu-Sin who gladdens Enlil's heart,
Give me, pray, of your caresses.

Your place goodly as honey, pray lay (your) hand on it,
Bring (your) hand over it like a gishban-garment,
Cup (your) hand over it like a gishban-sikin-garment,

It is a balbale-song of Inanna.

5. The Development of Excavation in Mesopotamia

THE extracts in this section illustrate in various ways the natural background to life in Mesopotamia, the history of the valley and the relationship between these factors and the problems confronting archaeologists working there. It shows, too, how archaeological research cut further and further down into time. First the comparatively recent Assyrian period was revealed, then the Babylonian and Akkadian. Presently it was realized that before the Semitic peoples had ruled the valley, there was a more ancient civilization —that of the Sumerians. Then the Sumerian culture was seen to be rooted in that of the prehistoric people represented at al 'Ubaid. At the time Leonard Woolley wrote, he had to say, "It is impossible to assign even an approximate date to the village settlement of al 'Ubaid"—but now it is securely assigned to the fourth millennium B.C. Seton Lloyd tells how the hunt was then pushed even further back with the recognition of the Tell Halaf, Samarra and Hassuna cultures, best known through their painted pottery and now dated to the fifth and sixth millennia B.C. He says that with Hassuna the story of exploration in Mesopotamia can be ended, for it "has now reached a point beyond which it seems impossible to pass with any certainty." Yet it has already been seen (p. 251, I) how at Jarmo it was taken even further back, revealing the life of villagers who had not yet learnt the art of potting, and how at Jericho the link was finally made with the Mesolithic hunters of ten thousand years ago.

SETON LLOYD

A History of Excavation
in Mesopotamia

THE name Mesopotamia, with its habitual associations, applies strictly only to the lower reaches of the Tigris and Euphrates. Both rivers have their sources high up among the mountains of Anatolia, and the Euphrates, passing diagonally across north Syria, has run well over half its course when it crosses the border into Iraq. Even then it is still separated from the Tigris by a considerable tract of desert, and it is not until a point is reached a little north of Baghdad that the two draw together and combine to irrigate the land which was once Babylonia. This point marks an important geographical dividing line, for to the north lies the country anciently called Assyria, which possesses climatic characteristics in marked contrast to the south.

Babylonia is economically dependent upon the rivers. The rainfall during an average winter is very unreliable and apt at times to be almost negligible, while the scorching heat of the summer persists from March to October. The whole of the southern plain, like the delta of the Nile, consists of alluvium brought down and deposited by the rivers. It now stretches for many miles on either side of them, and produces a potentially fertile soil, but, unlike the Nile valley with its conveniently perennial floods, the waters of the Tigris and Euphrates need to be artifically distributed over the countryside. In a country of this sort wood as well as stone for building and other purposes must be imported from elsewhere. Date-palms will grow and certain shrubs, but other trees do not repay the water and labour necessary to irrigate them. Sun-dried brick, or, for greater permanence, the kiln-baked variety, will invariably be the material used for building. Arches and vaults will be used to avoid the necessity for roofing timbers. And above all,

From *Mesopotamia*, pp. 1-26.

earthenware will have taken its primary place in everyday life, so that one form or another of pottery will be used for every conceivable domestic purpose.

In the north, partly owing to the proximity of the mountains, the winters are bitterly cold. Heavy frosts occur for three months in the year and rainstorms lasting sometimes from ten to fifteen days. Moreover, the land is traversed by tributaries of the greater rivers, the two Zabs to the east and the Khabur to the west. Thus cereal cultivation is made possible without resorting to irrigation. Here the date-palm is out of its element, but vines and fruit-trees take its place. Also there is a supply of building stone and wood which can be obtained, without much difficulty, from the neighbouring foot-hills.

During the period since the War, excavations in Iraq have been mainly concentrated in the south. For here, long before the beginnings of written history, there was created a civilization now known as Sumerian, destined to dominate the history of the land for over three thousand years. More recently, however, as will be seen later, there has been an increase of archaeological interest in the pre-Assyrian remains of the north; and whether these investigations reveal Sumerian colonies or collateral cultures within the sphere of Sumerian influence, certain discrepancies in the finds are easily explicable in view of the above considerations.

We must picture southern Mesopotamia, then, at the height of Sumerian prosperity as a flat plain traversed by a complex system of irrigation canals such as would do credit to a modern engineer. During most of this period it was divided into a number of city-states, of which each in turn, and occasionally two at the same time, produced a dynasty of kings to hold nominal authority over the whole land. Each state's period of hegemony began and ended in war, and hardly a reign passed without inter-state quarrels, usually arising from irrigation disputes. Furthermore, the whole history of this epoch is punctuated by the raids, and occasionally the partial domination, of mountaineer races from the north and east, who cast covetous eyes upon the fertile lowlands. In this way city after city was sacked and destroyed, only to be rebuilt shortly afterwards. Sometimes this happened as often as twice in a generation, to judge from the results of excavations, and each time the town rose a little higher above the level of the plain. An example of the process carried to its logical conclusion may be seen in the town of Erbil, once called Arbela, which claims to be the oldest still-inhabited city in the world. Here in the course of time the building level has risen, until half of the modern Erbil is perched upon the crest of a mound a hundred feet high, covering the remains of innumerable earlier cities. The other half, since the population has greatly increased, straggles away into the plain from its foot. So in antiquity each town would soon find itself standing upon a little hill.

Similarly, the canals continually needed to be enlarged or replaced, and each new one added to the already complicated network of irrigation works. In a land which depends upon artificial irrigation for its very existence, these canals become vital arteries. In addition to being the subject of continual inter-state quarrels in antiquity, their vulnerability in more modern times eventually led to the ruin of the entire land. This began in 1258 A.D. with the invasion of the Mongol hordes under Hulagu, and was later completed by Tartar and Ottoman Turks. It seems probable that it was not a process of wholesale destruction, caused by the deliberate breaching of canals and barrages, but rather a slow deterioration of the irrigation system for lack of proper upkeep and administration. The people were conquered and dispirited, and no longer possessed the individual energy or the requisite organization to maintain it. There was no longer anything to prevent a peasant from making a breach in the bank of a high-level canal and drawing off water to work his mill, or from allowing the breach to enlarge itself beyond the limits of safety. Moreover, in the course of years the beds of the rivers themselves had sunk deep in the alluvium, and now ran between steep banks four or five metres beneath the level of the plain they used to irrigate. This necessitated the extra labour of pumping, where a barrage would no longer serve to divert the water into the canals.

Soon the breakdown of the system was complete, and was followed at once by the gradual desiccation of the country, so that to-day the cultivated portion of south Iraq consists mainly of strips of ploughland and palm-groves following the courses of the rivers. Here and there a modern canal has been dug, sometimes along the line of an ancient one. Such is the case of the Shatt-el-Hai (Shatt al Hai), which is known to have been constructed by Entemena, Governor of Lagash, to bring water from the Tigris, owing to the constant interference of the neighbouring state of Umma with the water supply from the Euphrates. But the other great artificial waterways of Babylonian times, such as the Shatt-en-Nil and the Nahr-Awan, like their smaller tributaries, can now only be traced as a double row of mounds with a slightly raised or sunken area between. Their great width is still impressive, and when crossing them in a car it seems as though minutes elapse between leaving one "bank" and arriving at the other.

With the canals no longer bringing water, the towns which were dependent upon them were abandoned. The action of wind and rain soon brought about the collapse of mud-brick buildings, and the effect of dust-storms, which increased in frequency as the cultivated land turned again to desert, ultimately converted what had once been prosperous cities into forgotten mounds. The rapidity with which this process of immolation seems to have taken place is remarkable. The sites of certain great cities were for one reason or another completely abandoned in antiquity, and within the space of a few years nothing remained but a group of brick-strewn mounds to bear witness to their one-time pomp and prosperity. In Assyria, for instance, King Sargon, like Akhenaten in Egypt, transplanted his capital from Nineveh to Khorsabad. Here he built a gigantic new city, square in plan and surrounded by a wall twenty metres high with seven great gateways. His palace was built upon a vast platform of sun-dried brick level with the tops of the walls, and included three separate temples and a ziggurat tower. Yet when he died and, like the city of Akhenaten, the new capital was abandoned, his son Sennacherib did not even find it worth while to remove the innumerable sculptured reliefs with which the palace and the gateways of the town had been adorned; so that soon these became no more than a verbal tradition among the people of Nineveh, while fifteen miles away peasants grazed their flocks upon the slopes of a mound which had once been Sargon's palace and ziggurat. Nineveh itself was destined to suffer a similar fate; though at the height of its prosperity under Sennacherib it ranked as the greatest city in the world. Its actual extent has probably been exaggerated, and when Jonah spoke of "an exceeding great city of three days' journey," he was probably including Nimrûd, twenty miles to the south, and Khorsabad, as suburbs of Nineveh. Diodorus says it had walls 100 feet high, with room for three chariots to drive abreast and there were 1500 towers 200 feet high. It is now established that at the time of Sennacherib the city had a circuit of 7½ miles and fifteen gateways. A passage from a letter written by Henry Layard when he was excavating Sennacherib's palace will give some idea of the scale on which it was conceived. "In this magnificent edifice," he says, "I had opened no less than 71 halls, chambers and passages, whose walls had almost without exception been panelled with sculptured slabs of alabaster. By a rough calculation about 9880 feet, or nearly two miles of bas-reliefs, with 27 portals formed by colossal winged bulls and lion sphinxes . . ." This was Nineveh, which fell in 607 B.C., when the Medes took advantage of the flooding of the Euphrates to bring their battering-rams against the walls upon rafts. They razed every building to the ground and massacred the Assyrians so thoroughly that the entire city was abandoned. Less than 200 years later, Xenophon, in his celebrated retreat, passed over the sites of Nineveh and Khorsabad without even remarking their existence. And later, in 150 A.D., Lucian, living nearby in Syria, asserted "Nineveh has perished. No trace of it remains, and one would never know that it had existed."

This is the explanation of the mounds of Iraq and the *tells* with which modern archæologists are mainly concerned. They are often lower and less extensive than the ancient repute of the city which they cover would lead one to expect, owing to a gradual rise in the level of the surrounding plain. Many traces of ancient occupation appear upon the surface—small objects of bronze or pottery, beads, cylinder seals and occasionally an inscribed tablet. But there are two most important elements in establishing the period to which a site belongs or even in connecting a group of mounds with the name of an ancient city already known to have existed, from references in texts, though not yet accurately located. These are the potsherds and the inscribed bricks. There is no need here to enlarge upon the archaeological importance of pottery. It is sufficient to remember that in Egypt, for instance, such exhaustive studies have now been made of the historical development of ceramics, that it is usually only necessary to walk over a mound and observe the potsherds lying on the surface in order to date the ruins beneath. During the last few years this has almost come to apply equally to Iraq. The habit of stamping an inscription containing the name of a king and a short dedication upon every brick of an important building seems to have existed from the middle of the third millennium right down to Neo-Babylonian times. It can well be imagined what enormous value these inscriptions have for archaeologists in relation to the buildings in which they occur. Here, for instance, is a brick-stamp found during the first few days of excavating Tell Asmar, a previously unexplored mound near Baghdad:

"IBIQ-ADAD
MIGHTY KING
ENLARGER OF ESHNUNNA
SHEPHERD OF THE BLACK-HEADED PEOPLE
BELOVED OF TISHPAK
SON OF IBALPEL."

There in a moment one has the name of the ancient city: the name of a governor of the city and his father, and therefore the beginnings of a genealogical table; a reference to "black-headed people," an epithet commonly used in connection with the Sumerians; and the name of the local deity. In this case it was similarly stamped bricks found on the surface which had enabled the mound to be identified as Eshnunna, a city state already known from extraneous evidence to have played an important part in the history of Mesopotamia at a certain period. There are, for instance, in the Louvre magnificent statues inscribed with the names of governors of Eshnunna. These were found by a French expedition in Persia, whither they had apparently been carried as booty by the Elamites after a successful raid upon the cities of the plain.

Now, the bricks found on the surface at Tell Asmar afforded sufficient evidence to justify the concentration of an archaeological expedition upon the site. And it only needed a single season's digging in the ruins of this one building to prove its assumed identity correct, and even to establish a complete chronological table of local governors. This was simply a matter of collecting the information provided by the stamped bricks, since each governor in turn seemed to have found it necessary to repair or completely rebuild the palace, and each had added his name and a new dedication upon the bricks. The neighbouring site of Khafaje, where digging was begun simultaneously, has only recently, after five years' systematic excavation, begun to be associated by scholars with the name of an ancient city, Akshak. This is because so far only that portion of the mound has been investigated which contains remains dating from a period before stamped bricks came into use.

In the case of the most important cities, the ruins of a ziggurat constitute a landmark which can be seen for many miles around. On many of these larger sites enormous masses of brickwork are accessible directly below the surface of the mound, and since the baked bricks themselves are of excellent quality and usually well preserved, they prove something of a temptation to the modern Arab, who is perpetually in need of building materials. Sometimes, particularly in the case of the Assyrian sites in the north, limestone is available, and whether it appears in the form of foundation blocks or sculptured reliefs, it is equally serviceable for burning into cement or patching the wall of a house. In this way natives of modern Mosul in their search for limestone slabs were the true discoverers of the ruins of Nineveh, and the brick-robbers from Hilla were originally responsible for the identification of the mounds which covered Babylon. This type of pilfering greatly decreased with the advent of the first archaeologists.

Half a dozen great names are inseparably connected with the early history of excavating in Mesopotamia. Rawlinson, Layard, Place, Botta, Koldewey and Loftus each in turn assisted in providing the nuclei of the great Assyrian and Babylonian collections of Europe. The conditions under which this older school of archaeologists worked, and their excavating methods, make an interesting contrast with the better subsidized, and consequently better equipped, digging expeditions which have taken the field since the War.

To-day efficient rail and motor services link Mosul and Baghdad with Basra on the Persian Gulf. To a point north of Mosul on the Iraq-Syrian border one travels by wagon-lit on the unfinished Berlin-to-Baghdad railway. From Damascus one reaches Baghdad in something under twenty-four hours, crossing the 500 miles of Syrian desert in one of the great eighteen-wheeled coaches which are now used on that route. Or one lands at the Baghdad Aerodrome three days and two nights after leaving Croydon. But when Botta began digging at Nineveh in 1841, and a little later, in 1845, when Layard tackled Nimrûd, both using Mosul as their base, it still required a journey of many weeks, mostly on horseback, to reach that town. Wallis Budge had a Turkish inspector sent from Istanbul to supervise his work at Nineveh, and this gentleman, being unable to ride even a donkey, was compelled to travel almost the entire distance in a "takh tarawan," an elementary wooden litter swung on poles between a pair of mules. As one might expect, he arrived more dead than alive.

In those days establishing one's claim to a new mound was rather on the principle of rival groups of colonists racing to plant their flags upon the shores of a new continent, and polite but spirited altercations were always taking place in connection with priority of claim to certain mounds. One such difference of opinion occurred when Layard conceived the idea of using some of the money given him by Stratford Canning to continue Botta's excavations at Nineveh. This was resented by the French consulate, who were sceptical of his claim to have obtained Botta's permission. In this case the argument must have reached a deadlock, for Budge describes how for some time "Layard continued to open trenches in the south side of the mound, and the French consul went on digging little pits a few feet deep in another direction." On a later occasion Layard's Chaldaean assistant Rassam was anxious to attack the northern corner of the Kuyunjik mound, but found the Frenchman Victor Place already at work. He was apparently undaunted, for "using strategy, he began to work there by night, and on the third night discovered the palace of Ashur-bâni-pal and the splendid set of sculptures which form the 'Lion Hunt' now in the British Museum."

It can be imagined that under these conditions the standard of excavating technique could not reach very great heights. In fact, in these very early days digging consisted mainly in the hurried looting of large semi-indestructible objects, such as sculptures in stone, and the preservation of such tablets or smaller objects as were not destroyed in the process. Moreover, once extracted from their mounds, the transport of these heavier finds to European museums presented a tremendous problem. As recently as 1929 a great winged bull was unearthed at Khorsabad, and though it was already broken into several pieces, it required all the resources of an American University to enable it to be transported by boat down the Tigris to Basra, where a steamer waited to take it across the Atlantic. Actually nothing better than an old three-ton lorry could be found for the first stage of its journey, a distance of fifteen miles from Khorsabad to the Tigris; and as the largest fragment weighed over fourteen tons, it was hardly surprising that, having got to within 200 yards of the river, the engine collapsed under the strain. A series of cables were then fixed to the remains of the chassis with the idea of dragging it the remaining distance by means of a donkey-engine on the paddle-boat. So firmly was the lorry stuck, however, that when the engine began to work, it was the boat which moved and began slowly to ascend the bank of the river. It had to be refloated before a second and more successful attempt could be made.

In the middle of the last century the only river craft suitable for work of this sort were rafts, known as *keleks,* supported on inflated skins. These are still used for the transport of grain, etc., down both rivers. An average raft consists of 300 to 500 skins, and is steered by a series of immensely long willow-pole oars. When it reaches its destination the skins are deflated, so that they may be packed on donkeys and carried back whence they came. The wooden framework is sold for firewood. Each of the great stone sculptures from Nineveh, Nimrûd and Khorsabad would be laid in turn upon a mud-bank close to the river, and piece by piece one of these rafts would be constructed beneath it. After this it was a matter of waiting for the first flood to set it afloat; but when afloat it would be a fairly safe method of transport. Only once, in 1855, a catastrophe occurred, at Kourna, where a raft was capsized and its load of Khorsabad bas-reliefs abandoned at the bottom of the Tigris.

In view of these difficulties, the number and size of the sculptures which came to view directly the Assyrian palaces were excavated proved disconcerting. Often it became necessary to leave them in place at the end of a season's digging for lack of transport facilities, and in this case it seemed advisable as far as possible to rebury them as a protection against the Arabs and Kurds, who are always on the look-out for limestone that can be used for burning into cement. Sometimes, however, this was impracticable owing to shortage of funds or shortage of time. In this manner many fine sculptures met an unworthy fate. Though only a small proportion of them had ever reached a museum, by 1891 there was only one winged bull left *in situ* at Kuyunjik, the palace mound of Nineveh. A year later its head was removed and taken to mend a peasant's wall, and subsequently the whole monument was "sold for the sum of three and sixpence by the Vali of Mosul and burnt into lime by its purchaser."

Similarly with metal objects; in one room of the Khorsabad palace, Place unearthed nearly 160 tons of iron implements, including hoes and other agricultural tools. A few of these were sent home, and most of the remainder found their way into the Arab village at the foot of the palace mound, where for many years they continued to be used for the purpose for which they were made in the eighth century B.C.

The evolution during recent years of a proper system of scientific excavation and the preservation of antiquities has progressed rapidly. Excavating methods depend directly upon ancient building methods, and therefore vary according to the country in which one is working. Egypt has always been an excavator's paradise, first because so many monuments of first-rate importance are either built of stone or cut in the solid rock; secondly because in a climate where rain is hardly known most types of antiquity are found in a perfect state of preservation. At a site like Tell el Amarna, where the buildings are of sun-dried brick, or in some cases of stone, it is only necessary to rake away the accumulated sand and a quantity of easily distinguishable fallen brickwork; after which one has the ground plan with walls standing up to about a metre high. Sometimes, even, there are decorations on the plaster with the colours as bright as on the day they were applied. Wood and ivory are preserved where white ants have not had access, and quite frequently cloth and wicker-work.

In Mesopotamia very different conditions prevail. Brick is the universal material, and, as we have seen, the sun-dried variety has been used from the fourth millennium onwards for almost every type of building from palace to a hovel. When these buildings are abandoned the roofs, constructed of mud upon poles and matting, are the first to collapse; then gradually the walls crumble, filling the rooms up to a certain height. Sometimes the site is not again occupied, in which case the ruin then becomes shaped to the curve of a mound. But more often old occupants return or new ones arrive and rebuild houses and temples, using as foundations the carefully levelled remains of the previous buildings. The continual repetition of this process produces an elaborate stratification, sometimes showing evidence of a succession of cultures lasting over a period of several thousands of years. For the archaeologist this provides a fine source of historical information and material for scientific deduction, but it also makes his work enormously complicated in comparison, for instance, with the Tell el Amarna type of site, which has been occupied only once. Added to this is the detrimental effect of heavy rainstorms in the winter, which gradually bring about the decay of almost every material except stone, metal and earthenware. There is also a tendency for standing walls and fallen rubbish to become welded together into such a homogeneous mass that only a practised eye can distinguish one from the other. Thus the craft of "wall-tracing" has gradually assumed a position of great importance among the various processes connected with excavating. It varies in its degree of technical difficulty from the gigantic walls of the Assyrian and late Babylonian palaces, whose faces often have a coating of plaster several centimetres thick, to those of the smaller buildings of the very early Sumerian periods. These are seldom plastered at all and have, in most cases, been buried beneath so many metres of superimposed later occupations that they are only with extreme difficulty distinguishable from the "room fillings" and surrounding debris.

Probably the first serious attempt at wall-tracing was made by Messrs. Place and Thomas, who patiently and systematically recorded the plan of Sargon's vast palace complex at Khorsabad. Here the walls stood too high to make trenches practicable, and an elaborate system of tunnelling was resorted to. But together with other processes, wall-tracing only began to reach a proper standard of efficiency in 1899, when the German school of excavators under Koldewey and Andrae started work on the ruins of Babylon. By the time they turned their attention to Ashur their methodical accuracy in recording had become a byword, and their plan of campaign in investigating a mound had been reduced to a system which has only recently begun to be improved upon by their successors. Amongst the Germans the architectural functions of an excavator had become pre-eminent. The disentangling of ground-plans and possible reconstruction of the upper parts of buildings had assumed an importance which was possibly a reaction against the earlier method of excavating, which consisted, as we have already seen, mainly in looting objects without paying proper attention to the evidence provided by their context. There are those who think that the new tendency was unduly exaggerated at that period, since this method of excavating supplies a minimum of historical information. It is true that the tremendously extensive excavations of the Deutsche Orient Gesellschaft at Babylon between 1899 and 1914 were concerned with a single period only, and produced few finds of primary importance beyond the magnificent glazed-brick portals of the Ishtar gate now in the Berlin Museum. Yet later at Ashur the same excavators were the first to follow the plan of a temple down through a most complicated succession of rebuildings to the remains of its original foundation in an extremely archaic period. The value of this system of excavations, and the importance of this particular piece of work, cannot be exaggerated, since it is a means of establishing a chronological sequence of cultures which can be checked on other sites. Also it suffers nothing from the meticulous care with which each successive plan, and in point of fact the position of every single brick, was noted and recorded.

These same excavators have maintained an equally high standard of efficiency during the post-war years at Warka (Uruk, Biblical

Erech), while in Sir Leonard Woolley's camp at Ur the technique of extracting valuable objects from the ground, preserving and interpreting them, and finally the artistry connected with their publication, reached a very high degree of accomplishment.

Each of these groups of excavators, however, has been in one way or another hampered by shortage of funds, and in this respect the larger American universities which have put expeditions into the field in recent years have been able to set a new standard. There can be no question that a body of archaeologists when approaching an important piece of excavating will benefit by being properly constituted, so that each may have his appropriate work allotted to him according to his specialized training. And it is equally certain that no amount of scientific equipment or amenities of living for the excavators can do otherwise than enhance the standard of their work and increase their capacity for thoroughness. Published results speak for themselves, and the advantage of no longer needing to be deflected from one's original plan of campaign, in order to force sensational finds with a view to increasing one's next year's budget, is something which yearly becomes more obvious. The Oriental Institute of the University of Chicago now have camps of this type in Iraq, Syria, Palestine and Egypt. Each is carefully staffed with experts, and provided with photographic studios, scientific laboratories and even, in certain cases, a library. All these units cooperate in collating their results, and there is a continual interchange of personnel among the various expeditions, so that individual workers become apprised of the wider scientific aims of the whole organization.

H. V. HILPRECHT

America Awakens

THE importance of the study of Semitic languages and literature was early recognized in the United States. Hebrew, as the language of the Old Testament, stood naturally in the centre of general interest, as everywhere in Europe; and the numerous theological seminaries of the country and those colleges which maintained close vital relations with them were its first and principal nurseries. But in the course of time a gradual though very visible change took place with regard to the position of the Semitic languages in the curriculum of all the prominent American colleges. The German idea of a university gained ground in the new world, finding its enthusiastic advocates among the hundreds and thousands of students who had come into personal contact with the great scientific leaders in Europe, and who for a while had felt the powerful spell of the new life which emanated from the class rooms and seminaries of the German universities. Post-graduate departments were organized, independent chairs of Semitic languages were established, and even archaeological museums were founded and maintained by private contributions. Salaries in some cases could not be given to the pioneers in this new movement. They stood up for a cause in which they themselves fully believed, but the value of which had to be demonstrated before endowments could be expected from the liberal-minded public. They represented the coming generation, which scarcely now realizes the difficulties and obstacles that had to be overcome by a few self-sacrificing men of science, before the present era was successfully inaugurated.

The study of the cuneiform languages, especially of Assyrian, rapidly became popular at the American universities. The romantic story of the discovery and excavation of Nineveh so graphically told by Layard, and the immediate bearing of his magnificent results upon the interpretation of the Old Testament and upon the history of art and human civilization in general, appealed at once to the re-

From *Explorations in Bible Lands*. Edinburgh: T. & T. Clark; 1903, pp. 289-90.
By permission of T. & T. Clark.

ligious sentiment and to the general intelligence of the people. The American Oriental Society and the Society of Biblical Literature and Exegesis became the first scientific exponents of the growing interest in the lands of Ashurbânapal [Ashur-bani-pal] and Nebuchadrezzar [Nebuchadnezzar]. The spirit of Edward Robinson, who more than sixty years before had conducted his fundamental researches of the physical, historical, and topographical geography of Syria and Palestine, was awakened anew, and the question of participating in the methodical exploration of the Babylonian ruins, to which De Sarzec's extraordinary achievements at Tello had forcibly directed the public attention, began seriously to occupy the minds of American scholars. "England and France have done a noble work in Assyria and Babylonia. It is time for America to do her part. Let us send out an American expedition,"—was the key-note struck at a meeting of the Oriental Society which was held at New Haven in the spring of 1884.

H. V. HILPRECHT

A Bad Beginning:
Battle at Nippur

Soon after we had reached Nuffar [Nippur, the site selected by the Americans] Dr. Peters had made us acquainted with the low ebb in the finances of the expedition. It was, therefore, decided to close the excavations of the first campaign at the beginning of May. But the working season was brought to a conclusion more quickly than could have been anticipated. The trouble started with the Arabs. The methodical exploration of the ruins had proceeded satisfactorily for about nine weeks till the middle of April, tablets being found abundantly, and the topography of ancient Nippur becoming more lucid every day. Notwithstanding those countless difficulties which, more or less, every expedition working in the interior

Ibid., pp. 313-17.

of Babylonia far away from civilization has to meet at nearly every turn, we began to enjoy the life in the desert and to get accustomed to the manners of the fickle Arabs, whose principal "virtues" seemed to consist in lying, stealing, murdering, and lasciviousness. And the 'Afej, on the other hand, had gradually abandoned their original distrust, after they had satisfied themselves that the Americans had no intention of erecting a new military station out of the bricks of the old walls for the purpose of collecting arrears of government taxes. But there existed certain conditions in our camp and around us which, sooner or later, had to lead to serious complications. Hajji Tarfâ, the supreme sheikh of all the 'Afej tribes, a man of great diplomatic skill, liberal views and far-reaching influence, was unfortunately absent in the Shamîye when we commenced operations at Nuffar. His eldest son, Mukota, who meanwhile took the place of his father, was a sneaking Arab of the lowest type, little respected by his followers, begging for everything that came under his eyes, turbulent, treacherous, and a coward, and brooding mischief all the while. Two of the principal 'Afej tribes, the Hamza and the Behahtha, both of which laid claim to the mounds we had occupied, and insisted on furnishing workmen for our excavations, were at war with each other. At the slightest provocation and frequently without any apparent reason they threw their scrapers and baskets away and commenced the war-dance, brandishing their spears or guns in the air and chanting some defiant sentence especially made up for the occasion, as, e. g., "We are the slaves of Berdi," "The last day has come," "Down with the Christians," "Matches in his beard who contradicts us," etc. The Turkish commissioner and the zabtîye (irregular soldiers),—whose number had been considerably increased by the gâimmaqâm of Dîwânîye, much against our own will,—picked frequent quarrels with the natives and irritated them by their overbearing manners. The Arabs, on the other hand, were not slow in showing their absolute independence by wandering unmolested around the camp, entering our private tents and examining our goods, like a crowd of naughty boys; or by squatting with their guns and clubs near the trenches and hurling taunting and offensive expressions at the Ottoman government.

It was also a mistake that we had pitched our tents on the top of the ruins. For as the mounds of Nuffar had no recognized owner and yet were claimed by the Turks, the Bedouins, and the Ma'dân tribes at the same time, we were practically under nobody's protection, while by our very conspicuous position we not only suffered exceedingly from hot winds and suffocating sand storms, but invited plundering by every loiterer and marauder in the neighborhood. Moreover, unacquainted as we all were then with the peculiar customs of Central Babylonia, we had not provided a mudhîf or lodg-

ing-house, a spacious and airy *sarifa,* which in every large village
of the country is set apart for the reception of travellers and guests.
What wonder that the simple-minded children of the desert and the
half-naked peasants of the marshes, who noticed our strange mode
of living and saw so many unknown things with us for which they
had no need themselves, shook their heads in amazement. On the
one hand they observed how we spent large sums of money for uncovering old walls and gathering broken pottery, and on the other
they found us eating the wild boar of the jungles, ignoring Arab
etiquette, and violating the sacred and universal law of hospitality
in the most flagrant way,—reasons enough to regard us either as
pitiable idiots whom they could easily fleece or as unclean and
uncouth barbarians to whom a pious Shiite was infinitely the superior.

Repeated threats to burn us out had been heard, and various attempts had been made to get at our rifles and guns. One night our
bread-oven was destroyed, and a hole was cut in the reed-hut which
served as our stable. Soon afterwards four sheep belonging to some
of our workmen were stolen. The thief, a young lad from the Saʿîd, a
small tribe of bad repute, half Bedouin and half Maʿdân, encouraged
by his previous success, began to boast, as Berdi told me later, that
he would steal even the horses of the Franks without being detected.
Though he might have suspected us to be on the alert, he and a few
comrades undertook to execute the long-cherished plan in the night
of the fourteenth of April. Our sentinels, who had previously been
ordered to occupy the approaches to the camp night and day, frustrated the attempt and opened fire at the intruders. In an instant
the whole camp was aroused, and one of the thieves was shot
through the heart. This was a most unfortunate occurrence, and
sure to result in further trouble. No time was therefore lost to inform
the ʿAfej chiefs, to despatch a messenger to the next military station,
and to prepare ourselves for any case of emergency. Then followed
a period of anxious suspense. Soon the death wail sounded from a
village close beneath us, indicating that the body of the dead Arab
had been carried off to the nearest encampment. Then a signal
fire was kindled. This was answered by another and another, until
the whole plain was clothed with little lights, while through the still
night came the sounds of bustle and preparation for the attack.
On the next morning we decided to avoid the consequences of the
severe laws of Arab blood revenge by paying an adequate indemnity
to the family of the fallen man. But our offer was proudly rejected
by the hostile tribe, and an old Saʿîd workman, employed as a go-
between, returned with torn garments and other evidences of a beating. The American party was equally prompt in refusing to give up
the "murderer." The days and nights which followed were full of

exciting scenes. Mukota, Berdi, and other 'Afej sheikhs, who professed to come to our assistance, had occupied the spurs around us. Thirty irregular soldiers, with six hundred rounds of cartridges, were sent from Dîwânîye and Hilla, and others were expected to arrive in the near future. There were constant alarms of an attack by the Sa'îd. The 'Afej, not concealing their displeasure at seeing so large a number of *zabtîye* in their territory, were evidently at heart in sympathy with the enemy. Besieged as we practically were, we were finally forced to withdraw our laborers from the trenches and make arrangements for quitting Nuffar altogether. On Thursday, April 18, long before the sun rose, the whole expedition was in readiness to vacate the mounds and to force their way to Hilla, when upon the treacherous order of Mukota, an Arab secretly set fire to our huts of reeds and mats and laid the whole camp in ashes in the short space of five minutes. For a while the utmost confusion prevailed, the *zabtîye* got demoralized, and occupied a neighboring hill; and while we were trying to save our effects, many of the Arabs commenced plundering. Half the horses perished in the flames, firearms and saddle-bags and $1000 in gold fell into the hands of the marauders, but all the antiquities were saved. Under the war-dance and yells of the frantic Arabs the expedition finally withdrew in two divisions, one on horseback, past Sûq el-'Afej and Dîwânîye, the other on two boats across the swamps to Daghâra, and back to Hilla, where soon afterwards the governor-general of the province arrived, anxious about our welfare and determined, if necessary, to come to our rescue with a military force.

LEONARD WOOLLEY

Before the Sumerians

OF the three elements the Sumerians were probably the last to enter the south country. They came from a distance and were not likely to be tempted to migrate so far until the land was sufficiently formed

From *The Sumerians*, pp. 12-16.

to offer reasonable facilities for agriculture and for commerce, whereas the Semitic nomads were on the spot and would naturally have moved down on to the fertile soil as it appeared. "Mankind when created did not know of bread for eating or garments for wearing. The people walked with limbs on the ground, they ate herbs with their mouths like sheep, they drank ditch-water," says a Sumerian hymn, and the description, which scarcely fits the Sumerians themselves as the apostles of civilization, would be apt enough for the despised dwellers in the swamps whom the new-comers found on their arrival and enslaved to their service.

The account given by the Babylonians of how civilization was introduced implies that there were already people in the land and that their manner of life must have been very much that described in the hymn.

A glimpse of these marsh-dwellers is afforded by the excavation at al 'Ubaid near Ur of a primitive settlement of the painted pottery age. Upon a low mound rising above the level of the flooded land there was planted a village made up of little huts whose walls were of reed matting stretched between wooden uprights and waterproofed with pitch or with a thick mud plaster; their roofs were flat, of mud spread over mats supported by cross beams, or else arched like those of many modern huts in the district, in which bundles of tall reeds tied together serve instead of the wooden uprights and the tops of each facing pair are bent inwards and lashed together so as to form a series of arches, then horizontal ribs of reed are tied to these and reed mats laid over the whole. The huts had wooden doors whose hinge-poles revolved on sockets of imported stone, and the hearths were either holes in the beaten mud floor or were built up with bricks of unbaked mud. Cows, sheep, goats and pigs were kept; barley was grown, and the people ground it in rough querns or pounded it in mortars to make a kind of porridge, and fish was a staple article of food. Copper was known, but was still a luxury; for most purposes stone was used, and small knives, saws, the cutters of the threshing-machines, arrow-heads and so on were chipped out from flint or chert picked up in the high desert or from translucent obsidian, like bottle-glass, imported from the far-off Caucasus. Indeed metal was so rare that the sickles for cutting the barley were made of baked clay, and because these so quickly broke or grew blunt and were thrown away we find hundreds of them strewing the ancient sites. Bone was used for awls and netting-needles. Besides the painted pots, there were coarser clay wares, sometimes with incised decoration, and food-bowls of limestone for those that could afford such. The villagers went on the marshes in narrow canoe-shaped boats with high curled prows made of reeds tied together. They wore garments of sheepskin or of homespun cloth, and judging from the painted marks on a clay figurine they may have tattooed their bodies: their ears were pierced to take studs of bone, bitumen or baked clay, and the women wore heavy necklaces of beads roughly chipped from crystal, carnelian and shell and dressed their hair in a "bun" at the back of the head; the men seem to have had long pointed beards. They buried their dead in the earth lying on one side with the knees bent, and as they placed with them offerings of food, personal ornaments, tools, etc., we may suppose that they had some kind of belief in the continuation of life after death.

It is impossible to assign even an approximate date to the village settlement of al 'Ubaid; only the presence of the painted pottery shows that it must have flourished very long before the semi-historic age which is illustrated by the excavations of Kish and Ur and can be brought into relation with the written records of the Sumerians. But it does throw some light upon the conditions of life in the delta when human occupation was still in its early phases, conditions which otherwise we can only deduce from the natural course of events and from what we find to have evolved in later times.

———

SETON LLOYD

Further Into the Past

EARLY in 1940 the first full-scale government excavation was undertaken on a pre-historic site called Tell 'Uqair, fifty miles south of Baghdad. A sensational discovery was made. This mound represented the well-preserved remains of a temple dating from the proto-Sumerian period and its walls were covered with painted frescoes. Its publication two years later in Chicago was the first intimation to archaeologists in their wartime *diaspora* that in Iraq at least excavations were still in progress. In the years which followed, other sites were selected for excavation in such a way that the periods

From *Foundations in the Dust*, pp. 236-9.

which they represented should fall into sequence and eventually cover the whole panorama of Mesopotamian history. The training of staff was thus greatly facilitated, and by 1943 their standard of competence could be considered equal to that of most Western expeditions. It was under these circumstances that the site called Hassuna was discovered.

As early as 1928 Dorothy Garrod had found in the Kurdish mountains traces of Palaeolithic man. But a prodigious gap existed between these cave-dwellers of the Mousterian and Aurignacian periods and the settled agricultural communities of Tell Halaf and Samarra, with their evidence of copper-smelting and other advanced processes. Working at Nineveh in 1931, Mallowan found indications of a culture preceding Samarra, but at such a depth beneath the surface that little evidence of its character could be recovered. Twenty miles south of Nineveh, at Hassuna, the Department now discovered a little mound whose surface, amidst the grass and flowers, was littered with broken fragments of this pre-Samarra pottery. Its seven metres of superimposed settlements in fact ended on the surface at almost the exact point beyond which the great pit at Ninevch had been unable to penetrate.

During the months that the mound was under excavation the horizon of pre-history once more receded several centuries. Revealed in the simplest terms of archaeological evidence was a new and earliest chapter in the history of what may reasonably be called civilized man. As a nomad he had first ventured out from the mountains on to these grassy uplands above the Tigris. Here at the junction of two streams he had first camped and remained long enough to reap a store of wild barley. In the lowest stratum at Hassuna were the ashes of his campfires, and grouped around them the simple paraphernalia of his household—flint weapons, bone implements, and the first crude pottery vessels. At the next stage he had learned to sow as well as reap, and his nomadic habits were forgotten. Primitive adobe houses began to appear, and the improved pottery was ornamented with painted designs. Near the surface was a well-built village with the practical economy of an agricultural community almost completely developed. Seventy centuries later the modern village of Hassuna is run on much the same lines.

The discovery of Hassuna makes a fitting end to this story of Mesopotamian exploration. For in archaeology the elucidation of the country's history has in some sense been reversed. The writings of the Assyrians and Babylonians led to the discovery of the Sumerians and Akkadians. But the search for the remoter origins of the Sumerians themselves and their predecessors has now reached a point beyond which it seems impossible to pass with any certainty.

Meanwhile the way is open for a new generation of diggers to enrich and amplify the results of previous research. They will no longer have the role of explorers in a neglected and half-savage country, but will find working conditions little different from those at home. They will also for the first time be able to benefit from the collaboration of their locally-born colleagues.

The British Residency in Baghdad changed its quarters more than once during the early years of the present century. In the modern Embassy building, which stands on the west bank of the Tigris, there is a vestibule which serves as a miniature portrait gallery. Here at a glance one may see the whole saga of British representation, first in Turkish Arabia and later in the kingdom of Iraq. Here is Rich, the first great orientalist, with his look of sober responsibility; Taylor, the recluse, in his library of Arabic books and manuscripts; Rawlinson, the soldier-scholar, absorbed in the enigma of cuneiform writing; Tweedie, whose interest was divided between the men and the horses of Arabia; and others whose names have been omitted from these pages. Their faces are summoned from the past—a company of witnesses to Great Britain's century-long association with Iraq in the realm of culture. Facing them in striking counterpoint are the High Commissioners and Ambassadors of more recent years; men whose concern was for the welfare of the modern state, and whose preoccupation with its future transcended their interest in its past. And always between the two groups stands, in one's imagination, the figure of Gertrude Bell, who alone watched the transition from bondage and retrospection to this new freedom, and to whose clear vision the tradition of Mesopotamian research owes its perpetuation in a new form.

6. *Palestine*

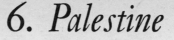

CHARLES WARREN

Early Excavations in Jerusalem

THE Palestine Exploration Fund was established in England in 1865, and two years later Charles Warren, a young ordnance officer, was sent out to excavate at Jerusalem. Although his work laid the foundations for future researches, there were as yet no reliable means of dating what he uncovered, and nearly all his conclusions have been disproved. Passages have therefore been selected to illustrate his methods, adventures—and lively style. One suspects that the young man deliberately modelled himself in the likeness of Henry Layard. His archaeological ambitions were frustrated, but he rose in the army to become Major-General Sir Charles Warren.

WE had started at 7 A.M. and expected to arrive at Jerusalem soon after noon, but we did not reach it till 8 P.M.; we were thus seventeen hours between Jaffa and Jerusalem on the track, a distance of thirty-six miles, which since the coach road has been made I have ridden over in less than four hours. While en route a queer-looking person put in an appearance mounted on an Arab horse and saddle, and gave herself out to be Mrs. Ducat; she wore a kind of hat, her eyes were streaming with tears, owing to the violence of the wind, and she rode her horse like a man. A Russian widow of a German savant, she stated she was in possession of the oldest Hebrew copy of the Pentateuch in existence, written by a son of Aaron. She asked me to examine it on my arrival, and I did so.

It has a long legend, which can be seen in the photograph of the

From *Underground Jerusalem*. London: Richard Bentley; 1876, pp. 35-7, 140-1, 149-52.

Palestine Exploration Fund, in which the name of the writer is stated. It is called the "Fire tried," there being a tradition that it had been exposed to the flames and escaped unhurt during the time of the Jewish captivity. Mrs. Ducat's method of riding without side-saddle was novel to me, but when I mentioned it to some American ladies the next day I noticed sufficient embarrassment to cause me to change the subject; and on making inquiry afterwards I found that these ladies also were journeying in the same manner, and that it was not an uncommon sight in the Holy Land to see ladies galloping about Amazon fashion.

With the continual interruptions our road appeared to be interminable.

> "Where wilds immeasurably spread,
> Seem lengthening as I go."

Goldsmith's lines were intensely applicable on this occasion. When at last we arrived near the city we had no time to feel disappointed at the intrusive appearance of the Russian buildings situated on the site of Titus's camp and overlooking the city; our thoughts were centred upon the hurrying up our animals to the gates before they were closed for the night; this we just succeeded in doing.

Our approach in some manner became known in the city, and soon several dragomen came out to greet us, bringing bonbons in their pockets to comfort our weary souls.

My interview with Izzet Pasha over, I had lost no time in commencing work at the water passages, under the eastern of the two ancient gates of Herod's Temple, facing the midday sun. Fortune favoured our enterprise, and in a few hours an old parting wall in the rock-hewn aqueduct yielded to our efforts, and we found ourselves in the substructures of the Temple itself; among the piers supporting the vast vaults, called the Stables of Solomon; below where once stood the palace of that great king. Our progress through these passages had been rapid, but unhappily the hammerblows, resounding through the hollow walls in so unwonted a manner, alarmed the modern representative of the High Priest. Infuriate with anger, the fine old sheikh would listen to no reasoning: but repairing to the south-east angle of the old Temple enclosure, mounted its battlements and summoned the Sheikh of Siloam to stand forth and answer for his misdeeds. With full turban and long flowing robes, edges tipped with fur, the old man stood, on the edge of the steep masonry, stamping his feet with rage and bellowing imprecations.

Accordingly, I picked out a spot along the south wall, about eighty feet from the south-west angle, concealed behind some prickly pears, where we worked down along the wall in security;

at the same time I also commenced another shaft at the south, about forty feet from the wall in the open, for at that distance it was not supposed I could get near the wall itself. We mined in this case down to the rock, and then run along its surface until we reached the great wall, and there we commenced our work, examining the masonry. All this time our men were being threatened by the Pasha with imprisonment and driven away; but after they discovered that I looked after their interests, they came back again, though sometimes intimidated, for a few days: all except the nervous ones—men that were not required.

The people of Siloam are a lawless set, credited with being the most unscrupulous ruffians in Palestine; perhaps such qualities make them good workmen in dangerous places. This at least I can say for them, that they were industrious, willing, and good-tempered, easily made to laugh.

Siloam and Lifta, villages north of Jerusalem, supplied our works, from twenty to fifty men daily; we also employed a few Nubians and men from the city. They were not allowed to work by families, but were mixed up as much as possible, so that in case anything was found they would not be able to keep it secret. In the hands of these men we were constantly intrusting our lives, and always felt secure with them so far as their intentions were concerned; but the accidental dropping of a stone, or even a crow-bar down a shaft, at the bottom of which we were working, was rather treated as a joke among them than as a matter for serious consideration.

It took many weeks to drill these men into order; at first they would do just as they chose, but gradually they learnt obedience. First it was necessary to establish three rates of pay, so as to encourage the industrious: and this was a very difficult matter to arrange, for it was contrary to their feeling of justice. Allah had made one man stronger than another; why should the weak receive less than the strong? This had to be met in their own form. "Allah had made one man stronger than other, therefore, Allah intended that one man should receive more wages than another." Though this did not satisfy them at first, they gave way by our perseverance.

Our first result was a general strike, and most of them took themselves off; but next week those who came in their place were paid at a lower rate than some who had remained and knew what to do, and so the strike assisted our efforts. When everything worked fairly, the rates were about 1s. 3d. to 1s. 5d. per diem for work from sunrise to sunset. We paid about a penny a day more than the market price, so as to secure our men, and soon found that a tight hold could be kept over them, especially when they discovered that they received the full amount, instead of having a percentage deducted by a middleman.

Praying was a favourite excuse. A man, when he got tired of shouldering the basket, would suddenly face Mecca, and go through his formulae. Now we observed that they never prayed either before or after hours, or when they were working for themselves; in fact, that it was only an excuse for idleness; and accordingly they were mulct pay for each prayer until they desisted. The villagers do not frequently go to the Friday prayers in the mosque, but they found they should like to do so while with us; this was very undesirable, because, when there, they were liable to be cross-questioned by the Turkish authorities. I therefore arranged that one of their number, the head of a family, who enjoyed the distinction of wearing a green turban, should take the sins of the whole party each Friday, and carry them to the mosque: this had a very good effect, for he was paid for this service, and he liked it, and being of the family of the Prophet he was much respected, and had influence among his clan. A little deference thus paid to the old heads of families allowed me to be stricter with the younger branches.

The fellahs, or villagers, have a very simple dress, a white skull cap, with a handkerchief rolled round it of red and yellow or white, to form a turban; a cotton shirt fastened at the waist by a leathern pouch, and over this a woollen abba. Sometimes they wear a coloured cotton waistcoat under the abba, and in cold weather a sheep-skin coat, wool inside, with the leather coloured bright blue or crimson; leather slippers completed their costume. When they go beyond their villages they always carry arms, generally a very long gun with a flint lock. When working hard they take off the abba and throw down their shirt, which remains suspended by the leather band, and in extreme heat they work naked.

The fellahîn, like other Easterners, do not know the use of the spade; they only use the mattock; striking towards them when they work: thus the muscles for throwing from them are not developed, neither are those for wheeling a barrow; the consequence was that those men who were initiated into English working ways complained bitterly at first that they felt as though they had been well beaten; gradually, however, the younger ones became used to the work, and were proud of their proficiency. A great deal of the work, however, had to be done according to the manners of the people: that is to say, by means of a mattock and basket and rope. The baskets are made of rushes at Lydd, and will carry about 25 lbs. of earth; the man draws the earth into the basket with the mattock, and then carries it off on his head, or fastens a rope to it, and allows it to be hauled up by his companion.

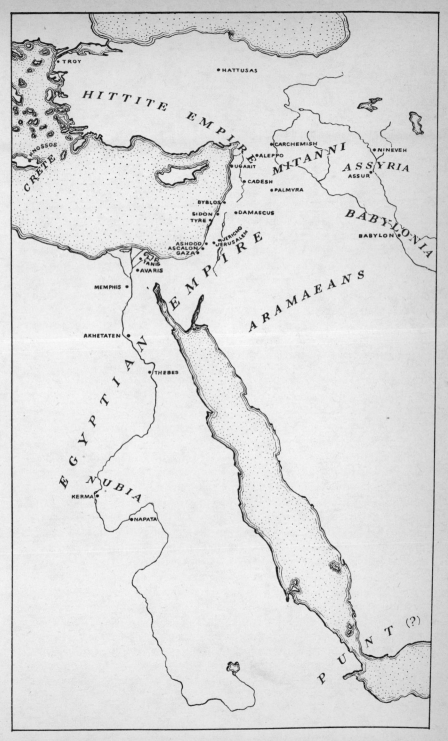

THE NEAR EAST IN THE MIDDLE YEARS OF THE SECOND MILLENNIUM B.C.

CHARLES WARREN

Failure at Jericho

CHARLES WARREN went to explore various mounds, hoping, as
he frankly admits, to find treasures that would rival those which
had recently made Layard famous. Among them he sampled the
tell at Ain es Sultan, which he rightly identified with Jericho. As
he delved in helpless ignorance in the mass of mud brick, bitterly
disappointed though he was, he had the wit to see that there might be
"monuments of the greatest importance" there if they could be
tackled "in some special manner." In 1954, when Kathleen Kenyon
was making her revolutionary exploration of the *tell*, she was able
to identify one of Warren's soundings.

❧

ON this night of my arrival at Ain es Sultan, I was too full of the
prospects of opening up the mounds to suffer from the heaviest
supper. Grand visions of what existed in the interior dimly shadowed
themselves forth and excluded every other view: the colossal figures
which emanated from my excited imagination far exceeded anything
obtained from Nineveh by Layard. And now that the dream of
bringing them to England is over, now that this draw in the lottery of
life is a blank, can I say they were not met with, that others do
not yet exist within those mounds? In truth, I cannot. In excavating
those remains of a bygone race, we were groping in a land of
shadows and phantoms; ever and anon, as the pick opened up the
soil, the half-light revealed to us objects which evaded our grasp,
which, on being brought to the strong daylight, vanished from view
and returned into the dust from which they were constructed. The
very bricks ceased to exist as bricks when exposed to the air. It
cannot, then, be said that in these mounds, so thoroughly ripped
open, there are not monuments of the greatest importance yet
existing, but if so, they must be obtained in some special manner,

From *Underground Jerusalem*, pp. 169-70, 196-7.

for a few seconds sufficed to take away their appearance and leave but a yellow marly clay.

As a general result on the completion of these excavations it may be said for a certainty that these mounds are artificial throughout, and that they probably are the remains of ancient castles.

There is scarcely a doubt that the Ain es Sultan is that which Elisha healed on his return with the mantle of Elijah: and therefore these mounds surrounding it are probably the remains of the Jericho of that date. If this be so, I have to suggest whether it would not be worth while shifting the whole mound with the prospect of finding among the remains some record of the past; this could be executed for £400.

J. M. ALLEGRO

Discovery of
the Dead Sea Scrolls

MANY people will be found to disagree with some of the interpretations and judgments given in this very frank and lively description of the now world-famous discovery of the "Dead Sea Scrolls." It is unlikely that it will ever be possible to give an absolutely objective and undisputed account of these fascinating but tangled events. Since this initial discovery, many other caves in the region have yielded further manuscripts.

THE dust had hardly settled over the battlefields of the world, when newspapers began to carry reports of a sensational new discovery in the field of biblical archaeology. It was announced that, in the

From *The Dead Sea Scrolls*. Harmondsworth: Penguin Books Ltd.; 1956, pp. 15-34. By permission of Penguin Books Ltd.

summer of 1947, a cave had been found near the Dead Sea which had produced manuscripts of the book of Isaiah older by something like a thousand years than any previously known Hebrew copy of the Old Testament. Later examination was to show that of the scrolls found in this cave, the biblical manuscripts were probably the least important of what appeared to be the remains of a Jewish sectarian library dating from shortly after the time of Jesus Christ. More discoveries in this region followed in the ensuing years, and before long the world was in possession of the remains of hundreds of scrolls covering a period which had hitherto been one of the most sparsely documented, yet important, periods in Man's history. Questions which had been hammering at the door of scholarship since the beginning of critical research into Christian origins could now be answered. This little book is an attempt to trace the general outline of results so far achieved and where further research may be expected to lead as this exciting new material becomes generally available. But first let us see how the discovery was made, and to do so we must travel to the wilderness of Judaea, to a point amongst the mountains bordering the Dead Sea, a few miles south of Jericho.

Muhammad Adh-Dhib had lost a goat. The lad was a member of the Ta'amireh tribe of semi-Bedouin who range the wilderness between Bethlehem and the Dead Sea, and he had been out all this summer's day tending the animals entrusted to his care. Now one of them had wandered, skipping into the craggy rocks above. Muhammad pulled himself wearily up the limestone cliffs, calling the animal as it went higher and higher in search of food. The sun became hotter, and finally the lad threw himself into the shade of an overhanging crag to rest awhile. His eye wandered listlessly over the glaring rocks and was suddenly arrested by a rather queerly placed hole in the cliff face, hardly larger than a man's head. It appeared to lead inwards to a cave, and yet was too high for an ordinary cave entrance, of which there were hundreds round about. Muhammad picked up a stone and threw it through the hole, listening for the sound as it struck home. What he heard brought him sharply to his feet. Instead of the expected thud against solid rock, his sharp ears had detected the metallic ring of pottery. He listened a moment, and then tried again, and again there could be no doubt that his stone had crashed among potsherds. A little fearfully the Bedouin youth pulled himself up to the hole, and peered in. His eyes were hardly becoming used to the gloom when he had to let himself drop to the ground. But what he had seen in those few moments made him catch his breath in amazement. On the floor of the cave, which curved back in a natural fault in the rock, there were several large, cylindrical objects standing in rows. The boy pulled himself up again to the hole, and holding on until his arms and fingers were numb, saw, more clearly this time, that they were large, wide-necked jars, with broken pieces strewn all about them. He waited no longer, but dropped to the ground and was off like a hare, his goat and flock forgotten in a frantic desire to put as much distance between himself and this jinn-ridden cave as possible. For who else but a desert spirit could be living in such a place with an entrance too small for a man?

That night Muhammad discussed his discovery with a friend who, being the elder, was entitled to scoff at the superstitions of his junior. He urged Muhammad to take him to the spot, and the next day the two of them went to the cave, and this time squeezed through the hole and dropped inside. It was just as the younger lad had described. The jars stood in rows on each side of the narrow cave, and, in the middle, broken sherds lay amidst debris fallen from the roof. There were seven or eight of the jars all told, and some had large, bowl-like lids. They lifted one and peered in, but found it empty. And so with another, and another, until in the third they saw a bundle or rags and under it two more. If they had hoped for the glitter of gold and precious stones they were sorely disappointed, for the bundles crumbled at a touch, and, pulling away some of the folds, they could see only some black tarry substance and, below that, folds of smooth brown leather. When, later, the boys had taken this booty back to their camp, they took off all the wrappings from the large bundle, and unrolled the scroll it contained, until, as they later recounted wonderingly, it stretched from one end of the tent to the other. It seems certain that this must have been the larger of the two manuscripts of Isaiah, the news of which was to set the biblical world astir. However, at the time it evoked little interest among its new owners who could neither read the strange writing inscribed on it, nor think of anything useful to which they could put the leather, fragile as it was. So for a time the Bedouin carried the scrolls about with them as they pastured their flocks and made what trade they could with their neighbours. These Bedouin have no real home. The world is their prey and usually their enemy. This tribe had been in the vicinity since the seventeenth century, and they have managed to eke out a sparse enough living with their few animals, now and again putting their detailed knowledge of the territory to better gain in smuggling. Until the area became effectively policed by the Arab Legion, they practised highway robbery when they could, and always found a ready market for their trading, legal or illegal, in Bethlehem. It was to this town that they made regular visits to sell their milk and cheese, and there, one market day, they took the three scrolls. Their general dealer happened to be an Assyrian Christian, by name

Khalil Iskander Shahin, known locally as Kando, who, besides the small general store patronized by the Ta'amireh, owned a cobbler's shop next door. When the Bedouin showed him the scrolls, he evinced little interest, but thought they might serve as raw material for his cobbler's business. Later, after they had been kicking about the floor of the shop for some days, he picked one up and looked more closely at the surface. The writing was as meaningless to him as to the Bedouin, but it occurred to him that his spiritual guardians in Jerusalem might know more about it, and accordingly one day when he was going up to the city, he took the scrolls along with him, to the Syrian Convent of St. Mark in the Old City. This much is certain, but it must be confessed that from here on the story begins to disintegrate, as love of truth on the parts of the chief actors in the drama gives way before fear and cupidity. One thing is certain, however; Kando began to realize that the scrolls had some monetary value and found out that the Bedouin had by no means cleared the cave. He and his accomplice George accordingly launched a minor archaeological expedition to the cave indicated by the Bedouin and collected at least a number of large fragments and probably at this time the remainder of the scrolls, making seven in all. After they had taken all they could find, they seem to have let the Syrian authorities of St. Mark's into the secret. In any case the Metropolitan organized his own expedition to the cave, which proceeded to ransack the place, making a large opening near the ground, and pulling out everything they could lay their hands on. Of course, it will be realized that all such excavations were and are completely illegal under the laws of the country, whether of the Mandate or of the succeeding Jordan Government. All such archaeological material remains the property of the country in which it is found, until the Government directs otherwise. So complete secrecy shrouded all these operations, and much harm was done as a result. It is certain that the Syrians found some more fragments, but valuable archaeological data like linen wrappings and sherds from the broken jars they threw on to a rubbish dump outside. Kando had meanwhile deposited the scrolls in his possession with the Metropolitan, on a security, he now says, of £24; and these and some fragments the Church leader began to hawk round the various scholastic institutions of Jerusalem to get an idea of their worth. It seems that one of the scrolls was shown to the late Professor E. L. Sukenik of the Hebrew University, who kept it for some time and then set about finding the rest of the scrolls, which he had realized were very old and of considerable value. He made a perilous journey to Bethlehem, for by now the Jewish-Arab hostilities had become open warfare following on the withdrawal of the Mandate. There he seems to have contacted Kando and brought away three more scrolls.

This gentleman now began to get scared since he was afraid that the news of the illegal excavations would leak out, and he would rightly be held responsible by the authorities. He therefore took the precaution of burying some of the largest fragments from the cave in his garden at Bethlehem! Unfortunately, the soil of Kando's back garden is somewhat different from the parched dust of the Qumrân caves, and when later he went to retrieve them he found only several lumps of sticky glue.

Meanwhile, in Jerusalem, the Syrian Metropolitan was continuing his rounds trying to discover if the scrolls were really old. Finally, on 18 February 1948 he called up the American School of Oriental Research and spoke to Dr. John C. Trever, who had been left in temporary charge of the establishment during the absence of the Director. He told Trever that during a clear-out of his library at the Convent, he had found some old Hebrew manuscripts on which he would like his advice. An appointment was made for the next day, and the Metropolitan sent round the scrolls packed in an old suitcase, by the hand of a Father Butros Sowmy and his brother. After some hasty comparing of pictures of other ancient Hebrew manuscripts . . . (Trever) discovered that he was looking at a scroll of Isaiah, and that as far as he was able to tell, it was genuinely very old. He asked permission to make photographs of the scroll, and after some negotiations did so. As he worked he became more and more excited, for if it was as old as a favourable comparison with a photograph of a pre-Christian Hebrew papyrus fragment would seem to indicate, then he was handling the oldest manuscript of the Bible ever known. It was only with great difficult that Trever could restrain his impatience when, half way through the work of photography, he had to fulfil a long-standing engagement with the Curator of the Palestine Museum, then Mr. Harry Iliffe, to go to Jericho and take photographs of a local excavation. However, he seems to have restrained both his impatience and his tongue, for neither then nor at any other time was any mention of the discovery made to the authorities responsible for the control of antiquities in Palestine, who alone could have taken adequate and immediate steps to safeguard the treasures and seal the cave until a properly organized expedition could learn its secrets. Rather did Trever urge the Metropolitan to take the documents out of the country, since the situation was fast deteriorating, and war was beginning to stalk the streets and hills of that unhappy land. It was not until November of 1948, when the April copies of the *Bulletin of the American Schools of Oriental Research* reached Jerusalem, that Mr. G. Lankester Harding, newly responsible for the archaeological interests of Arab Palestine as well as Trans-Jordan, learnt that eighteen months before, a fabulous discovery had been made by the Dead Sea. By now photographs of the scrolls had been examined by competent palaeographers like Professor W. F. Albright and pronounced definitely pre-Christian, probably dating to the first or second centuries before our era. Excitement ran high all over the scholarly world, and in Jordan, Harding was now faced with an extremely difficult and urgent problem. The source of these scrolls had to be found, and if any related archaeological material remained, it had to be expertly examined at the first opportunity, not only to confirm the palaeographical dating but to determine the community from whose library they had come. Furthermore, it seemed not improbable that there might be more scrolls, and certainly fragments, since apparently some of the documents found were in a fragile condition with pieces missing from the outside and edges. But the original discovery had taken place so long ago that the chances of finding the source relatively free from tampering were very slight. The Metropolitan had succeeded in smuggling the scrolls in his possession out of the country, and had taken them to America. The Jordan Government, of course, demanded their immediate return, but by now the monetary values being accorded them in the popular Press were so astronomical as to persuade the Syrian Church leader that the chances of his returning were well worth sacrificing for the sake of the money he could expect to raise in their sale. The one bright light in the whole miserable affair at this stage was that he had agreed with Trever and the American Schools to allow them to photograph and publish the scrolls immediately whilst their sale was being negotiated. The Americans had told him, apparently, that if they were published quickly their value would be much enhanced. In fact, it declined, since once they were readily available in printed form the need for the originals became less urgent. The American scholars did, in fact, publish them, extraordinarily well and quickly, putting the scholarly world greatly in their debt.

Back in Jordan, Harding had gone immediately to the Palestine Archaeological Museum in Jerusalem, and in his capacity as Acting Curator instructed Joseph Saad, the new Secretary, to spare no effort in discovering the whereabouts of the fabulous cave and any other information he could about the find and the personalities involved. Saad's first call was to the American School, and there Dr. O. R. Sellers, that year's Director, immediately offered all the help in his power. Together they went to St. Mark's Monastery, despite the extremely dangerous nature of the journey through the Old City, where Jewish shells and sniping were making it near suicide to be out of doors during daylight. Slipping from shelter to shelter they finally arrived at the building which backs on to the dividing wall between Arab and Jewish Jerusalem, and there interviewed a person by the name of George Isaiah. It became clear from the beginning that he was not going to be very helpful, and, although he did not deny that the Monastery had organized an excavation of the cave, refused point-blank to disclose its whereabouts. Saad argued, cajoled, and bullied, but all to no effect, and he was just about to give up hope of gaining any useful information at all when, out of the corner of his eye, he saw one of the Syrian fathers approaching, a venerable saint called Father Yusif. When the old man had drawn quite near, Saad suddenly turned from George and asked Yusif what he knew about the cave. Before George could stop him, the old man began to describe the excavations and their whereabouts. George turned on him fiercely, but could not silence him before he had given at least a general idea of the cave's position. It seemed that it was somewhere south of the Junction of the roads to Jericho and the Dead Sea, amongst the cliffs which border the Sea to the west. Now those limestone cliffs are honeycombed with caves and clefts in the rock, and the mountains rise nearly a thousand feet from the marly plateau, so that with a southern limit at Ras Feshkha about six miles to the south, a good deal more detailed pin-pointing was going to be necessary for the cave to be discovered. As Saad and his companion retraced their steps through the Old City, they discussed the next move. It seemed obvious that they would have to try the great stand-by of the East, bribery. Most things out there have their price, and it only remained to find out how high it was going to be. So on their return, negotiations with George Isaiah were opened, on the general principle that, if he would lead a party to the cave, he would receive a cash payment and the custody of any further scrolls found would be equally shared between them. These negotiations took a considerable time, involving many trips to the Monastery through gun-fire. Finally, when it seemed that arrangements were sufficiently far advanced, Saad arranged for the mayor of Jerusalem and his dignitaries to accompany them to St. Mark's to witness the formal agreement. The party arrived on the day appointed and took their seats. Everybody asked after everybody else's health, and were asked in return, and Allah duly thanked. Coffee was passed round, and, after that, the customary small talk ensued, without which no Arab meeting is considered opened. Sellers was beginning to get restless, but Saad, raised in the traditions of the East, played the game in all its formality and was patient. At last, after the seventh round of thanking Allah for their individual good health, the main subject was broached, the terms stated, and nothing but the clasping of hands remained to seal the bargain. And George Isaiah would have nothing to do with it.

Sellers and Joseph parted gloomily at the gates of the American

School, and Saad carried on to the Museum. Weeks of negotiation had produced practically nothing and, apart from its general locality, they knew little more about the cave than what had been learnt from the American *Bulletin*. Now it happened that the Museum at this time was in the hands of the Arab Legion, and Saad had to pass a ring of sentries to reach his quarters. He made a perfunctory greeting to the man on duty at the gate and then something prompted him to hesitate and look at the soldier more closely. He was a lean, dark-skinned Arab of the desert, of the type Glubb always chose for his picked troops, and Saad studied his face for a moment, noticing his long, straight Semitic nose, his short curly beard, and black smouldering eyes. He was a true son of the desert from the sandy wastes of the Hijaz, trained from his boyhood in desert lore and with eyes as keen as an eagle's. It occurred to Saad that if anybody could find that cave, given general directions as to its whereabouts, men like this soldier could. They would be able to perceive from an amazing distance any disturbance of the ground round the illicit excavations, and so detect the cave perhaps even from ground level. The idea crystallized into a plan of campaign, and waiting only to collect Sellers from the American School, Saad went in search of the officer in charge of the troops in the Jerusalem area, a Major-General Lash. He found this officer well prepared, for only a night or two before he had been discussing the problem with a Belgian United Nations observer, Captain Lippens, and had that day telephoned to Harding in Amman, asking if he would like him to send a few of his desert troops down to the area and search for the caves. Harding had agreed, and now with the added information Saad was able to provide, no further time was lost and a detachment of troops under the direction of an English officer, Brigadier Ashton, and a Jordanian Captain (now Major) Akkash el Zebn, was sent down to the road junction by the Dead Sea. Deploying from this point, in such a way that as far as possible no section of the cliffs at all visible from the littoral plain would miss their scrutiny, they set off slowly, working their way south. Within seventy-two hours, Akkash was on the phone reporting that they had found the cave, and asking for further instructions. Whilst waiting for Harding's arrival, Ashton plotted the cave and started collecting the pottery which lay round about, making accurate notes and drawings which were of the greatest help to the excavators later. Then Harding arrived, and together they made the first preliminary excavation. Harding confesses that when he first saw the cave he was dubious of its being the source of the scrolls, but the presence of undoubtedly ancient pottery made it worth investigating further. He asked Ashton to mount a guard on the cave until such time as a properly equipped archaeological party could be assembled. This was done, but the expedition was dogged by bad luck for days. Every time they gathered at the road junction it rained, which made the tracks completely impassable to their transport, and once it even snowed! Ashton could not leave his men standing about outside a cave by the Dead Sea for long, however, and it became urgent to mount the expedition, which finally started work on 15 February 1949, a fortnight after the rediscovery of the cave. Father De Vaux of the French School of Archaeology, Joseph Saad, and two others joined the excavation, and the early finding of scores of small inscribed fragments of leather, together with pieces of the linen wrappings, and the sherds of dozens of the characteristic large scroll jars, in which it was said that the original scrolls had been found, soon made it plain that this was certainly a scroll cave, if not the original one. The damage caused by illegal excavations was all too plain; no hope could now be entertained of any stratification of the remains, and some of the most valuable of the pottery and wrappings had been tossed outside on to a dump. The number of jars originally placed in the cave was now seen to have been between forty and fifty, and if, as it was then thought, each of those jars had held several scrolls, then it became a matter of extreme urgency to find the rest which might still be in the country and perhaps suffering damage. In any case, there must clearly have been hundreds of fragments and these had also to be found and studied together, if they were to be of any use at all.

Another detective inquiry was instituted, and Saad given *carte blanche* to find and, if necessary, buy those pieces regardless of cost. It was clear now, as more and more reports came in from scholars studying the first scrolls, that every word of these documents was going to be worth its weight in gold, and, indeed, that was just about what they were going to cost before they were all finally in safe hands.

Saad went again to the Monastery of St. Mark's, this time accompanied by Harding himself. The object of this inquiry was to find out the name of the dealer in Bethlehem who had continually cropped up in reports, but had never been named. If there were more scrolls and fragments about, he was the most likely person to know about them, and he would also know the names and tribe of the Bedouin who had found the cave. George Isaiah was a little more informative this time, but could not or would not describe the cave in sufficient detail to make its identification with the Legion's discovery certain, and refused to disclose the name of the dealer. Saad knew better this time than to waste much time over him. After the inevitable coffee, and inquiries after each other's health, with no more useful information forthcoming, they rose to leave, keeping their eyes open all the time for Father Yusif. It was as they were leaving the gate of the Monastery that they saw the frail figure approaching, and immediately engaged him in conversation on the cave. Unfortunately, they now seemed to know more than he, and still they lacked tho name of the Bethlehem dealer. Then they had an amazing piece of luck. Harding had noticed that as they had been speaking to Father Yusif, a woman across the road had been showing keen interest in their conversation. Finally, she came across to them and spoke. Were they talking about the excavations of the Dead Sea cave which George Isaiah had organized about a year ago? Her husband had taken part in the "dig," and had even been rewarded for his pains with a leather fragment, which the priests had told him was most valuable, although he had not yet discovered a way of converting it into hard cash. However, if they would like to wait a moment she would see if she could find him; he could not be far away. Saad and Harding looked at each other, and then to heaven. They finally ran the man, Jabra by name, to earth in a nearby coffee shop, and induced him to come along to the Museum. In the basement, the spoils of the official excavation of the cave were arranged on large trestle tables, and, bringing him near, Harding asked Jabra if he could see anything there that he recognized. The man looked long and earnestly over the table, and then a broad smile lit his face. Yes, this. Amidst the broken pottery and linen wrappings, the Roman lamp and the cooking pot, he had spied his own dear, long-lost but never forgotten cigarette roller. So another link in the chain was forged, the cave was now definitely identified, and it now remained to find out how much more Jabra knew. An Arab who realizes that he has partaken, however, unwittingly, in an illegal act, is a wary creature. Harding and Saad had somehow to win his confidence, if they were to obtain the information they so desperately wanted. Bribery was of course inevitable, and a generous tip went far towards loosening Jabra's tongue. He admitted that they had found some scroll fragments, and the Metropolitan had taken most of them away with him when he left. They tackled him about the name of the Bethlehem dealer; but at once he shut up like a clam, and for a long time would say nothing on the subject. Harding saw the fear of death in his eyes, and the man confessed that he was literally scared for his life. It took a great deal of alternate threatening and reassuring before they finally forced the truth from him, and when they had let him scurry off home, Saad and Harding sat down and faced one another. Events now had taken a sinister turn. If Jabra's fears were justified, it meant that this dealer and his confederates were willing to go to any length to avoid interference in their territory. It was clear that from now on the game would be played to very high stakes, perhaps to higher values than mere money.

The journey to Bethlehem was an adventure in itself. To-day it takes only half an hour of smooth driving on a new tarmac road to go from Jerusalem to Bethlehem, and before the troubles a more direct road took only half that time. In 1949, with this in Jewish hands, as it still is, the make-shift route was long and dangerous, a dirt track which snaked far out into the Judaean hills by the monastery of Mar Saba. Transport was by donkey, and the journey took half a day. The morning following the interview with Jabra, Saad set out, taking with him two of the Museum guards, and reached Bethlehem shortly after midday. Leaving the guards and the animals on the outskirts of the town, he walked into the centre, feeling suddenly lonely and unprotected. From now on he would be working alone; any sign of official support, and every way would be blocked; the dealer, scrolls, and everything else would go underground and nothing ever recovered. But Bethlehem in those days, cut off from a central government by the fighting, was no place for an unprotected man to face a gang of desperate brigands, and Joseph hesitated a moment outside the shop which had been pointed out to him as Kando's. It opened, like all such eastern shops, straight on to the street, and behind the piles of vegetables and hanging kuffiyas, the bright sunlight did not penetrate. Joseph peered into the shadows but could see nothing from outside. Then he entered.

His eyes took a little time to accustom themselves to the gloom, so he did not at first see the men standing at the back of the room, watching him. One of them was rather portly, heavy-jowled, and dressed in the long Arab nightshirt type of garment, with a red tarbush on his head. His companion was an older man who stared at Joseph suspiciously from beneath heavy eyebrows, and glanced from time to time at his companion and the door standing ajar behind him. Saad realized from their manner that news of his arrival had preceded him and came straight to the point. He had heard that Kando knew something about the scrolls which had been found in a cave, and furthermore, had some of the illegally excavated fragments in his possession. There was a moment's heavy silence, and then the old man flew at him, calling him a government spy, traitor, and worse, pushing Saad against the wall as he hurled abuse at him. Joseph raised his arms to fend off his assailant, but, even as he did so, saw the other man slip out of the open door and shut it behind him. Almost immediately the old man calmed down, glancing behind him to ensure that Kando had got clear, but Saad knew now that there was nothing to be gained by waiting longer and left the shop to return to his friends. Now the fat was really in the fire. Kando knew what he was after and suspected him of being in league with the Government. The chances were that either he would try and silence Saad, or smuggle the incriminating evidence out of the country and make off, until things had quietened down. The safest thing for Saad to do would have been to make tracks for Jerusalem and his well-guarded Museum. Instead he sent his men away, and took lodgings in Bethlehem, determined to try and win his way into Kando's confidence. It was the act of a brave man.

Day after day Joseph returned to the little shop, engaging Kando in conversation at first on anything but the scrolls. He made the acquaintance of George, who appeared to be Kando's right-hand man, and had certainly co-operated with him in the illicit digging. Slowly he won their confidence, and one day brought up the subject of the scrolls again. He hastened to reassure them that no ill would come to them from working with him; indeed, if they would trust him he would find them a market for their fragments which would pay well and be perfectly safe. After all, if they tried to smuggle them out of the country they might lose everything, including their freedom. They would lose nothing doing things Saad's way. The logic of Joseph's reasoning gradually had its effect, and the first suspicion gave way to a wary, but nevertheless, genuine friendship. When he finally left Bethlehem, it was with a promise from Kando that he would come and visit him at the Museum. On the journey back, Joseph reflected rather ruefully that he had not seen a single fragment during all those days in Bethlehem; yet, on balance, he was not displeased with progress.

Kando kept his word and soon after appeared at Jerusalem, and Saad in due course paid a return visit. This went on for some weeks without further mention being made of the fragments, and Joseph was almost beginning to wonder if Kando had already sold them or, indeed, had ever possessed any. Then one day, in the gardens of the Museum, Kando took Saad over to a shady corner, looked at him hard, and then thrust his hand into the grimy "night-shirt" and brought out a wallet. Inside, as he slowly opened it, there lay a piece of inscribed parchment, about the size of three or four fingers. Saad took the piece in his hand and studied it. There could be no doubt that the writing was very similar to that on the fragments he had already seen and the leather on which it was written was genuinely old. He replaced it carefully in the folds of Kando's wallet, knowing that one false move now could forfeit in a moment all the confidence he had built up over these trying weeks. Nevertheless, as he watched the wallet go back into its home, he wondered if he would ever see that precious fragment again. However, the game had to be played out the hard way; if Kando had that piece he would probably have a lot more, and Harding had told him to get the lot. Saad showed his interest in buying the piece and any more that Kando might have, and on this they parted, Joseph reporting the new development to Harding. In a few days Kando returned, ready to take negotiations further. Who was Saad acting for? Joseph answered that an English

Professor visiting the country was anxious to buy these fragments, but wanted more than this one piece; how much had he to offer? Kando, rather warily replied that he had "quite a lot," and arranged a rendezvous at which Saad would bring the "English Professor" and where Kando would have all the pieces in his possession. The place appointed was to be in Jericho, and, when the date and time had been arranged, Saad went off to find the mythical financier. It so happened that, working with Harding at this time as a non-technical assistant, was an Englishman, Mr. Richmond Brown, who willingly agreed to take the part. At a preliminary meeting Harding handed over a thousand pounds in one dinar notes (1 Jordan dinar = the pound sterling), but told Saad to try and obtain all the fragments in Kando's possession for eight hundred pounds. The absolute maximum was fixed at a pound per square centimetre of fragment, but to try and ascribe any monetary value at all to this priceless material was extremely difficult. If this price seems outrageously high, it must be remembered that, at that time, the Syrian Metropolitan was asking something like a million dollars for the scrolls in his possession, and reports to this effect were being heard all over Jordan on the radio. The Bedouin and Kando were now well aware that these scrolls were considered beyond price by the outside world, and that their recovery was worth almost any amount of money. It should be also recognized that behind all these negotiations there lay the shadow of irresponsible people who were willing to buy illegally smuggled pieces for their collections or as souvenirs, or in order to make a profit on a further transaction. The danger of such loss was ever present forcing the pace, and thus raising the price. It was bad enough that the complete scrolls should be taken from the country, but at least they could be published as a unity, as the American scholars were doing so admirably. But with fragments, it was different. They could only be made of use to scholarship if they were kept together, and as far as possible reunited with their parent documents. A small piece of Dead Sea Scroll may look very nice framed and hung over the mantelpiece, but it may well ruin the value of other larger pieces, depending for their sense on the inscription on the "souvenir." Furthermore, irresponsibility is not the sole prerogative of tourists and dealers. At a later stage, one world-famous museum was willing to consider buying fragments smuggled from Jordan in order to have them in their cases, even though to have taken them would have delayed the publication of thousands of others, or, at least, reduced their value for want of the additional evidence. Happily the possibility was then foiled by the more responsible attitude of an Eastern University who procured the fragments and returned them immediately to Jordan. Thus at this stage there was little quibbling about price; the main thing was to rescue the fragments and give them to the world in as complete a form and as soon as possible.

Kando's choice in hotels ran pretty low. This was a dirty, fifth-rate hovel, and, as the two drew near, Saad could see that Kando was fearing a trap and taking no chances. Lounging on both sides of the street and round the entrance were some of the grimmest, toughest-looking characters one could wish not to meet anywhere, and they watched Saad and his companion through every move and gesture as they approached. Joseph felt the thick wad of notes bulging in his pocket, and thought they could not have been more conspicuous if he had carried them in his hand. The hairs on their necks bristled as they walked through the porch, trying to look unconcerned. Casually they asked a shifty-looking proprietor if Kando was there, and he motioned them to a room leading off the main entrance hall. Saad put his hands on the notes in his pocket, squared his shoulders, and the two of them walked in.

Kando was standing with George at the far side of the room. A table covered with a greasy cloth stood in the centre, and Saad noticed that, as usual, Kando had prepared for a quick exit with a window standing wide open behind him. It idly crossed Joseph's mind to wonder if they were as well prepared. A brief greeting did nothing to relieve the tension, and Saad asked abruptly if Kando had got the fragments. The man nodded and raised his eyebrows questioningly in return. In answer, with studied carelessness, Joseph brought out the bundle of notes, stripped off the band, and fanned them out on to the table. It was a magnificent gesture and Kando hesitated no longer but laid on to the table beside the notes a pile of decrepit-looking pieces of skin, torn and rotted at the edges, and covered with a fine white dust through which the ancient writing could just be seen. Saad passed them over to the "English professor" who at once began measuring them with a pocket rule. The tension had now decreased considerably, and whilst Richmond Brown was at work, Saad engaged Kando in conversation. Brown's calculations actually brought the figure to 1,250 sq. cm., but following his instructions he said "I can only give eight hundred pounds for this lot." Saad looked at Kando expectantly, but the latter jerked his head and gave the click of the tongue which is the Arabic refusal. Then he began to collect the fragments together, and Saad after a while did the same with the notes. Each delayed the process as long as possible, hoping for the other to give way, but when they both had finished the silence remained unbroken. Saad walked to the door, followed by Brown, both wondering if Kando would let them go through that grim circle of henchmen with a thousand pounds in their pockets. However, they passed unmolested and started to walk towards the Winter Palace Hotel where Harding awaited them. Certainly they were alive, and had handled the precious fragments, but were they to lose them all for the sake of two hundred pounds? Harding, however, having heard their story supported their action, and was sure that the next day would see Kando at the Museum with his pieces, more than willing to sell them for eight hundred pounds.

The next day sure enough, Kando appeared. But he seemed curiously certain of his ground, and would not go below a thousand pounds. Saad said he would go and ask the "professor" and stepped next door to where Harding sat in the Board Room, awaiting developments. Harding agreed to the price and Saad returned and gave Kando the money. Then part of the cause of his confidence became apparent, for as Kando handed him the fragments, he looked at Joseph and said, "and give my greetings to Mr. Harding." Saad remembered then that, when the three of them had left the Winter Palace in Jericho that day, a bystander had stared curiously into the windows of the car. Of course, Kando now knew the secret of Saad's relationship with the Director of Antiquities, and probably realized that the "English professor" had been a fake. He knew too that the Government meant to deal leniently with him so long as he played their game. Indeed, Harding still had much to learn about the finding of that cave, and wanted badly to know the names of the Bedouin lads who had climbed through the hole. It was by no means certain that with Kando's collection all the fragment material from the cave had been exhausted, and there was always the possibility that new caves in the vicinity might be found any day, now that the Bedouin were on the look-out.

Eventually, Kando told Saad the names of the Bedouin and their tribe, and in due course they were persuaded to leave their desert camps and come to Amman. There Harding learned the full story of the discovery, and the Bedouin found a new friend in the Director of Antiquities. Well dined and liberally tipped, the lads returned to their shepherding to enliven the camp fires of their tribe with marvellous tales of the great city across the Jordan, and of an English official of their Government who spoke their tongue as well as they, and knew their customs and their lore better than any foreigner they had ever met. The wise administrator knows when to put the letter of the law into second place, and to the fact that Harding is such a person, the world owes much of the light which further discoveries in the Judaean desert were to throw upon this important Jewish sect by the Dead Sea.

EDMUND WILSON

The Monastery of Qumrân

THE American literary critic Edmund Wilson went to Jordan to visit the site of the discovery of the scrolls, to make his own estimate of some of the characters involved, and to judge the meaning of the discoveries for the history of Christianity. While there he went with Père Roland de Vaux, director of the *École Biblique* at Jerusalem, to visit the ruins known as Khirbet Qumrân that lie on the plateau between the Dead Sea and the cliffs, about a thousand yards south-east of the first of the "scroll" caves. Père de Vaux and Lankester Harding had been excavating them since 1951 and had proved them to be those of a monastery of a Jewish community— now almost universally identified with the Essene Sect. Jars were found there exactly like others used to contain the manuscripts in the caves, helping to prove that the brotherhood had owned the Qumrân library. The excavations also proved the monastery to have been occupied from the latter part of the second century B.C. until its destruction at the time of the First Jewish Revolt (A.D. 66-70), save for about thirty years coinciding with the reign of Herod the Great, when it was temporarily deserted.

❧

HE was delighted to take people there, but the very idea made me giddy. It even made me giddy to climb with him to the top of the monastery's highest wall—fifteen feet above the ground—and to perch there, clinging to the stones, while Père de Vaux expounded the building to us. He was giving us a bird's-eye view. The main structure presents a large rectangle, ninety-eight by a hundred and twenty feet, made of rudely cut blocks of stone joined with earthen mortar. There are windows, and the walls inside are plastered. The floor has been paved with pebbles. Layers of ashes seem to show

〰〰〰〰〰〰〰〰〰〰

From *The Scrolls from the Dead Sea*. London: W. H. Allen & Company; 1955, pp. 64-7. By permission of Edmund Wilson and W. H. Allen & Co.

that the roofing, probably made out of the Dead Sea reeds, had eventually been burned, and the empty mould left by the trunk of a palm suggests that it was used as a beam or for some kind of central support. In the northwestern angle stood a two-story tower, evidently used for defence, the basement of which was a storehouse. Inside the monastery proper, there are a kitchen, which has been identified by the oven and the hole in the wall for a flue; and what was presumably the refectory of the sacred repasts, close to which were found neatly stacked about a thousand jars and bowls. Another chamber, seventy-two feet long, has the look of an assembly room, with a platform of stone at one end that may perhaps have served as a pulpit from which the sacred books were read. A room with tables and benches constructed of plaster and brick was evidently a *scriptorium,* where the scrolls were copied out. Three inkwells were also found here—one of bronze, which has turned green, and two of terra cotta, turned black—in which there is still some dried ink. The brotherhood presumably made their pens from the reeds that grew by the lake-shore. There is a pottery, with a kind of round nest of stones, which may have held the potter's wheel; and a mill for grinding grain, of which the two parts, for some reason not known, turned up in different rooms. Lying about in various places were nails, locks and keys, hoes, scythes and pruning knives. There was a jar which resembles exactly the jars in which the first lot of scrolls were preserved, as both resemble the fragments found in 1952 in the newly discovered caverns; and there are lamps which match those in the caves.

Among the most striking features of the monastery are the six large cisterns, with steps leading down into them, upon which the inmates depended for water. Into these cisterns they evidently canalized the rains that descended by a trough from the hills and of which the supply was undoubtedly scant. Père de Vaux says that only twice in all the months of the three years he has worked here has he seen any water come down from these hills. The Essenes must have had to store, in the relatively rainy season, all their water for the rest of the year. And they had, also on the surface level, seven smaller cisterns—of which some of the piping can still be seen—which must have been used for "lustrations" and the baptisms of which so much is said in the literature of the sect (seven, for the Jews, was a mystical number). There are even two little cupped hollows in the room where the scrolls were copied, which must have been basins for washing in connection with this holy work. Another basin is probably a cesspool. Unaccountably, one finds here and there the traces of some more pretentious building: square stone and sections of column that must once have been the parts of a portico or colonnade, and two queerly placed bases of columns set close together in the ground, as if they had been stands for something. Scattered about the building were about four hundred coins. No coins have been found in the Qumrân caves; and this perfectly fits in with what we are told by Philo and Josephus: that the finances of the Essene brotherhood were entirely handled by a manager. De Vaux has concluded that the members of the community lived in the nearby caves, and also in huts or tents—since pottery and large forked poles have been found stuck away in crevices or sheltered by overhanging rocks in a way which would seem to indicate that they had been concealed or stored by people who were living outside the caves. The building would have been their centre, to which they would have been fully admitted only after they had completed their probation.

NELSON GLUECK

Solomon's Mines

DR. GLUECK discovered the mines in the Wadi Arabah during the great survey of Transjordan which he directed between 1933 and 1943. When he excavated Ezion-geber on the Gulf of Aqabah, he proved it to be not only Israel's one seaport but also a leading metallurgical centre.

IT was only after I had finished exploring the Wadi Arabah and had discovered Solomon's copper mines in it, that it was possible to understand fully why this great fissure, extending between the southern end of the Dead Sea and the northern end of the Gulf of Aqabah, must have served as the chief bone of contention between

From *Rivers in the Desert*. London: George Weidenfeld and Nicolson Ltd.; 1959, pp. 154-6. By permission of George Weidenfeld and Nicolson Ltd. and Farrar, Straus & Cudahy, Inc., New York. © 1959 by Nelson Glueck.

Judah and Edom. Its importance as a natural highway was long
known. The Israelites of the Exodus had trekked through it as far
north as Punon on its east side. To retrace the ancient pilgrimage
and trade-route through it was one of the main purposes of our
expedition. Riding camel-back, we spent weeks crisscrossing its
width many times, as we moved steadily southward, halting at
every spring and water-hole, and examining every "khirbeh" or
ancient ruin, no matter how poor its remains or insignificant its
appearance.

Our guide and chief assistant was Sheikh Audeh ibn Jad of the
Injadat Arabs. In name, which reflects that of the tribe of Gad, and
in appearance, he could have been one of the Israelite chieftains
who had journeyed with Moses and the children of Israel during
that part of the Exodus which led through the Wadi Arabah, before
they turned eastward to circumvent Edom and Moab to reach the
Promised Land. As we advanced slowly towards the Red Sea, eating
the unleavened bread he baked for us each night and sleeping on
the ground wrapped in our *abayehs* wherever darkness overtook
us, it was sometimes hard for me to remember that he was really
not a member of the ancient tribe of Gad and that he himself had
not been a companion of the Biblical pilgrims, showing them, as
did the Kenites, the best trails and camping places in the Negev
and the Arabah.

And then, one day, we came across a great copper mining and
smelting site, called Khirbet Nahas (the Copper Ruin), which we
could date by pottery fragments on the surface of the ground to the
time of Solomon and of the kings who followed him down to the
sixth century B.C. It possessed the features which we found to be
characteristic of all the other mining sites discovered subsequently
on both sides of the Arabah as far south as the hills overlooking
the present shoreline of the Gulf of Aqabah. The raw ores dug in
open mines in the vicinity were given a preliminary "roasting" in
numerous small, stone-block furnaces. The waste slag was thrown
aside, forming the large, black piles that had first attracted our
attention as we neared the site. Both the furnaces and the slag piles
were contained within a strongly walled enclosure, which could
have served no other purpose than to prevent the slave labour employed in the mines and at the furnaces from escaping. It was killing work for expendable human beings, who must have suffered
greatly under the fierce heat and miserable living conditions.

The fate of captives taken by the Judaeans and Edomites in the
relentless war they waged against each other was literally to be con-
signed to the mines. It is in this light, perhaps, that we can understand more fully than hitherto the prophet's excoriation of Edom,
which was the prelude to his condemnation of Judah and Israel:

"Thus saith Jehovah, For three transgressions of Edom, yea, for four, I will not turn away the punishment thereof; because he did pursue his brother with the sword, and did cast off all pity, . . . and he kept his wrath forever" (Amos 1.11). We learn from the fourth century A.D. writings of Eusebius, bishop of Caesarea in Palestine, that early Christians and criminals were herded together in slave camps in the Wadi Arabah, for the purpose of mining and smelting its ores.

We believe that the Arabic name of the first great copper and iron mining and smelting site we discovered in the Wadi Arabah, namely Khirbet Nahas (The Copper Ruin), may well be the same as the 'Ir Nhash (the City of Copper) mentioned in the Bible, and that the Ge-harashim (the Valley of the Smiths), referred to in connection with it, was used interchangeably in Biblical times for the Arabah itself (I Chronicals 4:12.14). Above all, however, the demonstration of the existence of these ores in large quantities in the Wadi Arabah, underscores once again the amazing accuracy of the historical memory of the Bible. Every syllable of the hitherto enigmatic description in the Bible of the Promised Land as being, among other things, a land "whose stones are iron and out of whose hills thou canst dig copper" (Deuteronomy 8:9), has now been proven to be literally correct.

These mines also furnish the explanation of one of the chief sources of Solomon's fabulous wealth. The mineral deposits of the Wadi Arabah had also been worked in previous ages, in fact as early as the time of Abraham and before that in the Chalcolithic period, too. Never, however, were they worked as intensively and in as coordinated a fashion as from Solomon's time on. It is revealed now that not only was he a great ruler of legendary wisdom, and a highly successful merchant prince and shipping magnate, but that he was also a copper king of the first rank, who transformed Israel into an industrial power. The elaborate copper smelter and manufacturing center constructed by him at Ezion-geber is the largest that has thus far been discovered.

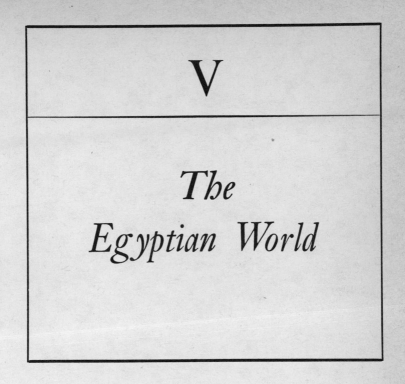

V

The Egyptian World

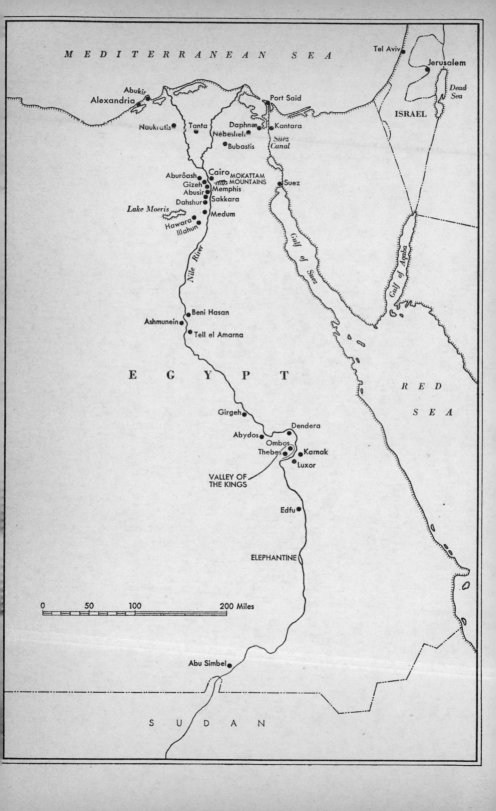

INTRODUCTORY

AS a result of Greek respect for ancient Egyptian learning and of the conspicuous survival of its great monuments, Egypt was long believed to be the cradle of human civilization. Indeed, fanatical diffusionists believed it to be the centre from which all civilization was carried to the rest of the world. Archaeological studies have proved otherwise. Both in the beginning of farming in Neolithic times and in the first development of true civilization, Egypt played a role secondary to that of western Asia.

While farming was already being practised in some parts of Asia as early as 7000 B.C., the earliest Neolithic predynastic cultures of Egypt are usually dated to about 5000 B.C. At that time, although the population of the Nile valley seems to have been of native north African stock, they probably got not only the idea of farming but domesticated stock and seed grain from their Asiatic neighbours. It has already been seen (p. 283, I) that further definite influences from Asia affected the late predynastic Gerzean culture of the fourth millennium B.C., and there seems also to have been a considerable influx of people at this time. As a higher civilization began to emerge, Mesopotamian architectural traditions made themselves felt in Egypt, as did certain principles of writing.

In about 3200 B.C., the legendary Menes, who can probably be identified with the historic King Narmer, founder of the First Dynasty, united Upper and Lower Egypt by conquest and created the unified kingdom under a single divine king which was to endure (with brief interruptions) through pharaonic times. Indeed, in the famous Narmer palette the whole political, religious and artistic "form" of Egyptian civilization is already manifest.

Not very much is known of the history of the first two dynasties ruling from Narmer's newly-established capital at Memphis. But with the beginning of the Third in 2780, the great age known as the Old Kingdom began, and art and architecture rose quickly to their greatest heights. The second pharaoh of the dynasty, Djoser, had working for him Imhotep, a man of genius who among his many achievements could count the building of the step pyramid at Sakkara for his divine master—an architectural inspiration which quite rapidly developed into those titanic mausolea of the Fourth Dynasty: the pyramids of Gizeh.

During the Old Kingdom there was not only a wonderful flowering of the arts and of religious philosophy, but also a tremendous confidence. All was well with Egypt and would remain so. Then the Sixth Dynasty collapsed, and revolution and anarchy destroyed that confidence for ever. During the First Intermediate Period (2180-2080 B.C.), internal struggles, and foreign invasion encouraged by the breakdown of government, wrecked what had seemed an immutable order (p. 592, I), and although peace and order were restored with the Middle Kingdom (2080-1640 B.C.), the Egyptian outlook was never quite the same. There was a new streak of pessimism, while Osiris, the god of the underworld, who could look after the welfare of the dead, began to be of more importance relatively to the lord of life, the Sun God, Re. Nevertheless this profound psychic upheaval also had power to stimulate, and the finest Egyptian literature was written during the Middle Kingdom. Some of these writings show a remarkable deepening of personal and social morality.

With the end of the Thirteenth Dynasty, Egypt as a united kingdom again collapsed. It is no longer thought that the Hyksos rulers of the resulting Second Intermediate Period (1640-1570 B.C.) represent the invasion of a conquering horde of Asiatics. The name seems to mean Rulers of the Uplands, and they were wandering groups of Semites who had long come to Egypt for trade and other peaceful purposes. With the breakdown of central government, Semites and other Asiatics probably came in larger numbers into the Delta. Presently they seized Memphis and became the absolute rulers of Lower Egypt, with some degree of power over surviving Egyptian princes in Thebes and an alliance with princes of Kush in the extreme south.

The Hyksos interlude at least admitted fresh cultural influences from the eastern Mediterranean and Asia. Bronze at last fully displaced the copper which had lingered for so long in Egypt (beside flint) for tools and weapons, and there was an improvement in the technique of weaving and other crafts. The fighting chariot was adopted, together with more effective weapons and armour.

The overthrow of the Hyksos and the re-establishment of Egyptian independence took place rapidly. Strong princes came to power in Thebes, defeating both the foreign rulers in the north and their allies in Kush. By 1570, the Eighteenth Dynasty Pharaoh Ahmosis

was in undisputed control of a reunited kingdom. Thebes had been
the capital during a part of Middle Kingdom times and a few Pharaohs had been buried there. Now, with the New Kingdom (1570-
1075 B.C.), it came into its full glory, monarch after monarch
enriching temples and palaces on both sides of the Nile and furnishing superb tombs in or near the Valley of the Kings.

Among notable builders of the New Kingdom were the formidable
Hatshepsut who contrived to make herself pharaoh and built the
beautiful temple of Deir el Bahari (Deir el Bahri) in western Thebes,
enriched with reliefs of her great trading expedition to the Land of
Punt; Amenophis III who built temples on the east bank at Thebes
and a new palace on the west bank; Amenophis's son, the extraordinary young Pharaoh Akhenaten who created a new faith and a
new capital further to the north at the site to be known as el Amarna;
Tutankhamen, who returned to Thebes, but would have been of no
special interest if it had not been for the chance preservation of his
tomb; and finally Ramses II, a tremendous builder who has left
temples up and down the Nile valley, including the vast Hypostyle
Hall in eastern Thebes (Karnak) and the rock-hewn temples of
Abu Simbel.

Much of the wealth that made all this building and tomb-furn-
ishing possible came from Egypt's tributary states. For the desire
to prevent further Asiatic incursions by extending their own frontiers, accompanied by a new nationalist fervour, had led the pharaohs of the New Kingdom into imperial conquest in south-west
Asia. Repeated campaigns and marriage alliances extended Egyptian power or political influence to Syria and beyond. The New
Kingdom rulers also extended their territory southward. The Old
Kingdom frontier had been at Elephantine on the First Cataract,
though trading interests had extended further; then Middle Kingdom pharaohs built forts well to the south of the Second Cataract. Now the frontier was established at Napata near the Fourth
Cataract, and the whole of these dependencies of Nubia and Kush
(known to the Greeks and in the Bible as Ethiopia) were put under
a viceroy known as the King's Son of Kush. This became an important office, and as Egypt went into decline, Ethiopia became a virtually independent kingdom, and in the eighth century a Kushite line
succeeded to the throne of pharaoh as the Twenty-fifth Dynasty.
Later still Ethiopia drifted apart from Egypt proper and set up a
new capital at Meroë, which became an important iron-working
centre. Its rulers were still buried under pyramids (p. 452, I) and a
form of Egyptian culture lingered on, mixed with African elements.
In Graeco-Roman times, however, the northern part of the area,
Upper Nubia, was prosperous, and the island of Philae with its
sanctuary of Isis was crowned with temples (p. 527, I).

Archaeological literature concerning Egypt is very different from that concerning Mesopotamia. Egyptian civilization lasted long enough to be admired and recorded by Herodotus and other classical writers. Its massive stone architecture remained largely intact, and the Nile valley is more accessible to European travellers than that of the Two Rivers. So Egyptian civilization was never forgotten, and very many of its famous monuments have been visited and described again and again through the centuries.

Furthermore, there is a quite exceptional amount of information about the Egyptian way of life. The very dry climate has preserved countless possessions of men and women of all classes that elsewhere would have perished. The Egyptians themselves left models and painted and carved scenes from their everyday life in their tombs. Finally they created a far richer literature than the Sumerians or their followers, and so can address us directly.

So in the following pages the emphasis will be less on the historical development of archaeology and the knowledge derived from it and more on Egyptian life and its enduring monuments. The spectacular discoveries that have helped to reveal that life, also, of course, find a place.

I. *Travelling and Excavating*

RICHARD POCOCKE

Harlots and Pyramids

POCOCKE was an English cleric with a passion for travel. He visited Egypt in 1737-8, going up the Nile as far as Philae.

IT WAS on my way from Faiume [Fayum] that I went to Saccara [Sakkara], going out of the direct road to Cairo, soon after we had passed the sandy deserts; and travelling about five miles north west, we came to Dashour, where there is a cane, in which there are public harlots, who are professed Mahometans, as I was inform'd they are also in many other parts. These women are always unveil'd; and knowing that we were Europeans, they came and stared at us, and were very impudent, insomuch that my servant was obliged to drive them away. From this place we travelled along by the western canal, and after two miles we came to a village call'd Elmenshieh Dashour, being opposite to the great pyramid to the south; the pyramid built of brick being in a line with Dashour. We soon after came to the sandy desert, having a large canal to the east of us; we after passed between the melon gardens, and came to a wood of Acacia trees, which extends about a mile north to the groves of palm trees that are near Saccara, which is a poor village at the foot of the hills. Having letters of recommendation, I went to the house of the Sheik, who according to custom, set of their fare before us, and promised after he had been at the mosque at noon, it being friday, to go with me to the pyramids that were near. Accordingly we went half a mile to the south, there being a small lake on that part of the town. We came to a causeway made of great stones thirty-five feet wide, leading westward up the hills . . . This day and the two following I made the observations, in which I am the more exact, as few persons have described any

From *A Description of the East.* 1743, p. 49.

thing particularly here except the catacombs. The ascent is short to
a sandy plain, that may extend four or five miles to higher hills.
The pyramids are built from north to south along the brow of the
hill, extending from the three northern ones which are three or
four miles from Saccara, for eight or nine miles to the south. About
half a mile east of the pyramid that appears at a distance to be
built of great steps, is a little descent to a sort of a round plain with
a rising in the middle; bones and skulls are seen almost all over
this spot, under which are the catacombs of the mummies, extending near to this pyramid, the whole country being a rocky soil,
cover'd over with sand five or six feet deep. About half a mile
to the north of the same pyramid, are the catacombs of the birds. In
this part I found about the sands many of those little earthen statues
of Osiris, that are cover'd with a sort of green enamel or paint. I
saw here several heaps of ruins, and a sort of fossee which goes all
round to the south of Saccara; so that probably this place was formerly enclosed.

VIVANT DENON

With Napoleon's Army
to Philae

VIVANT DENON was a writer, archaeologist and artist who was
among those experts and savants whom Napoleon took with him
to Egypt in 1798. While his soldiers conquered Egypt, this party was
to record its geography and antiquities. This combination of purposes is shown in Denon's account of the visit to the island of
Philae made when he accompanied General Desaix into Upper
Egypt.

From Travels in Egypt. London: Longman and Rees; 1803, Vol. I, Dedication Page
to Napoleon; Vol. II, pp. 46-51.

DEDICATION.

TO BONAPARTE.

To combine the lustre of your Name with the splendour of the Monuments of Egypt, is to associate the glorious annals of our own time with the history of the heroic age; and to reanimate the dust of Sesostris and Mendes, like you Conquerors, like you Benefactors.

Europe, by learning that I accompanied you in one of your most memorable Expeditions, will receive my Work with eager interest. I have neglected nothing in my power to render it worthy of the Hero to whom it is inscribed.

VIVANT DENON.

WE could only keep our persevering enemy at a distance from us by starving the country between us and them. We therefore bought up all the cattle, paid for the green crops on the land, and the inhabitants assisted us themselves in pulling up from the ground every source of provision, and followed us with their domestic animals. Thus carrying off with us the whole population, we left behind us nothing but a desert. In returning, I was again struck with the sumptuous appearance of the edifices of Philöe; and I am persuaded that it was to produce this effect upon strangers entering their territory, that the Egyptians had collected upon their frontier such a splendid group of monuments. Philöe was the entrepot of a commerce of barter between Ethiopia and Egypt; and wishing to give the Ethiopians a high idea of their resources and their magnificence, the Egyptians had raised so many sumptuous edifices on the confines and natural frontier of their empire, Syene and the Cataracts. We had another parley with the inhabitants of Philöe, and it was more explicit: they signified to us, that if we were to come there every day for two months successively, they would never let us land. We were obliged to submit this time to their determination; but as it would have given a bad example to the country to allow a handful of peasants to brave us with such insolence close by our establishments, we resolved on the next day to try if we could not make them change their determination. Accordingly on the morrow, we returned with two hundred men; as soon as they saw us, they put themselves in a posture of defence, and defied us in the manner of savages, with loud cries, which the women repeated. The inhabitants of the neighbouring larger island, immediately collected in arms, which they made to glitter in the sun like sword-players; some of them were quite naked, holding in one hand a sabre, and in the other a buckler, others had rampart-musquets with matchlocks, and long pikes, and in a moment all the east side of the rock was covered with enemies. We still cried out to them that we were not coming to do them any harm, and we only wanted to enter amicably into their island; they answered that they would never let us approach, or furnish us with the means of landing on their shores, and that they were not Mamelukes, to fly before us: this bragging speech was closed with loud shouts which resounded on all sides; they wished for the fight; they had defended themselves against the Mamelukes; they had defeated their neighbours; and they now wished to have the glory of resisting us, and even giving us defiance. Immediately the order was given to our sappers to level the huts on the shore, to furnish us with wood for a raft: this act was a declaration of war; they fired on us, and posting themselves in the clefts and caves of their rocks, they kept up a brisk and well-directed fire on us. At this moment one of our field-pieces came up, the first sight of which carried their rage to the highest pitch; but from this time the communication between Philöe and the larger island was broken, the people of the latter drove off their herds and cattle, made them cross an arm of the river, and followed them into the desert.

We found that the palm-tree wood was too heavy and took water, which compelled us to defer the descent till the next day; and in the mean time our troops remained on the shore, and every necessary was collected in order to construct a raft to hold forty men. This business employed us the whole of the following day, and this delay encreased the insolence of these wretches, who dared to propose to the general to pay a hundred piastres to be allowed to come alone and disarmed into the island. The scene, however, was soon changed, when on a sudden they saw the larger island covered with our volunteers, whose descent had been protected by grape shot: terror succeeded, as usual, to headstrong rashness; men, women, and children, all threw themselves into the river to escape by swimming; and preserving their ferocious character, we saw mothers drowning their children whom they could not carry away with them, and mutilating the girls to save them from the violence of the victors. When I entered on the island the next day, I found a young girl seven or eight years old, who had been cut with brutal cruelty in such a manner, as to prevent her from satisfying the most pressing necessity of nature, and it was only by a counter-operation and a bath, that I was able to save the life of this unfortunate little creature, who was very pretty. Others of a more advanced age had not recourse to such severities, and chose for themselves companions from among the victors. In a word, the population of the island was dispersed in a few minutes, having suffered a most serious and irreparable loss.

They had pillaged the boats which the Mamelukes had not been able to get above the falls, and had formed magazines of this booty, which had made them immensely rich, in comparison with their neighbours, and might have secured to them repose and easy circumstances for a number of years; in a few hours they were reduced to beggary, destitute of support, both for the present and the future, and were obliged to go and solicit an asylum from those on whom they had made war a few days before. Our soldiers were employed the rest of the day in evacuating the magazines of the larger island, and I made use of this time in making drawings of the rocks and antiquities.

The ruins in this island consist of a small sanctuary, faced by a portico of four columns with very elegant capitals, to which had been added at a later period another portico, which doubtless was attached to the circumvallation of the temple. The most ancient part, which was also constructed with more care, was ornamented in a higher degree than the rest; the use made of it in the rites of the catholic religion has impaired the original character, by adding square arched door-ways. In the sanctuary, close to the figures of Isis and Osiris, may still be seen the miraculous impression of the feet of St. Anthony, or St. Paul the hermit.

The next day was the finest to me of my whole travels: I possessed seven or eight monuments in the space of six hundred yards, and could examine them quite at my ease, for I had not by my side any of those impatient companions who always think they have seen enough, and are confidently pressing you to go to some other object, nor had I in my ears the beating of drums as a signal to muster, or to march, nor Arabs nor peasants to torment me; I was alone in full leisure, and could make my drawings without interruption. This was my sixth visit of Philöe; the five first I had employed in taking views of the shores of the vicinity.

G. A. HOSKINS

Journey to
the Meroë Pyramids

HOSKINS did well to penetrate up the Nile so far as Meroë, and to survey the ruins. He was quite wrong in supposing the pyramids and other ruins to belong to a very early phase of Egyptian history. They date from the last millennium B.C.

❧

Feb. 1, 1833.   HAVING spent twelve months in the valley of the Nile, I had designed to leave Thebes this week, and return to Cairo. To this long period had an intended stay of a few weeks been protracted, in consequence of my daily increasing devotion to the fascinating but laborious study of Egyptian antiquities. I cannot, however, escape some uncomfortable feelings when I contrast the prospect now before me, of privation and dreariness in a long journey through the desert, with the hopes I had indulged of returning now to Europe, to the enjoyments of social and domestic intercourse, and the refinements and comforts of civilised life. My boat was ready, and all preparations made for my voyage down the Nile, when its direction was changed by the arrival of Signor Bandoni, a skilful Italian artist, whom I had long anxiously expected. I then immediately determined to proceed with my projected journey to the antiquities of Meroë, and thus complete my investigation of the architectural wonders of the Nile. Wearied, however, with my previous labours at Thebes, and in the Oasis Magna, I had felt reluctant to make this arduous attempt without the assistance of an artist. Had I now lacked courage, the redoubtable appearance of my Lucchese ally would have inspired me with

From *Travels in Ethiopia*. London: Longman, Rees, Orme, Brown, Green & Longman; 1835, pp. 2-4, 17-20, 32-3, 36-7, 68-70, 73, 82-3.

resolution to encounter the wildest Bishareen of the Nubian desert, or the hungriest lion of Ethiopia. The Signor brings with him his bosom companion, a double-barrelled Spanish *escopette*, of awe-inspiring calibre, the destructive powers of which, he assures me, have been frequently proved upon the turtle doves in the palm groves of the Nile: he animates me also with the assurance, that *"non ha niente paura;"* nor, since his landing in these barbarous regions, has he yet known bodily fear, except once, and that by mistake, when scared by the *lion-like* roar of a buffalo, near the base of Pompey's Pillar. The valley of the Nile, as far as Wadi Halfah, has been described by many. Only six or seven Europeans have penetrated beyond that cataract; and, unfortunately, all even of those were not sufficiently acquainted with Egyptian antiquities, and competent, as artists, to give a satisfactory description and correct delineations of the interesting remains which still exist in those remote regions. In using the term acquainted, I do not mean to state that any person has penetrated very deeply into the mysteries of Egyptian lore, much less can I pretend to have lifted "the veil of Isis which no mortal has yet raised;" but even a slight knowledge of the recent discoveries in hieroglyphics gives to the traveller of the present day an advantage over, perhaps, even the most learned travellers who visited this country before the discoveries of Young, Wilkinson, Champollion, and Rosellini. Egypt is no longer a field for speculative ingenuity and brilliant imagination. The daylight has appeared, and the efforts of talent and perseverance have cleared away many of the difficulties which obstructed the first labourers in this rich mine of antiquarian research. Enough is already known of hieroglyphics to make the subject be duly appreciated by literary men, and we may confidently expect important information from that source. The drawings which have hitherto been made in Upper Nubia are considered to be very inaccurate; much has been left undone, and the hieroglyphics have been but partially and imperfectly copied; while many of the inscriptions are totally unknown. Aware of these circumstances, and also that not a drawing or description of the antiquities of Meroë has yet been published in England, and hoping that my labours may be of some service to those interested in these subjects, I leave Thebes to encounter again the fatigues and perils of the desert; but Meroë is before me, the probable birth-place of the arts and sciences.

The Great Nubian Desert.—Feb. 16. This morning, at eight o'clock, we left Korosko, and entered the Desert. Having omitted until now giving a description of my caravan, I may mention, as useful to future travellers, the provisions and equipments which may be considered as necessary for a journey of this description. Both my artist, Signor B. and myself, wear the Turkish Nizam uniform. A traveller might, without much risk, retain his European dress; but it is most prudent and desirable to adopt the Turkish, as being the best suited, not only to the climate, but also to serve the important object of commanding respect. Those travellers who refuse this tribute to the customs of the country pay dear for their prejudice. If it does not expose them to frequent insult, they are at all events less esteemed by the natives; and they lose a decided advantage, in not having the comfort and luxury of a dress so admirably suited to the climate and manners of the East. Our unnatural tight trousers, waistcoats, and coats, with their padding, braces, straps, starch, stiffners, and stocks, in a tropical country would be intolerable. Another advantage of this comfortable and graceful costume is, that it enables you to repose with ease in any position. To sit bolt upright, on a hard chair, in such a latitude as this, is what no one could endure, who had experienced the luxurious ease of the Turkish divan. The rest of my caravan consisted of a guide (Habeer) on his dromedary; a very picturesque-looking fellow. Besides the usual arms of the Arabs, the long spear, sword, and shield of the hippopotamus, he had also a brace of pistols attached to his saddle, which he took great pride in displaying. He was very independent, and conscious of the importance of his office, so that I was afraid at starting he would not have been so manageable as I afterwards found him. My dragoman, Mahomet Abdini, a native of Cairo, was the cleverest servant I ever knew in any country: his wily tongue and insinuating address were often of more service to me than my piastres. I had, besides, a Greek servant, named Ibrahim, alias Michele; a Mahometan with the Arabs and Turks, and a Christian with his own countrymen. He speaks Italian fluently, and also the Turkish, Greek, and Arabic. He is the musician of the party; and his singing, accompanied by his fiddle, is vastly agreeable to the natives, but, being in the harsh style of the modern Greeks, is grating to my ears. I had, besides, a Copt, who had served me long and usefully at Thebes, in the dignified station of umbrella-bearer. Including, therefore, our Ababdehs, owners of the camels, the full complement of my little caravan amounts to twelve persons and eleven camels. My stock of provisions chiefly consists of a large sack of Cairo biscuit, and another of rice. Besides these two chief requisites, and also charcoal, I have a good supply of groceries, tea, sugar, coffee, and wax candles, and last, but most important, twenty geerbahs of water, which I expect will be amply sufficient for the eight days of desert journey, though the Signor has fore-warned me, most anxiously, more than fifty times, *che beve molto*. This is the desert in which Bruce and Burckhardt suffered so much. They took the easterly and more direct track, which com-mences at Derouch, a little below Assuan, and therefore had a

longer space to traverse, with, however, the advantage of meeting
repeatedly with good water. At a quarter past six, P.M., we encamped. Our road this day has been through a succession of narrow
valleys, called Akaba, or mountain passes, and small plains, bounded
by low picturesque hills. The valleys are covered with sand, in some
places two feet deep, but generally much less, and sometimes the
bare rock is visible. Sandstone forms the base of the valley and
of the hills. There are, however, some of slate, varying from
150 to 180 feet in height. I observed a great variety in their forms.
We have already met with a few of the horrors of the desert,
particularly numbers of dead camels, some of which had perished
lately, and vultures were feeding on their carcases. They seem also
to have attracted the hyaenas from their dens, as I discerned on
the sand numerous traces of those animals. Some of our water-
skins, I am sorry to find, are bad. I marvel Signor B. did not perceive
this at Korosko, as he took an active part in tying them up. The
journey from Assuan has injured them, yet, with care, I hope to
have a sufficient supply. This evening the camel men objected to
pitching my tent, saying that they were afraid of robbers. I did not
yield to their alarms, as sleeping in the open air is an Eastern
custom which I am not much inclined to try at this season of the
year. I cannot conceive a tent to be much additional attraction
to Arab plunderers, if there are any; but the depredations upon
the water, I fear, are by my own Ababdehs, as their own supply is
small. I have, therefore, caused all the geerbahs to be carried into
my tent. If we run short, and have to suffer, it shall not be for
want of precautions. While my camel men were thus occupied, one
of them asked me why I was subjecting myself to the danger of
fatigue of such a journey, when I was rich enough to stay at home.
The Arabs are now not so much surprised at travellers going to
Wadi Halfah. So many make that journey, that it is no longer a
novelty; besides that, the Cangias (boats of the Nile), though any
thing but agreeable to Europeans, appear luxurious to the peasants.
They can easily conceive the pleasure of sailing in what they
consider delightful conveyances, listening to the songs of the
boatmen, smoking all the day, and eating and drinking of the best
the villages can afford; but that travellers should voluntarily expose
themselves to the fatigues and heat of the desert, apparently for
the sake of a few old stones, is to them quite incomprehensible.

Desert.—*Feb.* 17. A fearful accident has befallen us. To our
utter dismay, four of our largest geerbahs are empty, the water
having leaked out during the night. The skins are old, although the
best we could procure at Assuan. The rest seem good: Heaven grant
that they may prove so! the consequences of another such accident
might be fatal. We have passed to-day the bodies of seven human

beings who have doubtless recently perished from thirst and fatigue; we have seen also dead camels without number.

Arrival at the Nile. Village of Abouhammed.—Feb. 23. We left this morning at seven, and reached the banks of the Nile in five hours. There is no apparent descent from the desert. Our fatigues and sufferings were all forgotten, and every one seemed to bless his stars, and think it luxury to quaff again the delicious waters of this most noble of streams, uncontaminated by the taste of the geerbah skins, and no longer confined to the scanty allowance of the caravan. The Ababdehs have found here many relations and friends, and there seems to be no end to *salamats* and *taip eens*, to shaking of hands and embracing. At their request I have consented that the remainder of the day shall be devoted to repose and festivity. My servants have killed the fattest sheep they could find; part of which, and a small backsheesh (present of money), I have given to the Ababdehs to complete their happiness. They are already at work, drinking the bouza; and I observe that some pretty Berber women with their jests and charms are increasing their hilarity. We have been eighty-six hours in this route:—

                                                                    Miles.

33 hours in the valleys, at 2¾ miles per hour - - 91¾
53 hours on the plains, which I calculate at 3 miles
    per hour .- - - - - - - - - - - - - 159
This agrees very satisfactorily with the known difference
    of latitude.   250

Gagi.—Feb. 24. We set out this morning at eight, and encamped at the village of Gagi at five,—nine hours. Here, and in the island of the same name adjoining, they number fifty men, all of the Ababdeh tribe. In the island are six sakkeas, for each of which they pay to the government fourteen dollars and two ardebs of wheat. We are encamped, as usual, near the house of the sheikh. I walked into his harem without ceremony, and chatted with his wives and female slaves. Some of them were very beautifully formed; and being almost naked, they displayed finely shaped busts, and, I may say, almost perfect symmetry of shape; their features very regular, and their full dark eyes exceedingly expressive. The little drapery worn by them is adjusted with great taste, and they possess a natural ease of manner, neither bashful nor yet too forward, which is very engaging. The slaves were employed in making basket-work, and the wives reposing on their angareebs. I could not, in Egypt, have taken the liberty of entering a harem in this manner; but here, apparently, more freedom is permitted, for they did not seem at all offended; on the contrary, they gave me as much encouragement as I could desire. They examined my arms and dress, and were profuse in their admiration of my beard, and in exclamations, as, "Odjaib, whallah! wonderful, God is great! but he is a tall man." The sheikh was smoking under the shade of some doum trees. He saw me enter, but had the politeness not to interfere.

Never were my feelings more ardently excited than in approaching, after so tedious a journey, to this magnificent Necropolis. The appearance of the pyramids, in the distance, announced their importance; but I was gratified beyond my most sanguine expectations, when I found myself in the midst of them. The pyramids of Geezah [Gizeh] are magnificent, wonderful from their stupendous magnitude; but for picturesque effect and elegance of architectural design, I infinitely prefer these of Meroë. I expected to find few such remains here, and certainly nothing so imposing, so interesting, as these sepulchres, doubtless of the kings and queens of Ethiopia. I stood for some time lost in admiration. From every point of view I saw magnificent groups, pyramid rising behind pyramid, while the dilapidated state of many did not render them less interesting, though less beautiful as works of art. I easily restored them in my imagination; and these effects of the ravages of time carried back my thoughts to more distant ages.

The porticoes on the east side of each pyramid soon attracted my attention, and I passed eagerly from one to the other, delighted to find in several of them monuments of sculpture and hieroglyphics, which, few as they are, have, I trust, given us the assurance of the locality, and will, I hope, throw some light upon the mythology and arts of the Ethiopians. There are the remains and traces of eighty of these pyramids: they consist chiefly in three groups. The principal and most imposing, at which I arrived first, is situated on a hill, two miles and a half from the river, commanding an extensive view of the plain. This group is arranged nearly in the form of a bow, the string of which is 1050 feet.

Thus, the façade of [one] portico faces about north-east, while the generality of the other porticoes vary from east to south-east. The circumstance of the porticoes fronting generally towards the east, and not one to the north and south-west, proves a religious observance; but that there was no astronomical object in view, in their porticoes facing the rising sun, is certain from the variation in the directions, and from there being no attempt at mathematical precision. Although we cannot attribute to them the scientific object conceived by some to have been contemplated in the location of the pyramids of Memphis, still a happier combination of position could not be imagined for producing upon the mind those impressive feelings which the royal cemeteries of kings of an age so distant, and of a nation once so great and powerful, naturally inspire.

It is evident that, from motives of curiosity, or perhaps avarice, attempts have been made to open many of the pyramids, but without success. From the appearance of those which have been partially broken into, I do not perceive the slightest probability that any of them contain galleries. Probably they are constructed over wells in which the bodies are deposited. That they are places of sepulture cannot be doubted, from their position, number, and, most particularly, from the subjects of the sculpture on the walls, which I will presently describe. One of the porches or porticoes is most interestingly curious, the roof being arched, in a regular masonic style, with what may be called a keystone. This arch consists of four and five stones alternately; but, notwithstanding this irregularity, the principle is the same, the stones being held together only by lateral pressure. I trust to be able to establish, beyond dispute, that the arch has its origin in Ethiopia. The style of the sculpture in this portico, and the hieroglyphic names of kings on porticoes ornamented in a similar style, being, as I hope to prove, much more ancient than any in Egypt, where there is no specimen of a stone arch constructed in so regular a manner, we may consider such proficiency in architectural knowledge as a decided proof of the advanced state of the arts, at a very remote period, in this country.

A question which has long engaged the attention of literary men is, whether the Ethiopians derived their knowledge of the arts from the Egyptians, or the latter from the former. One of these hypotheses must be admitted, as the similarity of the style evidently denotes a common origin. These pyramids belong, without doubt, to the remotest age.

At the extremity of each portico, as before observed, is the representation of a monolithic temple, above which are the traces of a funeral boat filled with figures, but all too defaced to be distinctly made out. In the centre of each boat is the sphere in the usual concave socket; and I was able, with much difficulty, to distinguish the divinities Kneph and Anubis. On each side of the boat is a pedestal on which is the bird with a human face representing the soul: one has a sphere on its head. Diodorus mentions that some of the Ethiopians preserved the bodies of their relations in glass (probably alabaster) cases, in order to have them always before their eyes. These porticoes may have been used to contain such cases.

I have carefully described this interesting and magnificent cemetery; but how shall I attempt to express the feelings of the traveller on treading such hallowed ground? One who, in passionate admiration for the arts, had visited the chief galleries of Europe, gazed upon the breathing image of divinity in the Apollo of the Vatican, or the deep expression of the most poetical of statues, the

The ancient Egyptians were fond of wine. Painting of a grape harvest from the Theban tomb of Nakht, who was a Scribe of the Granaries during the XVIIIth Dynasty. Fifteenth century B.C.

Scenes of ploughing, hoeing and tree-felling, also from painted murals in the tomb of Nakht. The artist liked to show a ground-line even if he had to bend it to fit into the available space.

This bas-relief of the Pharaoh Akhenaten and Queen Nefertiti worshipping the life-giving sun disk, or Aten, illustrates some of the curious mannerisms that were part of the artistic revolution accomplished under this "heretic" Pharaoh. Akhenaten ruled from 1367-1350 B.C.

The anteroom in the Tomb of Tutankhamen crowded with funerary furniture, including chariots, stools and lion frames for a bed. Tutankhamen died in 1339 B.C.

Two life-size effigies of Tutankhamen stand guard at the entrance to the inner chamber of his tomb. The outermost wooden sarcophagus of the Pharaoh can be seen through the still partially sealed entrance.

Neith, Isis and Serqet, three of the four goddesses whose golden effigies were set to guard the vessels containing Tutankhamen's heart and other organs.

An over-ripe yet still charming art style is manifest in this gold and calcite model of a funerary boat from Tutankhamen's Tomb.

Queen Nefertari appears as a tiny figure beside the right leg of one of the colossal statues of her husband, Ramses II, before the Great Temple at Abu Simbel. A figure (upper left) of the falcon-headed sun god, Horus, with the sun disk on his head, fills a niche above the entrance. Ramses II ruled 1290-1224 B.C.

The Great Temple of Abu Simbel is cut from solid rock. In the main hall two lines of huge columns show Ramses II as Osiris, holding the crook and flail.

Ritual wailing accompanied the burial of the Egyptian dead. This painting of women mourners from the tomb of Ramses II still shows much of the life and individuality of the art style initiated by Akhenaten.

Dying Gladiator of the Capitol; who had beheld and felt the pictorial creations of a Raphael and a Correggio, and, with delight, contemplated Grecian, Roman, and modern sculpture, could not be unmoved at finding himself on the site of the very metropolis where those arts had their origin. The traveller who has seen the architectural antiquities of Rome, and has admired the magnificent use that nation has made of the arch, making it the chief ornament of their baths, palaces, and temples, would be further deeply interested at finding here the origin of that discovery. These emotions would be felt with peculiar force by one who, like myself, had been fortunate enough to trace art through her earliest creations,—from the splendid Gothic edifices of the north to the ruins of the Eternal City—from Rome to Magna Graecia—from the magnificent Temple of Neptune at Paestum to the still purer antiquities of Sicily, particularly at Girgenti, where nature and art seem to have vied with each other— from that interesting island to the Morea and the city of Minerva, where the knowledge of the arts, sown in the most genial soil, produced the perfection of elegance, chasteness, and magnificence. But the seeds of the knowledge of the Greeks were derived from Egypt; and the Egyptians received their civilisation from the Ethiopians, and from Meroë, where I now am writing. The beautiful sepulchres of that city afford satisfactory evidence of the correctness of the historical records. Where a taste for the arts had reached to such perfection, we may rest assured that other intellectual pursuits were not neglected, nor the sciences entirely unknown. Now, however, her schools are closed for ever, without a vestige of them remaining. Of the houses of her philosophers, not a stone rests upon another; and where civilisation and learning once reigned, ignorance and barbarism have reassumed the sway.

AMELIA EDWARDS

With Amelia Edwards
to Abu Simbel

MISS AMELIA EDWARDS was a Londoner, and during her younger days a novelist. The whole direction of her life was changed when in 1873-4 she went up the Nile in the agreeable kind of houseboat known as a *dahabeah*. Her party went as far as the Second Cataract. Miss Edwards was so enthralled by the ancient monuments, and at the same time so shocked by the damage she saw being done to them, that she determined to take action. She contrived to raise funds, and when Maspero succeeded the tyrannical Mariette (p. 51, I), the Egypt Exploration Society was founded, Miss Edwards became its first joint secretary, and Flinders Petrie its chief excavator. In 1889-90 she made a triumphantly successful lecture tour in the United States, but died only about a year later.

❧

AMPÈRE has put Egypt in an epigram. "A donkey-ride and a boating-trip interspersed with ruins" does, in fact, sum up in a single line the whole experience of the Nile traveller. Apropos of these three things—the donkeys, the boat, and the ruins—it may be said that a good English saddle and a comfortable dahabeah add very considerably to the pleasure of the journey; and that the more one knows about the past history of the country, the more one enjoys the ruins.

Of the comparative merits of wooden boats, iron boats, and steamers, I am not qualified to speak. We, however, saw one iron dahabeah aground upon a sandbank, where, as we afterwards learned, it remained for three weeks. We also saw the wrecks of three steamers between Cairo and the First Cataract. It certainly

From *A Thousand Miles up the Nile*. London: George Routledge & Sons; 1891, pp. ix-x, xii-xiv, 49-52, 96-7, 259-61, 292-329.

seemed to us that the old-fashioned wooden dahabeah—flat-bottomed, drawing little water, light in hand, and easily poled off when stuck—was the one vessel best constructed for the navigation of the Nile. Other considerations, as time and cost, are, of course, involved in this question. The choice between dahabeah and steamer is like the choice between travelling with post-horses and travelling by rail. The one is expensive, leisurely, delightful; the other is cheap, swift, and comparatively comfortless. Those who are content to snatch but a glimpse of the Nile will doubtless prefer the steamer. I may add that the whole cost of the Philae—food, dragoman's wages, boat-hire, cataract, everything included except wine— was about £10 per day.

Of the fascination of Egyptian travel, of the charm of the Nile, of the unexpected and surpassing beauty of the desert, of the ruins which are the wonder of the world, I have said enough elsewhere. I must, however, add that I brought home with me an impression that things and people are much less changed in Egypt than we of the present day are wont to suppose. I believe that the physique and life of the modern Fellâh is almost identical with the physique and life of that ancient Egyptian labourer whom we know so well in the wall-paintings of the tombs. Square in the shoulders, slight but strong in the limbs, full-lipped, brown-skinned, we see him wearing the same loin-cloth, plying the same shâdûf [water-hoist] ploughing with the same plough, preparing the same food in the same way, and eating it with his fingers from the same bowl, as did his forefathers of six thousand years ago.

The household life and social ways of even the provincial gentry are little changed. Water is poured on one's hands before going to dinner from just such a ewer and into just such a basin as we see pictured in the festival-scenes at Thebes. Though the lotus-blossom is missing, a bouquet is still given to each guest when he takes his place at table. The head of the sheep killed for the banquet is still given to the poor. Those who are helped to meat or drink touch the head and breast in acknowledgment, as of old. The musicians still sit at the lower end of the hall; the singers yet clap their hands in time to their own voices; the dancing-girls still dance, and the buffoon in his high cap still performs his uncouth antics, for the entertainment of the guests. Water is brought to table in jars of the same shape manufactured at the same town, as in the days of Cheops and Chephren; and the mouths of the bottles are filled in precisely the same way with fresh leaves and flowers. The cucumber stuffed with minced-meat was a favourite dish in those times of old; and I can testify to its excellence in 1874. Little boys in Nubia yet wear the side-lock that graced the head of Ramses in his youth; and little girls may be seen in a garment closely resembling the girdle worn by young princesses of the time of Thothmes the First. A sheikh still walks with a long staff; a Nubian belle still plaits her tresses in scores of little tails; and the pleasure-boat of the modern Governor or Mudîr, as well as the dahabeah hired by the European traveller, reproduces in all essential features the painted galleys represented in the tombs of the kings.

In these and in a hundred other instances, all of which came under my personal observation and have their place in the following pages, it seemed to me that any obscurity which yet hangs over the problem of life and thought in ancient Egypt originates most probably with ourselves. Our own habits of life and thought are so complex that they shut us off from the simplicity of that early world. So it was with the problem of hieroglyphic writing. The thing was so obvious that no one could find it out. As long as the world persisted in believing that every hieroglyph was an abstruse symbol, and every hieroglyphic inscription a profound philosophical rebus, the mystery of Egyptian literature remained insoluble. Then at last came Champollion's famous letter to Dacier, showing that the hieroglyphic signs were mainly alphabetic and syllabic, and that the language they spelt was only Coptic after all.

If there were not thousands who still conceive that the sun and moon were created, and are kept going, for no other purpose than to lighten the darkness of our little planet; if only the other day a grave gentleman had not written a perfectly serious essay to show that the world is a flat plain, one would scarcely believe that there could still be people who doubt that ancient Egyptian is now read and translated as fluently as ancient Greek. Yet an Englishman whom I met in Egypt—an Englishman who had long been resident in Cairo, and who was well acquainted with the great Egyptologists who are attached to the service of the Khedive—assured me of his profound disbelief in the discovery of Champollion. "In my opinion," said he, "not one of these gentlmen can read a line of hieroglyphics."

Then again the colouring!—colouring not to be matched with any pigments yet invented. The Libyan rocks, like rusty gold—the paler hue of the driven sand-slopes—the warm maize of the nearer pyramids which, seen from this distance, takes a tender tint of rose, like the red bloom on an apricot—the delicate tone of these objects against the sky—the infinite gradation of that sky, soft and pearly towards the horizon, blue and burning towards the zenith—the opalescent shadows, pale blue, and violet, and greenish-grey, that nestle in the hollows of the rock and the curves of the sand-drifts—all this is beautiful in a way impossible to describe, and alas! impossible to copy. Nor does the lake-like plain with its palm-groves and corn-flats form too tame a foreground. It is exactly what is wanted to relieve that glowing distance.

And now, as we follow the zigzags of the road, the new pyramids grow gradually larger; the sun mounts higher; the heat increases. We meet a train of camels, buffaloes, shaggy brown sheep, men, women, and children of all ages. The camels are laden with bedding, rugs, mats, and crates of poultry, and carry, besides, two women with babies and one very old man. The younger men drive the tired beasts. The rest follow behind. The dust rises after them in a cloud. It is evidently the migration of a family of three, if not four generations. One cannot help being struck by the patriarchal simplicity of the incident. Just thus, with flocks and herds and all his clan, went Abraham into the land of Canaan close upon four thousand years ago; and one at least of these Sakkara pyramids was even then the oldest building in the world.

It is a touching and picturesque procession—much more picturesque than ours, and much more numerous; notwithstanding that our united forces, including donkey-boys, porters, and miscellaneous hangers-on, number nearer thirty than twenty persons. For there are the M. B.s and their nephew, and L. and the writer, and L.'s maid, and Talhamy, all on donkeys; and then there are the owners of the donkeys, also on donkeys; and then every donkey has a boy; and every boy has a donkey; and every donkey-boy's donkey has an inferior boy in attendance. Our style of dress, too, however convenient, is not exactly in harmony with the surrounding scenery; and one cannot but feel, as these draped and dusty pilgrims pass us on the road, that we cut a sorry figure with our hideous palm-leaf hats, green veils, and white umbrellas.

But the most amazing and incongruous personage in our whole procession is unquestionably George. Now George is an English north-country groom whom the M. B.s have brought out from the wilds of Lancashire, partly because he is a good shot and may be useful to "Master Alfred" after birds and crocodiles; and partly from a well-founded belief in his general abilities. And George, who is a fellow of infinite jest and infinite resource, takes to Eastern life as a duckling to the water. He picks up Arabic as if it were his mother tongue. He skins birds like a practised taxidermist. He can even wash and iron on occasion. He is, in short, groom, footman, housemaid, laundry-maid, stroke oar, gamekeeper, and general factotum all in one. And besides all this, he is gifted with a comic gravity of countenance that no surprises and no disasters can upset for a moment. To see this worthy anachronism cantering along in his groom's coat and gaiters, livery-buttons, spotted neckcloth, tall hat, and all the rest of it; his long legs dangling within an inch of the ground on either side of the most diminutive of donkeys; his double-barrelled fowling-piece under his arm, and that imperturbable look in his face, one would have sworn that he and Egypt were friends of old, and that he had been brought up on pyramids from his earliest childhood.

It is a long and shelterless ride from the palms to the desert; but we come to the end of it at last, mounting just such another sand-slope as that which leads up from the Gizeh road to the foot of the Great Pyramid. The edge of the plateau here rises abruptly from the plain in one long range of low perpendicular cliffs pierced with dark mouths of rock-cut sepulchres, while the sand-slope by which we are climbing pours down through a breach in the rock, as an Alpine snowdrift flows through a mountain gap from the ice-level above.

And now, having dismounted through compassion for our unfortunate little donkeys, the first thing we observe is the curious mixture of debris underfoot. At Gizeh one treads only sand and pebbles; but here at Sakkara the whole plateau is thickly strewn with scraps of broken pottery, limestone, marble, and alabaster; flakes of green and blue glaze; bleached bones; shreds of yellow linen; and lumps of some odd-looking dark brown substance, like dried-up sponge. Presently some one picks up a little noseless head of one of the common blue-ware funereal statuettes, and immediately we all fall to work, grubbing for treasure—a pure waste of precious time; for though the sand is full of debris, it has been sifted so often and so carefully by the Arabs that it no longer contains anything worth looking for. Meanwhile, one finds a fragment of iridescent glass—another, a morsel of shattered vase—a third, an opaque bead of some kind of yellow paste. And then, with a shock which the present writer, at all events, will not soon forget, we suddenly discover that these scattered bones are human—that those linen shreds are shreds of cerement cloths—that yonder odd-looking brown lumps are rent fragments of what once was living flesh! And now for the first time we realise that every inch of this ground on which we are standing, and all these hillocks and hollows and pits in the sand, are violated graves.

"*Ce n'est que le premier pas que coûte.*" We soon became quite hardened to such sights, and learned to rummage among dusty sepulchres with no more compunction than would have befitted a gang of professional body-snatchers. These are experiences upon which one looks back afterwards with wonder, and something like remorse; but so infectious is the universal callousness, and so over-mastering is the passion for relic-hunting, that I do not doubt we should again do the same things under the same circumstances. Most Egyptian travellers, if questioned, would have to make a similar confession. Shocked at first, they denounce with horror the whole system of sepulchral excavation, legal as well as predatory; acquiring, however, a taste for scarabs and funerary statuettes, they soon begin to buy with eagerness the spoils of the dead; finally, they forget all their former scruples, and ask no better fortune than to discover and confiscate a tomb for themselves.

It was, I think, towards the afternoon of this second day, when strolling by the margin of the river, that we first made the acquaintance of that renowned insect, the Egyptian beetle. He was a very fine specimen of his race, nearly half an inch long in the back, as black and shiny as a scarab cut in jet, and busily engaged in the preparation of a large rissole of mud, which he presently began laboriously propelling up the bank. We stood and watched him for some time, half in admiration, half in pity. His rissole was at least four times bigger than himself, and to roll it up that steep incline to a point beyond the level of next summer's inundation was a labour of Hercules for so small a creature. One longed to play the part of the *Deus ex machina*, and carry it up the bank for him; but that would have been a dénouement beyond his power of appreciation.

We all know the old story of how this beetle lays its eggs by the river's brink; encloses them in a ball of moist clay; rolls the ball to a safe place on the edge of the desert; buries it in the sand; and when his time comes, dies content, having provided for the safety of his successors. Hence his mythic fame: hence all the quaint symbolism that by degrees attached itself to his little person, and ended by investing him with a special sacredness which has often been mistaken for actual worship. Standing by thus, watching the movements of the creature, its untiring energy, its extraordinary muscular strength, its business-like devotion to the matter in hand, one sees how subtle a lesson the old Egyptian moralists had presented to them for contemplation, and with how fine a combination of wisdom and poetry they regarded this little black scarab not only as an emblem of the creative and preserving power, but perhaps also of the immortality of the soul. As a type, no insect has ever had so much greatness thrust upon him. He became a hieroglyph, and stood for a word signifying both To Be and To Transform. His portrait was multiplied a millionfold; sculptured over the portals of temples; fitted to the shoulders of a God; engraved on gems; moulded in pottery; painted on sarcophagi and the walls of tombs; worn by the living and buried with the dead.

Every traveller on the Nile brings away a handful of the smaller scarabs, genuine or otherwise. Some may not particularly care to possess them; yet none can help buying them, if only because other people do so, or to get rid of a troublesome dealer, or to give to friends at home. I doubt, however, if even the most enthusiastic scarab-fanciers really feel in all its force the symbolism attaching to these little gems, or appreciate the exquisite naturalness of their execution, till they have seen the living beetle at its work.

We were now only thirty-four miles from Abu Simbel; but making slow progress, and impatiently counting every foot of the way. The heat at times was great; frequent and fitful spells of Khamsîn wind alternating with a hot calm that tried the trackers sorely. Still we pushed forward, a few miles at a time, till by and by the flat-topped cliffs dropped out of sight and were again succeeded by volcanic peaks, some of which looked loftier than any of those about Dakkeh or Korosko.

Then the palms ceased, and the belt of cultivated land narrowed to a thread of green between the rocks and the water's edge; and at last there came an evening when we only wanted breeze enough to double two or three more bends in the river.

"Is it to be Abu Simbel to-night?" we asked, for the twentieth time before going down to dinner.

To which Reïs Hassan replied, "*Aiwah*" (certainly).

But the pilot shook his head, and added, "*Bûkra*" (tomorrow).

When we came up again, the moon had risen, but the breeze had dropped. Still we moved, impelled by a breath so faint that one could scarcely feel it. Presently even this failed. The sail collapsed; the pilot steered for the bank; the captain gave the word to go aloft —when a sudden puff from the north changed our fortunes, and sent us out again with a well-filled sail into the middle of the river.

None of us, I think, will be likely to forget the sustained excitement of the next three hours. As the moon climbed higher, a light more mysterious and unreal than the light of day filled and overflowed the wide expanse of river and desert. We could see the mountains of Abu Simbel standing as it seemed across our path, in the far distance—a lower one first; then a larger; then a series of receding heights, all close together, yet all distinctly separate.

That large one—the mountain of the Great Temple—held us like a spell. For a long time it looked a mere mountain like the rest. By and by, however, we fancied we detected a something—a shadow —such a shadow as might be cast by a gigantic buttress. Next appeared a black speck no bigger than a porthole. We knew that this black speck must be the doorway. We knew that the great statues were there, though not yet visible; and that we must soon see them.

For our sailors, meanwhile, there was the excitement of a chase. The Bagstones and three other dahabeahs were coming up behind us in the path of the moonlight. Their galley fires glowed like beacons on the water; the nearest about a mile away· the last a spark in the distance. We were not in the mood to care much for racing to-night; but we were anxious to keep our lead and be first at the mooring-place.

To run upon a sandbank at such a moment was like being plunged suddenly into cold water. Our sail flapped furiously. The men rushed to the punting poles. Four jumped overboard, and shoved with all the might of their shoulders. By the time we got off, however, the other boats had crept up half a mile nearer; and we had hard work to keep them from pressing closer on our heels.

At length the last corner was rounded, and the Great Temple stood straight before us. The façade, sunk in the mountain-side like a huge picture in a mighty frame, was now quite plain to see. The black speck was no longer a porthole, but a lofty doorway.

Last of all, though it was night and they were still not much less than a mile away, the four colossi came out, ghost-like, vague, and shadowy, in the enchanted moonlight. Even as we watched them, they seemed to grow—to dilate—to be moving towards us out of the silvery distance.

It was drawing on towards midnight when the Philæ at length ran in close under the Great Temple. Content with what they had seen from the river, the rest of the party then went soberly to bed; but the painter and the writer had no patience to wait till morning. Almost before the mooring-rope could be made fast, they had jumped ashore and begun climbing the bank.

They went and stood at the feet of the colossi, and on the threshold of that vast portal beyond which was darkness. The great statues towered above their heads. The river glittered like steel in the far distance. There was a keen silence in the air; and towards the east the Southern Cross was rising. To the strangers who stood talking there with bated breath, the time, the place, even the sound of their own voices, seemed unreal. They felt as if the whole scene must fade with the moonlight, and vanish before morning. . . .

The relative position of the two Temples of Abu Simbel has been already described—how they are excavated in two adjacent mountains and divided by a cataract of sand. The front of the small Temple lies parallel to the course of the Nile, here flowing in a north-easterly direction. The façade of the Great Temple is cut in the flank of the mountain, and faces due east. Thus the colossi, towering above the shoulder of the sand-drift, catch, as it were, a side view of the small Temple and confront vessels coming up the river. As for the sand-drift, it curiously resembles the glacier of the Rhone. In size, in shape, in position, in all but colour and substance, it is the same. Pent in between the rocks at top, it opens out like a fan at bottom. In this its inevitable course, it slants downward across the façade of the Great Temple. For ever descending, drifting, accumulating, it wages the old stealthy war; and, unhasting, unresting, labours grain by grain to fill the hollowed chambers, and bury the great statues, and wrap the whole Temple in a winding-sheet of golden sand, so that the place thereof shall know it no more.

It had very nearly come to this when Burckhardt went up (A.D. 1813). The top of the doorway was then thirty feet below the surface. Whether the sand will ever reach that height again, must depend on the energy with which it is combated. It can only be cleared as it accumulates. To avert it is impossible. Backed by the illimitable wastes of the Libyan desert, the supply from above is inexhaustible. Come it must; and come it will, to the end of time.

The drift rose to the lap of the northernmost colossus and half-way up the legs of the next, when the Philæ lay at Abu Simbel. The doorway was clear, however, almost to the threshold, and the sand inside was not more than two feet deep in the first hall. The whole façade, we were told, had been laid bare, and the interior swept and garnished, when the Empress of the French, after opening the Suez Canal in 1869, went up the Nile as far as the Second Cataract. By this time, most likely, that yellow carpet lies thick and soft in every chamber, and is fast silting up the doorway again. . . .

We hurried on to the Great Temple, without waiting to examine the lesser one in detail. A solemn twilight reigned in the first hall, beyond which all was dark. Eight colossi, four to the right and four to the left, stand ranged down the centre, bearing the mountain on their heads. Their height is twenty-five feet. With hands crossed on their breasts, they clasp the flail and crook; emblems of majesty and dominion. It is the attitude of Osiris, but the face is the face of Ramses II. Seen by this dim light, shadowy, mournful, majestic, they look as if they remembered the past.

Beyond the first hall lies a second hall supported on four square pillars; beyond this again, a transverse chamber, the walls of which are covered with coloured bas-reliefs of various Gods; last of all, the sanctuary. Here, side by side, sit four figures larger than life— Ptah, Amen-Ra, Ra, and Ramses deified. Before them stands an altar, in shape a truncated pyramid, cut from the solid rock. Traces of colour yet linger on the garments of the statues; while in the walls on either side are holes and grooves such as might have been made to receive a screen of metal-work.

The air in the sanctuary was heavy with an acrid smoke, as if the priests had been burning some strange incense and were only just gone. For this illusion we were indebted to the visitors who had been there before us. They had lit the place with magnesian wire; the vapour of which lingers long in these unventilated vaults.

To settle down then and there to a steady investigation of the wall-sculptures was impossible. We did not attempt it. Wandering from hall to hall, from chamber to chamber; now trusting to the faint gleams that straggled in from without, now stumbling along by the light of a bunch of candles tied to the end of a stick, we preferred to receive those first impressions of vastness, of mystery, of gloomy magnificence, which are the more profound for being somewhat vague and general.

Scenes of war, of triumph, of worship, passed before our eyes like the incidents of a panorama. Here the King, borne along at full gallop by plumed steeds gorgeously caparisoned, draws his mighty bow and attacks a battlemented fortress. The besieged, some of whom are transfixed by his tremendous arrows, supplicate for mercy. They are a Syrian people, and are by some indentified with the Northern Hittites. Their skin is yellow; and they wear the long hair and beard, the fillet, the rich robe, fringed cape, and embroidered baldric with which we are familiar in the Nineveh sculptures. A man driving off cattle in the foreground looks as if he had stepped out of one of the tablets in the British Museum. Ramses meanwhile towers, swift and godlike, above the crowd. His coursers are of such immortal strain as were the coursers of Achilles. His sons, his whole army, chariot and horse, follow headlong at his heels. All is movement and the splendour of battle.

Farther on, we see the King returning in state, preceded by his prisoners of war. Tied together in gangs, they stagger as they go, with heads thrown back and hands uplifted. These, however, are not Assyrians, but Abyssinians and Nubians, so true to the type, so thick-lipped, flat-nosed, and woolly-headed, that only the pathos of the expression saves them from being ludicrous. It is naturalness pushed to the verge of caricature.

A little farther still, and we find Ramses leading a string of these captives into the presence of Amen-Ra, Maut [Mut], and Khons—Amen-Ra weird and unearthly, with his blue complexion and towering plumes; Maut wearing the crown of Upper Egypt; Khons by a subtle touch of flattery depicted with the features of the King. Again, to right and left of the entrance, Ramses, thrice the size of life, slays a group of captives of various nations. To the left Amen-Ra, to the right Ra Harmachis, approve and accept the sacrifice. In the second hall we see, as usual, the procession of the sacred bark. Ptah, Khem, and Bast, gorgeous in many-coloured garments, gleam dimly, like figures in faded tapestry, from the walls of the transverse corridor.

But the wonder of Abu Simbel is the huge subject on the north side of the Great Hall. This is a monster battle-piece which covers an area of 57 feet and 7 inches in length, by 25 feet 4 inches in height, and contains over 1100 figures. Even the heraldic cornice of cartouches and asps which runs round the rest of the ceiling is omitted on this side, so that the wall is literally filled with the picture from top to bottom.

Fully to describe this huge design would take many pages. It is a picture-gallery in itself. It represents not a single action but a whole campaign. It sets before us, with Homeric simplicity, the pomp and circumstance of war, the incidents of camp life, and the accidents of the open field. We see the enemy's city with its battlemented towers and triple moat; the besiegers' camp and the pavilion of the king; the march of infantry; the shock of chariots; the hand-to-hand melée; the flight of the vanquished; the triumph of the Pharaoh; the bringing in of the prisoners; the counting of the hands of the slain. A great river winds through the picture from end to end, and almost surrounds the invested city. The king in his chariot pursues a crowd of fugitives along the bank. Some are crushed under his wheels; some plunge into the water and are drowned. Behind him, a moving wall of shields and spears, advances with rhythmic step the serried phalanx; while yonder, where the fight is thickest, we see chariots overturned, men dead and dying, and riderless horses making for the open. Meanwhile the besieged send out mounted scouts, and the country folk drive their cattle to the hills.

A grand frieze of chariots charging at full gallop divides the subject lengthwise, and separates the Egyptian camp from the field of battle. The camp is square, and enclosed, apparently, in a palisade of shields. It occupies less than one sixth part of the picture, and contains about a hundred figures. Within this narrow space the artist has brought together an astonishing variety of incidents. The horses feed in rows from a common manger, or wait their turn and impatiently paw the ground. Some are lying down. One, just unharnessed, scampers round the enclosure. Another, making off with the empty chariot at his heels, is intercepted by a couple of grooms. Other grooms bring buckets of water slung from the shoulders on wooden yokes. A wounded officer sits apart, his head resting on his hand; and an orderly comes in haste to bring him news of the battle. Another, hurt apparently in the foot, is having the wound dressed by a surgeon. Two detachments of infantry, marching out to reinforce their comrades in action, are met at the entrance to the camp by the royal chariot returning from the field. Ramses drives before him some fugitives, who are trampled down, seized, and dispatched upon the spot. In one corner stands a row of objects that look like joints of meat; and near them are a small altar and a tripod brazier. Elsewhere, a couple of soldiers, with a big bowl between them, sit on their heels and dip their fingers in the mess, precisely as every Fellah does to this day. . . .

We are despaired of ever seeing a crocodile; and but for a trail that our men discovered on the island opposite, we should almost have ceased to believe that there were crocodiles in Egypt. The marks were quite fresh when we went to look at them. The creature had been basking high and dry in the sun, and this was the point at which he had gone down again to the river. The damp sand at the water's edge had taken the mould of his huge fleshy paws, and even of the jointed armour of his tail, though this last impression was somewhat blurred by the final rush with which he had taken to the water. I doubt if Robinson Crusoe, when he saw the famous footprint on the shore, was more excited than we of the Philæ at sight of this genuine and undeniable trail.

As for the Idle Man, he flew at once to arms and made ready for the fray. He caused a shallow grave to be dug for himself a few yards from the spot; then went and lay in it for hours together, morning after morning, under the full blaze of the sun,— flat, patient, alert,—with his gun ready cocked, and a Pall Mall Budget up his back. It was not his fault if he narrowly escaped sunstroke, and had his labour for his reward. That crocodile was too clever for him, and took care never to come back.

Our sailors, meanwhile, though well pleased with an occasional holiday, began to find Abu Simbel monotonous. As long as the Bagstones stayed, the two crews met every evening to smoke, and dance, and sing their quaint roundelays together. But when rumours came of wonderful things already done this winter above Wadi Halfeh—rumours that represented the Second Cataract as a populous solitude of crocodiles—then our faithful consort slipped away one morning before sunrise, and the Philæ was left companionless.

At this juncture, seeing that the men's time hung heavy on their hands, our painter conceived the idea of setting them to clean the face of the northernmost Colossus, still disfigured by the plaster left on it when the great cast was taken by Mr. Hay more than half a century before. This happy thought was promptly carried into effect. A scaffolding of spars and oars was at once improvised, and the men, delighted as children at play, were soon swarming all over the huge head, just as the carvers may have swarmed over it in the days when Ramses was king.

All they had to do was to remove any small lumps that might yet adhere to the surface, and then tint the white patches with coffee. This they did with bits of sponge tied to the ends of sticks; but Reïs Hassan, as a mark of dignity, had one of the painter's old brushes, of which he was immensely proud.

It took them three afternoons to complete the job; and we were all sorry when it came to an end. To see Reïs Hassan artistically touching up a gigantic nose almost as long as himself; Riskalli and the cook-boy staggering to and fro with relays of coffee, brewed "thick and slab" for the purpose; Salame perched cross-legged, like some complacent imp, on the towering rim of the great pschent overhead; the rest chattering and skipping about the scaffolding like monkeys, was, I will venture to say, a sight more comic than has ever been seen at Abu Simbel before or since.

Ramses' appetite for coffee was prodigious. He consumed I know not how many gallons a day. Our cook stood aghast at the demand made upon his stores. Never before had he been called upon to provide for a guest whose mouth measured three feet and a half in width.

Still, the result justified the expenditure. The coffee proved a capital match for the sandstone; and though it was not possible wholly to restore the uniformity of the original surface, we at least succeeded in obliterating those ghastly splotches, which for so many years have marred this beautiful face as with the unsightliness of leprosy. . . .

The thing that now caught the painter's eye, however, was a long crack running transversely down the face of the rock. It was such a crack as might have been caused, one would say, by blasting.

He stooped—cleared the sand away a little with his hand—observed that the crack widened—poked in the point of his stick; and found that it penetrated to a depth of two or three feet. Even then, it seemed to him to stop, not because it encountered any obstacle, but because the crack was not wide enough to admit the thick end of the stick.

This surprised him. No mere fault in the natural rock, he thought, would go so deep. He scooped away a little more sand; and still the cleft widened. He introduced the stick a second time. It was a long palm-stick like an alpenstock, and it measured about five feet in length. When he probed the cleft with it this second time, it went in freely up to where he held it in his hand—that is to say, to a depth of quite four feet.

Convinced now that there was some hidden cavity in the rock, he carefully examined the surface. There were yet visible a few hieroglyphic characters and part of two cartouches, as well as some battered outlines of what had once been figures. The heads of these figures were gone (the face of the rock, with whatever may have been sculptured upon it, having come away bodily at this point), while from the waist downwards they were hidden under the sand. Only some hands and arms, in short, could be made out.

They were the hands and arms, apparently, of four figures; two in the centre of the composition, and two at the extremities. The two centre ones, which seemed to be back to back, probably represented gods; the outer ones, worshippers.

All at once, it flashed upon the painter that he had seen this kind of group many a time before—*and generally over a doorway*.

Feeling sure now that he was on the brink of a discovery, he came back; fetched away Salame and Mehemet Ali; and, without saying a syllable to any one, set to work with these two to scrape away the sand at the spot where the crack widened.

Meanwhile, the luncheon bell having rung thrice, we concluded that the painter had rambled off somewhere into the desert; and so sat down without him. Towards the close of the meal, however, came a pencilled note, the contents of which ran as follows:—

"Pray come immediately—I have found the entrance to a tomb. Please send some sandwiches—A. M'C."

To follow the messenger at once to the scene of action was the general impulse. In less than ten minutes we were there, asking breathless questions, peeping in through the fast-widening aperture, and helping to clear away the sand.

All that Sunday afternoon, heedless of possible sunstroke, unconscious of fatigue, we toiled upon our hands and knees, as for bare life, under the burning sun. We had all the crew up, working like tigers. Every one helped; even the dragoman and the two maids. More than once, when we paused for a moment's breathing space, we said to each other: "If those at home could see us, what would they say!"

And now, more than ever, we felt the need of implements. With a spade or two and a wheelbarrow, we could have done wonders; but with only one small fire-shovel, a birch broom, a couple of charcoal baskets, and about twenty pairs of hands, we were poor indeed. What was wanted in means, however, was made up in method. Some scraped away the sand; some gathered it into baskets; some carried the baskets to the edge of the cliff, and emptied them into the river. The Idle Man distinguished himself by scooping out a channel where the slope was steepest; which greatly facilitated the work. Emptied down this shoot and kept continually going, the sand poured off in a steady stream like water.

Meanwhile the opening grew rapidly larger. When we first came up—that is, when the painter and the two sailors had been working on it for about an hour—we found a hole scarcely as large as one's hand, through which it was just possible to catch a dim glimpse of painted walls within. By sunset, the top of the doorway was laid bare, and where the crack ended in a large triangular fracture, there was an aperture about a foot and a half square, into which Mehemet Ali was the first to squeeze his way. We passed him in a candle and a box of matches; but he came out again directly, saying that it was a most beautiful *Birbeh,* and quite light within.

The writer wriggled in next. She found herself looking down from the top of a sandslope into a small square chamber. This sand-drift, which here rose to within a foot and a half of the top of the doorway, was heaped to the ceiling in the corner behind the

door, and thence sloped steeply down, completely covering the floor.
There was light enough to see every detail distinctly—the painted
frieze running round just under the ceiling; the bas-relief sculptures
on the walls, gorgeous with unfaded colour; the smooth sand,
pitted near the top, where Mehemet Ali had trodden, but undisturbed elsewhere by human foot; the great gap in the middle of
the ceiling, where the rock had given way; the fallen fragments on
the floor, now almost buried in sand.

Satisfied that the place was absolutely fresh and untouched, the
writer crawled out, and the others, one by one, crawled in. When
each had seen it in turn, the opening was barricaded for the night;
the sailors being forbidden to enter it, lest they should injure the
decorations.

W. M. FLINDERS PETRIE

To the Turquoise Mines
of Sinai

FROM Old Kingdom times onwards the Egyptians went regularly
to the Sinai peninsula for turquoise. The mountains there came to
be known as the Turquoise Terraces (the Egyptian word rendered
as turquoise included malachite and other forms of green stone).
Many sculptures and inscriptions of historical importance were left
in the quarries. Flinders Petrie led the expedition, which he describes in such a lively fashion, in 1904-5.

From *Researches in Sinai*. London: John Murray; 1906, pp. 1-4, 46-7. By permission
of John Murray.

THE conditions of travelling and of working in Sinai are very different from those of life in a fertile country such as Egypt, and are still further from the ways of any European land. In Egypt most long distances can be traversed on the railway, and to go a few miles from a station means only an hour or two of donkey ride; whereas in Sinai the tedious camel is the only vehicle, and you may well spend six days on a distance which would be crossed in two or three hours in a train. In Egypt there is always water of some quality near at hand, and it only needs boiling before use; in Sinai the water sources are a day's journey apart, and you may be glad to be within such a distance that a camel can go to the water and back in the day. The beginning is the worst of all, for on the road down is the serious bar of three days without water. In Egypt the rich fertility of the land provides an abundance everywhere; excellent birds, fish, good native bread, eggs, milk, and vegetables are almost always to be had. But in Sinai grim nature gives you the stone and the serpent instead of the bread and the fish, and the utmost that can be obtained from the desert valleys is an occasional tough sheep or goat.

And if the conditions are thus different, so also are the people. In Egypt the fellah is one of the pleasantest of good fellows, where yet uncursed by the tourist: always obliging and friendly, and being generally intelligent within the scope of his ideas, he is capable of being trained to a high degree of care and skill; moreover, his industry is amazing, and can always be had by good treatment and pay. But the poor Bedawy of the desert is a very different man: he has been on short commons for untold generations, and has parted with every ounce of his anatomy, and every thought from his mind, that was not essential in his hard struggle. The simplest reckoning puzzles him; he is incapable of foresight or of working for a given end, and he is physically unfit for any continuous labour except that of slowly wandering on foot all day with his camel. A few more persevering men are found, who drift to the turquoise mines and spend a few hours a day, with many rests between, in rude blasting and breaking up the rock. One or two important chiefs show more capacity; by far the strongest of these is Sheikh Mudakhel, who has developed a good character and power of business in his dealings at Tor. So different are these people from the Egyptians, that our men from Upper Egypt consorted with us far more than with the Bedawyn [Bedouin]; and, indeed, they had benefited by some years of training, so that they were much nearer to us mentally than they were to the men around. The natives were incessantly quarrelling over trying to get the better of one another, while a squabble was unknown among our Egyptians.

Without the Egyptians we could have done nothing in excavation, for it was only on their steady work and skill that we could rely. We wrote to our old friends at Quft, in Upper Egypt, selecting about thirty of the strongest among them; and Mr. Currelly headed them across more than three hundred miles of the deserts and the Red Sea, up to our camp in Sinai . . .

Having a camp of thirty-four persons is a serious responsibility in the midst of such a wilderness. The ordinary traveller goes through with perhaps one or two men beside the Bedawyn, and those men are generally his providers, who look after him, instead of his having to think about looking after their needs. Very few, if any, travellers have been through here without having everything arranged for them by a dragoman; and certainly no such party as thirty men staying for some months has ever been here since the old mining expeditions of the Egyptians, which came to an end three thousand years ago. To read most narratives of visitors to Sinai is only to hear of the inevitable fat Mūsa or Suleyman, who was so devoted, yet so domineering; who cheated over the tents, and doled out such versions of the way as he thought would interest the helpless employers who paid him. The negotiations in a grand hotel in Cairo, the days of delay while the retinue was being collected at Suez, the bargains and contracts with official sheikhs, all these form the threshold of most narratives. Here I shall state the steps of a very different way of proceeding, without any of those complications which are useless if you have a small knowledge of Arabic, and give some outline of the management which is required when dealing with a large camp in such a life.

Our stores were a vital question, and we carefully planned them, and had them sent from England to Suez. Such details as may be useful, regarding rations for natives and the food needful for good health, have been stated in the preface. The essential facts are that it is cheaper and better to have everything—even flour—out from England; and that by properly assorting the boxes, and planning their storage until required, everything can be at hand without encumbering the movements of the party to a serious extent.

The dominant factor in every arrangement is the camel—how much it can carry, how long it will take on the road, and how its loads can be arranged. And the camel-driver is the next factor, as his tariff will determine what is worth while in transport, and how to plan affairs, and his possibilities of peculation will settle how much you will receive of what he brings. Very few camel-men can resist taking toll from food in sacks—sometimes a large proportion, worth nearly as much as their wages; so it is needful to secure all stores in nailed-up boxes, which they have not the tools or the wits to tamper with.

When we reached the valley [of Magháreh] we found that most of the monuments previously known had been destroyed or injured about three years before. A company had been formed which had taken out of the hands of the natives their ancient resource of turquoise hunting, in order to "develop" it for the benefit of English shareholders. Everything gave way to the greed for dividends, with the result that the promoters lost their money, the natives lost their turquoises, and the world lost many of its most ancient monuments. No care seems to have been taken by the department which gave the concession to prevent injury to the monuments; no inspector or guardian took charge of the historical remains; and ignorant engineers destroyed what was, in the European market of museums, worth far more than all the turquoises which they extracted. The Khufu [Cheops] sculptures were smashed up. The half-dozen Assa inscriptions were all destroyed or buried. The Pepi inscriptions were annihilated. The whole of the Amenemhet inscriptions at the mines have likewise disappeared. The Snefru scene has been brutally bashed about with a hammer, and the only portrait of Snefru has been destroyed. The Sahura scene and the Men·kau·hor tablet have both been partly blasted away. The Ra·n·user tablet has had pieces knocked off it. Only the Semerkhet scene, high up above the quarries, the second Snefru scene, and the tablet of Tahutmes III [Thutmose, Thotmes] have escaped the wanton mischief done by the ignorant savagery of so-called educated man. The Goths, who protected and preserved the monuments of Rome, were cultivated in comparison with the dividend-hunting Englishman. To find a parallel to the destruction by speculating companies and engineering we must look to the Turkish destruction on the Acropolis of Athens, or Mehemet Aly's wrecking of temples to build factories and magazines. In all these cases a little extra proportion of cost or labour would have attained exactly the same benefits without doing any injury. But the destroyers had not that education which would enable them to understand or value what they unluckily had the inclination to waste. Thus perishes year by year what might so easily be preserved by a little foresight and care. Had any one proposed to carefully transfer these sculptures—the oldest scenes in the world—to a European museum, he would have met with reprobation for appropriating what had stood in position for six thousand years, unaltered and unharmed; and certainly onerous terms would have been demanded of him by the Government. But to abandon the whole to mere savage destruction was the easy course of neglect which befell them.

WALLIS BUDGE

An Excavation by the Military

SIR WALLIS BUDGE, emissary of the British Museum, gives an amusing picture of excavation by artilleryman. (Sir R. Wingate had succeeded Kitchener as Sirdar of the Egyptian army and Governor General of the Sudan.) The pyramids raised as tombs by the "Ethiopians" can be compared with those at Meroë (p. 452, I).

❦

WE stayed the night in the railway mess, which thanks to its large and commodious quarters, built by the Royal Engineer officers, is the most comfortable in the Sudan, and the following day I went to Khartum [Khartoum] to meet Sir R. Wingate. In a brief interview he explained the arrangements he had made for the excavations at the Pyramids of Bagrawiya. He had decided to form a camp of exercise at the pyramids, and about one hundred and eighty artillerymen, under the command of two British officers, Captain W. H. Drake, R.F.A., and Captain H. F. F. Lewin, R.F.A., were to do the digging. The performance of some manoeuvres and a review to be held at Mutmîr, in which these officers and men were to take part, would prevent our beginning the work for a few days, but as soon as these were over the men would be drafted to Bagrawiya, near which they would encamp. The camp was to be as near the pyramids as possible, so that the men might march out to them in the morning, and return in the evening. A few days later accordingly we went to Kabushîa, the station on the railway nearest the pyramids we intended to excavate, and rode from there to the place which Captain Lewin had chosen for the camp. This spot was close to the railway, on the west side of it, and was, as the crow flies, about three miles from the pyramids; it was about half a mile from the river, and was thus very convenient for watering the horses. In

From Wallis Budge: *The Egyptian Sudan*. London: Kegan Paul, Trench & Trubner; 1907, pp. 331-6. By permission of Routledge & Kegan Paul Ltd.

order to get the best results possible from our work, Captains Lewin and Drake decided to have their tents and mine pitched on the hill just below the pyramids, and to live there whilst the excavations were going on. This was an excellent arrangement, for it enabled us to begin work soon after sunrise, and to continue, with an interval for food and rest in the middle of the day, until sunset. So soon as the two batteries were encamped we rode out early one morning to the pyramids, and before the day was ended our tents were pitched on the hill, and the men who were with us had established themselves in their tents in the little valley between the two groups of pyramids to the south of us. With the loose stones on the hill-side a kitchen was built, and so soon as wood arrived the cook was able to get to work. His stoves were primitive and were made of stones, but in spite of the high winds which blew through the crevices in the walls and made it at times very difficult to keep the fire going, he managed very well. At the further end of the kitchen was a raised bench of stones, which, with a sheepskin upon it, served him for a bed; the soldier-servants lived in a little tent pitched close by.

All the arrangements necessary for supplying us with food and water were made by Captain Lewin. Early every morning mules arrived, each carrying two of the little regulation tanks filled with water, which was at once emptied into the large water jars that stood on wooden frames on the north sides of the tents, as much in the shade as possible. The mules returned to the camp near the river for the day, and came back in the evening with another load. Milk was supplied by the native women near the river, who sent it out to us each morning. Chickens were very scarce, and eggs scarcer still, but so soon as the women in the villages began to realize that we paid for things on the spot, they looked after their chickens, and fed them sometimes, and by degrees a fair supply of eggs was produced. At first the women thought that they would be expected to provide the officers with eggs, poultry, and sheep for nothing, and every inquiry for eggs was met by the answer that the "chickens would not lay." One day Captain Lewin interviewed the black matrons in the village, and having told them that they would be paid for their goods, he made them a few little presents, and left them to consider the matter. A little later in the day one of the Egyptian officers also visited the matrons, and told them that the Sirdar had given orders that the hens were to lay, and that if they did not, he, i.e., the officer, would not be surprised if great trouble fell on the village. The result was satisfactory, whatever may have been the cause, for the very next day six good eggs appeared instead of two, as was usually the case, and the supply increased until the last day we were at the pyramids, several weeks later, when the number of eggs brought in the morning was forty-four. The Sudani eggs, like the Egyptian, are, however, very small. The experiment was interesting, as showing that the natives are quite willing to work when ready money is to be obtained. Fresh meat could generally be obtained by buying a sheep, which cost from fifteen to twenty piastres, and every few days we obtained a basket of vegetables, i.e., the egg plants, mulûkhîa, tomatoes, etc. with occasionally a large water melon, from Mr. Morgan, an *employé* of a land company in the Sudan whose headquarters were near Bagrawîya. Bread we obtained from a Greek merchant at Shendî who for some weeks sent it regularly by train to Kabûshîa, whence it was brought to the pyramids by the men. One day, however, he went to Khartum and got married, and for several days no bread appeared; but when he returned to his shop he made up for his neglect by sending us at one time fourteen four-pound loaves, two for each of the days he was away!

For the first fortnight or so a body of artillerymen used to march out to the pyramids at sunrise, and work there all day, and time their departure in the afternoon, so that they might reach their camp near the river at sunset. Captains Lewin and Drake decided, however, that this arrangement was not a good one, for the men having walked about three and a half miles in the morning before they began their work, and having the same distance to go after they had ended it, naturally spared themselves during the day. The new plan which these officers made was a much better one. The men came out on shifts of three days, and then went back to the river for three days, and in this way duties connected with the care of the horses and the labour of digging were distributed equally among all the men in the two batteries. It necessitated an increase in the transport work, but a great deal more digging was done than would have been possible under the first arrangement. One or other of the British officers, and sometimes both, rode into the camp near the river each day to see that all was right with the men, guns, and horses, and they were indefatigable in the discharge of both their military and antiquarian duties. That more constant supervision might be given to their men two heliostats were obtained from Khartum, and thus instant communication between the camp on the river and that at the pyramids was established; at night, signals were made between the camps with lamps. By means of these instruments much time was saved, and supplies of all kinds were obtained quickly.

A word may be said about the weather which we had at the pyramids. The nights were very cold, so cold that we cordially welcomed the sunrise; as we were some miles from the river there was no damp in the air, and we escaped the bitter cold which is always felt in a camp pitched close to the Nile, even when there is no vegetation near. The first two or three hours of the day were generally pleasant, but from eleven in the morning to three in the afternoon the heat was tremendous. The hill on which the pyramids stand is of stone, and by noon the air near the surface was moved into waves by the heat reflected from it, as by a heated furnace. The only thing to do then was to take refuge in some pyramid chapel, but even there the absence of moving air would make the atmosphere inside it stifling. Towards sunset a breeze would often begin to blow from the north, but when, as was frequently the case, the gentle breeze turned into a strong wind, we were glad to seek the shelter of the tents. Occasionally the absence of wind would tempt Captain Lewin to arrange for us to dine in the open air, but more often than not we were driven into our tents by the wind by nine o'clock. When the weather is propitious nothing is more lovely than a Sudan night, especially if there be a moon. The whole desert becomes flooded with brilliant white light, the rugged face of the desert disappears, the shrubs and small trees turn into shapes of mystic beauty, and the whitish blue of the sky casts a reflection of soft beauty over the remote stretches of the desert which are filled with dimly seen silver-grey mountains, and turns them into Fairyland. At certain times of the month several reaches of the river, which were many miles away, revealed themselves by moonlight, and when seen under these circumstances they looked like lakes of silver mingled with white fire. When there is no wind the "outgoings of the morning and evening" are things of great beauty, but in a strong, continuously blowing north wind, the deserts of the Sudan are unbearable. In February, 1903, a fierce wind blew from the north for three days, and on the third day we could not see the sun: the air was filled with sand to such a degree that we felt as if we were shut in by walls of sandstone, and the fine sand got into the food and water, and filled the eyes, and ears, and nostrils, and made life most uncomfortable. For several days after the gale had blown itself out, the atmosphere was charged with fine dust stirred up from the desert, and though this made the sunsets glorious, every one was thankful when the hills resumed their wonted clear-cut outlines, and it became again a pleasure to breathe the wonderful Sudan air. On the whole, the climate of the Sudan in January and February is good, and the air is dry and invigorating, but care must be taken to guard against chills, which are very easily contracted in the early morning, and against the heat of the sun between noon and three o'clock. In February the alternate spells of heat and cold are trying, but they need cause no inconvenience to the traveller, especially if he takes care to keep warm at night, or can sleep in a

thick-walled mud hut. Many of the native huts are very comfortable, especially those possessing an inner room which is inaccessible to the north wind. It would be unfair to judge the Sudan climate
in the early spring from the weather which we experienced on the
hill of the pyramids, for there we were exposed for several weeks
to the full heat of the sun by day, and to the whole force of the
wind by night. There was on the hill no soil into which to drive
the tent-pegs, and our tents were only kept in position by tying the
ends of the ropes to large stones. Thus by night the north wind
blew under the tents and made them very cold inside, and by day
they were filled with hot air which came in in the same way; and
when a storm was raging outside, every object inside was soon
covered with a thick layer of sand, and the air was charged with
dust. The Sudan Government has, very wisely, spared neither pains
nor money in providing for the housing of the officials, and in
building rest-houses for the use of inspectors when journeying
through their districts, but it seems a pity that sun-dried bricks
are not more frequently used in the construction of the houses built
for the officials at Khartum. Walls made of burnt bricks absorb
much heat by day, and radiate it by night to the great discomfort
of those who live within them.

2. *Famous Discoveries*

GASTON MASPERO

A Windfall of Royal Mummies

IMPORTANT antiquities mysteriously flooding the antique dealing market roused the suspicion of the authorities that the villagers of Kurna (on the site of western Thebes) had discovered some exceptional hoard. Maspero, then Director of Antiquities, describes how in 1881 he took action and succeeded in screwing information from the village family concerned. The truth was that in a deep shaft grave near Deir el Bahari dug for the obscure queen Inha'py they had come upon a great cache of mummies and coffins. Maspero's researches soon showed that high priests of the Twenty-first Dynasty, appalled by the accelerating plunder of tombs in the Theban Necropolis, decided to collect all the important bodies they could find and conceal them. So there went into Inha'py's burial place the mortal remains and coffins of many of the pharaohs of the New Kingdom, including such famous rulers as Thutmose III, Sethos I and Ramses II, together with those of some of their queens, of lesser princes and high priests. All had already been robbed of their precious ornaments, but identification was easy. There were even dockets giving details of the reburials. The opportunity to see the features, however withered, of so many famous men and women, roused great popular excitement.

FOR SOME YEARS it had been known that the Arabs of el-Qurna had dug out one or two royal tombs, whose location they refused to reveal. In the spring of 1876 an English general named Camp-

Gaston Maspero: *Rapport sur la trouvaille de Deir-el-Bahari*, 1881. Translation by W. R. Trask, in *The Treasures of Time*, 1961, edited by Leo Deuel, pp. 38-43. Reprinted by permission of The World Publishing Company, New York, and Souvenir Press Ltd., London. Copyright © 1961 by The World Publishing Company.

bell had shown me the hieratic ritual of the High Priest Pinotem, purchased at Thebes for four hundred pounds. In 1877 Monsieur de Saulcy, on behalf of a friend in Syria, sent me photographs of a long papyrus that had belonged to Queen Notemit, mother of Hrihor (the end of it is now in the Louvre and the beginning in England). Monsieur Mariette had also arranged to purchase from Suez two other papyri, written in the name of a Queen Tiuhathor Henttaui. About the same time the funerary statuettes of King Pinotem appeared on the market, some of them delicate in workmanship, others coarse. In short, the fact of a discovery became so certain that as early as 1878, I could state of a tablet belonging to Rogers-Bey that "it came from a tomb in the neighborhood of the as yet unknown tombs of Hrihor's family"; its actual source is the hiding place at Deir el Bahari, where we found the mummy for which it had been written.

To search for the site of these royal vaults was, then, if not the first, at least one of the primary objects of the journey that I made in Upper Egypt during March and April 1881. I did not plan to take borings or to start excavations in the Theban necropolis; the problem was of a different nature. What had to be done was to extract from the fellahs the secret that they had so faithfully kept until then. I had but one fact to proceed on: the leading merchants of antiquities were a certain Abd-er-Rassul Ahmed, of El-Sheikh Abd-el-Qurna, and a certain Mustapha Aga Ayad, vice-consul of England and Belgium at Luxor. To go after the latter was not easy: protected as he was by diplomatic immunity, he could not be prosecuted by the excavations administration. On April 4th I sent the chief of police at Luxor an order to arrest Abd-er-Rassul Ahmed, and I telegraphed to His Excellency Daud Pasha, Mudir [governor] of Qena, as well as to the Ministry of Public Works, asking to be authorized to conduct an immediate inquiry into his actions. Questioned on shipboard first by Monsieur Emile Brugsch and then by Monsieur de Rochemonteix, who was kind enough to put his experienced help at my disposal, he denied everything with which I charged him according to the almost unanimous testimony of European travelers—the discovery of the tomb, the sale of the papyri and the funerary statues, the breaking of the coffins. I accepted his proposal to have his house searched, less in the hope of finding anything compromising there than to give him an opportunity to think it over and come to terms with us. Gentleness, threats—nothing availed; and on April 6, the order to open the official investigation having arrived, I sent Abd-er-Rassul Ahmed and his brother Hussein Ahmed to Qena, where the Mudir was demanding their appearance for trial.

The investigation was energetically carried on but, on the whole, failed of its object. The interrogations and arguments, conducted by the magistrates of the mudiria [province] in the presence of our delegate, the official inspector of Dendera, Ali-Effendi Habib, resulted only in bringing out considerable testimony in favor of the accused. The notables and mayors of el-Qurna declared several times, on oath, that Abd-ed-Rassul Ahmed was the most loyal and disinterested man in that part of the country, that he had never excavated and would never excavate, that he was incapable of diverting the most insignificant antique, still less of violating a royal tomb. The only interesting detail revealed by the investigation was the insistence with which Abd-er-Rassul Ahmed asserted that he was the servant of Mustapha Aga, vice consul of England, and that he lived in the latter's house. He thought that by making himself out to belong to the vice consul's household, he gained the advantage of diplomatic privileges and could claim some sort of protection from Belgium or England. Mustapha Aga had encouraged him in this mistaken belief, together with all his associates; he had convinced them that by sheltering themselves behind him they would thenceforth be safe from the agents of the native administration; and it was only by this trick that he had succeeded in getting the entire trade in antiquities in the Theban plain into his own hands.

So Abd-er-Rassul Ahmed was given provisional freedom, on the recognizance of two of his friends, Ahmed Serur and Ismaïl Sayid Nagib, and went home with the certificate of spotless honor conferred on him by the leading men of el-Qurna. But his arrest, the two months he had spent in prison, and the vigor with which the inquiry had been conducted by His Excellency Daud Pasha, had clearly shown that Mustapha Aga was unable to protect even his most faithful agents; then too, it was known that I planned to return to Thebes during the winter and that I was determined to reopen the matter myself, while the mudiria would also begin further investigations. Some timid accusations reached the Museum, we learned a few more details from abroad, and, even better, disagreement arose among Abd-er-Rassul and his four brothers: some of them thought the danger had passed forever and that the Museum directorate had been defeated; others considered that the wisest course would be to come to terms with the directors and reveal the secret to them. After a month of discussions and quarreling, the eldest of the brothers, Mohammed Ahmed Abd-er-Rassul, suddenly decided to speak up. He went secretly to Qena and informed the Mudir that he knew the site that had been fruitlessly sought for a number of years; the tomb contained not merely two or three mummies but about forty, and most of the coffins were marked with a small snake, like the one displayed on the head-dresses of the pharaohs. His Excellency Daud Pasha immediately referred the information to the Ministry of the Interior, which transmitted the dispatch to His Highness the Khedive. His Highness, to whom I had spoken of the matter on my return from Upper Egypt, at once recognized the importance of this unexpected declaration and decided to send one of the Museum staff to Thebes. I had just returned to Europe, but I had left Monsieur Emile Brugsch, assistant curator, the necessary powers to act in my stead. As soon as the order arrived he set out for Thebes, on Saturday July 1st, accompanied by a friend on whom he could rely and by Ahmed Effendi Kamal, Secretary-Interpreter to the Museum. On reaching Qena, he found a surprise awaiting him: Daud Pasha had searched the premises of the Abd-er-Rassul brothers and had seized several precious objects, among them three papyri of Queen Maekere, Queen Isimkheb, and Princess Neskhonsu. It was a promising beginning. To ensure the success of the delicate undertaking that was about to begin, His Excellency put at our agents' disposition his *wekil* and several other employees of the mudiria, whose zeal and experience proved to be of great service.

On Wednesday the 6th, Messrs. Emile Brugsch and Ahmed Effendi Kamal were led by Mohammed Ahmed Abd-er-Rassul directly to the spot where the funeral vault opened. The Egyptian engineer who had excavated it long ago had laid his plans in the most skillful manner possible—never was hiding place more effectively concealed. The chain of hills that here separates the Biban el-Muluk from the Theban plain forms a series of natural basins between the Asasif and the Valley of Queens. Of these basins, the best known hitherto was the one in which stands the monument of Deir el Bahari. In the rock wall that divides Deir el Bahari from the following basin, directly behind the hill of El-Sheikh'Abd el-Qurna, and some 60 metres above the level of the cultivated ground, a vertical shaft was sunk 11½ metres deep by 2 metres wide. At the bottom, in its western wall, was cut the entrance to a corridor 1.4 metres wide by 80 centimetres high. After running for 7.4 metres, the corridor turns suddenly northward and continues for some 60 metres, but not remaining of the same dimensions throughout—in some places it reaches a width of 2 metres, at others it is only 1.3 metres wide. Toward the middle of it, five or six roughly hewn steps reveal a marked change in level, and, to the right, a sort of uncompleted niche shows that the architect had once considered changing the direction of the gallery yet again. It finally leads into a sort of irregular oblong chamber about 8 metres long.

The first thing Monsieur Emile Brugsch saw when he reached the bottom of the shaft was a white and yellow coffin bearing the name of Neskhonsu. It was in the corridor, some 60 centimetres from the entrance; a little farther on was a coffin whose shape suggested the style of the XVIIth Dynasty, then Queen Tiuhathor Henttaui, then Seti I [Sethos I]. Beside the coffins and scattered over the ground were boxes with funerary statuettes, canopic jars, libation vessels of bronze, and, farther on, in the angle formed by the corridor where it turns northward, the funeral tent of Queen Isimkheb, folded and crumpled, like something of no value that a priest in a hurry to get out had carelessly thrown into a corner. All along the main corridor were the same profusion of objects and the same disorder; he was forced to crawl, never knowing upon what hand or foot might be set. The coffins and mummies, fleetingly glimpsed by the light of a candle, bore historic names, Amenophis I, Thutmose II, in the niche near the stairway, Ahmose I and his son Siamun, Soqnunrî, Queen Ahhotpu, Ahmose Nefertari, and others. The confusion reached its height in the chamber at the end, but no more than a glance sufficed to reveal that the style of the XXth Dynasty was predominant. Mohammed Ahmed Abd-er-Rassul's report, which at first seemed exaggerated, was actually far short of the truth. Where I had expected to find one or two obscure kinglets, the Arabs had disinterred a whole vault of pharaohs. And what pharaohs! perhaps the most illustrious in the history of Egypt, Thutmose III and Scti I, Ahmose the Liberator and Ramses II the Conqueror. Monsieur Emile Brugsch, coming so suddenly into such an assemblage, thought that he must be the victim of a dream, and like him, I still wonder if I am not dreaming when I see and touch what were the bodies of so many famous personages of whom we never expected to know more than the names.

Two hours sufficed for this first examination, then the work of removal began. Three hundred Arabs were quickly got together by the Mudir's officials and set to work. The Museum's boat, hastily summoned, had not yet come; but one of the pilots was present, Rais Mohammed, a reliable man. He went to the bottom of the shaft and undertook to bring out its contents. Messrs. Emile Brugsch and Ahmed Effendi Kamal received the objects as they emerged from underground, transported them to the foot of the hill, and placed them side by side, never relaxing their vigilance for an instant. Forty-eight hours of energetic work were enough to bring up everything; but the task was only half finished. The convoy had to be conducted across the Theban plain and beyond the river to Luxor; several of the coffins, lifted only with the greatest effort by twelve or sixteen men, took seven or eight hours to travel from the mountain to the river bank, and it is easy to imagine what such a journey was like in the dust and heat of July.

Finally, on the evening of the 11th, mummies and coffins were all at Luxor, carefully wrapped in mats and cloth. Three days later the Museum's steamboat arrived; no sooner was the load aboard than it started back to Bulaq with its cargo of kings. Strangely enough, from Luxor to Qift, on both banks of the Nile fellah women with their hair down followed the boat howling, while the men fired shots as they do at funerals. Mohammed Abd-er-Rassul was rewarded with five hundred pounds sterling, and I thought it proper to appoint him *reïs* of the excavations at Thebes. If he serves the Museum with the same skill that he used so long to its detriment, we may hope for more fine discoveries. . . .

THEODORE DAVIS

The Parents of a Queen: the Tomb of Iuya and Tuyu

IUYA and Tuyu were the parents of Queen Tiye, wife of Amenophis III and mother of Akhenaten. Both were old people when they died.

IN the "Valley of the Kings," on the west side of the Nile at Thebes, there is a narrow lateral valley, nearly half a mile long, leading up to the mountain. At the mouth of this valley there is a foothill about

From Theodore Davis: *The Tomb of Iouiya and Touiyou*, London: Constable & Co. Ltd.; 1907, pp. xxv-xxx.

sixty feet high, in the side of which Ramses III commenced a tomb, and beyond which Ramses XII excavated his tomb. In the winters of 1902 and 1903 I undertook to clear and explore this valley, commencing just above the tomb of Ramses XII, and continuing my work until I reached the mountain. It resulted in the discovery of the tombs of Thoutmôsis IV [Thutmose IV] and of Queen Hâtshopsitû [Hatshepsut].

On the 20th of December, 1904, I resumed my explorations in the lower end of the lateral valley, which I was enabled to do owing to the kindness of Mr. J. E. Quibell, the Chief Inspector at Thebes, who, with the approval of Monsieur Maspero, Director-General of the Cairo Museum, undertook the employment and superintendence of my workmen, pending my arrival in the valley.

On my arrival in January, 1905, I found that the work on the location selected had yielded nothing and gave no promise. Consequently I abandoned the site, and transferred my workmen to the unexplored space between the tombs of Ramses III and Ramses XII, heretofore described.

The site was most unpromising, lying as it did between the Ramses tombs, which had required many men for many years; therefore it did not seem possible that a tomb could have existed in so narrow a space without being discovered. As an original proposition I would not have explored it, and certainly no Egyptologist, exploring with another person's money, would have thought of risking the time and expense. But I knew every yard of the lateral valley, except the space described, and I decided that good exploration justified its investigation, and that it would be a satisfaction to know the entire valley, even if it yielded nothing.

From the 25th of January, 1905, until the 5th of February, the work progressed without sign of promise. My daily visits were most discouraging, but on my arrival at the work on the 6th February, I was greeted by my *reïs* (Captain) and workmen with great acclamation. I quickly made my way to the spot, where I saw a few inches of the top of a well-cut stone step, which promised steps below and the possible existence of a tomb.

From the 6th of February until the 11th my workmen were hard at work removing the overhanging *débris* which concealed the door; but before the night of the 11th a small portion of the doorway was exposed, and from that moment the opening was guarded day and night by policemen and valley guards. At the close of the twelfth day the door was entirely cleared—a most satisfactory sight! It was cut in the solid rock, and was 4.02 metres high and 1.35 wide, with a decorated lintel. The doorway was closed within eighteen inches of the top with flat stones, about twelve inches by four, laid in Nile mud plaster. This opening clearly indicated that, at some early

date, the tomb had been entered and probably robbed—a most unwelcome indication! Although it was nearly dark, I concluded to
have a look through the opening. Mr. Arthur Weigall, the appointed
but not formally confirmed Chief Inspector in succession to Mr.
Quibell, had ridden out to the valley with me, and was invited to
join me in the first sight of the corridor of the tomb. The opening
was chin high, but we could dimly see a few yards of the corridor,
which seemed to be about five feet wide and high, with a steep decline. As soon as my eyes became used to the semi-darkness, I saw
what I thought to be a cane, or small club, lying on the floor a few
feet from the doorway. Neither of us could get up to the opening, nor
through it, without a ladder—which did not exist in the valley—
so I selected a small native boy and had him lifted up to the opening, through which he entered. We watched the boy closely and
saw him pick up the cane; then he came towards us, picked up two
other objects and passed them to me. They proved to be a wooden
staff of office, a neck yoke, and a large stone scarab, covered more
or less with gold-foil, which made it seem, at first glance, to be solid
gold.

Happily, Monsieur Maspero was on his dahabeah at Luxor, and,
as soon as I reached mine, I wrote him a note asking him to come
over and see something worth looking at. Shortly thereafter he
came, followed by Professor Sayce, and we not only enjoyed the
discoveries of the day, but were even more interested in the ownership of the tomb, as to which we had not the slightest clue. Monsieur Maspero requested me to open and enter the tomb next day,
that he might show it to H. R. H. the Duke of Connaught and party,
who were expected to arrive on the following afternoon.

Consequently, next morning, Monsieur Maspero and Mr. Weigall
joined me at the tomb, and I at once set the men to work taking
down the wall which barred the outer door. It was very slow work,
as every stone had to be examined for hieroglyphs and signs, and
every basket of sand and *débris* sifted and examined for objects of
interest which might be concealed in the deposit. However, nothing
was found, and, in the course of an hour or so, the doorway was
cleared.

The electric wire had been installed at the outer doorway, but as
the introduction down the corridor would have required the services
of electricians, we concluded that it would be safer to use candles
for our entry and examinations. Monsieur Maspero and I and, at
my invitation, Mr. Weigall, each with a candle, started down the
corridor, which proved to be 1.75 metres wide and 2.05 metres
high, cut out of the solid rock and descending so sharply as to require care not to fall. It was neither painted nor inscribed. After
descending about twenty feet, we found a shelf cut into one side

of the wall and on it a large ceremonial wig made of flax and dyed black, also an armful of dried flowers which doubtless were offerings to the dead (as is done in our day and generation). Passing on some 9 metres, we came to another flight of stone steps descending almost perpendicularly, at the bottom of which we found a doorway 2.10 metres high and 1.20 metres wide, closed with stones set in Nile mud plaster, with an opening at the top of about the same size as was found in the first doorway, confirming our fears of a robbery. The face of the wall was plastered with mud and stamped from top to bottom with seals.

On either side of this doorway, carefully placed to escape injury, stood a reddish pottery bowl about twelve inches wide, showing the finger-marks of the man who with his hands gathered the mud and plastered it on the doorway wall. In each bowl was a wide wooden stick, evidently used to scrape the mud from his hands. Having copied the seals, we investigated the possibility of entry without taking down the wall. We found that the opening which the robber had made was too high and too small to allow of Monsieur Maspero getting through without injury. Though we had nothing but our bare hands, we managed to take down the upper layer of stones, and then Monsieur Maspero and I put our heads and candles into the chamber, which enabled us to get a glimpse of shining gold covering some kind of furniture, though we could not identify it. This stimulated us to make the entry without further enlarging the opening. I managed to get over the wall and found myself in the sepulchral chamber. With considerable difficulty we helped Monsieur Maspero safely to scale the obstruction, and then Mr. Weigall made his entry. The chamber was as dark as dark could be and extremely hot. Our first quest was the name of the owner of the tomb, as to which we had not the slightest knowledge or suspicion. We held up our candles, but they gave so little light and so dazzled our eyes that we could see nothing except the glitter of gold. In a moment or two, however, I made out a very large wooden coffin, known as a funeral sled, which was used to contain all the coffins of the dead person and his mummy and to convey them to his tomb. It was about six feet high and eight feet long, made of wood covered with bitumen, which was as bright as the day it was put on. Around the upper part of the coffin was a stripe of gold-foil, about six inches wide, covered with hieroglyphs. On calling Monsieur Maspero's attention to it, he immediately handed me his candle, which, together with my own, I held before my eyes, close to the inscriptions so that he could read them. In an instant he said, "Iouiya." Naturally excited by the announcement, and blinded by the glare of the candles, I involuntarily advanced them very near the coffin; whereupon Monsieur Maspero cried out,

"Be careful!" and pulled my hands back. In a moment we realized that, had my candles touched the bitumen, which I came dangerously near doing, the coffin would have been in a blaze. As the entire contents of the tomb were inflammable, and directly opposite the coffin was a corridor leading to the open air and making a draught, we undoubtedly should have lost our lives, as the only escape was by the corridor, which would have necessitated climbing over the stone wall barring the doorway. This would have retarded our exit for at least ten minutes.

As soon as we realized the danger we had escaped, we made our way out of the chamber and, seating ourselves in the corridor, sent for workmen, who took down the door blocking the doorway. Then the electricians brought down the wires with bulbs attached, and we made our second entry into the chamber, each of us furnished with electric lights which we held over our heads, and we saw that every foot of the chamber was filled with objects brilliant with gold. In a corner stood a chariot, the pole of which had been broken by the weight of a coffin lid that the robber had evidently deposited upon it. Within a foot or two of the chariot stood two alabaster vases of great beauty and in perfect condition.

From the neck of one of the vases hung shreds of mummy-cloth which had originally covered the mouth of the vase. Evidently the robber, expecting the contents to be valuable, tore off the cloth. Three thousand years thereafter I looked into the vase with like expectation; both of us were disappointed, for it contained only a liquid which was first thought to be honey, but which subsequently proved to be natron.

The mummies of Iouiya and Touiyou were lying in their coffins. Originally each mummy was enclosed in three coffins; the inner one holding the body. Evidently the robber had taken the inner coffins out and then had taken off their lids, though he did not take the bodies out of their coffins, but contented himself with stripping off the mummy-cloth in which they were wrapped. The stripping was done by scratching off the cloth with his nails, seeking only the gold ornaments or jewels. At least that seems to have been the manner of robbing the bodies, as we found in both coffins, on either side of the bodies, great quantities of mummy-cloth torn into small bits. Among the shreds were found numerous valuable religious symbols, several scarabs, and various objects of interest and beauty. In lifting the body of Iouiya from his coffin, we found a necklace of large beads made of gold and of lapis lazuli, strung on a strong thread, which the robber had evidently broken when scratching off the mummy-cloth, causing the beads to fall behind the mummy's neck.

The robber had also overlooked a gold plate about the size of the palm of a man's hand, which had been inserted by the embalmer to conceal the incision he had made in extracting the dead man's heart for special mummification.

When I first saw the mummy of Touiyou she was lying in her coffin, covered from her chin to her feet with very fine mummy-cloth arranged with care. Why this was done no one can positively state, but I am disposed to think that the robber was impressed by the dignity of the dead woman whose body he had desecrated. I had occasion to sit by her in the tomb for nearly an hour, and having nothing else to do or see, I studied her face and indulged in

speculations germane to the situation, until her dignity and character so impressed me that I almost found it necessary to apologize for my presence.

From all the evidence furnished by the acts of the robber, it seems reasonable to conclude that the entry into the tomb was made within the lifetime of some person who had exact knowledge of its location. Evidently the robber had tunneled through the overlying *débris* which concealed the door of the tomb; otherwise he would have been compelled to remove a mass of rock and soil which would have required many days, and would also have exposed the robbery to the first passer-by. When the robber found the outer doorway barred by a wall, he took off enough of it to enable him to crawl through; and when he reached the second and last door-way, he found a corresponding wall, which he treated in the same manner. He seems to have had either a very dim light or none at all, for when he was in the burial chamber he selected a large stone scarab, the neck-yoke of the chariot, and a wooden staff of office, all of which were covered with thick gold foil, which evi-dently he thought to be solid gold: he carried them up the corri-dor until he came to a gleam of daylight, when he discovered his error and left them on the floor of the corridor, where I found them.

When the robber got out of the tomb, he carefully concealed the doorway and his tunnel with stones and *débris*, and did it so effec-tively, that it was not disturbed until its discovery three thousand years later.

HOWARD CARTER AND A. C. MACE

The Tomb of Tutankhamen: the Opening of the Tomb

TUTANKHAMEN ruled from 1347 until 1339 B.C. He was only about eighteen at the time of his death, and therefore a mere child when he came to the throne. He seems to have been hurried back to Thebes after the final overthrow of Akhenaten's regime at el Amarna. Some people have thought that he was Akhenaten's son

From Howard Carter and A. C. Mace: *The Tomb of Tutankhamen*. London: Cas-sell and Company Ltd.; 1923, Vol. I, pp. 86-99, 178-88. By permission of Cassell and Company Ltd.

by some woman other than Nefertiti, some have suggested he was his brother—a late child of Amenophis III. There is in fact no clear evidence for Tutankhamen's parentage, and he may well have owed the throne to his (undoubted) marriage to a daughter of Akhenaten and Nefertiti. After his long search for the tomb, Howard Carter came upon it late in 1922.

❦

THIS was to be our final season in The Valley. Six full seasons we had excavated there, and season after season had drawn a blank; we had worked for months at a stretch and found nothing, and only an excavator knows how desperately depressing that can be; we had almost made up our minds that we were beaten, and were preparing to leave The Valley and try our luck elsewhere; and then —hardly had we set hoe to ground in our last despairing effort than we made a discovery that far exceeded our wildest dreams. Surely, never before in the whole history of excavation has a full digging season been compressed within the space of five days.

Let me try and tell the story of it all. It will not be easy, for the dramatic suddenness of the initial discovery left me in a dazed condition, and the months that have followed have been so crowded with incident that I have hardly had time to think. Setting it down on paper will perhaps give me a chance to realize what has happened and all that it means.

I arrived in Luxor on October 28th, and by November 1st I had enrolled my workmen and was ready to begin. Our former excavations had stopped short at the north-east corner of the tomb of Ramses VI, and from this point I started trenching southwards. It will be remembered that in this area there were a number of roughly constructed workmen's huts, used probably by the labourers in the tomb of Ramses. These huts, built about three feet above bed-rock, covered the whole area in front of the Ramesside tomb, and continued in a southerly direction to join up with a similar group of huts on the opposite side of The Valley, discovered by Davis in connexion with his work on the Akhenaten cache. By the evening of November 3rd we had laid bare a sufficient number of these huts for experimental purposes, so, after we had planned and noted them, they were removed, and we were ready to clear away the three feet of soil that lay beneath them.

Hardly had I arrived on the work next morning (November 4th) than the unusual silence, due to the stoppage of the work, made me realize that something out of the ordinary had happened, and I was greeted by the announcement that a step cut in the rock had been discovered underneath the very first hut to be attacked. This seemed too good to be true, but a short amount of extra clearing revealed the fact that we were actually in the entrance of a steep cut in the rock, some thirteen feet below the entrance to the tomb of Ramses VI, and a similar depth from the present bed level of The Valley. The manner of cutting was that of the sunken stairway entrance so common in The Valley, and I almost dared to hope that we had found our tomb at last. Work continued feverishly throughout the whole of that day and the morning of the next, but it was not until the afternoon of November 5th that we succeeded in clearing away the masses of rubbish that overlay the cut, and were able to demarcate the upper edges of the stairway on all its four sides.

It was clear by now beyond any question that we actually had before us the entrance to a tomb, but doubts, born of previous disappointments, persisted in creeping in. There was always the horrible possibility, suggested by our experience in the Thothmes III valley, that the tomb was an unfinished one, never completed and never used: if it had been finished there was the depressing probability that it had been completely plundered in ancient times. On the other hand, there was just the chance of an untouched or only partially plundered tomb, and it was with ill-suppressed excitement that I watched the descending steps of the staircase, as one by one they came to light. The cutting was excavated in the side of a small hillock, and, as the work progressed, its western edge receded under the slope of the rock until it was, first partially, and then completely, roofed in, and became a passage, 10 feet high by 6 feet wide. Work progressed more rapidly now; step succeeded step, and at the level of the twelfth, towards sunset, there was disclosed the upper part of a doorway, blocked, plastered, and sealed.

A sealed doorway—it was actually true, then! Our years of patient labour were to be rewarded after all, and I think my first feeling was one of congratulation that my faith in The Valley had not been unjustified. With excitement growing to fever heat I searched the seal impressions on the door for evidence of the identity of the owner, but could find no name: the only decipherable ones were those of the well-known royal necropolis seal, the jackal and nine captives. Two facts, however, were clear: first, the employment of this royal seal was certain evidence that the tomb had been constructed for a person of very high standing; and second, that the sealed door was entirely screened from above by workmen's huts of the Twentieth Dynasty was sufficiently clear proof that at least from that date it had never been entered. With that for the moment I had to be content.

While examining the seals I noticed, at the top of the doorway, where some of the plaster had fallen away, a heavy wooden lintel. Under this, to assure myself of the method by which the doorway had been blocked, I made a small peephole, just large enough to insert an electric torch, and discovered that the passage beyond the door was filled completely from floor to ceiling with stones and rubble—additional proof this of the care with which the tomb had been protected.

It was a thrilling moment for an excavator. Alone, save for my native workmen, I found myself, after years of comparatively unproductive labour, on the threshold of what might prove to be a magnificent discovery. Anything, literally anything, might lie beyond that passage, and it needed all my self-control to keep from breaking down the doorway, and investigating then and there.

One thing puzzled me, and that was the smallness of the opening in comparison with the ordinary Valley tombs. The design was certainly of the Eighteenth Dynasty. Could it be the tomb of a noble buried here by royal consent? Was it a royal cache, a hiding-place to which a mummy and its equipment had been removed for safety? Or was it actually the tomb of the king for whom I had spent so many years in search?

Once more I examined the seal impressions for a clue, but on the part of the door so far laid bare only those of the royal necropolis seal already mentioned were clear enough to read. Had I but known that a few inches lower down there was a perfectly clear and distinct impression of the seal of Tutankhamen, the king I most desired to find, I would have cleared on, had a much better night's rest in consequence, and saved myself nearly three weeks of uncertainty. It was late, however, and darkness was already upon us. With some reluctance I re-closed the small hole that I had made, filled in our excavation for protection during the night, selected the most trustworthy of my workmen—themselves almost as excited as I was—to watch all night above the tomb, and so home by moonlight, riding down The Valley.

Naturally my wish was to go straight ahead with our clearing to find out the full extent of the discovery, but Lord Carnarvon was in England, and in fairness to him I had to delay matters until he could come. Accordingly, on the morning of November 6th I sent him the following cable:—"At last have made wonderful discovery in Valley; a magnificent tomb with seals intact; re-covered same for your arrival; congratulations."

My next task was to secure the doorway against interference until such time as it could finally be re-opened. This we did by filling our excavation up again to surface level, and rolling on top of it the large flint boulders of which the workmen's huts had been composed. By the evening of the same day, exactly forty-eight hours after we had discovered the first step of the staircase, this was accomplished. The tomb had vanished. So far as the appearance of the ground was concerned there never had been any tomb, and I found it hard to persuade myself at times that the whole episode had not been a dream.

I was soon to be reassured on this point. News travels fast in Egypt, and within two days of the discovery congratulations, inquiries, and offers of help descended upon me in a steady stream from all directions. It became clear, even at this early stage, that I was in for a job that could not be tackled single-handed, so I wired to Callender, who had helped me on various previous occasions, asking him if possible to join me without delay, and to my relief he arrived on the very next day. On the 8th I had received two messages from Lord Carnarvon in answer to my cable, the first of which read, "Possibly come soon," and the second, received a little later, "Propose arrive Alexandria 20th."

We had thus nearly a fortnight's grace, and we devoted it to making preparations of various kinds, so that when the time of re-opening came, we should be able, with the least possible delay, to handle any situation that might arise. On the night of the 18th I went to Cairo for three days, to meet Lord Carnarvon and make a number of necessary purchases, returning to Luxor on the 21st. On the 23rd Lord Carnarvon arrived in Luxor with his daughter, Lady Evelyn Herbert, his devoted companion in all his Egyptian work, and everything was in hand for the beginning of the second chapter of the discovery of the tomb. Callender had been busy all day clearing away the upper layer of rubbish, so that by morning we should be able to get into the staircase without any delay.

By the afternoon of the 24th the whole staircase was clear, sixteen steps in all, and we were able to make a proper examination of the sealed doorway. On the lower part the seal impressions were much clearer, and we were able without any difficulty to make out on several of them the name of Tutankhamen. This added enormously to the interest of the discovery. If we had found, as seemed almost certain, the tomb of that shadowy monarch, whose tenure of the throne coincided with one of the most interesting periods in the whole of Egyptian history, we should indeed have reason to congratulate ourselves.

With heightened interest, if that were possible, we renewed our investigation of the doorway. Here for the first time a disquieting element made its appearance. Now that the whole door was exposed to light it was possible to discern a fact that had hitherto escaped notice—that there had been two successive openings and re-closings of a part of its surface: furthermore, that the sealing originally discovered, the jackal and nine captives, had been applied to the re-closed portions, whereas the sealings of Tutankhamen covered the untouched part of the doorway, and were therefore those with which the tomb had been originally secured. The tomb then was not absolutely intact, as we had hoped. Plunderers had entered it, and entered it more than once—from the evidence of the huts above, plunderers of a date not later than the reign of Ramses VI— but that they had not rifled it completely was evident from the fact that it had been re-sealed.

Then came another puzzle. In the lower strata of rubbish that filled the staircase we found masses of broken potsherds and boxes, the latter bearing the names of AkhenAten, SmenkhkaRe and Tutankhamen, and, what was much more upsetting, a scarab of Thothmes III [Thutmose III] and a fragment with the name of Amenhotep III. Why this mixture of names? The balance of evidence so far would seem to indicate a cache rather than a tomb, and at this stage in the proceedings we inclined more and more to the opinion that we were about to find a miscellaneous collection of objects of the Eighteenth Dynasty kings, brought from Tell el Amarna by Tutankhamen and deposited here for safety.

So matters stood on the evening of the 24th. On the following day the sealed doorway was to be removed, so Callender set carpenters to work making a heavy wooden grille to be set up in its place. Mr. Engelbach, Chief Inspector of the Antiquities Department, paid us a visit during the afternoon, and witnessed part of the final clearing of rubbish from the doorway.

On the morning of the 25th the seal impressions on the doorway were carefully noted and photographed, and then we removed the actual blocking of the door, consisting of rough stones carefully built from floor to lintel, and heavily plastered on their outer faces to take the seal impressions.

This disclosed the beginning of a descending passage (not a staircase), the same width as the entrance stairway, and nearly seven feet high. As I had already discovered from my hole in the doorway, it was filled completely with stone and rubble, probably the chip from its own excavation. This filling, like the doorway, showed distinct signs of more than one opening and re-closing of the tomb, the untouched part consisting of clean white chip, mingled with dust, whereas the disturbed part was composed mainly of dark flint. It was clear that an irregular tunnel had been cut through the original filling at the upper corner on the left side, a tunnel corresponding in position with that of the hole in the doorway.

As we cleared the passage we found, mixed with the rubble of the lower levels, broken potsherds, jar sealings, alabaster jars, whole and broken, vases of painted pottery, numerous fragments of smaller articles, and water skins, these last having obviously been used to bring up the water needed for the plastering of the doorways. These were clear evidence of plundering, and we eyed them a-skance. By night we had cleared a considerable distance down the passage, but as yet saw no sign of second doorway or of chamber.

The day following (November 26th) was the day of days, the most wonderful that I have ever lived through, and certainly one whose like I can never hope to see again. Throughout the morning the work of clearing continued, slowly perforce, on account of the delicate objects that were mixed with the filling. Then, in the middle of the afternoon, thirty feet down from the outer door, we came upon a second sealed doorway, almost an exact replica of the first. The seal impressions in this case were less distinct, but still recognizable as those of Tutankhamen and of the royal necrop-olis. Here again the signs of opening and re-closing were clearly marked upon the plaster. We were firmly convinced by this time that it was a cache that we were about to open, and not a tomb. The arrangement of stairway, entrance passage and doors reminded us very forcibly of the cache of Akhenaten and Tiy material found in the very near vicinity of the present excavation by Davis, and the fact that Tutankhamen's seals occurred there likewise seemed al-most certain proof that we were right in our conjecture. We were soon to know. There lay the sealed doorway, and behind it was the answer to the question.

Slowly, desperately slowly it seemed to us as we watched, the remains of passage debris that encumbered the lower part of the doorway were removed, until at last we had the whole door clear before us. The decisive moment had arrived. With trembling hands I made a tiny breach in the upper left hand corner. Darkness and blank space, as far as an iron testing-rod could reach, showed that whatever lay beyond was empty, and not filled like the passage we had just cleared. Candle tests were applied as a precaution against possible foul gases, and then, widening the hole a little, I inserted the candle and peered in, Lord Carnarvon, Lady Evelyn and Callen-der standing anxiously beside me to hear the verdict. At first I could see nothing, the hot air escaping from the chamber causing the candle flame to flicker, but presently, as my eyes grew accustomed to the light, details of the room within emerged slowly from the mist, strange animals, statues, and gold—everywhere the glint of gold. For the moment—an eternity it must have seemed to the others standing by—I was struck dumb with amazement, and when Lord Carnarvon, unable to stand the suspense any longer, inquired anxiously, "Can you see anything?" it was all I could do to get out the words, "Yes, wonderful things." Then widening the hole a little further, so that we both could see, we inserted an electric torch.

I suppose most excavators would confess to a feeling of awe—embarrassment almost—when they break into a chamber closed and sealed by pious hands so many centuries ago. For the moment, time as a factor in human life has lost its meaning. Three thousand, four thousand years maybe, have passed and gone since human feet last trod the floor on which you stand, and yet, as you note the signs of recent life around you—the half-filled bowl of mortar for the door, the blackened lamp, the finger-mark upon the freshly painted surface, the farewell garland dropped upon the threshold—you feel it might have been but yesterday. The very air you breathe, unchanged throughout the centuries, you share with those who laid the mummy to its rest. Time is annihilated by little intimate details such as these, and you feel an intruder.

That is perhaps the first and dominant sensation, but others follow thick and fast—the exhilaration of discovery, the fever of suspense, the almost overmastering impulse, born of curiosity, to break down seals and lift the lids of boxes, the thought—pure joy to the investigator—that you are about to add a page to history, or solve some problem of research, the strained expectancy—why not confess it?—of the treasure-seeker. Did these thoughts actually pass through our minds at the time, or have I imagined them since? I cannot tell. It was the discovery that my memory was blank, and not the mere desire for dramatic chapter-ending, that occasioned this digression.

Surely never before in the whole history of excavation had such an amazing sight been seen as the light of our torch revealed to us. . . . imagine how [it] appeared to us as we looked down from our spy-hole in the blocked doorway, casting the beam of light from our torch—the first light that had pierced the darkness of the chamber for three thousand years—from one group of objects to another, in a vain attempt to interpret the treasure that lay before us. The effect was bewildering, overwhelming. I suppose we had never formulated exactly in our minds just what we had expected or hoped to see, but certainly we had never dreamed of anything like this, a roomful—a whole museumful it seemed—of objects, some familiar, but some the like of which we had never seen, piled one upon another in seemingly endless profusion.

Gradually the scene grew clearer, and we could pick out individual objects. First, right opposite to us—we had been conscious of them all the while, but refused to believe in them—were three great gilt couches, their sides carved in the form of monstrous animals, curiously attenuated in body, as they had to be to serve their purpose, but with heads of startling realism. Uncanny beasts enough to look upon at any time: seen as we saw them, their brilliant gilded surfaces picked out of the darkness by our electric torch, as though by limelight, their heads throwing grotesque distorted shadows on the wall behind them, they were almost terrifying. Next, on the right, two statues caught and held our attention; two life-sized figures of a king in black, facing each other like sentinels, gold kilted, gold sandalled, armed with mace and staff, the protective sacred cobra upon their foreheads.

These were the dominant objects that caught the eye at first. Between them, around them, piled on top of them, there were countless others—exquisitely painted and inlaid caskets; alabaster vases, some beautifully carved in openwork designs; strange black shrines, from the open door of one a great gilt snake peeping out; bouquets of flowers or leaves; beds; chairs beautifully carved; a golden inlaid throne; a heap of curious white oviform boxes; staves of all shapes and designs; beneath our eyes, on the very threshold of the chamber, a beautiful lotiform cup of translucent alabaster; on the left a confused pile of overturned chariots, glistening with gold and inlay; and peeping from behind them, another portrait of a king.

By the middle of February our work in the antechamber was finished. With the exception of the two sentinel statues, left for a special reason, all its contents had been removed to the laboratory, every inch of its floor had been swept and sifted for the last bead or fallen piece of inlay, and it now stood bare and empty. We were ready at last to penetrate the mystery of the sealed door.

Friday, the 17th, was the day appointed, and at two o'clock those who were to be privileged to witness the ceremony met by appointment above the tomb. They included Lord Carnarvon, Lady Evelyn Herbert, H. E. Abd el Halim Pasha Suleman, Minister of Public Works, M. Lacau, Director-General of the Service of Antiquities, Sir William Garstin, Sir Charles Cust, Mr. Lythgoe, Curator of the Egyptian Department of the Metropolitan Museum, New York, Professor Breasted, Dr. Alan Gardiner, Mr. Winlock, the Hon. Mervyn Herbert, the Hon. Richard Bethell, Mr. Engelbach, Chief Inspector of the Department of Antiquities, three Egyptian inspectors of the Department of Antiquities, the representative of the Government Press Bureau, and the members of the staff—about twenty persons in all. By a quarter past two the whole company had assembled, so we removed our coats and filed down the sloping passage into the tomb.

In the antechamber everything was prepared and ready, and to those who had not visited it since the original opening of the tomb it must have presented a strange sight. We had screened the statues with boarding to protect them from possible damage, and between them we had erected a small platform, just high enough to enable us to reach the upper part of the doorway, having determined, as the safest plan, to work from the top downwards. A short distance back from the platform there was a barrier, and beyond, knowing that there might be hours of work ahead of us, we had provided chairs for the visitors. On either side standards had been set up for our lamps, their light shining full upon the doorway. Looking back, we realize what a strange, incongruous picture the chamber must have presented, but at the time I question whether such an idea even crossed our minds. One thought and one only was possible. There before us lay the sealed door, and with its opening we were to blot out the centuries and stand in the presence of a king who reigned three thousand years ago. My own feelings as I mounted the platform were a strange mixture, and it was with a trembling hand that I struck the first blow.

My first care was to locate the wooden lintel above the door: then very carefully I chipped away the plaster and picked out the small stones which formed the uppermost layer of the filling. The temptation to stop and peer inside at every moment was irresistible, and when, after about ten minutes' work, I had made a hole large enough to enable me to do so, I inserted an electric torch. An astonishing sight its light revealed, for there, within a yard of the doorway, stretching as far as one could see and blocking the entrance to the chamber, stood what to all appearance was a solid wall of gold. For the moment there was no clue as to its meaning, so as quickly as I dared I set to work to widen the hole. This had now become an operation of considerable difficulty, for the stones of the masonry were not accurately squared blocks built regularly upon one another, but rough slabs of varying size, some so heavy that it took all one's strength to lift them: many of them, too, as the weight above was removed, were left so precariously balanced that the least false movement would have sent them sliding inwards to crash upon the contents of the chamber below. We were also endeavouring to preserve the seal-impressions upon the thick mortar of the outer face, and this added considerably to the difficulty of handling the stones. Mace and Callender were helping me by this time and each stone was cleared on a regular system. With a crowbar I gently eased it up, Mace holding it to prevent it falling forwards; then he and I lifted it out and passed it back to Callender, who transferred it on to one of the foremen, and so, by a chain of workmen, up the passage and out of the tomb altogether.

With the removal of a very few stones the mystery of the golden wall was solved. We were at the entrance of the actual burial-chamber of the king, and that which barred our way was the side of an immense gilt shrine built to cover and protect the sarcophagus.

It was visible now from the Antechamber by the light of the standard lamps, and as stone after stone was removed, and its gilded
surface came gradually into view, we could, as though by electric
current, feel the tingle of excitement which thrilled the spectators
behind the barrier. We who were doing the work were probably less
excited, for our whole energies were taken up with the task in hand
—that of removing the blocking without an accident. The fall of
a single stone might have done irreparable damage to the delicate
surface of the shrine, so, directly the hole was large enough, we
made an additional protection for it by inserting a mattress on the
inner side of the door-blocking, suspending it from the wooden lintel
of the doorway. Two hours of hard work it took us to clear away
the blocking, or at least as much of it as was necessary for the
moment; and at one point, when near the bottom, we had to delay
operations for a space while we collected the scattered beads from
a necklace brought by the plunderers from the chamber within and
dropped upon the threshold. This last was a terrible trial to our
patience, for it was a slow business, and we were all of us excited to
see what might be within; but finally it was done, the last stones
were removed, and the way to the innermost chamber lay open
before us.

In clearing away the blocking of the doorway we had discovered
that the level of the inner chamber was about four feet lower than
that of the Antechamber, and this, combined with the fact that
there was but a narrow space between the door and shrine, made
an entrance by no means easy to effect. Fortunately, there were
no smaller antiquities at this end of the chamber, so I lowered
myself down, and then, taking one of the portable lights, I edged
cautiously to the corner of the shrine and looked beyond it. At the
corner two beautiful alabaster vases blocked the way, but I could
see that if these were removed we should have a clear path to the
other end of the chamber; so, carefully marking the spot on which
they stood, I picked them up—with the exception of the king's
wishing-cup they were of finer quality and more graceful shape
than any we had yet found—and passed them back to the Antechamber. Lord Carnarvon and M. Lacau now joined me, and, picking our way along the narrow passage between shrine and wall,
paying out the wire of our light behind us, we investigated further.

It was, beyond any question, the sepulchral chamber in which
we stood, for there, towering above us, was one of the great gilt
shrines beneath which kings were laid. So enormous was this
structure (17 feet by 11 feet, and 9 feet high, we found afterwards)
that it filled within a little the entire area of the chamber, a space
of some two feet only separating it from the walls on all four sides,
while its roof, with cornice top and torus moulding, reached almost

to the ceiling. From top to bottom it was overlaid with gold, and upon its sides there were inlaid panels of brilliant blue faience, in which were represented, repeated over and over, the magic symbols which would ensure its strength and safety. Around the shrine, resting upon the ground, there were a number of funerary emblems, and, at the north end, the seven magic oars the king would need to ferry himself across the waters of the underworld. The walls of the chamber, unlike those of the Antechamber, were decorated with brightly painted scenes and inscriptions, brilliant in their colours, but evidently somewhat hastily executed.

These last details we must have noticed subsequently, for at the time our one thought was of the shrine and of its safety. Had the thieves penetrated within it and disturbed the royal burial? Here, on the eastern end, were the great folding doors, closed and bolted, but not sealed, that would answer the question for us. Eagerly we drew the bolts, swung back the doors, and there within was a second shrine with similar bolted doors, and upon the bolts a seal, intact. This seal we determined not to break, for our doubts were resolved, and we could not penetrate further without risk of serious damage to the monument. I think at the moment we did not even want to break the seal, for a feeling of intrusion had descended heavily upon us with the opening of the doors, heightened, probably, by the almost painful impressiveness of a linen pall, decorated with golden rosettes, which drooped above the inner shrine. We felt that we were in the presence of the dead King and must do him reverence, and in imagination could see the doors of the successive shrines open one after the other till the innermost disclosed the King himself. Carefully, and as silently as possible, we re-closed the great swing doors, and passed on to the farther end of the chamber.

Here a surprise awaited us, for a low door, eastwards from the sepulchral chamber, gave entrance to yet another chamber, smaller than the outer ones and not so lofty. This doorway, unlike the others, had not been closed and sealed. We were able, from where we stood, to get a clear view of the whole of the contents, and a single glance sufficed to tell us that here, within this little chamber, lay the greatest treasures of the tomb. Facing the doorway, on the farther side, stood the most beautiful monument that I have ever seen—so lovely that it made one gasp with wonder and admiration. The central portion of it consisted of a large shrine-shaped chest, completely overlaid with gold, and surmounted by a cornice of sacred cobras. Surrounding this, free-standing, were statues of the four tutelary goddesses of the dead—gracious figures with outstretched protective arms, so natural and lifelike in their pose, so pitiful and compassionate the expression upon their faces, that one felt it almost sacrilege to look at them. One guarded the shrine on each of its four sides, but whereas the figures at front and back kept their gaze firmly fixed upon their charge, an additional note of touching realism was imparted by the other two, for their heads were turned sideways, looking over their shoulders towards the entrance, as though to watch against surprise. There is a simple grandeur about this monument that made an irresistible appeal to the imagination, and I am not ashamed to confess that it brought a lump to my throat. It is undoubtedly the canopic chest and contains the jars which play such an important part in the ritual of mummification.

There were a number of other wonderful things in the chamber, but we found it hard to take them in at the time, so inevitably were one's eyes drawn back again and again to the lovely little goddess figures. Immediately in front of the entrance lay the figure of the jackal god Anubis, upon his shrine, swathed in linen cloth, and resting upon a portable sled, and behind this the head of a bull upon a stand—emblems, these, of the underworld. In the south side of the chamber lay an endless number of black shrines and chests, all closed and sealed save one, whose open doors revealed statues of Tutankhamen standing upon black leopards. On the farther wall were more shrine-shaped boxes and miniature coffins of gilded wood, these last undoubtedly containing funerary statuettes of the king. In the centre of the room, left of the Anubis and the bull, there was a row of magnificent caskets of ivory and wood, decorated and inlaid with gold and blue faience, one, whose lid we raised, containing a gorgeous ostrich-feather fan with ivory handle, fresh and strong to all appearance as when it left the maker's hand. There were also, distributed in different quarters of the chamber, a number of model boats with sails and rigging all complete, and, at the north side, yet another chariot.

Such, from a hurried survey, were the contents of this innermost chamber. We looked anxiously for evidence of plundering, but on the surface there was none. Unquestionably the thieves must have entered, but they cannot have done more than open two or three of the caskets. Most of the boxes, as has been said, have still their seals intact, and the whole contents of the chamber, in fortunate contrast to those of the Antechamber and the Annex, still remain in position exactly as they were placed at the time of burial.

How much time we occupied in this first survey of the wonders of the tomb I cannot say, but it must have seemed endless to those anxiously waiting in the Antechamber. Not more than three at a time could be admitted with safety, so, when Lord Carnarvon and M. Lacau came out, the others came in pairs: first Lady Evelyn Herbert, the only woman present, with Sir William Garstin, and

then the rest in turn. It was curious, as we stood in the Antechamber, to watch their faces as, one by one, they emerged from the
door. Each had a dazed, bewildered look in his eyes, and each in
turn, as he came out, threw up his hands before him, an unconscious
gesture of impotence to describe in words the wonders that he had
seen. They were indeed indescribable, and the emotions they had
aroused in our minds were of too intimate a nature to communicate,
even though we had the words at our command. It was an experience which, I am sure, none of us who were present is ever likely
to forget, for in imagination—and not wholly in imagination either
—we had been present at the funeral ceremonies of a king long
dead and almost forgotten. At a quarter past two we had filed
down into the tomb, and when, three hours later, hot, dusty, and
dishevelled, we came out once more into the light of day, the very
Valley seemed to have changed for us and taken on a more
personal aspect. We had been given the Freedom.

February 17th was a day set apart for an inspection of the tomb
by Egyptologists, and fortunately most of those who were in the
country were able to be present. On the following day the Queen of
the Belgians and her son Prince Alexander, who had come to Egypt
for that special purpose, honoured us with a visit, and were keenly
interested in everything they saw. Lord and Lady Allenby and a
number of other distinguished visitors were present on this occasion. A week later, for reasons stated in an earlier chapter, the
tomb was closed and once again re-buried.

So ends our preliminary season's work on the tomb of King
Tutankhamen. Now as to that which lies ahead of us. In the coming
winter our first task, a difficult and anxious one, will be the dismantling of the shrines in the sepulchral chamber. It is probable,
from evidence supplied by the Ramses IV papyrus, that there will
be a succession of no fewer than five of these shrines, built one
within the other, before we come to the stone sarcophagus in which
the king is lying, and in the spaces between these shrines we may
expect to find a number of beautiful objects. With the mummy—if,
as we hope and believe, it remains untouched by plunderers—there
should certainly lie the crowns and other regalia of a king of Egypt.
How long this work in the sepulchral chamber will take we cannot
tell at present, but it must be finished before we tackle the innermost
chamber of all, and we shall count ourselves lucky if we can accomplish the clearing of both in a single season. A further season
will surely be required for the Annex with its confused jumble of
contents.

Imagination falters at the thought of what the tomb may yet
disclose, for the material dealt with in the present volume represents
but a quarter—and that probably the least important quarter—of

the treasure which it contains. There are still many exciting moments in store for us before we complete our task, and we look
forward eagerly to the work that lies ahead. One shadow must
inevitably rest upon it, one regret, which all the world must share
—the fact that Lord Carnarvon was not permitted to see the full
fruition of his work; and in the completion of that work we, who
are to carry it out, would dedicate to his memory the best that in
us lies.

HOWARD CARTER AND A. C. MACE

The Tomb of Tutankhamen: the Opening of the Coffins

MANY strange scenes must have happened in the Valley of the
Tombs of the Kings since it became the royal burial ground of the
Theban New Empire, but one may be pardoned for thinking that
the present scene was not the least interesting or dramatic. For ourselves it was the one supreme and culminating moment—a moment
looked forward to ever since it became evident that the chambers
discovered, in November, 1922, must be the tomb of Tutankhamen,
and not a cache of his furniture as had been claimed. None of us
but felt the solemnity of the occasion, none of us but was affected
by the prospect of what we were about to see—the burial custom of
a king of ancient Egypt of thirty-three centuries ago. How would
the king be found? Such were the anticipatory speculations running
in our minds during the silence maintained.

The tackle for raising the lid was in position. I gave the word.
Amid intense silence the huge slab, broken in two, weighing over
a ton and a quarter, rose from its bed. The light shone into the
sarcophagus. A sight met our eyes that at first puzzled us. It was
a little disappointing. The contents were completely covered by

Ibid., pp. 51-3, 70-84.

fine linen shrouds. The lid being suspended in mid-air, we rolled back those covering shrouds, one by one, and as the last was removed a gasp of wonderment escaped our lips, so gorgeous was the sight that met our eyes: a golden effigy of the young boy king, of most magnificent workmanship, filled the whole of the interior of the sarcophagus. This was the lid of a wonderful anthropoid coffin, some 7 feet in length, resting upon a low bier in the form of a lion, and no doubt the outermost coffin of a series of coffins, nested one within the other, enclosing the mortal remains of the king. Enclasping the body of this magnificent monument are two winged goddesses, Isis and Neith, wrought in rich gold-work upon gesso, as brilliant as the day the coffin was made. To it an additional charm was added, by the fact that, while this decoration was rendered in fine low bas-relief, the head and hands of the king were in the round, in massive gold of the finest sculpture, surpassing anything we could have imagined. The hands, crossed over the breast, held the royal emblems—the Crook and the Flail—encrusted with deep blue faience. The face and features were wonderfully wrought in sheet-gold. The eyes were of aragonite and obsidian, the eyebrows and eyelids inlaid with lapis lazuli glass. There was a touch of realism, for while the rest of this anthropoid coffin, covered with feathered ornament, was of brilliant gold, that of the bare face and hands seemed different, the gold of the flesh being of different alloy, thus conveying an impression of the greyness of death. Upon the forehead of this recumbent figure of the young boy king were two emblems delicately worked in brilliant inlay—the Cobra and the Vulture—symbols of Upper and Lower Egypt, but perhaps the most touching by its human simplicity was the tiny wreath of flowers around these symbols, as it pleased us to think, the last farewell offering of the widowed girl queen to her husband, the youthful representative of the "Two Kingdoms." . . .

The Antechamber freed of its beautiful furniture, the Burial Chamber denuded of its golden shrines, leaves the now open stone sarcophagus in the centre with its coffins within alone retaining their secret.

The task before us now was to raise the lid of the first outermost coffin, as it rested in the sarcophagus.

This great gilded wooden coffin, 7 feet 4 inches in length, anthropoid in shape, wearing the *Khat* head-dress, with face and hands in heavier sheet-gold, is of *Rishi* type—a term applied when the main decoration consists of a feather design, a fashion common to coffins of the preceding Intermediate and Seventeenth Dynasty Theban periods. During the New Empire, in the case of burials of high officials and commoners, the style of decoration of coffins completely changes at the beginning of the Eighteenth Dynasty; but in the case of the royal coffin, as we now see, the older fashion still survived, with only very slight modification, such as the addition of figures of certain tutelary goddesses. This is a complete inversion of the usual order of things—fashion generally changing more rapidly with the upper than with the lower stations in life. May not this connote some religious idea in connexion with a king? There may be tradition behind it. The goddess Isis once protected the dead body of Osiris by taking him within her wings, thus she protects this new Osiris as represented by the effigy.

After careful study of the coffin it was decided that the original silver handles—two on each side—manifestly made for the purpose, were sufficiently well preserved still to support the weight of the lid, and could be used without danger in raising it. The lid was fixed to the shell by means of ten solid silver tongues, fitted into corresponding sockets in the thickness of the shell (four on each side, one at the head-, and one at the foot-end) where they were held in place by substantial gold-headed silver pins. Could we remove the silver pins by which the lid was fixed to the shell of the coffin without disturbing the coffin in the sarcophagus? As the coffin filled up nearly the whole of the interior of the sarcophagus, leaving only the smallest space, especially at the head- and foot-ends, it was by no means easy to extract the pins. By careful manipulation, however, it was found possible to withdraw them, with the exception of the pin at the head-end where there was only space enough to pull it half out. It had therefore to be filed through before the inner half could be withdrawn.

The next step was to place in position the hoisting tackle necessary for lifting the lid. This tackle consisted of two sets of three sheaf pulley-blocks provided with automatic brakes, fixed to an overhead scaffold, the pulleys being slung so as to come immediately above the centre of the lid opposite each pair of handles. The tackle was attached to the handles of the lid of the coffin by means of slings, and thus a correct centralization of its weight was assured, otherwise there would have been a danger of the lid bumping against the sides of the sarcophagus the moment it became free and pendent.

It was a moment as anxious as exciting. The lid came up fairly readily, revealing a second magnificent anthropoid coffin, covered with a thin gossamer linen sheet, darkened and much decayed. Upon this linen shroud were lying floral garlands, composed of olive and willow leaves, petals of the blue lotus and cornflowers, whilst a small wreath of similar kind had been placed, also over the shroud, on the emblems of the forehead. Underneath this covering, in places, glimpses could be obtained of rich multicoloured glass decoration encrusted upon the fine gold-work of the coffin.

Some time was spent in the previous summer working out the methods to be followed in this undertaking, and in providing the necessary appliances, thus it was completed in one morning when otherwise it would have occupied several days at least. The tomb was closed, everything being left undisturbed to await Mr. Harry Burton's photographic records.

Thus far our progress had been fairly satisfactory, but we now became conscious of a rather ominous feature. The second coffin which, so far as visible through the linen covering, had every appearance of being a wonderful piece of workmanship, showed distinct signs of the effect of some form of dampness and, here and there, tendency for its beautiful inlay to fall away. This was, I must admit, disconcerting, suggesting as it did the existence of former humidity of some kind within the nest of coffins. Should this prove the case, the preservation of the royal mummy would be less satisfactory than we had hoped.

On October 15, Mr. Burton arrived, and on the 17th, early in the morning, he successfully completed the photographic records of the shroud and floral garlands that covered the second coffin, as it rested within the shell of the first, in the sarcophagus.

These records complete, we had now to consider how best to deal with the second coffin, as well as the shell of the first. Manifestly, our difficulties were increased on account of the depth of the sarcophagus, and it was evident that the outer shell and the second coffin, neither of which was in a condition to bear much handling, must be raised together. This was eventually accomplished by means of pulleys as before, attachment being attained by means of steel pins passed through the tongue-sockets of the first outermost shell. In this way hoisting was possible with the minimum of handling.

In spite of the great weight of the coffins—far heavier than at first seemed possible—they were successfully raised to just above the level of the top of the sarcophagus, when wooden planks were passed under them. In the confined space, and with the restricted head-room available, the task proved one of no little difficulty. It was much increased by the necessity of avoiding damage to the fragile gesso-gilt surfaces of the outermost coffin.

Further records having been taken, I was then able to remove the chaplet and garlands, and roll back the covering shroud. It was one more exciting moment. We could now gaze, with admiring eyes, upon the finest example of the ancient coffin-maker's art ever yet seen—Osiride, again in form, but most delicate in conception, and very beautiful in line. As it now lay in the outer shell which rested upon the modern improvised trestles, it presented a wonderful picture of Majesty lying in State.

The chaplet and garlands placed upon the shroud in memory of "the wreaths given to Osiris on his triumphant exit from the Judgment-hall of Heliopolis," which, as Dr. Gardiner remarks, reminds us of the "crown of righteousness" (2 Tim. iv. 8), were but illustration of Pliny's description of ancient Egyptian wreaths. When the care and precision with which these are fashioned is recognized, there is strong reason for the belief that this particular occupation with the ancient Egyptians, as in later days, must have been a specialized trade.

This second coffin, 6 feet 8 inches in length, sumptuously inlaid on thick gold-foil with cut and engraved opaque glass, simulating red jasper, lapis lazuli and turquoise respectively, is similar in form and design to the first. It symbolizes Osiris, it is *Rishi* in ornament, but it differs in certain detail. In this case the king wears the *Nemes* headdress, and in place of the protective figures of Isis and Nephthys, the body is embraced with the wings of the vulture Nekhebet and of the serpent Buto. The arresting feature is the delicacy and superiority of the conception, which confer upon it at once the position of a masterpiece.

We were now faced by a complicated problem, not unlike the one we had to solve two seasons before when the covering shrines were dismantled. It was again a case of the unexpected happening. Conclusions drawn from former evidence or example are not to be trusted. For some unknown reason the reverse too often proves to be the case. On seeing that there were handles on the outer coffin for lowering or raising it, we were led to expect similar metal handles on the second coffin. There was none, and their absence placed us in a dilemma. The second coffin proved exceedingly heavy; its decorated surface very fragile; it fitted the outer shell so closely that it was not possible to pass one's little finger between the two. Its lid was fixed, as in the case of the outer coffin, with gold-headed silver pins which, as the coffin lay in the outer shell, could not be extracted. It was evident that it would have to be lifted in its entirety from the outer shell before anything further could be done. Thus the problem which confronted us was to discover a method of doing this with the minimum risk of damage to its delicate inlay, that had already suffered from some kind of humidity, the origin of which was then unknown.

It may be, under the strain of such operations as these, that one is too conscious of the risk of irreparable damage to the rare and beautiful object one desires to preserve intact. Much in the early days of Egyptian archaeological research has undoubtedly been lost to us by too eager or careless handling, more still from want of necessary appliances at the right moment; but against ill luck, even when every possible precaution has been taken, no man is secure. Everything may seem to be going well until suddenly, in the crisis of the process, you hear a crack—little pieces of surface ornament fall. Your nerves are at an almost painful tension. What is happening? All available room in the narrow space is crowded by your men. What action is needed to avert a catastrophe? There is, too, another danger. As the lid is being raised, the excitement of seeing some new and beautiful object may attract the workmen's attention; for a moment their duty is forgotten and irreparable damage in consequence may be done.

Such are often the anxious impressions uppermost in the archaeologist's memory when his friends inquire what his emotions in these thrilling moments may have been. Only those who have had to handle heavy yet fragile antiquities in circumstances of similar difficulty, can realize how exacting and nerve-racking the strain and responsibility may become. Moreover, in the case before us, we could not be sure that the wood of the coffin was sufficiently well preserved to bear its own weight. However, after long consultations, and having studied the problem for nearly two days, we devised a plan. To remove the second coffin from the shell of the first, some points of attachment were necessary. There were, it will be remembered, no handles, so it was judged best to make use of the metal pins which fastened down the lid.

Inspection showed, however, that although the space between the shell of the outer coffin and the second coffin was insufficient to enable us to withdraw these pins entirely, they could still be pulled out about a quarter of an inch, so as to permit stout copper wire attachments to be fixed to them and to the overhead scaffold. This we did successfully. Strong metal eyelets were then screwed into the thickness of the top edge of the shell of the outer coffin, so as to enable it to be lowered from the second coffin by means of ropes working on the pulleys.

On the following day, after these preparations, we were able to proceed with the next stage. It proved to be one of the most important moments in the dismantling of the tomb. The process adopted was the reverse of that which might at first appear to be the natural order of things. We lowered the outer shell from the second coffin, instead of lifting the second coffin out of the first. The reason for this was that the head-room was insufficient, and the weight being stationary, there would be less risk of undue stress upon those ancient silver pins. The operation proved successful. The shell of the outer coffin was lowered once more into the sarcophagus, leaving for a moment, the second coffin suspended in mid-air by means of the ten stout wire attachments. A wooden tray sufficiently large to span the opening of the sarcophagus was then passed under it, and thus the second coffin strongly supported, stood before us free and accessible. The wire attachments having been severed, the overhead gear removed, Mr. Burton made his records, and we were able to turn our energies to the raising of its lid.

The entire inlaid surface was indeed, as already mentioned, in a very fragile condition, and any handling, so far as possible, had to be avoided. In order therefore to lift the lid without causing injury, metal eyelets, to serve as handles, were screwed into it at four points where there would be no danger of permanent disfigurement. To these eyelets our hoisting tackle was fixed, the gold-headed silver nails were extracted and the lid was slowly raised.

There was at first some slight tendency for the lid to stick, but gradually it rose from its bed and, when high enough to clear the contents of the coffin, it was lowered on to a wooden tray placed at the side to receive it.

This revealed a third coffin which, like its predecessors, was Osiride in form, but the main details of the workmanship were hidden by a close-fitting reddish-coloured linen shroud. The burnished gold face was bare; placed over the neck and breast was an elaborate bead and floral collarette, sewn upon a backing of papyrus, and tucked immediately above the *Nemes* head-dress was a linen napkin.

Mr. Burton at once made his photographic records. I then removed the floral collarette and linen coverings. An astounding fact was disclosed. This third coffin, 6 feet 1¾ of an inch in length, was made of solid gold! The mystery of the enormous weight, which hitherto had puzzled us, was now clear. It explained also why the weight had diminished so slightly after the first coffin, and the lid of the second coffin, had been removed. Its weight was still as much as eight strong men could lift.

The face of this gold coffin was again that of the king, but the features though conventional, by symbolizing Osiris, were even more youthful than those on the other coffins. In actual design it reverted to that of the outermost coffin, inasmuch as it was *Rishi*, and had engraved upon it figures of Isis and Nephthys, but auxiliary to this design were winged figures of Nekhebet and Buto. These latter protective figures, emblematic of Upper and Lower Egypt, were the prominent feature, for they are superimposed in gorgeous and massive cloisonné work over the richly engraved ornament of the coffin—their inlay being natural semiprecious stones. In addition to this decoration, over the conventional collarette of "the Hawk"—again in auxiliary cloisonné work—was a double detachable necklace of large disk-shaped beads of red and yellow gold and blue faience, which enhanced the richness of the whole effect. But the ultimate details of the ornamentation were hidden by a black lustrous coating due to liquid unguents that had evidently been profusely poured over the coffin. As a result this unparalleled monument was not only disfigured—as it afterwards proved, only temporarily—but was stuck fast to the interior of the second coffin, the consolidated liquid filling up the space between the second and third coffins almost to the level of the lid of the third.

These consecration unguents, which had obviously been used in great quantity, were doubtless the cause of the disintegration observed when dealing with the outer coffins which, as they were in a practically hermetically sealed quartzite sarcophagus, cannot have been affected by outside influences. As a further result it may be mentioned that the covering shroud and floral collarette mingled with blue faience beads had suffered, and although these at first appeared to be in good condition, they proved so brittle that the material broke the very instant it was touched.

We raised the third coffin contained in the shell of the second, which now rested on the top of the sarcophagus, and moved them into the Antechamber where they were more accessible, both for examination and manipulation. It was then that the wonder and magnitude of our last discovery more completely dawned upon us. This unique and wonderful monument—a coffin over 6 feet in length, of the finest art, wrought in solid gold of 2½ to 3½ millimetres in thickness—represented an enormous mass of pure bullion.

How great must have been the wealth buried with those ancient Pharaohs! What riches that valley must have once concealed! Of the twenty-seven monarchs buried there, Tutankhamen was probably of the least importance. How great must have been the temptation to the greed and rapacity of the audacious contemporary tomb robbers! What stronger incentive can be imagined than those vast treasures of gold! The plundering of royal tombs, recorded in the reign of Ramses IX, becomes easily intelligible when the incentive to these crimes is measured by this gold coffin of Tutankhamen. It must have represented fabulous wealth to the stonecutters, artisans, water-carriers and peasants—to contemporary workers generally, such as the men implicated in the tomb robberies. These plunderings occurred in the reigns of the later Ramessides (1200–1000 B.C.) and are recorded in legal documents now known as the Abbott, Amherst, Turin, and Mayer papyri, discovered in Thebes about the beginning of last century. Probably the thieves, who made their practically ineffectual raid on Tutankhamen's tomb, were aware of the mass of bullion covering the remains of the young Pharaoh under its protective shrines, sarcophagus and nested coffins.

Our first object now was to protect from injury and, so far as was possible for the moment, to conserve the delicate inlay on the shell of the second coffin. The process used we knew to be effective. It was, therefore, lightly brushed to remove loose dust, sponged with warm water and ammonia, and when dry, the whole surface covered with a thick coating of paraffin wax applied hot with a long brush. This wax as it cooled and solidified held the inlay securely in position so that the coffin could be handled with impunity. The great advantage of this system is that the wax coating may be removed by heat at any time should further restoration be considered necessary, and the mere reheating of the wax has also a cleansing quality.

The next problem for consideration, requiring a certain amount of experimental work, was to ascertain the most satisfactory, and at the same time the most expeditious manner, of dealing with those ancient consolidated consecration unguents, that not only covered the body of the coffin but completely filled the space between the two, thus sticking them fast and for the moment preventing further progress in investigation. Mr. Lucas made a preliminary analysis of this substance. In appearance it was black, and resembled pitch; in those places where the layer was thin, as on the lid of the coffin, the material was hard and brittle, but where a thicker layer had accumulated, as was the case under and between the coffins, the interior of the material was soft and plastic. Its smell when warm was penetrating, somewhat fragrant, not unpleasant, and suggestive of wood-pitch. Naturally a complete chemical analysis was not then possible, but, as a result of a preliminary examination, it was found to contain fatty matter and resin. There was no mineral pitch or bitumen present, and even the presence of wood-pitch, which was suggested by the smell, could not then be proved. There can be little doubt from the manner in which this material had run down the sides of the third coffin and collected underneath, that it was in a liquid or semi-liquid condition when employed.

On account of its nature, it follows that this substance could be melted by heat and dissolved by certain solvents, but neither of these methods in the existing circumstances was practicable. So we decided to raise the lid and examine the contents before any further procedure, and before applying any drastic measures. Luckily the line of junction between the lid and the coffin was visible and, with difficulty, accessible, except at the extreme foot-end where the second and third coffins practically touched.

The lid was fastened to the shell by means of eight gold tenons (four on each side), which were held in their corresponding sockets by nails. Thus, if the nails could be extracted the lid could be raised. In the narrow space between the two coffins ordinary implements for extracting metal pins were useless, and others had to be devised. With long screwdrivers converted to meet the conditions, the nails or pins of solid gold, that unfortunately had to be sacrificed, were removed piecemeal. The lid was raised by its golden handles and the mummy of the king disclosed.

At such moments the emotions evade verbal expression, complex and stirring as they are. Three thousand years and more had elapsed since men's eyes had gazed into that golden coffin. Time, measured by the brevity of human life, seemed to lose its common perspectives before a spectacle so vividly recalling the solemn religious rites of a vanished civilization. But it is useless to dwell on such sentiments, based as they are on feelings of awe and human pity. The emotional side is no part of archaeological research. Here at last lay all that was left of the youthful Pharaoh, hitherto little more to us than the shadow of a name.

Before us, occupying the whole of the interior of the golden coffin, was an impressive, neat and carefully made mummy, over which had been poured anointing unguents as in the case of the outside of its coffin—again in great quantity—consolidated and blackened by age. In contradistinction to the general dark and sombre effect, due to these unguents, was a brilliant, one might say magnificent, burnished gold mask or similitude of the king, covering his head and shoulders, which, like the feet, had been intentionally avoided when using the unguents. The mummy was fashioned to symbolize Osiris. The beaten gold mask, a beautiful and unique specimen of ancient portraiture, bears a sad but calm expression suggestive of youth overtaken prematurely by death. Upon its forehead, wrought in massive gold, were the royal insignia--the Nekhebet vulture and Buto serpent—emblems of the Two Kingdoms over which he had reigned. To the chin was attached the conventional Osiride beard, wrought in gold and lapis-lazuli-coloured glass; around the throat was a triple necklace of yellow and red gold and blue faience disk-shaped beads; pendent from the neck by flexible gold inlaid straps was a large black resin scarab that rested between the hands and bore the *Bennu* ritual. The burnished gold hands, crossed over the breast, separate from the mask, were sewn to the material of the linen wrappings, and grasped the Flagellum and Crozier—the emblems of Osiris. Immediately below these was the simple outermost linen covering, adorned with richly inlaid gold trappings pendent from a large pectoral-like figure of the *Ba* bird or soul, of gold cloisonné work, its full-spread wings stretched over the body. As these gorgeous trappings had been subjected to the consecration unguents, their detail and brilliance were hardly visible, and to this must be attributed the disastrous deterioration which we discovered to have taken place in the case of many of the objects.

But through this obstruction it could be faintly seen that these trappings, made of heavy gold plaques held together by threads of beads, bore welcoming speeches of the gods—for example, on the longitudinal bands down the centre, the goddess of the sky, Nût, the Divine Mother, says:—"I reckon thy beauties, O Osiris, King Kheperu·neb·Re; thy soul livest: thy veins are firm. Thou smellest the air and goest out as a god, going out as Atum, O Osiris, Tutankhamen. Thou goest out and thou enterest with Ra . . ." The god of the earth, the prince of the gods, Geb, says:—"My beloved son, inheritor of the throne of Osiris, the King Kheperu·neb·Re; thy nobility is perfect: Thy Royal Palace is powerful; Thy name is in the mouth of the Rekhyt, thy stability is in the mouth of the living, O Osiris, King Tutankhamen, Thy heart is in thy body eternally. He is before the spirits of the living, like Re he rests in heaven." While the texts upon the transverse bands open with words, such as "Honoured before Anubis, Hapy, Kebeh·sen·uef, Dua·mutef," and "Justified before Osiris."

3. *Famous Monuments*

HERODOTUS

Pyramid-Building
According to Herodotus

Up to the time of Rhampsinitus, Egypt was excellently governed and very prosperous; but his successor Cheops (to continue the account which the priests gave me) brought the country into all sorts of misery. He closed all the temples, then, not content with excluding his subjects from the practice of their religion, compelled them without exception to labour as slaves for his own advantage. Some were forced to drag blocks of stone from the quarries in the Arabian hills to the Nile, where they were ferried across and taken over by others, who hauled them to the Libyan hills. The work went on in three-monthly shifts, a hundred thousand men in a shift. It took ten years of this oppressive slave-labour to build the track along which the blocks were hauled—a work, in my opinion, of hardly less magnitude than the pyramid itself, for it is five furlongs in length, sixty feet wide, forty-eight feet high at its highest point, and constructed of polished stone blocks decorated with carvings of animals. To build it took, as I said, ten years—including the underground sepulchral chambers on the hill where the pyramids stand; a cut was made from the Nile, so that the water from it turned the site of these into an island. To build the pyramid itself took twenty years; it is square at the base, its height (800 feet) equal to the length of each side; it is of polished stone blocks beautifully fitted, none of the blocks being less than thirty feet long. The method employed was to build it in tiers, or steps, if you prefer the word—something like battlements running up the slope of a hill; when the base was complete, the blocks for the first tier above it were lifted from ground level by cranes or sheerlegs, made of short timbers; on this first tier there was another lifting-crane which raised the

From *The Histories*. Book II, 5th century B.C. Translated by Aubrey de Sélincourt. London: Martin Secker & Warburg Ltd.; 1954, pp. 151-2. By permission of David Higham Associates Ltd.

blocks a stage higher, then yet another which raised them higher still. Each tier, or story, had its crane—or it may be that they used the same one, which, being easy to carry, they shifted up from stage to stage as soon as its load was dropped into place. Both methods are mentioned, so I give them both here. The finishing-off of the pyramid was begun at the top and continued downwards, ending with the lowest parts nearest the ground. An inscription is cut upon it in Egyptian characters recording the amount spent on radishes, onions, and leeks for the labourers, and I remember distinctly that the interpreter who read me the inscription said the sum was 1600 talents of silver. If this is true, how much must have been spent in addition on bread and clothing for the labourers during all those years the building was going on—not to mention the time it took (not a little, I should think) to quarry and haul the stone, and to construct the underground chamber?

But no crime was too great for Cheops: when he was short of money, he sent his daughter to a bawdy-house with instructions to charge a certain sum—they did not tell me how much. This she actually did, adding to it a further transaction of her own; for with the intention of leaving something to be remembered by after her death, she asked each of her customers to give her a block of stone, and of these stones (the story goes) was built the middle pyramid of the three which stand in front of the great pyramid. It is a hundred and fifty feet square.

Cheops reigned for fifty years, according to the Egyptians' account, and was succeeded after his death by his brother Chephren. Chephren was no better than his predecessor; his rule was equally oppressive, and, like Cheops, he built a pyramid, but of a smaller size (I measured both of them myself). It has no underground chambers, and no channel was dug, as in the case of Cheops' pyramid, to bring to it the water from the Nile. The cutting of the canal, as I have already said, makes the site of the pyramid of Cheops into an island, and there his body is supposed to be. The pyramid of Chephren lies close to the great pyramid of Cheops; it is forty feet lower than the latter, but otherwise of the same dimensions; its lower course is of the coloured stone of Ethiopia. Both these pyramids stand on the same hill, which is about a hundred feet in height. Chephren reigned for fifty-six years—so the Egyptians reckon a period of a hundred and six years, all told, during which the temples were never opened for worship and the country was reduced in every way to the greatest misery. The Egyptians can hardly bring themselves to mention the names of Cheops and Chephren, so great is their hatred of them; they even call the pyramids after Philitis, a shepherd who at that time fed his flocks in the neighbourhood.

JOHN GREAVES

The Calife, the Englishman and the Pyramid of Cheops

THE Arab tradition concerning the opening of the Great Pyramid quoted by John Greaves is of considerable interest. Greaves himself was an English mathematician and was in Egypt in 1638-9. As for the note about Dr. Harvey and the oxygen supply—there *are* ventilating shafts in the pyramid of Cheops. This physician was, of course, William Harvey, discoverer of the circulation of the blood.

❧

"AFTER that Almamon the Calife entrcd Aegypt, and saw the Pyramids, he desired to know what was within, and therefore would have them opened: they told him it could not possibly be done: he replyed, I will have it certainly done. And that hole was opened for him, which stands open to this day, with fire, and vinegar. Two smiths prepared, and sharpned the iron, and engines, which they forced in, and there was a great expense in the opening of it: the thicknes of the wall was found to be twenty cubits, and when they came to the end of the wall behind the place they had digged, there was an ewer (or pot) of green Emrauld, in it were a thousand dinars very waighty, every dinar was an ounce of our ounces: they wondred at it, but knew not the meaning of it. Then Almamon said, cast up the account, how much hath been spent in making the entrance: they cast it up, and lo it was the same summe which they found, it neither exceeded, nor was defective. Within they found a square well, in the square of it there were doores, every doore opened into an house (or vault) in which there were dead bodies wrapped up in linnen. They found towards the top of the Pyramid a chamber in which there was an hollow

From *Pyramidographia*. London: George Badger; 1646, pp. 83-4, 95, 101.

stone: in it was a statue of stone like a man, and within it a man, upon whom was a breast-plate of gold set with jewels, upon his breast was a sword of unvaluable price, and at his head a Carbuncle, of the bignesse of an egge, shining like the light of the day, and upon him were characters written with a pen, no man knows what they signify. After Almamon had op'ned it, men entred into it for many years, and descended by the slippery passage, which is in it; and some of them came out safe, and others dyed." Thus farre the Arabians: which traditions of theirs, are little better than a *Romance,* and therefore leaving these, I shall give a more true, and particular description, out of mine own experience, and observations. . . .

Within this glorious roome (for so I may justly call it) as within some consecrated Oratory, stands the monument of Cheops, or Chemmis, of one peece of marble, hollow within, and uncovered at the top, and sounding like a bell. Which I mention not as any rarity, either in nature, or in art (For I have observed the like sound, in other tombs of marble cut hollow like this) but because I find modern Authors to take notice of it as a wonder. Some write, that the body hath been removed hence whereas *Diodorus* hath left above sixteen hundred yeeres since, a memorable passage concerning Chemmis the builder of this Pyramid, and Cephren the Founder of the next adjoyning. "Although" (saith hee) "these Kings intended these for their Sepulchers, yet it hapened that neither of them were buried there. For the people being exasperated against them, by reason of the toilsomnesse of these works, and for their cruelty, and oppression, threatned to teare in pieces their dead bodies, and with ignominy to throw them out of their Sepulchers, Wherefore both of them dying commanded their friends privately to bury them, in an obscure place." This monument in respect of the nature, and quality of the stone, is the same with which the whole roome is lined: as by breaking a little fragment of it, I plainly discovered, being a speckled kind of marble, with black, and white, and red spots as it were equally mixt, which some writers call *Thebaick marble.* . . .

Thus have I finished my description of all the inner parts of this Pyramid: where I could neither borrow light to conduct me, from the Ancients: nor receive any manuduction from the uncertaine informations of modern travailers, in those dark, and hidden paths. We arc now come abroad into the light, and Sunne, where I found my Janizary, and an English Captain, a litle impatient to have waited above* three houres without, in expectation of my

* That I and my company, should have continued so many houres in the Pyramid, and live (whereas we found no inconvenience) was much wondred at by Doctor

return: who imagined whatsoever they understood not, to be an impertinent, and vain curiosity.

WILLIAM BROCKEDON

In Egypt and Nubia

WILLIAM BROCKEDON was an English painter and writer. The following pieces are from among the texts which he wrote to accompany David Roberts's fine watercolour studies of Egyptian monuments.

The Sphinx

No monument in existence strikes the observer with a greater impression of vastness than the Sphinx near the Pyramids of Gizeh: when brought by the judgment of an observer into comparison with the human head, which it represents (for this part alone of the figure appears above the level of the rock, out of which it rises), it overwhelms by its immensity all other colossal imitations. If the head of a man be taken at a length of ten inches from the top to the chin, it is here sculptured of the enormous length of twenty-eight fcet six inches, which presents a bulk nearly 40,000 times greater than its original.

This marvellous figure is cut out of the solid rock from a mass that projects above the general level of the bed of a rather soft greyish-white limestone, upon which the Pyramids are built, which

From D. Roberts and W. Brockedon: *Egypt and Nubia*. London: Moon; 1846.

Harvey, his Majesties learned Physician. For said he, seeing we never breath the same aire twice, but still new aire is required to a new respiration (the *Succus alibilis* of it being spent in every expiration) it could not be but by long breathing we should have spent the aliment of that small stock of aire within, and have been stifled; unless there were some secret tunnels conveying it to the top of the Pyramid, whereby it might passe out, and make way for fresh aire to come in, at the entrance below.

extends up the valley of the Nile at a general elevation of about one hundred and fifty feet above the level of the river and in some places one hundred and twenty feet above the sandy plain around it.

It is remarkable that Herodotus, who has furnished us with details of the Pyramids, has been altogether silent on the great Sphinx: that it was in existence when he was in Egypt there cannot be a doubt. On its breast a granite tablet was found, bearing the cartouche of Thothmes IV., in the date of whose reign, 1561 B.C., chronologists agree; but they differ widely upon that of Suphis, or Cheops, whose cartouche, found within the Great Pyramid, confirms the statement of Herodotus that he was its founder. Wathen, by close and powerful argument, places the reign of Cheops in 941 B.C., 620 years later than the age of the Sphinx; but Wilkinson, who is profound in the subject, carries it back to 2123 B.C., thus making the Pyramids 562 years older than the Sphinx. As, however, this stupendous figure existed 1100 years before the visit of the Greek historian to Egypt, 470 B.C., the omission of all mention of the Sphinx by him, may, perhaps, be accounted for by the probability that the text of Herodotus is imperfect. It is known that Aristotle refers to passages in this author which are not to be found in the text which has descended to us.

About twenty years ago M. Caviglia succeeded in accomplishing what the French attempted but did not complete, the laying open of the whole front of the Sphinx. When the sand, after immense labour, was removed, this stupendous figure was disclosed in all its height from the top of the head to the floor of the Temple between its paws, above one hundred feet: its total length is one hundred and forty-six feet; the breadth across the shoulders thirty-four feet; height to the top from the sand in front forty-four feet six inches; height from the back of the shoulders to the top of the head twenty-seven feet. The whole is cut from the solid rock, except the fore legs, or paws, which are of masonry, and project fifty feet from the breast of the figure; between them lies a small Temple. By these excavations an approach from the rocky plain above was laid open before the figure, nearly three hundred feet in length, first by a long and gradual incline, and then by two descending flights of steps to the platform of the Temple, where altars and many other antique fragments were found that are now deposited in the British Museum.

The head of the Sphinx is so much broken and injured, that the different opinions upon its expression and character have had free scope: Langles, in his "Notes on Norden," says it was thus mutilated by a fanatic sheikh of the Sofi sect in 1379. From what remains, there appears to have been the quiet repose and dignity of expression, which generally characterised the colossal sculpture of that remote but, in this art, highly advanced period.

The Great Hall at Karnak

"NEXT to the Pyramids," says Wathen, "the most wonderful relic of Egyptian art is, undoubtedly, the Great Hall of the Temple-Palace of Karnak. From the inscriptions we learn that this Hall was founded by Menepthah-Osiri I. [This was Sethos I. The great hall was in fact built by him and his son Ramses II. They ruled from 1309–1224 B.C.] father of the Great Ramses, who was on the throne about the middle of the fifteenth century B.C. Its superficial area, three hundred and forty-one feet by one hundred and sixty-four, is sufficiently spacious for a large quadrangle. Majestic in ruin, what must it have been when perfect? The massive stone roof is supported by a phalanx of one hundred and thirty-four giant columns, ranged in sixteen rows; most of these are nine feet in diameter, and nearly forty-three feet high; but those of the central avenue are not less than eleven feet six inches in diameter, and seventy-two feet high. The diameter of their capitals at their widest spread is twenty-two feet. The walls, columns, architraves, ceilings —every surface exposed to the eye is overspread with intaglio sculptures—gods, heroes, and hieroglyphics, painted in once vivid colours. It is easy to detail the dimensions of this building, but no description can convey an idea of its sublime effect. What massive grandeur in its vistas of enormous columns! what scenic effects in the gradations of the chiaro-scuro, and the gleamings of accidental lights athwart the aisles!"

The roof is formed of ponderous blocks, stretching across the aisles. The three central avenues rise above the general level, and the spaces between the upper piers are filled with close-set loopholes: besides these, the only openings for the light appear to have been the great doorways at the ends of the middle avenue, and a few slits in the roof of the remote aisles. Thus, while a solemn gloom reigned through the interior generally, the nave was strongly lighted, and brought into prominence as a master line bisecting the hall.

Impressive as Karnak is when visited, Roberts laughs at the affected enthusiasm of the French army, as narrated by Denon— stopping *en masse*, and clapping their hands in an ecstasy of delight. In the vast plain of Thebes these ruins, enormous as they are, are mere patches, and nothing could have been distinguished at the distance whence these are first seen to create such enthusiasm, or make this show of it a praiseworthy *performance*. "It is only," says our Artist, "on coming near that you are overwhelmed with astonishment: you must be under these stupendous masses—you must look up to them, and walk around them—before you can feel that neither language nor painting can convey a just idea of the emotions they excite. That such masses could ever have been displaced, seems to be as surprising as that they were ever erected; but there is abundant evidence that fire was one of the means of destruction employed; at least in the closer passages and corridors, where the stones are splintered by this element in every direction."

The Temple of Abu Simbel

THE first discovery of this extraordinary Temple was made by the celebrated Burckhardt on his return from Mahass, after an ineffectual attempt to reach Dongola in the spring of 1813. He had visited the Temple of Isis, the lesser Temple of Abu Simbel; and having, as he supposed, seen all the antiquities here, he was about to ascend the sandy side of the mountain by the same path that he had descended, when "having," he says, "luckily turned more to the southward, I fell in with what is still visible of four immense colossal statues, cut out of the rock, at a distance of about two hundred yards from the lesser Temple: they stand in a deep recess excavated in the mountain; but it is greatly to be regretted that they are now almost entirely buried beneath the sands, which are blown down here in torrents. The entire head and part of the breast and arms of one of the statues are yet above the surface."

In 1816 Belzoni ascended the Nile into Nubia, with the intention of opening the great Temple of Abu Simbel, and commenced his undertaking; but the chiefs of the country threw so many obstacles in his way, that at length his funds failed, and he was obliged to discontinue, but not until he had cleared downwards twenty feet in the front of the Temple. It is remarkable that this is the first time the natives learnt the use of money as a recompense for labour.

In the spring of 1817 he returned to his excavations at Abu-Simbel, accompanied by Mr. Beechey. At Philae they had the good fortune to be joined by Captains Irby and Mangles, then on their journey in the East. The united exertions of these gentlemen accomplished the entrance to the Great Temple in defiance of the dangers and difficulties thrown in their way, and which are most interestingly narrated in Irby and Mangles' Travels. Belzoni and his friends removed forty feet of sand, which had accumulated above the top of the door before the recent excavations; but they carried them no farther than three feet below the top of the entrance, when they effected their passage into this Temple, and saw the most extraordinary work that remains to us of the age of Ramses II. Belzoni describes its façade as one hundred and seventeen feet wide and eighty-six feet high (Wilkinson says, ninety to one hundred feet), the height from the top of the cornice to the top of the door being sixty-six feet six inches, and the height of the door twenty feet. Each of these enormous statues—the largest in Egypt or Nubia, except the Sphinx of the Pyramids—measures from the shoulder to the elbow fifteen feet six inches, the face seven feet, the ears three feet six inches, across the shoulders twenty-five feet four inches. Their height as they sit is about fifty-one feet, not including the caps, which are about fourteen feet. These, the most beautiful colossi yet found in any of the Egyptian ruins, represent Ramses II.; they are seated on thrones attached to the rock. On the sides, and on the front angles of the thrones, and between the legs of the statues, are sculptured female figures, supposed to be of his wife and children; they are well preserved, though the material is a coarse, friable gritstone. During the execution, defects in the stone were filled and smoothed with stucco, and afterwards painted, of which traces yet remain. The upper part of the second figure has fallen, but the faces of these colossi exhibit a beauty of expression the more striking as it is unlooked for in statues of such dimensions.

Roberts, in his Journal, complains indignantly of the way in which "Cockney tourists and Yankee travellers" have knocked off a toe or a finger of these magnificent statues. "The hand," he says, "of the finest of them has been destroyed (not an easy matter, since Wilkinson says the forefinger is three feet long) by these contemptible relic-hunters, who have also been led by their vanity to smear their vulgar names on the very foreheads of the Egyptian deities."

The Island of Philae

THERE is no object on the Nile so beautiful as the island of Philae, with its temples and trees seen amidst the wild desolation of the vast rocks which here bound the river above the first cataract of the Nile.

On whichever side this charming island is approached, nothing can exceed its beauty. The picturesque forms of its temples, its romantic situation, and its fertility, are the themes of every traveller. It is the first object lying in the beauty of repose which presents itself to those who ascend the river after the turmoil and dangers of the cataract. But with all these natural advantages, and the emotions excited by the charm of contrast, it acquires a vast increase of beauty if it be seen at sunset, against the blaze of the last rays of an Egyptian sun; it is then that the light breaking through the elegant temple called the Bed of Pharaoh, enriches the scene with the character of fairy land.

W. M. FLINDERS PETRIE

Petrie and the Great Pyramid

FLINDERS PETRIE went to Egypt in 1880. His survey at Gizeh was the first considerable work he undertook there.

∞☙∞

THE small piece of desert plateau opposite the village of Gizeh, though less than a mile across, may well claim to be the most remarkable piece of ground in the world. There may be seen the very beginning of architecture, the most enormous piles of building ever raised, the most accurate constructions known, the finest masonry, and the employment of the most ingenious tools; whilst among all the sculpture that we know, the largest figure—the Sphinx—and also the finest example of technical skill with artistic expression— the Statue of Khafra—both belong to Gizeh. We shall look in vain for a more wonderful assemblage than the vast masses of the Pyramids, the ruddy walls and pillars of the granite temple, the titanic head of the Sphinx, the hundreds of tombs, and the shattered outlines of causeways, pavements, and walls, that cover this earliest field of man's labours.

But these remains have an additional, though passing, interest in the present day, owing to the many attempts that have been made to theorise on the motives of their origin and construction. The Great Pyramid has lent its name as a sort of by-word for paradoxes; and, as moths to a candle, so are theorisers attracted to it. The very fact that the subject was so generally familiar, and yet so little was accurately known about it, made it the more enticing; there were plenty of descriptions from which to choose, and yet most of them were so hazy that their support could be claimed for many varying theories.

Here, then, was a field which called for the resources of the

From W. M. Flinders Petrie: *The Pyramids and Temples of Gizeh*. London, 1883, pp. 1-2. By permission of the Department of Egyptology at University College, London.

present time for its due investigation; a field in which measurement and research were greatly needed, and have now been largely
rewarded by the disclosures of the skill of the ancients, and the
mistakes of the moderns. The labours of the French Expedition,
of Colonel Howard Vyse, of the Prussian Expedition, and of Professor Smyth, in this field are so well known that it is unnecessary
to refer to them, except to explain how it happens that any further
work was still needed. Though the French were active explorers,
they were far from realising the accuracy of ancient work; and
they had no idea of testing the errors of the ancients by outdoing
them in precision. Hence they rather explored than investigated.
Col. Vyse's work, carried on by Mr. Perring, was of the same nature,
and no accurate measurement or triangulation was attempted by
these energetic blasters and borers; their discoveries were most
valuable, but their researchers were always of a rough-and-ready
character. The Prussian Expedition sought with ardour for inscriptions, but did not advance our knowledge of technical skill, work,
or accuracy, though we owe to it the best topographical map of
Gizeh. When Professor Smyth went to Gizeh he introduced different
and scientific methods of inquiry in his extensive measurements,
afterwards receiving the gold medal of the Royal Society of Edinburgh in recognition of his labours. But he did not attempt the
heaviest work of accurate triangulation. Mr. Waynman Dixon, C.E.,
followed in his steps, in taking further measurements of the inside
of the Great Pyramid. Mr. Gill—now Astronomer Royal at the Cape
—when engaged in Egypt in the Transit Expedition of 1874, made
the next step, by beginning a survey of the Great Pyramid base,
in true geodetic style. This far surpassed all previous work in its
accuracy, and was a noble result of the three days' labour that he
and Professor Watson were able to spare for it. When I was engaged in reducing this triangulation for Mr. Gill in 1879, he impressed on me the need of completing it if I could, by continuing
it round the whole pyramid, as two of the corners were only just
reached by it without any check.

When, after preparations extending over some years, I settled
at Gizeh during 1880-2, I took with me, therefore, instruments of
the fullest accuracy needed for the work; probably as fine as any
private instruments of the kind. The triangulation was with these
performed quite independently of previous work; it was of a larger
extent, including the whole hill; and it comprised an abundance of
checks. The necessary excavations were carried out to discover the
fiducial points of the buildings, unseen for thousands of years. The
measurements previously taken were nearly all checked, by repeating them with greater accuracy, and, in most cases, more
frequency; and fresh and more refined methods of measurement

were adopted. The tombs around the pyramids were all measured, where they had any regularity and were accessible. The methods of workmanship were investigated, and materials were found illustrating the tools employed and the modes of using them.

I. E. S. EDWARDS

A History of the Pyramids

THE important developments in the Mastaba from the IVth Dynasty onwards were a direct result of the realization that the measures which had been taken to defeat the elements and the robber had also defeated their own ultimate object, namely the preservation of the body. An inevitable consequence of burying the body in a deep chamber far from the drying influence of the hot sand was that it decomposed unless some method of embalmment were employed. The earliest mummy hitherto discovered is one dating from the Vth Dynasty found by Sir Flinders Petrie at Meidum in the season 1891-2. Even during the Early Dynastic Period, however, attempts were sometimes made to imitate the external form of the living body by wrapping each limb separately and inserting under the wrappings linen pads soaked in resin and moulded to the shape of the individual members. A further development, for which evidence is available from the IVth Dynasty, was the painting in green of the facial features on the outside of the wrappings covering the head, while in some cases, although rarely before the Vth Dynasty, a coat of plaster was applied either to the head alone or to the entire body and modelled to the required shape.

There can be no doubt that the Egyptians were fully aware of the inadequacy of their precautions to preserve the body from molestation and decay. As an additional safeguard for the continuation of life after death they therefore resorted to magic.

In the cult of the dead, the Egyptians believed that, without de-

From I. E. S. Edwards: *The Pyramids of Egypt*. Harmondsworth: Penguin Books Ltd.; 1961, rev. ed., pp. 29-32, 49, 53-4, 87-9, 103-7, 151-2, 212-17, 229-30. By permission of Penguin Books Ltd.

priving the deceased person of the virtues of the prototype, a model could be substituted for any article which it was not practicable to supply in actuality. For instance, in some IInd Dynasty Mastabas dummy vases were used instead of vessels filled with provisions and were thought to be equally beneficial to the owner of the tomb. Similarly, a statue or even a figure carved in relief was considered to be an effective substitute for the human body in the event of its destruction. One of the best known Mastabas of the IIIrd Dynasty was provided with figures of the deceased owner, a high official named Hesy-Re, carved in relief on wooden panels which fitted into the recesses on the east side of the superstructure. The figures were certainly intended to enable Hesy-Re to leave and re-enter his tomb. Outside panels of this kind were, however, very vulnerable and the Serdab was devised so as to give the figure better protection without any corresponding loss of efficacy. Even greater security was obtained by the introduction of stone figures to take the place of those made of wood. As a variant to the complete figure in the Serdab, but not necessarily instead of it, a stone representation of the head of the dead person was sometimes, in the IVth and Vth Dynasties, placed in the burial-chamber. These so-called reserve heads were undoubtedly portraits of their owners, perhaps given by the king to privileged members of the court, male and female, as a mark of special favour. The ears, in the surviving examples, are invariably broken off and in some instances an incision has been scored in a line running from the top to the back of the skull, but the reason for these deliberate mutilations is unknown. Presumably the owner's intention was that the reserve head should serve as substitute for the actual head if the latter were destroyed or damaged.

When once the principle of substitution by means of a representation had been recognized, it was but a step to extend its scope to cover not only individual objects, such as food-vessels or statues, but also composite scenes illustrating episodes in the life of the deceased which he wanted to enjoy again in the After-life. Scenes depicting him hunting, fowling or inspecting his estates were therefore believed to provide him with the means to continue these pursuits after his death. Likewise, scenes of harvesting, slaughtering of animals, brewing and baking were thought to guarantee a constant supply of the commodities thus produced.

In order to eliminate any risk of the spirit of the deceased failing to recognize his statue, it was usually inscribed with his name and titles in hieroglyphs. Similarly, in the scenes carved in relief, short explanatory inscriptions were inserted as a kind of commentary, often giving the names of the persons represented and sometimes describing the actions which they performed. These persons were generally relatives of the deceased or his servants, who were thus assured of an After-life in the service of their master.

In spite of all the different devices for securing subsistence which were included in the equipment of the tomb, a regular supply of fresh provisions was always thought essential for the well-being of the deceased. They were laid on a low flat altar, which stood in front of the false door built into the west wall of the offering-room constructed on the east side of the superstructure. This position probably resulted from the practice of building Mastabas on the high desert west of the Nile, so that the deceased, when looking out of the false door, would be facing the valley whence the offerings were usually brought.

Possibly the first offerings were presented by a son who, in providing for his deceased father's needs, symbolized Horus, the son of Osiris. Subsequent offerings would generally be brought by mortuary priests (like Shery mentioned above in connection with the royal tombs of the IInd Dynasty) who were engaged by written contract and paid for their services. Payment took the form of land bequeathed by the deceased to the priests. As an instance, one of the sons of Chephren, the builder of the second Pyramid at Gizeh, bequeathed at least twelve towns as a mortuary endowment of this kind. Such land, having become the property of the priests, would be passed on by them to their heirs, who would also inherit the accompanying obligations with respect to the tomb. Experience must, however, have shown that even the most binding contracts would not be observed for longer than a limited period and, at an early date, the so-called funerary stela was introduced into the tomb to serve as a substitute for the actual offerings. This stela contained a magic formula declaring that the deceased had received the daily offerings in abundance; above the formula there was generally a scene, carved in relief, showing him seated at a table heaped with offerings presented to him by members of his family. While not intended to dispense with the regular supply of fresh provisions, the stela, by means of the magic power of its written word, provided the deceased with a valuable method of reinsurance against starvation and neglect.

However primitive and materialistic the Egyptian conception of the After-life may seem, it must be conceded that it was responsible for the production of some of the greatest artistic masterpieces in antiquity. Without the impetus provided by a practical motive, it is doubtful whether a fraction of the statues, reliefs or inscriptions which are now so universally admired would ever have been produced.

To review the Step Pyramid as a whole: it is certainly not an exaggeration to describe it as one of the most remarkable architectural works produced by the ancient Egyptians. That later generations regarded it with exceptional esteem is clear, not only from the veneration which they accorded to Imhotep, but also from hieratic graffiti on the passage walls of the northern and southern buildings, which record the admiration felt by some Egyptians who visited the monument more than a thousand years after it was built. No other known Pyramid was surrounded with such an array of imposing buildings to supply the needs of the king in his After-life. In their place the kings who ruled two dynasties later were content with pictorial representations carved in relief. As an example, the Pyramid complex of Sahure, the second king of the Vth Dynasty, contains only reliefs of the *heb-sed;* it has no court with buildings specially designed for use in the ceremony.

Doubts have sometimes been entertained whether so high a degree of architectural perfection could have been achieved without having been preceded by a long process of development. There is, however, no evidence that stone had been employed in any earlier building, except for the construction of isolated parts. Moreover, the Step Pyramid displays many features which suggest that its builders lacked experience in the use of stone. Small blocks which could be easily handled were used instead of the massive slabs found in later buildings, showing that the technique of quarrying and manipulating heavy pieces of stone had not then been mastered. Again, engaged columns were probably not the outcome of artistic preference, but of doubt regarding the strength of the free-standing pillar. In decoration too the patterns chosen were copied from the wood, reed or brick elements of earlier buildings; independent forms suited to stone had not yet been evolved.

Size, architectural design and decorative elements were not the only respects in which Zoser's Pyramid excelled the tombs of his predecessors. It was also equipped on a scale never attempted before. In spite of being subjected to plundering over a period of at least four thousand years, it has yielded in the course of excavation thousands of beautifully shaped vases and dishes made of alabaster, schist, porphyry, breccia, quartz crystal, serpentine and many other stones. Considerable quantities still await removal from the tombs of the royal family, where they may be seen lying in heaps reaching from the floor to the ceiling. No food or other commodity was placed in most of these vessels; their very presence, possibly in conjunction with the recitation of a magic formula by the priest, was enough to ensure a constant supply of their appropriate contents for the king.

Before its destruction, the enclosure must have contained a considerable number of statues. Only the seated figure of Zoser in the Serdab has been preserved substantially intact, but fragments of other statues have also been found. At the northern end of the *heb-sed* court there is a limestone pedestal on the top of which are carved eight human feet; it must therefore have supported a group of four statues, possibly those of the king, queen and two princesses. In the same court there were found three large monolithic figures, only one of which had been finished. At first sight these figures resemble caryatides, but it is highly unlikely that they were designed to stand as independent columns; they were probably intended to be built into niches. Fragments of other statues, including at least one of the king, were discovered outside the enclosure wall and in a recess in the south wall of the entrance colonnade. All these statues, and possibly several more which have now disappeared without trace, were made not to commemorate the persons whom they represented, but to provide their spirits with a substitute for their bodies during the various ceremonies performed within the Pyramid enclosure. Since only two royal statues dating from an earlier period—both representing a predecessor of Zoser, Khasekhem—have hitherto been discovered, it is highly probable that Zoser's reign marked a big advance in the production of sculpture in the round. The figure in the Serdab, if it may be regarded as typical, suggests that the collection of statues once contained in the enclosure was of a quality comparable with the finest masterpieces of the succeeding dynasties. . . .

Seneferu's [Snefru] son and successor to the throne was Khufu, better known as Cheops, the Greek form of his name. Inspired possibly by the magnitude of his father's constructions, he chose a plateau, situated on the edge of the desert above five miles west of Gizeh, and erected at its north-west corner a Pyramid of even vaster dimensions. Two later kings of the IVth Dynasty, Chephren and Mycerinus, followed his example by building their Pyramids on the same plateau, a short distance to the south. Together, these three Pyramids constitute possibly the most celebrated group of monuments in the world.

The Pyramid of Cheops, or the Great Pyramid, marks the apogee of Pyramid-building in respect of both size and quality. No exact computation of the amount of hewn stone contained in it is possible, because the centre of its core consists of a nucleus of rock, the size of which cannot be precisely determined. It has, however, been estimated that, when complete, the core of local stone and the outer facing of Tura limestone were composed of about 2,300,000 separate blocks, each averaging some two and a half tons in weight and reaching a maximum of fifteen tons.

Many attempts have been made by writers on the Great Pyramid to illustrate its size by comparison with other famous buildings. It has, for instance, been calculated that the Houses of Parliament and St. Paul's Cathedral could be grouped inside the area of its base and still leave considerable space unoccupied. According to another estimate there would be room for the Cathedrals of Florence, Milan and St. Peter at Rome, as well as for Westminster Abbey and St. Paul's Cathedral. It has also been reckoned that, if it were sawn into cubes measuring a foot in each dimension and these cubes were placed in a row, they would extend over a distance equal to two-thirds of the earth's periphery at the Equator. One computation of this kind has been attributed to Napoleon during his campaign in Egypt. When some of his Generals returned from climbing to the top of the Pyramid, Napoleon, who had declined to make the ascent himself, greeted them with the announcement that, according to his calculations, the three Pyramids on the Gizeh plateau contained enough stone to build a wall, measuring 10 feet in height and 1 foot in width, around the whole of France. The mathematician Monge, who was among the savants accompanying Napoleon on this campaign, is alleged to have confirmed this calculation.

No monument in Egypt has been surveyed and measured so often and with so much care as the Great Pyramid. Even before the theories regarding the supposed esoteric significance of its angles and dimensions had been invented, Edmé-François Jomard, another of Napoleon's staff of savants, Colonel Howard Vyse and J. S. Perring (1837-8) and other pioneers of Egyptian archaeology had measured the monument with as high a degree of accuracy as is required by most modern excavators. The first exhaustive survey of the monument was, however, conducted by Sir Flinders Petrie, who spent the greater part of two seasons (1880-2) at the task. His published results remained the standard work on the subject until 1925, when they were partly superseded by a fresh survey undertaken with the help of more modern instruments by J. H. Cole of the Survey Department of the Egyptian Government. From this survey it was ascertained that the following were the original measurements of the four sides at the base: north, 755.43 feet; south, 756.08 feet; east, 755.88 feet; west, 755.77 feet. While, therefore, no two sides were absolutely identical in length, the difference between the longest and the shortest was only 7.9 inches. Each side was oriented almost exactly in line with true north and south or east and west, the following being the estimated errors: north side, 2′28″ south of west; south side, 1′57″ south of west; east side, 5′30″ west of north; west side, 2′30″ west of north. As the accuracy of this orientation implies, the four corners were almost perfect right angles, their exact measurements being: north-east, 90°3′2″; north-west, 89°59′58″; south-east, 89°56′27″ and south-west, 90°0′33″. When complete, it rose to a height of 481.4

feet, the top 31 feet of which are now missing. Its four sides incline at an angle of about 51°52' to the ground. The area covered by its base is 13.1 acres.

Although the Great Pyramid, when viewed from a distance, gives the impression of being preserved substantially intact, closer observation reveals that it has suffered severely at the hands of despoilers. About a dozen courses and the capstone, possibly made of granite, have been removed from the apex. The whole of the outer facing of Tura limestone, with the exception of a few pieces at the base, has been stripped off the sides. In the north face, a little below the original entrance, there is a large aperture roughly cut in the core. According to Moslem tradition, this aperture was made during the latter part of the ninth century at the command of the Caliph Ma'mun, son of Harun al-Rashid of Arabian Nights fame, in the mistaken belief that the Pyramid contained hidden treasure. Until that time the Pyramid, though doubtless robbed of its former contents, had probably remained structurally intact. Subsequently it became a copious and convenient quarry, providing the stone required for bridges over irrigation canals, houses, walls and other buildings in the neighbourhood of Gizeh and Cairo. . . .

South of the Causeway, close to the first of the subsidiary Pyramids, the Boston-Harvard expedition directed by Reisner found in 1925 the only undisturbed tomb-chamber of the Old Kingdom hitherto known. It lay at the bottom of a vertical shaft which had been blocked with masonry to its entire depth of 99 feet. Within this chamber were stored the fine alabaster sarcophagus and funerary equipment of Queen Hetepheres, wife of Seneferu and mother of Cheops. Although the sarcophagus proved to be empty, the viscera, which had been removed from the body to help in its preservation, were found in an alabaster chest—the so-called canopic chest. To explain the absence of the body, since the chamber had never been plundered, Reisner suggested that Hetepheres was buried in a tomb at Dahshur near the northern stone Pyramid, which he ascribed to Seneferu, but that soon after her burial robbers had broken into the tomb and removed the body with its jewellery and gold ornaments. Before they were able to steal the remainder of the equipment, however, news of the violation of the tomb had reached the king. Hoping to prevent further despoilment, Cheops, who may not have been told of the disappearance of the body, decided to transfer his mother's tomb—possibly in secret—to Gizeh, where it would receive the same degree of protection as his own Pyramid. As an additional precaution not only was no superstructure built above the new tomb, but a coating of plaster was spread over the stones covering the mouth of the shaft and finally the whole cavity was overlaid with a layer of limestone gravel so that no trace of its presence was visible. The fact that it remained undetected until the twentieth century, when the American excavators literally swept the sand from the rock-bed, is the best testimony to the success of the stratagem.

Among the smaller objects found in this chamber were alabaster vessels, a copper ewer, three gold vessels, gold razors and knives, copper tools and a gold manicure instrument, pointed at one end for cleaning the nails and curved at the other end for pressing down the quick; a toilet-box contained eight small alabaster vases filled with unguents and kohl. Inside a jewel-case were twenty silver anklets, each inlaid with dragonflies of malachite, lapis lazuli and carnelian. The larger objects included a canopy-frame made of wood cased with gold, and two armchairs and a bed which were partly cased with gold sheeting. On the foot-board of the bed was a panel of gold inlaid with a blue and black floral design. A carrying-chair, also made of wood partly cased with gold sheeting, bore an inscription, written in hieroglyphs of gold set in ebony panels and repeated four times, which read: "The mother of the King of Upper and Lower Egypt, follower of Horus, she who is in charge of the affairs of the harem (?), whose every word is done for her, daughter of the god (begotten) of his body, Hetepheres."

No description can do justice to the artistic excellence and technical perfection of the equipment of Hetepheres; in comparison with its exquisite simplicity of design, much of the tomb furniture used in the later periods appears tawdry. Only the woodwork had suffered with the passage of time; inevitably it had either become decayed or shrunk to such a degree that it could not be used when the objects were reconstructed by the experts of the Boston-Harvard expedition before being delivered, in accordance with the terms of the excavators' agreement, to the Cairo Museum. Reisner was of the opinion that at least some of the objects had been used by Hetepheres during her lifetime. There is nothing improbable in the suggestion. Belongings of a personal kind were certainly not placed in the tomb until the time of the funeral, although vases and jars containing stores were often made expressly for the tomb and may well have been deposited there in advance. Whether the objects actually formed part of the furnishings of the queen's apartments in the palace is, however, a matter of only secondary importance. The real interest of the discovery lies in the light which it throws on the practical and artistic achievements of the IVth Dynasty and in the concrete evidence which it provides of the kind of equipment which was once to be found in other contemporary royal tombs.

Not the least significant of the various elements designed to add to the impressive effect of the Great Pyramid was its architectural setting. Other Pyramids were surrounded by the tombs of officials and relatives of their owners, but little attention seems to have been given to their lay-out. East and west of the Great Pyramid enclosure wall, however, large cemeteries of Mastabas were arranged in parallel rows several feet apart. South of the Pyramid only a single row was built, while on the north there were none. The ownership of the tombs was also carefully planned, those in the eastern cemetery being allotted to close relatives of the king and those in the western cemetery—the larger—to officials. Although most of these Mastabas have now lost their entire outer casing, it must be supposed that they were all originally faced with Tura limestone; their colour therefore would have been uniform with that of the vast Pyramid rising in their midst. H. Junker, who excavated a part of the western cemetery, has aptly remarked that the Egyptian conception of the dead ruler continuing in the After-life to be surrounded by his relatives and loyal followers has never found so vivid an expression as in the arrangement of the tombs in this necropolis. It may be claimed, with equal truth, that the difference between the divine majesty of the ruler and his mortal subjects was never more strongly emphasized than in the contrast between the towering Pyramid and the simple flattopped Mastabas.

Cheops's obvious wishes for the architectural setting of his tomb appear to have commanded little respect from subsequent generations. Already in the Vth and VIth Dynasties the symmetry of the original design was being destroyed by the construction of smaller Mastabas in the spaces between the rows. The owners of these tombs were either officials of the necropolis or mortuary priests who, during their lifetime, had performed the various duties deemed necessary for securing the well-being of the dead king and his associates. In later times, particularly under the Saites, burial in the vicinity of the three Gizeh Pyramids was believed to confer special benefits on the dead, with the result that the whole area became honeycombed with tombs and the regularity of the earliest design must have been obscured beyond recognition.

South of the Great Pyramid complex and near the Valley Building of the Second Pyramid lies the Giant Sphinx. A knoll of rock, which had been left by the builders of the Great Pyramid when quarrying stone for its inner core, was fashioned in the time of Chephren into a huge recumbent lion with a human head. It was probably overlaid with a coating of plaster and painted. The length of this colossus is about 240 feet, its height 66 feet and the maximum width of the face 13 feet 8 inches. On the head is the royal head-dress; other emblems of royalty are the cobra on the forehead, and the beard, now largely missing, on the chin. Although the face has been severely mutilated, it still gives the impression of being a portrait of King Chephren and not merely a formalized representation. A figure, possibly of the king, was carved in front of the chest, but scarcely any trace of it now remains. Between the outstretched paws stands a large slab of red granite bearing an inscription which purports to record a dream of Thutmosis IV of the XVIIIth Dynasty before he ascended the throne. According to this inscription the prince, when hunting, decided to rest at midday in the shadow of the Sphinx. During his sleep the Sphinx, which was regarded at that time as an embodiment of the Sun-god Harmachis, promised him the Double Crown of Egypt if he would clear away the sand which had nearly engulfed its body. Unfortunately, the latter part of the inscription is too badly weathered to be legible, but it may be surmised that it related how the god's wish was fulfilled and how the prince was finally rewarded with the Crown of the Two Lands. In addition to clearing away the sand, Thutmosis IV may have repaired damaged portions of the body by the insertion of small blocks of limestone—an operation which was repeated in Ptolemaic or Roman times, when the sand was once more removed and an altar was erected in front of the figure. The first excavation of the Sphinx in modern times was conducted by Captain Caviglia in 1818 at a cost of £450. Sixty-eight years later it was again freed of sand by Gaston Maspero and lastly, in 1925, the *Service des Antiquités* undertook once more its clearance and restoration. . . .

More notable, however, than the structural innovations of this Pyramid [of Unas] are the vertical columns of hieroglyphic inscription which entirely cover the walls of the vestibule and the limestone portions of the walls of the burial-chamber. Every hieroglyph has been filled with a blue pigment, so that it stands out clearly against the white background. These inscriptions are known as the Pyramid texts. They are found not only in this Pyramid, but also in the VIth Dynasty Pyramids of Teti, Pepi I, Merenre and Pepi II, in the Pyramid of a king named Ibi, whose date is uncertain, and in the Pyramids of Pepi II's three queens. They do not form a continuous narrative, but consist of a collection of spells assembled in no fixed order. Although most of the spells occur in more than one Pyramid, very few are repeated in all the Pyramids in which the texts are found; in the Pyramid of Unas, for instance, only two hundred and twenty-eight spells are included out of a known total exceeding seven hundred.

The purpose of the Pyramid texts, like that of every other element in the Pyramid complex, was to secure for the king or queen a happy After-life. So powerful was the magic of the written word that its presence alone provided a sufficient guarantee that the thought expressed would be realized. Doubtless the spoken word, if delivered by a qualified person, possessed at least equal virtue, but its utterance was dependent on the goodwill or diligence of other people. A text which is generally inscribed on the north wall of the burial-chamber reproduces the ritual which the priests used to recite every day in the Mortuary Temple when laying the provisions on the altar in front of the false door. By having this ritual in writing and supplies of provisions in the magazines of his temple, the king believed that he would eliminate the risk of suffering hunger and thirst, even if the priests should neglect to perform their duties. Many of the texts describe the journey of the king to the Other World, situated in the sky beyond the eastern horizon, and his activities on arrival. It is clear that the king could count on little assistance from the gods when making this journey, but, armed with the magic power of the texts, he might expect to overcome successfully its many hazards. With their help, moreover, his association with the Sun-god in his daily voyage across the sky was assured. Among the texts were also collections of hymns to the gods and prayers on behalf of the dead king. . . .

At the same time as the preliminary work was being conducted on the Pyramid site, other preparations for building were being made elsewhere. The foundation of the Causeway, composed of stone quarried in the locality, was being laid so that it could be used for the passage of material when constructional work on the Pyramid began. Fine limestone blocks for the outer casing of the building were being quarried on the east bank of the Nile at Tura in the Muqattam hills. The men employed on this work painted the names of their gangs in red ochre on the blocks before they were taken from the quarry; although these names were very often erased in the course of subsequent operations, enough remain to perpetuate many of the gangs. As examples, the following names, found by Alan Rowe, occur on casing-blocks of the Meidum Pyramid: "Stepped Pyramid Gang," "Boat Gang," "Vigorous Gang," "Sceptre Gang," "Enduring Gang," "North Gang" and "South Gang." A block in the Great Pyramid bears the name: "The Craftsmengang. How powerful is the White Crown of Khnum Khufu!" Why these names were placed on the stones is not evident, unless it was with the intention of facilitating the task of keeping a tally of the work done by each gang. Far away to the south, at Aswan, another group of men were quarrying granite for columns, architraves, door-jambs, lintels, casing-blocks and sometimes the outer sarcophagus.

Limestone, whether obtained from the surface of the rock, as at Gizeh, or extracted by tunnelling, as at Tura, presented the Pyramid builders with no serious difficulties in its quarrying. A discovery by W. B. Emery in the early dynastic cemetery of Sakkara has shown that even in the Ist Dynasty the Egyptians possessed excellent copper tools, including saws and chisels, which were capable of cutting any kind of limestone. As an aid to sawing, a wet abrasive material such as moistened quartz sand, which is plentiful in Egypt, may have been employed, but there is no positive evidence either of the material used or of the practice. Chisels and wedges were, however, the tools most favoured for quarrying limestone, the former for cutting the blocks away from the rock on every side except the bottom and the latter for detaching the blocks at the base. In a tunnel-quarry, for instance, a deep hollow resembling a shelf and extending across the whole breadth of the passage was first cut between the roof and the block to be detached. The purpose of this hollow was to allow a quarryman to crawl across the top of the block and separate it from the rock behind by chipping vertically downwards with a chisel struck by a wooden mallet. At the same time other quarrymen made similar vertical cuttings down the two sides. Finally, wedges were inserted into holes cut at the bottom in order to make a horizontal split in the rock, which freed the block entirely. Sometimes the wedges were composed of wood, and the split was achieved by wetting the wood and so causing it to expand. The process was afterwards repeated on the rock below, without the necessity of cutting the initial hollow, until floor-level had been reached; a new series of cuttings, starting at roof-level, was then begun deeper in the tunnel. Surface-quarrying was carried out by exactly the same method. It possessed a great advantage over tunnel-quarrying, in so far as the space for working was not so confined and a greater number of men could therefore be employed at one time. On the other hand, the finest limestone often lay in strata buried deeply beneath the surface, and tunnelling offered the only practical means of access.

The methods employed in the Pyramid Age for quarrying granite and other hard stones are still a subject of controversy. One authority even expressed the opinion that hard stone quarrying was not attempted until the Middle Kingdom; before that time, the amount needed could have been obtained from large boulders lying loose on the surface of the ground. It seems difficult, however, to believe that a people who possessed the degree of skill necessary for shaping the colossal monoliths built into the granite Valley Building of Chephren were not also able to hew rough blocks of this stone out of the quarry, particularly since tunnelling was never adopted. Furthermore, on the backs of the slabs roofing Mycerinus's burial-chamber marks made by the insertion of wedges may still be seen, and the natural inference appears to be that the operation denoted by these wedge-marks was the splitting of the slabs from the rock in the quarry. This method of quarrying was certainly practised in later times, as is demonstrated by the countless rows of wedge-slots still visible today in the Aswan quarries; there is nothing to suggest that quarrymen were not detaching blocks by the same device in the Old Kingdom. The slots may have been made either by rubbing an abrasive powder with stone or by a metal tool. Since copper is the only metal for tools known to have been available in Egypt before the Middle Kingdom, it has been supposed that the Egyptians had mastered a process, now lost, of giving copper a very high temper, but this surmise has not yet been proved.

An alternative and more laborious method of quarrying granite was by pounding the rock around the block to be detached with balls of dolerite—a hard greenish stone found over a wide area of the eastern desert near the Red Sea. An unfinished obelisk dating from the New Kingdom, which still lies at Aswan, was undoubtedly quarried by this method, and there is no inherent improbability in the supposition that quarrymen were already acquainted with the technique in Pyramid times.

By whatever method of quarrying the granite blocks were obtained, the procedure for reaching stone of the quality required, if it were not available in the uppermost stratum, would have been similar. Granite, like many another stone, if heated to a high temperature and then suddenly cooled, will develop superficial cracks, and the face, when subjected to the slightest friction, will immediately crumble away. A fire lit on the rock to be pared down would soon raise its temperature to the requisite degree, and the application of cold water would cause the disintegration of the surface, which could then be rubbed away with the aid of a small stone scraper. If necessary, the process could be repeated many times until stone of the desired hardness had been reached.

By no means the least remarkable achievement of the Pyramid builders was the transport of the blocks from their quarries to the site of the Pyramid. Some of the heaviest pieces of local limestone embodied in the Mortuary Temple of Mycerinus, according to Reisner's estimate, weigh about 200 tons. In comparison with this amount, the casing-blocks of the Great Pyramid, which average only about 2½ tons, and the 50-ton granite roof-slabs of the King's Chamber may seem trivial, but it must be remembered that the latter required not only to be loaded on barges and subsequently unloaded, but also, for the most part, to be raised at the end of their journey to a very considerable height above ground-level. The navigation of these megaliths, probably undertaken in the main during the inundation season, may well have been the least formidable part of the whole task, though the control of heavily laden barges on a fast-flowing river must always have been a hazardous operation requiring great skill. Moreover, the journey from Aswan, although free from cataracts, involved negotiating the difficult waters and shifting sandbanks near Gebel Abu Foda, about ninety miles south of Sakkara. For transport over land, the method employed was probably the same whether the weight to be moved was 200 tons or 2½ tons, the number of men being regulated by the amount of the weight. What was this method? It is highly improbable that wheeled vehicles were used, because, although some of the carrying possibilities of the wheel had been realized at least as early as the Vth Dynasty, scenes in tombs of the XVIIIth Dynasty demonstrate that, even after a lapse of a thousand years, statues and heavy blocks of stone were not moved by wheeled transport. Instead, sledges were employed, and there can be little doubt that the Pyramid builders also used this method. Each block was probably levered on the sledge either directly from the ground or by way of a low ramp composed of brick or stone. Both sledge and block, lashed together by ropes, may then have been raised again by means of levers, in order that wooden rollers might be placed underneath. The loaded sledge would subsequently be dragged over a way paved with baulks of timber by men pulling on ropes attached to the sledge. An illustration of the actual process of transport was included by Djehutihotep, a nobleman of the XIIth Dynasty, in his tomb at El-Bersheh. In this scene an alabaster statue of Djehutihotep, which probably weighed about 60 tons, is mounted on a sledge pulled by 172 men. Water or some other liquid is poured on the ground to lessen the friction and thus facilitate haulage. . . .

In the face of so many unknown or unconfirmed factors, speculations regarding the number of men required for building one of the larger Pyramids and the time needed for the work may perhaps appear vain. Certainly, any estimate based on the evidence now available must lack precision and can only serve to convey an approximate idea. Herodotus claims to have been informed that the Great Pyramid was built in twenty years. Levies numbering one hundred thousand men, he says, were employed for "periods of three months" on transporting the stones from the quarry to the Pyramid. Herodotus seems to have intended his readers to understand that the aggregate of men engaged annually was 400,000—four separate groups of 100,000, each group being employed for three months in the year. Such a number would, however, have been unnecessarily large, as a simple mathematical calculation will demonstrate. If the estimated total of 2,300,000 separate blocks in the Pyramid is approximately correct, the average number of blocks to be transported annually for twenty years would have been 115,000. The mean weight of the blocks is about

2½ tons, a weight which Petrie believed could have been handled by a gang of eight men. Assuming that Petrie was right and that only 100,000 men were employed in a year, each gang would have been required to move ten blocks in twelve weeks. Such a task would almost certainly have been within the ability of a gang, bearing in mind that the distance to be traversed, especially by the core blocks, was not very great. Moreover, as Petrie pointed out, the work could have been done during the inundation season, between the end of July and the end of October, when the land could not be cultivated and the majority of the population would have been idle.

There can be little doubt but that, in addition to the men levied annually for the special purpose of transporting the blocks of the Great Pyramid, a large number of whole-time workers must have been engaged in building the Pyramid. These men, consisting of skilled masons and an attendant body of labourers, were continuously employed preparing and laying the blocks and erecting or dismantling the ramps and foot-hold embankments. They lived, it may be presumed, in the buildings found by Petrie lying west of the Pyramid of Chephren. About 4,000 men, according to Petrie's estimate, could have been housed in these barracks, and that figure would therefore represent the total number of permanent workers. The chips of stone cast away by the masons were dumped over the side of the cliffs both north and south of the Pyramid. Commenting on the size of the dumps, Petrie wrote: "They are probably equal in bulk to more than half of the Pyramid."

4. *Life in Egypt*

WALLIS BUDGE

The Peasant and the Official

THIS extract from what is sometimes called the tale of the Wronged
Peasant, or the Eloquent Peasant, gives a glimpse of the riverside
fields of the Middle Kingdom. They are still much the same today.
Anyone who has walked near the Nile knows these narrow paths
on balks between crops and irrigation channels. The peasant won
his case in the end.

THE text of these appeals is written in hieratic on papyri preserved
in Berlin. These papyri belong to the period of the Middle Empire
and were inscribed about 2000 B.C., probably in the reign of King
Nebkaura. The principal interest of the appeals is the high-flown
and elegant language in which they are couched.

[HOW THE APPEALS CAME TO BE MADE]

There was a certain man whose name was Khunanpu, and he was
a field-labourer in Sekhet-hemat (i.e. Salt-Field), and he had a
wife whose name was Merit. And this peasant said unto his wife:
"Behold I am going down to Egypt in order to bring back food for
my children. Go into the grain-shed and measure the grain which
remaineth there, and tell me how many measures there are." And
his wife went and measured the grain, and found that there were
eight measures. Then this peasant said unto his wife: "Behold, thou
shalt keep two measures of grain for the support of thyself and thy

From *Egyptian Tales and Romances*. London: Thornton Butterworth & Co. Ltd.;
1931, pp. 48-51, 213-14. By permission of the Estates Bursar of University College,
Oxford, and Eyre and Spottiswoode Ltd.

children, and the remaining six measures thou shalt make into bread and beer which shall serve for my food day by day whilst I am on my journey."

[THE PEASANT SETS OUT FOR EGYPT]

And the peasant went down into Egypt, having laden his asses with natron and salt and muriate of soda, and twigs from the Oasis of Farafrah, and skins of leopards and wolves, and doves and other birds of the Oasis, and medicinal plants, coriander seed, aniseed, wild thyme, narcissus and certain fruits, and precious stones, and every kind of useful object produced in the Oasis of Salt Field.

[THE PEASANT MEETS THE OFFICIAL DJEHUTI-NEKHT]

And this peasant journeyed towards the South, with his asses, towards Ahnas, and he arrived in the district of Per-Fefa, which lay to the north of Metnit. There he found standing on the dyke a man called Djehuti-Nekht. He was the son of a man whose name was Asri, and was one of the subordinate officials of the chief steward Rensi, the son of Meru. And when this man Djehuti-Nekht saw the asses of the peasant, of which his heart highly approved, he said: "Would that I had with me the image of some god (i.e. amulet or charm) that through it I might filch the possessions of this peasant from him!"

Now the house of this Djehuti-Nekht stood upon a platform of earth by the side of a foot-path, which was narrow and not wide, and was only as broad as a kerchief (or, napkin); on the one side of it was the water (of the canal), and on the other a crop of *dhura* (millet?) was growing. And Djehuti-Nekht cried out to his servant: "Make haste (or run) and fetch me a sheet from my house," and the sheet was brought unto him forthwith. Then he spread out the sheet over the surface of the path, and one end of it fluttered over the water, and the other end of it over the growing millet.

And the peasant advanced on the path which was used by the people generally, and Djehuti-Nekht said unto him: "Take care, O peasant, wouldst thou dare to walk over my sheet?" And the peasant said unto him: "I will do whatsoever pleaseth thee, so that my road is a good one." And the peasant went along on the landward side of the path [to avoid the sheet]. And Djehuti-Nekht said unto him: "What is this? Wouldst thou turn my grain-field into a highway?" And the peasant said unto him: "My road is a proper one. The slope is steep and the grain hath grown over the path, and thou hast covered it up with thy sheet. Wouldst thou prevent us from travelling on the path altogether?" And at the very moment when he spake thus one of the asses bit off a mouthful of the grain with the stalk. Thereupon Djehuti-Nekht said: "Look you, peasant, I shall seize thy ass for he is eating up my grain, and he shall in return for his boldness tread out the grain."

Then this peasant said: "My road is a proper one (or, is the right one). Inasmuch as one side of the path was impassable, I have been obliged to drive my ass along on the other. And now thou wouldst seize him because he hath filled his mouth with the grain and the stalk. But I know the lord of this farm, and it belongeth to the chief steward Rensi, the son of Meru. He hath suppressed every highway robber in all this district, and am I to be robbed on his estate?" And this Djehuti-Nekht said: "Doth not a proverb which the people use run, 'The name of the peasant is only uttered (or, mentioned) at his lord's will.' It is I who am speaking to thee, but it is of the chief steward of whom thou art thinking." Then Djehuti-Nekht snatched up a cudgel of tamarisk wood, and beat every member of his body therewith, and he seized the peasant's asses and drove them into his own farmyard.

Then the peasant began to weep bitterly and to cry out aloud through the beating which had been inflicted upon him. And this Djehuti-Nekht said unto him: "Lift not up thy voice so loudly, O peasant, for behold, thou art in the district of the Lord of Silence." And this peasant said: "Thou hast beaten me and robbed me of my goods; wouldst thou now also rob me of the cry which my mouth uttereth? Lord of Silence forsooth! Give me back my possessions, and then I will not cry out and disturb thy Silence (or Peace)." And during the next ten days this peasant passed his whole time in making entreaty to Djehuti-Nekhat [for his goods], but this man paid no heed thereto.

HERODOTUS

Egypt According to Herodotus

THE Egyptians before the reign of Psammetichus used to think that
of all races in the world they were the most ancient; Psammetichus,
however, when he came to the throne, took it into his head to settle
this question of priority, and ever since his time the Egyptians have
believed that the Phrygians surpass them in antiquity and that they
themselves come second. Psammetichus, finding that mere inquiry
failed to reveal which was the original race of mankind, devised an
ingenious method of determining the matter. He took at random,
from an ordinary family, two newly born infants and gave them
to a shepherd to be brought up amongst his flocks, under strict
orders that no one should utter a word in their presence. They were
to be kept by themselves in a lonely cottage, and the shepherd was
to bring in goats from time to time, to see that the babies had
enough milk to drink, and to look after them in any other way that
was necessary. All these arrangements were made by Psammetichus
because he wished to find out what word the children would first
utter, once they had grown out of their meaningless baby-talk. The
plan succeeded; two years later the shepherd, who during that time
had done everything he had been told to do, happened one day to
open the door of the cottage and go in, when both children, running
up to him with hands outstretched, pronounced the word "becos."
The first time this occurred the shepherd made no mention of it;
but later, when he found that every time he visited the children to
attend to their needs the same word was constantly repeated by
them, he informed his master. Psammetichus ordered the children
to be brought to him, and when he himself heard them say "becos"
he determined to find out to what language the word belonged. His
inquiries revealed that it was the Phrygian for "bread," and in consideration of this the Egyptians yielded their claims and admitted
the superior antiquity of the Phrygians. That this was what really
happened I myself learnt from the priests of Hephaestus at Memphis—though the Greeks have various improbable versions of the

From *The Histories*, Book II, pp. 102-4, 115-18, 131, 132-4, 137.

story, such as that Psammetichus had the children brought up by women whose tongues he had cut out. The version of the priests, however, is the one I have given. There were other things, too, which I learnt at Memphis in conversation with the priests of Hephaestus, and I actually went to Thebes and Heliopolis for the express purpose of finding out if the priests in those cities would agree in what they told me with the priests at Memphis. It is at Heliopolis that the most learned of the Egyptian antiquaries are said to be found. I am not anxious to repeat what I was told about the Egyptian religion, apart from the mere names of their deities, for I do not think that any one nation knows much more about such things than any other; whatever I shall mention on the subject will be due simply to the exigencies of my story. As to practical matters, they all agreed in saying that the Egyptians by their study of astronomy discovered the solar year and were the first to divide it into twelve parts—and in my opinion their method of calculation is better than the Greek; for the Greeks, to make the seasons work out properly, intercalate a whole month every other year, while the Egyptians make the year consist of twelve months of thirty days each and every year intercalate five additional days, and so complete the regular circle of the seasons. They also told me that the Egyptians first brought into use the names of the twelve gods, which the Greeks took over from them, and were the first to assign altars and images and temples to the gods, and to carve figures in stone. They proved the truth of most of these assertions, and went on to tell me that the first man to rule Egypt was Min, in whose time the whole country, except the district around Thebes, was marsh, none of the land below Lake Moeris— seven days' voyage up river from the sea—then showing above the water. I have little doubt that they were right in this; for it is clear to any intelligent observer, even if he has no previous information on the subject, that the Egypt to which we sail nowadays is, as it were, the gift of the river and has come only recently into the possession of its inhabitants. The same is true of the country above the lake for the distance of a three days' voyage: the priests said nothing to me about it, but it is, in fact, precisely the same type of country.

About Egypt itself I shall have a great deal more to relate because of the number of remarkable things which the country contains, and because of the fact that more monuments which beggar description are to be found there than anywhere else in the world. That is reason enough for my dwelling on it at greater length. Not only is the Egyptian climate peculiar to that country, and the Nile different in its behaviour from other rivers elsewhere, but the Egyptians themselves in their manners and customs seem to have reversed the ordinary practices of mankind. For instance, women attend market and are employed in trade, while men stay at home and do the weaving. In weaving, the normal way is to work the threads of the weft upwards, but the Egyptians work them downwards. Men in Egypt carry loads on their heads, women on their shoulders; women pass water standing up, men sitting down. To ease themselves they go indoors, but eat outside in the streets, on the theory that what is unseemly but necessary should be done in private, and what is not unseemly should be done openly. No woman holds priestly office, either in the service of goddess or god; only men are priests in both cases. Sons are under no compulsion to support their parents if they do not wish to do so, but daughters must, whether they wish it or not. Elsewhere priests grow their hair long; in Egypt they shave their heads. In other nations the relatives of the deceased in time of mourning cut their hair, but the Egyptians, who shave at all other times, mark a death by letting the hair grow both on head and chin. They live with their animals—unlike the rest of the world, who live apart from them. Other men live on wheat and barley, but any Egyptian who does so is blamed for it, their bread being made from spelt, or Zea as some call it. Dough they knead with their feet, but clay with their hands—and even handle dung. They practise circumcision, while men of other nations—except those who have learnt from Egypt—leave their private parts as nature made them. Men in Egypt have two garments each, women only one. The ordinary practice at sea is to make sheets fast to ring-bolts fitted outboard; the Egyptians fit them inboard. In writing or calculating, instead of going, like the Greeks, from left to right, the Egyptians go from right to left—and obstinately maintain that theirs is the dexterous method, ours being left-handed and awkward. They have two sorts of writing, the sacred and the common. They are religious to excess, beyond any other nation in the world, and here are some of the customs which illustrate the fact: they drink from brazen cups which they scour every day—everyone, without exception. They wear linen clothes which they make a special point of continually washing. They circumcise themselves for cleanliness' sake, preferring to be clean rather than comely. The priests shave their bodies all over every other day to guard against the presence of lice, or anything else equally unpleasant, while they are about their religious duties; the priests, too, wear linen only, and shoes made from the papyrus plant—these materials, for dress and shoes, being the only ones allowed them. They bathe in cold water twice a day and twice every night—and observe innumerable other ceremonies besides. Their life, however, is not by any means all hardship, for they enjoy advantages too: for instance, they are free from all personal expense, having bread made for them out of the sacred grain, and a plentiful daily supply of goose-meat and beef, with wine in addition. Fish they are forbidden to touch; and as for beans, they cannot even bear to look at them, because they imagine they are unclean (in point of fact the Egyptians never sow beans, and even if any happen to grow wild, they will not eat them, either raw or boiled). They do not have a single priest for each god, but a number, of which one is chief-priest, and when a chief-priest dies his son is appointed to succeed him. Bulls are considered the property of the god Epaphus—or Apis—and are therefore tested in the following way: a priest appointed for the purpose examines the animal, and if he finds even a single black hair upon him, pronounces him unclean; he goes over him with the greatest care, first making him stand up, then lie on his back, after which he pulls out his tongue to see if that, too, is "clean" according to the recognized marks—what those are I will explain later. He also inspects the tail to make sure the hair on it grows properly; then, if the animal passes all these tests success-fully, the priest marks him by twisting round his horns a band of papyrus which he seals with wax and stamps with his signet ring. The bull is finally taken away, and the penalty is death for anybody who sacrifices an animal which has not been marked in this manner. The method of sacrifice is as follows: they take the beast (one of those marked with the scal) to the appropriate altar and light a fire; then, after pouring a libation of wine and invoking the god by name, they slaughter it, cut off its head, and flay the carcase. The head is loaded with curses and taken away—if there happen to be Greek traders in the market, it is sold to them; if not, it is thrown into the river. The curses they pronounce take the form of a prayer that any disaster which threatens either themselves or their country may be diverted and fall upon the severed head of the beast. Both the liba-tion and the practice of cutting off the heads of sacrificial beasts are common to all Egyptians in all their sacrifices, and the latter explains why it is that no Egyptian will use the head of any sort of animal for food. The methods of disemboweling and burning are various, and I will describe the one which is followed in the worship of the goddess whom they consider the greatest and honour with the most important festival. In this case, when they have flayed the bull, they first pray and then take its paunch out whole, leaving the intestines and fat inside the body; next they cut off the legs, shoul-ders, neck, and rump, and stuff the carcase with loaves of bread, honey, raisins, figs, frankincense, myrrh, and other aromatic sub-stances; finally they pour a quantity of oil over the carcase and burn it. They always fast before a sacrifice, and while the fire is consum-ing it they beat their breasts. That part of the ceremony done, they serve a meal out of the portions left over.

All Egyptians use bulls and bull-calves for sacrifice, if they have passed the test for "cleanness": but they are forbidden to sacrifice cows, on the ground that they are sacred to Isis. The statues of Isis show a female figure with cow's horns, like the Greek representations of Io, and of all animals cows are universally held by the Egyptians in the greatest reverence. This is the reason why no Egyptian, man or woman, will kiss a Greek, or use a Greek knife, spit, or cauldron, or even eat the flesh of a bull known to be clean, if it has been cut with a Greek knife.

They have a curious method of disposing of dead bulls and cows: cows are thrown into the river, but bulls are buried on the outskirts of towns, with one horn, or sometimes both, sticking out from the ground to mark the place. In due time, when the carcase has rotted, a barge comes from the island called Prosopitis to collect the bones. This island is part of the Delta and is nine *schoeni* in circumference; it contains a number of towns, the one from which the barges come being Atarbechis, where there is a temple of much sanctity dedicated to Aphrodite. From Atarbechis many people go round to the various towns to dig up the bones, which they take away and bury again all together in one spot. Other cattle which die a natural death are disposed of in the same way as bulls—for that is the law. None of them are slaughtered.

The Egyptians who live in the cultivated parts of the country, by their practice of keeping records of the past, have made themselves much the best historians of any nation of which I have had experience. I will describe some of their habits: every month for three successive days they purge themselves, for their health's sake, with emetics and clysters, in the belief that all diseases come from the food a man eats; and it is a fact—even apart from this precaution—that next to the Libyans they are the healthiest people in the world. I should put this down myself to the absence of changes in the climate; for change, and especially change of weather, is the prime cause of disease. They eat loaves made from spelt—*cyllestes* is their word for them—and drink a wine made from barley, as they have no vines in the country. Some kinds of fish they eat raw, either dried in the sun, or salted; quails, too, they eat raw, and ducks and various small birds, after pickling them in brine; other sorts of birds and fish, apart from those which are considered sacred, they either roast or broil. When the rich give a party and the meal is finished, a man carries round amongst the guests a wooden image of a corpse in a coffin, carved and painted to look as much like the real thing as possible, and anything from eighteen inches to three feet long; he shows it to each guest in turn, and says: "Look upon this body as you drink and enjoy yourself; for you will be just like it when you are dead.". . .

The clothes they wear consist of a linen tunic with a fringe hanging round the legs (called in their language *calasiris*), and a white woollen garment on top of it. It is, however, contrary to religious usage to be buried in a woollen garment, or to wear wool in a temple. They agree in this with those who are known as the followers of Orpheus and Bacchus (actually followers of the Egyptians and of Pythagoras); for anyone intitiated into these rites is similarly debarred from burial in a garment of wool. They have a religious doctrine to explain the reason for this.

The Nile boats used for carrying freight are built of acantha wood —the acantha resembles in form the lotus of Cyrene, and exudes gum. They cut short planks, about three feet long, from this tree, and the method of construction is to lay them together like bricks and through-fasten them with long spikes set close together, and then, when the hull is complete, to lay the deck-beams across on top. The boats have no ribs and are caulked from inside with papyrus. They are given a single steering-oar, which is driven down through the keel; the masts are of acantha wood, the sails of papyrus. These vessels cannot sail up the river without a good leading wind, but have to be towed from the banks; and for dropping downstream with the current they are handled as follows: each vessel is equipped with a raft made of tamarisk wood, with a rush mat fastened on top of it, and a stone with a hole through it weighing some four hundredweight; the raft and the stone are made fast to the vessel with ropes, fore and aft respectively, so that the raft is carried rapidly forward by the current and pulls the "baris" (as these boats are called) after it, while the stone, dragging along the bottom astern, acts as a check and gives her steerage-way. There are a great many of these vessels on the Nile, some of them of enormous carrying capacity.

When the Nile overflows, the whole country is converted into a sea, and the towns, which alone remain above water, look like the islands in the Aegean. At these times water transport is used all over the country, instead of merely along the course of the river, and anyone going from Naucratis to Memphis would pass right by the pyramids instead of following the usual course by Cercasorus and the tip of the Delta.

GASTON MASPERO

Egyptian Houses

THE soil of Egypt, periodically washed by the inundation, is a black, compact, homogeneous clay, which becomes of stony hardness when dry. From immemorial time, the fellaheen have used it for the construction of their houses. The hut of the poorest peasant is a mere rudely-shaped mass of this clay. A rectangular space, some eight or ten feet in width, by perhaps sixteen or eighteen feet in length, is enclosed in a wickerwork of palm-branches, coated on both sides with a layer of mud. As this coating cracks in the drying, the fissures are filled in, and more coats of mud are daubed on until the walls attain a thickness of from four inches to a foot. Finally, the whole is roofed over with palm-branches and straw, the top being covered in with a thin layer of beaten earth. The height varies. In most huts, the ceiling is so low that to rise suddenly is dangerous both to one's head and to the structure, while in others the roof is six or seven feet from the floor. Windows, of course, there are none. Sometimes a hole is left in the middle of the roof to let the smoke out; but this is a refinement undreamed of by many.

At the first glance, it is not always easy to distinguish between these huts of wattle and daub and those built with crude bricks. The ordinary Egyptian brick is a mere oblong block of mud mixed with chopped straw and a little sand, and dried in the sun. At a spot where they are about to build, one man is told off to break up the ground; others carry the clods, and pile them in a heap, while others again mix them with water, knead the clay with their feet, and reduce it to a homogeneous paste. This paste, when sufficiently worked, is pressed by the head workman in moulds made of hard wood, while an assistant carries away the bricks as fast as they are shaped, and lays them out in rows at a little distance apart, to dry in the sun. A careful brickmaker will leave them thus for half a day, or even for a whole day; after which the bricks are piled in stacks in such wise that the air can circulate freely among them; and so

From *Egyptian Archaeology*. Translated by Amelia Edwards. London: Grevel & Co. Ltd.; 1887, pp. 1-4, 6-10, 170-7.

they remain for a week or two before they are used. More frequently, however, they are exposed for only a few hours to the heat of the sun, and the building is begun while they are yet damp. The mud, however, is so tenacious that, notwithstanding this carelessness, they are not readily put out of shape. The outer faces of the bricks become disintegrated by the action of the weather, but those in the inner part of the wall remain intact, and are still separable. A good modern workman will easily mould a thousand bricks a day, and after a week's practice he may turn out 1,200, 1,500, or even 1,800. The ancient workmen, whose appliances in no wise differed from those of the present day, produced equally satisfactory results. The dimensions they generally adopted were 8.7 x 4.3 x 5.5 inches for ordinary bricks, or 15.0 x 7.1 x 5.5 for a larger size, though both larger and smaller are often met with in the ruins. Bricks issued from the royal workshops were sometimes stamped with the cartouches of the reigning monarch; while those made by private factories bore on the side a trade mark in red ochre, a squeeze of the moulder's fingers, or the stamp of the maker. By far the greater number have, however, no distinctive mark. Burnt bricks were not often used before the Roman period nor tiles, either flat or curved. Glazed bricks appear to have been the fashion in the Delta. The finest specimen that I have seen, namely, one in the Boulak Museum, is inscribed in black ink with the cartouches of Ramses III. The glaze of this brick is green, but other fragments are coloured blue, red, yellow, or white. . . .

The lower classes lived in mere huts which, though built of bricks, were no better than those of the present fellaheen. At Karnak, the Pharaonic town; at Kom Ombo, in the Roman town; and at Medinet Habu, in the Coptic town, the houses in the poorer quarters have seldom more than twelve or sixteen feet of frontage. They consist of a ground floor, with sometimes one or two living-rooms above. The middle class folk, as shopkeepers, sub-officials, and foremen were better housed. Their dwellings were frequently separated from the street by a narrow court, beyond which the rooms were ranged on either side of a long passage. More frequently, the court was surrounded on three sides by chambers; and yet oftener, the house fronted close upon the street. In the latter case, the façade consisted of a high wall, whitewashed or painted; and surmounted by a cornice. The door was the only opening, save perhaps a few small windows pierced at irregular intervals. Even in unpretentious houses, the door was often made of stone. The door-posts projected slightly beyond the surface of the wall, and the lintel supported a painted or sculptured cornice. Having crossed the threshold, one passed successively through two dimly-lighted entrance chambers, the second of which opened into the central court;

the ground-floor offices were used as stabling for donkeys or cattle, and as storerooms for grain and provisions, as well as for cellarage and kitchens. Wherever the upper floors still remain standing, they reproduce the ground-floor plan with scarcely any differences. These upper rooms were reached by an outside staircase, steep and narrow and divided at short intervals by small square landings. The rooms were oblong, and were lighted only from the doorway; when it was decided to open windows on the street, they were mere air-holes near the ceiling, pierced without regularity or symmetry, fitted with a lattice of wooden cross bars, and secured by wooden shutters. The floors were bricked or paved, or consisted still more frequently of merely a layer of rammed earth. The walls were whitewashed, and occasionally painted with bright colours. The roof was flat, and made probably, as at the present day, of closely laid rows of palm-branches covered with a coating of mud thick enough to withstand the effects of rain. Sometimes it was surmounted by only one or two of the usual Egyptian ventilators; but generally there was a small washhouse on the roof, and a little chamber for the slaves or guards to sleep in. The terrace and the courtyard played an important part in the domestic life of the ancient Egyptians; it was there that the women gossiped, cooked, and made their bread. There, also, the whole family was wont to sleep in summer, under the shelter of mosquito nets.

The mansions of the rich and great covered a large space of ground. They most frequently stood in the midst of a garden, or of an enclosed court planted with trees; and, like the commoner houses, they turned a blank front to the street, consisting of bare walls battlemented like those of a fortress. Thus, home-life was strictly secluded, and the pleasure of seeing was sacrificed for the advantages of not being seen. The door was approached by a flight of two or three steps, or by a porch supported on columns and adorned with statues, which gave it a monumental appearance, and indicated the social importance of the family. Sometimes this was preceded by a pylon-gateway, such as usually heralded the approach to a temple. Inside the enclosure it was like a small town, divided into quarters by irregular walls. The dwelling-house stood at the farther end; the granaries, stabling, and open spaces being distributed in different parts of the grounds according to some system to which we as yet possess no clue. These arrangements, however, were infinitely varied.

GASTON MASPERO

Egyptian Art

THEIR conventional system differed materially from our own. Man or beast, the subject was never anything but a profile relieved against a flat background. Their object, therefore, was to select forms which presented a characteristic outline capable of being reproduced in pure line upon a plane surface. As regarded animal life, the problem was in no wise complicated. The profile of the back and body, the head and neck, carried in undulating lines parallel with the ground, was outlined at one sweep of the pencil. The legs also are

well detached from the body. The animals themselves are lifelike, each with the gait and action and flexion of the limbs peculiar to its species. The slow and measured tread of the ox; the short step, the meditative ear, the ironical mouth of the ass; the abrupt little trot of the goat, the spring of the hunting greyhound, are all rendered with invariable success of outline and expression. Turning from domestic animals to wild beasts, the perfection of treatment is the same. The calm strength of the lion in repose, the stealthy and sleepy tread of the leopard, the grimace of the ape, the slender

Ibid., pp. 170-7.

grace of the gazelle and the antelope, have never been better expressed than in Egypt. But it was not so easy to project man—the whole man—upon a plane surface without some departure from nature. A man cannot be satisfactorily reproduced by means of mere lines, and a profile outline necessarily excludes too much of his person. The form of the forehead and the nose, the curvature of the lips, the cut of the ear, disappear when the head is drawn full face; but, on the other hand, it is necessary that the bust should be presented full face, in order to give the full development of the shoulders, and that the two arms may be visible to right and left of the body. The contours of the trunk are best modelled in a three-quarters view, whereas the legs show to most advantage when seen sidewise. The Egyptians did not hesitate to combine these contradictory points of view in one single figure. The head is almost always given in profile, but is provided with a full-face eye and placed upon a full-face bust. The full-face bust adorns a trunk seen from a three-quarters point of view, and this trunk is supported upon legs de-

picted in profile. Very seldom do we meet with figures treated according to our own rules of perspective. Most of the minor personages represented in the tomb of Khnumhotep seem, however, to have made an effort to emancipate themselves from the law of malformation. Their bodies are given in profile, as well as their heads and legs; but they thrust forward first one shoulder and then the other, in order to show both arms, and the effect is not happy. Yet, if we examine the treatment of the farm servant who is cramming a goose, and, above all, the figure of the standing man who throws his weight upon the neck of a gazelle to make it kneel down, we shall see that the action of the arms and hips is correctly rendered, that the form of the back is quite right, and that the prominence of the chest—thrown forward in proportion as the shoulders and arms are thrown back—is drawn without any exaggeration. The wrestlers of the Beni Hassan tombs, the dancers and servants of the Theban catacombs, attack, struggle, posture, and go about their work with perfect naturalness and ease. These, however, are exceptions. Tradition, as a rule, was stronger than nature, and to the end of the chapter, the Egyptian masters continued to deform the human figure. Their men and women are actual monsters from the point of view of the anatomist; and yet, after all, they are neither so ugly nor so ridiculous as might be supposed by those who have seen only the wretched copies so often made by our modern artists. The wrong parts are joined to the right parts with so much skill that they seem to have grown there. The natural lines and the fictitious lines follow and complement each other so ingeniously, that the former appear to give rise of necessity to the latter. The conventionalities of Egyptian art once accepted, we cannot sufficiently admire the technical skill displayed by the draughtsman. His line was pure, firm, boldly begun, and as boldly prolonged. Ten or twelve strokes of the brush sufficed to outline a figure the size of life. The whole head, from the nape of the neck to the rise of the throat above the collar-bone, was executed at one sweep. Two

long undulating lines gave the external contour of the body from the armpits to the ends of the feet. Two more determined the outlines of the legs, and two the arms. The details of costume and ornaments, at first but summarily indicated, were afterwards taken up one by one, and minutely finished. We may almost count the locks of the hair, the plaits of the linen, the inlayings of the girdles and bracelets. This mixture of artless science and intentional awkwardness, of rapid execution and patient finish, excludes neither elegance of form, nor grace of attitude, nor truth of movement. These personages are of strange aspect, but they live; and to those who will take the trouble to look at them without prejudice, their very strangeness has a charm about it which is often lacking to works more recent in date and more strictly true to nature.

We admit, then, that the Egyptians could draw. Were they, as it has been ofttimes asserted, ignorant of the art of composition? We will take a scene at hazard from a Theban tomb—that scene which represents the funerary repast offered to Prince Horemheb by the members of his family. The subject is half ideal, half real. The dead man, and those belonging to him who are no longer of this world, are depicted in the society of the living. They are present, yet aloof. They assist at the banquet, but they do not actually take part in it.

Horemheb sits on a folding stool to the left of the spectator. He
dandles on his knee a little princess, daughter of Amenhotep III.,
whose foster-father he was, and who died before him. His mother,
Souit, sits at his right hand a little way behind, enthroned in a large
chair. She holds his arm with her left hand, and with the right she
offers him a lotus blossom and bud. A tiny gazelle which was probably buried with her, like the pet gazelle discovered beside Queen
Isi-em-Kheb in the hiding-place at Deir el Bahari, is tied to one of
the legs of the chair. This ghostly group is of heroic size, the rule
being that gods are bigger than men, kings bigger than their subjects, and the dead bigger than the living. Horemheb, his mother,
and the women standing before them, occupy the front level, or
foreground. The relations and friends are ranged in line facing their

deceased ancestors, and appear to be talking one with another. The
feast has begun. The jars of wine and beer, placed in rows upon
wooden stands, are already unsealed. Two young slaves rub the
hands and necks of the living guests with perfumes taken from an
alabaster vase. Two women dressed in robes of ceremony present
offerings to the group of dead, consisting of vases filled with flowers,
perfumes, and grain. These they place in turn upon a square table.
Three others dance, sing, and play upon the lute, by way of accom-
paniment to those acts of homage. In the picture, as in fact, the
tomb is the place of entertainment. There is no other background
to the scene than the wall covered with hieroglyphs, along which
the guests were seated during the ceremony. Elsewhere, the scene
of action, if in the open country, is distinctly indicated by trees and
tufts of grass; by red sand, if in the desert; and by a maze of reeds
and lotus plants, if in the marshes. A lady of quality comes in from
a walk. One of her daughters, being athirst, takes a long draught

from a "goullah;" two little naked children with shaven heads, a boy
and a girl, who ran to meet their mother at the gate, are made happy
with toys brought home and handed to them by a servant. A trelissed
enclosure covered with vines, and trees laden with fruit, are shown
above; yonder, therefore, is the garden, but the lady and her daughters have passed through it without stopping, and are now indoors.
The front of the house is half put in and half left out, so that we
may observe what is going on inside. We accordingly see three attendants hastening to serve their mistresses with refreshments. The
picture is not badly composed, and it would need but little altera-
tion if transferred to a modern canvas. The same old awkwardness,
or rather the same old obstinate custom, which compelled the
Egyptian artist to put a profile head upon a full-face bust, has,
however, prevented him from placing his middle distance and background behind his foreground. He has, therefore, been reduced to
adopt certain more or less ingenious contrivances, in order to make
up for an almost complete absence of perspective. . . .

J. G. WILKINSON

Everyday Things

SIR John Gardner Wilkinson deserves a considerable place among
the pioneers of Egyptology. He first went to Egypt in 1821 and
worked and travelled there and in Nubia for the next twelve years.
On his return to England (made necessary by his health) he wrote
a number of works, of which the *Manners and Customs* is the most
important.

wwwwwwwwwwwwwww
From *Manners and Customs of the Ancient Egyptians*. London: John Murray; 1837,
Vol. III, pp. 380-3, Vol. I, p. 281, Vol. II, pp. 418-20, 426-8.

Eye Shadow

THE custom of staining the eyelids and brows, with a moistened powder of a black colour, was common in Egypt from the earliest times; it was also introduced among the Jews and Romans, and is retained in the East to the present day. It is thought to increase the beauty of the eye; which is made to appear larger by this external addition of a black ring; and many even suppose the stimulus its application gives to be beneficial to the sight. It is made in various ways. Some use antimony, black oxide of manganese, preparations of lead, and other mineral substances: others the powder, or the lamp black of burnt almonds, or frankincense; and many prefer a mixture of different ingredients.

Mr. Lane is perfectly correct in stating that the expression "painted her face," which Jezebel is said to have done, when Jehu came to Jezreel, is in the Hebrew, "painted her eyes"; the same is again mentioned in Jeremiah and Ezekiel; and the lengthened form of the ancient Egyptian eye, represented in the paintings, was probably produced, as Mr. Lane supposes, by this means.

Such is the effect described by Juvenal, Pliny and other writers, who notice the custom among the Romans. At Rome it was considered disgraceful for men to adopt it, as at present in the East, except medicinally; but, if we may judge from the similarity of the eyes of men and women in the paintings at Thebes, it appears to have been used by both sexes among the ancient Egyptians.

Many of these *kohl* bottles have been found in the tombs, together with the bodkin used for applying the moistened powder. They are of various materials, usually stone, wood, or pottery, sometimes composed of two, sometimes of four and five separate cells, apparently containing each a mixture, differing slightly in its quality and hue, from the other three. Many were simple round tubes, vases, or small boxes: some were ornamented with the figure of an ape, or monster, supposed to assist in holding the bottle between his arms, while the lady dipped into it the pin, with which she painted her eyes; and others were in imitation of a column made of stone, or rich porcelain of the choicest manufacture. . . .

Wooden Pillows

. . . and their head, says Porphyry, was supported by a half cylinder of wood, in lieu of a pillow.

The same mode of resting the head was common to all the Egyptians, and a considerable number of these stools have been found

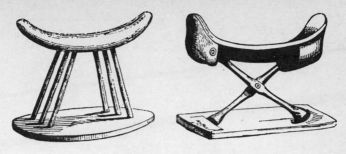

WOODEN PILLOWS

in the tombs of Thebes: generally of sycamore, acacia, or tamarisk
wood; or of alabaster, not inelegantly formed, and frequently ornamented with coloured hieroglyphics. In Abyssinia, and in parts of
Upper Ethiopia, they still adopt the same support for the head; and
the materials of which they are made are either wood, stone, or
common earthenware. Nor are they peculiar to Abyssinia and the
valley of the Nile: the same custom prevails in far distant countries;
and we find them used in Japan, China, and Ashanti, and even in
the island of Otaheite, where they are also of wood, but longer and
less concave than those of Africa.

Games and Toys

The same antiquity may be claimed for the game of draughts, or,
as it has been erroneously called, chess. As in the two former, the
players sat on the ground or on chairs, and the pieces, or men, being

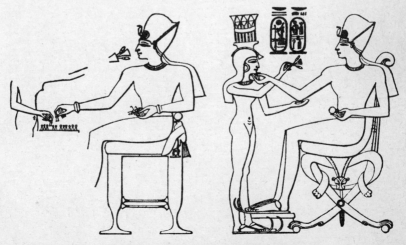

RAMSES III PLAYING AT DRAUGHTS

ranged in line at either end of the table, probably moved on a chequered board, as in our own chess and draughts; but, the representations being always given in profile, it is impossible to ascertain the exact appearance, or the number, of squares it contained.

The pieces were all of the same size and form, though they varied on different boards, some being small, others large with round summits: many were of a lighter and neater shape, like small ninepins, probably the most fashionable kind, since they were used in the palace of King Ramses. These last seem to have been about one inch and a half high, standing on a circular base of half an inch in diameter; and one in my possession, which I brought from Thebes, of a nearly similar taste, is one inch and a quarter in height, and little more than half an inch broad at the lower end. It is of hard wood, and was doubtless painted of some colour, like those occurring on the Egyptian monuments.

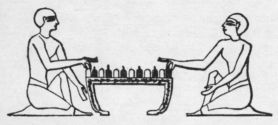

GAME OF DRAUGHTS WITH PLAYERS
SEATED ON THE FLOOR

They were all of equal size upon the same board, one set black, the other white or red, standing on opposite sides, and each player raising it with the finger and thumb advanced his piece towards those of his opponent; but though we are unable to say if this was done in a direct or a diagonal line, there is reason to believe they could not take backwards, as in the Polish game of draughts, the men being mixed together on the board.

It was an amusement common in the houses of the lower classes and in the mansions of the rich; and King Ramses is himself portrayed on the walls of his palace at Thebes, engaged in the game of draughts with the favourites of his *harem*. . . .

The games and amusements of children were such as tended to promote health by the exercise of the body, and to divert the mind by laughable entertainments. Throwing and catching the ball, running, leaping, and similar feats, were encouraged, as soon as their age enabled them to indulge in them; and a young child was amused with painted dolls, whose hands and legs, moving on pins, were made to assume various positions by means of strings. Some of

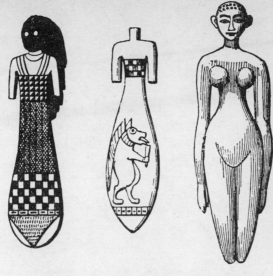

WOODEN DOLLS

these were of rude and uncertain form, without legs, or with an imperfect representation of a single arm on one side. Some had numerous beads, in imitation of hair, hanging from the doubtful place of the head; others exhibited a nearer approach to the form of a man; and some, made with considerable attention to proportion, were small models of the human figure. They were coloured

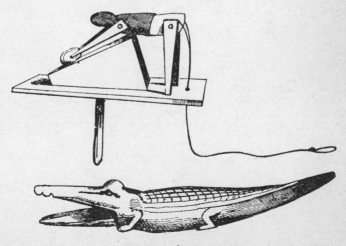

CHILDREN'S TOYS

according to fancy; the most informous had usually the most gaudy appearance, being intended to catch the eye of an infant; but a show of reality was deemed more suited to the taste of an older child; and the nearer their resemblance to known objects, the less they partook of artificial ornament. Sometimes a man was figured washing, or kneading dough, the necessary movement indicative of the operation being imitated by pulling a string; and a typhonian monster, or a crocodile, amused a child by its grimaces, or the motion of its opening mouth; plainly showing that children, in all ages, delight in the frightful, and play with objects which, if real, they would shudder to behold.

ALAN GARDINER

Hieroglyphs and Other Writing

MAN'S successive discoveries, at very great intervals, of the respective techniques of speech and writing, have been the two main stages passed by him on his long road to civilization. The use of

From *Egypt of the Pharaohs*. Oxford: The Clarendon Press; 1961, pp. 19-24. By permission of The Clarendon Press, Oxford.

articulate sounds enabled him to interchange thoughts, wishes, and questionings with his fellow men. Writing, building upon the same basis, substituted visible for audible signs, and so extended the range of his communications in both space and time. In our attempt to outline the history of one of the oldest, and certainly the most splendid, of all Eastern civilizations it is fitting to begin with some account of the impact upon it of these two techniques, so far as it can be known. Unfortunately the origin of the EGYPTIAN LANGUAGE lies so far back in the uncharted past that only little that is certain can be said about it. Since it is generally agreed that the oldest population of Egypt was of African race, it might be expected that their language should be African too. And in fact many affinities with Hamitic and in particular with Berber dialects have been found, not only in vocabulary, but also in verbal structure and the like. On the other hand, the relationship with Semitic (Hebrew, Arabic, etc.) is equally unmistakable, if indeed not greater. In this matter there have been wide differences of opinion among scholars, and even if some measure of agreement could be reached as to the place or places of origin, there would still remain the problems of date. We therefore turn without further delay to the consideration of the EGYPTIAN WRITING, the evolution of which can be witnessed in detail.

The decorations of vases and other objects of common use were a sort of visual communication, this growing even more obvious when the images of men, animals, ships, and so forth were introduced. Writing began when there were added visible signs which absolutely compelled translation into the sounds of language. In Egypt this innovation becomes observable shortly before the advent of Menes, when it is marked by the introduction of isolated miniature images clearly distinguishable from the surrounding purely pictorial representations. The images are the same in both cases, mirroring all kinds of material objects such as weapons, plants, animals, human beings, and even the gods themselves. The emergence of HIEROGLYPHS, as the miniature signs are called, was due to the fact that there was much which people wished to communicate that could not be exhibited visually, such as numbers, proper names, and mental phenomena. This supplementary character persisted, side by side with others, throughout the whole of Egyptian history, so that when, as often happened, the scenes in sculptural reliefs were furnished with explanatory hieroglyphic legends, the latter might be fairly said to illustrate the former rather than vice versa. There were, however, many important further developments which it will be our next business to explain, and there even came a time, not long before the Christian era, when three different kinds of Egyptian script were in simultaneous use for different purposes, while the Greeks, who by then had taken possession of the land, employed their own alphabet for all the main business of life.

The three kinds of script just mentioned are still called by the names given to them by Champollion and his contemporaries, though derived from different sources and strictly applicable only to the Graeco-Roman period. The term HIEROGLYPHIC used by Clement of Alexandria in a famous passage above alluded to, means literally "sacred carvings" and deserves its name solely because in the latest times it was almost exclusively employed for the inscriptions graven on temple walls. It is now applied, however, to all Egyptian writing which is still truly pictorial, ranging from the

TOP: HIEROGLYPHIC
MIDDLE: HIERATIC
BOTTOM: DEMOTIC

detailed, brightly coloured signs found adorning the tombs down to the abbreviated specimens written with a reed-pen in papyri of religious content. Hieroglyphic is, of course, the original variety of writing out of which all the other kinds were evolved; sometimes it reads from top to bottom, sometimes from right to left, but sometimes also from left to right, this being the form adopted in our printed grammars; when the writing is from right to left the signs face towards the right.

The name HIERATIC, Clement tells us, was given to the style of writing employed by the priestly scribes for their religious books. This is a derivative of the abbreviated hieroglyphic mentioned in the last paragraph, but Egyptologists have extended the use of the term to several still more shortened varieties of script found in literary or business texts; ligatures, i.e. signs joined together, are frequent, and in the most cursive sort all but the initial signs are apt to be reduced to mere strokes. For scholarly convenience Hieratic is customarily transcribed into Hieroglyphic, though this practice becomes well-nigh impossible in extreme cursive specimens. The direction of writing is normally from right to left.

For the third kind of Egyptian writing, called Enchorial "native" on the Rosetta Stone and Epistolographic "letter-writing" by Clement, modern scholars have retained Herodotus's name DEMOTIC "popular." This was evolved out of Hieratic only about the time of the Ethiopian Dynasty, from *c.* 700 B.C. It presents many peculiarities and demands intensive specialist study. In the Ptolemaic and Roman ages it was the ordinary writing of daily life, and its range of employment is best described as non-religious.

Between the two extremes of Hieroglyphic and Demotic there are many intermediate varieties, the main motive discernible being the desire for increased speed. This could be achieved only by a gradual diminution of the pictorial character, with the result that the principles underlying the system at length faded out of sight. Another factor that assisted in the evolution was the writing surface involved. Hieroglyphic was essentially monumental, cut into stone with a chisel or painstakingly executed in ink or paint upon carefully prepared walls. Hieratic was practically as old as Hieroglyphic, but was employed like Demotic for writing on papyrus, on wooden boards covered with a stucco wash, on potsherds, or on fragments of limestone.

When Christianity began to supersede the Pharaonic paganism, a medium more easily intelligible became required for the translations of Biblical texts. That was the reason for the introduction of COPTIC, already mentioned as the latest phase of the Egyptian language. This was written in Greek characters with a few additional letters taken over from Demotic. The literature of Coptic is full of Greek words, and indeed the entire set-up proclaims it to be more of a semi-artificial jargon than a direct lineal descendant of the old language; for this state of affairs modern Palestinian Hebrew may be quoted as an analogy.

The serious student will not be content without some further account of the hieroglyphs, the more so since it is only through Champollion's discovery that an orderly and historically accurate picture of the ancient civilization has become possible. It has already been intimated that hieroglyphic writing was an offshoot of direct pictorial representation. In this respect it resembled the original Babylonian script, and indeed it is not improbable that there was actual relationship between them, though it may have amounted to no more than a hearsay knowledge that the sounds of language could be communicated by means of appropriately chosen pictures. The subsequent development, however, differed very considerably in the two cases. Babylonian writing, using cuneiform (wedge-shaped) characters, quickly ceased to be recognizable as pictures, whereas the Egyptian hieroglyphs retained their pictorial appearance throughout the centuries, only losing it, and then only partially, in their derivative hieratic and demotic forms. By virtue of this fact many signs continued to mean what they represented, though of course when the things in question were referred to in speech, they bore their Egyptian names; signs so used are called Ideograms and examples are 𓀀 *iaw* "old man," ⊙ *rē* "sun." However, many signs like ⊏⊐ *pōr* "house" (this is the ideographic use) could also be employed in words whose sound was similar, but whose signification had no connexion whatsoever with the object depicted; when so employed the hieroglyphs are termed Phonograms or Sound-signs; thus ⊏⊐ is found in the hieroglyphic spelling of *pery* "go forth," *proyet* "winter," *peret* "seed." Egyptian writing, like Hebrew and Arabic, normally did not indicate the vowels, so that the pronunciations which for once we have supplied are not strictly justifiable, being merely a concession to those by whom the more scientific *pry*, *pr(y)t*, and *prt* would be found unpalatable. It will be seen that in our three examples ⊏⊐ has the common consonantal value *p+r*, and is consequently a Biliteral sign. The underlying principle is that of the rebus or charade; one thing is shown, but another meant. By this method the Egyptians very early evolved a whole body of Uniliteral signs, in fact an alphabet of twenty-four letters; for example ◇, depicting a mouth and when accompanied by a simple stroke ◇ often conveying the word *rā* "mouth," gave them their letter *r*; other alphabetic signs will be quoted further on. There were also Triliteral signs like 𓄤 *nfr* and 𓆢 *hpr*. Now one disadvantage of the hieroglyphic system of writing was that the miniature pictures which it used were apt to be ambiguous in both sound and meaning; thus the sign 𓏞 depicting a scribe's palette, water-jar, and reed-case might represent not only that entire outfit, for which the word was *mnhd*, but also the activity of writing (*sš*), the professional writer or scribe, and other things besides. To ease this situation some other sign or signs were apt to be added; when pictorial, as in 𓏞𓀀 *sš* "scribe" the additional sign served as a Determinative, but when phonetic, as in 𓄤 *nfr* (strictly *nfr+f+r*) "good" "beautiful" or as in 𓆣 *hpr* (*hpr+r*) "become" the additional sign or signs are known as Phonetic Complements. There are three kinds of Determinatives, (1) Specific, as in the word for "scribe" just quoted, (2) Generic, when the sign indicates only the kind of notion that was meant, as 𓀜, a striking man, employed not only in the word 𓁷 *hwi* "strike," but also in such words as 𓏶𓀜 *ith* "drag"; or again ⊙, "the sun" as in 𓇳 *hrw* "day," 𓅱 *wbu* "shine forth," (3) Phonetic, a rarer variety, like the sign 𓄊representing a kid in the verb 𓂧𓄊 *ibi* "be thirsty" which inserts the entire word *ib* "kid" in front of the generic determinatives for water and for actions performed by the mouth.

In sum, the hieroglyphic writing of the Egyptians was a mixed system comprising both sound-signs and sense-signs. The following short sentence accompanied by transliteration and translation will suggest that the analysis above is more or less exhaustive:

Ḫd·n·f r Nỉwt h̲r inw nb nfr

Fared downstream he to (the) City with presents all (sorts of) goodly Here , , , , and are the alphabetic signs for *f, n, r, ẖ, t,* and *d* respectively; , and are biliterals for *in, nb* and *h̲r*, and a triliteral for *nfr;* the *r* after *h̲r* is a phonetic complement, and the *f+r* after *nfr* are two such; , , and are determinatives; lastly , depicting a village with intersecting streets, is an ideogram.

Students must not be deluded into thinking that hieroglyphic writing has anything particularly mysterious about it. It is a genuine script, containing many complexities it is true, but possessing the advantages of appealing to the eye as well as to be the mind. Since the absence of written vowels makes it unpronounceable, some might conclude that it does not represent a language at all, or else that the language is one without grammar. Nothing could be more untrue, though it must be confessed that our ignorance of the underlying vocalization is a serious handicap. The subtleties of tense and mood can be deduced only from the context, or mostly so, since these nuances were conveyed more often by internal changes than by prefixes and affixes. To classical scholars accustomed to traditional vocabularies Egyptian is apt to be disconcerting. Coptic has proved less helpful than might have been hoped; but for establishing word-meanings, as well as for the division of one word from another, the determinatives have rendered important service. So too have the scenes which the accompanying legends were intended to explain. Most valuable of all, especially in historical texts and stories, is the logic of the situation.

5. *Death in Egypt*

HERODOTUS

Burial Rites
According to Herodotus

THE practice of medicine they split up into separate parts, each doctor being responsible for the treatment of only one disease. There are, in consequence, innumerable doctors, some specializing in diseases of the eyes, others of the head, others of the teeth, others of the stomach and so on; while others, again, deal with the sort of troubles which cannot be exactly localized. As regards mourning and funerals, when a distinguished man dies all the women of the household plaster their heads and faces with mud, then, leaving the body indoors, perambulate the town with the dead man's female relatives, their dresses fastened with a girdle, and beat their bared breasts. The men too, for their part, follow the same procedure, wearing a girdle and beating themselves like the women. The ceremony over, they take the body to be embalmed.

Embalming is a distinct profession. The embalmers, when a body is brought to them, produce specimen models in wood, painted to resemble nature, and graded in quality; the best and most expensive kind is said to represent a being whose name I shrink from mentioning in this connexion; the next best is somewhat inferior and cheaper, while the third sort is cheapest of all. After pointing out these differences in quality, they ask which of the three is required, and the kinsmen of the dead man, having agreed upon a price, go away and leave the embalmers to their work. The most perfect process is as follows: as much as possible of the brain is extracted through the nostrils with an iron hook, and what the hook cannot

From *The Histories*, Book II, pp. 132-4.

reach is rinsed out with drugs; next the flank is laid open with a flint knife and the whole contents of the abdomen removed; the cavity is then thoroughly cleansed and washed out, first with palm wine and again with an infusion of pounded spices. After that it is filled with pure bruised myrrh, cassia, and every other aromatic substance with the exception of frankincense, and sewn up again, after which the body is placed in natron, covered entirely over, for seventy days—never longer. When this period, which must not be exceeded, is over, the body is washed and then wrapped from head to foot in linen cut into strips and smeared on the under side with gum, which is commonly used by the Egyptians instead of glue. In this condition the body is given back to the family, who have a wooden case made, shaped like the human figure, into which it is put. The case is then sealed up and stored in a sepulchral chamber, upright against the wall. When, for reasons of expense, the second quality is called for, the treatment is different: no incision is made and the intestines are not removed, but oil of cedar is injected with a syringe into the body through the anus which is afterwards stopped up to prevent the liquid from escaping. The body is then pickled in natron for the prescribed number of days, on the last of which the oil is drained off. The effect of it is so powerful that as it leaves the body it brings with it the stomach and intestines in a liquid state, and as the flesh, too, is dissolved by the natron, nothing of the body is left but the bones and skin. After this treatment it is returned to the family without further fuss.

The third method, used for embalming the bodies of the poor, is simply to clear out the intestines with a purge and keep the body seventy days in natron. It is then given back to the family to be taken away.

When the wife of a distinguished man dies, or any woman who happens to be beautiful or well known, her body is not given to the embalmers immediately, but only after the lapse of three or four days. This is a precautionary measure to prevent the embalmers from violating the corpse, a thing which is said actually to have happened in the case of a woman who had just died. The culprit was given away by one of his fellow workmen. If anyone, either an Egyptian or a foreigner, is found drowned in the river or killed by a crocodile, there is the strongest obligation upon the people of the nearest town to have the body embalmed in the most elaborate manner and buried in a consecrated burial-place; no one is allowed to touch it except the priests of the Nile—not even relatives or friends; the priests alone prepare it for burial with their own hands and place it in the tomb, as if it were something more sacred than the body of a man.

WALLIS BUDGE

Embalmment, Mummification, Burial: the Story of an Interment

AN attempt may now be made to describe briefly what happened after death to the body of a man of high rank who departed this life at Thebes towards the end of the XVIIIth or beginning of the XIXth Dynasty, that is to say about 1400 B.C. The facts are all known, and therefore nothing need be invented; it is only necessary to gather them together and to bring them to a focus on the person of one man. We must imagine then that we are living on the east bank of the Nile, near the temple of Ámen-Rā, "lord of the thrones of the earth," in the fifteenth century before Christ. One morning before the day has dawned, even before the officials who conduct the early services in the temples are astir, we are awakened by loud cries of grief and lamentation, and on making inquiries we are told that Ani the great scribe of the offerings of the gods in the temple of Ámen-Rā, is dead. As he was the receiver of the revenues of the gods of Abydos, as well as of Ámen-Rā of Thebes, first prophet of Ámen, and the precentor who stood on the threshold of the temple morning by morning to lead off the hymn of praise to the sun, his death naturally causes great excitement in the temples and the immediate neighbourhood; as his forefathers for five or six generations have been temple officers of the highest rank, it is certain that his funeral will be a great event, and that numbers of the hereditary aristocracy and government officials will assist at the ceremony. He leaves no wife to mourn for him, for she is already dead, and is now lying in a chamber of a splendid tomb, not yet finished, however, nine miles away across the river, awaiting the coming of her husband. She was

From *The Mummy*. Cambridge: Cambridge University Press; 1893, pp. 157-73. By permission of Cambridge University Press.

called Tutu, and belonged to one of the oldest and most honourable families in Thebes; she was a member of the famous college of singers of Ámen-Rā, and also a member of the choir of ladies, each one of whom carried a sistrum or a tambourine in the temple of that god. Ani began to hew out the tomb for himself and his wife many years ago, and during his lifetime he spared neither pains nor expense in making it one of the largest and finest ever known for a person of lower rank than a king. Ani was not a very old man when he died, although his step was slow and his back somewhat bent; in stature he was of middle height, and his features had a kind but dignified look, and though comparatively few loved him, all respected him for his uprightness and integrity. He was a learned man, and knew the literature of Egypt well; he himself wrote a fine, bold hand, and was no mean artist with his pencil. He was a tried servant of the king, and loved him well, but he loved his god Ámen more, and was very jealous for his honour, and the glory of his worship in the temple of the Apts. All his ancestors had been in the service of the god, and it was even said that the oldest of them had seen Ámen, who, until the expulsion of the Hyksos by the kings of Thebes, had occupied the position of a mere local deity, suddenly become the national god of Egypt. Whether Ani believed in his innermost heart any or all of the official religion is another matter; his official position brought him into contact with the temporal rather than the spiritual affairs of the Egyptian religion, and whatever doubts he may have had in matters of belief, or concerning the efficacy of the magic of his day, etc., etc., he said nothing about them to any man.

For some days past it had been seen that Ani's death was to be expected, and many of his colleagues in the temple had come to see him from time to time, one bringing a charm, another a decoction of herbs, etc., and a few had taken it in turns to stay in his room for some hours at a time. One night his illness took a decidedly serious turn, and early in the morning, a short time before daybreak, when, as the Orientals say, the dawn may be smelled, Ani died. The news of his death spreads rapidly through the quarter, for all the women of his house rush frantically through the streets, beating their breasts, and from time to time clutching at their hair, which is covered with handfuls of the thick dust of the streets, after the manner of Ánpu in the *Tale of the Two Brothers*, and uttering wailing cries of grief. In the house, parties of mourning women shriek out their grief, and all the members of the house add their tears and sobs. The steward of the house has, however, sent across the river to the *cher-ḥeb* or priest who superintends and arranges the funerals of the wealthy and great, and informed him of Ani's death, and as quickly as possible this official leaves his house near the Valley of the Tombs of the Kings, and together with his assistants, makes his way with all haste to Ani's house. Having arrived there he takes Ani's body into his charge, and proceeds to discuss the method by which the body shall be preserved, and the style of the funeral. While his assistants are taking away the body to the embalming house, he sends quickly to the western bank of the Nile, and summons his chief mason to his presence; after a short time he arrives, and the *cher-ḥeb* instructs him to go to Ani's tomb with a body of men, and to finish hewing whatever chambers and pillars remain in a half completed state, to plaster the walls, and to paint upon them scenes for which he supplies him with details and notes. The *cher-ḥeb* knows that for many years past Ani, and one or two of his friends among the scribes, had been writing and illuminating with vignettes a fine copy of the "Book of the Dead"; he remembers that this work remains unfinished, and he therefore sets a skilful scribe to finish it in the style in which Ani would probably have finished it. Parties of professional mourners are next organized, and these go round about the city at stated times, singing in chorus, probably accompanied by some musical instrument, funereal dirges, the subjects of which were the shortness of life and the certainty that all must die, and the virtues of the dead man. These dirges were sung twice daily, and Ani's friends and colleagues, during the days of mourning, thought it to be their duty to abstain from wine and every kind of luxury, and they wore the simplest and plainest garments, and went quite unadorned.

Meanwhile it was decided that Ani's funeral should be one of the best that money could purchase, and as while he was alive he was thought to be in constant communion with the gods, his relatives ordered that his body should be mummified in the best possible way, so that his soul and his intelligence when they returned some thousands of years hence to seek his body in the tomb, might find his *ka* or "genius" there waiting, and that all three might enter into the body once more, and revivify it, and live with it for ever in the kingdom of Osiris. No opportunity must be given for these four component parts of the whole of a man to drift away one from the other, and to prevent this the perishable body must be preserved in such a way that each limb of it may meetly be identified with a god, and the whole of it with Osiris, the judge of the dead and king of the nether world. The tomb must be made a fit and proper dwelling-place for the *ka*, which will never leave it as long as the body to which it belongs lies in its tomb. The furniture of the tomb must be of the best, and every material, and the workmanship thereof, must also be of the best.

The *cher-ḥeb* next goes to the embalming chamber and orders his assistants to begin their operations upon Ani's body, over which formulae are being recited. The body is first washed and then laid upon the ground, and one of the assistants traces with ink on the left side, over the groin, a line, some few inches long, to indicate where the incision is to be made in the body; another assistant takes a knife, probably made of flint, and makes a cut in the body the same length as the line drawn in ink by his companion. Whether this man was then driven away with sticks, and stones thrown after him, as Diodorus states, or not, is a moot point upon which the inscriptions give us no information. The chief intestines and the heart and lungs were then carefully taken out and washed in palm wine, and stuffed with sweet smelling spices, gums, etc. They were next smeared all over with an unguent, and then carefully bandaged with strips of linen many yards long, on which were inscribed the names of the four children of Horus who symbolized the four cardinal points and of the four goddesses who took the intestines under their special protection. While this was being done a set of four alabaster jars was brought from the stores of the *cher-ḥeb's* establishment, and in each of these one of the four packets of embalmed intestines was placed. Each jar was inscribed with a formula, and all that was wanted to make it the property of Ani was to inscribe his name upon it in the blank spaces left for the purpose. Each jar had a cover made in the form of the head of the child of Horus to whom it was dedicated. The jar of Mesthà had the head of a man, and in it was placed the stomach; it was under the protection of Isis. The jar of Ḥāpi had the head of an ape, and in it were placed the smaller intestines; it was under the protection of Nephthys. The jar of Ṭuamāutef had the head of a jackal, and in it was placed the heart; it was under the protection of Neith. The jar of Qebḥsennuf had the head of a hawk, and in it was placed the liver; it was under the protection of Serqet. The inscriptions on the jars state that the part of the deceased in it is identified with the child of Horus to whom the jar is dedicated, and that the goddess under whose charge it is protects it. The covers of the jars are fastened on by running in liquid plaster, and they are finally set in the four divisions of a coffer on a sledge with a vaulted cover and a projecting rectangular upright at each corner. It was of the greatest importance to have the intestines preserved intact, for without them a man could not hope to live again. The brain is next removed through the nostrils by means of an iron rod curved at one end, and is put aside to be dried and buried with the body; at every step in these processes religious formulae are recited. The body thus deprived of its more perishable parts is taken and laid to soak in a tank of liquid natron for a period of seventy days. At the end of this time it is taken out and carefully washed and dried, and it is seen that it is of a greenish-grey colour; the skin clings to the bones, for the flesh beneath it has shrunk somewhat, but the hair of the body is well preserved, the nails of the hands and feet still adhere to the skin, and the face, though now drawn and very thin, has changed but little. Longitudinal slits are next made in the fingers and toes and the fleshy parts of the arms, thighs and legs, which are then stuffed with a mixture of sweet spices and natron, and sewn up again. The cavity in the skull is now filled up with a mixture of spices, powdered plaster and natron, and the nostrils through which it was inserted are plugged up with small linen pledgets dipped in some astringent; obsidian eyes are also inserted in the eyesockets. Large quantities of gums, spices, natron, as well as a very little bitumen, are pounded and well mixed together, and with them the breast and stomach are carefully packed through the slit in the side; while certain formulae are being recited, a gold plate inscribed with the *utchat,* or eye of Horus, is laid upon it to indicate that this god watched over this body as he did over that of his father Osiris. The nails of the hands are stained with *henna* and on the little finger of the left hand is placed Ani's gold ring, in the bezel of which is mounted a handsome steatite scarab inscribed on the base with his name and titles. The ring was supposed to confer upon the deceased some power, but what that power was is not yet exactly made out; it is certain, however, that no one was buried without one or more, and if the relatives of the deceased were not able to buy them in gold or silver, they made use of faience rings, glazed various colours, and even of small strings of beads which they tied on the fingers in lieu of rings. The legs are then brought closely together, and the arms are laid on the body with one wrist crossed over the other. The *cher-ḥeb* next provides a large and handsome scarab made of green basalt which is set in a frame of gold, over the back of it is a horizontal band of the same metal, at right angles to which, on the side of the tail of the beetle, runs another band which joins the frame; at the head of the scarab is a gold loop through which is now threaded a thick gold wire sufficiently long to go round Ani's neck. This scarab was part of the stock in trade of the *cher-ḥeb,* and all that was necessary to do to make it Ani's property was to inscribe his name and titles upon it in the blank line left for the purpose at the head of the flat base. This done the scarab was covered with a thin gold leaf and laid upon Ani's breast at the neck. The inscription upon it was one of the verses of the 30th chapter of the Book of the Dead, and contained a prayer, addressed by Ani to his heart, that there might not be brought against him adverse evidence when it was weighed in the balance in the judgment hall of Osiris, that he might not be obstructed or driven back, and that his name might not be overthrown by those powers who made it their business to harass the newcomers among the dead in the nether-world. The prayer ends with a petition that no false evidence may be borne against him in the presence of the god.

And now the bandaging begins. The body is first of all smeared all over with unguents. Pieces of linen are then torn into strips about three inches wide, and one edge of each strip is gummed. On one end of each of these the name of Ani has been written in hieratic characters to facilitate the identification of the mummy during the process of bandaging; a number of these strips are dipped in water, and the embalmers having bandaged the fingers, hands, and arms, and toes separately, begin to bandage the body from the feet upwards. The moist bandages cling tightly to the body, and the gummed edge enables each fold of the bandage to obtain firm hold; the little irregularities are corrected by small pledgets of linen placed between the folds and gummed in position. These linen bandages are also held in position by means of narrower strips of linen wound round the body at intervals of six and eight inches, and tied in a double knot. Over these fine linen bandages passages from the Book of the Dead, and formulae which were intended to give power to the dead, are written. One end of a very thick bandage of eighteen to twenty-five folds of linen is laid under the shoulders, and the other is brought over the head and face, and rests on the upper part of the chest; this is held in position by a bandage wound round the neck, and tied in a double knot at the back of the neck. The same plan is adopted with respect to the feet, but before the bandage which secures all is tied, thick pads of linen are laid on the top of the feet to prevent any injury happening to them when the mummy is made to stand upright. The bandaged arms having been pressed closely into the sides, and the fore-arms and hands having been laid upon the stomach, the bandaging goes on again, while formulae are recited by the *cher-heb*. Each bandage had a special name, each bandage gave power to the deceased, and was inscribed with words and figures of gods, which also gave him power, and the adjustment of each in its proper position required both care and judgment. More folds of linen are laid on the body perpendicularly, and more bandages are wound round the body horizontally, until, little by little, it loses its shape beneath them. When a length of about three hundred cubits has been used in folds and bandages, a coarse piece of linen is laid on the body, and is sewn up at the back. Over this again a saffron-coloured linen sheet is laid, and this having been deftly sewn over the head, down the back, and under the feet, is finally held in position by a perpendicular bandage of brownish coloured linen, passing from the head to the feet and under them up the back to the head, and by four horizontal bandages of the same coloured linen, one round the shoulders, one round the middle of the body, one round the knees, and one round the ankles. Thus the mummy is complete.

During the seventy days which have been spent in embalming

Ani's body, the coffin makes have not been idle, and they have made ready a covering of wood to be laid on the mummy, and two beautiful coffins. The covering, in the form of a mummy, is slightly vaulted, and has a human face, bearded, on it; it is handsomely painted outside with collar, figures of Nut, Anubis, and Ap-uat, the full names and titles of Ani in perpendicular lines of inscription, the cartouches of the king in whose time he lived, and scenes in which Ani is adoring the gods. On the inside of the cover, on the purple ground, are painted in a light yellow colour pictures of the horizon, the spirits of the East, in the form of apes, adoring Rā, the lion gods of the morning and evening with a disk on their united backs, etc., etc. The inner coffin is equally handsome, and carpenter and artist have expended their best labour upon it; before Ani was embalmed he was measured for it, and due allowance having been made for the bandages, it fits the mummy exactly. It is in the form of a mummy, and the sycamore planks of which it is made are about two inches thick; the bottom is in one piece, as is also each of the sides, the rounded head-piece is cut out of a solid piece of wood, and the foot-piece is also separate; all these parts are pegged together with wooden pegs about two inches long. On the cover is pegged a solid face, carved out of hard wood, which is thought to have a strong resemblance to that of Ani; bronze eyelids and obsidian eyes are fixed in it, and a carved wooden beard is fastened to the chin. Solid wooden hands are next fastened to the breast. The whole coffin, inside and out, is next covered with a thin layer of plaster; over this a coat of light yellow varnish is painted, and the scenes and inscriptions are painted on it in red, light and dark green, white and other colours. At the head is Nephthys, and at the foot is Isis, each making speeches to Ani, and telling him that she is protecting him. On the cover outside is Nut, and between two series of scenes in which Ani is represented worshipping the gods, are two perpendicular lines of inscriptions recording his name and titles; at the foot of these are figures of Anubis and Ap-uat. The sides of the coffin are ornamented with figures of gods in shrines, the scene of the weighing of the heart, Ani drinking water from the hands of a goddess standing in a tree, Shu lifting up Nut from the embraces of Seb, etc. Inside the coffin are painted figures of a number of gods and genii with instructions referring to them, and the goddesses Nut and Hathor; the first covers Ani with her wings, and the second, as mistress of the nether-world, receives Ani into her arms. Around the edge of the coffin near the cover, from head to foot, run two lines of inscription, one on each side, which repeat at considerable length the name and titles of Ani. The outer edge of the coffin, and the inner edge of the cover are "rabbeted" out, the one to fit into the other, and on each side, at regular intervals, four rectangular slots about 1½in. x 2in. x ⅜in. are cut; to fasten the coffin hermetically, tightly fitting wooden dowels, four inches long, are pressed into the slots in the coffin, and pegs driven from the outside of the coffin through them keep them firmly in position. Ani's body having been placed in this coffin, the cover is laid upon it, the ends of the dowels fit into the slots in the sides, and coffin and cover are firmly joined together; wooden pegs are driven through the cover and dowels, the "rabbets" fit tightly, the little space between the coffin and cover is "stopped" with liquid plaster, and thus the coffin is sealed. Any injury that may have happened to the plaster or paintings during the process of sealing is repaired, and the whole coffin is once more varnished. This coffin is, in its turn, placed inside an outer coffin, which is painted, both inside and outside, with scenes similar to those on the inner coffin; the drawing is, however, more free, and the details are fewer. The outer coffin being sealed in the same way as that inside it, Ani is now ready to be carried to his everlasting home in the Theban hills.

On a day fixed by the relatives and friends, all the various articles of funereal furniture which have been prepared are brought to Ani's house, where also the mummy in its coffins now lies awaiting the funeral; the *cher-ḥeb* sees that the things necessary for a great man's funeral are provided, and arranges for the procession to start on the first auspicious day. This day having arrived, the *cher-ḥeb's* assistants come, and gathering together the servants and those who are to carry burdens, see that each has his load ready and that each knows his place in the procession. When all is ready the funeral train sets out from Ani's house, while the female servants wail and lament their master, and the professional mourners beat their breasts, feign to pull out their hair by handfuls, and vie with each other in shrieking the loudest and most often. They have not a great distance to go to reach the river, but the difficulties of passing through the narrow streets increase almost at every step, for the populace of Thebes loved the sight of a grand funeral as much as that of any European country to-day. After some few hours the procession reaches the river, and there a scene of indescribable confusion happens; every bearer of a burden is anxious to deposit it in one of the boats which lie waiting in a row by the quay; the animals which draw the sledge, on which Ani's bier is laid, kick out wildly and struggle while being pushed into the boats, people rush hither and thither, and the noise of men giving orders, and the shouts and cries of the spectators, are distracting. At length, however, the procession is embarked and the boats push off to drop with the current across the Nile to a place a little north of the Temple of Thothmes III, opposite Asâsif. After an hour spent in disembarking, the procession reforms itself in the order in which it will march to the tomb, and we see for the first time what a splendid funeral has been provided. In the front walk a number of men bearing tables and stands filled with vases full of wine, beer, oil, perfumes, flowers, bread, cakes, ducks, haunches of beef, and vegetables; one man carries Ani's palette and box of instruments which he used for writing and drawing, another carries his staff, another his bed, another his chair, others bring the *ushabtiu* figures in a box with a vaulted cover and made like a tomb; and following them comes the stele recording his name and titles and prayers to the gods of the nether-world; and behind them, drawn by two men, is a coffer surmounted by a jackal, on a sledge decorated with lotus flowers, in which stand the four jars which contain Ani's intestines. Next follow the men bearing everything which Ani made use of during his life, as, for example, the axe which he carried when he followed his king to war in order to keep the accounts of the army and to make lists of all the precious things which were brought to his lord as gifts and tribute, and the harp on which he played in his leisure hours. Next comes the chest in which is laid the mummy of Ani, placed in a boat which is mounted on a sledge drawn by four oxen; at the head of the chest is a figure of Nephthys, and at the foot a figure of Isis, the boat is supplied with oars as if it were really destined to row down to Abydos, so that the body might be buried there, and its soul pass into the nether-world through the "Gap," the place whence, according to the Egyptian belief, souls, under the guidance of Osiris, set out on their last journey. At the head of the boat stands a white-robed *Sam* priest wearing a panther skin; he holds a bronze instrument for burning incense in the left hand, and with the right he scatters water on the ground from a libation vase. Behind the boat follow a number of white-robed priests, one of whom has his head powdered. Next follow more funereal offerings and flowers carried in boxes suspended from the ends of poles which the men who carry them balance on their shoulders. After these come a number of women with breasts uncovered and dishevelled hair, who in their wailing lamentations lament the dead and praise his virtues. Among these would probably be the female servants of Ani's house, whose grief would be genuine, for they would feel that they had lost a good master and a comfortable home.

Meanwhile the procession has moved on and has entered one of the rocky defiles to the north of Deir el Baḥari, whence, winding along through the valley of the kings, they hope to reach a remote place in the western valley. The progress of the train is slow, for the ground is rough and rocky, and frequent halts have to be made; on the right hand and on the left, kings and nobles are buried in splendid tombs, and almost every hill which they climb hides the mummy of some distinguished Egyptian. A few miles further on, at some little distance upon a hill, a rectangular opening is seen, and when the procession arrives at the foot of it, a number of workmen, attendants, tomb-guardians and others are seen assembled there. The mummy in its coffin is lifted out of the chest, and carried up the hill to the rectangular opening, which proves to be the mouth of Ani's tomb; there it is set upright, and before it the attendants pile up tables with sepulchral offerings and flowers, and animals for sacrifice are also brought there. The wailing women and the distant relatives of Ani here take farewell of him, and when they have descended the hill, the coffin is let down the slanting passage by ropes into the chamber, where it is hoped that Ani's friends will bring sepulchral offerings to his *ka*, at the appointed seasons. This chamber is rectangular and has two rows of square pillars in it. From it there leads a passage about six feet wide by seven feet high, and passing through this we see to the right and left a series of chambers upon the walls of which are painted in vivid colours the pictures of Ani and his wife Tutu making offerings to the gods, and inscriptions recording his prayers and their answers. The walls of some rooms are occupied entirely with scenes drawn from the daily events of his life. As he was a scribe, and therefore no mean artist, we are probably right in assuming that he superintended the painting of many of them himself. Some of the rooms have their walls unornamented, and it would seem that these were used for the living rooms of the priests who visited or lived in the tombs for the purpose of carrying out the various sepulchral rites at their appointed times. We pass through or by seventeen chambers, and then arrive at a flight of steps which leads down to the chamber in which the mummy and coffin are to be placed. Hewn in the wall just above the top of the flight of steps is a square niche, in which, seated on one seat, are two stone figures of Ani and his wife; he has an open roll of papyrus on his knees, and holds a palette in his hand, and she has lotus flowers in both hands, which rest on her knees. The plinth of the statues is inscribed with the names and titles of Ani and Tutu. Beneath, let into the wall, is a stone stele, the surface of which is divided into two parts; the upper part contains a representation of Ani adoring the sun-god Rā, and the lower contains about thirty lines of inscription in which Ani prays that Rā, Osiris and Anubis will cause all kinds of sepulchral goods to be supplied for his *ka* or genius; that they will grant his coming forth from and going into the nether-world whenever he pleases; that his soul may alight on the trees which he has planted; that he may drink cool water from the depths of the Nile when he pleases, etc.

The mummy in its coffin has been brought down the steps, and is now carried into a large chamber on the left, where its final resting place is to be. As we pass into this room we see that a part of it is already occupied with a coffin and the funereal furniture belonging to it. When we come nearer we find that it is the coffin of Tutu, Ani's wife. Close by her is a table of alabaster covered with shapely vessels of the same substance, filled with wine, oil, and other unguents; each of those fragile objects is inscribed with her name. On the table are spoons made of ivory of the most beautiful workmanship. They are shaped in the form of a woman. The body is stained a deep creamy colour, the colour of the skin of the Egyptian lady, who guarded herself from the rays of the sun; the hair is black, and we see that it is movable; when we lift it off we see the name of "Tutu, the sistrum bearer," engraved beneath. On a second stand, made of wood, we find the articles for her toilet, mirror, kohl pot in obsidian, fan, etc., and close by is the sistrum which she carried in the temple of Åmen-Rā upon earth, and which was buried with her, so that she might be able to praise that god with music in his mansions in the sky. Chairs and her couch are there too, and stands covered with dried flowers and various offerings. Removing the lid of the coffin we see her mummy lying as it was laid a few years before. On her breasts are strings of dried flowers with the bloom still on them, and by her side is a roll of papyrus containing a copy of the service which she used to sing in the temple of Åmen in the Apts, when on earth. Her amethyst necklace and other ornaments are small, but very beautiful. Just over her feet is a blue glazed steatite *ushabti* figure. While we have been examining Tutu's general furniture, the servants of the *cher-ḥeb* have brought down the coffin, which is placed on a bier along the east wall, and the chairs and couch and boxes and funereal offerings, and arranged them about the chamber. In a square niche in the wall, just over the head of the coffin, Ani's writing palette and reeds are placed, and by its side is laid a large roll of papyrus nearly 90 feet long, inscribed in hieroglyphics during his lifetime and under his direction, with the oldest and most important chapters of the "Book of the Dead"; the vignettes, which refer to the chapters, are beautifully painted, and in some as many as thirteen colours are used in this chamber; and in every work connected with Ani's tomb there is a simple majesty which is characteristic of the ancient Egyptian gentleman. At each of the four corners or sides of the bier, is placed one of the so-called canopic jars, and at the foot are laid a few stone *ushabtiu* figures, whose duty it was to perform for the deceased such labours as filling the furrows with water, ploughing the fields, and carrying the sand, if he were called upon to do them. When everything has been brought into this chamber, and the tables of offerings have been arranged, a priest, wearing a panther skin, and accompanied by another who burns incense in a bronze censer, approaches the mummy, and performs the ceremony of "opening the mouth" while a priest in white robes reads from a roll of papyrus or leather. The act of embalming has taken away from the dead man all control over his limbs and the various portions of his body, and before these can be of any use to him in the nether-world, a mouth must be given to him, and it must be opened so that his *ka* may be able to speak. When the mouth of the deceased had been opened, his *ka* gained control of his speech, intelligence and limbs, and was able to hold intercourse with the gods, and to go in and out of his tomb whenever he pleased. When the formulae are finished and all rites performed, Ani's relatives and near friends withdraw from the mummy chamber and make their way up the stairs, through the long passage and into the first chamber, where they find that animals have been slaughtered, and that many of the assistants and those who accompanied the funeral are eating and drinking of the funereal offerings. When the last person has left the mummy chamber, masons bring along slabs of stone and lime which they have ready and wall it up; the joints between the stones are so fine that the blade of a modern penknife can with difficulty be inserted to the depth of half an inch. We have seen Ani's body embalmed, we have watched all the stages of the manufacture of his coffin, we have seen the body dressed and laid in it, we have accompanied him to the tomb, we have gone through it and seen how it is arranged and decorated, and we have assisted at the funereal ceremonies; in his beautiful tomb then, let us leave him to enjoy his long rest in the company of his wife. Ani did not cause such a large and beautiful tomb to be hewn for him merely to gratify his pride, with him, as with all educated Egyptians, it was the outcome of the belief that his soul would revivify his body, and was the result of a firm assurance in his mind of the truth of the doctrine of immortality, which is the foundation of the Egyptian religion, and which was as deeply rooted in them as the hills are in the earth.

G. ELIOT SMITH

Tomb Robbers and Mummies

PROFESSOR Eliot Smith wrote this piece after the tomb of Tutankhamen had been found but before the coffins were opened. His prediction that "jewellery of great value" would be found on the body was overwhelmingly fulfilled.

❦

IN the late Lord Amherst's collection, which was recently sold in London, there was a judicial papyrus of the reign of Ramses IX (about 1125 B.C.), reporting the trial of eight "servants of the High Priest of Amen," who were arraigned for plundering the tomb of King Sebekemsaf of the thirteenth dynasty. The written depositions of the prisoners set before the pharaoh by the vizier, the lieutenant, the reporter, and the mayor of Thebes were translated by Professor Percy Newberry in these terms: "We opened the coffins and their wrappings, which were on them, and we found the noble mummy of the king. There were two swords and many amulets and necklaces of gold on his neck: his head was covered with gold. We tore off the gold that we found on the noble mummy of this god [i.e. the dead king who was identified with Osiris]. We found the royal wife also. We tore off all that we found from her mummy likewise, and we set fire to their wrappings. We took their furniture of gold, silver and copper vases, which we found with them." The prisoners who made this confession were found guilty, and sentenced "to be placed in the prison of the temple of Amen," to await "the punishment that our lord the pharaoh shall decide." There are several other famous papyri reporting trials of desecrators of the royal tombs. In the Abbott papyrus (in the British Museum) inspectors submit a report on the tombs that were said to have been plundered, but the only one that had actually been robbed was that referred to in the confession just quoted from the Amherst papyrus. The two Mayer papyri in the Liverpool Free Public

From *Tutankhamen*. London: Routledge & Kegan Paul Ltd.; 1923, pp. 75-84. By permission of Routledge & Kegan Paul Ltd.

Museums relate to plundering in the Valley of the Tombs of the Kings. One of these is of special interest at the present moment because it relates to the violation of the tomb of Ramses VI, which is immediately above that of Tutankhamen. The robbers were discovered as the result of quarrels among themselves about the division of the spoil. This was one of the most disgraceful incidents in the whole history of tomb-plundering. The robbers, in their haste to get at the gold and jewels upon the mummies, usually chopped through the bandages, and mutilated the mummy in the process. But when, in 1905, I removed the wrappings from the mummy of Ramses VI (which in ancient times had been removed to the tomb of Amenhotep II, where it was discovered by M. Loret in 1898), the body was found to be hacked to pieces. This was no mere accidental injury, but clearly intentional destruction of a malicious nature. It makes one realize the sort of vandalism Tutankhamen's tomb so narrowly escaped.

Hiding the Mummies

The discovery of the royal mummies in 1881—and this applies with special force to the remains of the famous pharaohs Seti I and Ramses II—gave us the other side of the story, for it revealed the measures taken to protect the bodies of these kings from further injury, and the persistence with which the protectors of the tombs moved the mummies from one place to another in their endeavour to save them. The condition of affairs revealed in the tomb of Tutankhamen brings proof of what has long been suspected, that the work of the plunderer began soon after the closing of the chambers. But during the twentieth and twenty-first dynasties, when there was a rapid weakening of the Administration, tomb-robbing assumed proportions it had never attained before. The record inscribed upon the coffins of Seti I and Ramses II throws a lurid light on the extent of this loss of control. For a century and a half their mummies were moved from one hiding-place to another in the attempt to secure their safety. The mummy of the great Ramses was moved to the tomb of his father, Seti I, whose body for some time remained in its own alabaster sarcophagus, which is now in Sir John Soane's Museum in Lincoln's Inn Fields. But in the reign of Siamon (976-58 B.C.) the two mummies were hidden in the tomb of a queen called Inhapi, and about ten years later were moved again, this time to a tomb that had been originally prepared for Amenhotep I at Deir el Bahari. Here they, together with more than thirty other royal mummies, remained undisturbed for more than twenty-eight centuries, until about fifty years ago they were rediscovered, and the successors of the ancient tomb-robbers of Thebes once more resumed the old process of depredation. But the late Sir Gaston Maspero had not studied the papyri of the twentieth dynasty in vain, for he obtained a confession that is worthy of being set beside those recorded in the Amherst and Mayer papyri.

The story of the ill-treatment of the royal mummies and of their repeated removal from one hiding-place to another prepared us in some measure for the discoveries that were made when the shrouds and linen bandages were removed. But in spite of this the investigation was full of surprises. Several of the mummies after being hastily rewrapped (in the twentieth or twenty-first dynasty) were put into the wrong coffins. So that, for example, when the mummy supposed to be Ramses I (of the nineteenth dynasty) was unwrapped, an old white-haired lady was found embalmed in a way distinctive of the early part of the eighteenth dynasty. And again, when the mummy in the coffin of Setnakht (the first king of the twentieth dynasty) was examined, it was found to be that of a woman embalmed in the manner distinctive of the time of Setnakht's predecessor (Seti II, of the nineteenth dynasty); and it is probable that she is Queen Tausret, the wife in turn of the two kings, Siptah and Seti II. Such discoveries reveal the need for caution in claiming that the Valley of the Tombs of the Kings has yielded up all its hidden secrets. For there are many royal mummies that we know to have been buried there which have yet to be recovered.

If the examination of the royal mummies reveals the thoroughness with which the tombs have been rifled—not one of the series has ever been found undisturbed—they also give us some idea of the value of the jewellery and amulets which excited the greed of the robbers thirty centuries ago. The torn and mutilated wrappings of the mummies often bear the impressions of magnificent pectoral ornaments, and of amulets on the forehead, neck, or limbs; and the occasional finding of fragments of these, made of gold, lapis lazuli, or carnelian, gives us some idea of the value and beauty of this extravagant equipment of the dead. But I have known only one instance of an object of any considerable intrinsic value escaping the diligent searching of these experienced robbers. During the examination (in 1909) of the badly plundered mummy of Queen Hontaui I found a large and beautifully embossed plate of pure gold, unique in size and in the elaboration of its design.

From these considerations we can safely predict that if, as seems now to be certain, the unplundered mummy is found in the tomb of Tutankhamen, jewellery of great value and beauty of design will probably be found on it. The superb workmanship displayed in making these ornaments and amulets is known to us from the discoveries made by M. de Morgan in the Pyramids at Dashur in

1893. These gold pectoral ornaments inlaid with precious stones were wrought with an amazing perfection of technical skill many centuries before the time of Tutankhamen; but the jewellery of the eighteenth and nineteenth dynasties now exhibited in many museums (especially the Cairo Museum and the Louvre) reveals that the skill in making such works of art had not been lost. The quality of the workmanship revealed in the objects found in the first chamber of Tutankhamen's tomb should prepare us for the discovery on the mummy of ornaments even surpassing those of Ramses II in the Louvre.

But the chief interest in the discovery should be in the mummy itself, for the welfare of which all the elaborate arrangements were made. It is not merely because the mummies enable us to form some idea of the physical features of the kings and queens, and by appealing to our common humanity give their personalities a reality they would not otherwise possess; nor is it because they often reveal evidence of age and infirmities; their chief interest is the light they throw on the history of the period and upon the development of the art of embalming.

Perhaps I can best make plain what is meant by this statement if I refer to specific illustrations of the former kind of contribution the study of mummies makes to the fuller understanding of history.

When in 1907 the bones were found that had once formed part of the mummy wrongly assumed to be the famous Queen Tiy, I discovered that they were the remains of a young man's skeleton, for which, if it had been normal, it was difficult to admit an age of more than twenty-six years, if indeed as much. Now the archæological evidence seems to leave no loophole of escape from the conclusion that these bones are actually the skeleton of King Akhenaten; but, on the other hand, the historical evidence seems to demand an age of at least thirty years (or, according to a recent memoir by Professor Kurt Sethe, thirty-six years) for the famous heretic pharaoh. This apparent conflict between the two classes of evidence has stimulated an intensive study of the historical data and of the medical history of Akhenaten himself; and the final outcome of the investigations is likely to provide a most illuminating revelation of the inner meaning of perhaps the most human and dramatic incident that has come to us from ancient times. The peculiar features of Akhenaten's head and face, the grotesque form assumed by his legs and body, no less than the eccentricities of his behaviour, and his pathetic failure as a statesman, will probably be shown to be due to his being the subject of a rare disorder, only recently recognized by physicians, who have given it the cumbrous name *Dystocia adiposo-genitalis*. One of the effects of this condition is to delay the process of the consolidation of the bones. Studying the history of modern instances of this affection the possibility suggests itself that Akhenaten might well have attained the age of thirty or even thirty-six years, although his bones are in a condition which in the normal individual is appropriate to the years twenty-two to twenty-six. It is tempting to speculate on the vast influence on the history of the world, not merely the political fate of Egypt and Syria in the fourteenth century B.C., but the religious conceptions of Palestine and the whole world for all time, for which the illness of this pacifist poet may have been largely responsible.

WALLIS BUDGE

Mummies and Mortality

THIS anecdote is translated from the Coptic. It concerns a visit by Christian monks to some ancient Theban tomb.

[THIS story is related by John the Elder and Moses, Bishop of Captos, a friend and fellow-monk of Bishop Pisentius, each speaking in turn.]

When my father Pisentius was still living with me in the mountain of Djemi (Western Thebes), he said to me one day: "John, my son, rise up and follow me, and I will show thee the place where I take my repose and pray and meditate, so that thou mayest visit me every Sabbath and bring me a little food to eat and a little water to drink, enough only for the support of my body." And my father rose up, and walked before me, and he was meditating on the Holy Scriptures of the Spirit of God. And when we had walked a distance which appeared to me to be about three miles, we came

From *Egyptian Tales and Romances*, pp. 213-15.

to a passage in the rock which was open. And when we had gone through the passage we came to a chamber which seemed to have been hewn out of the rock, and six pillars supported the roof. The chamber was fifty-two cubits (78 feet or 86 feet 8 inches square), and its height was in proportion to its length and breadth. A large number of mummified bodies were in it, and even when walking out into the passage thou couldst smell the odour of the sweet spices that had been used in making them. (This is literally true. Some tombs when first opened smell strongly of *anti*, or gum, which was used freely in making mummies. W.B.) And we took the coffins and piled them up one on top of another to the full height of the chamber. The first mummy that lay near the doorway was swathed in pure silk, similar to that which is used by kings. It was that of a very large man, and his fingers and toes were bandaged separately. And my father Pisentius said: "How many years is it since these people died? And from what homes do they come?" And I answered: "Only God knows." And my father said to me: "Get thee gone, my son. Sit in thy monastery and take heed to thyself, for this world is a thing of vanity, and we may be removed from it at any moment. Take heed to thy perilous state. Continue thy fastings with strict regularity. Pray thy prayers hour by hour, even as I have taught thee, and come not here except on the Sabbath."

And when he had said these things to me, and I was turning round to leave his presence, my eyes wandered over one of the pillars, and I found attached to it a small roll of parchment. And my father unrolled it and read it, and he found written therein the names of all the people who were buried in that chamber: then he gave it to me and I put it back in its place. And I saluted my father, and came away from the chamber, and I walked on, and as he showed me the way he said to me: "Be thou diligent in the work of God that He may show mercy to thy wretched soul. Thou seest these mummies: needs must that everyone shall become like unto them."

6. *Religion and Morality*

J. H. BREASTED

The New Morality
of the Feudal Age

As we have so often said, it is not easy to read the spiritual and
intellectual progress of a race in monuments so largely material
as contrasted with literary documents. It is easy to be misled and
to misinterpret the meagre indications furnished by purely material monuments. Behind them lies a vast complex of human
forces and of human thinking which for the most part eludes us.
Nevertheless it is impossible to contemplate the colossal tombs of
the Fourth Dynasty, so well known as the Pyramids of Gizeh, and
to contrast them with the comparatively diminutive royal tombs
which follow in the next two dynasties, without, as we have before
hinted, discerning more than exclusively political causes behind
this sudden and startling change. The insertion [into the royal
tombs] of the Pyramid Texts themselves during the last century
and a half of the Pyramid Age is an evident resort to less material
forces enlisted on behalf of the departed Pharaoh as he confronted
the shadow world. On the other hand, the Great Pyramids of Gizeh
represent, as we have said before, the struggle of titanic material
forces in the endeavor by purely material means to immortalize the
king's physical body, enveloping it in a vast and impenetrable husk
of masonry, there to preserve forever all that linked the spirit of
the king to material life. The Great Pyramids of Gizeh, while they
are to-day the most imposing surviving witnesses to the earliest
emergence of organized man and the triumph of concerted effort,

Extracts from *Development of Religion and Thought in Ancient Egypt* by James
H. Breasted are used by permission of Charles Scribner's Sons. Copyright 1912
Charles Scribner's Sons; renewal copyright 1940 Charles Breasted. New York, 1959,
pp. 178-84, 322-4, 334-6, 339-43.

are likewise the silent but eloquent expression of a supreme endeavor to achieve immortality by sheer physical force. For merely physical reasons such a colossal struggle with the forces of decay could not go on indefinitely; with these reasons political tendencies too made common cause; but combined with all these we must not fail to see that the mere insertion of the Pyramid Texts in itself in the royal tombs of the last century and a half of the Pyramid Age was an abandonment of the titanic struggle with material forces and an evident resort to less tangible agencies. The recognition of a judgment and the requirement of moral worthiness in the hereafter was a still more momentous step in the same direction. It marked a transition from reliance on agencies external to the personality of the dead to dependence on inner values. Immortality began to make its appeal as a thing achieved in a man's own soul. It was the beginning of a shift of emphasis from objective advantages to subjective qualities. It meant the ultimate extension of the dominion of God beyond the limits of the material world, that he might reign in the invisible kingdom of the heart. It was thus also the first step in the long process by which the individual personality begins to emerge as contrasted with the mass of society, a process which we can discern likewise in the marvellous portrait sculpture of the Pyramid Age. The vision of the possibilities of individual character had dimly dawned upon the minds of these men of the early world; their own moral ideals were passing into the character of their greatest gods, and with this supreme achievement the development of the five hundred years which we call the Pyramid Age had reached its close.

When Egypt emerged from the darkness which followed the Pyramid Age, and after a century and a half of preparatory development reached the culmination of the Feudal Age (Twelfth Dynasty), about 2000 B. C., the men of this classic period looked back upon a struggle of their ancestors with death—a struggle whose visible monuments were distributed along a period of fifteen hundred years. The first five hundred years of this struggle was still represented by the tombs of the first two dynasties in Abydos and vicinity, but it was veiled in mist, and to the men of the Feudal Age its monuments were mingled with the memorials of the gods who once ruled Egypt. Of the thousand years which had elapsed since the Pyramid Age began, the first five hundred was impressively embodied before their eyes in that sixty-mile rampart of pyramids sweeping along the margin of the western desert. There they stretched like a line of silent outposts on the frontiers of death. It was a thousand years since the first of them had been built, and five hundred years had elapsed since the architects had rolled up their papyrus drawings of the latest, and the last group of workmen had gathered up their tools and departed. The priesthoods too, left without supper, had, as we have already seen, long forsaken the sumptuous temples and monumental approaches that rose on the valley side. The sixty-mile pyramid cemetery lay in silent desolation, deeply encumbered with sand half hiding the ruins of massive architecture, of fallen architraves and prostrate colonnades, a solitary waste where only the slinking figure of the vanishing jackal suggested the futile protection of the old mortuary gods of the desert. Even at the present day no such imposing spectacle as the pyramid cemeteries of Egypt is to be found anywhere in the ancient world, and we easily recall something of the reverential awe with which they oppressed us when we first looked upon them. Do we ever realize that this impression was felt by their descendants only a few centuries after the builders had passed away? and that they were already ancient to the men of 2000 B.C.? On the minds of the men of the Feudal Age the pyramid cemetery made a profound impression. If already in the Pyramid Age there had been some relaxation in the conviction that by sheer material force man might make conquest of immortality, the spectacle of these colossal ruins now quickened such doubts into open scepticism, a scepticism which ere long found effective literary expression.

Discernment of moral requirements had involved subjective contemplation. For the first time in history man began to contemplate *himself* as well as his destiny, to "expatiate free o'er all this scene of man." It is a ripe age which in so doing has passed beyond the unquestioning acceptance of traditional beliefs as bequeathed by the fathers. Scepticism means a long experience with inherited beliefs, much rumination on what has heretofore received unthinking acquiescence, a conscious recognition of personal power to believe or disbelieve, and thus a distinct step forward in the development of self-consciousness and personal initiative. It is only a people of ripe civilization who develop scepticism. It is never found under primitive conditions. It was a momentous thousand years of intellectual progress, therefore, of which these sceptics of the Feudal Age represented the culmination. Their mental attitude finds expression in a song of mourning, doubtless often repeated in the cemetery, and as we follow the lines we might conclude that the author had certainly stood on some elevated point overlooking the pyramid cemetery of the Old Kingdom as he wrote them. We possess two fragmentary versions of the song, one on papyrus, the other on the walls of a Theban tomb. But the papyrus version was also copied from a tomb, for the superscription reads: "Song which is in the house (tomb-chapel) of King Intef the Justified, which is in front of the singer with the harp." The song reads:

"How prosperous is this good prince!
It is a goodly destiny, that the bodies diminish,
Passing away while others remain,
Since the time of the ancestors,
The gods who were aforetime,
Who rest in their pyramids,
Nobles and the glorious departed likewise,
Entombed in their pyramids.
Those who built their (tomb)-temples,
Their place is no more.
Behold what is done therein.
I have heard the words of Imhotep and Hardedef,

(Words) greatly celebrated as their utterances.
Behold the places thereof;
Their walls are dismantled,
Their places are no more,
As if they had never been.

"None cometh from thence
That he may tell (us) how they fare;
That he may tell (us) of their fortunes,
That he may content our heart,
Until we (too) depart
To the place whither they have gone.

"Encourage thy heart to forget it,
Making it pleasant for thee to follow thy desire,
While thou livest.
Put myrrh upon thy head,
And garments on thee of fine linen,
Imbued with marvellous luxuries,
The genuine things of the gods.

"Increase yet more thy delights,
And let (not) thy heart languish.
Follow thy desire and thy good,
Fashion thine affairs on earth
After the mandates of thine (own) heart.
(Till) that day of lamentation cometh to thee,
When the silent-hearted hears not their lamentation,
Nor he that is in the tomb attends the mourning.

"Celebrate the glad day,
Be not weary therein.
Lo, no man taketh his goods with him.
Yea, none returneth again that is gone thither."

Such were the feelings of some of these men of the Feudal Age as
they looked out over the tombs of their ancestors and contemplated
the colossal futility of the vast pyramid cemeteries of the Old
Kingdom

J. H. BREASTED

Faith and Revolution:
Akhenaten

FINDING Thebes embarrassed with too many theological traditions,
in spite of its prestige and its splendor, Ikhnaton [Akhenaten]
forsook it and built a new capital about midway between Thebes
and the sea, at a place now commonly known as Tell el Amarna.
He called it Akhetaton, "Horizon of Aton." The name of the Sun-

Ibid., pp. 322-4.

god is the only divine name found in the place, and it was evidently intended as a centre for the dissemination of Solar monotheism. Here several sanctuaries of Aton were erected, and in the boundary landmarks, imposing stelae which the king set up in the eastern and western cliffs, the place was formally devoted to his exclusive service. A similar Aton city was founded in Nubia, and in all likelihood there was another in Asia. The three great portions of the Empire, Egypt, Nubia, and Syria, were thus each given a centre of the Aton faith. Besides these, sanctuaries of Aton were also built at various other places in Egypt.

This was, of course, not accomplished without building up a powerful court party, which the king could oppose, to the evicted priesthoods, especially that of Amon. The resulting convulsion undoubtedly affected seriously the power of the royal house. The life of this court party, which now unfolded at Akhetaton, centred about the propagation of the new faith, and as preserved to us in the wall reliefs which fill the chapels of the cliff tombs, excavated by the king for his nobles in the face of the low cliffs of the eastern plateau behind the new city, it forms, perhaps, the most interesting and picturesque chapter in the story of the early East. It is to the tombs of these partisans of the king that we owe our knowledge of the content of the remarkable teaching which he was now propagating. They contain a series of hymns in praise of the Sun-god, or of the Sun-god and the king alternately, which afford us at least a glimpse into the new world of thought, in which we behold this young king and his associates lifting up their eyes and endeavoring to discern God in the illimitable sweep of his power—God no longer of the Nile valley only, but of all men and of all the world.

It is this recognition of the fatherly solicitude of Aton for all creatures which lifts the movement of Ikhnaton far above all that had before been attained in the religion of Egypt or of the whole East before this time. "Thou art the father and the mother of all that thou hast made" is a thought which anticipates much of the later development in religion even down to our own time. The picture of the lily-grown marshes, where the flowers are "drunken" in the intoxicating radiance of Aton, where the birds unfold their wings and lift them "in adoration of the living Aton," where the cattle dance with delight in the sunshine, and the fish in the river beyond leap up to greet the light, the universal light whose beams are even "in the midst of the great green sea"—all this discloses a discernment of the presence of God in nature, and an appreciation of the revelation of God in the visible world such as we find a thousand years later in the Hebrew psalms, and in our own poets of nature since Wordsworth.

It is evident that, in spite of the political origin of this movement, the deepest sources of power in this remarkable revolution lay in this appeal to nature, in this admonition to "consider the lilies of the field." Ikhnaton was a "God-intoxicated man," whose mind responded with marvellous sensitiveness and discernment to the visible evidences of God about him. He was fairly ecstatic in his sense of the beauty of the eternal and universal light. Its beams enfold him on every monument of his which has survived. He prays, "May my eyes be satisfied daily with beholding him, when he dawns in this house of Aton and fills it with his own self by his beams, beauteous in love, and lays them upon me in satisfying life for ever and ever." In this light—which more than once, as here, he identifies with love, or again with beauty, as the visible evidence of the presence of God—he revels with an intoxication rarely to be found, and which may be properly compared to the ecstatic joy felt by such a soul as Ruskin in the contemplation of light. Ruskin, as he sees it playing over some lovely landscape, calls it "the breathing, animated, exulting light, which feels and receives and rejoices and acts—which chooses one thing and rejects another—which seeks and finds and loses again—leaping from rock to rock, from leaf to leaf, from wave to wave, glowing or flashing or scintillating according to what it strikes, or in its holier moods absorbing and enfolding all things in the deep fulness of its repose, and then again losing itself in bewilderment and doubt and dimness, or perishing and passing away, entangled in drifting mist, or melted into melancholy air, but still—kindling or declining, sparkling or still—it is the living light, which breathes in its deepest, most entranced rest, which sleeps but never dies." That is the loftiest modern interpretation of light, a veritable gospel of the beauty of light, of which the earliest disciple was this lonely idealist of the fourteenth century before Christ. To Ikhnaton, too, the eternal light might sleep, when he that made the world has "gone to rest in his horizon," but to him also as with Ruskin it "sleeps but never dies."

In this aspect of Ikhnaton's movement, then, it is a gospel of the beauty and beneficence of the natural order, a recognition of the message of nature to the soul of man, which makes it the earliest of those revivals which we call in the case of such artists as Millet and the Barbizon school, or of Wordsworth and his successors, "a return to nature." As the earliest of such movements known to us, however, we cannot call it a "return." We should not forget also that this intellectual attitude of the king was not confined to religion. The breath of nature had also touched life and art at the same time, and quickened them with a new vision as broad and untrammelled as that which is unfolded in the hymns. The king's charmingly natural and unrestrained relations with his

family, depicted on public monuments without reserve, is another example of his powerful individuality and his readiness to
throw off the shackles of tradition without hesitation in the endeavor to establish a world of things as they are, in wholesome
naturalness. The artists of the time, one of them indeed, as he says,
under the king's own instructions, put forth works dominated by the
same spirit. Especially do they reflect to us that joy in nature which
breathes in the religion of Ikhnaton. We have come to speak habit-
ually of an Amarna age, in religion, in life, in art,. and this fact
of itself is conclusive evidence of the distinctive intellectual attitude of Ikhnaton.

Such fundamental changes as these, on a moment's reflection,
suggest what an overwhelming tide of inherited thought, custom,
and tradition had been diverted from its channel by the young king
who was guiding this revolution. It is only as this aspect of his
movement is clearly discerned that we begin to appreciate the
power of his remarkable personality. Before his time religious documents were usually attributed to ancient kings and wise men, and
the power of a belief lay chiefly in its claim to remote antiquity
and the sanctity of immemorial custom. Even the social prophets
of the Feudal Age attribute the maxims of Ptahhotep to a vizier
of the Old Kingdom, five or six centuries earlier. Until Ikhnaton
the history of the world had been but the irresistible drift of tradition. All men had been but drops of water in the great current.
Ikhnaton was the first individual in history. Consciously and deliberately, by intellectual process he gained his position, and then
placed himself squarely in the face of tradition and swept it aside.
He appeals to no myths, to no ancient and widely accepted versions
of the dominion of the gods, to no customs sanctified by centuries—
he appeals only to the present and visible evidences of his god's
dominion, evidences open to all, and as for tradition, wherever it
had left material manifestations of any sort in records which could
be reached, he endeavored to annihilate it. The new faith has but
one name at Amarna. It is frequently called the "teaching," and this
"teaching" is attributed solely to the king. There is no reason to
question this attribution. But we should realize what this "teaching"
meant in the life of the Egyptian people as a whole.

Here had been a great people, the onward flow of whose life,
in spite of its almost irresistible momentum, had been suddenly
arrested and then diverted into a strange channel. Their holy places
had been desecrated, the shrines sacred with the memories of
thousands of years had been closed up, the priests driven away,
the offerings and temple incomes confiscated, and the old order
blotted out. Everywhere whole communities, moved by instincts
flowing from untold centuries of habit and custom, returned to

their holy places to find them no more, and stood dumfounded before the closed doors of the ancient sanctuaries. On feast days, sanctified by memories of earliest childhood, venerable halls that had resounded with the rejoicings of the multitudes, now stood silent and empty; and every day as the funereal processions wound across the desert margin and up the plateau to the cemetery, the great comforter and friend, Osiris, the champion of the dead in every danger, was banished, and no man dared so much as utter his name. Even in their oaths, absorbed from childhood with their mothers' milk, the involuntary names must not be suffered to escape the lips; and in the presence of the magistrate at court the ancient oath must now contain only the name of Aton. All this to them was as if the modern man were asked to worship X and swear by Y. Groups of muttering priests, nursing implacable hatred, must have mingled their curses with the execration of whole communities of discontented tradesmen—bakers who no longer drew a livelihood from the sale of ceremonial cakes at the temple feasts; craftsmen who no longer sold amulets of the old gods at the temple gateway; hack sculptors whose statues of Osiris lay under piles of dust in many a tumble-down studio; cemetery stone-cutters who found their tawdry tombstones with scenes from the Book of the Dead banished from the cemetery; scribes whose rolls of the same book, filled with the names of old gods, or even if they bore the word god in the plural, were anathema; actors and priestly mimes who were driven away from the sacred groves by gendarmes on the days when they should have presented to the people the "passion play," and murmuring groups of pilgrims at Abydos who would have taken part in this drama of the life and death and resurrection of Osiris; physicians deprived of their whole stock in trade of exorcising ceremonies, employed with success since the days of the earliest kings, two thousand years before; shepherds who no longer dared to place a loaf and a jar of water under yonder tree and thus to escape the anger of the goddess who dwelt in it, and who might afflict the household with sickness in her wrath; peasants who feared to erect a rude image of Osiris in the field to drive away the typhonic demons of drought and famine; mothers soothing their babes at twilight and fearing to utter the old sacred names and prayers learned in childhood, to drive away from their little ones the lurking demons of the dark. In the midst of a whole land thus darkened by clouds of smouldering discontent, this marvellous young king, and the group of sympathizers who surrounded him, set up their tabernacle to the daily light, in serene unconsciouness of the fatal darkness that enveloped all around and grew daily darker and more threatening.

In placing the movement of Ikhnaton against a background of

popular discontent like this, and adding to the picture also the far
more immediately dangerous secret opposition of the ancient priesthoods, the still unconquered party of Amon, and the powerful military group, who were disaffected by the king's peace policy in Asia
and his lack of interest in imperial administration and mainte-
nance, we begin to discern something of the powerful individuality
of this first intellectual leader in history. His reign was the earliest
age of the rule of ideas, irrespective of the condition and willing-
ness of the people upon whom they were to be forced. As Matthew
Arnold has so well said, in commenting on the French Revolution:
"But the mania for giving an immediate political application to all
these fine ideas of the reason was fatal. . . . Ideas cannot be too
much prized in and for themselves, cannot be too much lived with;
but to transfer them abruptly into the world of politics and practice,
violently to revolutionize the world at their bidding—that is quite
another thing." But Ikhnaton had no French Revolution to look
back upon. He was himself the world's first revolutionist, and he
was fully convinced that he might entirely recast the world of religion, thought, art, and life by the invincible purpose he held, to
make his ideas at once practically effective. And so the fair city
of the Amarna plain arose, a fatuous island of the blest in a sea
of discontent, a vision of fond hopes, born in a mind fatally forget-
ful that the past cannot be annihilated. The marvel is that such
a man should have first arisen in the East, and especially in Egypt,
where no man except Ikhnaton possessed the ability to forget. Nor
was the great Mediterranean world which Egypt now dominated
any better prepared for an international religion than its Egyptian
lords. The imperial imagination of Ikhnaton reminds one of that
of Alexander the Great, a thousand years later, but it was many
centuries in advance of his age.

We cannot wonder that when the storm broke it swept away
almost all traces of this earliest idealist. All that we have to tell
us of him is the wreck of his city, a lonely outpost of idealism, not
to be overtaken and passed till six centuries later those Bedouin
hordes who were now drifting into Ikhnaton's Palestinian provinces
had coalesced into a nation of social, moral, and religious aspira-
tions, and had thus brought forth the Hebrew prophets.

Index

A NOTE ON THE TYPE

THE TEXT of this book was set on the Linotype in a new face called PRIMER, designed by *Rudolph Ruzicka*, earlier responsible for the design of Fairfield and Fairfield Medium, Linotype faces whose virtues have for some time now been accorded wide recognition. The complete range of sizes of Primer was first made available in 1954, although the pilot size of 12 point was ready as early as 1951. The design of the face makes general reference to Linotype Century (long a serviceable type, totally lacking in manner or frills of any kind) but brilliantly corrects the characterless quality of that face.